LORD BURGHLEY
and
QUEEN ELIZABETH

WILLIAM CECIL, LORD BURGHLEY

LORD BURGHLEY
and
QUEEN ELIZABETH

by

CONYERS READ

JONATHAN CAPE
THIRTY BEDFORD SQUARE
LONDON

FIRST PUBLISHED 1960
© 1960 BY CONYERS READ

PRINTED IN GREAT BRITAIN IN THE CITY OF OXFORD
AT THE ALDEN PRESS
ON PAPER MADE BY JOHN DICKINSON & CO.
BOUND BY A. W. BAIN & CO. LTD, LONDON

CONTENTS

ILLUSTRATIONS

PREFACE

FOUR years ago I sent to press *Mr. Secretary Cecil and Queen Elizabeth*. It was designed as the first volume of a life of William Cecil, Lord Burghley. This is the second volume and carries the story to Burghley's death. Roughly speaking, volume i deals with Cecil as a commoner and Secretary, volume ii with him as a peer and Lord Treasurer. As Lord Treasurer, he not only administered the royal finances, but he presided as well over the Court of Exchequer. In that capacity, as also in his Mastership of the Court of Wards, he occupied an important place in the English judiciary. But he was above all things a counsellor; the oldest, in point of service, of all Elizabeth's counsellors and the one upon whom she leaned most heavily. It may almost be said that Elizabeth never made an important decision in matters of policy without first consulting him. And much of the policy which emerged from those consultations was based upon his advice.

On that account it has not been easy to write his life without writing as well the history of the first forty years of her reign, not only in matters political but in matters religious and economic as well.

He grew physically feeble as he grew older. During the last five years of his life he had to be carried wherever he went, and in the last year or two he was very deaf. But his mental powers apparently remained undiminished until the very last. Within six months of his death, in his seventy-eighth year, he was still sitting with the Privy Council, still presiding in the Court of Exchequer and the Court of Wards. But after his son Robert's appointment as Principal Secretary in 1596, he took over virtually all the routine business of government and Burghley's activities in administration became reduced to an occasional memorandum and an occasional letter. For that reason I have, in the concluding chapters, been less concerned with the detailed consideration of public events.

The one part of Burghley's public life which I intended to write but have not written was his relations to the Irish problem. I think I have read all his extant dispatches on Irish affairs. Those to Sir Henry Sidney in the 'sixties, preserved in the Public Record Office; those to Sir William Fitzwilliam in the 'seventies, among the Carte MSS. in the Bodleian Library, and those to Nicholas White in the Lansdowne MSS. at the British Museum, are numerous. But they all deal either with English news or with details of Irish administration. On one occasion Burghley observed that the Flemings had no such cause to protest against Spanish oppression as the Irish against the tyranny of England; on another he rejected the policy of Ireland for the Irish. He wrote to Nicholas White: 'I think a great part of the misorders in that [Irish] government hath arisen by such as have been more inclined to private commodity and to singularities than to the public benefit.' But this was the string Burghley harped upon in every department of administration.

9

I find no memoranda from him on the Irish problem analogous to those which he prepared on almost every other matter of royal concern.

Ireland was for him a drain on English resources and a convenient base of operations for England's enemies. What he strove for there was the restoration of order in the English interest. But he does not appear, even in those terms, to have proposed any programme for action. In short, I have found little or nothing in the record of Burghley's relations to Ireland to throw fresh light either upon the history of the island or of the man.

I should perhaps apologize for my neglect of Burghley as Master of the Court of Wards. This aspect of his career has been so well presented by Joel Hurstfield in *The Queen's Wards*, published last year, that I could have done little more than paraphrase his findings. Upon the thorny question of Burghley's profits from the office, though commonly regarded by his contemporaries as the chief source of his wealth, the evidence is too scanty to justify any positive estimate.

My benefactors in the preparation of this volume were those who helped me with volume i. A second fellowship from the Guggenheim Foundation and a generous grant-in-aid from the American Philosophical Society enabled me to spend two more summers in the English archives. Once again I have to thank the officials of the Public Record Office and the British Museum for their courtesy and helpfulness. Lord Salisbury has kept the doors of Hatfield House open to me and his new librarian, Miss Clare Talbot, has placed me deeply in her debt. It is pleasant to record that the present Marquess of Exeter, whom Americans will always think of as Lord Burghley, one of the fastest runners and finest sportsmen who ever participated in American games, has opened to me also the doors of Burghley House and has undertaken a systematic examination of his archives there under the competent direction of Mr. P. I. King, archivist of the Northamptonshire Record Society. The survey is not yet finished, but Mr. King's first report reveals little or nothing pertinent to the life of the first Lord Burghley.

My old friend Sir John Neale has increased my indebtedness to him by reading and improving my manuscript before it went to press.

My wife once again has shared with me the pains and the pleasures of writing this book, and her contributions have added lustre to every page of it.

CONYERS READ

Villa Nova, Pennsylvania
May 1st, 1959

FOREWORD

WILLIAM CECIL, Lord Burghley, was Queen Elizabeth's Principal Secretary during the first thirteen years of her reign. He was largely responsible for Elizabeth's decision to break with Rome and establish a Church which retained the ecclesiastical hierarchy of the old Church but made important concessions to the Protestant theology. To the Queen herself the Anglican Church was neither Protestant nor Catholic, but pure English. Cecil would have preferred a Church more distinctly Protestant, but he accepted the Elizabethan establishment because he believed that the Queen would go no further. Indeed, during the first decade of her reign, one of his besetting fears was that she would accept some form of reconciliation with the Roman communion. Elizabeth herself preferred an ambiguous position. She was not a zealot of any creed. Her choice of a modified Protestantism was no doubt due in part to the circumstances of her birth, in large measure to the fact that during her sister's reign she had come to be regarded as the hope of the English Protestants. On the other hand, she realized that her two principal neighbours, France and Spain, were both Catholic, and that any pronounced Protestant leanings might expose her to a joint attack by her Catholic neighbours, particularly since her heir presumptive, Mary Stuart, was at hand to supply a focus to their efforts and a Roman Catholic alternative to a heretical English queen. Actually the issue turned upon the force of religion in international affairs. No doubt the reaction against the Protestant Reformation was growing stronger. The Counter Reformation was well under way. Elizabeth herself was disposed to discount its force. She thought that in the long run national interests would prevail over the religious issue. And she proved to be right. But her confidence was not shared by her councillors.

At the time of Elizabeth's accession, Mary Stuart was the wife of the French Dauphin and was presently to become Queen of France. This fact strengthened Mary's position both in France and in Scotland. On the other hand it made Philip II of Spain reluctant to take sides against Elizabeth. On the whole he preferred a heretic queen in England to a Roman Catholic one who might well unite France, Scotland and England under one banner and cut right across his line of communications with the Low Countries.

Elizabeth's position was considerably strengthened when Mary's French husband died and she went to her Scottish kingdom. Her mother-in-law, Catherine de Medicis, who took over French affairs, was on the whole anti-Marian in her attitude. The consequence was that Mary could no longer count upon French support, though Mary's uncles, leaders of the House of Guise, remained important factors in French affairs and brought constant pressure upon the French Crown to espouse Mary's cause.

In Scotland Mary's arrival was greeted with doubtful enthusiasm. For Scotland under the leadership of John Knox had broken with Rome and established a Protestant Church. But Catholicism was still strong in Scotland, particularly in the north, and was strengthened by Mary's presence.

All these considerations determined Elizabeth's policy both towards Scotland and towards France. In Scotland the Protestants were her natural allies. In France the House of Guise was her natural enemy, the Politiques and the Huguenots her natural friends. Cecil strongly urged her to cultivate her friends and oppose her enemies in both countries — to strengthen her bonds with her co-religionists and organize their combined strength against the Catholics in both countries. But Elizabeth was not willing to make definite commitments. She lent aid underhand to the Scottish Protestants, and did the same thing for the French Huguenots. Indeed, she sent armies both into Scotland and into France in support of her partisans. Her military intervention in France was a flat failure. In Scotland it was more successful, but it never went far enough to assure the domination of the Protestant government there. Mary might, indeed, have prevailed had she not alienated the affections of her subjects by her involvement in the murder of her second husband and her subsequent marriage to his murderer. As it was, she had to flee the land and take refuge in England. There she remained, occupying a position somewhere between that of royal guest and royal prisoner. At the end of the decade Elizabeth had not yet made up her mind what to do with her.

Spain presented an analogous problem. Philip II, King of Spain, was Elizabeth's brother-in-law. He had intervened actively on her behalf during her sister Mary's reign and when Mary died had proposed marriage to Elizabeth. She rejected the proposal, but succeeded in persuading Philip that she might be won back to the Roman faith and so for a time preserved his good will or at least his neutrality.

Philip was also Duke of Burgundy, which meant the Low Countries; and the Low Countries were old allies of England, an alliance strengthened by intimate and very profitable trade relations. England, of course, commanded communications by sea between Philip and his Netherlands. It was therefore important to Philip to keep England, his old ally, friendly and France, his old enemy, from securing control of both sides of the Channel.

But the Low Countries were not Spanish. They resented the government of a Spanish king. This resentment was quickened by oppressive taxation and by the spread of Protestantism in the Netherlands, particularly in the northern provinces of Holland and Zeeland. The outcome was open revolt against Spanish rule followed by Spanish efforts to suppress the revolt by blood and iron. Here again, Protestant rebels offered a channel through which Elizabeth might strike at the overwhelming power of Spain.

Relations between her and her Spanish brother-in-law were strained by reason of her seizure in 1568 of Spanish ships, laden with money to pay Alva's troops in the Low Countries, which had taken refuge in English harbours. Trade relations between England and the Low Countries had been stopped, and something like a cold war ensued.

Meanwhile in England there was considerable discontent, both on the left which wanted to go further in the direction of Protestantism and on the right which wanted to go back, with Cecil leaning towards the left and his mistress towards the right. There was factional discontent — the old nobility against the 'new men' — following more or less the lines of religious cleavage and accentuated by the personal rivalry between Cecil the administrator and Leicester the favourite, with the Queen pulled one way by her emotions and the other way by her reason, prompted always by her father's example, to divide and rule.

The end of the decade was marked by an effort on Leicester's part to get rid of Cecil, which failed, and an effort by the northern Earls to overthrow what they were pleased to regard as the Cecilian régime, which also failed.

None of the problems with which Cecil had to wrestle were solved after ten years. But they were at least defined. The time of probation was ended. Elizabeth had not only established firmly her right to rule but had proved her competence to rule. Cecil, beyond peradventure, was recognized as her first minister. She and he in partnership were the constant factors in the English government for thirty years to come. Others came and went, but the Queen remained always the dominant figure, and always at her right hand her devoted servant.

LORD BURGHLEY
and
QUEEN ELIZABETH

CHAPTER I

THE CAPTIVE QUEEN OF SCOTS, 1570

THE beginning of the year 1570 found William Cecil, in his fiftieth year, secure in office, secure in the royal confidence, secure in the leadership of Elizabeth's Council. As he had grown in political stature he had grown also in affluence. From the revenues and perquisites of the Court of Wards he was becoming rich. We hear no more about his poverty. He had moved from his town house in Cannon Row to his much more pretentious residence in Covent Garden. He had relinquished his country place at Wimbledon to his son, Thomas, and was rapidly transforming his family seat at Stamford Baron into one of the most imposing of Elizabethan country mansions. And he had already begun an even more imposing structure at Theobalds in Hertfordshire. He had two sons and two daughters. His first-born had been a disappointment, but he had made a good marriage and was by way of becoming, if not a distinguished, at least a reputable country gentleman. His second son, Robert, was still a young boy, a rather sickly boy with a crooked back, who had not yet revealed the abundant promise which was in him. His daughters, Ann and Elizabeth, were unmarried, though plans were well advanced for a match between Ann and young Philip Sidney, the son of Cecil's old friend, Sir Henry Sidney, and the nephew of the Earl of Leicester.

In January 1570 Elizabeth was conscious of a sense of security such as she had rarely enjoyed since her accession. The crisis of 1568-69 had passed. Her chief rival, Mary Stuart, was a prisoner in England; her party in Scotland had been reduced to obedience by the firm and moderate government of the Regent Murray, governor for the young King, and the Protestant religion had been firmly established. Murray was a warm friend of Cecil and of the English alliance. So the 'postern gate' was in safe hands.

France meanwhile was deep in the Third Civil War which had dragged on for over a year and had effectively prevented any aggressive foreign policy. The French King knew well enough that Elizabeth was giving assistance underhand to the French Protestants and it did not increase his affection for her. He was powerless at the moment to retaliate, though he made it clear enough that he was in a mood to promote the pretensions of Mary Stuart so far as he dared. At the moment he could do no more than remonstrate; with Murray in Scotland and Mary a prisoner and the militant strength of Roman Catholicism crushed by the suppression of the Rising of the North, the prospects of successful intervention on his sister-in-law's behalf were reduced almost to the vanishing point.

The Spaniards were more menacing. Elizabeth was well aware that Northumberland and the northern rebels had been encouraged and assisted by the Spanish ambassador in England, Guerau de Spes. She was well aware that Mary herself and her Catholic supporters in England pinned their hopes to active intervention by Spain. And she realized that her bold seizure of the Spanish pay ships a year earlier had brought the Duke of Alva, the Spanish Governor in the Low Countries, almost to the point of war. But she realized also that Alva had his hands full with the Dutch revolt against his government, that his resources had been considerably reduced by the interruption of trade with England, and that what England had lost in the way of trade she had more than regained by the exploits of the English buccaneers against Spanish commerce in the Channel. Alva indeed, after his first ill-considered outburst of anger over the affair of the pay ships, had shown increasing eagerness to come to terms and increasing reluctance to participate in the belligerent purposes of Guerau de Spes. And his master, Philip II of Spain, was of the same mind. His efforts and energies at the moment were directed to the suppression of a menacing uprising of the Moriscos in Spain and to resistance against the advance of the Ottoman Turks in the Mediterranean. Spain like France clearly offered no immediate threat. As Cecil had pointed out in the spring of 1569, security from attack by Elizabeth's Catholic neighbours arose rather from their preoccupation with other problems than from any good will towards England. But at the moment all was reasonably well.

And then in mid-January 1570 came the murder of the Regent Murray. Scotland almost at once fell apart into contending factions, and Elizabeth again found herself faced by a distracted and unstable northern neighbour.

It is conceivable, though not certain, that had she decided to recognize formally the government of the young King, she might have restored order and stability there. But she was very reluctant to do so, partly because she thought Mary should be restored on terms, partly because she feared to antagonize both Spain and France by endorsing Mary's deposition. And those in Scotland who were of Mary's party were well aware of Elizabeth's position. William Maitland of Lethington hastened to utilize it, and in the disordered and uncertain state of affairs in Scotland succeeded in building up the Marian faction by spreading abroad the story that Elizabeth intended to restore Mary. Maitland asserted that Elizabeth had communicated with him personally, and there is evidence that she did conduct some correspondence with him unbeknown to her own councillors, though none of it appears to have survived.

The Earl of Sussex, who commanded the English army on the Scottish border, evidently feared that Elizabeth would fall under the spell of Maitland's wit and eloquence. He therefore took care to pass on to her some of the uncomplimentary remarks which Maitland was charged with having made of her. The most notorious of these was to the effect that he would make her 'sit on her tail and whine like a whipped hound'.[1] Probably Elizabeth had taken Maitland's measure, but she liked his wit and got a good deal of amusement out of crossing swords with him.

In any case Maitland grew steadily in power and prestige among the Scots.

They recognized that he knew more about English attitudes than any man among them, and when he claimed to have special knowledge of Elizabeth's purposes they were disposed to take him at his word.

The first response of the English government to the news of Murray's death was to strengthen the hand of the young King's party so far as it might be done without formal recognition. Immediately, the problem was to deal with the English rebels, Northumberland, Westmorland, Dacres and the rest, who had fled to Scotland after the Rising of the North and taken refuge among the wild tribesmen of the Scottish border side. Thence they were engaged in raids upon the English border. The Scottish government professed its inability to deal with them. Elizabeth laid the problem before a selected group of her councillors in March. Bacon, Cecil and Leicester were of the group.[2] They advised that the Earl of Sussex should march with an army to the frontier and take punitive action against the rebels, inviting the Scottish government to join in the enterprise. Sussex received his orders accordingly.

But before the army was ready, Maitland made a desperate effort to prevent it. He had written to Cecil late in January, laid before him the problems presented by Murray's death and invited his assistance in reconciling the warring factions in Scotland.[3] He followed this letter up with a second and a third, evidently hoping to re-establish an old familiar intercourse. But Cecil was wary. When Maitland wrote his first letter he was still in prison, charged with complicity in Darnley's murder, and though he was a little later cleared of the charge, he still had no official position. Cecil was not prepared to recognize his *de facto* position as leader of the Marians by discussing matters of policy with him, but contented himself with acknowledging Maitland's letters through Thomas Randolph, the English agent in Scotland.[4]

Maitland then directed his efforts to Leicester. Late in March, after Sussex had received his instructions, Maitland wrote a long letter to Leicester.[5] The gist of it was that those in Scotland who favoured Mary's cause were the principal men of the country, and that sooner than submit to the coercion of the King's party they would bring in the French. As Maitland presented the picture, the course for Elizabeth to pursue was not to apply force in support of the weaker against the stronger, 'but rather by way of treaty to bring the parties to an accord'.

If we are to believe the French ambassador in England, La Mothe Fénélon,[6] Leicester had already expressed his sympathy with the Queen of Scots. On March 17th, Fénélon, in a dispatch to his master, related a conversation with Leicester in which Leicester had expressed great desire to establish peace with France and to promote the interests of Mary Queen of Scots. In the course of the conversation Leicester had pointed to Cecil as the sworn enemy of Mary and the active agent in stimulating Elizabeth's jealousy of the Scottish Queen. According to Leicester, Cecil was strongly opposed to Mary's claims to the English succession, aimed to promote an heir presumptive of his own choosing and had pitched upon the young son of Catherine Grey,[7] who, after Mary, probably had the best claim.

Fénélon in his dispatches presented a picture of a divided Council, one group under Leicester favouring the restitution of Mary Queen of Scots, the other under Cecil favouring the formal recognition of Mary's son, James, as King of Scotland. Leicester told Fénélon that Cecil was trying to get rid of him as he had other councillors who favoured Mary. According to Fénélon, Leicester was responsible for the recall of the Earl of Arundel, one of Cecil's known enemies, to the Council.

It is always difficult to evaluate evidence of this sort. Leicester was certainly cultivating the French ambassador at this time. It was probably through Leicester that Fénélon was kept informed about the deliberations of Elizabeth's Council. There is very little other evidence on the subject, none from domestic sources and none from the Spanish ambassador whose complicity in the Norfolk marriage and in the Rising of the North had made him *persona non grata* at Court.

It is reasonably safe to assume, in view of Leicester's support of a projected marriage of Mary and the Duke of Norfolk in 1569, that he leaned towards the Scottish Queen. Cecil certainly leaned away from her. But what Fénélon wrote to his master on the subject must be taken with a grain of salt. His picture of a sharply divided Council lacks confirmation from other sources. Both Fénélon and De Spes agreed that Cecil was the dominant figure, though the evidence from Spanish sources is curiously contradictory. On August 1st a Spanish agent in London, Antonio de Guaras, wrote that Cecil was in despair, contemplated flight and had ordered his wife to pack up her jewels.[8] Only five days later De Spes wrote:[9] 'The Queen's own opinion is of little importance and that of the Earl of Leicester still less, so that Cecil unrestrainedly and arrogantly governs all.'

From Cecil himself we have nothing at all. He was certainly the dominant figure, but he met with considerable opposition from Leicester and from Arundel. Cecil and his brother-in-law, Sir Nicholas Bacon, the Lord Keeper, worked together. Of the other members of the Council there is no record. Fénélon says that Elizabeth herself favoured the Marians.[10] Certainly she gave him that impression. For the better part of a year she laboured to create that impression. But during the spring of 1570 she followed a vigorous course. The efforts of the opposition to induce her to recall her orders to Sussex were unavailing. In April he marched into Scotland and spread wholesale destruction in the border side. Ninety strong castles, houses and dwelling places with three hundred towns and villages were utterly destroyed.

But Elizabeth would go no further. Sussex on April 25th, after he got back to Berwick, wrote to Cecil: 'If her Majesty will presently enter into public maintenance of this King's authority and send money to entertain 1000 soldiers of their own for three months and command the forces here to aid them for that time, they will bring all Scotland in effect to obey that authority . . . and cause all Scotland to yield justice to England without the Queen's charge . . . If her Majesty . . . command me to join with them I will, with the allowance of 300 carriage horses, make all men within 30 miles of the border to obey that authority . . . and if her Majesty will command me I will with the help of Morton [leader of the opposition to Mary] deliver the castle of Edinburgh or any other in Scotland to the hands of any in Scotland whom Morton shall appoint to receive them.'

Sussex had heard persistent rumours of Elizabeth's intention to come to terms with Mary, and he plainly was afraid they were true. 'Therefore,' he added, 'good master Secretary, sound the Queen's mind fully, and if she intend to restore the Scottish Queen advise her to do it in convenient sort and suffer me not to put my finger in the fire without cause.'[11]

Elizabeth called a meeting of her Council together on April 29th to consider the situation. It is one of the few occasions on which Elizabeth is recorded to have sat with her Council and to have participated in their deliberations.

We have an account of this meeting from La Mothe Fénélon.[12] According to him Elizabeth laid before her councillors three problems:

1. The impending hostility of France and Spain.
2. The widespread Roman Catholic sentiment in England.
3. Mary Stuart.

Fénélon records that the Council divided sharply on all three of these questions. One group took the position that France and Spain were not basically hostile, that they had just grievances against England and that if these grievances were remedied all would be well. The opposing group insisted that France and Spain could not be trusted and that the only safe course for Elizabeth was to arm against them and to form a strong alliance with other Protestant princes. The same line of cleavage, by Fénélon's account, appeared on the religious question. The group seeking accommodation with France and Spain advocated a mild and tolerant attitude towards the English Catholics, holding that they would never jeopardize their lives and property by rebellion if they were reasonably well treated. The opposing group argued for a more rigorous enforcement of the laws against the Catholics. On the question of Mary Stuart, Fénélon reported that partisanship ran strong. He implied that no decision was reached on any one of the three questions. What he was at pains to point out was that there was a strong group in Elizabeth's Council who were convinced that the religious issue was the dominating one among Elizabeth's Catholic neighbours and among her own subjects. They favoured a course of action based on that assumption. Fénélon does not precisely say so but he implies that Leicester and Arundel were the leaders of one group, Bacon and Cecil the leaders of the other. The position of the other councillors is not revealed, though Fénélon speaks of the heads of the nobility as supporting Leicester, and of eight members of the Council as following Bacon. At a guess the principal members of Bacon's company were, beside Cecil, Bedford, Sadler, Mildmay and Knollys. Bacon appears to have been their spokesman.

We have a memorandum in Cecil's hand about this meeting which confines itself to the problem of Scotland and the Scottish Queen.[13] According to Cecil, Elizabeth opened the meeting by laying before it a report from Sussex on the Scottish problem and inviting each councillor to speak his mind. 'She assured them that she herself was free from any determined resolution and that she would first hear their advice and thereupon make choice of what she should think meetest for her honour.' Cecil's account makes it clear that there were two factions in the

Council and that the matter was debated at length. According to him the policy advocated by Sussex of supporting the King's party with money and reinforcements prevailed.

'This', Cecil wrote, 'was the opinion of the more part, according to the intelligence of the state of Scotland for the present to them notified, and time would reveal any alteration to the worse. Then according to the accidents they were to review their advices, which surely they much feared would ensue if speedy comfortable answer be not made. For that they perceived by sundry advertisements from the Earl of Sussex that the opinion, that was by Lethington and his party so resolutely reported, of the Queen's Majesty's intention to send home the Queen of Scots, was and is the principal cause of the decay of her Majesty's party.'[14]

Elizabeth hesitated. In a letter drafted by Cecil which she sent to Sussex the day after the Council meeting she said that she was still undecided. The French King, she wrote, had announced his determination to assist the Marian faction in Scotland, and she had news from France that forces were being raised. She was also fearful of intervention by Spain. Under the circumstances she thought the wise course was to comfort the King's party in Scotland and to hold the Marians there in check while the question of Mary's restitution was considered at leisure. And that was the course she elected to follow.

Early in May at Hampton Court the Privy Council undertook to define the terms upon which they were prepared to consider the restitution of the Queen of Scots.[15] Cecil in his agenda for the meeting proposed the following terms:

1. That Mary should renounce her present title to the English throne.
2. That she should accept a league betwixt England and Scotland.
3. That she would prevent the entry of all foreign forces into Scotland.
4. That she would surrender the English rebels.
5. That she would deliver hostages, to wit, the young prince, her son; the Earl of Argyle, Lord Herries and Lord Fleming, her principal supporters.
6. That she would surrender to England for occupation Hume Castle and Dumbarton.
7. That both the Scottish and the English Parliaments would agree that if Mary broke these terms she should surrender the Scottish throne to her son and forfeit all rights to the English succession.
8. That she would maintain the Protestant religion in Scotland.
9. That she would continue the leaders of the young King's party in their states and offices.

We have no record of the deliberations in the Council. In another memorandum of the same date Cecil recorded 'Articles to be performed by the Queen of Scots and devised by the Q. Majesty's commandment'.[16] They probably record the action taken at the Council meeting. In the main they conform to the terms set forth in Cecil's agenda paper. The only important deviation was that instead of sending the young Scottish King to England as a hostage he was to remain in Scotland, retain his title and rule jointly with his mother upon terms analogous to the joint rule in England of Philip and Mary. This alternative seems, however, to have been abandoned in the subsequent negotiations.

With some such terms in mind negotiations were opened with Mary's ambassador, the Bishop of Ross. They were interrupted almost at once by the untimely publication of two pamphlets, one of them a defence of Mary's innocence, the other a statement of her claims upon the English Crown. Bacon hastened to show them to Elizabeth and her yielding mood stiffened. The troops of Sussex were once more set in motion and an army under Sir William Drury crossed the border to join forces with the King's party in Edinburgh.

It does not appear, however, that Elizabeth intended any more than another punitive expedition against those who were sheltering her rebels, this time against the Hamiltons. Sussex told her that if she would give him leave he could capture Edinburgh and Dumbarton and bring all Scotland to her obedience in a matter of weeks. But she insisted upon confining his operations to a more limited objective, and she presently went forward with negotiations for Mary's release.

Fénélon was bringing constant pressure upon her to withdraw her forces from Scotland and to restore Mary. Elizabeth seems to have reached an informal agreement with him late in May[17] the essence of which was:

1. That the French King should induce the Hamiltons in Scotland either to surrender the English refugee rebels or at least to abandon their cause.

2. That France and England together should induce the warring factions in Scotland to lay down their arms and cease fighting.

3. That English troops should be withdrawn from Scotland, provided that the French King would send no troops there and withdraw any troops that he had sent.

4. That Mary would be allowed to send to her friends in Scotland and that negotiations should go forward for her release and restoration on the basis of the terms which Elizabeth had offered.

Fénélon transmitted the terms of this agreement to his master in a bundle of dispatches dated May 27th. He was apparently not then aware that two days before, on Corpus Christi Day, a papal bull excommunicating Elizabeth and absolving her subjects from their allegiance had been found nailed to the door of the Bishop of London's house in St. Paul's Churchyard.[18] It came apparently as a complete surprise, though it bore the date February 25th and copies of it had reached England early in May. But no one of the government appears to have been aware of it, nor had Cecil any advance warning of it.

The bull called forth at once ballads, proclamations and vigorous retorts in pamphlets, probably officially inspired, a grave sermon by Bishop Jewel and a refutation by Bullinger. Cecil himself attempted a pamphlet on the subject, entitled *England Triumphant*,[19] in which he undertook to trace the history of England's relations to the Papacy and to show that England had never admitted the papal supremacy. He began with the mythical Brutus of Troy, accepted the legend of Joseph of Arimathea and designated Lucius of Britain as the first Christian King of

Britain. Cecil's style was as bad as his history. The whole composition was a tedious, long-winded affair. It was fortunately never published. Possibly even Cecil got bored with it. But it reveals what became increasingly apparent as time went on, that he had an itching hand for the pen with no marked aptitude in the use of it.

The bull was in effect a declaration of war against Elizabeth. It put an end to any hope of reconciling her with Rome. It put an end also to her ambiguities which had won for her twelve precious years to solidify her position. Thereafter she was committed, willy-nilly, to the Protestant cause. At the same time it made of every English Catholic who recognized papal supremacy a potential traitor.

The bull was evidently intended to support the hands of the northern rebels but it came too late. Though actually neither the French nor the Spanish King approved of the bull, Elizabeth and her councillors found it impossible to believe that the Pope had put it forth without the consent and approval of the two Catholic monarchs. Elizabeth affected to make light of it, but she was worried, and it may well have been the impelling factor in the resumption of negotiations for Mary's release.

Early in June she summoned her Council to discuss the situation. Bacon, who, doubtless at Cecil's prompting, had taken on the role of chief spokesman of the opposition to Mary, declined to attend. In fact he was on his way out of town when Arundel intercepted him and urged him to remain for the meeting. Bacon replied that it was useless, that the Queen did not recognize good counsel when she got it. Arundel retorted that he had better come, and observed that he and Cecil alone were holding up everything. Bacon returned.[20]

His position, in the role that Cecil usually played, is interesting. Probably Cecil had decided that he could accomplish more with his difficult mistress if he avoided the appearance of partisanship. Fénélon reported that during the interval between the calling of the Council and its assembling Cecil worked hard to divert Elizabeth from her purpose and told her flatly, in Leicester's presence, that she would presently be abandoned by her wisest councillors if she insisted upon exposing herself and her realm to the certain peril entailed in the liberation and restitution of the Scottish Queen.

She turned upon him sharply and asked him for his reasons, observing that all he had so far displayed was passion and hate. Cecil did not answer, but Leicester interjected: 'You see, Madam, what a fellow this secretary is; for yesterday in London he assured us that he would recommend the restitution of the Scottish Queen.' 'Quite so,' Elizabeth replied, 'and he often tells me things about you which turn out to be quite wrong.' Then, turning to Cecil: 'Master Secretary,' she said, 'I want to get out of this business and meet the French King's wishes, and not to play along any more with your "brothers in Christ".'

It is difficult to appraise the significance of this episode. It all comes to us from Fénélon and it may very well have been arranged for Fénélon's benefit. Elizabeth's objective was to persuade the French King that she seriously intended to release Mary and to restore her to her throne. She wanted to prevent active intervention by France on Mary's behalf and she did succeed in convincing Fénélon that under the circumstances French intervention would be ill-advised. Her attack upon Cecil may have been staged to give verisimilitude to the role she had decided to play.

But Cecil was not sure. He knew well enough that his mistress had never reconciled herself to the idea of holding Mary a prisoner and of supporting her rebels against her. It was a position almost without precedent. It ran counter to her basic ideas of the relations of the sovereign to her subjects. She found it difficult to justify it either to herself or to her neighbouring sovereigns. More or less against her will she had been forced into it by the exigencies of the situation. But she was always casting about for an alternative. And Cecil could never be sure that her feints in the direction of liberating Mary would not turn out to be realities. He himself harboured strong doubts about it in his own mind. He also believed in the sanctity of kingship. And, as he told Fénélon late in July, he realized that in the event of Elizabeth's death without children, Mary had the best claim to succeed her. As he had demonstrated already in the case of another Mary, Elizabeth's predecessor, he held fast to the principle of legitimacy in the succession. Mary, in short, might some day be his mistress, and in the meanwhile she was entitled to the consideration due to the heir presumptive.

Whatever Elizabeth intended, certainly she behaved as though her mind were made up. In an interview with Fénélon on May 22nd she promised to withdraw her forces from Scotland and to open negotiations with Mary forthwith. Fénélon reported this to the Privy Council which professed great alarm at her decision. They waited upon her and one of their number made what Fénélon called a marvellously insolent speech. Froude assumes that Bacon was the spokesman and he probably was, though Fénélon does not say so. The essence of the speech, as Fénélon reported it, was that Elizabeth was deceived and misled; that she was following the advice of those who were banded together against her in favour of the Scottish Queen; that Fénélon spoke for the Guises, not for the French King, who was too busy with affairs at home to contemplate an aggressive policy abroad; that if she pursued a resolute course she could bring all Scotland to her devotion; that her great father, Henry VIII, would never have followed such a craven course; and that so far as he, the spokesman, was personally concerned, he was quite prepared, if the French invaded, to go himself and cut off Mary's head.[21] He ended by directly accusing Leicester of infidelity to his mistress.

Leicester defended himself, and Elizabeth in anger swore that Bacon's advice was rash and dangerous, that she would never hold her crown at the expense of her Scottish cousin's life; she charged the speaker at his peril to indulge no more in such language.

Arundel thereupon urged reason and moderation, and made an eloquent defence of the case for accommodation. And with that policy Elizabeth announced her concurrence.

If this was play-acting, it seems to have been convincing to the onlookers, including Cecil himself. The day after his interview with Fénélon, Cecil wrote to

Norris: 'God send her Majesty a good issue of this Scottish matter, wherein the issue is easy, but the passage within doubtful, and I fear the end will be monstrous.'[22] From these ambiguous words we can at least gather that Cecil was alarmed. He added: 'By your letters of late time it hath seemed that your opinion was for the Queen's Majesty to be delivered of the Scottish Queen. But surely few here amongst [us] conceive it feasible with surety.'

The course of action which Elizabeth proposed was:

1. To open negotiations with Mary.
2. To impose an armistice upon the contending factions in Scotland.
3. To invite both parties in Scotland to send commissioners to participate in the negotiations for Mary's restoration.

In pursuit of the first she released Mary's ambassador, the Bishop of Ross, from restraint and allowed him to confer with his mistress. She promised to recall her forces from Scotland if the Marians would either surrender the English rebels or abandon their cause and if the French King would send no troops to Scotland.[23] She invited the French King's co-operation in this policy and urged him to send an envoy into Scotland to secure the acquiescence of the Marian party there.[24]

And so the negotiations with Mary were resumed. The Bishop of Ross was the principal instrument and Mary showed herself willing to agree to almost any terms. Maitland so advised her. Elizabeth seems to have convinced both Ross and Fénélon of her good intentions, yet at the very time she was writing to Sussex directing him to advise the King's party in Scotland[25] that though she felt in honour bound to hear Mary's case she did not intend to do anything 'whereby to make alteration of the young King's estate'. A little later Fénélon wrote that Sussex and Cecil together were conspiring to drag out the matter at length.[26] Fénélon believed that this was unknown to Elizabeth. But the probabilities are that she was playing a double game. Early in July she approved the choice of Lennox as Regent and on the 26th authorized a raid on the west borders.[27]

In an interview with Ross on September 1st[28] Elizabeth announced her intention of sending Cecil and Mildmay to negotiate with Mary. The choice is significant. Both of them belonged to the party opposing Mary's release.

On the same day Ross had a conference with Cecil, complained of the delay and called for action. According to the Bishop's report of the interview, Cecil had told him that 'as long as the Queen of Scots pressed to pull down the Queen his mistress and set herself up, he gave counsel to maintain his own mistress. When he sees the Queen of Scots willing to yield and be content with her own and not to press to pull down his mistress, he will leave nothing undone, that may stand within his duty, for the Queen of Scots and so far she may trust him and no further, for he was not subject to any faction and there was never yet one in England that heard him speak an evil word of the Q. of Scots, for she is a Princess born and tender to his mistress. Therefore he had given counsel plainly to the Queen his own mistress to deal with the Q. of Scotland's self by her own Councillors and make end with her'.[29]

Cecil did not relish the task of conferring with Mary. He relished it still less when Elizabeth told him that he must be careful not to succumb to Mary's charms as so many others had done.[30] He tried to beg off and rather opportunely, as Fénélon thought, fell sick.

Whether he was sick or not, he recovered rapidly when he got word that Elizabeth had decided to send Sir Francis Knollys in his place.[31] According to Fénélon, he prepared his own instructions and had them approved by his mistress. Fénélon thought them severe and De Spes pronounced them intolerable,[32] and believed that they were not seriously intended. According to Fénélon, some members of the Council were in favour of moderating them, but Cecil insisted upon handling the matter in his own terms and his own way. But he was not sanguine about the outcome. His only recorded observation is in a letter to Norris, September 25th:[33] 'I am thrown into a maze at this time, that I know not how to walk from dangers. Sir Walter Mildmay and I are sent to the Scottish Queen ... God be our guide for neither of us like the message.'

Just before he left Court he received a letter from Lady Margaret Lennox, enclosing two intercepted letters from Maitland to Mary and to Ross[34] which her husband, the Scottish Regent, had forwarded to her from Scotland. The letters were in cipher, but Cecil had them deciphered, and no doubt conveyed them rapidly to Elizabeth. The sum and substance of the advice to Ross was to accept any conditions however hard so that Mary regained her liberty. 'If', Maitland added, 'she were once at liberty I fear not that means shall be found to make both England and Scotland loathe to enterprise far against her.' To Mary he wrote that Elizabeth was not to be trusted, that she never meant to come to terms but that Mary should continue to treat with her and 'give her words as she does you'.

There is unhappily no record of Elizabeth's reaction to these revelations, but they must have served Cecil's purpose to increase her distrust of Mary's good intentions.

Cecil left the Court at Reading, in company with Mildmay, on September 26th. He ran into floods on the way[35] and did not reach Chatsworth in Derbyshire, where Mary was living in the custody of the Earl of Shrewsbury, until October 1st. He carried with him proposals for a treaty with Mary which followed closely the terms agreed upon by the Council in May: a league with England, and no offensive alliance with other powers against England; confirmation of the Treaty of Edinburgh; renunciation of all present title to the English throne; surrender of the English rebels; amends for border outrages against the English; pursuit of the murderers of Darnley and of the Earl of Murray; no marriage without the consent either of Elizabeth or of the present Lords of the Scottish Parliament; the fulfilment of these terms to be secured by six Scottish hostages, the surrender of the young King to English care and the delivery of Hume Castle, Fort Castle and a third stronghold in western Scotland to English garrisons.

These terms were considered by Mary in conference with the Bishop of Ross and the two English commissioners. She made her answer in writing on October 5th. In that answer she acquiesced in most of the demands, though she asked that her chief councillors should be excluded from the hostages and she declined to deliver the strongholds to English garrisons. She showed great reluctance to surrender the English rebels, but was prepared to do so if Elizabeth would pardon them.[36]

How Cecil impressed Mary and how Mary impressed Cecil is not recorded. There is nothing from Mary, and Cecil's written reports confine themselves to the details of the negotiations between them. He does speak often of her resort to tears, but he gives no inkling of his own appraisal of her.[37] The Bishop of Ross, who assisted her at the conference, wrote to the Duke of Norfolk that Mary had 'dealt with' Cecil 'firmly, in such sort that he has promised to be her friend'. According to Ross, Cecil 'liked her nature very well and confirmed his opinion that Lethington's saying to him was true, which was that the Queen of Scots was of a clement and gentle nature and was disposed to be governed by counsel of them in whom she reposeth her trust. He promises to travail that she and the Queen of England shall speak together and hath given her counsel how she should behave herself in that case to win the Queen of England's favour'.[38] Evidently Cecil laid himself out to be agreeable. According to Ross he even intimated that he would promote the Mary-Norfolk match. It is impossible to say whether Cecil was trying to pull wool over the eyes of Mary and Ross, or Ross trying to quicken the ardour of Norfolk. Certainly Cecil must have smiled when the Bishop's letter fell into his hands.

On October 5th Cecil and Mildmay sent to Elizabeth their first detailed report on the negotiations. It contained a statement of their demands and of Mary's rejoinders.[39] Elizabeth laid it before her Council and dispatched her reply on October 13th.

During the interval Cecil slipped away for a few days to take the baths at Buxton.[40] He resumed negotiations with Mary when he had received Elizabeth's letter.[41] What she said substantially was that she would entertain none of Mary's objections. She insisted that Mary should accept her terms virtually unaltered. She evidently thought, however, that Mary's general acquiescence justified a further consideration of the problem of Mary's relations with her subjects. And so the second part of the conference was directed to these two considerations:

  1. Mary's reply to Elizabeth's reply.
  2. Mary's relations to her subjects.

On the first point Mary conceded almost everything. Her only significant objection was to the surrender of Scottish strongholds, Hume Castle and the rest, to English garrisons.

On the second point Cecil had come instructed. He proposed that Mary's abdication should be cancelled, but that all the public acts in Scotland since should be accepted as good and lawful, subject to the adjudication of a committee of twelve to be chosen in part by Mary and in part by Lennox. In matters religious all laws and regulations during the regency should be accepted without review. All property seized by the warring factions should be returned to its owners, and all clergymen should remain undisturbed in their parishes; there was to be a general action of oblivion for all political offenders, and a Privy Council of twelve should be established of which Lennox was to be a member.

The provisions for the security of the King's party seem rather inadequate. But it was understood that they were subject to revision when commissioners for the King's party came to negotiate. Mary accepted them, taking issue only with the religious acts under the regency.[42]

And so the conference ended. Cecil and his colleagues left Chatsworth on October 15th and were back at Court on the 25th.[43]

Elizabeth's announced intentions were to lay the tentative arrangements with Mary before commissioners for the Marians and for the King's party who were called upon to assemble in London.

And then follows a long tedious interval when nothing was done, awaiting the arrival of the commissioners of the King's party. The delay was intentional, while Elizabeth was engaged in mending her fences with France.[44]

CHAPTER II

CECIL BECOMES LORD BURGHLEY, 1571

B Y midsummer of 1570 it was reasonably clear that the Third French Civil War was drawing to its close. Negotiations for peace had begun in January and had dragged on through the spring and summer. By August 1st the end was in sight. Sentiment in England on the subject was divided. Fénélon represented Cecil and his following as opposed to the peace, fearing that it would be followed, as it had been followed in the First Civil War, by a resolute and united attack upon England. In any case Elizabeth decided to send an envoy to France, before the negotiations were finished, with the idea of offering her services as a mediator and of urging the Huguenots not to accept unfavourable terms. The man selected for the mission was Francis Walsingham.

He was, without much question, Cecil's choice,[1] but he was evidently well regarded by Leicester. His Protestant sympathies were pronounced and outspoken, his hostility to Mary Queen of Scots well known. These very attributes commended him to Cecil. Fénélon regarded him as a trouble-breeder.

Cecil drafted his instructions, which directed him to the French King to plead for a stable peace based upon toleration for the Huguenots. It was anticipated that the King would express surprise at Elizabeth's plea for toleration when she herself did not tolerate Roman Catholicism. And this gave Cecil the opportunity to turn the papal bull to advantage. The Huguenots were loyal subjects. The English Catholics, by papal decree, had become political traitors. In response to any inquiries about Mary Stuart, Walsingham was to say that negotiations for her release and restoration were well advanced. He was also to establish contacts with the Huguenots and to urge them to stand fast for their terms, though he was to offer them no further aid in money.[2]

These instructions are interesting as setting forth the official position of England at the time. They turned out to be largely irrelevant because news came before Walsingham left London that the Peace of St. Germain had been signed in France.

But since the objective of his mission was to sound out French attitudes and to assure the French Huguenots of Elizabeth's continuing solicitude, he went nevertheless, was kindly received at Court and, though the King and his mother both showed some curiosity about Mary Queen of Scots, they accepted his assurances in good part. In a brief appraisal of the French situation to Leicester[3] Walsingham weighed the prospects of the peace, finding as the most favourable sign the hostility of the King to the house of Guise and the increase in favour of the Montmorencis. He thought that the attitude of the King's brother, the Duke of Anjou, was one of the unfavourable auspices.

The pro-English party in France two years before had suggested that the easiest way to divert Anjou from his hostile purposes towards England was to hold out hope of a marriage with the Queen of England herself.[4] At the time Elizabeth had not been much interested. She was busy pursuing her affair with the Archduke Charles. But the following summer, after the collapse of the German courtship, she began to consider favourably the idea of a French marriage, and she intimated as much to Fénélon. The French at first were not responsive.

After the re-establishment of civil peace in France the Cardinal Châtillon, Admiral Coligny's brother, broached the matter to Anjou himself. Catherine de Medicis wrote to Fénélon about it on October 20th.[5] She raised doubts about Elizabeth's sincerity in matters of courtship, and expressed the opinion that probably Elizabeth did not intend to marry at all. Her suggestion to Fénélon was that he discuss secretly with Cecil the possibilities of inducing Elizabeth to name a female as her successor and then arrange a marriage between that lady and Anjou. The suggestion was naïve to say the least. Even more naïve were her observations about Cecil. She understood, he said, that he was allied to a house which had always opposed the Queen of Scots.[6] What she plainly had in mind was the Suffolk line. Fénélon was to urge Cecil to induce Elizabeth to name *quel femme ou fille* of that line to succeed her, letting him understand that if he were successful he might win glory for his house, eternal fame for himself and more authority than ever in the English government. Catherine de Medicis had in mind Catherine Grey, forgetting that she was dead and that she had left no daughters behind her.

Fénélon[7] in his reply set her right about the facts but went on to say that another Huguenot refugee in England, the Vidame de Chartres, had made an analogous suggestion to Cecil earlier in the summer. Fénélon observed that though sentiment at Court was definitely favourable to a match between Elizabeth and Anjou, the opposition was strong against any presumptive claims of the Suffolk line. It is to be remarked that Catherine de Medicis took no account of the presumptive claims of Mary Queen of Scots. Fénélon had not forgotten them, though he was discreet enough not to allude to them in his letter to the Queen Mother.

In some such wise the Anjou marriage project got started, with the French sceptical and the English eager.

On Cecil's attitude at this juncture contemporary opinion varies. When Guido Cavalcanti, one of those ubiquitous Italians who was serving at the time as a non-official agent for the Queen Mother, broached the matter to Cecil in December, Cecil received him kindly, but confessed that since he had been away from the Court sick for a long time and had not spoken with his mistress, he was out of touch with affairs.[8] We hear nothing otherwise of this protracted illness. Certainly he was entertaining a group of councillors at his house in Covent Garden early in December.[9]

Leicester told Fénélon that Cecil was strongly opposed — indeed opposed to any husband for Elizabeth, except himself, who was more king than she was queen.[10]

Fénélon was still doubtful of Cecil's position when he wrote to Catherine early in February, and nearly a month later he wrote: 'I hear that Cecil, although he has spoken honourably about the match, does not want it and does not hope for it.'[11] Cecil had told him that the Cardinal Châtillon and the Vidame de Chartres had both urged the matter upon the Queen and that she had listened to them, but had not yet responded; that he did not think the matter could be agreed upon soon nor for a long time accomplished, and that outside the point of religion, the jealousy of other princes and other major difficulties, Anjou was too near successor to the throne of France and, if he did succeed, England would cease to be a kingdom and would become a province of France.

It was not indeed until April 15th that Fénélon was satisfied that Cecil definitely favoured the match.[12]

All of which may be taken to mean that Cecil was not disclosing his position and that Leicester was trying to keep the French marriage in his own hands by misrepresenting Cecil's attitude towards it.

Early in March, Cecil wrote to Walsingham:[13]

'Her Majesty repeated again unto me that I should write you of the great matter which I desired might be in a letter from herself to you, but her Majesty thought it sufficient to be imparted unto you in this sort following. If any person of value shall deal with you to understand your mind in the case of her Majesty's marriage you may say that at your coming from hence, upon some common bruit of such a matter concerning her Majesty and Monsieur D'Anjou, you sought what to think or report thereof, and this you are assured, that at your coming out of England, her Majesty, upon consideration of the benefit of her realm and to content her subjects, resolved to marry if she should find a person in estate and condition fit for her to match withal, and that she meant not to marry but with a person of the family of a prince, and you may add that you cannot by any means perceive that her Majesty is altered from that disposition, so as you may conclude that if any such matter be moved to you by any meet person to deal therein, you will advertise her Majesty thereof. . . .

'If God shall order this marriage, or any other to take place you may well judge no time would be wasted, otherwise than honour may require. I am not able to discern what is best, but surely I see no continuance of her quietness without a marriage. And therefore I remit the success to Almighty God.'

It may have been about this time[14] that Cecil drew up one of his characteristic memoranda on the subject. He began by arguing strongly, as he had always argued, in favour of the Queen's marriage. His great fear had always been that Elizabeth would die without offspring and that England would be plunged into another War of the Roses among candidates competing to succeed her. He recognized that even if Elizabeth married she might yet be childless, but, he went on, if she were married 'there would long be the possibility of children, the people would still cling to the hope that the Crown would remain in the line of King Henry VIII, and the curious and dangerous question of the succession would in the minds of quiet subjects, be, as it were, buried — a happy funeral for all England'.[15]

Then Cecil turned to the question of the bridegroom. Should she, in short, marry Anjou?

He stated first the reasons against it. Anjou was scarcely more than a boy. He was obviously much more Catholic than he was Protestant. As a Frenchman he would be unwelcome to the English. The old Anglo-Burgundian alliance would be ruptured. If the French King died without offspring the offspring of a match between Elizabeth and Anjou would unite the two kingdoms. If there were no offspring, Anjou might 'encroach upon the Crown, by colour perhaps of gift from the Pope, Elizabeth's life might be prematurely shortened, Anjou might then marry the Scottish Queen and so bring three kingdoms under himself'.

On the other hand:

France and England would be joined together in close alliance and the King of Spain would no longer take liberties with English subjects. 'The Pope's malice with his bulls and excommunications . . . would be suspended and vanish in smoke. Ireland would no longer be in daily peril of revolt, the Duke would bring a handsome revenue from his duchies and if he did, as perhaps he might, accept the English faith, Protestantism would be established in France and throughout Christendom.' Cecil dreamed also of the recovery of Calais, and even of a balanced budget. In a word, the result to be expected from a marriage was security at home against civil war, security abroad against crusading combinations of Catholic powers.

He evidently counted on Elizabeth's acquiescence, but he advised her to feign reluctance in order to obtain better terms. He advised her also to proceed as though yielding to the suit of her nobility, in order to escape the popular odium to a French match.

He recognized that a major difficulty would be the religious one, and he proposed to allow Anjou the private use of his religion though he should attend Elizabeth at her daily services, conceding that the service might be in Latin. And Anjou was to agree to be instructed of the truth and sufficiency of the Church of England and to avoid public scandal in the private exercise of his own faith.

Cecil was, in short, prepared to go far in the matter of religion. There can be no doubt of his zeal for the match.

Meanwhile on February 25th, 1571, Elizabeth had raised Cecil to the peerage as Baron of Burghley.[16] The reasons of the creation as set forth in the Letters Patent ran as follows:

'As well for the long services in the time of our progenitors, kings of England, as also for the faithful and acceptable duty and observance which he hath always performed from the very beginning of our reign, and ceaseth not daily to perform many ways, not only in the great and mighty affairs of Council but generally also in all other enterprises for the realm, and also for his circumspection, stoutness, wisdom, dexterity, integrity of life, providence, care and faithfulness.' (Circumspectionem, strenuitatem, prudentiam, dexteritatem, vitae integritatem, providentiam, curam et fidelitatem.) The words are hardly extravagant.

We have a contemporary account of the 'rites and ceremonies' attending this creation. It took place in the Presence Chamber at Westminster. A procession formed outside the door of the chamber, first the heralds, two and two together,

B

followed by Garter King of Arms walking alone and carrying the charter of crea-tion in his hands. After that came Lord Hunsdon, carrying the baron's cloak, and after that Cecil himself, escorted by the Earl of Leicester on his right and Lord Cobham on his left. In this colourful array the procession entered the Presence Chamber, 'making their obeisance'. Then Garter King of Arms presented the charter to the Lord Chamberlain, who handed it to the Queen. She delivered it to John Wooley, her Latin Secretary (it was of course in Latin) to be read. At the appropriate place in the reading, Elizabeth herself took the cloak from Hunsdon and hung it around Cecil's shoulders and pronounced him Baron of Burghley. She then handed him the charter of his appointment.

Cecil responded with words of thanks. The trumpet blew, the procession re-formed and went off to dinner, the Queen probably along with them. During dinner the heralds gathered and, having first proclaimed Elizabeth's title in Latin, French and English, drew a little further off and repeated the title of the new baron 'in these words, "*Du très noble Seigneur Guilliaume Cecil, chevalier Baron de Burgh-ley*"'. After that the heralds made their obeisance and, uttering their customary cry for *largesse*, withdrew. And so the ceremony ended.[17]

Leicester wrote to Walsingham[18] that the intention was to make the new peer Lord Privy Seal, but in the meantime he would remain Secretary with Sir Thomas Smith to assist him. Cecil himself wrote to Walsingham on March 3rd: 'Sir Thomas Smith I trust shall be admitted to the Council tomorrow and shortly after to be Secretary.'[19] Smith was named a councillor, but his appointment to be Secretary was deferred for over a year.[20]

The Spanish ambassador in London reported to his master that Elizabeth had raised Cecil to the peerage so that he might be more useful in Parliament and about the Queen of Scotland.[21] But this is hardly plausible. Certainly Cecil's value in the turbulent House of Commons was much greater than in the subservient House of Lords. Probably the best explanation is in Elizabeth's desire to recognize his unique services and his increasing disability, by reason of the gout, which almost incapacitated him in the early winter of 1570-71.

Cecil, in writing to his friend, Nicholas White, on March 2nd remarked: 'My style is Lord of Burghley, if you mean to know it for your writing, and if you list to write truly, the poorest Lord in England.'[22] Hereafter he signed his name William Burghley.

He affected to take the matter lightly, but rank and station and prestige meant far too much to him to be careless of a distinction which Elizabeth was very chary about conferring. Camden remarks that in the first twelve years of Elizabeth's reign she had created only three peers before him. He must have been very reluctant to give up the office of Secretary, which in his hands had become little short of prime minister, and through which he had drawn all the reins of the ad-ministration into his own hands. It was that reluctance very likely, plus a marked improvement in his bodily health, that led him to hang on for another year.

Doubtless his reluctance was increased by the uncertainties of the Scottish situation and its repercussions on Anglo-French relations. It is clear that one strong reason for his support of the Anjou match was that he regarded it as an easy way to dispose of the menace of Mary Stuart.

As French interest in the Anjou match developed, interest in the welfare of Mary Stuart seems to have declined.

Early in January 1571 Mary's commissioners from Scotland arrived, and Elizabeth named a committee from the Council, including Bacon, Leicester, Sussex, Cecil and Mildmay to deal with them.[23]

There was vigorous debate on the subject in Council before the king's commissioners arrived. Cecil wrote a ten-page memorandum in which he rehearsed the conventional arguments against Mary's restoration, and he drew up a 'Note of reasons remembered in Council to move the Q. Majesty not to release the Queen of Scots'[24] which was probably intended for Elizabeth's perusal.

Once again he rang the familiar charges against Mary, from her failure to ratify the Peace of Edinburgh to her assistance of the rebellious earls in the Rising of the North. Once again he made reference to her lack of faith, to her hostile intentions, to the danger that she might become the head of a Catholic league against England, to her certain overthrow of Elizabeth's friends in Scotland.

Upon one consideration Cecil laid considerable stress. 'If', he wrote, 'the Queen's Majesty shall put her [Mary] to liberty, whereby she must needs come to government, she shall then, by implication, discharge her of her heinous crime, whereof she was accused before her Majesty and to the which she never did make any plain answer for her acquittal. For after she be restored to government, the Queen's Majesty shall never have opportunity to denounce her former faults and crimes.'

In short, Cecil felt that by the liberation of Mary the whole basis upon which her trial and her retention had been justified would be destroyed.

The final passage in the memorandum is significant since it suggested the course which Elizabeth elected to follow: 'If it were found necessary to deliver Mary, it may be that the protracting of some terms in the treaty, which may be allowable in a matter of so great moment, specially in treating upon the [matter] of assurances, may percase otherwise do good. For haste herein may hinder other things in hand. And if the Queen of Scots shall either not be willing, or shall pretend disability to satisfy the Queen's Majesty in her reasonable demands, her Majesty may then, both in honour and reason, answer the French King and all others that the default of delivery of the Queen of Scots groweth not of lack of good will in her Majesty but for lack of assurance from the Q. of Scots.'

No course was more congenial to Elizabeth than one of procrastination.

In this course she was assisted by the dilatory tactics of the King's party in Scotland. Their delegation did not arrive until late in February, they objected strongly to Mary's restoration, insisted that they were not authorized to accede to any such terms and demanded permission to return to Scotland and consult Parliament on the subject. Elizabeth allowed them to go.

Fénélon, in despair, informed his master that he thought this concession marked the end of the hopes of a treaty.

And so indeed it did. Fénélon was of the opinion that Elizabeth's volte-face was brought about by a report from Walsingham in France, that a project was afoot there to marry Mary to the Duke of Anjou.[25] This may have been a factor, but the most important factor was the growing evidence of a conspiracy to release Mary by force and to set her upon the English throne.

At just about the time that Burghley got the first inklings of this conspiracy, Elizabeth called Parliament together. Her object was to get money. The expenses involved in suppressing the Rising of the North and the subsequent punitive expedition against the Scottish borders had been met by forced loans, but they merely postponed the day of reckoning. Burghley indeed had recognized the necessity of summoning Parliament a year earlier,[26] but Elizabeth, recalling the stormy sessions of the previous Parliament, postponed the evil day as long as she might. She remembered too well the efforts of her previous Parliament to get some commitment from her in the matter of the succession and of her marriage. On that occasion she had made promises which she had not fulfilled, and she no doubt feared that they would once more be called forcibly to her attention. Her fears in that particular turned out to be groundless. The one dominant interest in the Parliament of 1571 was religion. It had been broached in the previous Parliament, but without passionate bitterness and with no results. Puritanism had gained headway in the interval and it was a House of Commons dominated by Puritan ideas that presented bill after bill in an effort to secure further reform of the Church.

Burghley of course was no longer in the Commons. In this Parliament he made his début as a peer of the realm. He was certainly very active in parliamentary business. La Mothe Fénélon refers to one speech which he delivered in the Lords,[27] apparently on a bill to enforce attendance in the Established Church and to compel the taking of Communion at least once a year. It was of course directed against the crypto-Catholics who were systematically evading the Act of Uniformity. According to Fénélon, Burghley's speech was in support of the bill and followed the line that, in the interest of order, obedience to the laws regulating religious observance must be enforced. But there is no mention of it elsewhere, although the official journal names Burghley as a member of the committee to which the bill was referred after the second reading.[28] The bill in amended form subsequently passed the Lords, went back to the Commons and after two conferences with the Lords was finally passed. But it was vetoed by the Queen. The interesting fact about the matter was that Burghley apparently supported a position in matters religious not in accord with the royal wishes. But the evidence is too scant to be conclusive.

Apart from his activity in the Lords he also interested himself with what was going on in the Commons. The Queen wanted the Commons to get on with the subsidy and go home. In a message on April 10th she tried to quicken their proceedings. On the 21st Burghley got from the Speaker a list of the bills current in the House, and learned that though twenty-one bills had passed first reading and to the second reading, only one had gone to the Lords, and the subsidy bill had not yet been presented. Burghley commented on the situation in a letter to Walsing-ham early in May:[29]

'Our Parliament is daily new with child with projects for laws, that I was never so weary.' Apparently it was part of his business to follow procedure in the Commons and to keep his royal mistress fully posted.[30]

One of the interesting features of the session was the close co-operation between the Lords and the Commons, and the frequent conferences on points of disagreement between them. Quite conceivably this was evidence of Burghley's guiding hand. At any rate, in the closing speech, Bacon, the Lord Keeper, while he castigated the lower House for meddling with matters of religion, took special occasion in the Queen's name to compliment the Lords on their 'diligence, discretion and orderly proceedings, . . . much to their honour and commendation and much to her comfort and consolation'. Maybe De Spes was not altogether wrong after all when he declared that Elizabeth had elevated Burghley to the peerage in order that he might be more useful in Parliament.

It was against the background of a rampant Puritan House of Commons that the Ridolfi Plot gradually unfolded.

CHAPTER III

THE RIDOLFI PLOT, 1571-72

BURGHLEY himself wrote the story of the Ridolfi Plot in its earlier stages,[1] intended probably for publication but apparently never published. He did not tell the complete story. Parts of it involved disloyal behaviour by some important people whom it was not expedient to expose and techniques which it was not desirable to reveal. He began with Robert Ridolfi, a Florentine banker resident in London, who was an ardent Catholic and had wide acquaintance among the great ones at the English Court. Ridolfi knew the Duke of Norfolk well, and Mary's ambassador, the Bishop of Ross, and the Spanish ambassador — was engaged in banking business with all of them. In the autumn of 1569, at the time when Norfolk first fell under suspicion, Ridolfi was arrested, 'as one that had been seen and known very conversant and in practices with the Bishop of Ross, and that had also not long before received great sums of money from Flanders by bills of exchange, . . . suspiciously paid to the said Ross and other the Queen of Scots' ministers, and part to some servants of the Duke of Norfolk'. Having been arrested, Ridolfi was committed to the custody of Francis Walsingham, as shrewd a man as anyone in Burghley's service. He admitted that he had conveyed money from overseas for the use of the Scottish Queen, that he had loaned money to Ross and to Norfolk, but protested that it was all in the way of his banking business. It is sufficient testimony to his cleverness that he hoodwinked both Walsingham and Burghley, was subsequently released and on occasion consulted about government banking problems. In the spring of 1571 he announced his desire to go to Italy on private business, talked with Elizabeth herself at Greenwich and secured from her a 'very favourable' passport under her own hand.

At this time the English government accepted him at his face value, and there is no evidence that he was suspected of any nefarious intentions. The air, however, was full of rumours of hostile purposes, some from Spain, some from the Catholic refugees in the Low Countries,[2] and Burghley was keeping careful watch at the ports and particularly upon the goings back and forth of the messengers of the Bishop of Ross.

Early in April two men were picked up at Dover coming from the Low Countries, one of them Charles Bailly, a Scotsman in the employ of the Bishop of Ross. He was examined and searched. A portmanteau containing prohibited books was found upon him and a packet of letters for Ross. These were sent up to London to Lord Cobham, Warden of the Cinque Ports. He delivered the books to Burghley, but secretly, at the instigation of a renegade brother, withheld the letters. Burghley ordered Bailly's imprisonment and arranged to place a spy in the same prison. The spy in question was William Herle, a dissolute cousin of the Lady

Northumberland who had been arrested for complicity in the northern rebellion — a cunning fellow who lent himself eagerly to Burghley's purpose. He was a Welshman by birth and later claimed descent from the same Welsh family as the Cecils. Herle managed to worm his way into Bailly's confidence and discovered that he was exchanging letters in cipher with the Bishop of Ross and conferring secretly with the secretary of the Spanish ambassador. 'Whereupon,' Burghley relates, 'suspicion was then conceived that this Charles had some greater matter in charge than the bringing in of . . . books. And so, after Charles had sent 4 or 5 small letters to the Bishop and had received as many or more, all which, written in cipher, were intercepted, it was thought good suddenly to attack Charles and cause him to decipher these letters, for that as they passed there were true copies kept of some of them.' Thereupon Charles was removed to the Tower and by order of the Privy Council[3] put to the rack. Partly by torture and partly by bribery he was induced to give up the keys of his cipher.

'In the end,' Burghley wrote, 'after much ado with Charles, an alphabet was gotten and about a week after Easter (April 15) it was perceived by those letters that Charles had brought over with him certain packets of letters from Ridolfi and from the Earl of Westmorland and the Countess of Northumberland and others.' It was discovered also that these letters had been withheld by Cobham and sent to the Bishop of Ross who prepared forged letters instead for Burghley's perusal. Burghley in his narrative suppressed Cobham's part in the business, though he wrote to his friend, the Earl of Shrewsbury, in October 1571: 'My Lord of Cobham is in my house a prisoner, who otherwise should have been in the Tower. I loved him well and therefore am sorry at his offence.'[4] Later, Burghley's son, Robert, was to marry Cobham's daughter.

Further examination of Charles revealed the fact that among these letters were three special letters in cipher, one directed to Ross, the other two without address but endorsed 'with 2 algorism figures [arabic numerals] one to 40 the other to 30'. Charles at first denied any knowledge of their contents, but later admitted that 30 and 40 were two English noblemen and that the letters concerned a plot inviting the King of Spain, the Duke of Alva and the Pope 'to cause war in this realm and to have a force of strangers enter into the realm'. 'Hereupon,' Burghley continued, 'her Majesty, conferring with her Council and finding this to be a dangerous enterprise, meet to be discovered and withstood, and presuming certainly [that] the Bishop of Ross knew these two Lords and the practice, it was thought convenient by the whole Council that the bishop should be charged therewith and forced to disclose what he knew.'

What Burghley did not write was that he himself had interrogated Charles three times without result, had threatened him with death and disfigurement and had sent him to the rack. Charles afterwards admitted to the Spanish ambassador that he had been persuaded to confess by one who called himself Dr. Story, who was in fact one of Burghley's agents. Charles's confession does not appear to be preserved, but we gather from two letters which he wrote to Burghley early in May that his tale was substantially what Burghley reported it to be.

Burghley's narrative went on: 'So four of the Council, the Earl of Essex, Burghley, Sir Ralph Sadler and Sir Walter Mildmay, were sent to speak with him [Ross] whom they found in his bed, as he said, sick. And being herewith charged, after many vehement denials of most of the things plainly confessed by Charles, yet in the end, perceiving that his dealings with Charles by his letters sent to him both in the Marshalsea and the Tower were discovered, he confessed that indeed Charles brought letters from Ridolfi, and that there were two such letters entitled with 40 and 30. And that 40 was to the Queen of Scots and 30 to the Spanish ambassador[5] ... Therefore it was thought good that he should be guarded and so he was by Mr. Skipwith and H. Kingswill ... In the meantime both the Queen of Scots was enquired of such letters[6] and the Spanish ambassador, who precisely denied the receipt of any such, or any at all from Ridolfi since his departure, as my Lord of Shrewsbury can tell for the Queen of Scots' answer and Sir Walter Mildmay and Sir Thomas Smith for the Spanish ambassador.

'Well, whereupon the Bishop, continuing his sickness, was newly charged by the Earl of Sussex, the L. Burghley, Sir Ralph Sadler and Sir Walter Mildmay with the denial of the Scottish Queen and of the Spanish ambassador, whereupon he answered first, that he was not to answer in matters concerning his affairs as ambassador, but, being told that he must answer for his dealings with any of the Queen's subjects concerning rebellions, at length he said that indeed the Q. of Scots had not her letter of 40 and that he had destroyed it and the alphabet of the cipher also ... And so no more knowledge could be got of the Bishop, who was also the more favourably dealt with because he kept his bed as a sick man. After this, when he was amended, he was conveyed to the Bishop of Ely's palace in Holborn.[7]

'Then after this, both in parliament time [April 2nd to May 29th] and afterwards great care was taken by the Council for the understanding who these two Lords should be. And from the other side of the seas daily intelligence was given of the rebels' [Catholic refugees] reports that before summer should end they should be in their former estates ... Many terrible speeches [were] reported by secret intelligence out of Flanders to her Majesty both before and whilst she was in her Progress. Whereupon she was moved by her Council that she would remain about London, only upon doubt of some great trouble both inward and beyond the seas. But her Majesty would not forbear her Progress, so as it might be near to London. Now, after St. Bartholomew's tide [August 24th], even while her Majesty was at the Duke of Norfolk's house by Walden [in Essex][8] where great means were used to her Majesty to put him to full liberty ... whereunto her Majesty seemed to give favourable ear, specially upon asseverations that he was thought that he would become a good subject and that he had foresaken the matter of the Q. of Scots and that he was not then suspected of her Majesty to be any of the two Lords ciphered with 40 and 30.

'Even then was it found by a good hap that he [Norfolk] had sent towards Bannister his man, being in Shropshire, certain money in gold to be conveyed into Scotland.'

The discovery of this transaction was a mere accident. Norfolk sent the money, some £600 in gold, by his secretary to a carrier, Thomas Browne, a Welsh draper bound for Shrewsbury, with instructions to deliver it to Bannister, Norfolk's steward. The secretary told Browne that the package contained some 50 pounds of silver. But Browne's suspicions were aroused. He opened the package, discovered that it contained not only £600 in gold but letters in cipher. He conveyed the news forthwith to Burghley.[9]

'Upon the taking of this money,' Burghley's narrative continues, 'and sundry letters therewith, whereof some were in cipher and some out of cipher, by those out of cipher it was first found that one Higford, the Duke of Norfolk's secretary, had written to Bannister at the same time and that it was likely that he was privy to the ciphered letters. Whereupon he was taken from the Duke without his knowledge and being straightly examined, he confessed that the Duke himself had sent that money.'

Burghley turned over the examination of Higford to Sir Thomas Smith and Dr. Thomas Wilson. Higford deciphered the ciphered letters as well as he could and told his examiners that the key to the cipher would be found at Howard House, 'under a mat, hard by the window's side where the map of England doth hang'.[10] Thereupon Norfolk was confined to his own house.

Smith and Wilson directed Sir Henry Neville, who was in charge of Norfolk, to find the cipher. He did not find it, and Smith and Wilson concluded that the Duke himself had been forewarned and had 'gotten away' with it. Neville did find a letter in cipher in the place of concealment, but the key to it was wanting.[11]

With that information Burghley wrote in haste to Sir Ralph Sadler to repair at once to Howard House. The letter pulled Sadler out of bed at one o'clock in the morning. He reached Howard House at eight, and found that Sir Henry Neville, acting no doubt under instructions, had confined the Duke to his room. Sadler reported that Neville was handling the situation admirably.

According to Burghley's narrative, Norfolk was examined by Sadler, Smith and Wilson while still at Howard House, 'and denied upon his oath . . . the knowledge of any part of the money or of the sending thereof in any sort. And so he was committed to the Tower where he began to confess that which he had before denied'.

At this point Burghley's narrative ends. The striking thing about it is that he made no claim to personal activity in the matter. As he tells the story, the discovery of the plot was due to two accidents, the accident of Bailly's capture with incriminating documents, and the accident of the Welsh draper, Thomas Browne, who deserves more credit than he has received.

We can follow the story easily from other sources. The seriousness of the situation seems to have impressed Norfolk when he learned of his impending imprisonment. 'He seemeth now very humble,' Sadler reported, 'and showeth as though he will come to open all.'

'So, having prepared a foot-cloth[12] nag for him, I, Sir Ralph Sadler on the one side and I, Dr. Wilson coming immediately after, with only our servants and friends accompanying us, he was betwixt four and five of the clock quietly brought into the Tower without any trouble, save a number of idle, rascal people, women, men, boys and girls, running about him, as the manner is, gazing at him.'

He was examined on the 8th. He admitted to the sending of the money to Scotland. He even admitted to correspondence with the Scottish Queen. But he told no more. He asked for an opportunity to confer privately with Burghley and Sadler, promising that he would reveal everything. Sadler urged that the request be granted. 'Indeed,' he wrote to Burghley, 'though it be painful to your Lordship to come hither, yet in my opinion it will serve to good purpose, for I perceive by the Duke that he will disclose to you that which, as I can guess by his manner of speech, he thinketh not meet to be uttered to others. And again, your Lordship being best acquainted with the matter of Ridolfi and all their practices, can best oppose the Duke, whereby the whole truth may be the same and better known, and so, expecting your Lordship's coming, I end.'[13]

But Burghley did not go. He had already received news that Norfolk's secretary had confessed that the Norfolk cipher key was concealed under the tiles at Howard House. Dr. Wilson found it there, and discovered that it was the key to the cipher letter which Neville had found earlier under the mat. The letter turned out to be one written in February by Mary to Ross. The gist of it was that Ridolfi was about to depart, that Mary thought he would be the best man to send to Spain, but that she left the decision to the Duke of Norfolk.[14] It made clear the close connection of Mary and Norfolk with Ridolfi's plans and purposes.

All this Burghley conveyed to Elizabeth, who directed that Norfolk's two secretaries, Higford and Barker, should be sent to the rack.[15] At this juncture she seems to have been vindictive to a degree. Probably the fact that Norfolk's implication was revealed just at the time she was visiting him at Audley End had something to do with it.

Barker in fact, under repeated pressure, revealed the whole story, part of it on September 19th, the rest of it on October 10th.[16]

Three days after that the Privy Council called the Mayor and Aldermen of London together and told them that the Pope and the King of Spain were involved with the Duke of Norfolk in a plot to dethrone Elizabeth and put Mary Queen of Scots in her place. The Mayor passed the news on to the London companies and it was presently common talk in the streets.[17] About the same time an account of the plot, probably officially inspired, was published.[18] With all the evidence in hand Norfolk was once again examined, this time by a committee of the Privy Council which included Clinton, Bedford, Burghley, Smith and the Attorney- and Solicitor-Generals.[19] Norfolk still insisted that he had seen Ridolfi only once, and had declined to ratify his plans. He denied that he had ever received a letter from Ridolfi — that is the famous No. 40 letter, the contents of which Barker had revealed in considerable detail. Norfolk admitted knowledge of a plan devised by Hugh Owen, servant of the Earl of Arundel, to steal Mary away, and implicated Sir Henry Percy, brother of the rebel Earl of Northumberland, in an analogous plan.

It was one of the shabbier aspects of the whole business that Norfolk, who was fighting a losing battle to save his own skin, seems to have had no qualms about betraying his friends.

From this point onward the investigation was directed chiefly to the confirmation of Barker's story, which smelt a little too much of the torture chamber, and to tracing the domestic ramifications of the Ridolfi Plot.

All the accumulated evidence revealed that Mary's ambassador, the Bishop of Ross, was deeply implicated. He had been examined in May when Bailly was taken and had been placed in custody of the Bishop of Ely at his town house in London. Later, when Parliament assembled, he had been removed to the country in order to keep him from intrigue with the assembled M.P.s.[20] He was, however, an ambassador and presumably enjoyed the immunities of an ambassador. Burghley submitted the problem of international law involved to five distinguished civilians in October. The sum and substance of their findings was that an ambassador who sought to procure rebellion against the prince to whom he was accredited lost his immunities and could be punished.[21]

Ross was accordingly examined by a committee of the Council, of which Bedford, Clinton, Burghley, Knollys and Smith were the principal figures. He apparently concluded that the game was up. He told the whole story of the plot, of his part in it, of his mistress's part in it, of the Spanish ambassador's part in it, of Norfolk's part in it. He told the story of Owen's plan to release Mary, of the involvement of Stanley and Percy and a number of lesser personages, of the hanky-panky with Bailly's packet.[22] In short, he left nothing untold.

Ross explained his betrayal to his mistress in a letter which he wrote to her on November 8th. He had discovered, he said, that Burghley knew everything anyway, and that the Privy Council had informed him that if he did not make a complete confession he would be punished for his participation. Ross appears to have been frightened out of his life. He even went so far as to tell Wilson that he was glad the whole matter had been exposed, that he thought Mary was not fit for any husband, that she had poisoned the French King, her first husband, had been party to the murder of her second and that she would not have kept faith with the Duke even if she had married him. Wilson observed in a letter to Burghley, 'Lord, what people are these! What a Queen! What an ambassador!'[23]

Ross took no account of the fact that his testimony served to confirm testimony otherwise suspect because it had been elicited under torture or the fear of torture. Without doubt it was his evidence most of all that secured Norfolk's subsequent conviction of high treason.

The case against Norfolk was complete by November 1st. At that point the further pursuit of it was delayed by one of Burghley's bad attacks of gout. He was about again before the end of the month.[24]

It is worth noting that all his efforts in the Ridolfi affair were directed towards the participation of English conspirators. Whether or not he had decided that if civil conspiracy were nipped foreign invasion would not be attempted, he proceeded on that assumption. And it proved to be sound. Philip II wrote to his ambassador in England on October 31st expressing grief at the news of Norfolk's imprisonment, '. . . because it frustrates a matter of so much importance . . . The thread of the business now being cut, there is no more to say to you about it'.

According to De Spes, Leicester and Burghley informed Elizabeth early in December that the case against Norfolk was complete, but Elizabeth as usual procrastinated and postponed action until after the holidays.[25] Norfolk was brought to trial on January 16th, 1572.

It is unfortunate that except for Burghley's memorandum we have almost nothing from him directly on the subject.[26] He made occasional references to it in his letters to Walsingham in France, and he kept Shrewsbury informed, but they add nothing to what we know already from other sources. No doubt he was the principal agent in pursuit of the investigation, though most of the detailed work was done by Smith and Wilson. There is little or no evidence of the effectiveness of any secret service. Even William Herle, who managed to ingratiate himself for a time both with Charles Bailly and with the Bishop of Ross, seems to have provoked the distrust of both of them before anything of great moment was revealed.

Before Norfolk was brought to trial, Elizabeth decided to get rid of the Spanish ambassador. Burghley set forth the case against him in his draft of a letter which went off from the Queen to the Duke of Alva on December 15th:

'We need not much to repeat to you how long we have misliked Guerau de Spes, whom the king, our good brother, sent hither in place of Signor Guzman de Silva . . . and how indeed by our letters and messages to the said king required that some other of better quality might be sent to revoke him . . . But why, either this unmeet and ungrateful person is not revoked, or no meeter sent, we know not. This we find most certainly and manifestly proved, that the said de Spes hath not amended his qualities but increased his practices to disturb our state, to corrupt our subjects, to stir up rebellion, to promise that which we trust he is not able to perform, to such as he findeth evil disposed, that the king, our good brother, will aid them and maintain them against us, with a multitude of such like. So as we can no more endure him to continue than a person that would secretly seek to inflame our realm with fire brands, and hereupon we have given him order to depart, without entering into any particular debate, whereunto he is naturally given.'[27] Burghley's own account of the affair appears in a letter he wrote to Sir Thomas Smith, in France on other business, two weeks later:

'Since your departure from hence there hath no new thing of value happened but the discharge of the late Spanish ambassador, who hath both in office and out of office used himself very crookedly, perniciously and maliciously against the state and namely and openly against me, not forbearing but in open Council, directing his speech to me, saying that I had been and was the cause of all the unkindness that had chanced betwixt the king his master and the Queen's Majesty. Whereunto, as it became me for truth's sake, I answered with more modest terms than he deserved and referred myself to all the Lords in Council to report of me whether anything had been said or done by me from the beginning of these broils concerning him or his master, or the arrest, that had not been ordered and directed by

THOMAS HOWARD, 4TH DUKE OF NORFOLK

her Majesty in Council, all of which the whole Lords did affirm, and my Lord of Sussex, in the Italian tongue, did very plainly and very earnestly confirm it. But yet his choler would not be so tempered, and so he was dismissed and Mr. Knollys appointed to tend on him at his house.

'This was done the 13th[28] of this month, until the 24th he could not be gotten out of town and then he went to Greenwich and on St. Stephen's Day [December 26th] to Gravesend, where he yet remaineth, but this day or tomorrow he is to remove to Canterbury and John Hawkins (with whom he is well enough agreed notwithstanding the brawl that hath been for Hawkins' spoil of the Indies) is now appointed to pass him over at Dover to Calais.'[29]

When De Spes got home he wrote an account of his embassy in which he included a pen portrait of Burghley:

'The principal person in the Council at present is William Cecil, now Lord Burghley, a Knight of the Garter. He is a man of mean sort but very astute, false, lying and full of all artifice. He is a great heretic and such a clownish Englishman as to believe that all the Christian princes joined together are not able to injure the sovereign of his country, and he therefore treats their ministers with great arrogance. This man manages the bulk of the business and by means of his vigilance and craftiness, together with his utter unscrupulousness of word and deed, thinks to outwit the ministers of other princes. This, to a certain extent, he hath hitherto succeeded in doing.'[30]

De Spes said that the English wanted to get him out of England before Norfolk was brought to trial. Froude on the other hand has maintained that De Spes tried to prolong his leave-taking until the fruition of a plot against the life of Burghley himself.[31]

On January 4th, Burghley received a letter, unsigned. The important part of it ran as follows:

'Of late I have, upon discontent, entered into a conspiracy with some others to slay your Lordship, and, the time appointed, a man with a perfect hand attended you three several times in your garden to have slain your Lordship. The which not fallen out, and continuing in the former mischief, the height of your study window is taken towards the garden, minding, if they miss this means, to slay you with a shot upon the terrace, or else, in coming late from the Court, with a pistolet. And being touched with some remorse of so bloody a deed I warn your Lordship of their evil and desperate meaning.'[32]

The result of this warning was that two hare-brained young men, Kenelm Berney and Edmund Mather, were captured and examined. The intervening steps can only be guessed at. It does appear, however, that William Herle was a party to their deliberations, the same William Herle who had been used as a stool-pigeon against Charles Bailly. Probably Herle disclosed the plot to Burghley. He wrote a somewhat ambiguous letter to Burghley on December 18th, 1571, in which he reported an interview with a person not named. Apparently Herle had won the confidence of the person in question by pretending to be an enemy of Burghley. The substance of Herle's report was a virulent attack by the unknown upon

Burghley—his tyranny and his ambition, his domination of his Queen, his opposition to her marriage lest it would diminish his own power, his support of the Suffolk claim to the succession, and so forth. This sounds like either Berney or Mather.[33]

From their confessions it appeared that Mather was the active spirit, impelled, so he said, by a desire to save the Duke of Norfolk. According to Mather he was in frequent conference with the Spanish ambassador, Guerau de Spes. Mather declared that De Spes suggested the idea of assassinating Burghley, and De Spes's steward, Borghese, actively promoted it.

On January 23rd Burghley wrote to Walsingham:[34] 'Mather hath in presence of my Lord of Leicester, Mr. Treasurer, Mr. Mildmay, manfully charged Borghese the Spanish ambassador's secretary, that his master and he both enticed Mather to murder me; and Borghese denying it, Mather hath offered to try it, *con la spada* etc.'

At the time the plot was discovered, De Spes was on his way out. But Burghley sent a quick message to Henry Knollys, who had attended De Spes in Canterbury, to arrest Borghese. He was arrested and sent to London in the custody of the Mayor of Canterbury.

Berney and Mather were executed on February 10th. It had been the day fixed for Norfolk's execution. All the preparations had been made on Tower Hill and a crowd of many thousands had gathered to view the spectacle. But the Queen at the last minute granted a reprieve, and the assembled Londoners had to be satisfied with much smaller fry.[35]

Borghese,[36] after a cautious examination and something like a month of what De Spes called intermingled threats and promises, was released and went overseas to join his master in Brussels.

It is hard to take this conspiracy seriously. We have no account of the trial. All the available evidence is based upon the confession of the two culprits, exacted no doubt under torture or the threat of torture. Herle may have testified against them at the trial, but he was hardly a man to be trusted. The plans of the conspirators seem to have been vague in the extreme. The story that they got so far as to lie in wait for Burghley does not come out in their testimony. The complicity of the Spanish ambassador, by the extant evidence, rests upon Mather's mere word. One cannot avoid the suspicion that William Herle fell in with a couple of discontented, ambitious, hare-brained young fellows, who talked rashly of what they might do, rather than of what they meant to do. By their own account, De Spes's part in the business went no further than to encourage them in their aspirations to get rid of Burghley. There was apparently no one else involved. But it added up to something like treason and placed Burghley in the position of having risked his life in the service of his mistress. In a less critical time it would probably not have been taken so seriously.

Norfolk was brought to trial on January 16th, 1572.[37] There was some fear of a popular demonstration in his favour. Guards were posted in all the streets and Norfolk was brought from the Tower by water.[38] He was tried in Westminster Hall before a court of his peers, with the Earl of Shrewsbury presiding as Lord

Steward. Twenty-six peers formed the court, among them were Leicester, Sussex, Bedford and Burghley. Both Chief Justices were present, and a number of members of the Queen's household and of her Privy Council.

Norfolk was denied counsel, but he was courteously treated and the case against him completely documented. Of all the peers present, Burghley was the only one to take any active part in the proceedings — once to correct the prosecuting attorney on a matter of fact, once on an ambiguity of date and once to ask Norfolk a question.

'My Lord,' said Burghley, 'did you ever desire to have any proofs or witnesses produced for your part to prove anything that might make for you? And were you denied?'

Norfolk replied: 'I have divers times prayed that if anything were denied to be true which I said, I might be driven to my proof of it.'

At which Burghley observed: 'I ask it because I have not heard it reported to her Majesty that you made any such request to have any special witnesses examined or proofs heard on your part.'

Norfolk's reply, if he did reply, is not recorded. His case, so far as he made any case, was to admit knowledge of the conspiracy but to deny complicity in it. Actually, in view of the evidence, which was produced at length in the trial, the fact of his treason can hardly be gainsaid. There can be little doubt that he was a reluctant traitor. He stood ready to profit by treason, but he was never an active agent in Ridolfi's plans and purposes and, as he himself pointed out in his trial, he never took any steps to organize his very considerable following in support of domestic rebellion. The verdict was a foregone conclusion. He was found guilty and condemned to a traitor's death.[39]

But the verdict could not be carried out without royal warrant. It was rumoured that he was to be executed on the last day of January. But the Queen hesitated. Twice the people flocked to the Tower and twice they were disappointed.[40] It was currently rumoured that Elizabeth was softening. Certainly she was hesitating. On January 23rd Burghley wrote to Walsingham:

'The Queen's Majesty hath been always a merciful lady and by mercy she hath taken more herein than by justice, and yet she thinks that she is more beloved in doing herself harm.'

On February 11th Burghley wrote again to Walsingham: 'I cannot write you what is the inward cause of the stay of the Duke of Norfolk's death, only I find her Majesty diversely disposed. Some time when she speaketh of her danger, she concludeth that justice should be done, another time she speaketh of his nearness of blood, of his superiority of honour, etc., she stayeth. As upon Saturday she signed a warrant ... for his execution on Monday, and so all preparations were made ... and concourse of many thousands yesterday in the morning, but their coming was answered by another, ordinary execution ... And the cause of the disappointment was this. Suddenly, on Sunday, late in the night, the Queen's Majesty sent for me and entered into a great misliking that the duke should die the next day and said she was and should be disquieted and said she would have a new warrant made that night to the sheriffs, to forbear until they should hear further. And so they did. God's will be fulfilled and aid her Majesty to do herself good.'[41]

A fortnight later a new warrant went to the sheriff for Norfolk's execution on the last day of February. Once again the warrant was recalled, only two hours before the day of execution.[42]

So February passed into March, and nothing was done. It looked, indeed, as though Norfolk was to be spared. Then, late in the month, Elizabeth had a sudden seizure, colic followed by fever. For several hours her life was despaired of.[43] According to Fénélon, Leicester and Burghley together spent three entire nights at her bedside. Elizabeth told Fénélon afterwards that she attributed it to some fish she had eaten. Burghley wrote of it to Smith and Walsingham in France on the 20th. Unfortunately his letter is missing, but Smith's reply to it gives some measure of the panic it created among Elizabeth's faithful servants.

'Your Lordship's letters of the 20th of March made us, both Mr. Walsingham and me in the reading, for we read them both together, in a marvellous agony; but having the medicine ready, that her Majesty was within an hour recovered,[44] it did in part heal us again. But, as your Lordship writeth, the care doth not yet cease in you, you may be assured it doth as little cease in us, calling to our remembrance and laying before our eyes the trouble, the uncertainty, the disorder, the peril and danger which had been like to follow if at that time God had taken from us that stay of the Commonwealth and hope of our repose, that lantern of our light next God, whom to follow, nor certainty where to light another candle. But if the Queen's Majesty do still continue in extremities to promise, in recoveries to forget, what shall we say but as Italians do, *Passato il pericolo gabbato il santo*.'[45]

But the fight was not without its compensating advantages. It made some action imperative. We do not know whose idea it was to call Parliament, nor what pressure was exerted upon Elizabeth to consent.[46] But the writs went out on March 28th and Parliament gathered accordingly on May 8th. The reason for its assembling, as stated in the opening speech by the Lord Keeper, was to provide laws adequate to deal with the great treasons and conspiracies but just revealed.[47]

It had not been long in session before it became a clamorous voice to deal with Mary Stuart as she deserved and to make short work of Norfolk. Elizabeth found the pressure irresistible. On June 2nd in the morning Norfolk went to the block. 'His head was at one chop cut off[48] and showed to all the people.'

Burghley entered in his diary June 2nd, 'The duke of Norfolk suffered'.[49] It is his only surviving comment on the successful termination of all his care and trouble over the Ridolfi Plot. No doubt his emotions were mingled, for Norfolk had been his friend and one of his staunch supporters in his long running fight with Leicester. Even to the very end Norfolk still regarded him as a friend. In his first letter to the Queen after his condemnation, he wrote:

'If that, with your Majesty's most gracious license, I might be so bold as to the poor orphans to adopt a father, who might bridle and rule their young inexperienced years, I would hope that my very good Lord Burghley, for the old love good will and friendship that he hath borne to me, their woeful father, would be entrusted to extend his charitable and friendly favour now in fathering them, who are otherwise destitute, and I would hope that they should be as obedient to him as ever they were to me.'

Two days later he wrote again, thanking the Queen for granting his request 'for my poor orphan children, and yet no orphans now considering it hath pleased your Majesty to christen them with such an adopted father as my good Lord Burghley is, for the which I do even upon my knees most humbly thank your Highness, thanking my good Lord also, not a little to requite the old good will and friendship which I have heretofore borne him, in receiving the poor infants under his most friendly care'.[50]

There was so much that was lovable in Norfolk! Burghley's eyes must have filled as he read those letters. But he never wavered. As between love for a friend, even though he were the first peer of England, and the service of his mistress and his country, neither now nor at any other time did he ever waver.

The Duke was dead, but she whom Walsingham called the 'bosom serpent' still lived in comparative freedom. Parliament had been called to deal with the whole problem of the conspiracies which circled about her. Norfolk was simply one aspect of the problem. Parliament assembled on May 8th. And almost at once a clamour arose in the Commons for the dispatch of the Scottish Queen. That was the preferred answer to the whole problem. As one Commoner put it — Cut off her head and make no more ado about it.

Thanks to Professor Neale's recovery of the diary of one Commoner we have a remarkable record not only of the proceedings in the Commons but of many of the speeches. Burghley, of course, was no longer in the Commons. He sat in the Lords. Undoubtedly he played the leading role in the debates in the Lords. But unfortunately we have only the barest outline of what happened in that House. Except in the list of those present Burghley's name never appears in the official journals.[51] And no member of that august body appears to have kept any diary of its proceedings. At least none has been found. So of Burghley's functioning we have no more than a few observations in his correspondence with Walsingham.

The intentions of the Parliament were savage. A joint committee of the two Houses proposed two alternate courses for dealing with the Scottish Queen. The preferred course was her execution as a traitor, the alternative was her exclusion from the succession. They presented these suggestions to the Queen.[52] She pushed aside the first suggestion, 'partly for honour, partly for conscience, for cause of herself knowing', expressing her preference for the alternative course.

The news came as a good deal of a shock to the Commons. But they proceeded to pass a bill in accordance with the royal wishes. It passed both Houses and was ready for royal approval on June 26th.[53] But the Queen even declined to take immediate action on that. So, as far as Mary was concerned, nothing more was accomplished than to make clear to Elizabeth the overwhelming sentiment in Parliament in support of immediate and drastic action.

Burghley's views about the matter are set forth in his correspondence with Walsingham.

On May 21st, just before Elizabeth sent her reply to the joint petition,[54] he wrote:

'I doubt not but others do certify to you of our Parliament proceedings wherein there can be found no more soundness than in the Common House, and no lack appearing in the higher house, but in the highest person such slowness in the offers of surety and such stay in resolution as it seemeth God is not pleased that the surety shall succeed. To lament that secretly I cannot forbear and thereby with it and such like I am overthrown in heart as I have no spark almost of good spirits left in me to nourish health in my body; being every third day thrown down to the ground, so as now I am forced to be carried to the Parliament house and to her Majesty's presence. And to lament it openly is to give more comfort to the adversaries. These are our miseries and such as I see no end thereof. And amongst others, shame doth as much trouble me as the rest, that all persons shall behold our follies, as they may think, imputing these lacks and errors to some of us that are accounted inward Councillors, where indeed the fault is not. And yet they must be so suffered and so imputed for saving the honour of the highest.'[55]

On June 6th, he wrote again: 'The Scottish Queen shall be touched with an Act of Parliament, but it will not draw her to any more fear to offend than words will do.'[56]

Both of these letters make it clear that Burghley at this time was in complete sympathy with the views of Parliament about Mary. He was evidently in very bad health, but he insisted on attending the House of Lords though he had to be carried there. He saw little merit in the bill to limit the succession, though it was better than nothing. Evidently he expected Elizabeth to accept it. When in the end she refused to go even that far, he was completely discouraged.

Just after Parliament rose he wrote to Walsingham:[57] 'Now for our Parliament, I cannot write patiently. All that we laboured for and had with full consent brought to fashion, I mean a law to make the Scottish Queen unable and unworthy to wear the crown, was by her Majesty neither assented to nor rejected, but deferred until the feast of All Saints. But what all other wise and good men may think thereof you may guess. Some here have, as it seemeth, abused their favour about her Majesty, to make herself her worst enemy. God amend them. I will not write to you who are suspected. I am sorry for them and so would you also, if you thought the suspicion to be true.'

There is no inkling of those whom Burghley had in mind. In a previous letter he had exonerated the Council. And Leicester seems to have shared his sentiments.[58] It is idle to speculate. In any case, the Queen's behaviour in the matter is so characteristic that she needed little active stimulus to act as she did.

CHAPTER IV

FRENCH MARRIAGE PROJECTS, 1571-72

T HROUGHOUT the year 1571 the negotiations for the French marriage continued on both sides of the Channel. Francis Walsingham handled the negotiations in France, Leicester and Burghley in England. The matter as we have seen was broached towards the end of the year 1570, and was favourably considered both at the French and at the English Courts. Obviously the initiative had to come from France. But the French were wary, knowing Elizabeth's ways in courtship, and Elizabeth got impatient. On March 10th Burghley wrote to Walsingham a letter in cipher[1] of which the key to some of the most important symbols is missing. This much we can make of it: 'I am commanded especially to write to you that certain reports are made there, as she thinketh by practice from hence of such as *do not like of her marriage with Anjou*, that *she meaneth not to marry*. And if L [?] shall by any occasion deal with you *she* will that you do so assure him for she knoweth not of any . . [?] . . that should mislike hereof. Herein I am commanded to write very earnestly unto you and to will you by no means to hinder the proceeding, for it is meant, as to me it appeareth, very earnest and some offence here taken with H. [?] for an opinion of cold dealing.'

A formal proposal came from France about a week later. Along with it came the suggestion from Catherine de Medicis that the preliminaries should be handled by her councillor, Paul de Foix, and Walsingham. She expressly requested that the matter be kept secret and that La Mothe Fénélon, the French ambassador in England, be excluded from the negotiations. Evidently she wanted to keep the affair on the level of diplomacy and to prevent the introduction of those coy feminine factors in which Elizabeth delighted. She would have liked Elizabeth's answer to be in the form of definite proposals.

But Elizabeth intended to play the game her own way. In her reply she gave thanks for Anjou's offer, but with some show of maiden modesty declined to propose conditions until she knew exactly what was offered. She consented to the discussion of preliminaries between De Foix and Walsingham, but with some reluctance, for she directed Walsingham, 'as of herself', to advise Catherine that much time would be saved if someone were sent over at once to England. She agreed to keep the matter secret from all her councillors save Leicester and Burghley, although she confessed that she saw no need for concealment.

Though Elizabeth wished to avoid definite commitments she told Walsingham that she was willing to accept the articles of marriage between her sister, Mary, and Philip of Spain as the basis for negotiations. She made, however, one important exception. 'Of necessity', she wrote to Walsingham, 'it must be especially prejudged that Monsieur shall not have authority to exercise the form of religion in England that is prohibited by the laws of our realm.'

The same post which carried these instructions to Walsingham carried personal letters to him from both Leicester and Burghley. Both agreed that Elizabeth was favourably disposed. Leicester wrote: 'The person of Monsieur is well liked of. I see her Majesty misliketh not his estate, for she is of mind to marry with the greatest . . . The conditions will be all, wherein I am right glad, and we are bound to thank God to see her Majesty so well to stand to the maintenance of the cause of religion.'

Leicester, in short, knowing Walsingham's pronounced Protestant predilections, emphasized the religious obstacle. Burghley's comment was briefer, in cipher, undeciphered. It seems to read: 'If I be not much deceived, *her Majesty* is *earnest* in this, wherefore you shall do well not to be oversuperstitious . . . I am in doubt that, if this matter for religion be not well conceived by them there, the adversaries to the marriage will take great advantage thereof and urge the persistence in it of purpose to dissolve the same. So as I had rather the speech hereof might have come from the Queen Mother or the others to you . . . than to begin abruptly of yourself.'

In short, Leicester wanted the religious obstacle stressed, Burghley wanted it toned down.

It appears from a second letter that Burghley wrote to Walsingham on the same day that he was very uncertain of Leicester's attitude.[2]

'I am also', he wrote, 'to ascertain you that, though the contrary may be reported, my Lord of Leicester, finding just occasion thereto, doth by all good means to my knowledge further the marriage. And therefore I think it reason that by such good means as yourself may think meet, both the Queen Mother and M. de Anjou might understand his disposition, so as he may be well thought of herein. And if he find that his doing may be liked there (if God be content with the cause) it is very probable that it may take effect. You see how plain I deal with you and the rather because I find by my L. Buckhurst, that upon the hope you have of the amendment of Monsieur in religion, you do not mislike the matter. Surely if Monsieur be not rooted in opinion of evil religion, as by his young years is not likely, there might be agreement made that marriage here with England would be becoming a professor of the gospel . . . He may prove a noble conqueror of all popery in Christendom . . . I wish he were capable of such a design. You see still the more I write the more open I am and yet, considering the trust I have in your secrecy, I trust nothing hereof shall have light to do me any hurt.'

Obviously one must read between the lines of this rather cryptic epistle if only to understand why Burghley charged Walsingham to keep it secret. On the face of it there is nothing which calls for concealment. In writing it Burghley evidently had in mind two considerations: (1) to secure Leicester's support to the match; (2) to reconcile Walsingham, ardent Protestant as he was, to a temporizing attitude on the religious issue. It is an early indication of a developing combination of Leicester's Court favour and the left-wing Protestants on the one hand and, on the other, of Burghley's increasing disposition to subordinate religious to national considerations.

For the time being at any rate Walsingham was disposed to follow Burghley's lead rather than Leicester's. He accordingly conveyed Elizabeth's answer to Catherine without making any mention of the religious difficulty.[3] He induced Catherine to send to England one of her Italian agents, Guido Cavalcanti,[4] with a definite statement of her demands.

While Cavalcanti tarried, Burghley's old enemy, the gout, laid him by the heels again. He wrote to Walsingham on April 7th:[5] 'My hard case is such as either by business in health or by dolour in sickness I cannot account myself a free man, but a slave to serve or an offender to suffer torment. The will of God be fulfilled in me in His honour for otherwise I find no comfort in this world. Of this enough! I am forced to write this in my bed with my hand, whilst I groan for pain in my knee and foot, and therefore I must be short.'

Cavalcanti arrived early in April. He was met at Dunkirk by one of Burghley's men and conducted very secretly to Burghley's own house.[6] Of what passed between the two men we have no record. But Burghley thought well of him. In a letter to Walsingham he wrote: '[Cavalcanti] appeareth to me a very careful and honest gentleman and well devoted to the Queen's Majesty.'[7]

In his interview with the Queen, Cavalcanti presented Catherine's demands and received Elizabeth's answer. The one difficult point at issue appeared at once on the religious question. Catherine asked that Anjou and his household be allowed the free exercise of their religion in England. The most that Elizabeth was prepared to concede was that he would be excused from attending the Anglican service.[8]

Burghley evidently hoped that the religious divergence would not be pressed any further. What happened next is set forth in his letter to Walsingham of April 19th:

'Sir, after I had written my other letters yesterday there happened some alteration in the great matter of moment. Where the Queen's Majesty had determined (besides her answer to the French articles) to have sent you certain other articles to be demanded of them there, whereby the whole cause should be opened and nothing left behind in silence, so that both parties might have understood their mutual intentions; now suddenly her Majesty hath thought good at this time to send only the French articles and her answers. And for the rest she meaneth to reserve until she may understand how her answers are taken, and specially how the knotty point of religion will be smoothed. And the cause of this change (as I conjecture) groweth of some late intelligence brought thence that if the Queen's Majesty will stand earnestly upon that point for religion, it shall be assented unto, which causeth her to proceed thus confidently. And for my part I wish most heartily that it may succeed, but that only I must fear, except you shall moderate the matter better, they there will imagine that this matter of religion is but projected to colour the delay in breaking off; for indeed, in like cause, so did the Emperor for his brother, the Archduke Charles. As I cannot instruct you how to

dissolve this doubt there, but as cause shall be given, so I know your wisdom sufficient to invent sufficient answer to mollify their hard conceits.'[9]

All this was provoked by Elizabeth's instructions to Walsingham in which she
made clear that she would not allow to Anjou the use of his own religion even in
secret. It was the irony of the situation that Burghley himself was obliged to
draft this letter. No doubt he did his best to temper the positive tone of it. But
even so it expressly charged Walsingham to give the French 'no other comfort in
that behalf'.

Walsingham, when he received these instructions, had no choice but to thrash
out the religious question with De Foix. Both of them stood valiantly to their
positions, and when Walsingham spoke subsequently to Catherine de Medicis, he
found her resolute. She encouraged Walsingham to believe in Anjou's early
conversion but meanwhile she would not agree to cut him off suddenly from
the consolation of his own faith. And so the matter stood, though Walsingham in
a private letter to Burghley[10] expressed the belief that Catherine would concede the
point rather than allow the marriage project to collapse. He thought that the
French ambassador in England had led the French to believe that Elizabeth would
yield.[11]

Burghley's response on May 5th was not cheerful: 'Your letters for the matter of
D [of Anjou] have driven us to the wall and particularly offended the Q's Majesty.
But the French ambassador hath letters from the Queen Mother and from De Foix
wherein the matters are more tempered and I think he hath commission to qualify
that hard article that cannot be there digested. It is too true . . . that some comfort
here hath made you hardlier answered. Indeed I wish things were not subject to
sudden changes, but God's will be done, for I cannot tell how to satisfy doubts,
but must refer me to His power to direct me.'

A week later Burghley wrote again at length on the subject: 'Sir, by the Queen's
Majesty's letters you shall understand what you are directed to do and say, and
therefore I must forbear to deal therein with you, considering you are prescribed.
But I will friendly let you know how the answer hath proceeded, and so, the cause
and circumstance known, you may the better conceive the inward sense of the
message. At the first coming of your letters hither, with the answer from the
Queen Mother . . . A [her Majesty?] was very sorry to judge the matter so perplexed, and almost desperate. Whereby I then judged there was here a plain forward intention to proceed in the cause, if this let for religion should not be a stay.
After two days the French ambassador had letters, and the Queen's Majesty was
by some informed that saw the letters, that there was no such difficulty in that
matter of religion. Nevertheless, the ambassador himself being appointed to
confer with my Lord of Leicester and me, made the cause very hard, alleging
directly that Monsieur would never sustain that dishonour, as to come hither with
an account to the world that he should have no religion; and then I answered as is
contained in the Queen's Majesty's letters, setting out the nearness of ours [religion]
to such as was good and sound in the Roman, adding that we omitted nothing but
those which were impious and doubtful to be against the Scriptures . . . After this

I was by one of some value secretly informed that if this matter of religion were earnestly sticked unto and peremptorily pressed it would be obtained, whereupon the answer was conceived, and I commanded to report it to the French ambassador who, hearing it, seemed much dismayed and concluded that he saw not but this answer should make a breach and end of the whole. For, if the answer (saith he) be grounded upon the Queen's conscience, then saith he, there is no qualification to be hoped for. Thus I reported, and thereupon I saw her Majesty was perplexed, and wished I had forborne to have made the principal foundation upon her Majesty's conscience, which I was commanded to do and therefore no fault in me. And to remedy the matter I was willed speedily to advertise the ambassador secretly that I was larger in explication of her Majesty's conscience than I see since my speaking with him was meant, and that the principal reasons were the other, of the misliking of her good subjects and of the danger to lose their good wills, etc. And so did I by a little writing advertise him, whereby what conceit he gathered I know not, but by some others I hear that he still judgeth it broken. After this I was commanded also to temper the sentence in the Queen's Majesty's letters, as you perceive, for it is not as it was, an assertion of direct necessity, but of possibility. Thus, having some circumstances to give you some light, but what you shall find by your light, God knoweth. I doubt the worst, and so I have said, but yet the opinion conceived by her Majesty maketh her to believe the contrary.

'It were strange that any one man should give comfort to the ambassador in the cause, and yet the same man to persuade the Queen's Majesty that she should persist. Both these things are done, but I dare not affirm by any one, and thus I end.'

We can follow the further course of the negotiations in Burghley's own account of them to Walsingham. On June 5th he wrote:[12] 'You must bear with my slow dispatches in returning your servants, for that I cannot obtain such resolutions as may give cause to write, whereupon I am forced to bear here patiently the lack that I find and you must do the like on your part, hoping that *Deus dabit meliora*. Now I send away this bearer, meaning and hoping to send herewith the great answer, and to give you some light hereof. Thus it is, the French ambassador upon the receipt of his last answers, agreeable with your letters, pressed the Queen's Majesty to have the rest of the articles on her part, which in no wise she would agree unto, pretending that without a resolute answer to the article of religion this could not be; wherewith the ambassador was so wounded as indeed in conference with him I found him desperate in the matter and entered into passions. But after some speech used with him I pacified him, with hope that the Q. Majesty might be by further persuasions induced to show the rest of the articles. And so with some long laborious persuasions her Majesty was induced to agree that the articles should be made ready and showed, as things earnestly pressed by that King and his ambassador here, with which pretence her Majesty thought her honour saved well. Hereof I was appointed to inform the ambassador, and then was I also commanded to put the articles in readiness, which were not unready as I conceived. But ere I could finish them I was commanded to conclude them with a request to have Calais restored, a matter so inconvenient to bring forth a marriage as indeed I thought it meant to procure a breach. And so the matter continued in my opinion desperate, but with good help it was remedied. I desired that the Queen's Majesty would let my Lord Marquess, the Earls of Sussex and Leicester to see the articles, and so they did, and very honourably and wisely gave counsel to forbear that toy of Calais, and generally did further the prosecution of the marriage as a matter of all other most necessary at this time. And now we take it that her Majesty intendeth it earnestly, whereupon yesterday afternoon my Lord of Leicester and I have delivered unto the ambassador a copy of the articles, which at the first hearing he did not mislike. What he will do this day I know not, but certainly they are very reasonable.'

Early in July, the French King[13] dispatched M. D'Archant, captain of the Duke of Anjou's guard, to England. He and Fénélon together conferred with the Queen. They asked her consent for a more formal embassy from France to conclude the matter. She replied that she did not think matters had developed to a point where a formal embassy could function. The religious issue was still unsettled. She had said flatly that she could not grant Anjou 'liberty to exercise the Roman religion' in any matter contrary to her laws. Until the King agreed to this 'she saw it but labour lost to send any ambassadors'.

This was discouraging to say the least. Later in conference with Leicester and Burghley, the Frenchmen raised the religious issue again. Leicester and Burghley insisted that Elizabeth was adamant on the subject. If the French did not like the denying of it they must forbear to demand it. 'Hereupon', Burghley wrote in his account of the conference, 'there followed some opinions on both parts that if Monsieur should forbear to require it and thereby her Majesty should not grant it, but that the matter should be forborne and pass in silence, it might be that Monsieur's friends might retain their good opinion of him as of one that had not changed his religion, and likewise the Queen's Majesty's good subjects should continue their opinions of her Majesty as of a Prince that would not assent to anything against her religion.'[14]

In a subsequent interview with the Queen, the Frenchmen suggested this way out. She was prepared to accept it as a face-saving device, but she told the Frenchmen flatly that 'the forbearing of it by way of treaty would not content her, but also the forbearing of the use of it'. 'And so', she wrote to Walsingham, 'we require you to express the same plainly . . . for we cannot esteem it a plain dealing to pass it over in silence in the treaty and yet to be in doubt whether the same shall be used indeed.'

Burghley commented on the situation in a letter to Walsingham of July 9th:

'I am in doubt whether to write or not, for to write nothing were to discomfort you and to write something with uncertainty cannot comfort and yet in extremities the lesser is to be admitted. I assure you that I cannot assure you from hence what is to be looked for by the Q. Majesty's manner of answers at this time. She is not unwarned how dangerous it were if in her default the matter taketh not success, and she seemeth to concede and pretendeth that she seemeth, that if the matter of religion may be granted there will be no other difficulty; but whether she is persuaded that therein the breach will be on that side and so she to escape the reproof, I cannot tell. God direct the matter for I have done my uttermost and so hath other Councillors here. My Lord Keeper hath earnestly dealt in it and so hath my L. of Sussex; my Lord of Leicester hath in my dealings also joined earnestly with me and among the rest of the Councillors I know none directly against it.'

Burghley evidently had about decided that Elizabeth did not mean to marry, religion or no religion. He anticipated that if the French yielded on the point she would find other objections. And by the end of the month, Walsingham in Paris concluded that the game was up. He wrote to Burghley on July 27th that Anjou would have none of the marriage even if Elizabeth met his religious demands. Three days later he informed Burghley that the King and his mother most earnestly desired 'a strait amity' with England, and that it was thought De Foix would be commissioned to make some liberal offers to that end.[15]

De Foix came to England in August, and had his first audience with Elizabeth on the 15th. Burghley's comment on his mission was brief. 'I fear', he wrote to Walsingham on the 16th, 'the offers of so great amity will diminish or divert the former intention of the marriage without which the French amity shall serve to small purpose but to make us ministers of their appetites and, those fulfilled, to cast us off. Surely I could have wished that the extremity of the marriage had been seen before these baits of amity had been thrown before us.'[16]

He had apparently not yet entirely abandoned hope. On August 6th he prepared a memorandum for the Queen in which he set forth at length the advantages of the marriage.

'If', he wrote, 'Your Majesty shall marry with France upon reasonable conditions, many things now evil digested and dangerous shall, by God's goodness, prove easy and ordered, that is to say:

'(1) The perilous case of the Scottish Queen and of Scotland.

'(2) The discontention of a great number of the subjects upon sundry causes.

'(3) The unkindness and abstinence of traffic betwixt this realm and the K. of Spain's countries.

'(4) The dangerous and unmeasurable charge in retaining of Ireland.

'(5) The general uncertainty of events of your neighbours, by occasion whereof your Majesty hath been or shall be to stand upon your guard with unmeasurable expenses both by sea and land.'

It is questionable whether any marriage would have worked these miracles. It would certainly have served to alleviate the Scottish situation, and it would certainly have silenced the popular clamour for the Queen to marry. And it would, of course, have faced Spain with the united strength of France and England, at least for a season. But even Burghley could not have expected it to work miracles.

He went on to examine the alternative of a 'strait amity' with France. It would, he admitted, so long as the amity continued, which would be no longer than the

French found it profitable, 'diminish many inconveniences'. What it would not diminish was the danger from the Scottish Queen's pretensions, or satisfy the demands of Elizabeth's subjects for a marriage, or reduce the tension over the question of succession. It would not offer an attractive alternative to trade with the Low Countries, and it might well draw England, as she had been drawn once before in Mary's reign, into the long struggle between France and Spain.[17]

Walsingham thought differently. In a letter to Leicester of August 3rd, he discussed the question at some length. The great obstacle as he saw it to a league with France was the traditional league with Burgundy. But, as he pointed out, that league was formed at a time when Burgundy was far inferior to England in power and largely dependent upon her. Now, united with Spain, Burgundy (by which, of course, he meant the Low Countries) had lost its ancient character and had become an adjunct to the overwhelming power of Spain. He went on to recall Spanish malice towards England and the necessity of providing means to resist it. 'And though', he concluded, 'France cannot yield like profit that Flanders doth, yet may it yield some profit with less hazard and more safety. In this case two things I consider chiefly:

'First, that the House of Austria [Spain] is become the Pope's champion and professed enemy unto the Gospel, and daily practiseth the rooting out of the same and therefore we that are professors of the Gospel ought to oppose ourself against it.

'The other, that the entrance into a league with France will not only be the advancement of the Gospel there but elsewhere. And therefore, though it yieldeth not so much temporal profit, yet in respect of the spiritual fruit that thereby may ensue I think it worth the embracing.'

Walsingham, in short, saw the problem in terms of the advancement of the Protestant cause. In an earlier letter to Leicester, he had declared: 'I wish God's glory and next the Queen's safety.'[18] He did indeed identify the two. The welfare of England to his thinking depended upon the welfare of the Protestant cause. It is probable that Leicester was following Walsingham's lead in the matter, though Leicester knew his mistress too well to believe that she would accept Walsingham's analysis.

During the spring and summer of 1571 Walsingham had great hopes that the King of France would take advantage of the situation in the Low Countries to strike a shrewd blow at his old enemy. That was the foreign policy which the French Huguenots advocated. In pursuit of that policy they had assurance of support from the Grand Duke of Tuscany and from Saxony, the strongest of the German Protestant States.

In the summer of 1571, belligerent plans against the Low Countries centred upon the person of Louis of Nassau, the brother of the Prince of Orange, who had, after the disastrous failure of the campaign against the Duke of Alva in 1568, taken refuge in France. He had fought on the Protestant side in the Third French Civil War, and had afterwards established himself at La Rochelle. There he gathered together a small fleet of Dutch privateers and made systematic incursions upon

Spanish shipping. At the beginning of the year 1571 he was making plans for a maritime attack upon Alva in the Low Countries.

He needed money, and sent one of his agents to Walsingham to sound out the possibilities of help from England. Walsingham fell in with the idea and sent his brother-in-law, Robert Beale, to lay it before Elizabeth. Her initial response was sympathetic,[19] but when she learned that much money was needed, and the security for repayment dubious, she declined to participate, at least for the present. Burghley commented on the matter in a letter to Walsingham of April 14th: 'I am sorry that the Q. Majesty findeth occasion to pretermit this late motion whereof (it is likely) she might reap great fruit, to the quietness of her own countries. You must make the best that you can to content the parties.'[20]

We hear no more of Count Louis and his plans until midsummer when the Huguenot advisers at the French Court induced Charles IX to confer privately with him. They met on July 18th, and a second time five days later. Louis proposed an alliance of France, the German Protestant Princes and England, together with the Dutch rebels, against Spain. Together they were to drive the Spaniards out of the Low Countries, and then divide them up — Flanders and Artois, the old French provinces, going to France; Brabant, Guelders and Luxemburg, once fiefs of the Empire, to the Germans; Holland and Zeeland to England. It was anticipated that William of Orange would be chosen to govern the part assigned to the Germans.

Charles IX thought well of the plan, and submitted it to his Council, which approved it unanimously. But they advised the King to make sure of German and English participation before committing France.

It was this which brought Count Louis to Walsingham on August 6th.[21] Walsingham sent a long account of their interview to Burghley on the 12th.[22] In a letter to Leicester on the same day he argued strongly in favour of the plan. 'I do not doubt', he wrote, 'but that your Lordship will do what you may so to deal with her Majesty as that some of the Count's requests may take place, whereby the fire that is now akindling may grow a flame and we take comfort of the heat thereof. I perceive nothing will so much advance the matter as for her Majesty to give some countenance to the same. The proud Spaniard (whom God hath long used for the rod of his wrath) I see great hope that they will now cast him into the fire, that he may know what it is to serve against God.'

But Walsingham awaited in vain for a response. A month later he wrote to Burghley: 'Count Louis left a man here of purpose to attend her Majesty's answer ... The resolution of that enterprise stayeth only upon the expectation what her Majesty will do and it is feared that the matter will be so long protracted and the opportunity of the enterprise will be let slip.'

Leicester had written in enthusiastic support of the plan on the 16th, but Burghley's response[23] indicated that he regarded the proposal as another bait to divert Elizabeth from marriage. 'I see', he added with a sly thrust at Leicester, 'those [baits] be most liked by such as I could not find to like of the marriage.'

Burghley's attitude is made a little more explicit by a memorandum dated

August 22nd which he drafted on the matter of a league with France.[24] It may have been intended for Elizabeth. He argued against the league on the grounds:

(1) That France would hardly have proposed it unless she intended to break with Spain. It would therefore draw England into a war with Spain, which would do England more harm than France and might well entail the loss of Ireland.

(2) He discounted the prospect that England might gain some part of the Low Countries (a plain allusion to Count Louis's project). 'It were a great folly', he declared, 'for a Prince to venture the loss of a kingdom in possession to seek another country by conquest.'

(3) He feared that when England and Spain were engaged France might, by practice and cunning of the Pope and his faction, abandon England.

(4) He pointed out that trade with France would be a poor substitute for the well-established and mutually profitable trade between England and the Low Countries.

He saw advantages in a purely defensive league with France and the German Protestant Princes against religious aggression. But he wanted to exact a price for it, to wit: (1) That France should cease to aid the Marians in Scotland and support the regency there; (2) that France should reduce her trade with the Low Countries to the dimensions it had been before the stay of trade there with England.

There is certainly no indication in this memorandum of any zeal to thrust the proud Spaniard into the fire, or even to promote the Protestant cause. Indeed, there is no mention of religious issues at all, except purely defensive ones. In short, Burghley opposed any aggressive religious policy and any entangling foreign alliance. And yet he was still strong for the marriage. It might be supposed that he had before his eyes that old Hapsburg cliché: *Bella gerant alii; tu, felix Austria, nube* — others wage war; you, happy Austria, make marriages. Actually, his opposition to the league was probably based upon the fact that the league was offered as an alternative to the marriage, and he much preferred the marriage.

At the centre of his thinking was the question of the succession and the aspirations of Mary Queen of Scots. He was at the moment deeply engaged in ferreting out the ramifications of the Ridolfi Plot. This much he knew already, that a plot was afoot to depose Elizabeth and enthrone Mary, to be realized by domestic uprising and foreign invasion. The solution of the problem as he saw it was a royal marriage and a royal offspring. With a French marriage the French interest in Mary Stuart would be terminated. Towards Spain his position was a defensive one. He was trying to arrange terms for a restoration of trade relations with the Low Countries, which had been interrupted in 1569. Somewhat reluctantly he had come to share the widespread belief that the cloth trade with Antwerp was indispensable to the welfare of England. The alternative trade with Hamburg had grown and prospered, the religious disorders in Antwerp had driven away the merchants and bankers, and the cold war in the Channel had yielded a lucrative harvest to English privateers. Nevertheless, and despite Spanish intrigues, Burghley still favoured the old Burgundian alliance. He was prepared to accept as an alternative a French marriage, but not a French league.

As a matter of fact, the marriage project, which had been pronounced dead at the beginning of August, showed signs of coming to life again. As the French grew cold, Elizabeth grew warm. Fénélon wrote to his master on August 12th that the news of De Foix's coming had been received with enthusiasm, that the prospects of a successful outcome of the marriage were distinctly promising,[25] and that De Foix would be well advised to keep quiet about the alternative of a league.

De Foix arrived about the middle of August and negotiations for the marriage were resumed. It cannot have been altogether accidental that no news of what was going on in England went from Burghley to France until De Foix's departure early in September. Burghley knew that Walsingham preferred the league to the marriage, and Elizabeth wanted to keep the matter in her own hands.[26] Burghley's excuses for his silence in his letter to Walsingham of September 2nd are not convincing. 'I am assured', he wrote, 'you have not been out of trouble and care in that you have not of long heard from hence in what sort M. De Foix hath treated, or rather been handled. But this shall content you to think, and therefore I do assure you, that the negotiation hath had almost as many changes, though not in contrarities, yet in varieties as it hath had days of conference, and sometimes more. If I may truly report that in some one day's act, one part of the day hath not been so seasonable as the other, how dissonant the same might have been in your ears, how deformed in your eyes . . . Would you ask of me the just cause thereof if you were with me, I would not refuse to declare conjecturally as I might, but to write hereof I do forbear.' All of which, though polite, must have struck Walsingham as specious.

Burghley continued: 'M. de Foix hath had seven or eight special conferences with her Majesty and with us of her Council. And at the first he found such favourable answers as he accounted the matter his own . . . And if any of them [the Council] have principally or indirectly impugned the same, as I cannot affirm truly herein, he nor they shall have hereafter a quiet conscience. Indeed we have cause to think that some for proof, practising particularity, have troubled quiet waters. God give them grace to repent their errors.

'The answers have been, since they were first given in words, altered in writing, and directed so to be to the worse. And thereby the ambassador hath been greatly perplexed to find the latter harder than the first. And yet now, as you shall see the words for the point of religion, thus her Majesty is resolved, and so she doth pronounce to her Council, whom she seeth earnestly bent by all means to further this marriage for her own surety and for the avoiding of the inevitable ruin of this monarchy, that surely, so as Monsieur will forbear the mass, she will assent to the marriage. And this she confirmeth with all good speeches to give credit. But yet all of us are not so persuaded, not for doubt of her assertions, which surely are agreeable to her mind when she uttereth them, but for doubt that others, misliking the same, may indirectly draw her from her determination. If you require of me what you may say, her Majesty's letters will warrant you for words. But what you may hope will succeed, I can no more ascertain you than I can myself, who am now to expect at God's hands blessing or vengeance, for it is likely that his Majesty will no longer dissemble his determinations.

'M. de Foix hath good entertainment in all external offices . . . He dined at my house, as I doubt not but he and the resident ambassador have seen my hearty devotion to the marriage. And indeed, so is my judgment therein confirmed, as I am not ashamed to utter myself howsoever it may be perilous to me when it shall not take place.'[27]

Burghley evidently thought that Leicester had once more changed the Queen's mind. Fénélon reported that someone, he did not say who, had stirred up the Protestants against the match,[28] but he left it to De Foix to tell the story. The Spanish ambassador, De Spes, heard that the Queen's Council was divided on the subject, with Burghley and Bacon and Sussex favourable to a marriage to be followed by a league; Leicester, Clinton and Knollys opposed to the marriage but in favour of a league, offensive and defensive, with France. 'The Queen', he added, 'is, so to speak, driven to the marriage, but Burghley is so powerful in the government that she dares not oppose him.'[29]

De Spes, of course, was wrong again. Like so many of the Spanish ambassadors to England, he grossly overestimated both Burghley's power and his malevolence.

On September 2nd Burghley wrote to Walsingham: 'M. De Foix hath very earnestly moved her Majesty to send some one person of credit to the French king to affirm and justify the reasons of her answer; or rather, if the marriage shall not take place, to enter into the treaty of some straiter alliance and confederacy, which for my part I thought very reasonable and did assent and move the same. But, finding now that he hath secretly named me for that place, I do coldlier deal therein, knowing both my insufficiency and doubting of the success thereof. But whether any shall come, or who shall, I surely cannot guess.'[30]

During September Burghley's letters to Walsingham indicated an increasing interest of the Queen in the marriage. He wrote to Walsingham on September 8th and 9th that Elizabeth was even content to yield to toleration in religion.[31] On the 14th he wrote again that she wanted Walsingham to promote it.[32] On the 28th, in describing the unravelling of the Ridolfi Plot, Burghley added: 'Truly the more matters are discovered the more necessary it is seen that her Majesty should marry.'

Walsingham for his part appears to have been quite desperate about the matter. He wrote to Burghley on October 8th: 'Against the coming of him whom her Majesty meaneth to send I will do what I may to renew it, but to be plain with your Lordship I despair thereof and so do as many as wish it. My fear is that if you wade further, it will be discovered that her Majesty is forsaken.' He went on to say that he thought it wise to 'reserve to himself' Elizabeth's acquiescence in the matter of toleration unless he saw 'more towardness here'.

But Elizabeth still persisted. On October 19th she dispatched Burghley's brother-in-law, Henry Killigrew, to France, to take Walsingham's place during his illness. In Killigrew's instructions the marriage was still regarded as undecided;

Killigrew was directed to inform the French King that she meant to send someone to France to pursue the matter further as soon as she had finished her investigation of the Ridolfi Plot. On October 20th Burghley wrote that someone was coming. 'Surely', he added, 'there are many impediments why I cannot, but the principal is that I am far unmeet to treat of anything out of England, being as I am known, only meet to speak as my mother taught me.'[33]

Walsingham had long ago abandoned the marriage in favour of the league. But Burghley still persisted and Elizabeth herself seems to have come to the conclusion that marriage was essential. The revelations of the Ridolfi Plot clearly alarmed her. And the news of the Spanish victory at Lepanto in October, which reached England about November 1st, served to accentuate the Spanish danger. Walsingham and Killigrew were strongly urging that someone be sent quickly to negotiate the league. On December 5th Burghley wrote to Walsingham that Sir Thomas Smith had been selected for the mission and was on the point of departure.[34] Smith reached Paris on December 24th. Before he left, Burghley wrote, on December 9th, to Walsingham:[35] *'Her Majesty was never more earnestly bent to the marriage* than now. I am commanded to move you to advise some secret ways with Sir Thomas Smith how, if the *Admiral* [Coligny] be not at Court, he might secretly procure to be there at Sir Thomas Smith's being there, and also by secret means Sir Thomas Smith may understand his [the Admiral's] opinion in the greatest matter . . . All this I write by commandment, and that after Mr. Smith's departure from this place, so as I have not speedily informed him hereof, and therefore I pray you impart this to him, adding this caution that Mr. Smith do not appear to any others to deal with him . . . Now, Sir, you may think that I am not a little perplexed in this matter when I consider myself the doubtfulness that you have signified unto me of . . . [36] Anjou, whereof I never made her Majesty privy, nor any other almost, and now finding here a contrary intention, which surely is earnestly meant and not the less for the cause of *Norfolk* [?] I am doubly troubled and therefore the good order, either to conclude or break off must lie in the wisdom of the ministers there to whom I wish the assistance of God's spirit. Sir, my infirmity, as Sir Thomas Smith can inform you, hath been so lingering upon me as I have been though not an idle, yet an unprofitable servant.'

Interestingly enough, Leicester's letter to Walsingham of December 6th[37] confirms Burghley's view of the situation. If he was still secretly opposed to the match, he found it expedient to change his tune even in a letter to Walsingham. Since, however, he evidently wrote by the Queen's commandment, it may well be that she saw the letter before he dispatched it. So far as he was concerned, what he wrote may have been designed to convey to his mistress the fact that he conformed to her wishes in the matter. He may have felt that in any case the marriage was gone beyond recall.

Sir Thomas Smith's instructions are missing.[38] But we can be reasonably certain that he was directed to revive the marriage if he could and even to concede to Anjou the private use of his religion. Failing that, Smith was to begin negotiations for a league.

Smith reached the French Court on January 4th. Even before his first audience with the King he learned that Anjou was obstinate on the point of religion, and was deep in an affair with a lady at the French Court. Five days later at his first audience, Smith opened at once the question of marriage. Catherine de Medicis declared that the only obstacle was Anjou's obstinate stand on the religious issue. Smith wanted to know what he wanted, and hinted that if he would be satisfied with Mass in his private chapel, that might be accorded. But Catherine said that he must have open practice of his religion with all its ceremonies. 'Why, Madame,' quoth Smith, 'then he may require also the four orders of friars, monks, canons, pilgrimages, pardons, oil and cream, reliques and all such trumperies.' That he declared could never be agreed. And that was the end of the Anjou marriage project.

Two days later Catherine suggested that her younger son, the Duke of Alençon, 'a much less scrupulous fellow', might take his brother's place as suitor. She even offered to send him to England. She also invited Smith to join in negotiations for a league. Incidentally Smith distributed a few copies of George Buchanan's notable attack on Mary Stuart which had been published in London, with royal sanction, in the late autumn of 1571.[39] Smith said it did much to discredit her cause.

Smith himself was strong for the Alençon alternative. He wrote to Burghley on January 10th that the young man was not so tall or fair as his brother, but neither was he so pig-headed or so papistical. And Smith had heard that Alençon was more apt for the getting of children.[40]

Burghley's reaction is set forth in a letter to Walsingham of January 23rd:[41] 'In that matter of the third person newly offered, his age, and other qualities unknown, maketh me doubtful how to use speech thereof. The ambassador has dealt, as he saith, secretly with me, and I have showed no argument to one hand or other. As I may learn further from thence I will deal, but fear occupieth me more in this cause of her marriage, whom God hath suffered to lose so much time, than for my next fit. Yet truly I have more cause than before time, for it cometh of a great cold and a rheum fallen into my lungs where it is lodged as yet without moving. But in respect of other things I see and suffer I weigh not my own carcass.'

La Mothe Fénélon in his letter to Catherine de Medicis of January 25th[42] gives the details of the interview to which Burghley refers in his letter just cited. It occurred on January 21st. On that day, after audience with the Queen, Fénélon and Burghley retired to a room apart. There Fénélon opened the conversation with the statement that he had been charged by Catherine to speak with Burghley about the Alençon proposal, and with none other, and to be guided by Burghley's advice. Burghley thereupon inquired whether Fénélon had broached the matter to the Queen. Fénélon said no. Burghley then advised that it be kept secret from everyone until he and Fénélon should agree on procedure. Burghley went on to say that Smith had written sympathetically about the match and that thereupon in conversation with Elizabeth, Burghley had mentioned Alençon, inquiring about his age, at which she had remarked abruptly that such a match would resemble more a mother and son than a husband and wife. Burghley told Fénélon that he had not dared reply. He then asked Fénélon to find out the day and hour of Alençon's birth, and his height, and he, Burghley, would inquire about his morals and his health and would consider how the marriage project could be shifted from Anjou to Alençon with honour. He went on to say that Elizabeth's natural repugnance to marriage had been overcome by the qualities of Anjou and it would be difficult to attract her to an alternative. Fénélon proceeded to enlarge upon Alençon's virtues and showed to Burghley Catherine's letter on the subject. Burghley closed the interview by rising, hat in hand, and expressing his thanks to Catherine for the confidence she had shown in him. He made no other commitment.

Early in February, Burghley wrote to Walsingham: 'I have not been to see her Majesty these eight days, and this day I am in physic thoroughly sick.' Nothing on French affairs. Nine days later he wrote again,[43] apparently recovered, but still nothing about the Alençon affair.

During the interval Fénélon spoke again to Burghley about it.[44] Burghley said that he had hazarded to mention it to the Queen who had once again remarked abruptly that though all other considerations were favourable, nevertheless both age and stature were too unequal between them. She asked how tall Alençon was. Burghley answered about his own height. 'Say rather the height of your grandson', she replied, to which he had not ventured a reply. Burghley then observed that he discerned two qualities in Alençon that made him more desirable for England than his brother: (1) he was less immediately in line for the French throne, and (2) he was more accommodating in matters religious. One gets the impression that Burghley favoured the match but found little interest in it from his mistress.

Smith and Walsingham both continued to urge the marriage in their letters to Burghley during February and March.[45] Fénélon spoke with Burghley about it more than once, and Burghley opened the matter with Elizabeth again early in March. She remarked again the disparity of age and stature, and Burghley told Fénélon that although he had no cause for hope he had not abandoned hope. Ten days later Fénélon raised the question again. Burghley said he did not know the answer, that Fénélon would have to consult the great oracle. According to Fénélon, Leicester was strong for the match.[46] But we hear no more about it for months, and apparently nothing went from England to France about it. Smith wrote to Burghley on March 30th that he had never a word from England either about the league or the marriage for twenty-two days.[47]

CHAPTER V

FRENCH ALLIANCE AND DUTCH REVOLT, 1572

MEANWHILE Smith had been busy discussing the terms of the treaty of alliance, assisted first by Killigrew and late in February by Walsingham. In the first session with the French commissioners little more was done than to define the issues which the treaty was designed to settle. It was easily agreed that the treaty was to be a defensive one under the terms of which each party was to assist the other if attacked.[1] But a difficulty arose at this point. The English commissioners demanded that it should be expressly stated in the treaty, by what came to be known as an *etiamsi religionis causa* clause, that assistance should be rendered by one party to the other even if attacked under the pretence of religion. The French demurred.

Another serious difficulty arose over Scotland, the old bone of contention. By the flight of Mary Stuart into England in 1568, the Scottish government had passed into the hands of her half-brother, the Earl of Murray, as Regent for her young son, James. The murder of Murray in 1570 and the subsequent murder of his successor, the Earl of Lennox, by Mary's supporters in Scotland, precipitated civil war. Under the leadership of the Earl of Mar, who succeeded Lennox, the Protestant pro-English faction in Scotland steadily gained ground and the Marian faction, as an active combatant, was reduced to a handful of desperate men who had shut themselves up in Edinburgh Castle, ably led by Kirkaldy of the Grange, a very gallant and very competent soldier, and by Maitland of Lethington, the cleverest man in Scotland. After the discovery of Mary's complicity in the Ridolfi Plot, Elizabeth wrote to Mar, announced her determination to abandon Mary's cause and indicated that she meant to lend Mar her whole-hearted support.[2] She sent him enough money to pay a small army but she would not intervene by force in his favour and Mar was not strong enough to take Edinburgh Castle without her.

Elizabeth's efforts during the autumn of 1571 were directed towards the termination of the civil war in Scotland by inducing the Marian leaders to recognize and support the regency, by promising to protect them in their lives and in their property and by giving them some share in the government. But the Marians declined to accept these terms and they received enough aid from their friends in France, and enough encouragement from prospects of intervention by the Duke of Alva in their behalf, to induce them to persist. So the Scottish problem had reached an impasse when the French and the English commissioners addressed themselves to it. The Frenchmen proposed to include Scotland in the league, and the Englishmen were not opposed, but they could not agree together as to what the word

Scotland meant. The French maintained that it meant Mary and her following, the English that it meant Mar and the regency.

Upon these two issues, the issue of religion and the issue of Scotland, the negotiations which followed really turned. Other matters of dispute, to be sure, arose. There was some debate as to whether the ally who gave aid in case of need or the ally who received it should pay expenses. The nature of the privileges to be enjoyed by the English merchants in France — for one of the matters under consideration was the transfer of the English continental staple at Antwerp to some town in France — involved differences of opinion. The English made a suggestion that Spain should be included in the treaty. But all these minor matters were settled without much trouble. It was too obvious to be long denied that the ally who received aid should pay for it. The French were too anxious to gain the English trade to haggle much over conditions. And as for Spain, even Elizabeth was brought to see the folly of including in the league the enemy against whom it was chiefly directed.

Up to this point the negotiations had been carried on in France. Smith and his colleagues felt that they could go no further until they were instructed from home.

Elizabeth accordingly laid the matter before a selected group of her councillors — Bacon, Leicester, Clinton, Mildmay and Burghley.[3] They discussed at length the points at issue with La Mothe Fénélon. Presumably Burghley played the major role in these discussions, though there is no specific evidence on the point. Almost the only pertinent document from him at this juncture is a long 'Consideration of the Case of Scotland'[4] which he drew up on December 10th, 1571. It represented a considered attempt to find a basis for compromise between the contending factions there. He started out by insisting that the claims of the Scottish Queen should be ignored on the grounds of her implication in the Darnley murder and her participation in the Ridolfi Plot. He also insisted that the only sound basis for compromise was the acceptance by both parties of James as King and Mar as Regent. He was evidently of the opinion that the Marians might be induced to agree on both these points if their personal interests were well protected. He proposed to give them a share in the government by the establishment of a Council which would limit the arbitrary power of the Regent and upon which the Marians might have representatives. He proposed to protect their lives and property rights by the annulment of all attainders and forfeitures. He even suggested that those Marians who had lost their offices might receive some compensation.

Regarding Edinburgh Castle, Burghley maintained that it must return to the King's obedience. He would have allowed Kirkaldy to remain in command if he promised to hold it for the King and give hostages to support his promise. Burghley argued strongly against the assault of the castle by English forces.

This plan of compromise is particularly significant because with some modifications in detail it incorporated the policy which Elizabeth and her Council subsequently elected to follow. About a month later, on January 22nd, Burghley drew up a statement of Elizabeth's position in the matter which he entitled: 'The opinion and Advice of the Queen's Majesty Conceived by many Conferences with her

Council.' And this memorandum formed the substance of her instructions to two commissioners, Sir William Drury, Marshal of Berwick, and Thomas Randolph, both of them veterans in Scottish affairs, whom she sent to Scotland in February to deal with the contending factions.

In connection with these instructions, Burghley drew up 'An Addition of more secrecy',[5] in which he dealt specifically with Kirkaldy and Maitland, the head and front of the resistance. He suggested that Kirkaldy might at a pinch be allowed to retain Edinburgh Castle for a year provided he pledged himself to support the regency. As for Maitland, Burghley pointed out that he could hardly expect to be restored to the office of Secretary but agreed that he might share the profits of the office.

Such was the official attitude of the English government towards Scotland at the time the English and the French commissioners, engaged in the business of an Anglo-French alliance, were casting about to find a solution of the Scottish problem acceptable both to England and to France.

On February 13th Elizabeth sent instructions to Smith, Killigrew and Walsingham in which she set forth her position in matters under dispute.

On the question of the *etiamsi religionis causa* clause she took the stand that though she would prefer it to be included in the text of the treaty she was prepared to accept as a substitute *sub quocumque praetextu vel colore* and *quavis de causa nulla omnino qualecumque excepta* (under any pretext or colour whatsoever, without any manner of exception). But if they must accept this alternative they must earnestly press 'that some special promise may be made in secret writing betwixt the King and us, signed and sealed mutually with both our hands for that purpose expressly if any invasion should be made, as though the same had been expressed by treaty without which secret provision to be made, considering the matter hath been in question, we would be very loath that you should accord'.[6]

On the Scottish problem, Elizabeth wrote that 'she had no other intention in the matter of Scotland but to have the hostility and civil wars to cease and the government of the realm to be established to the contentation of the nation'. She had already sent commissioners to arrange for an armistice as the preliminary to an accord. If they did not achieve their purpose then she would be glad to attempt joint action with France. She had, she insisted, no desire to withdraw the Scots from their old alliance with France. What she aimed at was good friendship among all of them. When she had spoken in these terms to the French ambassador he had seemed well content with them. So she hoped the matter might be settled that way. She would have preferred to leave Scotland out of the picture altogether, but if the French insisted and would not name James as King, then she suggested that Scotland might be referred to as *regnum et status Scotiae*. Her attitude in short was definitely conciliatory and the expectation was that the terms of the treaty would be settled in short order.

When Smith received Elizabeth's instructions along with powers under the Great Seal to conclude the treaty, he felt that the matter was virtually finished. On the last of February Killigrew went to take leave of the French King. At this audience Smith, rather gratuitously, raised again the question of the *etiamsi religionis causa* clause, insisting that the King's private letter on the subject should be issued under the Great Seal. Charles IX in anger thereupon insisted that Mary Stuart should be included in the treaty. But this point was straightened out when Fénélon's letters arrived from England to confirm Mary's complicity in the Ridolfi Plot.[7] Charles exclaimed: 'Ah, the poor fool will never cease until she lose her head . . . I meant to help but if she will not be helped, *je ne puis mais.*'

Some difficulty arose also from the fact that Charles IX had dispatched an envoy, one Du Croc, to England with instructions to join with an envoy to be appointed by Elizabeth and then proceed to Scotland to settle the differences there. Unfortunately Charles directed him to request permission to visit the Queen of Scots and to demand her release and her return to France.

When Du Croc arrived in England on March 1st and delivered his message to Elizabeth on the 4th she expressed her pleasure at his arrival, but said she would like to read him a letter which had recently come to her hands. It was in cipher, signed by Mary Stuart and addressed to the Duke of Alva. Being in cipher, Elizabeth read a deciphered version. In it Mary urged Alva to hasten an expedition to Scotland and seize the young James, and went on to say that she committed her cause to Spain. With that prologue, Elizabeth proceeded to enumerate her grievances against Mary, and ended by observing that under the circumstances she could hardly believe that the French King had read the letter to her which he had signed. Fénélon reported that Elizabeth seemed to him more hostile towards the Scottish Queen than ever she had been.[8] He added that the news she had received of preparations in France for an expedition to Scotland had increased her distrust to a point at which she began to question the attitude of the French King towards her. Fénélon tried to pacify her, and to explain why his master felt constrained to speak for the Scottish Queen. The outcome was that Elizabeth, while she refused to allow Du Croc to speak with Mary, deferred answer to his request for a passport to Scotland until she heard further from her own commissioners there.

While he lingered, news came of the arrival of Lord Seaton in Scotland. The ship in which he came had been forced by the weather to take shelter in Harwich. He himself had escaped in the disguise of a merchant and had found his way through England to Edinburgh. His ship was seized, its cargo of miscellaneous weapons was confiscated and his dispatches were opened and read. They confirmed the intention of Mary to place her reliance in Spain and of plans afoot for a Spanish descent upon Scotland. This added fuel to the fire, especially since it presently appeared that Seaton's arrival in Edinburgh had strengthened the resolution of Kirkaldy and Maitland to reject all compromise offers. Elizabeth told Du Croc that he might either return to France or await further instructions from his master.[9]

Just at this juncture, Elizabeth thought it well to make a friendly gesture towards Spain. For months an agent of the Duke of Alva, M. de Sweveghem, had been in England trying to settle the dispute over the affair of the Spanish pay ships in 1568, which had led to an embargo of trade between England and the Low Countries. The Spaniards were more eager to settle than the English, because in the long cold war the English had fared better than their opponents. In the seizure of ships on both sides England had taken much more than she had lost, and her takings steadily increased as more and more Spanish ships, driven by the weather or by Channel pirates, had been forced into English harbours. De Sweveghem had made little or no progress, but Alva had directed him to remain in England and to represent the Spanish interest there after De Spes's expulsion in January.

There was another Spaniard in London at the time who had some ill-defined connection with Spain — Antonio de Guaras, a Spanish merchant and a leading member of the Spanish community in London. De Guaras wrote a letter to the Duke of Alva on March 26th.[10] The essence of it was that late in January he had been approached by a 'third person' who urged him strongly to do what he could to settle the differences between England and Spain. De Guaras was responsive, and his interlocutor said that he would convey the message to Lord Burghley. 'As your Majesty knows,' De Guaras continued, 'it is Burghley who rules the whole of this country.' Nothing came of it apparently until March 25th, when Burghley invited De Guaras to visit him. In the interview which followed, Burghley expressed the desire of the Queen and her Council to come to terms with Spain. De Guaras said some polite things about Burghley's influence, who thereupon declared that but for him there had been open rupture between the two countries. He then suggested that De Guaras convey to Philip and to Alva the good will of Queen and Council towards peace. According to De Guaras, the conversation took place in Burghley's room with no one else present.

When Alva got this message he responded sympathetically.[11] His letter is missing, but we gather that De Guaras was directed to ask Burghley to draft the basis of an agreement. De Guaras received Alva's reply on Easter Day and went at once to Court to let Burghley know. 'As Burghley was very ill,' De Guaras wrote to Alva, 'I could not speak with him, but the "third person" went after mid-day and I myself waited at Court . . . But the "third person" was unable to see him in consequence of his serious illness. It was said yesterday that he was in great danger, and the Queen had been to visit him with most of the Councillors. I have heard that last night he was with somewhat better hopes of recovery . . . Certainly if this man dies it will be very unfortunate . . . It is true that hitherto he has undoubtedly been the enemy of peace and tranquillity for his own bad ends, but I am convinced . . . he is now well disposed, which means that the Queen and Council are so, because he and no one else rules the whole of the affairs of state.'[12]

Two days later De Guaras was at Court again. He wrote to Alva on the same day: 'Lord Burghley . . . although in consequence of his illness, he is not attending to any business, as soon as he heard that I was in his lodgings he sent out word . . . that he would receive me . . . He was very weak and feverish . . .' But they discussed peace at some length and De Guaras left quite satisfied that Burghley was sincere in his intentions.

As De Guaras was taking a boat to return home he saw the Queen's barge approaching and waited to make his bow. Elizabeth espied him and called to him in Italian, asking him whether he had been to Court and whether he had seen Lord

Burghley. Whereupon he replied that he had just left Burghley. The Queen thereupon waved her hand and responded: 'That is all right.'

In such wise the Queen and her Secretary played their little game. It was clearly no more than a game, for when De Guaras saw Burghley again the atmosphere was changed, and Burghley complained that De Guaras had misrepresented him. We can follow the story no further at this juncture because the correspondence of De Guaras is missing until after the peace with France was signed.

Meanwhile, negotiations with France had been interrupted by the sudden illness of the Queen late in March and by the ensuing illness of Burghley. They were resumed on April 1st, between Fénélon and the English councillors. The religious difficulty was met by the English agreement to accept a private letter from the King in lieu of definite mention in the treaty. On Scotland the English insisted that Mary Stuart should not be mentioned in the treaty. They would have preferred to omit any mention of Scotland, but finally agreed to a joint Anglo-French commission provided the French recognized James as the *de facto* King. Fénélon objected, but Catherine de Medicis told Smith in France that no reasonable demand would be rejected.

The concluding stages in the negotiations took place in France. Burghley himself was laid by the heels during the first fortnight in April. He was taken ill again on Good Friday[13] and on Easter Day had such a violent seizure that Fénélon thought he would not recover. It was the same illness that had interrupted his dealings with De Guaras and brought Elizabeth herself to his bedside. But he was about again less than a week later.

Peace with France was finally signed on April 19th. It provided for common defensive action in case of attack, but its virtue lay rather in the promise of each confederate not to assist the enemies of the other than in any adequate promise of mutual aid.

On the crucial issue of Scotland the treaty accorded with English ideas. No mention was made of Mary Queen of Scots, and no provision whatever for her welfare. To avoid commitments on the conflicting claims of Mary and her son to the Scottish Crown, the treaty referred simply to the *regnum et status Scotiae*. And it provided for a joint Anglo-French commission with power to reconcile the warring Scottish factions and to restore civil peace there.[14]

The treaty definitely provided for the establishment of an English staple in France for the vent of both wool and cloth, and guaranteed to English merchants a fixed rate of tolls, Customs and port dues. But the place of the staple was not appointed and, though Sir Thomas Smith seems to have cherished the hope that the French market would in time prove to be a satisfactory substitute for the market in the Low Countries, English merchants were less sanguine,[15] and it may well be that the English designed the whole plan mainly as a threat to induce the Duke of Alva to raise the embargo on English trade. In any case, it came to nothing.

Burghley's only recorded comment on the treaty, embodied in a letter to Walsingham on April 22nd, is not enthusiastic:

'Now', he wrote, 'that this treaty is well concluded to the apparent contentation of her Majesty and with the good liking of the French King, I wish all good means used in all parts to nourish your planting that first the glory of God and next the two realms and princes may long see the fruits thereof.'[16]

What the French Huguenots would have liked and what Walsingham would have preferred, to wit, an offensive league directed against Spain in the Low Countries, neither Burghley nor Elizabeth seriously entertained.

And yet the opportunity to strike a shrewd blow at Spain in the Low Countries seemed uncommonly promising in the spring of 1572. The Huguenots and the Politiques both favoured such a course. Louis of Nassau was still in France carrying on a private war against Spanish shipping in the Bay of Biscay and the Channel. And his brother, William, Prince of Orange, the recognized leader of the Dutch rebels, was organizing an army in Germany. A considerable company of Dutch freebooters, currently known as 'Sea Beggars', were operating independently in and around the Straits of Dover under the leadership of Count Willem de la Marck. De la Marck carried a commission from William of Orange and claimed recognition as the admiral of a sovereign prince at war with Spain; but he was little better than a pirate who did not hesitate to pick up plunder sailing under any flag. At the time his tatterdemalion fleet was based in Dover and arousing the indignation of all legitimate traders. The Spanish agent in England protested and complained, but it was apparently merchants of the Hansa League[17] who finally persuaded Elizabeth to deprive him of accommodation in English ports. On February 10th she instructed her commissioners for the Cinque Ports to summon De la Marck before them and express her wish that he should get ready to leave her ports and her coasts. Eleven days later she instructed the Mayor of Dover to procure De la Marck's dispatch by all means in his power. Finally, on March 1st, Elizabeth issued a proclamation ordering all freebooters of any nation to depart on penalty of confiscation and imprisonment.

It has been rashly assumed, on the basis of Spanish testimony, that these orders were all designed to conceal Elizabeth's real intentions, and that she supported and was in a large measure responsible for De la Marck's subsequent procedure. But the evidence has been weighed and found wanting. Both Elizabeth and Burghley had been fighting piracy in the Channel for a decade at least, and the expulsion of De la Marck should probably be interpreted as a move in that fight.

In any case De la Marck gathered his ships together and, after cruising about for some weeks, descended suddenly on the town of Brill in Zeeland, which he captured on April 1st. Once there he wrote Elizabeth asking her to allow him help from the Flemish refugees to England together with arms and ammunitions.[18]

Burghley's first recorded comment on the situation is in a letter to Walsingham of April 22nd.[19]

'The matters of the Low Countries are now in farther terms to relieve them of Pharaoh's cruelties used by the Duke of Alva than when you wrote last hither of the communication which you had with the Count [Louis of Nassau].[20] Here is all covert means used to let them of the Low Countries pass home to the help of the liberty of the country, and I wish it were done rather by themselves than by others that percase would not suffer them long to enjoy the liberty when it should be recovered. Percase it will not be liked there. I cannot write more presently, for I do this in haste, being absent from the Court and I have not your cipher by me.'

Burghley was evidently more concerned about French occupation of the Low Countries than about Belgian liberties. It was largely to prevent the French that he gave free rein to the passage of volunteers from England — Walloons for the most part, but with an increasing number of Englishmen. The French ambassador late in May estimated the English volunteers as between four and five thousand. Not long after the fall of Brill, Flushing also fell into the hands of the rebels. According to Fénélon, the English Privy Council early in May showed a strong disposition to go openly to the assistance of Flushing. It was, he said, a convenient place to establish the English trade, much better than Hamburg. And the English had grievances enough against Alva. But it was finally decided to do nothing more than encourage the Dutch refugees to go to the assistance of their countrymen with such arms and equipment as they could buy.[21] We have no record of the Council meeting from other sources, nor any way of knowing what policy Burghley supported there. He wrote to Walsingham on May 21st:[22] 'The matters of the Low Countries were hot awhile but now the Flemings are become cold. The Duke encroacheth upon them of Zeeland having, by reason of the treason of the townsmen in Arnew [Armuyden], recovered it and put in garrisons of the Spaniards. None withstandeth but Flushing, which is not well governed for lack of a head. We have suffered as many of the strangers to depart from hence as would, but they are but a simple help. If the Prince of Orange doth not now follow this opportunity his case will never be recoverable hereafter.'

Evidently Burghley was sympathetic with the cause of the Dutch rebels, and he clearly recognized that the release of Dutch refugees for service was a simple help. A little later he took an active interest and exercised a directing hand on the bands of English volunteers that went over under Sir Humphrey Gilbert. We hear nothing from him of French aid, though Walsingham was writing about it in very optimistic terms from France.[23] Burghley at the moment was mainly concerned with preventing the French from getting a substantial foothold. That, indeed, was his chief preoccupation with Low Countries affairs for many years to come. He opposed official English intervention because it might well lead to war with Spain. He countenanced unofficial intervention because it would embarrass Spain and might serve to kindle a flame that would divert Spanish energies from English or Scottish enterprises. If the flame spread to a conflagration, so much the better. If it flickered out, England might withdraw without dishonour.

His attitude of mind came out strongly in a 'Memorial for Matters of Flanders' which he drew up early in June.[24] It was probably prepared for the consideration of the Council, and ran as follows:

'To send to Flushing to discover the intention of the people there and to understand the strength of the whole island; to search the passages by water up the river towards Antwerp . . . and to see what entries be into Zeeland otherways and what places may best defend those entries. . . .

'To send to Brill for the like. . . .

'To send to Count Ludwig [Louis of Nassau] to decipher fully his intention and to see and advertise his daily exploits. . . .

'To send to Cologne to understand the intentions of the Princes of Almayne [Germany] and to have intelligence from Christopher Mount what the Emperor purposeth or intendeth in the matter.

'If upon these and other intelligences it appear manifest that the Duke of Alva is sufficiently prepared and able to resist all attempts, so as he may detain his master's countries from the conquest of the French, then it is like to be best for England to let both sides alone for a time; otherwise the French may be offended and the Spaniard not made sure, and if they accord we shall be sure of neither.

'If it appear that the Duke is not able to defend his master's countries from the French and that the French begin to possess any part of them, and especially the maritime parts, then it is like that the French, increasing their dominance, may be too potent neighbours for us and therefore [it] may be good for us to use all the means that may conveniently be, to stay that course.

'If the French proceed to seek to possess the maritime coasts and frontiers it seemeth to be good that by some good means the Duke of Alva were informed secretly of the Queen's Majesty's disposition to assist the king his master by all honourable means she might in the defence of his inheritance, so as it may appear to her that he will discharge his subjects of their intolerable oppression, restore them to their ancient liberties, reconcile his nobility to him, deliver them from the fear of the Inquisition and continue with her Majesty the ancient league for amity and traffic in as ample sort as any others, dukes of Burgundy, heretofore have done.'

Sooner than France, Spain, but only on condition that Alva would restore ancient liberties and deliver them from the fear of the Inquisition — there is nothing at all about religious freedom or even religious toleration, nothing about the Protestant cause. Burghley no doubt hoped that Orange would triumph, but he was evidently not too sure of Orange's brother, Louis of Nassau. In any case the French must be kept out at all costs, even if Englishmen had to fight shoulder to shoulder with Alva's butchers.

He wrote further to Walsingham on the subject three days later: 'As to the matters of the king of Spain's Low Countries, we have great cause to bear jealous countenance thereto; for as being in the Spaniard's hands we lacked traffic with surety, so if the maritime parts come to those where you are, not only the traffic with those parts for our merchants will be regulated by them, but our sovereignty upon the Narrow Seas will be abridged with danger and dishonour.

'And notwithstanding this, I see lack of disposition to provide the remedy where it should chiefly be. And I trust, with importunity we that see into the perils shall obtain somewhat. If not, our consciences shall be quiet, though our minds shall not.'[25]

What exactly Burghley had in mind as the remedy is far from clear. Quite possibly it was meant to be far from clear. He may merely have wanted to appear vaguely sympathetic with what he knew to be Walsingham's desires. Certainly if he importuned the Queen to do something for the rebels there is no evidence of it. Probably he underestimated the potentialities of the Dutch revolt. Probably he favoured unofficial aid, secret loans and bands of volunteers. In any case he was very far from Walsingham's crusader position.

In this connection it is illuminating to compare the letters which Walsingham wrote to Burghley and to Leicester about the matter.[26] To Leicester he wrote: 'I hope it will manifestly appear unto you that upon the good success or evil success of this [enterprise depends] the common cause of religion.'

Three days later he wrote to Burghley: 'I perceive that if there be no assistance given underhand by her Majesty, they [the Dutch rebels] shall be drawn to yield such inconveniences as shall be laid upon them by this nation [the French].'

To Leicester the appeal was in the cause of religion; to Burghley in terms of preventing French occupation. The rift begins to appear between those who subordinated religion to national considerations and those who put religion first. It was to grow wider as time went on, with Burghley and Walsingham as the protagonists.

On June 7th the first of the English bands under Thomas Morgan arrived at Flushing.[27] About a month later Sir Humphrey Gilbert arrived with a force of about 1000 men.[28] Both Morgan and Gilbert opened correspondence with Burghley almost at once, and placed themselves at his direction. In the first of Gilbert's surviving letters he took occasion to thank Burghley 'for many favours that we find in the town at your Lordship's hands for victuals and many other things'.

It is clear enough that Burghley was recognized by the English volunteers as their friend at Court. A Spanish agent in London declared that the volunteers were raised secretly by Burghley's orders, and he designated Burghley as the chief advocate of active intervention in the Low Countries, with the Queen and Leicester reluctant. The same agent, one Antonio Fogaza, a Portuguese, reported in July[29] that the Queen was sending Captain Pelham, the Master of her Ordnance, to survey the situation, and that Sir Ralph Sadler followed after him. He was right about Pelham, wrong about Sadler. In general he seems to have been voluble but ill-informed. When he went on to say that 10,000 troops had gone to the Low Countries from England and that Elizabeth planned to send Leicester's brother, the Earl of Warwick, to direct the whole operation, Fogaza was very far wrong. The French ambassador ten days earlier estimated that 2000 had gone over, but he was careful to add that they went without royal commission 'or any apparent authority from the Queen or her Council'.[30]

On July 19th the Duke of Alva wrote a letter to Elizabeth, protesting against the presence of English soldiers and demanding their recall. He said they were boasting that they had come with the Queen's knowledge and by her orders.[31]

She had, of course, been careful to conceal her hand in the matter, and could always remind Alva that he was at the moment cherishing her rebels in the Low Countries. But it is clear that she began to weaken. In a letter to Walsingham late in July, Burghley observed: 'The Queen's Majesty is very irresolute in these Bas Country matters.'[32]

He wrote on the same subject to Leicester a fortnight later:[33]

'Our people in Zeeland and the Low Countries do not prosper. They fall to pillage, etc. And besides we see the French will prevent them of the town of Flushing which, if they shall do, there is no cause why they should continue there. We therefore do send over one Pickman, a captain of Berwick, being a very wise and valiant man, to confer with Sir Humphrey Gilbert upon the estate, and principally to devise how they may prevent the French in the taking of Flushing. The Duke of Alva hath written to the Queen's Majesty a complaint against her people being there and by virtue of the treaties requireth that they may be revoked. We are not hasty to answer.'

Pickman went with instructions to Gilbert to keep his men in order, to refrain from aggressive warfare and to confine his activities to the defence of Flushing and the recovery of Sluys. He was also to spread the word, so that it would come to Alva's ears, that he had come to the Low Countries without the Queen's knowledge or consent.[34]

The capture of Brill and the spread of revolt in Zeeland and Holland were currently regarded as premature. Burghley, being an opportunist, was quick to seize the opportunity, but to those who were dreaming in France of a co-ordinated attack upon the Low Countries it came before they were quite ready. Louis of Nassau contemplated an assault from three sides: William of Orange with his army of German *reiters* from the south-east; France from the south-west; and, it was hoped, England from the sea. The Anglo-French treaty had of course taken a purely defensive position. If co-ordinated aggression against Spain was discussed at all, it never found expression in the formal negotiations. But the Huguenots had hopes, and their hopes were clearly shared by Francis Walsingham, the English ambassador in Paris. So the involvement of England in the Dutch revolt following the capture of Brill, even if it was unofficial, seemed to give promise of better things to come.

But none of this revealed itself in the official relations of England and France. In June a distinguished delegation, headed by the Duke of Montmorenci, came to England to ratify the treaty of Blois. Outside their formal business their chief preoccupation was to promote the Alençon marriage. But there is nothing in either the English or the French dispatches to indicate that there was any consideration of Low Country affairs. Fogaza said that there was, but he was almost certainly misinformed.[35]

Burghley wrote a brief account of the French delegation to Walsingham on July 2nd, the day after they had left for France.

'Now', he wrote, 'that Duke Montmorenci is gone I thought good briefly to write somewhat to you ... The Duke with all his train, to the number of forty, have been entertained here for their meat and drink, each in their degrees, as it is to be affirmed that the like hath not been seen in any man's memory. The honour also done to him hath been such, as surely her Majesty could do no more, I mean in her courteous usage of him, in appointing sundry sorts of the nobility of the highest sort to attend on him, the difference from my Lord Admiral's[36] entertainment was that no other Lord but my Lord of Leicester did feast him, as in France was done, saving I did upon Midsummer's Even feast him and all his gentlemen with a collation of all things that I could procure, being not flesh, to observe their manner.'[37]

Burghley then went on to speak of the Alençon courtship:

'Afore their going hence they have done what they could in the matter of the Duke of Alençon, whereunto they had neither yea nor nay, but a delay only for one month which they interpreted diversely. They mentioned certain things which I do send you here in a paper enclosed[38] with that which was answered. . . .

'I am willed to require you to use all good means possibly to understand what you can of the Duke of Alençon, of his age in certainty, of his stature, of his condition, his inclination to religion, his devotion this way, the devotion of his followers and servitors. Hereof her Majesty seeketh speedily to be advertised that she may be resolved before the month. And surely I cannot see in her any lack towards this, but in opinion for his age, which defect, if it might be supplied with some recompense, it were meet to be thought of. I could wish we might have Calais to the issue of their bodies, and he to be governor thereof during his life, so as we might have security for our staple there. I wish also that secretly the Queen's Majesty might be assured, although there be no contract therefore, that he would hear no Mass after his marriage. If somewhat be not devised to recompense the opinion that her Majesty conceiveth, as that she should be misliked to make choice of so young a prince, I doubt the end.'

Three days later Burghley wrote again: 'I am sorry that the opinion groweth here of the French king's recoil from the Flanders enterprise. It breedeth coldness here. Some that are come home [from France] bear us in hand that her Majesty reneweth the Anjou match whereby the Alençon matter is hindered. I marvel much therefore. Indeed her Majesty is more given to Anjou than to Alençon. I am commanded to write to you hereof and to require some answer of your opinion which I pray you do with all good haste you can. I see no remedy by worldly means but in Alençon. God send it some way.'

Walsingham in his reply sent a description of Alençon which was flattering in the extreme. He was wise, stalwart, of a good and tractable disposition, not subject to French lightness but well balanced; in religion 'easily to be reduced to the knowledge of the truth'. He went on to say that the French would not entertain the concession of Calais. In his conversation with De Foix on the subject, De Foix suggested that, since the Queen had already a foot in Flushing, she might accept the whole isle of Walcheren, 'which would', he added, 'be more profitable to your country than ten Calaises'. Finally Walsingham dismissed the rumour of a renewal by the Queen of the Anjou courtship as altogether false and vain.[39]

No doubt Burghley passed on Walsingham's report for the Queen's perusal. But she had meanwhile received less favourable reports from another quarter. Clinton, the Lord Admiral, who had been sent to France with a retinue of courtiers to ratify the Treaty of Blois, got back early in July. He reported well of Alençon, but could not conceal the fact that Alençon was far from handsome.

Fénélon discussed the matter with Burghley, pointing out that Alençon was pock-marked, but making light of it. The defect, he said, could easily be corrected. Burghley bade him produce anyone in England who had been cured of pock-marks. Fénélon cited two and added that the doctor, a man of wide knowledge and experience, who had effected the cure, had found a remedy which was both simple and sure.

Two days later Fénélon said the same thing to Elizabeth who urged him to apply the remedy to the royal suitor as soon as might be. Fénélon thereupon wrote to Catherine de Medicis and offered to send the doctor in question to France if she would have it so. Evidently the doctor went. Catherine reported that she meant to let him try his skill. But it does not appear that he achieved any marked success.

Elizabeth, who was very sensitive to masculine beauty, was disturbed by the pock-marks. Burghley told Fénélon that she was more deterred by this than by any other consideration, though she made much of the disparity of age.[40] She now decided that she would make no commitment until she had seen Alençon face to face.[41]

As to the Low Countries, we hear little or nothing of them in the official negotiations between France and England. Walsingham, who had been very optimistic about French intervention there, received a sad shock when an expedition led by the Sr. de Genlis, marching to the relief of Louis of Nassau, besieged in Mons, was cut to pieces by the Spaniards.

In writing to Burghley of the defeat of de Genlis, Walsingham observed: 'Such of the religion as before slept in security begin now to awake and to see their danger, and do therefore conclude that unless this enterprise of the Low Countries have good success their cause groweth desperate ... The Admiral therefore requested me to desire your Lordship, as you tender God's glory and her Majesty's safety, to see if you can induce her, upon overture first to be made by the King in this behalf, to join with him in yielding assistance.'[42]

Walsingham saw that the maintenance of the Huguenots in power in France depended upon the acceptance of an aggressive policy against Spain. But he also saw that the French King was not committed, and what he asked of Burghley was to induce Elizabeth to join if she were asked to join.

But the Huguenots never succeeded in inducing Charles to make the request. It is therefore absurd to say that Elizabeth's indecision brought about all the calamities which followed. She was never officially asked to decide.

It is clear that Charles would have liked to see Elizabeth plunge into the Low Country wars and declare herself openly against the King of Spain. But it is equally clear, and Charles said so in so many words, that he would not attack the Spaniards unless they first attacked him. He expressly disclaimed any responsibility for the ill-fated expedition of de Genlis.[43] The fact is that the French King was as reluctant to start a war as the English Queen was. He might have been persuaded if Elizabeth had agreed to join with him. The Huguenots hoped and Walsingham hoped that he would be persuaded. But he became in fact more reluctant as time went on.

There is no evidence to indicate that he ever went even so far as to say that he would fight if she would. Indeed, it is by no means certain that he would have joined had she taken the initiative.

Elizabeth was certainly unwilling to declare open war on Spain. She was in no wise disposed to assist the French to make war if it should mean the annexing of the Low Countries to France. Even Burghley would go no further than encourage English intervention to assist the Dutch rebels. Like his mistress he believed that England's position would be in greater jeopardy from French occupation of the Low Countries than from the continuation of Spanish rule there.

The zealots like Walsingham may have believed that by some miraculous divine intervention Catholic France would be induced to fight the battle of Protestantism in the Low Countries and, having fought and won, to stand forth as a champion of the Protestant cause. But neither Elizabeth nor Burghley expected miracles. What they saw was another expression of the inveterate hostility of Habsburg and Valois, Burgundy and France. And on the whole they leaned towards the old Burgundian connection.

CHAPTER VI

ST. BARTHOLOMEW'S
AND ITS CONSEQUENCES, 1572

IN the midst of all these entanglements, Lord Burghley ceased to be Principal Secretary and became Lord Treasurer. The reason for the change was probably the general state of his health. He had been seriously ill in April, so ill that he had not been expected to recover and the Queen herself went to his bedside. It began to look as though he could not long endure the heavy strain of carrying all the details of administration upon his shoulders. The old Treasurer, the Marquess of Winchester, who had long ceased to function, died early in March. The French ambassador wrote on the 18th that Sussex and Burghley were the two outstanding competitors for the office.[1] A month later Fénélon wrote again: 'Leicester will be made grand master, having refused to be Lord Treasurer which is of higher rank. But because it requires learning and knowledge (*des lettres et du savoir*) the office is reserved to Lord Burghley, who for this reason has been elected to the Order [of the Garter]. It is also said that Sussex will be made Privy Seal. Mr. Smith [Sir Thomas] will have alone the charge of Secretary of State and will be Chancellor of the Garter.'[2]

So far as Burghley and Smith were concerned Fénélon was correctly informed, though we hear no more about the Grand Mastership, and Sussex was not created Lord Privy Seal. That office went to Lord Howard of Effingham, and Sussex took his place as Lord Chamberlain.

The first step in Burghley's progress was his election as Knight of the Garter on St. George's Day (April 27th). Nearly two months later, on June 18th, he was formally installed at Windsor. The account of the formalities has been preserved.

'On Wednesday the 18th day of June, anno 1572, the feast of St. George was honourably kept in the castle of Windsor. Robert, Earl of Leicester, being lieutenant at the same feast, assisted with these knights of the Order, Francis, Earl of Bedford, Sir Henry Sidney, William, Earl of Worcester, and Henry, Earl of Huntingdon; who, on Tuesday, the day before, brought those Knights following to their installation, viz: Francis, Duke of Montmorenci, Walter, Earl of Essex, William, Lord Burghley, Arthur, Lord Grey of Wilton and Edmund, Lord Chandos.

'On Tuesday, the 17th day of June, 1572, the lieutenant accompanied with the other Knights above named ... made his entry into Windsor Castle about two of the clock in the afternoon ... he himself sitting in a wagon or chariot of the Queen's with the Duke of Montmorenci on his right hand, all the other Knights on horseback, well attended on with goodly number of servants in their liveries and badges. And about five of the clock the Lord Lieutenant and the other four Knights already installed, rode from the Castle above down to the chapel in their kirtles and robes of the Order and went presently into the Chapter House and sent out two of the old Knights already stalled to bring into the same Chapter House the elected Knights, one after another; where as he had a kirtle put on and a band laid on his right shoulder and was from thence, in like manner between two Knights led into the choir to the uttermost stall, right before the stall where the elected Knight's banner doth hang, and Garter goeth directly before him bearing the robe of the Order and the officers of arms two and two before them. The Duke of Montmorenci was led to his stall between the Earl of Bedford and Sir Henry Sidney; the Earl of Essex was brought to his stall between the Earl of Worcester and the Earl of Huntingdon; the Lord Burghley was brought to his stall between the Earl of Bedford and Sir Henry Sidney ... At the arriving at the said nether stall, they having the oath given them by the Register of the Order, Garter putteth on the robe of the Order and so is the new Knight brought out of the nether stall and is enstalled in his own stall above under his hatchments.

'These five new Knights being all thus installed they proceeded orderly, according to their places, into the Chapter House ... where as they put on the collars of the Order over their robes and so did attend upon the said Lord Lieutenant into the choir to hear even song ... Even song being done in the like manner they returned to the south door where they mounted upon their horses with foot cloths and proceeded in the like manner to supper.'

The following day began with a procession on horseback to the chapel where the Duke of Montmorenci, for the Queen, and the other newly installed Knights, for themselves, made customary offerings. After that they returned to Windsor Castle for the formal dinner. After the second course, the Garter King of Arms and all the heralds at arms put on their coats, marched up to the table, made three reverences to the Lieutenant and then called for *largesse*, first from the Queen and then from the newly installed Knights. After that they returned to their places, removed their heralds' coats — and so the dinner finished.

Later in the afternoon the Knights rode again to the chapel for evensong and then returned to the castle for supper.

The third day began with morning prayer, to which the Knights went informally in their ordinary clothes, but with their servants standing ready with their robes at the chapel door, and so they entered in procession. At the end of the service the hatchments of the three Knights who had last deceased were delivered solemnly to the Bishop of Winchester, prelate of the Order, Essex and Burghley together offering the banner and the sword and the helm and the crest of the Marquess of Northampton. That finished, there was a further offering and a final benediction by the prelate of the Order. Then the Knights departed, put off their robes and went their way. 'Thus ended that St. George's feast.'[3]

It must have been very colourful. It was certainly expensive. Each of the newly installed Knights had to provide his own accoutrements. The bill which was rendered to the Earl of Essex on that occasion has been preserved. Since he was an earl, his expense probably ran a little higher than Burghley's, who was a baron, but the items are interesting.

(1) For a helmet of steel gilt with fine gold ... ... £3 6s. 8d.
(2) For his mantle of cloth of gold lined with satin ... £4 os. od.
(3) For two caps of burnished gold and two tassels of silk of his colours ... ... 10s.
(4) For his crest, carved and gilt ... ... 26s. 8d.
(5) For a large banner of his arms wrought with gold and silver ... ... £4 13s. 4d.
(6) For a staff painted for the banner of his colours ... 2s. 6d.
(7) For a sword, the sheath of cloth of gold, the hilt and pommel gilt ... ... 30s.
(8) For a plate of his arms with the beasts supporting, graven in copper and gilt ... ... £4 os. od.
(9) For a book of the statutes of the Order ... ... 40s.
(10) For carrying of the said hatchments to Windsor ... 10s.

In addition to these expenses there were certain gratuities to be met, fixed apparently by rank. We have the figures for the Earl of Essex, with indication of the slightly reduced fee (given in brackets) for a baron.

To the college of Windsor £6 13s. 4d. (£5)
To Mr. Garter, his gown and fee ... ... 40s.
To the usher ... ... 40s.
To the officers of arms £6 13s. 4d. (£5)
To the vicars and clerks ... ... 20s.
To the verger ... ... 6s. 8d.
To the sexton ... ... 13s. 4d.
To the choristers ... ... 5s.

Taking all these together, the ceremony cost Essex £43 10s. 10d., Burghley about £40, a tidy sum by sixteenth-century reckoning.

This admission to the Order was the prelude to Burghley's appointment as Lord Treasurer. According to Burghley's diary, this took place on July 15th.[4] Curiously enough there is no mention cf it in the Acts of Privy Council. Sir Thomas Smith had been appointed Principal Secretary on June 24th.

As Lord Treasurer, Burghley became the presiding head of the Court of Exchequer and the administrative head of the Treasury.

The Court of Exchequer had jurisdiction over cases arising out of the collection of taxes, Customs, and the administration of Crown lands, the debtors of the Crown and *quo minus* the debtors of the debtors of the Crown.[5] Its business greatly increased during Elizabeth's reign,[6] as indicated by the number of plea rolls, which were 40 in Henry VIII's reign and 171 under Elizabeth.[7] One factor in this increase of business was the dissolution of the Court of Augmentations and First Fruits and Tenths under Mary and the transfer of the lands and revenues under their sway to the Court of Exchequer.

As head of the Court of Exchequer, Burghley presided, or at least might preside, over its sittings. In many cases, parties to litigation before the Court requested his presence, and that the hearings be postponed until he did preside. How often he presided is not clear, but probably less and less as he grew older. Since the Court of Exchequer met almost daily during term time, regular attendance would have virtually monopolized Burghley's working hours. As it was, it added considerably to his burden, particularly since he also presided over the Court of Wards.

Immediately under him was the Chancellor of the Exchequer, regarded at the time as synonymous with the vice-Treasurer. Four barons, generally selected because of their knowledge of the law, together with the Lord Treasurer and the Chancellor, formed the Court for transaction of legal business. The numerous subordinate officials were some of them recorders, some of them accountants. In Burghley's time the chief administrative officer was Thomas Fanshaw, the Queen's Remembrancer, an office held by his uncle before him and by his son after him. Most of Burghley's surviving correspondence on Exchequer matters was with Fanshaw, and to him Burghley customarily referred petitions he received for action or for counsel.[8]

This was the same Fanshaw who wrote *The Practice of the Exchequer Court*, which was later published in 1658. In the published edition the treatise is represented as having been written at the request of Lord Buckhurst, Burghley's successor as Lord Treasurer. But the evidence is clear that it was originally composed in 1572 at Burghley's request when he assumed office.[9]

Fanshaw began his treatise with an exposition of the position of the Lord Treasurer. He presided over the Court and conducted the proceedings, examined, debated and finally pronounced the judgment, though the judgment itself was determined either by the barons or by privy seal from the Crown. Those were his functions in the Court. In the administration of the Treasury he watched over the receipts and he ordered expenditures; but, as Fanshaw added, 'can suffer no penny to go out but by privy seal or by writ from the court'.

He oversaw the collection of taxes, both clerical and lay, and had complete control over the Customs, appointing, directing and when necessary punishing the Customs officers. Over the Crown lands his authority was very extensive. He appointed all the escheators and all the custodians of Crown lands. He leased lands held by the Crown as security for debt. He gave orders for the sale of wood and for necessary reparation of houses on royal manors. In fact, he directed and managed all sources of royal revenue and royal expenditure.

In this department of the government his appointing power was very extensive. The more important officials in the Court were appointed by the Queen, but probably in most instances on his nomination.[10] His actual allowance was £368,[11] with £15 7s. 8d. in addition for his robes. No office of the royal household except the Lord Chancellor received so much. How much he got besides in the way of perquisites by the lease of Crown lands and the appointment of Crown officials there is no way of knowing, though it must have been considerable.

There are no indications that he made any basic changes in the Court of Exchequer, though he kept a watchful eye upon its proceedings, saw that the Queen's interests were safeguarded and that justice was done. There is no evidence that he ever accepted presents or other forms of favour from litigants.[12]

The same thing was true of the administration of the royal finances. He recognized the inequities in the assessment of direct taxes, but he did nothing more than try to prevent dishonesty and favouritism by assessors. In the collection of the Customs he was active in trying to prevent smuggling and trying to correct rampant corruption of Customs officials. It may have been on that account that he did not prevent, though he does not seem to have promoted, the farming of the Customs. He played a more active part in dealing with purveyance, the feudal levy which provided victuals and the carts to convey them for the royal household, allowing merchants and farmers who were liable to purveyance to compound for a specific quantity of victuals at a fixed price. As Dr. Woodworth points out, the merchants and farmers liked composition because it protected them from the rapacity of the purveyors. Burghley liked it because it ensured fixed costs during a period of price inflation. The idea was not original with him, but he recognized its value and was the first to apply it on a large scale. By 1580 he had brought at least fifteen counties under the new arrangement, but the greatest gains came after 1589, when in response to pressure from Parliament the process was extended. As a result, at the time of Burghley's death virtually every shire in England and every victualler had been compelled to compound.[13]

He was much concerned also with the management of the royal household, a duty which fell normally to the Lord Steward, but which concerned Burghley as guardian of the royal finances.

Here his efforts were persistently directed to the reduction of expenses, by eliminating corruption and by reducing personnel. His papers are full of memoranda on the subject. An examination of household expenses year by year during Elizabeth's reign reveals the fact that they did not vary much above an average of roughly £45,000. On only two occasions (1560, 1586) did they exceed £50,000, and they never dropped below £40,000.[14] In view of the general rise of prices during the reign, this may be accounted as something of an achievement, but hardly enough to counterbalance the irritation of the Queen and the antagonism of the courtiers.

What strikes one most forcibly about Burghley's administration of the royal finances is that he accepted the existing system as it was, never attempted any fundamental reforms and directed his efforts to the elimination of peculation and corruption.

Probably the major defect in the whole pattern of Elizabeth's financial administration was that officials from top to bottom were inadequately paid and had to eke out their sustenance in ways which were at best unorthodox and at worst scandalously corrupt.[15] Burghley himself knew this well enough and had known how to exploit it for his private profit. But he never struck at the root of the evil and constantly connived at irregularities on the grounds that the poor fellows must live. As for Elizabeth, she was in this particular, as in so many others, penny-wise and pound-foolish, holding over-tight to her purse strings while she dissipated her other assets to her favourites, her courtiers and, sparingly, to her most devoted servants. Burghley saw this if she did not, and he tried to dissuade her from this form of profligacy. But he never succeeded.

During the latter part of her reign Parliament became increasingly rebellious at the inequities of the levy of taxes, the evils of purveyance and the wholesale disregard of the national interest in the distribution of lucrative aids and grants to courtiers. The matter came to a head in the debate on monopolies in 1601. Elizabeth was shrewd enough in that particular to read the signs of the times, but she passed on to her successor a pattern of financial management which was largely responsible for the calamities which followed her.

So far as Burghley was concerned the change of office was a momentous one. He was relieved of the crushing load of detailed administration, and though he assumed responsibility for the national finances, he was primarily hereafter a counsellor. It became abundantly clear that Elizabeth was constantly dependent upon him for advice and would never take a positive step without consulting him. To the very end of his life he was in frequent attendance upon her and a regular attendant at meetings of the Council. Smith relieved him but never supplanted him. Nevertheless, from this time forward the story of his life changes in character. For one thing, his correspondence becomes much less voluminous; for another he had enough leisure to direct his attention to the consideration of more fundamental problems. He became, in short, an elder statesman, sure of his position, sure of his influence, beyond the reach of envy or Court intrigue — a unique figure in the political scene.

Burghley's first recorded observation on his changed position was in a letter to Walsingham of July 27th, 1572. 'I can write no more,' he wrote, 'and now [that] I am out of office of the secretary you shall do best to write to Sir Thomas Smith, the Secretary.'

'And yet', he added, 'I am not discharged from my ordinary care.'[16]

Immediately he was faced with the formidable business of entertaining the Queen, who spent three days at Theobalds with her courtiers, her ladies-in-waiting and a multitude of servants.[17]

He was still working hard on the Alençon match. On July 27th he wrote to Walsingham: 'I am presently so occupied as I cannot write much more than the Queen's Majesty hath done in her letters. By the first you may see what she intended, and by the second what she would to be amended. Surely she findeth the marriage necessary for her and yet the opinion of others, misliking of the party for his person, doth more hinder her purposes than her own conceit. I see such extremities on both sides as I can make no choice, for by no marriage all evil must be looked for and by marriage without liking, no good can be hoped. Therefore to God I leave it.'[18]

On July 27th M. Le Mole, a gentleman deep in Alençon's confidence, arrived in England with royal letters and royal instructions to do what he could to promote the marriage. According to Fogaza, Burghley visited him secretly the night after his arrival and talked with him until past midnight.[19] But a day or so later Burghley left Court for a visit to Burghley House in Northamptonshire. In his absence Fénélon thought it well to mark time, recognizing that no decision could be hoped for without his presence.[20] During the interval Le Mole was sumptuously entertained and had several interviews with the Queen, who found him much to her fancy.

On Burghley's return, Fénélon pressed him for a decision. Burghley said that the Queen would go no further than she had gone. He added that he thought Le Mole's visit had been very timely and the letters he brought with him very helpful, and that he had not ceased to hope for a favourable outcome.

What seems to have been the decisive interview with the Queen took place at Warwick on August 18th. Le Mole and Fénélon had presented to her the King's answer to her suggestion for an interview the day before. It was not favourable. She told Fénélon that she had laid it before her Council, that she had listened to the opinion of each one of them and still found herself perplexed.[21] They had led her to believe that the King would consent to an interview, but she now found that they were wrong. She then went on to elaborate her position at some length. We gather from two copies of a paper in Burghley's hand that he had carefully coached her for this speech.[22] The gist of it was that she could not commit herself to marriage until she and Alençon had had an opportunity to see each other. As Burghley put it in his memorandum: 'Nothing doth so much rule in marriage when the persons are to be considered how one may like the other, as to have their own opinion satisfied with a mutual sight.' Here, of course, Elizabeth was on strong ground, and so Le Mole returned home without apparently accomplishing anything. Fénélon himself felt that the interview would solve the problem. Those who favoured the marriage in England kept shouting in his ears 'Let the Duke come'.[23] Burghley's own comment on the subject was in the same vein. He wrote to Walsingham on August 22nd: 'This gentleman Le Mole hath well behaved himself here to the great contentation of her Majesty and her Court. And I think also he returneth with good liking for so hath the usage of him here well deserved. Surely the choice of him was good and, as it seemeth, the Queen's Majesty is come nearer to the matter than I hoped for. If there may now any amendment grow to his visage and that he would come, I assure you I see no cause to doubt, for in that matter consisteth the only apparent stay.'[24]

But before Walsingham had received this letter, dreadful things had happened in Paris. The story of St. Bartholomew's Massacre need not be told again. In brief it was the wholesale slaughter of Huguenot leaders, their families and their adherents gathered at Paris for the nuptials of the young King Henry of Navarre to the King's sister, Marguerite of Valois. The news of it was first brought to England by refugees. Walsingham's reporters were detained at Boulogne by contrary winds and did not reach London until September 3rd. By that time all

England was on fire with the news. 'It is incredible', Fénélon wrote to his master a little later,[25] 'how the confused rumours which began to come in on the 27th of August of the events in Paris have stirred the hearts of the English who, having heretofore shown a great affection for France, have suddenly turned to extreme indignation and a marvellous hatred against the French, reproaching loudly broken faith, with great execration of excesses and so many kinds of outrages, mixed with words of defiance by those who bear arms against those who would gainsay them ... Even when the matter has been explained, they are no more moderate ... holding that it was the Pope and the King of Spain who kindled the fire in France ... and that there is something evil afoot from all three of them against England.'

The Bishop of London wrote to Burghley on September 5th: 'These evil times trouble all good men's heads and make their hearts ache, fearing that this barbarous treachery will not cease in France but will reach over to us. Neither fear we the mangling of our body, but we sore dread the hurt of our head [the Queen] for therein consisteth our life and safety ... The citizens of London in these dangerous days had need prudently to be dealt withal.'

He enclosed a paper of things which he thought ought to be done. The first item on the list was 'Forthwith to cut off the Scottish Queen's head'.[26] Fogaza wrote to Alva from London on September 8th: 'Lord Burghley ... is coming to this city in a day or two for the purpose of pacifying it, as since the news from France the sectarians, who are the great majority here, are holding meetings and showing signs of a desire to make some movement against the Catholics as a retaliation on what was done to the Huguenots.'[27]

Burghley's first recorded comment on St. Bartholomew's was in a letter to the Earl of Shrewsbury on September 7th:

'These French tragedies,' he wrote, 'and ending of [an] unlucky marriage with blood and vile murders, cannot be expressed with tongue to declare the cruelties, whereof now it is said that the king taketh repentance and that he was abused to cause it to be committed by the duke of Guise and the faction of the papists. None of any name of the religion is left living but such as fled and escaped their pursuers ... These fires may be doubted that their flames may come hither and into Scotland, for such cruelties have large scopes. God save our gracious Queen who now assembles her Council that may come to consult what is to be done for some surety. We have sent H. Killigrew this day into Scotland. The French ambassador came yesterday to Oxford ... but the Queen's Majesty is not hasty to hear any of them. All men cry out against your prisoner [Mary Queen of Scots].'[28]

Indeed Elizabeth herself cried out against Mary. As Burghley remarked, she sent Henry Killigrew, Burghley's brother-in-law, to Scotland before she had even received the French ambassador. He went ostensibly to take Drury's place in the Anglo-French commission which had been working to bring the warring Scottish factions to terms. But Killigrew had another very secret mission, known only to himself, the Queen, Leicester and Burghley. It is set forth in secret instructions preserved at Hatfield House, written in Burghley's own hand, which run as follows:[29]

'Where you are by other instructions directed, first to treat both with the king's party and the others of the Castle . . . and next that, secretly to inform some of the principals of either part of the late horrible, universal murder in France and there-upon to move them to have good regard to that State, that the like be not there attempted.

'Although those matters are of reasonable moment . . . yet, upon a singular trust, you are chosen to deal in a third matter of a far greater moment, wherein all secrecy and circumspection is to be used. . . .

'It is found daily, more and more, that the continuance of the Queen of Scots here is so dangerous both for the person of the Queen's Majesty and for her state and realm as nothing presently is more necessary than that the realm might be delivered of her. And though by Justice this might be done in this realm, yet, for certain respects, it seemeth better that she be sent into Scotland to be delivered to the Regent and his party, so as it may be, by some good means wrought, that they themselves would secretly require it, . . . so they would without fail proceed with her by way of justice, so as neither that realm nor this should be dangered by her hereafter. For otherwise, to have her and to keep her, were of all other most dangerous . . . You may give the said party some likelihood to think that if there were any earnest means secretly made by the Regent and the earl of Morton to some of the Lords of the Council here to have her delivered to them, it might be at this time, better than any time heretofore, brought to pass that they might have her, so as there might be good surety given that she should receive that she hath deserved there by order of Justice, whereby no further peril should ensue by her escaping or by setting her up again . . . And for assurance none can suffice but hostages of good value, that is some children and near kinsfolk of the Regent and the Earl Morton.

' . . . The time requireth that celerity be used to have this done before the French enter any deeper there.'

Killigrew took his leave of the Queen at Woodstock. As he left she charged him to remember that none were aware of his secret mission but herself, Burghley and Leicester, and that if it leaked out he would be responsible. Killigrew replied that it should be to him 'as his life'.[30]

There is no telling who was responsible for the idea. It may have been the Queen herself. On a later occasion, in order to escape the responsibility, she tried to induce one of her servants to make away with Mary privately. As it turned out, the Scots did not rise to the bait, but the fact that it was offered reveals something of the panic which St. Bartholomew's had created in English minds, even in the cool mind of the Queen herself.

Burghley's final comment on Killigrew's secret mission appears in a letter to Leicester written in November:

'I now see the Queen's Majesty hath no surety but as she hath been counselled, for this way that was meant for dealing with Scotland is, you may see, neither now possible nor was by their articles made reasonable. If her Majesty will continue her delays in providing for her own surety by just means given to her by God, she and we all will vainly call upon God when the calamity shall fall upon us. God send her Majesty strength of spirit to preserve God's cause, her own life and the lives of millions [?] of good subjects, all which are manifestly in danger, and that only by her delays. And so, consequently, she shall be the cause of the overthrow of a noble crown and realm, which shall be a prey to all that can invade it. God be merciful to us.'[31]

Evidently Burghley had not been sympathetic to the Killigrew plan. He vastly preferred the solution offered by the House of Commons.

On September 8th at Woodstock Elizabeth received the French ambassador. She had kept him kicking his heels in Oxford for three days, awaiting her pleasure. He found her surrounded by her councillors and ladies-in-waiting. He was struck by the silence which greeted him. The Queen herself advanced to meet him as he entered, drew him aside and spoke with him apart in a window embrasure. He found her grave, stern, but not unfriendly. We have two accounts of the interview which followed, one from Fénélon himself in letters to the French King and his mother, the other from Burghley in a letter to Walsingham.[32] It would be unwise to take either letter at its face value. Fénélon sought to emphasize Elizabeth's friendliness, Burghley her scepticism. And Burghley did not tell the whole story. He simply used parts of it to emphasize his instructions to Walsingham, and may well have put words into the Queen's mouth less temperate than those she used.

According to Fénélon, Elizabeth began by asking him what she was to make of the terrible news from Paris. His reply set forth the official version of the massacre — the King's last-minute discovery of a conspiracy of the Huguenots against his life and the lives of his mother and his brothers, the sudden emergency which had forced him to take instant action without due process of law. Elizabeth replied that his tale was different from the one she had received from Walsingham, that she had the utmost faith in the King's integrity, but hoped that he would clear himself in the eyes of the world.

According to Burghley, she expressed at this point considerable doubt about the validity of the charge against the Huguenots. She found it hard to believe that with Admiral Coligny invalided and in bed, his house surrounded by the King's guards, it would have been difficult to deal with him by due process of law. As Burghley put it: 'It cannot be denied that the same forces which murdered so many might have more easily attached them all. Even if they were guilty, she could not allow the manner of cruelty used in any kingdom or government.' If they were innocent, and the information against them was simply the malicious invention of their enemies, 'as therein surely the manner of the circumstances do lead all indifferent persons to think', then she wished him grace and power to punish the offenders, 'whereby not only his honour, which is now much blemished, may be saved, but principally himself and surety'. 'If', she concluded, 'the King shall not use his power to make such amends for so much blood so horribly shed, God who seeth the hearts of all, princes as others, will show His justice in time and place.'

These were her words according to Burghley. If they were, Fénélon certainly toned them down in his story. One can never be sure about Elizabeth. In a private letter to Walsingham, Burghley said that Fénélon had convinced her of the King's innocence, which makes it unlikely that she was as forthright as Burghley in his official letter made her out to have been. She was certainly alarmed and certainly had no intention of breaking with France. The conventional story of her Court in mourning and her cold rebuke of the French King[33] is not supported by the evidence.

At this point Burghley's account of the interview terminates and we are dependent upon Fénélon's narrative for the rest of the story. In reply to Elizabeth's censure he reiterated the necessity of quick action. He swore that no religious issue was involved and that the King had no intention of revoking the edict of toleration. He expressed the hope that the Anglo-French alliance would not be disturbed. Elizabeth raised doubts on that subject. She expressed her fear that those who had induced the King to abandon his own subjects would presently induce him to abandon his English friends. Fénélon insisted that his master intended to stand firm in support of the alliance. He produced a royal letter inviting her to send an embassy to France, suggesting that either Leicester or Burghley would be welcome. She dismissed the suggestion with the remark that she dared not send either Leicester or Burghley, knowing how much their French enemies desired their deaths. Perhaps later she would consider it.

With that she dismissed Fénélon, and bade him confer with her Council. In his letter to the King he expressed great satisfaction with her friendly attitude. The Council proved to be much less amiable.

It does not appear who spoke for the Council. Whoever it was enlarged at length on the enormity of the massacre — nothing like it was known since Christ's coming, an act so full of blood, for the most part innocent blood, too obviously fraudulent, violating the safety of a great king, troubling the serenity of the marriage of his sister, insupportable to the ears of princes, abominable to subjects of all realms, and so forth and so forth. And by whom? The Council would be glad to be shown that it was done by subjects, and hoped that all Christendom could be convinced of it.

Fénélon answered as he had answered the Queen. He pleaded for the maintenance of the alliance. To this the Council replied that the Queen had done nothing to threaten it and would not if she found the King of the same mind. If he were otherwise disposed, then they felt constrained to warn him that those who found the massacre to their liking might lead him into even more disastrous courses. Immediately the Council asked for assurance that the English wine merchants on their way to Bordeaux would be well treated. They also wanted to know what they were to make of the French fleet assembled under Strozzi. Fénélon reassured them on both points, but they asked for royal confirmation of his assurances.[34]

In commenting on this conference to Catherine de Medicis, Fénélon expressed the opinion that if the French King did not proceed to extremities against the Huguenots, the English would adhere to the alliance. But he admitted that the English were very distrustful of the French and that the King had better be on his guard against what the English might do in alliance with the German Protestants, or the Huguenot rebels in France, or even the Duke of Alva.

Burghley commented on the situation in a letter to Walsingham of September 11th:[35] 'I see the Devil is suffered by the Almighty God for our sins to be strong in following the persecution of Christ's members. And therefore we are not only to be vigilant of our own defence against such traitorous attempts as lately have been put in use there in France, but also to call ourselves to repentance. Of the Queen's answer to this ambassador, I have at good length comprised the same in writing, which cometh now unto you signed by the Council,[36] which you are to use according as the time shall teach you. For although the ambassador hath seemed to gain so much credit here with her Majesty as she thinketh the king is not guilty of the murders otherwise than as he reporteth; and further, that although the ambassador sayeth that the king willed him to assure her Majesty that the navy prepared by Strozzi should not any way endanger her Majesty we have great cause in these times to doubt all fair speeches. And therefore we do presently put all the sea coasts in order [of] defence and mean to send the Queen's Majesty's navy to the seas with speed. And so continue until we see further whereunto to trust . . . If I could have had my mind you had been presently revoked and only a secretary left there.[37] I desire to have knowledge of as many of the principals as were slain, and whether any papists were by casualty slain, and what Protestants did escape. We are much perplexed with variety of reports . . . The whole Council shall be here by tomorrow, but beforehand we that are here have not been idle, I can well speak, to give orders to the realm. God keep you and comfort His afflicted church.'

The following day Burghley wrote again: 'Yesternight after your servant was departed, Faunt and my cousin Zouche came hither, and although I had before moved her Majesty that she should require the king to licence your return, yet I could not then obtain it, as I did this morning. And so now I have obtained a letter from her Majesty to the French king which Master Secretary sendeth to you.'[38]

Later in the month Burghley wrote again: 'We have understood by report from Rouen that on Thursday was seven night, there was a general slaughter made at Rouen of all that could be imagined Protestants, so as the very channels of the streets did run blood. We have heard diversely from La Rochelle, by some that it is sacked by Strozzi, by some that it holdeth out and that it is like so to do a long time. As to the ambassador's negotiation here with us, to seek to persuade us that the King was forced for safety of his own life to cause the execution to be done as it was, and that thereof we should see the proof by the Admiral's process, you may imagine how hard a thing it is to us to be so persuaded against all our natural senses.'[39]

There can be no doubt about Burghley's position. But neither he nor his mistress was prepared to break with France, and the French for their part were desperately anxious to maintain the English alliance. Fénélon did his best to persuade Elizabeth and her councillors that the King would remain loyal to his English friends. He worked hard to revive the Alençon courtship, and even went so far as to promise that Catherine de Medicis herself would bring her son to

England for an interview.[40] He found Elizabeth amicably disposed, but the Council suspicious and hostile. 'I can assure you, Madame,' he wrote to Catherine de Medicis, 'that the late accident has wounded the Queen and her subjects so deeply that only a very skilful surgeon and a very sovereign balm can effect a remedy.'[41]

Early in November Burghley wrote to Walsingham: 'Yesterday the French ambassador sent me word to declare to her Majesty that the French Queen hath brought forth a daughter and to know whether the Queen's Majesty would be content to christen it with her own name and to send my Lord of Leicester or me thither. Her Majesty's answer was, that she would not desire to christen it nor would send my Lord of Leicester or me, but if the king would desire her Majesty to be Godmother she would not refuse it but would send some person qualified.'[42]

The Earl of Worcester was in fact sent over later in the month, and a show of friendship maintained.

Meanwhile, French refugees had been crowding into England, and French Huguenot leaders were organizing support for the beleaguered La Rochelle. The most active among them was the Count Montgomery, the same Montgomery whose splintered lance in tournament had given the death blow to King Henry II in 1559. Montgomery had escaped the slaughter of St. Bartholomew's by sheer hard riding. He had English connections, was in fact the brother-in-law of Sir Arthur Champernowne, Vice-Admiral of Devon, who virtually controlled the shipping of the west ports. Montgomery set about organizing a fleet for the relief of La Rochelle. During the winter Fénélon was constantly at Court protesting against the assistance rendered to the Huguenots. Elizabeth denied it and Burghley swore a great oath that it was not so.[43] There is virtually no evidence on the subject from English sources, and certainly if Elizabeth was lending assistance to Montgomery, she managed to conceal her hand very skilfully. It is, however, clear enough that Burghley was in close touch with Montgomery.[44] Just before he left for La Rochelle, he wrote to Burghley from Plymouth, complaining of the delays in getting away. When he had established himself at Belle Isle, off the south Breton coast, north of La Rochelle, he wrote again, begging Burghley 'to be a means that she will not delay to send succour to so many good people who have placed themselves under her obedience'. And when he got back to Plymouth he wrote again asking Burghley to instruct him 'what he shall do next'.[45] So the probabilities are that Burghley had done far more to assist the Rochellese than he was prepared to admit.

Over against this must be set Burghley's own observations in a letter to Walsingham of March 20th:[46] 'She [the Queen] hath much ado to detain them [her subjects] from adventuring in great numbers to pass to La Rochelle at their own charges, and those are not of the popular, but noblemen and gentlemen of ancient and great livelihoods, who surely have offered of their own charges to find an army of 20,000 footmen and 2000 horsemen for six months in Gascony. And so earnest they have been, that it is already known to themselves both where the men are to be had and the money. Only they desire but a permission. And truly her

Majesty, hearing hereof, hath shown herself much offended herewith ... As for the stay of Montgomery, it was said that he desired to depart the realm, considering her Majesty refused to aid him, and therefore her Majesty thought it a cruel part to stay him when she was not disposed to aid ... And for the manner of departure the [French] ambassador can tell how much he was grieved that her Majesty hath caused all such as were on the sea for him and Rochelle to be apprehended and all that which they had taken from other the French king's subjects to be restored, as indeed the like speedy restitution hath not been made at any time.'

How much of this was true, how much of it devised for the satisfaction of the French King, it is impossible to say. In any event, the flocking of volunteers to support the French Huguenots recalls the analogous flocking to support the Dutch rebels. An increasing number of Englishmen were evidently eager to flesh their swords for the Protestant cause.

Burghley also got involved in a rather mysterious business with the young Duke of Alençon. On October 14th he wrote to Walsingham in cipher:

'Hither came one La Ferté sent hither from ——— where M. *Montgomery* is. The party sayeth that he was sent by *M. La Torrey* ——— to desire, as in the name of the *Duke of Alençon* and of *Montmorenci* that the *Queen's Majesty* would give succour to *La Rochelle.* For *Alençon* and *Montmorenci* with the *brothers* of Montmorenci were disposed, if *the Queen* would thereto incline *herself* to make a *party*, in ——— and other parts of France to *avenge* the death of the *Admiral* and the rest. And this *La Ferté*, being a servant of *Torrey*, saith it is desired that *the Queen* would by some trusty person, inquire their intentions, and that he that shall do so shall use only this word for a token — *St. Antony*, for in that place was the conference had of this purpose.

'Hereupon you shall do well speedily to cause some of yours of trust to repair secretly to *La Torrey* with the said word and to declare the foundation of the message sent by his man named *La Ferté*, who, I think, will come thither or [ere] you can cause this matter to be moved ... As I perceive, Alençon by this messenger should fear his own estate. And here is ———, who being acquainted herewith, saith that if the *Queen* will hearken to this matter not only ... but all *Gascony* and all other, *our old* possessions, shall be at the direction of the *Queen.*'[47]

Walsingham set about at once investigating the matter, and replied on October 25th 'that the party employed passed the bounds of his commission or that such as employed him have altered their purpose'.[48]

In reply Burghley wrote on November 3rd[49] that he was shocked, that La Ferté had offered to pledge his life in the matter. Furthermore, in the interval, another messenger named Maisonfleur had arrived from Alençon to explain his dangerous position in France and to request of the Queen that he be allowed to repair to England. Burghley was not impressed with Maisonfleur: 'He pretendeth great devotion in religion and yet we understand that he is of great levity and folly, meet for any dangerous enterprise ... wherefore her Majesty hath willed me with all haste to will you by some good means to understand the truth of the party himself, that is to say, of Alençon.'

Five days later Burghley wrote again that the Queen had spoken with Maison-fleur, and that he had convinced her of his good faith. 'But yet', Burghley continued, 'I cannot for certain reasons but be jealous of such practices and therefore I am willed to require you to use some secret means to understand the truth.'[50]

Walsingham replied five days later that he had known Maisonfleur for some time, that he was a Huguenot and reputed to be honest. Walsingham wrote that he had sent for Le Mole and questioned him about Maisonfleur and that Le Mole had declared Maisonfleur to be a bona-fide messenger.

There appears to have been no further development in the matter for some weeks to come. On December 11th Burghley wrote to Walsingham that Maisonfleur had come to him, informed him that the French had got news of his mission and that Alençon meant to fly to England. Maisonfleur asked Burghley to send a ship to St. Valéry at the mouth of the Somme in Normandy to take the Duke off.

Burghley sent the ship. He also sent to Walsingham an account of the interview with Maisonfleur. Walsingham investigated and discovered that Alençon had no thought of flight. And so the ship, after cruising about for over three weeks, returned without its passenger. Maisonfleur wrote to Burghley to explain, but what his explanation amounted to was that he had acted without warrant from Alençon. Leicester and Walsingham both reached the conclusion that the whole matter was nothing less than an artifice of the French Crown. 'I dare venture my arm to be cut off', Leicester wrote, 'that it will fall out a plain practice and in the end the [French] king may take his advantage against her Majesty when he list and say justly that she was willing to offer him such an injury by entertaining evil practice against him.'[51] Burghley, although not quite so positive, inclined to the same opinion.

In connection with this French business, we get a hint of Elizabeth's affectionate regard for Burghley's welfare. Sir Thomas Smith early in January told the Queen that he had sent for Burghley. In a letter to Burghley he related the conversation which followed. '"Why," saith she, "I beshrew you, why did you send for him [Burghley]?" "Marry" quoth I, "Madam I do wish him here at the departing or before of my L. of Worcester, to make perfect all things first that ways into France and then with my Lord of Desmond and Ireland." "Why," saith her Highness, "I knew before he would take physic at London and then recreate himself a while at Tongs. I beshrew you for sending for him."

' "There is no hurt done," quoth I, "Madam, I will send him word again this night, what your Majesty doth say, and I think he will not be hasty to come." '[52]

Late in January Alençon dispatched Le Mole secretly to England.[53] The visit was carefully concealed, and apparently Fénélon never got wind of it. Burghley wrote to Walsingham on January 29th:[54] 'I have received your last letter of the 20th of this month . . . concerning *Alençon* and was on Friday last with the party you made mention [Le Mole] to be sent from *Alençon*. He spoke with the *Queen* and *Maisonfleur* with him. I see there was a great misliking of our doings, for by *Maisonfleur's* writing of a ship sent to *Valéry*, *Alençon* imagining that the Queen had a meaning to provoke *him* to come hither, whereupon this last gentleman came to inquire of the *Queen* some assurance, if *Alençon* should so do *she would marry him*. This you must think must needs appear very strange. Whereupon, before *Maison-fleur*, I did declare that all that was done came of him with earnest and lamentable requests to have *Alençon* preserved, because he said that the *French King* had gotten such knowledge of the same, as the same should tend to the ruin of *Alençon*. And so the party that now was sent is departed, well certified of the truth, but not satisfied according to his request. It is good to deal warily herein, for I have some cause to mistrust that Maisonfleur and all his partners do nothing herein without the knowledge of the *Queen Mother*, and therefore it is in such sort herein ordered as there can be no advantage taken I trust.'

And so the matter ended. Burghley at the moment was particularly incensed against the French. Early in January[55] Walsingham sent him two books. Burghley wrote to him about them on January 14th:[56] 'This day I received your letters with two French books, the one of Carpenter the Apostate, the other by an unknown malicious French writer taught by a rebellious crafty priest of England, wherein, though he mean maliciously to the state, yet he vomiteth his choler and despite chiefly against me and my Lord Keeper by nicknames. God amend his spirit and confound his malice. And for my part, if I have any such malicious or malignant spirit, God presently confound my body to ashes and my soul to perpetual torment in Hell. I know not whether you shall be able to understand the author but if by the printer it might be found out, I would be glad to bestow any reward upon the discovery. If it cannot be found, then I wish that some means were used of yourself to the Queen Mother that the print might be destroyed. For otherwise we shall think ourselves, considering the places we do hold in this estate, not well considered by that estate ... The licentiousness to inveigh against men by name in printed books, that use not by books to provoke any, is in all good estates intolerable. God send this Estate no worse meaning servants in all respects than we two [Bacon and Cecil] have been, who have indeed spared no labour nor care to serve our Queen and Country. And if we had, we may truly avow, neither our Queen nor Country had enjoyed that common repose that it hath done. From my house at Theobalds where are with me Mr. Ralph Sadler and divers others, as Mr. Denny, your good friend.

'P.S. When I consider of this lewd book I think it will be replied unto you that it is reason that answer be made to such books as are published for the condemning of the Queen of Scots. And so for my part I yield that writers answer writers. But to have the cause of the Duke of Norfolk brought in question and us that are Councillors to the Queen to be so maliciously and falsely calumniated, may not well stand with the terms of the amity professed.'

About a fortnight later Burghley referred to the subject again:[57] 'I have imparted to the French ambassador my misliking of this lewd book, in that it hath been translated by Belleforest, a man of note in that Court, and he showeth himself ready to procure the suppression of it. What he will or can do herein I know not.'[58]

There can be no doubt at all that Burghley referred to a French translation of *The Treatise of Treasons*, which had been published in Antwerp in January 1572.[59]

It was an attack on the government for their dealings with the Duke of Norfolk, all of which it blamed upon Bacon and Cecil.

Its preface will give some notion of its contents. It began by comparing Sinon, who betrayed the Trojans, with the two English culprits.

'For baseness of parentage, for ambition of mind, for smoothness of tongue, for shameless face, for little honesty and no conscience, looking upon old Sinon you see the right retract of the new. Yea, their very names do so concur and resemble each other that both beginning with one syllable and each of them having but two in all, containing also like amount of letters and vowels.'

Referring specifically to Cecil the author went on to say that evil things 'have been contrived by him for satisfaction of his own thirst to heresy and ambition. Yea what child can show more base, abject and contemptible courage than he, whose insolency is intolerable, whiles authority fawneth on him and, for every one least thwart of his superiority, faineth either to be sick for sorrow or lame of the gout, and falleth to sighing and sobbing, crouching and kneeling, weeping and whining like a boy and a babe till his head be stroked and he comforted and called a good son again'.

Burghley is never mentioned by name, but the allusions to him are unmistakable. Naturally he was not amused. Throughout his life he was, for a veteran politician, exceptionally sensitive to personal attacks.

One inevitable consequence of English distrust of France was an increased disposition to repair the fences with Spain. As Fénélon pointed out in a dispatch to his master in October, English tradition favoured the old Burgundian alliance. Burgundy was the old friend, France the old enemy.[60] It had been made clear enough in the unravelling of the Ridolfi Plot that Spanish intentions towards England were far from amiable. But over against the Ridolfi Plot, which had originated in England, the English set St. Bartholomew's Massacre. After all, the Spaniards had not been any more responsive to the appeal of the English Catholics than the English had been to the appeal of the Dutch Protestants.

For four years there had been an embargo on trade between England and the Low Countries arising out of Elizabeth's seizure of the Spanish pay ships in 1568. Property had been seized on both sides, Spanish property in England, English property in the Low Countries. On top of the original seizure English privateers, or pirates as you choose to call them, had gathered a rich harvest of Spanish shipping in the Narrow Seas. A quick appraisal of profits and losses had easily revealed the fact that the English takings far exceeded in value the Spanish takings. Perhaps it was for that reason that the English were in no haste to come to terms. What happened was that the Duke of Alva, badly in need of money to pay his soldiers, had converted his seizures into cash. After some delay the English followed suit. Alva got more out of his seizures than he would have got out of the pay ships; Elizabeth got enough out of hers to settle the claims of her merchants and a handsome profit to boot. She also undertook to repay the Italian bankers to whom, she alleged, the money conveyed to Alva in the pay ships really belonged. So Alva was reasonably well satisfied and Elizabeth quite well satisfied. The only losers by the transaction were the Spanish merchants, who had to look for satisfaction to Alva who had spent all his takings on military operations.

So the principals involved had little reason to continue the quarrel. Of the two, Alva felt the pinch more than Elizabeth, for he lost all the revenue from the lucrative English trade, and trade elsewhere was in constant jeopardy from English freebooters, and, increasingly, from the Dutch 'Sea Beggars' established at the mouth of the Scheldt, the highway to Antwerp. The English merchants, to be sure, suffered from the closing of the Antwerp market, but they had found other fairly adequate alternatives at Emden and at Hamburg.

So the situation was ripe for an Anglo-Spanish rapprochement. On the negotiations which follow we have painfully little from English sources, and are dependent upon what the French ambassador wrote about them, which was little, and what the Spanish agents in England wrote about them. Of these we hear of two,[61] Antonio de Guaras, a Spanish merchant in London, who was recognized both by Alva and by Philip II as their agent, though he had no official status; Antonio Fogaza, a Portuguese, who served Alva as a news agent. He probably had more than one, but Fogaza's correspondence happens to survive.[62] He was a very voluble fellow and a very credulous one. Much of what he wrote was demonstrably untrue, but it has some usefulness.

It will be recalled that when negotiations for the Treaty of Blois were still pending Burghley had had some conversations with De Guaras on the subject of an Anglo-Spanish rapprochement. They came to nothing at the time, but they left the door open to further dealings.

Early in October 1572 De Guaras presented himself at Court with a letter from Alva to the Queen.[63] The letter itself was a friendly one, though it ended with the bad news of the capitulation of Louis of Nassau at Mons. In conversation with Burghley, De Guaras was at pains to point out that Louis had been allowed to march out of Mons with the honours of war. Burghley observed that it was nobly done. It was to be supposed, he added, that Alva would keep faith with Louis. De Guaras retorted that it would certainly not be kept in the French fashion. Burghley agreed and took occasion to condemn French practices in unmeasured terms, at the same time, according to De Guaras, speaking with great reverence of the Spanish King and of Alva. After that, Burghley insisted that De Guaras should stop and dine with him, but at that point Sussex and some of the other councillors turned up and further conversation with De Guaras was postponed until the morning.

In the morning Burghley and De Guaras talked together for an hour, and would have gone on longer if the Queen had not suddenly summoned Burghley to her presence. Burghley told De Guaras that Elizabeth was much pleased with Alva's letter, and bade De Guaras tell his master that she agreed that they should come to an understanding, and that both she and Burghley greatly desired it. He added that neither the Queen nor her Council was too sure of the Spanish King's sincerity, but if he were sincere then both the Queen and her Council were delighted. De Guaras insisted that Alva had spoken for Philip and that Alva's word was beyond question. Burghley seemed to acquiesce.

D

De Guaras then suggested that since both sovereigns were so well disposed it would be well to start the ball rolling by drawing up some heads of agreement. Burghley concurred, but pointed out that one difficulty in the way was the treatment of Englishmen in Spain by the Inquisition. De Guaras suggested that Englishmen going to Spain who carried with them heretical books should be subject to the Inquisition, that any Englishman spreading heresy should be banished. Burghley did not object. It was understood, however, that the rule simply applied to transient Englishmen and not to residents. At that point Burghley was interrupted by the summons from the Queen. As he left, De Guaras said he would send news of the conversation to Alva. To which Burghley replied: 'Do so and return at once to Court, and I will draft the heads of agreement as impartially as I can and you can afterwards send them to his excellency.'

De Guaras, in commenting upon the interview in his account of it to Alva, observed that the English were at the end of their tether. 'Since the French occurrences everybody at Court looks upon me as the instrument for their welfare and the people at large say the same, though previously they were ready to stone me.'[64]

For the next week De Guaras was in constant attendance at Court, discussing with Burghley the terms of agreement.[65] His observations on the situation must be received with caution. There was evidently a certain amount of window-dressing for his benefit. But they are worth noting.

'It is undoubted', he wrote to Alva on October 12th, 'that there is a great amount of hidden dissension in the Council, as some are friendly to our side and others lean towards the French. But the best Councillor of all of them is Lord Burghley as he follows the will and bent of the Queen, which is towards concord; as he is supreme in the country and in the Queen's estimation. In all the important councils which were held during the days that I was at Court, he, with his great eloquence, having right on his side, was able to persuade those of the Councillors who were opposed to him. He assured me privately that he had gained over the great majority of his opponents, and especially the Earl of Leicester who has always been openly in every affair, public or private, on the side of the French, following in this the example of his father, who was strongly attached to that side.

'He also told me that since the occurrence that had happened in France to the Admiral and the other Huguenots, the French were pressing more than ever ... Lord Burghley told me this very secretly whilst he was assuring me of the Queen's desire to arrange the differences with us ... Whilst I was at Court the French ambassador came ... and it was very evident that the Queen and Council placed but small reliance upon the negotiations because they treated him very coolly and are casting their eyes entirely upon us, turning their backs upon him and his promises.'[66]

At Burghley's request De Guaras prepared a written memorandum of his views about the terms of settlement. A copy of this memorandum is still preserved at the Public Record Office with corrections in Burghley's own hand.[67]

The main features of it were: (1) that trade should be re-established for a period of two years among England and Spain and the Low Countries on the same terms as it had been before the embargo; (2) that in the meanwhile commissioners should be appointed to discuss matters at issue, with the understanding that if differences were not composed within the two years, conditions should revert to the *status quo*. De Guaras also raised the thorny question of the persecution of Englishmen for their religion. He proposed that in the Low Countries Englishmen be permitted the use of their religion, secretly and privately in their houses, as they had been before the embargo. As to Englishmen in Spain, those who brought in prohibited books should be punished in the customary way, those who talked heretical talk should be banished.[68]

Burghley agreed with these terms except that in the matter of religious offences in Spain he proposed in all cases banishment.

He raised also certain other questions about refugees, suggesting that those who had merely fled for religious reasons should be undisturbed, those who had fled to escape punishment for capital crimes should be expelled.

He considered the question of the resumption of diplomatic intercourse by the exchange of ambassadors, and suggested that resident ambassadors of both princes should enjoy the private use of their religion; but that none but native Spaniards in England or native Englishmen in Spain should be admitted to these private services.[69]

Burghley drew up a résumé of these deliberations which wound up with the statement that in order to avoid delay the statement should be signed by councillors of both princes, 'for which purpose I, Wm. Lord Burghley, Knight of the Order of the Garter, Master of the Court of Wards, etc., with the knowledge, consent and allowance of my sovereign lady, Queen Elizabeth, by the Grace, etc., do subscribe and seal the same, promising on the faith I bear to Almighty God and the duty to my said Lady and Queen, that I will to the uttermost of my power further and advance the due observation of all the contents of the former articles in all parts'.[70]

It appears to have been Burghley's intention to deliver the résumé to De Guaras. At the same time he intended to draw up a statement of the matters actually agreed upon with De Guaras for the King's signature. According to De Guaras, Elizabeth herself was to have read this statement and to have handed it to him personally, 'promising me on her word of honour that when it was returned to her signed by the king she would sign another similar document in my presence'.

But suddenly the whole picture changed. When De Guaras presented himself to receive those documents Burghley did not deliver them. He said instead: 'You may well go to London now, where I shall shortly arrive and will tell you more. At present I can only say that I do not hand you the heads of agreement nor the other document for your king's signature as we have received news that your king, the King of France and other princes are determined to kill all those who do not belong to their religion that they possibly can, and that any Englishmen who go to Spain or Flanders will be murdered.'[71]

De Guaras attributed this sudden volte-face to the effect of two dreadful stories which reached England at just about this time.[72] One of these reported the slaughter of the defenders of Malines by Alva's bloody troops; the other, the massacre of the French Huguenots who, after they had been allowed by Alva to march out of Mons with the honours of war, were murdered to the last man by the forces of the Duke of Guise. Englishmen read in these enormities a clear indication of the intentions of the Catholic monarchs towards Protestantism at large. To the Queen and her Council these grim forebodings were accentuated by the dispatches of Walsingham from Paris. He wrote to Sir Thomas Smith on October 8th: 'The Admiral is now dead and the duke of Guise liveth, the Prince of Orange is retired out of Flanders but the duke of Alva remaineth there still. I need not to conclude for that to man's judgment it is apparent what will follow . . . As far as I can learn there is none yet sent to deal with the Princes of Germany and yet there is here almost daily conferences between the Pope's nuncio, the ambassador of Spain and them here. They omit nothing that may tend to our peril. I would we were as careful not to omit anything that may tend to our safety.' To Burghley the same day he wrote: 'It is the opinion of all men of judgment that her Majesty is to look for any mischief that either Spain or this Crown can yield.'[73] Without much doubt the Queen's councillors were alarmed. She was doubtless alarmed herself. Burghley's sudden breaking off of the promising negotiations with Alva was no doubt due to her prompting.

In any case, after a brief interval, Elizabeth ignored Walsingham's diagnosis of the situation. She still preferred to play the old game of setting Spain against France and subordinating religious to political considerations. Instead of undertaking to organize the forces of Protestantism she reverted again to the business of coming to terms with the Spaniards.

Burghley's attitude towards the situation is nowhere defined. At the moment he followed where the Queen led, but he did not sever his connections either with the Huguenots or with William of Orange. It may well be, as Fogaza suggested,[74] that he felt the pressure of English commercial interests to re-establish the old ways of trade with the Low Countries. In any case his distrust of France was even greater than his distrust of Spain and, as between the two, Spain had more to offer. He certainly had no disposition to fight them both.

For two weeks he had been steadily avoiding De Guaras. Then he sent word to De Guaras that he wanted to see him. On November 4th De Guaras wrote that he had talked with Burghley on October 29th.[75] Burghley told him that some members of the Council did not feel that they could trust the Spanish King, even if he did come to terms. Burghley said that neither the Queen nor he were of that opinion. He bade De Guaras write to Alva and invite his comments on the draft agreement which had been sent to him, and particularly upon the treatment of Englishmen in Flanders and Spain about matters religious. Unless, Burghley said, some reasonable agreement could be reached on that subject, it would be waste of time to carry the negotiations any further.

Burghley told him that the Queen had ordered the return of Sir Humphrey Gilbert and his troops. At the same time he observed that she would be glad to mediate between the Spaniards and the Prince of Orange.

Five days later De Guaras wrote again that Burghley had sent for him and handed him a draft proposal of terms which De Guaras said was practically identical with the earlier one, though somewhat shorter.[76] As a matter of fact, it was not only shorter, but considerably less specific on matters in controversy. On the religious issue for example, Burghley simply said: 'It is to be understood that none of the subjects of either part shall be molested by the manner of inquisition for matter of religion, so as they do not commit any open act to the contempt of the religion in the country of the other prince, which if they shall do the same shall be banished out of the same country without further corporal punishment.'

Burghley went on to provide that 'the rebels of one prince may not be received, favoured nor suffered to remain in the dominions of the other prince, . . . And that in like manner no kind of pirates be cherished or favoured directly or indirectly of the one or the other part, but that all diligence be used by both the princes to suppress them'.

These terms are significant because Alva subsequently accepted them and they formed the basis of the agreement which followed.

In his interview with De Guaras, Burghley said that religion, restitution and other points in controversy could be settled by the commissioners after the ports were open. He expressed the wish that they could be opened on December 29th, the fourth anniversary of the seizure of English ships in the Low Countries. De Guaras was of the opinion that the English were so eager for the re-establishment of trade that they would accept almost any terms. He even thought that the Queen could be induced to return to the obedience of the Pope. Evidently Burghley buttered him well.

Following this interview negotiations marked time awaiting Alva's answer.[77]

As Alva delayed, De Guaras, who was naturally eager to win for himself the kudos of making peace, became increasingly anxious, and Burghley managed to increase the anxiety. He invited no further conference but sent 'the third person' to say that the Queen was surprised that she had received no answer to her letter to the Spanish King in August. Straightway De Guaras wrote to Alva that he thought the success of the negotiation turned upon the King's reply, observing at the time that emissaries from the Prince of Orange were at Court, that supplies were being shipped to Holland and that some mischief was on foot.

A month passed and still nothing happened. De Guaras wrote on December 15th that though Burghley saw him he said nothing and took no notice of him. He heard that half a million crowns were being raised to support the Huguenots in France and Orange in the Low Countries, and that 7000 troops were being made ready to send to Flushing.

On December 20th Burghley sent for De Guaras to inquire whether he had heard from Alva.[78] De Guaras replied that he expected to hear any minute. Burghley then went on to say that many of his fellow councillors were trying to persuade the Queen that the Spaniards were deceiving them, and that in view of the fact that neither the King nor Alva had written, it was hard to deny it.

In any event, Alva wrote at last on January 1st. He accepted Burghley's terms and charged De Guaras to thank Burghley warmly for his efforts in bringing about an agreement, assuring him that he could count upon Alva's co-operation.

After that the matter was plain sailing. The one point upon which the Spaniards refused to yield was any religious concession to Englishmen in Spain. After some hesitation this point was referred to commissioners who were to meet and seek a settlement of all matters in dispute. Alva signed for his master and sent the agreement to England, where Burghley on April 5th signed for his mistress.[79] What the convention provided was the restoration of trade between England on the one side, Spain and the Low Countries on the other, the ejection of English rebels from the Low Countries and Dutch rebels from England and vigorous action against piracy in the Channel. It did not touch the fundamental issues at stake, but it opened up to English merchants their old markets, and it relieved the tension between the two countries.[80] This convention, plus the displacement of Alva late in the year by his much more peaceful successor, Don Louis de Reques-cens, re-established friendly relations between the two countries for some time to come. Not the least of its consequences was the discouragement of the English Catholics at what they regarded as the apostasy of Spain. It must be accounted a considerable achievement, though to the ardent Protestants it seemed like a betrayal of the faith and a league with the powers of darkness.

All the evidence we have on the subject indicates that Burghley carried on these negotiations almost single-handed. It is to be observed that although he was no longer Secretary, his hand was still on the helm of the ship of state. We hear little of Smith. He himself wrote to Burghley on October 15th: 'I well perceive her Highness is disposed to sign nothing except your Lordship be here.' And again a month later: 'Your hasty going hence hath made, as appeareth, all things here turn backwards. I have somewhat ado to get to the Queen and more to get anything signed ... I perceive, until that your Lordship come again, will be no good done.'[81] The new Secretary had clearly not displaced the old.

CHAPTER VII

SCOTLAND, 1572-73

WITH France deep in the Fourth Civil War and still trying desperately to make a marriage alliance with England, and Spain once more on friendly terms, Elizabeth and Burghley were freed of pressing dangers from the continent and could turn to deal with the Scottish problem. In the spring of 1572 the alliance of France and England at Blois and the subsequent abandonment of Mary Stuart's interests by the French King and his mother reduced the Marian defenders of Edinburgh Castle almost to despair. And the massacre of St. Bartholomew's went far to complete their prostration. Killigrew, who was representing English interests in Scotland at the time, wrote in September: 'Those that have any fear of God break out into open speeches of detesting the cruelty and have exhibited a supplication to the Regent to take counsel in time and prevent the danger apparent from drawing nearer. Every man crieth out to join with England in some straiter league.'[1]

At St. Andrews, John Knox, no longer able to walk unsupported, went Sunday after Sunday to the pulpit and thundered against Mary and her partisans. He returned to Edinburgh in August and raised his voice there again from his old pulpit. Killigrew had words with him in October, scarcely a month before his death, and Knox sent a friendly message through Killigrew to Burghley. The story as Killigrew tells it runs as follows: 'He [Knox] doth reverence your Lordship much and willed me once again to send you word that he thanks God he had obtained at His hands that the Gospel of Jesus Christ is truly and simply preached through Scotland, which doth so comfort him as he now desireth to be out of this miserable life. He said further that it was not long of your Lordship that he was not a great bishop in England,[2] but that effect grown in Scotland, he being an instrument, doth much more satisfy him. He withal desireth me to make his last commendations most humbly to your Lordship and with all that he prayed God to increase His strong spirit in you, saying there was never more need.'[3]

Shortly after his last sermon Knox had a paralytic stroke. But his fighting spirit was never daunted. From his bedside he sent a message to Kirkaldy in the castle: 'Tell him I warn him in the name of God to leave that evil cause, if not he shall be brought down over the walls with shame and hung against the sun.' A few weeks later, beside his grave, Morton in one pregnant sentence spoke his obituary: 'There lies one who never feared the face of mortal man.' As Froude remarks: 'No grander figure can be found in the entire history of the Reformation in this island, than that of Knox.'[4] He and Burghley never saw eye to eye on matters theological, but it was part of the wisdom of Knox that he saw in Burghley, albeit they differed vastly in temper and in technique, another great champion of the cause for which he fought to his last breath.

Elizabeth's policy towards Scotland at this juncture, as it had been for the year past, was to induce the contending factions to compose their differences. Burghley did not agree. In a memorandum which he drafted in April he insisted that the proper course was to support the King's party, and not to make any pretence of non-partisanship. Every prince in Europe, he observed, knew well enough that Elizabeth was giving secret aid to one party and seeking to discredit the other, but by declining to make any open commitment she discouraged her friends and encouraged her enemies. In consequence, the Scottish issue was allowed to drag on and the danger increased that either Spain or France would intervene. It was, Burghley pointed out, a profitless and an expensive policy, more expensive and far less profitable than frank and open intervention.[5]

But Elizabeth could not be persuaded. Her efforts at mediation got her nowhere. By the Treaty of Blois she agreed with France to try joint intervention. In pursuit of this policy a French and an English commissioner were appointed, Du Croc, sometime French ambassador to Scotland, for France, Sir William Drury, Marshal of Berwick, for England. They got to work in May and after two months' effort induced the contending parties to agree to an armistice. Then came St. Bartholomew's Massacre in France and the dispatch of Henry Killigrew on his secret errand anent the Queen of Scots. Killigrew's official instructions were to replace Drury and join with Du Croc in joint efforts for peace. They got no further than to extend the armistice to the end of the year.

The Scottish situation meanwhile was rendered more difficult by the death of the Regent, Mar, late in October. Burghley wrote to Walsingham on November 3rd:[6] 'The ninth and twentieth of the last, the good regent of Scotland died, as I think, by a natural sickness,[7] and yet the certainty is not known. This will make our cause worse in Scotland, for I fear the conveyance away of the King, and yet there is care taken of his safety. But I can almost hope for no good, seeing our evils fall by heaps. And why the heaps fall not upon ourselves personally I see no cause to the let thereof in ourselves. God be merciful unto us.'

It is not clear why Burghley was so depressed. We have indeed almost nothing from his pen during the autumn of 1572, though it is clear enough from the letters addressed to him that he was still carrying the burden of administration.

In Scotland there was no headway. Du Croc returned to France early in October. Increasingly liberal terms were offered to the Catholics, but they were obdurate, expecting assistance from France. The Earl of Morton succeeded Mar in the regency. He was Elizabeth's candidate and he wrote to Burghley on December 1st that he would never have accepted the charge except for his assured hope of her support of him and her financial assistance in maintaining his army.[8]

At the time Burghley was in London, probably in pursuit of his judicial duties at the Exchequer and the Court of Wards, and Elizabeth was at Windsor, Leicester with her. When the news of Mar's death reached Burghley, he wrote a letter to

Leicester. The letter itself is missing, but we have Leicester's response to it which gives some inkling of its contents. He wrote to Burghley on November 4th: 'Yesternight, about six of the clock, I received your letters and could not have present occasion to deal with her Majesty touching the centre of them for that she was at her wonted repose. As soon as time served I told her the effect of H. Killigrew's letters, of the certain death of the regent and the danger of the King's person to be surprised, the Duke [of Châtelherault] with divers of the best of the contrary part being very nigh the place where he is. And upon such sudden alteration, what practice may be wrought is greatly to be feared. And I did put her Majesty therefore in remembrance, with all expedition, to show herself careful for the maintenance of her friends, whose ruin, as she was well able to conceive, must needs turn to her present danger as well as theirs, and that time would not suffer any delay at all. She was willing to talk to and fro what was best. For my part I told her Majesty I thought it convenient in all speed to send either my Lord of Hunsdon or some nobleman down to the borders that it might appear to her friends there what care she had of them. And he to have not only authority to give them good words of comfort but powers indeed to give them all manner of relief as their need should require, as well with men as with money . . . She seemed to take the matter earnestly, and that she will do all things that shall be urgent, requisite for her, as well in sending my L. Hunsdon . . . as also all other matter of demonstration that may further the King's party there. And willed me that I should this morning write unto you her disposition and to ask your advice for this present what way you think meetest for her and what you think of sending forthwith my Lord of Hunsdon . . . and to return your mind thereof with all diligence, with any further advice that you may remember meet for the present. I showed her Majesty your earnest letter touching this cause which she noted well and confessed there is no time to spare. . . .

'There will little be done while you are away. If I say plainly as I think, your Lordship, as the case stands, shall do her Majesty and your country more service here in an hour than in all the courts there will be worth this seven years. Therefore I can but wish you here, yea to fly if you would, till these matters be fully dispatched. . . .

'For the rest of your letter, I see her Majesty begins to startle at it and doth believe it verily, for it hath been long, she saith, one of her fears. I answered her again that the fault was only her own, for never prince hath had more warnings, nor better advice than she hath had to prevent all this long ago, and said further that now she might see how convenient it is for a prince, yea the wisest, to trust faithful known Councillors . . . She willeth you, in any wise, to lay all the weight you can do to discover the truth, as she perceives by your letter you mean to do. My Lord, it is no small matter, and the greater for that I have learned here since you went that this house is no less infected and grown into such persons as you would never suspect.'⁹

It is unfortunate that Burghley's letter is missing. Leicester's references to it are somewhat obscure, particularly at the end. In any case it seems to have produced, at least temporarily, the desired result. Morton was induced to accept the regency, and Elizabeth very reluctantly lent him financial aid.

The armistice was terminated on January 1st, 1573, and desultory warfare between the Castilians and their besiegers was resumed. According to the reports from Walsingham, the French were sending money into Scotland and encouraging the Castilians to believe that if they held out until Whitsuntide they would have ample assistance from the Pope, from Spain and from France.[10] It became increasingly apparent that the Castilians would not yield except to force, and Elizabeth in January seems to have contemplated seriously the application of force. About the middle of the month engineers were dispatched from Berwick to survey the strength of the castle and they reported that the castle might be taken in twenty days. Indeed, one of them went so far as to 'jeopard his life' that with twelve cannon and six sakers he would beat down the castle in three days. Killigrew concluded that if the Queen would send the cannon without any men it would be sufficient, but he advocated some troops, perhaps a thousand. On February 5th he wrote to Smith that he thought the very news of cannon on the way and English troops on the march would induce the Castilians to surrender before a shot was fired.[11] Smith wrote to Burghley from Greenwich on February 12th that he had raised with the Queen the question of military assistance. Her first response was that she could do the trick without cost by writing a letter. Smith replied that such a procedure would simply protract the time which was exactly what the Castilians wanted. He pointed out that the preoccupation of the French with their internal troubles made the time particularly opportune. She agreed, and expressed her satisfaction that Burghley had made arrangements for the shipment of powder and other necessaries, told Smith that Burghley would be at Court at the end of the week and that she would decide the matter then.[12]

Meanwhile, in Scotland James Kirkaldy, who had been sent with money and promises from France, was captured and his money put to good use. Virac, a French agent, who had been dispatched by sea from France with commission to conciliate the Regent and strengthen the resistance of the Castilians was blown by contrary winds into Scarborough Harbour and detained there.[13] And Killigrew, who had been working hard to arrange an agreement between Morton and the foremost of Mary's supporters, Huntley and the Hamiltons, reported progress. One of the obstacles in the way was the insistence of the Marians that further pursuit of the murderers of the two Regents, Murray and Lennox, should be suspended for a season. Elizabeth was consulted upon the point and agreed. In consequence an agreement was signed at Perth on February 23rd, by which Huntley and the Hamiltons abandoned the Castilians and made their peace with Morton. In short, the Marian faction as a belligerent element in the situation was reduced to Kirkaldy and Lethington and the garrison of the castle.

But the more favourable the general situation in Scotland became the more reluctant was Elizabeth to take drastic action. She still hoped that she would achieve her purpose without armed intervention. The French ambassador was at pains to point out to her that if she sent troops she would break the Treaty of

Blois and would open wide the door for French intervention. Early in March Killigrew was in despair about the delay. He begged that if the Queen did not intend to keep faith he might be recalled. Drury wrote from Berwick that in his simple opinion the sooner the Queen undertook the siege of the castle the better. All that Burghley could do was to instruct Killigrew to leave no stone unturned to secure the castle by composition. He even went so far as to suggest to Killigrew that Kirkaldy might be allowed to keep the castle for the King, a proposition which Killigrew refused even to submit. He would rather, he said, go to Rome barefoot than propose it. At least that is what we can gather from Killigrew's letters. None of Burghley's survive. He even had some difficulty in persuading the Queen not to give Virac a passport for Scotland. In any event he went on with military preparations.

On March 12th he induced Elizabeth to commission Drury to go to the assistance of the Regent if he asked for it, and a week later authorized the appropriation of money for Drury's levies.[14] Early in April she told Fénélon that if the Castilians did not yield by treaty she would send forces to compel them. Fénélon discussed the matter with Burghley in mid-April, pointing out that the Queen could not without breach of treaty send forces into Scotland. Burghley bade Fénélon assure his master that the Queen would not do anything in Scotland or elsewhere except in pursuit of her own safety and the quiet of her realm. She hoped that she would achieve these things and still retain the King's friendship. But she was much perturbed by the Scottish situation, where all the nobility, excepting only the Castilians, were obedient to the young King. She hoped that the Castilians would accept the very generous terms offered to them. Fénélon still insisted that armed intervention was a breach of treaty, and suggested joint action with the French King in dealing with the Castilians. Burghley appeared to acquiesce and so the conference ended. 'Nevertheless,' Fénélon observed, 'I fear that help will be sent to the Scots, so much they have at heart the surrender of Edinburgh Castle.'[15]

Maitland in the castle sparred for time.[16] Knowing Elizabeth better than anyone in Scotland he was confident that he could drag the negotiations out until assistance came from France. And he came near to being right. But Burghley's influence prevailed. On April 17th Drury, having sent his artillery ahead by sea, set forth for Scotland. On the 25th he was in Edinburgh, calling upon the Castilians to surrender. Contrary to the general expectation, they would not yield. Two days later the English cannon arrived by ship.

It took the better part of a month to get them in position. Meanwhile, young Thomas Cecil, unbeknown to his father, arrived in Edinburgh.[17] Killigrew said that his presence was 'comfortable' to both the English and the Scots. Some of the guns were in place on May 17th, and the battery began. Ten days later the Castilians asked for terms, demanding surety of living and lives for all the garrison. What they got was pardon for all except Kirkaldy and Lethington and a few others whose fate would be referred to the Queen of England. They had no choice but to accept.

Maitland and Kirkaldy wrote jointly to Burghley on the day following the surrender, in chastened but not abject terms.[18] The letter was in Maitland's hand and was no doubt his composition. 'Although', he wrote, 'we doubt not but your Lordship is sore offended with us and perhaps not without cause ... yet seeing our fault is not so great but it is pardonable, we have taken the boldness, presuming upon your Lordship's old friendship liberally extended towards us, to have recourse to the same now in this our great necessity ... Although it may seem that our suit cometh too late, yet thus much we may say by the way, that if we had not had a special confidence in her Majesty's clemency and of your Lordship's favour ... we would have run a more desperate course than was convenient ... We pray your Lordship forsake us not in time of our misery.'

It is the last surviving piece of a correspondence between Burghley and Maitland which dated back to the very beginning of Elizabeth's reign. They had much in common, and Maitland was on one occasion referred to as the Scottish Cecil. He was one of the cleverest men in Scotland, but he lacked guiding principles, either of patriotism or of loyalty. Burghley had thought well of him earlier and they had talked together about the union of the two kingdoms. But later Burghley lost faith in him. As for the letter, it is preserved among the Cotton MSS. It bears no address and does not carry any endorsement either of Burghley's or of anyone else's. Presumably Burghley got it. Presumably he ignored it. No one knew better than he that Maitland, from the point of view of England's interest, was the most dangerous man in Scotland.

In any case Maitland did not survive for either mercy or punishment. On June 9th he was found dead in his bed.[19]

Burghley's only recorded comment is in a letter to Shrewsbury of June 14th:[20] 'It is written that Lethington is dead of his natural sickness, being also stricken with great melancholy which he conceived of the great hatred that he did see all his countrymen bear towards him since he came out of the castle.'

As for Kirkaldy of the Grange, a very gallant soldier, Elizabeth after some delay delivered him over to Morton for judgment. On August 3rd he was hanged, 'in the face of the sun', even as John Knox had prophesied.

And that was the end of Mary Stuart's party in Scotland. The Scottish problem was to plague Burghley for the rest of his life, but it was changed in character. Hereafter there was no question of displacing the regency and the young King by his mother. The problem was to control the government of the young King.

CHAPTER VIII

ANGLICAN AND PURITAN, 1572-75

THE overthrow of the Castilians in Scotland and the re-establishment of trade with the Low Countries, both of which took place almost simultaneously in the spring of 1573, were the last important administrative tasks which Burghley undertook to handle in person. Until the end of the year 1573 he appears to have been in fact the administrative head of the government. But after Walsingham's appointment as second Principal Secretary in December he gradually slipped out of it, though the lines were never accurately drawn, and Burghley remained until the end of his days the first minister of the Crown. Foreign agents of the government still found it expedient to communicate with Burghley as often as they communicated with Walsingham, and in certain departments of the government he still kept the reins firmly in his own hands.

This was notably so in matters religious. He and Matthew Parker, Archbishop of Canterbury, were old friends, and the correspondence[1] between them, which continued without interruption until Parker's death in 1575, reveals clearly, not only that they were in fairly close accord on religious problems, but that Burghley was the channel through which Parker tried to win and hold the Queen's erratic support.

Three major religious problems presented themselves simultaneously: (1) the Roman Catholics; (2) the Puritans; and (3) the shortcomings of the Anglican Church.

The menace of Roman Catholicism had, of course, been accentuated by the Rising of the North in 1569, the papal bull of excommunication in 1570 and the Ridolfi Plot in 1571. It was further accentuated by Elizabeth's indulgent treatment of the captive Mary Stuart, 'the bosom serpent'. There is little or no evidence in Burghley's attitude of any crusading zeal against Roman Catholicism as such. Nor was he ever altogether wedded to the position that the security of England depended upon a vigorous anti-Catholic policy both at home and abroad. But he felt much more strongly than his mistress that Mary Stuart's claim to the throne, the potential strength of latent Roman Catholicism in England, and the continuing efforts of the Papacy to organize a religious crusade against England were, taken together, the most serious menace to England's peace and security. In a memorandum which he drew up in April 1572 he dwelt at length upon those matters. The date is significant. It was at the time when the Ridolfi Plot had been revealed, Norfolk convicted of high treason, the writs for the assembling of Parliament issued, and Elizabeth still hesitating as to what should be done either with Norfolk or with the Queen of Scots.

The memorandum is in Burghley's own hand, and some parts of it are illegible. It is entitled 'Certain matters wherein the Queen's Majesty's forbearing and delays hath produced not only inconvenience and increase of expenses but also dangers'.

It may have been intended for the Queen's own eyes, or for consideration by the Privy Council, or simply for the clarifying of Burghley's own thoughts. I am disposed to believe that it was the last of these.

It began 'with her Majesty's coldness and forbearing to proceed in marriage' which he believed 'had wrought great decay in her reputation' and had led to 'the continual and daily revolting of some secretly, the [numbers] whereof are not known, partly by re[bellion], partly by pretence of religion, so that, if stay be not provided, her Majesty shall be deprived of the multitude of her subjects and if occasion shall move her to use and to try them, it shall be a hard matter to make account . . . [of whom she] . . . may trust, which is so dangerous that it is, to any . . . [public] . . . person, as terrible to think of as for a private person to imagine that he cannot tell how to sleep surely in his own house.

'Secondly: her Majesty has from the beginning showed her natural disposition to be such towards her subjects in the cause of religion that they who have been "repugnant or mislikers of her religion" have not lacked her favour. So that these inconveniences have followed: (1) the favourers of her religion both in ecclesiastical ministry and in civil government have been evil regarded and in many things slandered and, at the least, hindered; (2) the contrary have persisted in their obstinacy and have increased their number in all places, both in their own families and in towns and countries so that her Majesty cannot count that in thirteen years' government she has increased, but rather diminished her number of favourers of her religion, and that, by example, is to be seen, that for the space of nine or ten years her government had no outward show of repining, but about the eleventh or twelfth year numbers received the Pope's bull, departed from their allegiance and in the end grew so bold that in the North they made an open rebellion of 8000 or 10,000 persons openly in field, and how many more were thereto consenting or allowing in the rest is uncomfortable to be counted, and of some proof was the intended rebellion in Norfolk and practices in Lancashire and Staffordshire.

'The Third: as the continual doubtful dealing with the Queen of Scots, with whom her Majesty from the beginning, since she challenged her crown from her head, hath dealt in such sort that it may be seen she meant to reclaim her by gentleness and benefit. She is reputed in the realm, by the great number of such as are disposed to consider of so weighty a matter as the succession of the crown is, to be the next heir to the Queen's Majesty, and hard it is to guess by how many she is accounted to have a present right to that Crown . . . But sure it is that all they who do . . . and think that the church of Rome hath superiority [in] this realm, do undoubtfully hold her to be in[deed] rig[htful] Queen of this realm. Add to these all such [as] for malice, envy or misliking desire a change, and so the number is greater than there is reason to [be] known, either to themselves for their encouraging, although they use slights for that purpose, or to the good [subjects] for their discouraging.'

Burghley went on to lament Elizabeth's uncertain policy in Scotland and he wound up by complaining that Elizabeth was so chary about increasing the number of her nobility that she lacked sufficient men to govern her people.[2]

He did not undertake to prescribe remedies, but he clearly was of the opinion that Roman Catholicism was increasing in England and that the lenient policy towards Mary Stuart was giving it great encouragement. Since he had long since discovered that religious arguments carried small weight with his mistress, he took care to emphasize political and dynastic considerations. It seems not unlikely that he was mistaken in assuming that Roman Catholicism was growing stronger. The evidence points rather the other way.[3] He might, had he been so minded, have gathered cheer from the fact that the Rising of the North was limited to the north and that the sporadic attempts at rebellion elsewhere fizzled out rapidly. The average English Catholic was no crusader, and by and large never accepted the implications of the bull of excommunication. A few were prepared to die for their faith, a good many were prepared to suffer for their faith, but very few were ever ready to sacrifice their Queen and their country for their faith. Elizabeth herself divined that fact and Burghley was to realize it gradually. At the moment he was alarmed and for many years to come hammered at his mistress to deal with the Catholics more rigorously. In this connection it is worth recalling that the bill which had been introduced in the House of Commons a year earlier, imposing the obligation upon all Englishmen to partake of the Communion service at least once a year, with the idea of preventing the occasional conformity to which many Catholics resorted, though it was vetoed by the Queen, had his support.[4]

Actually, after the failure of the northern uprising, the religious disturbance in England shifted rather rapidly from the right to the left, and found expression in the resurgence of Puritanism.

In its earlier form, Puritanism had expressed itself in a voluble protest against the ritual and ceremonial and particularly against the vestments of the Established Church. There is good reason to believe that Burghley at the outset was not unsympathetic with this movement, but he realized that pressure from the left only had the effect of increasing Elizabeth's natural disposition towards the right, and so he took a definite stand against innovations. Since the University of Cambridge provided many of the leaders and much of the momentum of this vestiarian movement, Burghley was called upon to deal with it not only as chief minister of the Queen but also as Chancellor of the University. Parker wrote, in the last of all his surviving letters to Burghley, that he cared very little about such matters as 'a cap, a tippet, surplice, wafer bread' and the like but that he felt strongly that the law should be enforced, and feared that contempt for law and authority would 'be the end of us'.[5] It was substantially Burghley's own position.

It was Parker's business to enforce the law, and Burghley's business to see that it was enforced. The problem would not have been too difficult had it not been for the following considerations: (1) that Parker could not depend upon the support of the Queen; (2) that the Puritans had friends in high places; (3) that the Anglican Church was suffering from a woeful lack of personnel, particularly of preachers, and that the young, vigorous and eloquent clergymen were precisely those who were flocking to Puritan standards. It must be recalled also that the nomination of the parish clergy was largely in the hands of the country gentry, which meant that an attack upon a non-conforming clergyman involved not only a blow at property rights but also at influential patronage. Parker ignored these considerations. But Burghley was acutely conscious of them and was not prepared to press for rigid conformity except by royal warrant, which Elizabeth declined to give. Her attitude is a puzzling one. She was violently anti-Puritan but at this time she did not wish to assume the onus of active procedure against the Puritans. It may have been due to Leicester's influence; it may have been due to the Puritan temper of the House of Commons which had revealed itself definitely in the sessions of 1563, 1566, 1571 and 1572. She may well have decided that Puritanism in the country was stronger than, indeed, it was.

It is quite possible that Burghley himself contributed to her uncertainty. But there is no evidence at all upon the point. Parker at any rate was clearly not satisfied with Burghley's co-operation: 'If you, in your place and credit as you be, will suffer so much authority to be borne under foot . . . in my opinion your conscience shall never be excusable . . . Execution, execution, execution, of laws and orders must be the first and last part of good government . . . And hereafter, for God's love, never stir any alteration except it be fully meant to have them established, for else we shall hold us no certainty but be ridiculous to our adversaries, condemned of our own and give the adventure of more dangers.' And again: 'Surely if I draw forward and others draw backward what shall it avail but to raise exclamations and privy mutterings against your honour and against me by whom they think those matters be stirred.'[6]

And yet Parker's programme was on the whole successful. It was no thanks to Elizabeth, who blew hot and cold as the exigencies of her foreign problems prompted her. And it was no thanks to Burghley who followed the royal lead. One important factor was a letter from Henry Bullinger, leader of the Church at Zürich, endorsing the official position on apparel. The Puritans did not accept it but it was published and it did much to weaken their position. In any case Elizabeth herself lost interest, and a certain amount of latitude in the matter of vestments and ritual was allowed to creep in without official rebuke.[7]

After three years of comparative quiescence, Puritanism broke forth again in 1570, once more at Cambridge, but under different leadership and with emphasis upon more fundamental issues.

It developed out of the appointment of Thomas Cartwright as Lady Margaret Professor of Divinity there. He began a series of lectures on the Acts of the Apostles which led him into the organization of the early Church and to the acceptance of Presbyterianism as the pattern of church government established by Holy Writ. His lectures created a sensation in Cambridge academic circles and, presently, a band of enthusiastic followers. At this point the orthodox began to protest. The first official complaint took the form of a letter to Burghley[8] as Chancellor of the University from the Regius Professor of Divinity, on June 11th,

1570.[9] The burden of his song was that Cartwright was attempting 'to overturn and overthrow all ecclesiastical and civil government'. Others letters to Burghley followed, one from Grindal, Archbishop of York. Cartwright himself wrote to Burghley and enclosed testimonials from fifteen members of the University who had attended his lectures.

On August 3rd, Burghley wrote to the Vice-Chancellor and the heads of the college discussing the situation at Cambridge. He had, he wrote, 'received reports both from Cartwright's friends and his enemies. What mind he had in moving of these matters by himself, in communication I perceive the same not to be much reprehended, being as it seemeth not of any arrogancy or intention to move troubles, but as a reader of Scripture to give notes by way of comparison betwixt the order of the ministry in the time of the Apostles and the present time now in the Church of England'. Burghley, in short, chose to regard the matter rather as an academic exposition of Holy Writ than as a movement for Church reform. Possibly he hoped to persuade both parties to look at it in that light. Had he been merely Chancellor of the University he might have argued more strongly for academic freedom. It is to his credit that he gave voice to it at all. But he was also Elizabeth's Principal Secretary and he knew too well how she felt about Presbyterianism to venture more than a sentence in Cartwright's behalf. So he went on to say that he did not feel competent to adjudicate in the matter but would support any course of action which the Vice-Chancellor and the college heads agreed upon.[10] A little later Burghley was persuaded to authorize new statutes for the University which placed practically absolute power on the heads of the colleges.[11] Acting under these new powers, Cartwright early in December was deprived of his professorship and prohibited from preaching in the University.

Certainly Burghley delivered Cartwright to his enemies. But, under the circumstances, it is hard to see how he could have done otherwise. A letter which he received from Cartwright late in August made it abundantly clear that something much more than a mere exposition of the Scriptures was involved. Cartwright invited Burghley to consider the question of Church organization as a statesman. In short, he invited Burghley to examine and by implication to approve Presbyterianism.[12] After that Burghley really had no choice, though he was clearly well disposed towards Cartwright and many times in later life befriended him.

Burghley's support of those opposed to him at Cambridge exposed him almost at once to rebuke from the left. This found expression in a letter from Edward Dering, one of the most learned of English scholars,[13] and one of the most eloquent of Puritan preachers, who had not hesitated to castigate from the pulpit Elizabeth herself.[14] It was not a very coherent letter and a considerable part of it is devoted to the business of asserting the integrity of the author. Its principal charge against Burghley was that he had 'of late sent unrighteous statutes to Cambridge'. Dering did not indicate wherein the unrighteousness lay but went on to denounce the private life and morals of those at Cambridge who had imposed the statutes. 'And most heartily', he wrote, 'I beseech the living Lord to give unto you also pure eyes that you may see such enormities. I do wish you well, neither for your gold or silver nor for your great authority, because you can give me living, but because you have professed the Gospel, are a magistrate in the commonwealth where Christ is truly preached and yet now do sustain much hatred of the enemy. Because you are such a one I desire your prosperity and God will keep me from this great sin that I should cease to pray for you ... I thought thus to admonish you, both that you have dealt hardly with God's children and your brethren and that you should at the last look at so great abominations. If it cannot sink into your heart, or you will not, I am afraid in your behalf that God's judgment will overthrow you.'

The letter smacks of the arrogance and assurance of John Knox, and recalls the letter which he wrote to Burghley shortly after Elizabeth's accession.[15] There is no record of Burghley's reply, if he did reply.

Two years later Dering wrote to him again, once more on the subject of Cartwright who was in Geneva and wanted to come home,[16] but feared to offend if he came unannounced. Dering asked Burghley to signify in a word that Cartwright's return would not be displeasing to him, and further asked that Cartwright might be appointed to the vacant chair of Professor of Hebrew at Cambridge. But Dering, true to form, could not close his letter without a final harangue on Burghley's lack of true religion.

All this in elegant Latin. We find among Burghley's papers what was probably an English draft of his reply.[17] It begins as follows: 'Mr. Dering, Since I received from you, in a piece of paper, a biting letter, pretended (as by the beginning of a few of your lines appeareth) for Mr. Cartwright, whose name you reiterate, for that you will me not to be in heat at the memory of his name, I have been in doubt whether I should, either for wasting my time or for nourishing of your humour make you any answer by letter. But I have yielded as you see.

'As for so much as concerneth Mr. Cartwright I answer you, *sine excandescentia* (which is your term) that, *quo possum candore, reditus ejus erit mihi gratus, eique optime cupio et opto* [in all sincerity his return will be agreeable to me, and I most heartily desire it]. But as for the reading of a public lecture in Cambridge I can promise nothing of myself. For therein I know no power that I have. I know very well it is my duty to further all good learning and quietness in that university, that indecent contentions be excluded from thence.

'The rest of your pamphlet or letter (worse I will not name it) containeth diverse ejaculations against me. As one, that if I were so void of knowledge or Godliness as your words make me, I should be ashamed to live in the place where I do. But most of all I might be reputed as a pagan, without sense or knowledge of my God. But what I am indeed God only knoweth first, and secondarily myself, who am, as you may be for your self, partial. And therefore, except it may please God to direct good men to think better of me than you do, I shall not be in danger of any vain glory.'

In the rest of the letter Burghley draws on Scripture, citation after citation, to demonstrate that Dering's arrogant assumption of superiority, both in knowledge and in godliness, was not in accordance with Holy Writ.

The last paragraph is illuminating: 'And now to end, lest you may think me too copious in citing of Scripture to you, I may remember you somewhat of my years or of mine old service in the common weal. And then I trust hereafter, until I be very obstinate, as partly you note me, you will also remember St. Paul to Timothy, *Seniorem ne increpaveris, sed obsecra, ut patrem, juvenes, ut fratres.* [Rebuke not an elder, but intreat him as a father, the younger as brethren.][18]

'And so wishing to myself that which you judge that I do lack; and to yourself all that which you seem to have. And what you have, for the charity I bear you, I heartily wish you more than by your behaviour you seem to have. And both of us to require of God . . . to plant in our hearts true fear of Him and to transplant out of our hearts all seeds or roots of vainglory, directing you in all your contemplations and teachings and me in my cares and public labours, to the glory of His Son Jesus Christ.

'Yours to be taught, but not to be condemned,

W. B.'

In a postscript Burghley added '*Non alta sapientes sed humiliter consentientes.*'[19] [Mind not high things but condescend to men of low estate. Be not wise in your own conceits.]

It was on the whole a very temperate reply from a man who was Chancellor of the University and first minister of the Queen to an arrogant upstart scholar, at least twenty years his junior.

Dering answered it at length,[20] stiffly, arrogantly, but somewhat apologetically. At that point, so far as we know, the correspondence ended.

It is to be presumed that Dering's maladroit techniques were designed to win Burghley's support for the Puritan position. Another and much more subtle effort came at about the same time from another quarter. Parliament had been summoned in March 1572 to meet early in May. There is some reason to believe[21] that in advance of the meeting Puritan leaders had made their plans for attack upon the episcopal organization of the Church and had evoked the support of Theodore Beza, John Calvin's successor at Geneva, desiring him to write a letter 'to a great man in the land'. He did in fact write to Burghley.[22] The letter was not written until after Parliament had arisen, but that was accidental. It was certainly intended for Burghley's perusal before the session began. The gist of it was that the Anglican Church was sound in doctrine but there were grave doubts about its soundness in discipline. Beza did not elaborate, though he wrote that he would be glad to, if Burghley desired it. He thought the matter called for careful consideration, intimating that in the Elizabethan settlement many things should have been done which had been left undone. He suggested that the Queen and her Council should address themselves to the problem. If they did they might well command the support of those 'that were now in most places hinderers', an artful allusion to the Puritan opposition. He concluded by saying that he did not doubt that Burghley 'wanted neither will nor anything else to the bringing of these things to perfection', and was persuaded he had already begun the good work.

Beza's letter is a masterpiece. His assumed identification of Burghley with a movement for the reform of the Church in the Presbyterian direction was clearly wishful thinking, though he may at that have struck a responsive chord. In any case the prospect of progress in the direction of what Beza and the Puritans wanted was scotched if not killed by the violence of the debate on the subject in the Commons and by the publication of the well-known *Admonition to Parliament* while it was still in session. Burghley, of course, was not in the Commons, and of his activity in the Lords there is no record. During a considerable part of the session, which lasted less than two months, he was so stricken with the gout that he had to be carried to the Parliament house. His interest at the time was focused upon the fate of Mary Stuart and he left behind him no comment on the religious debate. Towards the end of the session the Archbishop of York and some of the bishops in the Lords had hopes of inducing the Queen to sponsor a bill, presumably along the lines of the one Burghley had supported in the session of 1571, imposing compulsory Communion as well as compulsory attendance upon the Established Church. They prepared the bill and wanted to read it to the Queen, but she pleaded business and referred them to Burghley.[23] We hear no more of it.

Following the prorogation of Parliament at the end of June, the chief concern of the Crown, so far as the Puritans were concerned, appears to have been with the authors and the printers of the *Admonition to Parliament*. It proved to be an effective piece of propaganda literature and ran through two editions before the year was out. The Puritans were much better at this sort of popular appeal than their Anglican opponents. Field and Wilcox, the joint authors of the *Admonition*, were sent to prison. But the printers could not be found. Archbishop Parker suspected that they were being deliberately concealed[24] by the London authorities whose Puritan sympathies were well known.

The government apparently hoped at first that popular interest would die out and refrained from controversy, but by mid-summer decided that the *Admonition* must be answered. John Whitgift, at the time Master of Trinity College, Cambridge, was assigned to the task. Whitgift indeed, from that time forward — and he became Archbishop of Canterbury ten years later — was the most pugnacious and most resolute of all those who took up the cudgels against the Puritans. He had been largely responsible for the ejection of Cartwright from his professorship. Whitgift published his reply to the *Admonition* in September and set off a literary controversy which kept the issue alive for years to come.

But Puritanism rather more than held its own. Cartwright returned from Geneva to play his part, and Field and Wilcox kept open house in prison, received their friends and even drew up a confession of faith which had some circulation in manuscript. The massacre of St. Bartholomew's, like most other expressions of belligerent Roman Catholicism, had the immediate effect of turning government attention from the left to the right. Archbishop Parker's correspondence with Burghley in the spring of 1573 was one long complaint of the support which the Puritans were receiving in high places. 'If', he wrote on March 12th, 'Her Highness with her Council (I mean some of them) step not to it, I see the likelihood of a pitiful commonwealth . . . If your honour knew how we be bearded and used you would think strange that we should be thus dealt with in so favourable a governance. And but that we have our whole trust in God, in her Majesty and in two or three of her Council, I see it will be no dwelling for us in England.'

In July he wrote again: 'Surely if this fond faction [Puritans] be applauded to or borne with, it will fall out to a popularity [beggarly democracy] and as wise men think it will be the overthrow of all the nobility . . . Both papists and precisians have one mark to shoot at, plain disobedience . . . I marvel what prudence it can be, first to hew thus at us, and certainly yourself will shortly follow.'

Parker was evidently quite aware that many members of the Council were sympathetic to the Puritan position. Leicester he singled out as the head and front of the offending. In any case, he called upon Burghley for action.[25]

And some action was taken. In June 1573 the Queen issued a proclamation commanding her subjects to abide by the prayer book and to turn over all Puritan writings to the bishop of the diocese or to the Council. And in October[26] she issued another in which she condemned the bishops and magistrates for lax enforcement of the law and threatened imprisonment of all who spoke against the Act of Uniformity.

A few days later, at the end of Michaelmas Term, Burghley spoke on the subject in Star Chamber to the assembled Justices. It was not unusual for the Queen to call together those Justices of the Peace and Judges of Assize who were in Westminster, sometimes at the beginning, sometimes at the end of a law term, and through the mouth of the Lord Chancellor to bring to their attention matters to which she wished them to direct their efforts. On this particular occasion Sir Nicholas Bacon, who would normally have spoken for the Queen, was away, and Burghley was charged with the task.

We have a copy of part of his speech in his own hand.[27] 'There are,' he said, 'in sundry parts of her realm entered into ordinary cures of souls, that is, into rectories, vicarages, and such like, and into places of preaching and reading, a number of persons young in years, but over-young in soundness of learning and discretion, which according to their own imaginations and conceits, and not according to the public order established by law, having not only in the common services of the church, and in the administration of sacraments, made sundry alterations, but also, by their example and teaching, have enticed their parochians, and their auditories, being her Majesty's subjects, to conceive erroneous opinions, in condemning the whole government of the Church and order ecclesiastical, and in moving her Majesty's good subjects to think it a burden of conscience to observe the orders and rites of the Church established by law; a matter pernicious to the state of government, that her Majesty cannot, for the charge committed to her by Almighty God, but by speedy good means procure the stay of the dangers that must needs follow.'

He pointed out that the Puritans not only disagreed with the Established Church but did not even agree among themselves. Likening England to a ship in a storm (one of his favourite similes) he figured forth the disasters likely to follow if the crew turned rebellious. He went on to remind his listeners that the Queen had issued injunctions commanding uniformity, and he called upon the Justices of the Peace to see that these orders were obeyed.

The speech was well phrased and probably, considering Burghley's reputation as an orator, well delivered. Perhaps Elizabeth had charged him with the business because his sympathy with the Puritans was widely assumed. He did not discuss the merits of their position. He simply elaborated upon the necessity for obedience and uniformity — basic principles in the political and religious credos of Tudor gentry of all denominations, probably well calculated to carry weight with the justices, even with those more or less tarred with the Puritan brush.

What Walsingham wrote years later to a too zealous Puritan probably comes near to reflecting Burghley's attitude. 'If you knew,' Walsingham wrote, 'with what difficulty we retain what we have and that the seeking of more might hazard (according to man's understanding) that which we already have, you would then deal warily in this time when policy carrieth more sway than zeal. And yet have we great cause to thank God for that we presently enjoy, having God's word sincerely preached and the Sacrament truly administered. The rest we lack we are to beg by prayer and attend with patience.'[28]

After 1572 the Puritans seem to have lost hope of winning Burghley's active co-operation, and looked more and more to others for countenance and support — to Leicester first, and a little later to Walsingham. In 1575 Parker, in writing to Burghley, could refer sardonically to himself as head of the Church and to Burghley as head of the State, as 'great papists'.[29]

One obvious way to deter the drift away from Anglicanism towards the right and towards the left was to correct the things which were obviously wrong in the Established Church. Burghley more than any other man was responsible for the Elizabethan settlement. He had known at the outset what the Queen wanted, how much of Protestantism she would probably accept, how much emphatically she would reject. And, working wisely within these limitations, he had defined and established her Church. He had therefore an almost paternal interest in its welfare.

He was never content simply with maintaining the Anglican Church against the assaults of its enemies. Being a deeply religious man he wanted a Church which would satisfy his religious needs and would serve adequately the religious needs of the average Englishman. He accepted the organization of the Church, the theology of the Church and the rites of the Church. But he recognized that there was a great deal wrong in the behaviour of the Church. There was no lack of disciplinary machinery. Ultimate power lay, of course, with the Crown, and was from time to time exercised by the Queen or by her Privy Council. But in the first years of her reign Elizabeth established the Court of High Commission which exercised most of the routine ecclesiastical power of the Crown. Beside that there was the ordinary machinery of Church government, headed by the two archbishops, and under them the bishops and under them the archdeacons. At each of these three levels the state of the Church was from time to time examined by visitors, metropolitan, episcopal, archidiaconal. Church matters which were a breach of the statute law, like Protestant dissent and Catholic recusancy, were normally the business of the ecclesiastical commissioners or of the courts of common law. We hear much about them but relatively little about those conditions within the Church which everyone agreed should be corrected. What they were was revealed by the reports of the visitations and by extensive correspondence between Burghley and the archbishops and bishops. Probably he knew more about them than anyone in England.

On at least one occasion he had undertaken to do something about it. In the House of Commons in 1563 he had taken an active interest in a bill to provide more adequate income for curates and vicars in the smaller parishes by establishing minimum compensation based upon the number of people in the parish.[30] The Speaker in his address to the Crown had dwelt upon the poverty of the lower clergy and placed the blame, where it clearly belonged, upon the plunder of the tithes by lay impropriations.[31] Burghley's bill, if it was indeed his, proposed to increase the income of the lower clergy either by a charge upon the impropriator of the parish tithe or by a tax upon the members of the parish. But it never got through a House of Commons, otherwise not a little preoccupied with religious reform. Everybody wanted reform, but nobody wanted to finance it, least of all the gentry who were the chief offenders in the matter of impropriations and who controlled the House of Commons. And yet a great many of the current evils of the Church sprang from the fact that the lesser clergy were so poorly paid that they had to augment their living, if they were to live at all, by holding more than one benefice at the same time. This in turn led to pluralism and to non-residence, old evils which long antedated the Elizabethan settlement. Burghley's bill struck at the root of the evil. It was not original with him but was based upon recommendations by the clergy in Convocation.[32] But the vested interests in the old bad state of things were too strong to be overcome.

In general Burghley was more disposed to point out evils in the Church than to propose remedies. In the 'Memorial on the State of the Realm' which he had drawn up in the spring of 1569 he had made much of the falling away in religion. At that time he had written: 'The service of God and the sincere profession of Christian religion is much of late decayed, and in place thereof partly popery and partly paganism and irreligion are crept in. And this happeneth as well by long prosperity as by negligence in superiors that should give good example not only in words but in deeds.' Later in the same 'Memorial' he spoke of 'the increase of numbers of irreligious and epicures'.[33] One cannot but hazard the opinion that in this particular his eye was rather on the Court than on the country.

Some two years later in the autumn of 1572 he drafted two memoranda, one of which had to do with reforms of all sort called for, the other specifically with the reform of the Church.[34] The second is virtually an elaboration of ecclesiastical reforms mentioned in the first. It ran as follows:

'The government of the church of England to be directed, not only in more uniformity according to the laws and orders established, but also in more reverence and devotion. For which and like abuses would be reform in this sort following:
'(1) The churches would be replenished with the proper parsons and vicars and

all pluralities resumed by general order, and commissioners to be appointed to examine the necessity of any dispensation, wherein for order's sake the archbishops would be in commission in their several provinces.

'(2) The churches also would be both repaired in their decays and ordered to be kept more cleanly and reverently for divine prayer.

'(3) The statute for resort to common prayer would be by some better order executed and the imperfections therein amended, so as none shall live as they do without any manner of service of God, which hath bred so many heathen atheists to the dishonour of God and to the danger of the realm.

'In this point there is better regard to be given to the Queen's Majesty's own household which is now a cover for no small number of epicures and atheists, because the Court is not comprehended within a parish but seemeth to be a lawless place.

'(4) The days of Sundays would be both by order and example more straitly kept.

'(5) The whole clergy would be restrained from alienation of their lands and from unreasonable leases, wastes of woods and grants of reversions and advowsons to any persons and namely to their wives and children, or to others for their use. And inquisition would be made in the register books what number of grants have been made within those 5 or 6 years to the disherison of the church and a resumption would be made thereof by Parliament.'

We learn nothing new about the state of the Church from Burghley's analysis. All the abuses of which he complains were well known and come out with painful reiteration in the reports of visitations and in the episcopal correspondence. The remedies which Burghley prescribes are on the whole the conventional ones, already provided but very inadequately administered. He was disposed to blame the chronic misbehaviour of the lower clergy upon the lack of diligence by the bishops in correcting the evils revealed by episcopal visitations, though he thought some legislation might be necessary to strengthen their hands. He was much disturbed by the neglect of elementary education, at the parochial level; even more by the shortage of parish clergy, due in part to the wholesale deprivations following the break from Rome, in part to the starvation rations of the lower clergy, and in some measure also to the official attacks upon clergymen Puritanically inclined.

The worst of it was that not only was there a shortage of clergymen but the calibre of the parochial clergy was far from inspiring. There was a notable lack of preachers and though some attempt was made as early as 1560 to supplement the ordained clergy by lay readers, the Anglican clergy by and large stood in sorry contrast with the Jesuit missionaries and the Puritan preachers in spiritual fervour and in effectiveness.

It was that aspect of the matter which troubled Burghley particularly — the problem of developing a Church which could compete successfully against the alternatives offered both from the right and from the left, and be established by general consent, not by official decree.

CHAPTER IX

THEOBALDS AND THE OXFORD MARRIAGE

THE relief from the daily grind of administrative details after Burghley gave up the office of Principal Secretary, and particularly after the appointment of Walsingham as second Secretary at the end of 1573, gave Burghley considerably more leisure to pursue his private affairs and his private interests. Among other things he could address himself to the erection of the most famous of all his mansions, Theobalds.

He was an indefatigable builder, not only in financing the construction of his various houses, but also in the detailed planning of them. Indeed, he has some claim to the distinction of being one of the foremost architects of his day. Altogether, during the course of his life, he built three pretentious mansions. The first of these in point of time was the rebuilding of the family seat at Stamford Baron — Burghley House as it is generally called.[1] The second was his house in Westminster, generally called Cecil House; and the third and most pretentious was Theobalds on the eastern side of Hertfordshire close to the London road north to Ware. He set to work on Burghley House during Mary's reign and carried it forward vigorously during the first six years of Elizabeth's reign. The Queen visited him there in 1566, or rather planned to visit him there but was diverted at the last moment because Cecil's daughter, Ann, suddenly came down with the smallpox. About Cecil House near the Strand and in the edge of Covent Garden, we know little. It was begun but not finished by Sir Thomas Palmer who was executed in 1553 because of his support of Lady Jane Grey. John Stow, the London tailor-historian, writing in 1598, said that Palmer 'began to build in brick and timber, very large and spacious, but of late time it hath been far more beautifully increased by the late Sir William Cecil'.[2] Burghley, writing in 1585,[3] spoke of it rather disparagingly, though he admitted that the building of it cost him lands of the value of £100 a year (say £2000). It was only partially finished when Queen Elizabeth visited him there in July 1561[4]. Three years later she was there again at the christening of Cecil's daughter, Elizabeth. From the early 'sixties until the end of his life Cecil House was his London residence. We need not think of it as in close quarters or on city streets. Covent Garden in those days was distinctly suburban; Cecil House certainly had a walled garden,[5] probably a spacious one. But Burghley always preferred the countryside and never lingered in or near London by choice.

In June 1563 he purchased the parsonage of Cheshunt in Hertfordshire; the manor of Theobalds the next year and Cheshunt Park in 1570.[6] It is currently believed that Burghley was prompted by a desire to provide for his son, Robert, who was born about the same time. The neighbourhood had many advantages. It was close to London, and on the highway from London to Burghley House at Stamford. There were three royal houses within easy range: Enfield (3 miles); Hertford Castle (8 miles); and Hatfield (9½ miles). His old friend, Thomas Smith, lived some 7½ miles away in Essex at Hill Hall; his father-in-law, Sir Antony Cooke, at Gidea Hall, 12 miles away, and his brother-in-law, Sir Nicholas Bacon, was just starting to build his house at Gorhambury, near St. Albans, 15 miles away.

The house which Burghley acquired was a moated manor house.[7] In his earlier planning for Theobalds he evidently contemplated an enlargement of the house, but later proceeded altogether independently of it. Probably the Theobalds to which Elizabeth paid a passing visit in July 1564 was the original house, certainly quite inadequate to entertain the Queen and her Court.

Burghley began his new building in 1564, and by degrees enlarged and beautified the structure during the next ten years.[8] His Theobalds was virtually complete in 1585. It then stood in a park some three miles long and some eight miles in circumference. The house stood at the east end towards the London Road. It was brick with stone trim and consisted of three courtyards following one another from east to west, with two lateral courtyards for service quarters. The original intention was to develop what became ultimately the innermost court, and the first structure completed subsequently formed the eastern part of that court with the Great Hall as its central feature. This so-called Hall block was probably completed when the Queen paid her second visit to Theobalds in September 1571, and probably a good beginning had been made on the second court of which the Hall formed the western side. Elizabeth on her second visit found herself undoubtedly in the midst of building operations.

At some point in the creation of Theobalds Burghley's purpose changed from that of providing a home for his second son to that of providing a palace for the entertainment of the Queen and her Court. The temptation is to synchronize the change with his elevation to the peerage, but it probably came somewhat earlier. In any case, it was in full swing in 1571-72 when his annual expenditures in the building leaped to £2700. The operations were pushed rapidly forward in that year and, when Elizabeth visited Theobalds again in July 1572, the Middle Court and the core of the palace were ready to receive her. After that year annual expenditures diminished, and in the ensuing decade were directed to the rebuilding of the Inner or Conduit or Fountain Court as it was variously called. This turned out to be the most magnificent part of the structure, expressly designed for royal entertainment. But Elizabeth seems to have preferred her old quarters in the Middle Court, and in her subsequent visits (of which there are ten on record, the last in 1598)[9] she always occupied them. According to his anonymous biographer, these royal visits cost him between £2000 and £3000 for each visit.[10] This is doubtless an exaggeration, but certainly royal entertainment bit deep into his purse.

Only a stone or two of all this magnificence remains. But there are plans in plenty, many of them with corrections and annotations in Burghley's own hand. For that part of it which was built before 1572 he was his own architect. The plans for the reconstructed Inner Court in 1572 were made by Henry Hawthorn, and may have been derived from a plan published by Sertio of a house in Naples. If so, they are the first English house plans we know of based directly on an Italian prototype.[11] But even in them Burghley was almost certainly the director. John Summerson, after an extensive study of the subject, concludes:

'As a piece of architecture Theobalds has been totally forgotten, yet I do not think it too much to claim that it was, with the possible exception of Longleat [Bath] and Wollaton [Willoughby], the most important architectural adventure of the whole of Elizabeth's reign. Certainly it was the most influential of all. Both Holdenby [Hatton] and Audley End [Norfolk] directly derived from it. Castle Ashby [Marquess of Northampton], Hardwick [Bess of Hardwick], Apthorpe [Mildmay], Rushton [Tresham] and Hatfield seem to owe it much. Slight as our knowledge of the house must necessarily remain, unless some happy discovery enlightens us, I do not see that the history of Elizabethan architecture can be written without consideration of the part played by William Cecil.'

We hear almost as much about the gardens at Theobalds as we do about the house. The anonymous biographer wrote: 'Burghley also greatly delighted in making gardens, fountains and walks, which at Theobalds were perfected most costly, beautifully and pleasantly, where one might walk two miles in the walks before he came to the end.'[12] And in the year Burghley died, the German traveller, Paul Hentzner, wrote after a visit to Theobalds: 'From the place one goes into the garden encompassed with a moat full of water, large enough for me to have pleasure of going in a boat and rowing between the shrubs. Here are great variety of trees and plants, labyrinths made with a great deal of labour, a jet d'eau with a basin of white marble and columns and pyramids of wood and other material up and down the garden. After seeing these we were led by the gardener into the summer house, in the lower part of which, built semi-circularly, are the twelve Roman emperors in white marble and a table of touch-stone. The upper part of it is set round with cisterns of lead into which the water is conveyed through pipes so that fish may be kept in them and in summer time they are very convenient for bathing.'[13]

From another source[14] we hear of four gardens — the Great Garden to the south, the Maze Garden or New Privy Garden to the west, the Cook's Garden to the north-west, and the Old Privy Garden on the north. Taken altogether they surrounded the palace on all sides except on the east where the main gateway stood at the end of an avenue of trees. Presumably the cook's garden was for herbs and such vegetables as were grown. Of the other gardens we know little more than what Hentzner has told us. We do know that John Gerard, the author of the Herbal, probably the best known of all the Elizabethan garden books, looked after Burghley's gardens, both at Covent Garden and at Theobalds. In 1597 he dedicated his Herbal to Burghley.

Some years later Burghley's nephew, Francis Bacon, wrote his essay on gardens. Like his distinguished uncle, Bacon was an enthusiastic gardener. Every garden lover will recall the first sentence of his essay: 'God Almighty first planted a garden and, indeed, it is the purest of human pleasures.' Bacon, whose paternal mansion at Gorhambury was only a few miles from Theobalds, was thinking of that neighbourhood, and it is fair to assume that what he wrote in some degree envisages what one would have seen in walking through the gardens at Theobalds.

Bacon set up as his ideal a garden which would be in leaf or flower all the year round, and he outlined a garden calendar in terms of that objective, beginning with evergreens in the winter months and continuing through to the mellow fruitfulness of the early autumn. The holly and the ivy, the yew and the cypress and the pine are followed in March by crocuses and tulips and violets and daffodils 'which come before the swallow dares', and primroses 'that die unmarried ere they can behold, bright Phoebus in his strength'. These in turn usher in April, and the flowering almond and the lilac and the plum and the cherry in bloom and the peach, and May with its apple blossoms and its roses, its columbine and its lilies; and July with all the varieties of gillyflower, and the plum tree in fruit and the fragrant lime tree in flower; and finally in August and September all the familiar fruits, the grapes and the apples and the peaches and the nectarines. All of these are familiar names; others which Bacon enumerates are less familiar, but all of them good English flowers, none of them exotic.

Bacon made much of fragrance, and wrote lovingly of the rose and the musk rose and bay and rosemary and lavender. He made much of green lawns. 'Nothing', he said, 'is more pleasant to the eyes than green grass finely shorn.' But that came later. We should not expect cropped green sward in Burghley's day. Bacon made much of fruit trees, espaliered against walls or planted in rows with a border of flowers, 'but sparingly, lest they deceive [draw nourishment from] the trees'. He made much of hedges, though he disliked the fantastic topiary-clipping fashionable in Elizabethan days. Of the larger shade trees Bacon said nothing. He seems to have regarded them as out of place in a garden and counted on arbours to provide shade. He endorsed the current taste in fountains and flowing water. But he rejected 'statuary and such things', which he observed added 'state and magnificence but nothing to the true pleasure of a garden'. On this last point Burghley was of another mind. He had his statues — those of the twelve Roman emperors and many others. And it is to be feared that he attached more importance to state and magnificence than his nephew would have sanctioned.

At the time when Burghley became Lord Treasurer his immediate family included his wife, two sons, Thomas and Robert, and two daughters, Ann and Elizabeth. Thomas was married and had his separate establishment. The other three lived at home. There were other residents in his household as well.[15] His anonymous biographer remarks that 'most of the principal gentlemen of England preferred their sons and heirs to his service', and goes on to say: 'I have numbered in his house attending on the table twenty of his retainers of a thousand pounds a year.'[16]

Without doubt Burghley took a great interest in the education of promising young Englishmen. His household indeed was currently regarded as the best training school for the gentry in England. Only a select few, the flower of English youth, gained admission. How many there were all told does not appear.

Upon a different, more intimate footing were Burghley's wards. We have record of only two such wards, neither of them of much significance. But to these must be added his guardianship of royal wards, of which eight were of the noblest families of England.[17] We might almost include young Philip Sidney in the number; though he was never formally a ward he spent considerable time in Burghley's household, and was at one time under consideration as the husband of Burghley's daughter, Ann.[18] Of the eight, the first in point of seniority was the young Earl of Rutland,[19] the second Edward de Vere, seventeenth Earl of Oxford. Among the rest were the Duke of Norfolk's son, Philip Howard, the Earl of Essex, Elizabeth's favourite in the 'nineties, and the Earl of Southampton. But we are concerned here only with the first two, Rutland and Oxford. Oxford was the younger man and he entered Burghley's household as ward in 1562, at the age of twelve. Rutland came the next year at the age of fourteen. Both of them went to Cambridge, probably to St. John's College, and both of them received the degree of M.A. in August 1564 when they accompanied the Queen on her visit to the University. Both of them for that matter received the M.A. degree from Oxford when they went with the Queen on her visit there in 1566.

Presumably both degrees were honorary. We hear nothing of the residence of Rutland at either University. But Oxford had matriculated at Cambridge.[20] It is clear enough that both of them were good scholars. Rutland later distinguished himself at the bar and came within an ace of being Lord Chancellor. Oxford distinguished himself as a classical scholar, showed considerable talent as a poet, took a great interest in the drama, and has since been put forth seriously as the author of Shakespeare's plays.[21]

Of Rutland little more needs to be said in this connection, but Oxford played an important part in Burghley's life for many years to come.

One gets a clear impression of his training in Burghley's household from a document called 'Orders for the Earl of Oxford's Exercises', which has been preserved.[22] It runs as follows:

7:00–7:30 — Dancing
7:30–8:00 — Breakfast
8:00–9:00 — French
9:00–10:00 — Latin
10:00–10:30 — Writing and Drawing
The common prayers and so to dinner
1:00–2:00 — Cosmography
2:00–3:00 — Latin
3:00–4:00 — French
4:00–4:30 — Exercises with his pen.

On holidays we are told that he is to read before dinner the Epistle and the Gospel in his own tongue and in the other tongue [Greek?] after dinner. All the rest of the day to be spent in riding, shooting, dancing, walking and other commendable exercises.

His tutor was Lawrence Nowell, Dean of Lichfield, a scholar of distinction. There can be little doubt that Oxford was a diligent student.

He lived well. One of Burghley's early accounts reveals expenditures on Oxford for rapiers, daggers and apparel between 1562 and 1566 of £627 15s. 6d.[23] Another account, later, when he was nineteen, speaks of four geldings which he maintained, and of board and diet paid to Burghley for himself, his tutor and his servants of £3 a week.

In 1567, following Burghley's pattern, he entered Gray's Inn. It was in July of the same year that Burghley made the following entry in his diary:[24]

'About this time Thomas Brincknell, an under-cook, was hurt by the Earl of Oxford at Cecil House in the Strand whereof he died, and by a verdict found *felo-de-se*, with running upon a point of a fence sword of the said Earl's.'

Later when Burghley was far less kindly disposed towards Oxford than he had been in 1567, he recorded a different version of the affair: 'I did my best', he wrote, 'to have the jury find the death of a poor man whom he [Oxford] killed in my house to be found *se defendendo*.'[25]

There is no other record of the affair. It was clearly something more than an accident arising out of a fencing match, enough more so that Burghley had to use his influence upon a jury, presumably a coroner's jury, to cover the matter up. In any case, the wardship of Oxford was not without its difficulties.

The first opportunity for military experience presented itself in the Rising of the North in 1569 when Oxford was nineteen. Burghley sent both his son, Thomas, and his ward, the young Earl of Rutland, north in November. It seems not unlikely that Oxford was intended to go with them. But he was taken sick. On November 29th he wrote to Burghley saying he was recovered and asking permission to go. He apparently did not get it until after the northern rebellion was over.[26] He is said to have participated in the enterprises of Sussex in Scotland in April and May. But there is no record of it, nor even of when he returned from the borders.

We hear of him next at the opening of Parliament in April 1571[27] when he appeared in his hereditary office of Lord Great Chamberlain, next in precedence after the Lord Chancellor, the Lord Treasurer, the Lord Privy Seal and the Duke of Norfolk, who was Earl Marshal. There is no evidence that he took any active part in the session.

Before Parliament rose, Oxford made his first recorded appearance at Court in a tournament at Westminster before the Queen. He was one of four challengers, the other three being Charles Howard, Sir Henry Lee and Christopher Hatton. John Stow, the chronicler, records that 'all did very valiantly but the chief honour was given to the Earl of Oxford'.[28]

Considering that Oxford was just twenty-one, and that the other contestants were much more experienced, it was an amazing performance — as one commentator put it, 'far above expectation of the world'.

Oxford, in short, when he became of age seemed to have everything. His family, the Veres, was one of the oldest and most distinguished in England. He was in person rather sturdy than tall, with hazel eyes and brown curly hair — a good dancer, a competent musician (Elizabeth liked to dance with him or to hear him play on the virginal), a first-rate scholar, a fine horseman and now, as it appeared, already a master at the foremost of all courtly exercises, the tourney.

No wonder that he speedily won for himself a high place in the royal favour.[29] But he never played the courtier's game enthusiastically. Within a month of his brilliant performance at Westminster he was thinking of marriage. Before the end of July he was engaged. Lord St. John in a letter to the Earl of Rutland late in July[30] wrote: 'The Earl of Oxford hath gotten him a wife, or at the least a wife has caught him; this is Mistress Ann Cecil, whereunto the Queen hath given her consent and the which hath caused great weeping and sorrowful cheer of those that had hoped to have that golden day.'

Did Oxford catch Ann, or did Ann catch Oxford? Ann is, indeed, something of a puzzle. She was very dear to her father's heart, and his friends, when they referred to her at all, spoke of her affectionately. She seems to have been a sweet, winsome lass, modest, obedient, a good Christian. One does not hear anything of her beauty, or of her wit[31] or of her learning. It is hard to envisage her as the aggressor in any affair with Oxford.

Burghley himself wrote about the matter to the young Earl of Rutland on August 15th, 1571:

'I think it doth seem strange to your Lordship to hear of a purposed determination in my Lord of Oxford to marry with my daughter. And so, before his Lordship moved it to me I might have thought it, if any other had moved it to me but himself. For at his own motion I could not well imagine what to think, considering I never meant to seek it nor hoped of it. And yet reason moved me to think well of my Lord, and to acknowledge myself greatly beholden to him, as indeed I do. Truly, my Lord, after I was acquainted of the former intention of a marriage with Master Philip Sidney,[32] whom always I loved and esteemed, I was fully determined to have of myself moved no marriage for my daughter until she should have been near sixteen,[33] that with moving I might also conclude. And yet I thought it not inconvenient, in the meantime, being free to harken to any motion made by such others as I should have cause to like. Truly, my Lord, my good will serves me to have moved such a matter as this in another direction than this is, but having more occasion to doubt of the issue of the matter, I did forbear. And in mine own conceit I could have as well liked there as in any other place in England. Percase your Lordship may guess where I mean, and so shall I, for I will name nobody.

'Now that the matter is determined betwixt my Lord of Oxford and me, I confess to your Lordship I do honour him so dearly from my heart as I do my own son, and in any case that may touch him for his honour and weal I shall think him mine own interest therein. And surely, my Lord, by dealing with him I find that which I often heard of your Lordship, that there is much more in him of understanding than any stranger to him would think. And for mine own part I find that whereof I take comfort in his wit and knowledge grown by good conversation.'[34]

This is a tantalizing letter. One wonders why it was written at all, from a man in Burghley's position to a lad of twenty-two, who had been for some seven years a ward in Burghley's household. It reveals, as all of Burghley's letters do on the subject of the marriage of his children, that their views about the matter never appear as a factor in his arrangements. It reveals also that Burghley would have preferred to match Ann elsewhere, perhaps to Rutland himself. It reveals, and this we must consider against the background of a long association of Rutland and Oxford as wards in Burghley's household, that Burghley felt it necessary to emphasize his affection and admiration of Oxford. Burghley's relations with Rutland were always on quite a different footing from those with Oxford. We can judge that from the surviving correspondence between them.[35] It may be that Rutland had fitted well into Burghley's household and that Oxford had been something of a maverick there. Under these circumstances Burghley may well have realized that the news of the approaching marriage between his favourite daughter and Oxford would come to Rutland as something of a shock. Burghley's letter, in short, suggests a situation which called for explanation and justification. We should not, I think, regard it as a genuine expression of affection and admiration for his prospective son-in-law.

As for Ann, she was only fifteen and no doubt dazzled by the brilliant young courtier, fresh from his tournament triumph at Westminster. They were married on December 19th, 1571, in Westminster Abbey with the Queen herself present. After the ceremony there was a great feast at Cecil House in Covent Garden. All the great men were there including La Mothe Fénélon, the French ambassador.[36] It was characteristic of Burghley that even on that festive day he wrote an official dispatch to Walsingham, though he apologized for its brevity.

'I can write no more', he wrote, 'for lack of leisure, being occasioned to write at this time divers ways and not unoccupied with feasting my friends at the marriage of my daughter who is this day married to the Earl of Oxford, to my comfort, by reason of the Queen's Majesty, who hath very honourably with her presence and great favour accompanied it.'[37]

At the time of the marriage the Duke of Norfolk was in the Tower, awaiting trial for complicity in the Ridolfi Plot. He and Oxford were first cousins;[38] Norfolk was the older man, fourteen years older, but they appear to have been good friends. Some months after the marriage and after Norfolk had been tried and found guilty of high treason, one of Burghley's agents in the Low Countries reported that the English refugees there had great hopes of Oxford. They were affirming that Oxford was pleading for Norfolk with the Queen, was very much displeased with Burghley's attitude in the matter and 'had put away from him the Countess his wife'.[39]

This, of course, was mere rumour. It had some support later from rather doubtful sources. In 1574, a woman not identified reported to the Privy Council that when Norfolk was in prison Oxford had prepared a ship to carry Norfolk overseas, and had tried to bribe her to assist in his escape.[40] There is no confirma-

SIR FRANCIS WALSINGHAM

tion of this story, though, for what it may be worth, La Mothe Fénélon[41] in December 1571 wrote to his master that Oxford was up to something. Finally, there is the charge made some ten years later by Henry Howard, younger brother of the Duke of Norfolk.[42] Howard, though Oxford's first cousin, was at the time his mortal enemy. His testimony is therefore of very doubtful validity. What he said was that Oxford had been Norfolk's supporter in his treasonable purposes and had urged him to fight rather than submit.

It seems not unlikely that Oxford did befriend Norfolk and was critical of Burghley's attitude. But the evidence of active support of Norfolk in his treasonable purposes or of plans to assist his escape is too flimsy to be seriously entertained. There is certainly nothing but the idle gossip of Catholic refugees to indicate that at this juncture Oxford 'had put his wife' from him.

In any case, Oxford and his father-in-law appear to have been on the best of terms less than a year later. In the autumn of 1572 he wrote two affectionate letters to Burghley protesting his devotion.

But things were not going so well between the two as these letters would seem to indicate. When he wrote from his country place at Wivenhoe in October,[43] he acknowledged a letter from his father-in-law, and added that it was the first he had received in which Burghley had revealed a good opinion of him. He hoped it would continue, 'after so many storms passed of your heavy grace towards me'. And he hoped that those who had made ill reports of him would not again 'undo your Lordship's beginnings of well meaning of me'.

We have nothing from Burghley at this juncture to explain his critical attitude. In a memorandum later he spoke of Oxford's slanders, lies, inhumanity towards his wife, wasting of his patrimony and contempt of God.[44] Some ten years later, Charles Arundel, later an English Catholic refugee overseas, became embroiled with Oxford, and made a vicious attack upon his character.[45]

The charges he listed include:

'A shameless liar.
'An habitual drunkard.
'A buggering of a boy that is his cook and many other boys.
'Blasphemy, a denial of Christ's nativity, the Trinity a fable, the Virgin a whore, Joseph a wittol [cuckold].'

Some of this is not provable, though there is evidence of Oxford's drunkenness, and Burghley agreed that he was a liar and a blasphemer. Sodomy must be dismissed as unproven. At this juncture he appears to have been on at least conventionally good terms with his wife.

The relations between Burghley and his son-in-law seem to have improved in the autumn of 1572, possibly because Oxford was apparently quite eager to get away from Court, either on a foreign mission or in the navy, and looked to Burghley to find him a place.

He was still about the Court when Gilbert Talbot wrote a letter full of Court gossip to his father, the Earl of Shrewsbury, on May 11th, 1573.[46]

E

'My Lord Treasurer,' he wrote, 'even after the old manner, dealeth with matters of the state only, and beareth himself very uprightly ... My Lord of Oxford is lately grown into great credit, for the Queen's Majesty delighteth more in his personage and his dancing and valiantness than any other. I think Sussex doth back him all that he can. If it were not for his fickle head, he would pass any of them shortly. My Lady Burghley, unwisely, has declared herself, as it were, jealous, which is come to the Queen's ear, whereat she has been not a little offended with her, but now she is reconciled again. At all these love matters my Lord Treasurer winketh and will not meddle in any way.'

All of this is in the main clear enough, but must be taken with a grain of salt. The young man who wrote it was only twenty years old, though already married and an M.P. His reference to Lady Burghley is obscure. Either he wrote Lady Burghley when he meant Lady Oxford, or we must take the word 'jealous' in its old sense of apprehensive rather than in its current meaning. This much is obvious, that Oxford was in very high favour at Court and with the Queen.[47]

But Court life was not to his fancy. When we hear of him again it is in connection with an obscure plot to send an English expedition to support Alva in his Low Countries wars.[48]

The whole matter is puzzling, though of Oxford's implication there can be no doubt. Probably the most charitable interpretation to place upon his behaviour is that he was bored to death with Court life and casting desperately about for action. He was probably quite without convictions on the issue in the Low Countries and ready to fight on either side that offered service. No doubt he was properly rebuked when the cat came out of the bag, but was quite unpenitent. Six months later the whole Court was startled by the news that Oxford, without permission and without warning, had suddenly fled overseas.[49]

Elizabeth was enraged and dispatched a messenger forthwith to bring him back. Walsingham wrote to Burghley on July 6th: 'I made her Majesty acquainted with my Lord of Oxford's arrival at Calais, who doth not interpret the same in any evil part. She conceiveth great hope of his return upon some secret message sent him.'[50]

But there was not a little fear that Oxford had joined up with the English Catholic refugees in the Low Countries. Burghley wrote on July 15th to Sussex, in answer to a letter which is missing: 'I must heartily thank your Lordship for your advertisement of my Lord of Oxford's cause wherein I am sorry that her Majesty maketh such haste ... My Lord, howsoever my Lord of Oxford be, for his own part, in matters of thrift inconsiderate, I dare avow him to be resolute in dutifulness to the Queen and his country.'[51]

It was revealed to Burghley later by one of his correspondents at Antwerp that there had been great rejoicing among the English refugees at his arrival, that the Earl of Westmorland, exiled leader of the Rising of the North, had planned to go to Bruges to meet him.[52] But they were disappointed — Oxford was back in England before the end of July.

Burghley's old friend, Sir Walter Mildmay, wrote to him on the 27th:[53] 'Of my Lord of Oxford's return I am glad to hear. I trust this little journey will make him

love home the better hereafter. It were a great pity he should not go straight, there
be so many good things in him to serve his God and Prince.'

Walsingham sent good news four days later. 'I find', he wrote, 'her Majesty
graciously enough inclined towards the Earl of Oxford, whose peace I think will be
both easily and speedily made, for that her Majesty doth conceive that his obedience in his return hath fully satisfied the contempt of his departure. And the rather
through his honourable and dutiful carriage of himself towards the rebels and
other undutiful subjects of her Majesty in that country — an argument of his
approved loyalty which, as opportunity shall serve, I shall not fail to lay before
her Majesty by acquainting her with your L. letters.'[54]

Burghley replied to this letter at length on August 3rd from Theobalds:[55]

'Yesternight your letters came to Master Benigfeld and me signifying her
Majesty's pleasure that my L. of Oxford should come to Gloucester now at her
Majesty being there. Whereof he, being advertised by us, was very ready to take
the journey, showing in himself a mixture of contrary affections although both
reasonable and commendable. The one, fearful and doubtful in what sort he shall
recover her Majesty's favour because of his offence in departure as he did without
licence, the other glad and resolute to look for a speedy and good end because he
had in his abode so notoriously rejected the attempts of her Majesty's evil subjects
and in his return set apart all his own particular desires of foreign travel and come
to present himself before her Majesty, of whose goodness towards him he saith he
cannot count. Hereupon he and Master Benigfeld departed this afternoon to
London where the earl, as I perceive, will spend only two days or less to make him
some apparel meet for the court, although I would have had him forbear that new
charge, considering his former apparel is very sufficient and he not provided to
increase a new charge. . . .

'I cannot be there [at Court] as soon as he for that on Friday or Saturday next I
am to attend at London for the celebration of the French King's funeral, so I am
in doubt whether I shall come to Gloucester before Wednesday following. . . .

'I must be bold by this my letter to require you in my name most humbly to
beseech her Majesty that she will regard his loyalty and not his lightness in sudden
joy over his confidence in her goodness and clemency, and not his boldness in
attempting that which hath offended her . . . I think it is sound counsel to be given
to her Majesty that this young nobleman, being of such a quality as he is for birth,
office and other notable valours of body and spirit, he may not be discomforted
either by any extraordinary delay or by any outward sharp or unkind reproof —
and that her favourable accepting of his submission may be largely and manifestly
declared unto him, to the confirmation of him in his singular loyalty . . . If he shall
not find comfort now in this amendment of his fault, I fear the malice of some
discontented persons, wherewith the Court is overmuch sprinkled, may set to
draw him to a repentance rather of his dutifulness in thus returning than to set in
him a contentation to continue in his duty. . . .

'I cannot well end, neither will I end, without also praying you to remember
Master Hatton to continue my Lord's friend as he hath manifestly been . . . And I

doubt not but Master Secretary Smith will remember his old love towards the earl when he was his scholar.'

Burghley's English is rather involved, but he was obviously fearful that if the Queen were not magnanimous to the young culprit, he might yet resume his wayward course. She seems to have acquiesced with surprising alacrity.

Walsingham wrote to Burghley on or about August 7th:

'I am sure you are not unadvertised how the Earl of Oxford is restored to her Majesty's favour, in whose loyal behaviour towards her Majesty's rebels in the Low Countries who sought conference with him, a thing he utterly refused, did very much qualify her contempt in departing without her Majesty's leave. The desire to travel is not yet quenched in him, though he dare not make any motion unto her Majesty that he may, with her favour, accomplish the said desire. By no means he can be drawn to follow the Court, and yet there are many cunning devices used in that behalf for his stay.'[56]

Oxford finally won the Queen's assent to travel overseas, and on January 7th he took his leave of the Court and was on his way to Paris.

Before he left, Burghley, too well aware of his profligate habits, induced him to make arrangements for his financial affairs during his absence. To discharge his debts, which he estimated to be £6000, he set aside some £500 annually; he assigned to his wife £300 for her living expenses and 1000 marks (£666.6.8) for her jointure, for his sister £100, and for his own use overseas £1000.[57]

Oxford had promised the Queen that he would be entirely guided by Burghley in the matter, but Burghley, who had the interest of his daughter chiefly at heart, was reluctant to press his claims. In a note intended for Sir William Cordell, Master of the Rolls, who apparently had charge of the business, he wrote: 'I am not so meet to press my Lord in anything for her as others may do.'

He went on to say: 'If my Lord allot her any good portion to maintain herself withal, I will order the same that she, being sometime in the Court, as much of that portion as can be spared shall be employed to provide necessary things for his household against his return, whereof he hath great lack. I would gladly that he would leave to her the house and domains of Wivenhoe, if upon occasion she should be compelled to live in the country, and that she might have the lodging in the Savoy.

'You may say to the Master of the Rolls that my Lord hath promised the Queen's Majesty to be wholly advised by me and to use his wife well and honourably and so he avoweth to me.'[58]

We need not follow in detail his adventure overseas. In March Burghley wrote that Ann expected a baby. Oxford replied on the 17th: 'I thank God therefore, with your Lordship, that it hath pleased God to make me a father ... But thereby to take an occasion to return, I am off from that opinion.'[59] He concluded the letter with a call for more money. 'Wherein,' he wrote, 'I perceive by your Lordship's letter how hardly money is to be gotten, and that my man writeth he would fain pay to my creditors some part of that money which I have appointed to be made over to me, good my Lord, let rather my creditors bear with me awhile and take their days assured according to that order I left, than I to want in a strange country. My revenue is appointed with the profits of my lands to pay them as I may and if I cannot yet pay them as I would yet as I can I will, but preferring my own necessity before theirs.'

By the same post Oxford wrote to Ann and sent her his portrait and two horses.[60] The portrait appears to have been the one now at Welbeck. It does not reveal an engaging countenance. The face is hard, cold, calculating, supercilious, with a mere shadow of a moustache and scarcely any eyebrows. Valentine Dale, the English ambassador in Paris at the time, who saw the portrait before it went to England, pronounced it a good likeness. George Chapman later described Oxford as 'the most goodly fashioned man I ever saw'. But the encomiums of impecunious playwrights must be taken with many reservations.[61]

The news of his first child, a daughter, in July, Oxford did not receive until September when he was in Italy. It did not stir him to return. Quite the contrary. In the same letter in which he gave thanks for his wife's delivery he asked Burghley to secure from the Queen licence for further travel. He also announced that he had borrowed money and desired Burghley to repay it out of the sale of his lands. Indeed, most of his letters to Burghley during the summer and autumn which survive seem to have dealt with his increasing expenses and the increasing exclamations of his creditors. He kept on urging Burghley to sell more land, and Burghley kept on trying to curb his extravagances if only in the interest of his wife and child. But Oxford was heedless. 'I have no help', he wrote,[62] 'but of mine own, and mine is made to serve me and myself, not mine.' He went on to say that he had lost all hope of help by her Majesty's service, 'considering that my youth is objected unto me and for every step of mine a block is found to be laid in my way. I see it but vain *calcitrare contra li busse* [to kick against the pricks] . . . That I am determined to hope for anything I do not. But if anything do happen, *praeter spem*, I think before that time I must be so old [that] my son, who shall enjoy them, must give the thanks. And I am to content myself according to the old English proverb "to starve like a horse whilst the grass doth grow"'.

This from a youth of twenty-six! To Oxford the only thing which really mattered was Oxford. The Queen, his father-in-law, his mother-in-law, and presently his wife were so many obstacles in the way of his desires. And yet what he really wanted is not at all clear. At the moment he wanted freedom from any sort of restraint.

His letter just quoted was written in Siena on January 3rd, 1576. Where he was during the three months following is not clear. One story places him in Germany, another in Italy, though in the previous September he professed that he had all of Italy he cared to have. Burghley heard that he had reached Paris at the last of March 1576.[63] It may have been that he heard that the Queen would not give him further licence to remain abroad.

In any case he started home, apparently in a fine rage, which was not alleviated by the fact that his ship was intercepted by pirates and he was stripped to his shirt.[64] Inevitably he poured the vials of his wrath upon his father-in-law.

Burghley summarized the situation in a memorial which he set down on April 25th as follows:

'No unkindness known on his [Oxford's] part at his departure. She [Ann] made him privy that she thought she was with child, whereof he said he was glad. When he was certified thereof at Paris he sent her his picture with kind letters and messages. He sent her two coach horses. When he heard she was delivered he gave me thanks by his letters for advertising thereof. He never signified any misliking of anything until the 4th of April in Paris, from whence he wrote somewhat that, by reason of a man of his, his receiver, he had conceived some unkindness, but he prayed me to let pass the same for it did grow by the doubleness of servants. I wrote to Paris to him to hasten him homeward. I sent for my son, Thomas Cecil, who was more than a hundred miles from London, to come in post and meet him at Dover, or in France, who came and was with him at Dover within two hours after my Lord Howard and others,[65] and that he carried my commendations and his wife's, and did not understand from him any point of misliking.

'My daughter went to Gravesend sooner than I would, for my advice was that by my son she should understand his contentation, but she thought long to do [became impatient] for my son's answer and looked that my Lord would be come near before she could have word, and so went with my Lady Mary [probably Oxford's sister, Mary] who had written to her at Theobalds requesting that she might go with her. All this while I knew of no misliking towards me or his wife; but I heard that his receiver [servant appointed to receive money due] had been at Dover to speak with him and he refused it, saying he would speak with him before me [i.e. in my presence].

'I sent letters to entreat him to take my house for his lodging, whereof I had no answer, and yet I wrote twice by ij several messengers. But my son [Thomas] sent me word that he found him disposed to keep himself secretly two or three days in his own lodging and yet that Edward Yorke told him secretly that his Lordship would come first to my house, but he would nobody knew thereof. Whereupon I was very glad but his wife gladder. And the contrary I knew not until he was landed and then my son told me how he did suddenly leave the barge and took a wherry and only with Rowland Yorke landed about Yorke's house.

'Hereupon I sent to welcome him and with request to take a lodging in my house, but thereto he answered that he meant to keep himself secret in his lodgings ii or iij days and then he would come and speak with me. And the messenger did come from his wife with request that if he should not come that night to her father's house she would come to him, for she desired to be one of the first that might see him. To it he answered neither yea nor nay, but said, "why, I have answered you," meaning that he would keep himself secret ii or iij days, as the messenger took it. Whereupon I thought it convenient she should forbear to go to him until we might see how others were suffered to come to him or he to resort to others. Within ii hours I heard by them that had been with him how many had been with him without any his misliking . . . and that there was a coach preparing for my lady his sister to come to him, which, being heard by my daughter she very importunately required me she might go to him. And yet I required her to stay until I might send to my Lord Howard from whom I would know whether he knew that my Lord her husband would go to Court . . . My Lord Howard sent me word that he as yet could not tell.'[66]

At this point the memorandum suddenly breaks off.

It is certain that even when Burghley wrote this memorandum he knew that Oxford was charging his wife with infidelity.

Oxford's first recorded communication to Burghley was dated two days later.

'Although', he wrote, 'I have forborne in some respect, which should [be] private to myself, either to write or to come unto your Lordship, yet had I determined, as opportunity should have served me, to have accomplished the same in compass of a few days . . . I must let your Lordship understand this much, that is, until I can better satisfy or advertise myself of some mislikes I am not determined, as touching my wife, to accompany her. What they are, because some are not to be spoken of or written upon as imperfections, I will not deal withal. Some that otherwise discontented me I will not blazon or publish until it please me. And last of all I mean not to weary my life any more with such troubles and molestations as I have endured; nor will I, to please your Lordship only, discontent myself.'

He went on to say that he entirely approved of Burghley's suggestion that Ann return to her father's house — 'for there, as your daughter, or her mother's, more than my wife, you may take comfort of her, and I, rid of the cumber thereby, shall remain well eased of many griefs'.

Oxford added that he would have preferred to have treated the whole matter privately and not to have exposed Ann to the disgrace of the world.

This is the letter of a cad if ever there was one. He would not charge his wife with anything, but he was well rid of her! It is rather shocking to discover that a young, unwhipped cub like Oxford could have dared to write in these terms to the chief minister of the Queen. But such was the prestige of the Veres that socially they were almost above reproach. The Cecils, of course, were parvenus in comparison.

Though Oxford declined to disclose his grievances against his wife, they were an open secret at Court. Even before he went abroad he had sworn openly in the Presence Chamber that if his wife was with child it was no child of his. It passed as the mere flippancy of a courtier at the time. But the Queen did not like it and said so.[67] And two years later, before Oxford had returned from his travels, Lord Henry Howard reported him to have said that Ann's child could not be his, because he had not lain with her for nearly a year before the child was born.[68]

But Burghley could get no satisfaction from his son-in-law. In despair he wrote to Elizabeth herself:

'Most sovereign lady, As I was accustomed from the beginning of my service to your Majesty until of late by the permission of your goodness and by occasion of the place wherein I serve your Majesty, to be frequently an intercessor for others to your Majesty, and therein did find your Majesty always inclinable to give me gracious audience; so now do I find in the latter end of my years a necessary occasion to be an intercessor for another next to myself in a cause godly, honest and just; and therefore, having had proof of your Majesty for most favours in causes not so important, I doubt not but to find the like influence of your grace in a cause so near touching myself as your Majesty will conceive it doth. . . . '

He went on, somewhat incoherently, to explain that his infirmity prevented him from coming to Court and that his daughter, the Countess of Oxford, was also, perforce, absent; and to remind the Queen that he was 'an old, worn servant, that dare compare with the best, the greatest, the oldest and the youngest, for loyalty and devotion', and that his daughter yielded to none 'in dutiful love and fear, yea, in fervent admiration of your graces'.

He then turned to the meat of the matter: '. . . and in the cause betwixt my Lord of Oxford and her, whether it be for respect of misliking in me or misdeeming of hers, whereof I cannot yet know the certainty, I do avow in the presence of God and of his angels whom I do call as ministers of his ire, if in this I do utter any untruth.

'I have not in his absence on my part omitted any occasion to do him good for himself and his causes, no, I have not in thought imagined anything offensive to him, but contrariwise I have been diligent for his causes to his benefit as I have been for my own, and this I pronounce of knowledge for myself, and therefore if, contrary to my desert, I should otherwise be judged or suspected, I should receive great injury. For my daughter . . . I did never see her in her behaviour in word or deed, nor ever could perceive by any other means, but that she hath always used herself honestly, chastely, and lovingly towards him; and now, upon expectation of his coming, so filled with joy thereof, so desirous to see the time of his arrival approach, as in my judgment no young lover rooted or sotted in love of any person could more excessively show the same with all comely tokens; and when, at his arrival, some doubts were cast of his acceptance of her true innocency, seemed to make her so bold as she never cast any care of things, but wholly reposed herself with assurance to be well used by him. And with that confidence, and importunity made to me, she went to him, and there missed of her expectation, and so attendeth, as her duty is, to gain of her hope some recompense.

'And now, lest I should enter further into the matter, and not meaning to trouble your Majesty, I do end with this humble request; that in anything that may hereof follow, whereof I may have wrong with dishonesty offered me, I may have your Majesty's princely favour to seek my just defence for me and mine; not meaning, for respect of my old service, nor of the place whereunto your Majesty hath called me (though unworthy), to challenge any extraordinary favour, for my service hath been but a piece of my duty and my vocation. And so I do remain constant to serve your Majesty in what place so ever your Majesty shall command, even in as base as I have done in great.'[69]

We get some echo in this letter of the charge which Oxford hurled against Burghley, that he had purposely roused the Queen's indignation against him (Oxford). At the same time he charged Lady Burghley with alienation of his wife's affection.

But though recriminations were exchanged, the situation for some months remained unaltered. Burghley wrote out another memorandum in which he condemned Oxford's rejection both of Ann and of her child, and defended himself against charges that he had mismanaged Oxford's affairs when he was out of the country. Burghley insisted that he had done his best to advance Oxford's political future and had even urged his appointment as Master of the Horse.

In conclusion he added: 'I desire that his Lordship will yield to her, being his wife, either that love that a loving and honest wife ought to have, or otherwise to be so used as all lewd and vain speeches may cease of his unkindness to her; and that with his favour and permission she may both come to his presence and be allowed to do her duty to her Majesty, if her Majesty therewith be content, and she shall bear as she may the lack of the rest.

'Or else his Lordship will notify some instant cause of her not deserving such favour and that she may be permitted to make her answer thereto before such as her Majesty may please to appoint.'[70]

In July Oxford consented that his wife should be brought to Court, 'with condition that she should not come when I was present nor at any time have speech with me. But,' he added, 'now I understand that your Lordship means this day to bring her to the Court and that you mean afterwards to prosecute the cause with further hope. Now if your Lordship shall do so, then shall you take more in hand than I have, or can promise, for always I have and I will still prefer mine own content before others.'[71]

At the moment Oxford seems to have been consumed with self-pity. In a poem which he published the same year he wrote:

> Framed in the front of forlorn hope past all recovery
> I stayless stand, to abide the shock of shame and infamy. . . .
>
> My spirites, my heart, my wit and force, in deep distress are drowned;
> The only loss of my good name is of these griefs the ground.

It is not easy to share his grief, considering the shame and grief to which he was exposing his distinguished father-in-law and his innocent, loving wife.

Burghley wrote to Oxford again early in the following year. 'I cannot, my Lord,' he wrote, 'see this old year passed with such disgraces and a new entered to record a concourse of graces, nor feel the burden of the griefs to grow as they daily do without appearance of amendment, but essay by reasonable means to seek relief, specially for my daughter, whose grief is the greater and shall always be in as much as her love is most fervent and addicted to you and because she cannot or may not, without offence, be suffered to come to your presence', and so forth. Burghley asked for permission to visit Oxford in his own chambers and to talk with him there. But apparently nothing came of it.

Later in the same year, Burghley's old friend, Katherine of Suffolk, got involved. Her son, Peregrine, later Lord Willoughby, fell in love with Oxford's sister, Mary. Katherine disapproved of the match, and, as it turned out, on sound grounds. But

Peregrine would not be denied. Katherine wrote several letters to Burghley on the subject, asking his advice. In December she interested herself in an attempt to bring Oxford and Ann together again, but without success.

It was not until 1582 that Oxford effected at least a formal reconciliation with his wife. They had a son in the spring of 1583 who died in infancy,[72] and later two daughters. Oxford wrote a pseudo-affectionate letter to Burghley in June of that year,[73] and all seemed to be well again. But three years later Burghley wrote to Walsingham:[74]

'I was so vexed yesternight very late by some grievous sight of my poor daughter's affliction whom her husband had in the afternoon so troubled with words of reproach of me to her . . . as she spent all the evening in dolour and weeping. . . .

'No enemy I have can envy me this match, for thereby neither honour nor land nor goods shall come to their children, for whom, being three already to be kept and a fourth like to follow, I am only at charge even with sundry families in sundry places for their sustenance. But if their father was of that good nature as to be thankful for the same, I would be less grieved with the burden.'

As it turned out, there were only three children. Ann gave birth to a daughter late in May, but she lost a daughter in September.

Ann died the following June and was buried with great pomp and circumstance in Westminster Abbey. After her death Burghley brought up her daughters in his own household, and eventually found good marriages for them all. But Oxford remained a thorn in his side for the rest of his life.

CHAPTER X

HUGUENOTS AND SEA BEGGARS, 1573-76

After St. Bartholomew's and more emphatically after the re-establishment of commercial relations with the Low Countries in 1573, English official policy took a definite pro-Spanish turn. Elizabeth withdrew her covert support of the English volunteers fighting on behalf of the Dutch rebels in the Low Countries. Many of them, including Sir Humphrey Gilbert, returned home, and of those who remained many, lacking their pay, contemplated offering their services to the Spaniards. Elizabeth did not altogether abandon the Dutch, but for the better part of a year she confined her efforts to offers of mediation in their behalf, in which she got little or no encouragement from the Spanish government.

Meantime, relations with France, though not ruptured by St. Bartholomew's, were badly strained. The French King and his mother continued to press for the Alençon marriage, and Elizabeth continued to find one excuse after another for procrastination. It was first Alençon's religion and then his pock-marked countenance, and then his participation in the siege of the beleaguered Huguenots in La Rochelle. In May 1573 she sent Burghley to tell the French ambassador that she could not contemplate a marriage alliance in France so long as the French King persisted in his policy of exterminating the Huguenots.[1]

The situation in France underwent a marked change in May 1573 when Henry of Anjou, brother of the French King and heir presumptive to the French throne — the same Anjou who had paid reluctant court to Elizabeth in 1571 — was elected King of Poland. As a condition of his election, his agent in Poland had been obliged to swear that Henry would maintain the peace between the different religions. And so Anjou made peace with the Rochellians in June. But the terms of the peace were not satisfactory to the French Huguenots at large. They refused to accept it, and continued in arms. Nevertheless, a peace was signed, and one of Elizabeth's emphatic objections to the Alençon match was removed.

Most of what we hear of Burghley during the summer and autumn of 1573 has to do with the Alençon match. It takes the form of conversations on the subject with La Mothe Fénélon, in which Burghley took the position that he was strong for the marriage, and promised that he would continue to urge it upon his mistress, but that he was not hopeful because of difference in age and religion, and the distastefulness of the Duke's person. He thought Alençon's pock-marked visage was the chief impediment. Fénélon got the impression that both Leicester and Burghley were enthusiastic for the match, and that the Council at large favoured it. According to Fénélon, Burghley told Elizabeth that her position was a precarious one, and that the only way of strengthening it was by marriage.[2] In a long memorandum on the subject which he prepared for the Marshal de Ritz, who came over from France late in August to press for the marriage, Burghley made much of the popular opposition to the match in consequence of the St. Bartholomew's Massacre.[3] The indications are that he still strongly favoured the match but that he had pretty well abandoned hope of it, and was simply playing the Queen's favourite game as she wanted it played.

In December Burghley was seized with an uncommonly severe attack of the gout. De Guaras wrote to Alva on the 15th that Burghley had had a bad seizure and that in consequence all negotiations at Court had ceased.[4] Nine days later Fénélon wrote: 'I am sorry that my Lord Treasurer is so unwell, and so stricken with the gout and other disorders . . . that he can neither give counsel nor participate in these marriage negotiations as he wishes to do.'[5] We get a vivid impression of the gravity of his condition by his absence from the meetings of the Privy Council, which he normally attended with great regularity, from December 3rd until the 24th of the following February.[6]

On February 5th, when he was somewhat better, he wrote to his old friend, Sir William Fitzwilliam, Lord Deputy of Ireland: 'I make my account now of the rest of my life to become as one subject to the cross, both of body and mind, for indeed I find no other likelihood here about a court. And yet I see I must abide with patience for I see no ordinary remedy except I should willfully leave service and incur indignation. . . .

'I am now brought to the Court, but not able as yet to use my feet for weakness, neither have I yet seen her Majesty but must be constrained to be carried to her when it shall please her to speak with me, as she seemeth desirous for many causes. . . .

'And I mean not to tarry but will return within five or six days to recover my feet, and so shall I more comfortably attend when her Majesty shall command me.'[7]

He was, indeed, persistently troubled with the gout during most of the year 1574, was absent for a month in March, for another month in June, for ten days in July, for the better part of August and for over a month in the early autumn.

Indeed, he was away so much that Walsingham in August ventured to remonstrate.

'The persuasion I have,' he wrote, 'that your Lordship is now of late so wholly dedicated to a private life as the hearing what course public affairs taketh, might rather breed unto you discontentment than otherwise, hath been cause why I have foreborne to write unto your Lordship.

'But when I consider how unfit it is for you to live long privately, for that your calling in this state may not allow of it, then do I think it necessary that your Lordship should be made acquainted with the state of both home and foreign matters, to the end that when you shall be employed, the ignorance of them may be no hindrance to your service.'[8]

In May he entertained the Queen at Theobalds.[9] In July we hear of him participating in a meeting of the Privy Council with La Mothe Fénélon, the French ambassador. Fénélon records that what he had to say on the subject Burghley translated into English for the benefit of those councillors who knew no French.[10] Evidently he had made considerable linguistic progress from the time when he declared that he knew no language except the one his mother had taught him.[11]

We hear of him again the following month in connection with the visit of Bernardino de Mendoza to England to strengthen the ties between England and Spain. Fénélon wrote at length about Mendoza's visit, of his long conferences with Burghley and Leicester and Hatton, of his elaborate entertainment — feasting and hunting, dining with the Queen; of expensive presents — gold chains and horses and greyhounds.[12] Walsingham's views about Mendoza's visit he set forth in a letter to Burghley of July 13th:[13]

'What Mendoza bringeth is yet unknown, but men of judgment think that the chief end of his coming is to entertain us with Spanish compliments to lull us asleep for a time until their secret practices be grown to their new and full ripeness.'

In any case Mendoza returned to the Low Countries convinced that official sentiment in England was altogether Spanish. Thomas Wilson, writing to Burghley later from Antwerp, reported that Mendoza was giving out 'that how straitly soever our nation is used in their demands there is no fear or doubt of any breach, for the Queen's Majesty and the Council also (sayeth he) are so desirous to live in peace that they will agree to any conditions, be they never so hard, rather than they will fall out with the King, giving out that the Queen's Majesty is very fearful, with other unmannerly speech of the Council and the whole nation'.[14]

Fénélon also got the idea that the English Court was strongly pro-Spanish. He set forth the reasons at some length in a dispatch to his master in August.[15] How Burghley felt about it is not recorded, but he was widely regarded as a Spanish sympathizer. Even Leicester, who had always been identified with the French interest, was at some pains to point out to Fénélon his indebtedness to the King of Spain.[16] It is clear enough that both Elizabeth and her courtiers set out to convince both the French and the Spanish that the Anglo-French alliance was a thing of the past, and England was to revert again to her old Burgundian connections.

It may well be that one of the impelling motives was the death of the French King, Charles IX, on May 30th. For the death of Charles meant the accession of his brother Henry (February 1575), who was currently regarded as hand in glove with the house of Guise and an enthusiastic supporter of the anti-English and anti-Protestant policy. Elizabeth asked Burghley, if he thought it appropriate, to arrange for obsequies in honour of Charles IX.[17] And so he did.[18] The ceremony was held in St. Paul's[19] on August 7th, with Burghley representing the Queen and many of the nobility in attendance. According to Fénélon it was a very magnificent affair.[20]

One of the most interesting of Burghley's activities during the year of comparative retirement was his development of contacts with English Catholic refugees in the Low Countries. We get early indications of this activity in the letters of John Lee which are preserved in the Public Record Office.[21] By Lee's own account he was an Englishman and a Roman Catholic, a merchant of sorts, who had left England in the late 'sixties and gone to Antwerp because of some sort of row with his wife's relations. He was apparently of the gentry.[22] He was corresponding with Burghley as early as March 1570, and sending him information about the movement of Catholic refugees in the Low Countries. He was deeply involved in the notorious abduction of Dr. Story in the same year,[23] quite possibly at Burghley's instigation. After the flight of the leaders of the northern rebels, the Countess of Northumberland, the Earl of Westmorland, Francis Norton (son of Old Norton) and the rest, to the Low Countries in 1570, Lee established contacts with them. From January 1571 to May 1573 his reports to Burghley are for the most part preserved. They concern themselves with his efforts to induce the rebels to plead for pardon, and to return home. He seems to have made considerable progress in that direction both with the Earl of Westmorland and with Francis Norton.[24] But in October 1572 he was arrested, at the instigation, he thought, of Dr. Story's wife,[25] and for some months was kept in prison without trial. Fortunately he had taken the precaution to conceal incriminating papers.[26] He was formally brought to trial in April 1573, and copies of his letters to Burghley were produced against him. Despite the vigorous efforts of both Burghley and Leicester, acting upon De Guaras, the Spanish agent in England,[27] Lee's chance of escape seemed slim. But fortunately for him the question of his fate arose at just about the time that Alva and Burghley had reached an agreement on the reopening of trade. So that finally a personal letter from Leicester to Alva on his behalf[28] secured his liberation. After that he disappears; obviously his usefulness was at an end.

His story has been worth telling because it serves as an introduction to Burghley's continuing efforts to maintain contact with the refugees. He seems to have persuaded them that he was their best friend beside the Queen, and he nourished that belief by securing for them various small favours.

At one time or another he exchanged letters with the Earl of Westmorland, with Lord Henry Morley, with Sir Francis Englefield, with Egremont[29] Radcliffe, the Earl of Sussex's renegade half-brother, and with Sir Thomas Copley. Unfortunately we have preserved only one side of this correspondence. The most voluminous is that of Sir Thomas Copley.[30] He was at the outset a zealous Protestant, but at some time during the first decade of Elizabeth's reign was converted to the Roman Church. He appears to have been imprisoned for some years as a recusant and left England without licence in 1570. He subsequently entered the service of the King of Spain. His efforts to secure permission to return to England, that he might enjoy his estate without compromising his religious beliefs, were futile. He finally died in Flanders in 1584.

One letter from Burghley to Copley, written on December 28th, 1574, survives, and is worth quoting at some length:

'For yourself, truly I always, before your departure hence, had a good opinion of you for your wisdom, virtue and other good qualities, having never heard you were touched with any spot of discourtesy or disworship. And I was also the more inclined to think well of you because I knew you were of blood and kin to my wife, so as your children and mine by her were to be knit in love and acquaintance by blood . . . And now Mr. Copley, why should you so fashion your conscience to condemn that which you did not in all King Edward's time, nor yet in a great part of her Majesty's reign? Wherein make you the difference so great in matters of religion here used, or that you here may use without peril, that you will for that lose the sweet benefits of your native soil, your friends, your kindred — yea, incur the infamies that wilful exile doth bring — to be accounted if not a traitor, yet a companion of traitors and conspirators, a man subject to all the curses and impre-cations of zealous, good subjects, your native countrymen, yea, subject to lack of living by your own and thereby compelled to follow strangers for maintenance, livelihood and food. The cause must needs be of great force to induce you thereto and indeed I think your only conscience enforceth you thereto. But yet you may do well sometime to examine the foundations thereof and not to be curious in condemning everything that by others is misliked, but what is by God's word condemned and what is allowed or tolerated.

'To examine and compare our estate with others in the matter of religion, both for doctrine, ceremonies and life and manners were too long a work for me and superfluous. But this I think, that no church on earth shall be, until the day of Judgment, when the good shall be separated from the evil and, as the Scripture saieth, the lambs from the goats, so clear and free either in doctrine, ceremonies or manners, from errors, superstitions and corruptions but that there must be a con-versation of the good with the evil, so as the good must always contend, by teaching and example, to amend and correct the evil. And this exercise of the good must continue to the end of the world, for otherwise men should do as the persons do that, being in a ship whereunto the Church of Christ is resembled, and per-ceiving some evil-conditioned persons, will, for misliking of these, leave the ship, to their own peril. But in this ship of England do you find such offenders as are not in the like abroad? Be there in this our ship blasphemers, heretics, irreligious, avouterers [adulterers] and such like, and be there not the like in other, yea, in all places in Christendom, the more is to be lamented? And be there not here also, think you, in this your native country, numbers that reverence and believe in the same God, the Father, the Son and the Holy Ghost, as you and others where you are do it receive, and uphold the same articles of the apostolic creeds that you and others do, that make as just estimation of the Holy Scriptures as you and others do, that prefer all moral virtues and condemn all vices as far as you and others do, that labour to preserve public peace by administration of justice with as great care as others do? I could, percase, say more in defence of this estate, being compared to others, but I know comparisons be odious and I myself may seem, being in office, though unworthy, yet no mean servant and minister, to be a partial preferer of the State wherein I serve. And yet I am not ignorant how maliciously this state hath been of late years slandered, perverting every accident to the worst by untruths, in which I have noted the excess of the slanders to be such as it was not regarded what was here done and deserved, but how evil and abominable reports might be with words, seeking and travailing rather how they may exceed in foul speeches than why or upon what grounds they may so exceed — a fault common now-a-days either in praising or dispraising, never to measure the subject whereupon they treat but to extend their own force to utter what they can, either with flattery or praise, or with spite and blasphemy, to dispraise and backbite.

'When I consider what spiteful and railing books and pamphlets are sewn abroad in the world and that, which is most unseemly, by such as make profession of Divinity, I do bewail this age, wherein I see none utter any work or treatise to procure an attunement and concord in the matters of the church, but rather by lies, slanders, opprobriums and backbitings to kindle the fires of dissension and schism, so void is this age of charity and sufferance. . . .

'And to conclude, I wish you to continue your advised manner of life there, that, seeing as I hear, you have some favour with that governor, of whose wisdom and temperance there is generally good report, that you be not seduced by such as were of this country, for their particular passions, do maintain themselves in their rebellious rancours against the Queen's Majesty.'[31]

At this point in the letter Burghley turned from the problem of Copley to an impassioned personal defence against the charges levied at him in the *Treatise of Treason*. After two years the matter still rankled.

The letter is a clever one. It did not, of course, touch upon the basic issue between the Roman and the Anglican position. But it dangled before Copley's eyes, wrestling in a foreign country with the problem of supporting a wife and seven children, with an eighth on the way, the blessings of his own country and his friends and his good repute. On the religious side it simply raised the question as to whether dissent in minor differences of faith was worth what it cost. Burghley's observations on the character of controversial literature may simply have been prefatory to his outburst on the *Treatise of Treason*. And yet it is evident that he was coming close to the Queen's own position which he had set forth so eloquently four years before,[32] a policy of 'attunement and concord', of 'charity and sufferance'.

Copley's reply was a masterpiece of polite disagreement.[33] The essence of it is distilled in a single sentence. 'I thought it better', he wrote, ' . . . to remit the answering of those arguments to your own wisdom and conscience than by using in that matter more words than needed to work none other effect than the offending of your Lordship.' But he remained steadfast in his faith and apparently loyal to his sovereign. Though he accepted service, and a pension, and even a title from the King of Spain, there is no evidence that he ever participated in any of the conspiracies against his country or his Queen. Ten years later he died in exile. There were many like him in England and not a few among the refugees overseas. It was part of the intuitive wisdom of Elizabeth that she realized that fact. It was part of her influence upon her wise old servant that by degrees she brought him to realize it.

Burghley's continued absence from Court at the end of 1574 was interfering with the dispatch of public business. 'We have great want of you here', Smith wrote to him on December 6th, 'for dispatching of matters.' Poor Smith, he was experiencing all of Cecil's earlier difficulties in getting any positive action from

Elizabeth, but he lacked Cecil's skill in dealing with them. He wrote again to Burghley early in March 1575:

'For matters of state I will write as soon as I can have any access to her Majesty, the which, as it was when your Lordship was here, sometime so, sometime no, and all times uncertain and ready to stays and revocation. So it is now . . . This irresolution doth weary and kill her ministers, destroy her actions and overcome all good designs and counsels — no letters touching Ireland, although read and allowed by her Majesty, yet can I get signed. I wait whilst I neither have eyes to see or legs to stand upon. And yet these delays grieve me more and will not let me sleep in the night . . . For private matters and suits I have the same success. They increase daily. Yea nor nay can I get, and as I hear her Majesty hath forbidden Mr. Hatton and my Lord of Leicester to move suits. Then had we need within a while to have a horse or an ass to carry bills after us, increasing daily and never dispatched.'[34]

Walsingham also felt the need of Burghley, and wrote to him on January 13th, 1575:

'By these enclosed your Lordship may perceive how her Majesty's great neighbours are affected towards her and what hollow friendship she is to look for at their hands. Your Lordship may perceive how unsound we are at home and how much it behooveth her Majesty to look unto her estate and not to slumber as she doth in a weak security . . . Her Majesty, at my departure from the Court, willed me to send such things as should come into my hands of importance unto herself . . . the same to be communicated unto you. And therefore your Lordship shall not need to take any knowledge to have had a former sight of this. I think it convenient to stay the sending of them unto her Majesty until such time as you shall be at Court. It may please you therefore, at the return of these enclosed to send me word of your return hither.'[35]

Evidently Walsingham felt that the best way to get action from the Queen was to get Burghley back beside her. He was back on January 21st.[36]

Meanwhile he had been interesting himself in a little adventure in alchemy, which took the form of an enterprise to convert iron into copper. Sir Thomas Smith appears to have been the promoter of it and he drew into the enterprise Burghley, Leicester and Sir Humphrey Gilbert.[37] On January 28th Smith wrote to Burghley that he had got the letters patent organizing the society signed and would make all haste to have it pass the Signet and Privy Seal and so to the Great Seal.[38] Smith asked Burghley to confer with Leicester about getting the work started. 'It hath long enough lain in suspense and no profit come of it but charges and expense to me and others. And your Lordship lacked both the profit and honour which I trust shall rise upon it.'[39] Leicester and Burghley had put £100 into the enterprise. It came, of course, to nothing. But it serves to show that like all his fellows even Burghley succumbed on occasion to the alluring promises of the alchemists.

In March Burghley was appointed Royal Exchanger. The grant gave him control over all exchange operations involving the conversion of foreign money into English money in England and the conversion of English money into foreign money for use overseas. He was empowered to create, license and control brokers of exchange. The grant was for twenty-three years with allowance to Burghley of one-half the receipts from fees, forfeitures and the like. In return he was to pay to the Crown £30 annually.[40]

It was probably a consequence of this grant that in September of the year following a proclamation was issued establishing a commission of three, two haberdashers and one grocer of London, to issue licences for exchange transactions. They were authorized to impose a charge both upon the payer and the payee of three farthings in the pound. They were directed to restrict their licences to the use of known merchants or such others as might receive licence from the Crown.

Government control of exchange transactions had a long history before Burghley's day.[41] It had been tried many times and abandoned many times. The mercantile interests opposed it; Thomas Gresham, who probably knew more about the intricacies of exchange than anyone in England, opposed it. Gresham believed that rates of exchange depended entirely upon matters of supply and demand and they in turn upon the balance of trade. But the impression was widespread in England that rates of exchange unfavourable to English merchants were due to the manipulation of continental bankers who undervalued English money and overvalued the money of other countries. To this school of thought Burghley evidently belonged. Here again we must number him among those who knew little and feared much of the machinations of the mercantile world.

The opposition in this case took the form of a protest by a group of Italian commission merchants.[42] They complained about the charges, they complained about the inquisitorial procedure involved, they complained about the lack of flexibility in the dealings between merchant and merchant. They anticipated a loss of business both in imports and exports and a consequent loss to the Queen in her Customs and the English in their trade. The issue was at bottom the perennial issue between government control and free enterprise, between orthodox mercantilism and an open market controlled only by market conditions. The protest was addressed to a commission appointed by the Privy Council to consider their arguments.[43]

Apparently the plan outlined in the September proclamation was applied for a season. We have an account of the fees collected by one of the haberdashers from September 27th, 1576, to July 11th, 1577.[44] It would be dangerous to argue that the end of the account marked the end of the enterprise. It certainly did not last long. Not for the first time orthodox mercantilism had to yield to the new economic forces at work.

During most of 1575 Burghley's surviving correspondence has mainly to do with the state of his health.

On April 11th he wrote to Walsingham, who was absent amending his own frail health: 'I heartily thank you for your Italian advices, wherein a man can see that the world is made of a round substance, that it cannot stand still. And here our little world, for lack of some profitable motions, may chance to further decay ... At my being at the Court, though myself was lame, yet with the help of others I have again set afoot the enterprise of Ulster, and her Majesty doth by her letters greatly commend, thank and comfort the Earl of Essex.[45] God send him as good speed as if he were mine own son.

'I did yesterday show to the Queen's Majesty the Regent's [of Scotland] letter to you, Mr. Secty. Smith being present. There was great and long talk for satisfying the Regent, but I fear there will be more smoke arise than fire.'[46]

Four days later from his house in Covent Garden he wrote to Walsingham again:

'I am right glad that you are at the Court where, though you cannot find things succeed as were to be desired, yet I doubt not but by your discretion and diligence other good things will come to effect or evil fall in defect. If my ability was I would gladly help the plough with you, whether in the ridge or furrow until I had the yoke pulled off from my neck ... I am in doubt what to do, whether to come to the Court on Friday, being not able, I fear, then to make the passage on foot. But if St. George's four nights should ride as he doth,[46a] I could better do my service. I begin to be able to go softly with help of one staff and if the weather shall not hinder more I would hope to do the same with a small staff. If you shall in any wise perceive what is looked for by the supreme I pray you advertise me.'[47]

He was still at Covent Garden on May 6th writing to Walsingham about minor administrative problems. His observations upon a letter which Walsingham had forwarded to him from Hubert Languet are worth recording. Languet had been in Paris representing the Elector of Saxony at the time of the St. Bartholomew Massacre. He had barely escaped with his life and had returned to Germany to represent Saxony at Vienna. He was an ardent Protestant and a close personal friend of Walsingham and young Philip Sidney.[48] Burghley wrote: 'I return to you your letter from Languet, for the which I thank you, for I take pleasure in all his letters, they are so full of good judgment.'[49]

Later in the same month Burghley had word that Matthew Parker, Archbishop of Canterbury, was critically ill, and he wrote to Walsingham regarding his successor: 'This day I heard of the danger of the Archbishop of Canterbury's life,[50] being almost speechless. And as in my cogitation I thought the meetest man to succeed him should be the Archbishop of York [Edmund Grindal], so you may perceive the opinion of a faithful wise man, Mr. Dean of Paul's.[51] I pray you if you know not the contrary of her Majesty's determination, to take my proxy for my poor voice for the Archbishop of York, both for knowledge of government and good proof of the same in the North and also for the place he holdeth next to the place in the South by degree.'[52]

This is a surprising letter. It is surprising in the first place that Burghley should have conveyed his opinion about such an important appointment through Walsingham rather than in conference with the Queen herself; surprising in the second place that Grindal, who had been, when Bishop of London, something of a thorn in the side of Parker because of his Puritan sympathies, should not only have been Burghley's nominee but also, some five months later, Elizabeth's selection. She soon had occasion to rue her choice, finding Grindal much less accommodating than his predecessor. Burghley's argument in Grindal's favour was that he was a good administrator. But Burghley must have been quite aware of Grindal's Puritan proclivities and presumably have endorsed them, though he was careful to base his support on quite other grounds.

In his next surviving letter to Walsingham he was once more preoccupied with his health. 'I perceive', he wrote, 'her Majesty meaneth to depart thence [on her Progress] about the 9th of the next month and that I am looked for to come thither shortly. Now Sir, how soon or how late it shall be mete for me to come, as you have answered for my intent so both I thank you and upon answer from you I will conform myself. But this I pray you understand that the longer her Majesty's service there shall permit me to continue here, the better I shall serve her Majesty here and content myself in doing some little things of my own. And indeed, since her Majesty went from my house[53] I assure you I have done little or nothing in mine own poor private cause, in which, on my faith I find myself greatly oppressed with heaviness of debt as I am many times in winter oppressed with sickness. But thereof I will make no boast.

'I and Sir Walter Mildmay have yet business in chequer matters, three or four days, and these done I would covet three or four here for myself at my house at Theobalds, where, though my wife and children are, yet have I not been but two nights since her Majesty went from there, a hard case to bridle my desire. Therefore if you shall think that I may tarry so as I may be there the 6th or 7th of June [July] I will purpose by God's leave to be there at that time. And, I humbly pray you, further my intentions to that end if it may be, if not I will not observe times. And because I desire answer with speed I send this by the post to have return by post.'[54]

The next letter from Burghley to Walsingham dated July 28th at Theobalds (clearly a mistake for June 28th) is interesting if only because of its reference to Henry Hawthorn, who was at the time doing architectural work for Burghley at Theobalds and quite possibly for Sussex and Leicester as well.[55]

'The bearer, H. Hawthorn, cometh very aptly to carry certain letters presently brought to me, directed to my Lords the earls of Sussex and Leicester and to me, which I do by him send to them. And being ready to deliver them to him your letters came to me, by which you have, I thank you, delivered me of some care, in that I knew not how long I might tarry here from the Court. And now I understand that if I be there by the 5th of July my duty shall be satisfied. And so I mean with God's leave. And so I thank you, praying you that my chamber [at Court] may understand the same.'[56]

Clearly Burghley was a very tired man when he wrote this letter. Early in August he left for the north to take the waters at Buxton. The healing waters of Buxton had been known and utilized as far back as the time when the Romans occupied Britain. William Camden, a contemporary of Burghley, wrote of them in his *Britannia*: 'George, Earl of Shrewsbury, lately beautified [Buxton] with buildings and so are they begun again to be resorted unto by concourse of the greatest gentlemen and of the nobility.'[56a] It was this Earl of Shrewsbury who, in 1575, was the keeper of Mary Queen of Scots at Sheffield, some twenty miles to the north-west. On several occasions Mary herself was allowed to visit Buxton. For a man of Burghley's stature a visit to Buxton involved a visit to Shrewsbury. It might even mean a visit to Mary herself.

We have two letters from him there, both written on August 7th to Walsingham. One of them shows that whatever the state of his body, his mind was running on public business.

'I most heartily thank you', he wrote, 'for your own and other letters which you have sent me. By the letters from France all things there seem very troublesome, but yet no attempts against the King nor any final success to the benefit of the attempters, the most part of them being discovered or disappointed whereof must needs follow evil fortune to their part.

'I am sorry to find Mauvissière[57] so near hitherward, for surely he can bring no good with him, he himself being no vessel to carry or hold any honesty ... I see the Queen is to be at Dudley the 18th where I am very sorry I cannot be, specially for satisfaction of my Lord and Lady Dudley, who I know would gladly have me there, the rather to further some of their suits, which, otherwise I shall be most willing to do and think it a very good deed to procure the enlarging of her Majesty's good.'[58]

The letter then goes on about problems of victualling Berwick.

Evidently he was keeping in close touch with Walsingham and public business. And he was hardly following otherwise anything in the nature of a rest cure. Two years later when he was contemplating another trip to Buxton, Leicester wrote to him that if he hoped to derive any benefit he must not do as he had done on his previous visit — eat freely, entertain company both at dinner and supper and take journeys of ten or twelve miles daily.[59]

One consequence of his visit to Buxton is set forth in a letter to Shrewsbury later in the year. Shrewsbury had evidently proposed marriage between his fourth son, Edward, and Burghley's daughter, Elizabeth. Burghley wrote:[60]

'I cannot sufficiently express in words the inward hearty affection that I conceive by your Lordship's friendly offer of the marriage of your younger son, and that in such a friendly sort, by your own letter, and as your Lordship writes, the same proceeding of yourself. Now, my Lord, as I think myself much beholden to you for this your Lordship's kindness, and manifest argument of a faithful good will, so must I pray your Lordship to accept mine answer, with assured opinion of my continuance in the same towards your Lordship. There are specially two causes why I do not in plain terms consent by way of conclusion hereto; the one, for that my daughter is but young in years; and, upon some reasonable respects, I have determined (notwithstanding I have been very honourably offered matches) not to treat of marrying of her, if I may live so long, until she shall be above fifteen or sixteen; and if I were of more likelihood myself to live longer than I look to do, she should not, with my liking, be married before she were near eighteen, or twenty. The second cause why I defer to yield to conclusion with your Lordship is grounded upon such a consideration as, if it were not truly to satisfy your Lordship, and to avoid a just offence which your Lordship might conceive of my forbearing, I would not by writing or message utter, but only by speech to your Lordship's self. My Lord, it is over true, and over much against reason, that upon my being at Buxton last, advantage was sought by some that loved me not, to confirm in her Majesty a former conceit which had been laboured to put into her head, that I was of late become friendly to the Queen of Scots, and that I had no disposition to encounter her practices; and now, at my being at Buxton, her Majesty did directly conceive that my being there was, by means of your Lordship and my Lady, to enter into intelligence with the Queen of Scots; and hereof at my return to her Majesty's presence, I had very sharp reproofs for my going to Buxton, with plain charging of me for favouring the Queen of Scots; and that in so earnest a sort as I never looked for, knowing my integrity to her Majesty; but specially knowing how contrariously the Queen of Scots conceived of me for many things past to the offence of the Queen of Scots. And yet, true it is, I never indeed gave just cause by any private affection of my own, or for myself, to offend the Queen of Scots; but whatsoever I did was for the service of mine own sovereign Lady and Queen, which if it were yet again to be done I would do. And though I know myself subject to contrary working of displeasure, yet will I not, for remedy of any of them both, decline from the duty I owe to God and my sovereign Queen; for I know, and do understand, that I am in this contrary sort maliciously depraved, and yet in secret sort; on the one part, and that of long time, that I am the most dangerous enemy and evil willer to the Queen of Scots; on the other side, that I am also a secret well willer to her, and her title, and that I have made my party good with her. Now, my Lord, no man can make both these true together; but it sufficeth for such as like not me in doing my duty to deprave me, and yet in such sort is done in darkness as I cannot get opportunity to convince them in the light. In all these crossings, my good Lord, I appeal to God, who knoweth, yea (I thank him infinitely) who directeth my thoughts to intend principally the service and honour of God, and, jointly with it, the surety and greatness of my sovereign Lady the Queen's Majesty; and for any other respect but it may tend to those two, I appeal to God to punish me if I have any. As for the Queen of Scots, truly I have no spot of evil meaning to her; neither do I mean to deal with any titles to the Crown. If she shall intend any evil to the Queen's Majesty, my sovereign, for her sake I must and will mean to impeach her; and therein I may be her unfriend, or worse.

'Well now, my good Lord, your Lordship seeth I have made a long digression from my answer, but I trust your Lordship can consider what moveth me thus to digress. Surely it behooveth me not only to live uprightly, but to avoid all probable arguments that may be gathered to render me suspected to her Majesty, whom I serve with all dutifulness and sincerity; and therefore I gather this, that if it were understood that there were a communication, or a purpose of marriage between your Lordship's son and my daughter, I am sure there would be an advantage sought to increase these former suspicions... Considering the young years of our two children... as if the matter were fully agreed betwixt us, the parents, the marriage could not take effect, I think it best to refer the motion in silence, and yet so to order it with ourselves that, when time shall hereafter be more convenient, we may (and then also with less cause of vain suspicion) renew it ... My Lord, I pray you bear with my scribbling, which I think your Lordship shall hardly read, and yet I would not use my man's hand in such a matter as this is.'

The letter hardly calls for comment. It will be noticed that Burghley says nothing about an interview with Mary. She herself says nothing of one in her surviving letters, though she wrote at length about Leicester's secret interview with her two years later.[61] Nor do we hear anything of Elizabeth's suspicions from any other source.

Burghley probably spent a fortnight at Buxton. We hear of him on September 16th taking refuge in Sir Thomas Gresham's house in London because of the plague in Westminster.[62] Later in September he was at Theobalds, writing to ask Walsingham when the Queen expected him at Court. Walsingham answered that he need not come before she returned to Windsor 'unless by some extraordinary accident (not yet thought of) your access hither shall be necessarily required'.[63]

A letter which he wrote to his friend, the Earl of Sussex, on September 27th gives a revealing picture of some of the minor problems with which he had to wrestle. It had to do with someone or other who had secured from the Queen a special licence to export butter and cheese. The details are unimportant, but the issue involved forecasts the whole struggle against monopolies later.

'The matter', he wrote, 'of the licence granted for the butter and cheese is not justly construed to be unto my liking. Such a matter was moved unto me as a thing that her Majesty meant to benefit the party withal, for his only butter and cheese that he should make in Lanam Park, and I was required not to be against her Majesty's disposition to do the party good. I answered that it would be a hard thing to be granted without common offence, but most hardest to be observed, that under colour of such a licence no more should pass, for hard it is and impossible for officers in ports to discern which were Lanam butter and cheese from others. Then it was answered that it should not be granted but with conditions ... I said if it might be so ordered as officers might see and mark it and to pass only at one port, the harm would be less. And so I ended with opinion that before her Majesty had granted it I might have been made privy to the devices[64] for avoiding of fraud. But I see particular gain excludeth all public regard of honour or good. And this indeed is the course of long time kept with me, to set abroad inconvenient suits and then when I show my misliking for certain reasons, then it is answered that those reasons shall be remedied and the Queen's Majesty is informed that I do not mislike the body of the suits. God send me some change of these courses, for they are very cross courses for me, who either must still suffer them or must oppose myself, with adventure of deadly hate. And yet no amendment to follow by her Majesty's order, who must needs believe them most that most occupy her ears. And this have I well felt in sundry things past, that when I have sought to stay such inconvenient grants, my doings have been interpreted as diminutions of her Majesty's prerogative, which your Lordship knoweth is so grateful to princes to maintain as in nothing more may a prince's displeasure be attained.'[65]

After his holiday at Buxton, Burghley seems to have taken a more active part in public affairs. At the moment Elizabeth and her Council were deep in consideration of Anglo-French relations. It had become apparent towards the end of 1573 that the French King was mortally ill. At the time his brother, Henry, was absent in Poland and his younger brother, Francis, Duke of Alençon, was virtually a prisoner at the French Court. If Henry was hand in glove with the house of Guise, Francis was in close touch with the Huguenot leaders, the King of Navarre and the Prince of Condé, and with the Montmorencis, leaders of that wing of the French Catholics which was opposed to the house of Guise. Henry was his mother's favourite, and she dominated the policy of the Crown. As it became evident that the throne would soon be vacant, she bent her energies to preventing Francis from assuming the leadership of the opposition. After Henry's departure for Poland she had kept her younger son and the Huguenot leaders, Navarre and Condé, in close surveillance. Her interest in an English marriage for Alençon blew hot and cold. Sometimes she favoured it as a way of getting rid of him; sometimes she feared it as a way of increasing his strength.

The approaching death of the French King had a profound effect upon Elizabeth's attitude towards France. She recognized that the accession of Henry of Anjou would almost inevitably mean the restoration of the Guises to power. She did not welcome the prospect. Nor did she forget that she had gone far in her efforts to conciliate Anjou earlier when he was a reluctant suitor for her hand. It is not unlikely that there was something in her attitude of a woman scorned.

In any event, we find her playing some part in the various attempts which were made in France during the years 1574 and 1575 to free Alençon from his mother's tutelage and to place him at the head of his partisans.

In Alençon's earlier efforts to escape from Court she apparently remained aloof. But in April 1574 she countenanced the sending of secret agents to France to report on the situation, and in May she dispatched an envoy, Captain Leighton, to the French Court to remonstrate. Both Charles and his mother asserted that they were on the best of terms with Alençon and that he was not a prisoner at all. But their actions belied their words. They gave Leighton permission to speak with the young duke, but saw to it that he dared not grant the interview. Leighton nevertheless contrived to communicate with Alençon secretly, and learned that Alençon was in fear of his life, but that he thought he might escape if he could find money to bribe his guards. He begged Elizabeth to send him money for the purpose.

Up to this point we hear nothing of Burghley's views about the matter. He was still talking to Fénélon about the marriage in the spring of 1574,[66] but seems to have had nothing to do with the undercover intrigue. None of his memoranda on the subject, if indeed he wrote any, seem to have survived. The first revelation of his attitude comes in a letter to Walsingham of May 26th, prompted apparently by Alençon's request for help.[67] Burghley wrote that something must be done to preserve Alençon's person, 'to counterpoise the tyrant that shall come from Poland'. He thought the best course was to provide money for bribery, but he urged the necessity of great secrecy and proceeded to outline a number of ways by which money in small parcels might be sent to France without arousing suspicion.[68] Nothing apparently came of it. Five days later Charles IX died and Catherine shut up the young Duke in the Louvre. There she held him fast until she left Paris on August 8th to meet the new King come from Poland.

When Anjou took his seat on the French throne as Henry III, it seemed as if Elizabeth's fears of him were to be realized. Dale, the English ambassador in Paris, reported manifold signs of the King's unfriendly disposition. English merchants, he wrote, were being tormented and English ships seized. There were rumours of a Catholic league between Henry III and the Pope. In London Fénélon reopened the old issues of Scotland and Mary Stuart, the broaching of which always suggested hostile intentions.

Meanwhile, the Huguenots under La Noue had broken out into open war again. The Prince of Condé had escaped into Germany and was negotiating for assistance with the German Protestant princes. And the Montmorencis had gone all the way over to the rebel camp. They all appealed to Elizabeth for aid — La Noue and the Montmorencis, and Condé from Germany. Elizabeth received them all graciously, but she sent no money and she sent no troops.

The war party in the Council led by Leicester and Walsingham clamoured for action. Walsingham wrote to Burghley on July 13th: 'The parties you wot of, hearing that the navy stayeth and that nothing is done in Germany to their favour and assistance, are much dismayed withal, whereon they builded much, and therefore, that hope removed, they think their case now desperate. If they quail, beside the dishonour, the danger that is like to light on us is evident. We seek neither to conserve friends nor to provide for withstanding our enemies. If this kind of government might carry continuance withal, then should we have less cause to lament. But surely it is so loose as in reason it cannot last. God be merciful unto us.'[69]

It is hard to see what there was in the situation to justify such grim forebodings. How Burghley felt about the matter is not recorded. Walsingham would hardly have written as he did unless he had felt reasonably sure of Burghley's acquiescence. Certainly Elizabeth did not favour drastic action. She chose instead to send an envoy to France, this time Lord North, one of Leicester's henchmen. Dale, the English ambassador in France, wrote that North was well received.[70] But Walsingham's agents told another tale, and when North got back he complained of the small dignities he had received and told the story that Catherine de Medicis had shown him two dwarfs dressed up to imitate Queen Elizabeth and in his presence had mocked at them.[71] Of this we hear nothing from Dale. It is at least possible that North, prompted by Leicester, did his best to discredit Elizabeth's pacific gestures.

According to La Mothe Fénélon, North's report, particularly his story of the dwarfs and their mockeries, quickened Elizabeth's belligerency. She called her war captains together and held long conferences with the agents of the French rebels. Fénélon advised his master to send an envoy to England and to drop any mention of Mary Stuart and her grievances.

Henry III followed the advice, and sent an envoy to England to invite Elizabeth to renew the Anglo-French treaty of alliance signed by his brother three years before. She did so and Henry in turn did so, and cordial relations with France appeared to be restored. But it was not so indeed. Elizabeth was very seriously considering a project to send money to Condé in Germany.

In February she sent Thomas Wilkes to Frederick III, the Count Palatine, the principal supporter of Calvinism in Germany. Wilkes was Walsingham's man, but it is interesting to note that his instructions were drafted by Burghley, the first indication we have of his active participation in the project.[72] Wilkes was directed to take counsel with Frederick about the desirability of military intervention, the prospect of its success and the general question as to whether more might not be gained by treaty than by force. If the Count still favoured military intervention, then Elizabeth undertook to underwrite a loan to assist in the enterprise. It was understood that she would not appear in the transaction at all. Frederick was to borrow the money from the Geneva bankers. Condé was to pledge himself that he would repay the loan and to keep the German forces in France until it was repaid. What Elizabeth agreed to do was to discharge the debt to the Geneva bankers upon condition that Frederick would repay her as soon as Condé paid him. In order to cover Wilkes's visit it was to be given out that he was sent to induce Frederick to suppress 'a certain horrid, damnable book lately made in Germany against Moses, Christ and Mohamet'.

This was not the first time nor was it to be the last time that Elizabeth sought to help the French Huguenots by lending them money to raise troops in Germany. It came to be accepted procedure and in pursuit of it she almost invariably resorted to the Palatinate — to Frederick the Pious while he lived, and after his death (1576), to his younger son, John Casimir. And she generally was at great pains to conceal her hand by some device or other which deceived nobody but seems to have salved her royal conscience, always troubled by the thought of helping rebels against their sovereign.

Wilkes brought back answer that Frederick saw no prospect of peace in France without military intervention, and asked for a loan of 150,000 crowns.

Elizabeth at first seems to have been disposed to meet the demand, though upon condition that Frederick would guarantee to restore Calais to her. But a little later she changed her tune, ignored Calais and reduced her offering to 50,000 crowns. Frederick said it was not enough, but decided to accept it. We hear of Burghley in the matter in connection with the providing of the money. Much of it he borrowed at Antwerp, making use of the service of James Harvey, a merchant.[73] Some of it (about £8000) he sent over from England. His correspondence with Harvey is missing, but he wrote to Walsingham: 'This day I was in London and there heard from Bruges that the money I sent over was safely past Bruges.'[74]

In the same letter Burghley set forth at some length an interview with Francesco Giraldi, the Portuguese ambassador. The letter has reference to the long-running quarrel between Portugal and England over English rights of trade in the Portuguese possessions in Africa. It had arisen in connection with the slaving voyages of John Hawkins to the Guinea coast in the 'sixties. In that connection Burghley had defined the English position as freedom of trade in Guinea except where the Portuguese were in effective possession. The issue regarding the Barbary Coast north of Cape Blanco was something else again. For over twenty years London merchants had established a flourishing trade with Barbary. It was, indeed, the chief source of sugar for England, and an increasingly important market for English cloth. The Portuguese complained that the English also sent arms and ammunition, and, what was still more shocking to the orthodox, Hebrew bibles to the Jews in Morocco. There was also a flourishing trade between England and Portugal in cloth one way, in spice the other, though the chief distributing centre for Portuguese spice in the markets of the north was the Portuguese staple at Antwerp. Through this channel also English cloth flowed in large quantities into the Portuguese market, estimated in 1569 at 2,050,000 ducats annually.[75]

Burghley wrote as follows:

'The Portuguese ambassador would needs speak with me and I would neither go to him nor have him come to me. But I appointed him Spinola's house in his garden near Shoreditch.[76] And so there he had longer talk with me than I can comprehend in writing ... The body and sum of his matter was to procure the stay of arrests and a restoring of free traffic, whereof I liked well. And indeed I see now, as it is used, ii or iii private persons have the gain from the universal. And otherwise of the arrests I see that certain persons privately make an excessive gain. But he and I differ in the means. He still harpeth to exclude us from Barbary and I altogether press to have no prohibition but to have traffic restored to liberty as it was before the restraint. And the matter of Barbary to remain also as it did, without any mention thereof. Thereupon, he, finding me as a private man (for so I protested my communication should be) obstinate in this opinion, he yieldeth that our men should go to Barbary, so as they would carry no artillery etc., and that they would touch in Portugal and register their lading there, and so to pass with the King's permission. This latter part I misliked as an innovation.

'Then he propounded a thing which he said I had an intention to bring to pass, that was to bring the staple of the Portuguese spices into England out of the Low Countries and France, and thereof I said as it was true I had thought it good for us, so now the troubles of the Low Countries and France being considered, he might think it best for the Portugales. And so with much long talk the evening made me break off, to come now hither.

'I doubt not but the fire illuminating heaven on Michelmas eve was seen there — such as I never saw for the time more fearful. God sendeth us such signs but for our erudition.'[77]

It is always something of a shock to find this mixture of astrology in one of the sanest of sixteenth-century Englishmen. John Stow records the same heavenly display, but in terms which suggest the Northern Lights rather than any special admonition from on high![78]

Burghley's informal conversation with Giraldi seems to have opened the door to further negotiations. The final upshot was a treaty signed[79] in 1576, which led to a resumption of normal trade between Portugal and England. No mention at all was made of Barbary and Guinea.

There is some doubt as to whether the treaty was ratified. In any case, it does not seem to have ameliorated the situation which remained unchanged four years later when Portugal was annexed to Spain and Anglo-Portuguese relations blended with the larger issue between England and Spain.

It may be by accident of survival, but from the evidence at hand it is clear that Burghley during the four years following St. Bartholomew's was much more interested and much more active in the problems of the Low Countries than in those of France.

Before St. Bartholomew's he had taken a sympathetic attitude towards the Dutch rebels and had encouraged English volunteers to go and fight on their behalf. But he had been fearful of French intervention there and had taken the stand, long traditional in English foreign policy, that sooner than see the French in possession in the Low Countries England should join with the Spanish to keep them out.

After St. Bartholomew's Elizabeth found herself faced with a choice among (1) taking the Dutch rebels under her protection; (2) acquiescing in their defeat by the Spaniards and the continuation of Alva's monstrous régime; (3) acquiescing in French intervention.

She rejected all three of them, set out to re-establish stable relations with Spain and dreamed of terminating the Dutch wars by personal intervention. The first-fruits of this policy was the convention of Nymegen in the spring of 1573, which restored commercial relations between England and the Low Countries and set up machinery for the settlement of other points at issue. As a corollary to the agreement, Elizabeth recalled, or affected to recall, English volunteers from the Dutch service and agreed that if the King of Spain would expel her Catholic rebels from the Low Countries, she would expel Dutch rebels from England. But the Dutch cause was not altogether abandoned. For over a year she continued to offer her service as mediator between the Spanish King and the Dutch. She received no encouragement either from Philip II or from his governors in the Low Countries — Alva and, after Alva's recall in December 1573, Requescens. Nevertheless, the relations between England and Spain during 1574 were definitely friendly, friendly even to the point of offering shelter and provisions to a Spanish fleet and allowing a Spanish minister to visit the Channel ports in preparation for it. When Mendoza paid his visit in July, he was sumptuously entertained and returned home with the impression that Spain could have anything she asked for from England.

In all of this Burghley played his part.

During the autumn of 1572 William of Orange had clearly regarded him as his best friend in England and addressed through him the various appeals he made to Elizabeth for support.[80] After Elizabeth came to terms with Spain in the spring of 1573, William, though he did not abandon all hope of English support, began to consider seriously the French alternative.[81]

It was at this point that William Herle, that confidential agent of Burghley whom we have heard of before in connection with the Ridolfi Plot and whom we are to hear of more than once again, appeared in the Low Countries. How he got there is not at all clear,[82] but it may be assumed that he was acting under Burghley's orders. In any case, he returned from the Low Countries at the end of May, bringing with him a letter from the Prince of Orange to Burghley, in which Orange asked for a continuance of Burghley's good will and gave assurance that no one in the world had greater desire to employ himself in Burghley's service. When Herle got to London, he wrote a long memoir, in which he reported on a number of conferences which he had held with Orange. The memoir was designed for the Queen, the Lord Treasurer and the Earl of Leicester. It was without much doubt written at Burghley's suggestion and under his oversight. How much of it Burghley himself inspired is past finding out.

According to Herle, Orange had addressed himself in the first place to a presentation of the reasons why Elizabeth could anticipate nothing but hostility from Spain. He pointed out that the best way for her to secure herself against Spanish attack was to retain the control of the seas. This she could hardly do unless she could command both her own naval resources and the naval resources of the Low Countries. He urged her to take the Low Countries under her sovereignty, assuring her that the revenue she would derive from them would more than compensate for the cost of defending them. If, however, she were indisposed to accept full sovereignty, she might assure the continued resistance of the Dutch against Spanish domination by a substantial loan, say, £50,000. If she would do neither, then he had no alternative but to accept French aid, which had already been offered in men and money.[83]

The memoir as printed runs to fourteen quarto pages and is a very persuasive document. We know nothing of its reception. It was badly timed, but from the point of view of the Dutch rebels the situation was too critical to admit of accurate timing. Elizabeth had just signed a peace with Spain. The markets of the Low Countries, after five years' embargo, had just been opened to English traders. Fears of French aggression had diminished almost to the vanishing point by the destruction of the French party in Scotland and by the renewal of civil wars in France itself. As to the Dutch rebels, they were rebels after all. Elizabeth could not altogether ignore the religious ties which identified their cause with hers, particularly in view of the enthusiasm for their cause in Protestant England. She would do what she could for them by mediation, but she had no notion, at least no immediate notion, of more active measures on their behalf. At the moment, though they were putting up one of the most gallant fights in human history in defence of Haarlem, the possibility of any long resistance appeared hopeless.

Something like that was the picture of the situation as Elizabeth saw it. As to how Lord Burghley saw it, we have no immediate indication. At any rate, through Herle's memoir he laid before her a strong case in favour of the Dutch. It was typical of the adroit way in which he handled her.

Meanwhile, formal relations with the Dutch got steadily worse. In October the English volunteers under Orange were thinking of offering their services to the enemy. In November Orange dismissed Thomas Morgan, one of the first of the English volunteer captains.[84] In January another one of them, Captain Chester, came back to England. He brought with him a letter from Orange to Burghley. In itself the letter was not very illuminating. It said no more than that Chester would convey a message and it asked Burghley to accredit it as if he, the Prince, had himself delivered it. Unhappily, we have no record of what passed between Chester and Burghley. All we know is that Chester was actively engaged the following spring in enlisting English volunteers for Orange, and that a year later he was acting as one of Burghley's agents in the Low Countries. What we may fairly assume is that even in 1573 Burghley had private channels of contact with Orange.

During the following year there is almost no record of direct relations between the English government and the Dutch. From Spanish sources we hear of a constant flow of reinforcements from England,[85] but this seems to have been organized and financed privately.

Meanwhile, serious difficulties arose over the Dutch blockade of Spanish ports. English trade with the Low Countries had scarcely been opened by treaty before it was closed by the Dutch, or at any rate rigorously controlled by the Dutch. Orange himself believed that he could starve the Spanish forces into submission. He told an English agent 'that if he could but hinder that in a year's space there come no salt into Flanders he could win such a peace as he asked for'. The important branch of the English trade was, of course, the export of cloth to Antwerp, monopolized by the Merchant Adventurers. It had become almost the vital factor in English industrial prosperity. As long as Orange cherished any hope of English intervention in his behalf, he did not attempt to cut it off. In May of 1573 he came to terms with the Merchant Adventurers. They were permitted to come up the Scheldt in fleets of four, drop anchor at Flushing, leave one of the four there as hostage for the other three, which might go on to Antwerp, dispose of their cargo and reload, provided that they did not take on their return voyage lace, canvas, mocados, bays and other commodities likely to compete with industries established by the Dutch refugees in England.[86] Orange made these concessions to the Merchant Adventurers with the understanding that other Englishmen trading in the Low Countries without his licence should be lawful prize. He made them also on the understanding that the Merchant Adventurers would lend him 50,000 florins (about £17,000).

The Merchant Adventurers seem to have accepted these terms, but other traders, notably the Staplers, were less acquiescent. They might purchase licences to trade but otherwise were subject to seizure. Elizabeth wrote to Orange in

March 1574 asking him to restore to the Staplers freedom of trade with their old headquarters at Bruges. Orange regretted that he could not oblige her.[87]

Elizabeth was outraged. She sent an envoy in June 1575 to tell Orange so in unvarnished terms, and reiterated her demands. Meanwhile, she dispatched Dr. Thomas Wilson, a distinguished civilian who was later to succeed Sir Thomas Smith as Principal Secretary, on a mission to Requescens, the Spanish governor in the Low Countries. Burghley himself drafted Wilson's instructions, which may be taken to confirm the impression that relations with Spain fell to Burghley's particular assignment. The purpose of the embassy was threefold:

(1) To secure the consent of Requescens to free trade with Antwerp; (2) to press for the expulsion of English refugees from the Low Countries; (3) to offer English mediation in the war with the Dutch.

Wilson's surviving correspondence is almost entirely directed to Burghley. He accomplished his chief objective. Requescens opened up the port of Antwerp at least so far as it was in his power to do so; and he expelled those English refugees who were demonstrably rebels as opposed to those who had merely left England for conscience sake. Wilson got nowhere in his offers of mediation, chiefly because the Emperor had already accepted that role, and as a result of his efforts a conference of delegates representing the opposing parties was assembled at Breda early in March 1575.[88] But even before Wilson's return it became evident that the Spanish King, though prepared to accord their ancient privileges to the Netherlanders, would yield no more on the essential religious issue than a choice between conformity and exile. Even on these terms Philip demanded that all the seaport towns should be restored to him. The Dutch indignantly rejected such terms and the Breda conference came to nothing.

In a letter to Burghley of March 13th, Wilson wrote: 'I did hear upon my return from Brussels . . . that your Lordship was very sick and therefore could not write to me, for the which I was very sorry. And I pray you, even for your country's sake, have a regard to your health. Do not, by overlaying yourself with affairs, shorten your days. You have run a goodly course and may run many years longer if your over much care do not shorten your race, which were an heavy loss to England. Your name is famous here, as the which is feared of the evil and honoured of the good. So deal and occupy your wits and body that you may long continue and England receive good fruit, from time to time for many years hereafter, of your worthy and noble travail.'

With William of Orange Wilson had nothing to do; 'fearing', as he wrote to Burghley, 'my doings should be known, unto which the Commendator [Requescens] hath had a vigilant eye'.

But just before he left for home Wilson had news that a ship on the way to Antwerp had been detained at Flushing. He forthwith sent off letters of protest to the Prince of Orange and to the governor of Flushing[89] by his secretary, Daniel Rogers.

Rogers seems to have spent about a fortnight with the Dutch, and then went back to England and then back to Holland again.[90] He was, it seems, dealing with

English grievances against the Dutch, chiefly their blockade, incidentally their piratical attacks on trade in the Channel. The governor of Flushing wrote a long letter to Elizabeth on May 28th in justification of the blockade.

This seems to have set Elizabeth in a fine rage. She sent Rogers back to Orange with a strong letter to the Prince. And she bade Rogers say that unless amends were made promptly she would not 'suffer the said injuries unavenged'.[91]

What apparently disturbed Elizabeth most was the fact, confirmed from many sources, that Orange was seeking aid in France and meant to surrender the Low Countries into French hands. His French proclivities appeared to have been accentuated by his marriage to Princess Charlotte of Bourbon at about the time of Rogers's departure (June 12th).[92] Upon this subject she instructed Rogers to say to the Prince 'that she findeth this dealing of his so perilous to her state as she neither may nor will in any case endure it, and that rather than it should so come to pass . . . she mindeth to bend all her forces to the assistance of the King of Spain'.

But she evidently did not intend this to be taken *au pied de la lettre*, since she went on to say that if the Prince did not respond to this treatment, Rogers was to point out to him that the French were not dependable and were more likely to turn out conquerors than protectors. He was to remind Orange of St. Bartholomew's and that the French King was at war with those in France defending the same religion that Orange was fighting for.

During September and October Burghley's two correspondents in the Low Countries kept hammering at the French menace. Orange, they wrote, was altogether French, his agent Calvart in London was French, and there was a whole company of French advocates in his entourage. Chester observed that the Estates of Holland and Zeeland preferred an English connection, and he came over to England with a secret message from three of the Dutch leaders,[93] asking for a loan of £12,000 a month and pledging in return the joint revenues of Holland and Zeeland, estimated at £100,000 annually.[94]

Meanwhile, in France events were taking shape which seemed to accentuate the menace of French intervention. In September 1575 the Duke of Alençon escaped from his mother's surveillance and joined the rebel leaders, Condé and Montmorenci. There were those who maintained that his flight would make French intervention in Dutch wars out of the question. But the prevalent view in England seems to have been that the King of France would seek to alleviate the domestic situation by the alternative of war against Spain. As far as Burghley's attitude was concerned, he seems to have discounted French intervention in dealing with Orange and to have stressed it in dealing with the Spaniards.

We have no record of deliberations in the Privy Council on the subject, but a memorandum in Burghley's hand dated October 17th[95] may have been prepared in that connection. His position was briefly as follows:

The Dutch must either submit to the King of Spain or obtain aid either from Elizabeth or from the King of France.

If they submit to Spain then must they be governed by Spaniards. 'And thereupon must needs follow that the realm of England shall be neighboured by such a nation as will take advantage many ways to offend this realm and to attempt for the cause of religion and other quarrels to make an alteration or rather a sub-version of this estate.'

If they seek and get adequate aid from France ' . . . in a short time they shall be so at commandment of the crown of France as, with the commodities of those countries and of their havens and ships, they shall command both England and Scotland and all the Narrow Seas as they may . . . a peril inevitable to the Crown of England'.

'The third way . . . is to be aided by England . . . by one of these two ways: either by secret relieving them with money . . . or else upon their acquitting of themselves for their obedience to the king of Spain to receive them into her Majesty's protection', which might either be done by financing their rebellion until such time as the King of Spain would restore to them 'their ancient privileges', or by accepting 'upon their own offer as subjects to Her Majesty . . . and to be governed by her Majesty as the dukes of Burgundy have heretofore done'.

With these basic considerations in mind, Burghley suggested:

(1) To consider what would be a just course.
(2) To consider what aid would be meet and necessary.
(3) What the outcome of aiding the Dutch would be likely to be.

On the first point he suggested that the cause of the failure of the conference of Breda should be investigated — whether 'the default be in the King's part, as refusing to grant them reasonable things, or in the subjects', being not content with reasonable things'.

He further suggested that the articles of their privileges as granted to them by the Duke of Burgundy and confirmed by the King should be examined in order to find out whether, if their ruler failed to observe the same, it were 'lawful for the people to withdraw their obedience and to become subjects of any other prince, and whether there are any examples of the like in the estates of Holland and Zeeland'.

Burghley then posed a number of practical questions:

(1) What nobles and what fortified towns adhere to the Prince, what to the King?
(2) What are the forces of the Prince at the moment, what had they been, where are they obtained, what are the monthly charges, how levied and how may their levies be continued?
(3) How many more soldiers are necessary to maintain the defence, where shall they be stationed and at what cost may they be maintained? How many ships are at the Prince's command, of what strength and tonnage, how manned, how victualled and how can they be employed? What is the fighting strength of the enemy by land and sea, which may be learned from the Prince and by Englishmen in the Spanish Low Countries?

F

Finally, if Elizabeth shall agree to relieve them until by mediation the King of Spain restored their liberty, how much money they will ask for and how to be paid, and upon what security for repayment. Or if her Majesty shall accept sovereignty, how much annually will it cost, and how much will the revenues of the country yield to her?

In a final paragraph Burghley suggested that the Queen call a meeting of noblemen and townsmen to consider not only whether the enterprise should be undertaken but how it might be maintained.

The immediate decision was to send an envoy — to Requescens and then to Orange — to try mediation. Sir Henry Cobham had already been instructed to proceed to Spain on the same mission, though he did not get away until late in August. On October 29th Robert Corbett was dispatched to Requescens and on the same day John Hastings to Orange.[96] It is to be remarked that Burghley drafted the instructions for all of them, a task which normally fell to the Principal Secretary.[97] This means, if it means anything, that Elizabeth distrusted Walsingham's too pronounced Protestant bias. As for Smith, the other Secretary, he was a very sick man, and had almost ceased to function. In any case, Burghley, who had almost withdrawn from public business for two years, slips again into the very centre of the administration.

The purpose of all these missions — Hastings to Orange, Corbett to Requescens, Cobham to Philip II — was exploratory. Hastings was to warn Orange against resort to France and to hint vaguely at aid from England. Corbett was to urge Requescens to come to terms with the Dutch by restoring to them their ancient liberties. Cobham was to carry the same suggestion to Philip in Spain. In view of the failure of the Emperor at Breda, Elizabeth could hardly have hoped to achieve peace by mediation. One gets the impression that she was simply marking time, partly perhaps wishing to emphasize her preference for a peaceful settlement. There is indeed no evidence that either Burghley or his mistress wanted to keep alive civil disorders in the Low Countries. England's commercial and financial interests were too deeply engaged there.

In any case, neither Hastings nor Corbett nor Cobham achieved any positive results. Cobham, indeed, had been very cavalierly treated in Spain. Peace by negotiation was not to be had. Elizabeth had to make up her mind either to help the Dutch herself or to allow them to be beaten into subjection by the Spaniards, or to stand aside and watch the French intervene.

De Guaras, the Spanish agent in London, presented a frantic picture of the Queen's state of mind. 'I have', he wrote, 'received trustworthy information that on Thursday last the Queen very loudly declared that she was against sending forces openly to Zeeland and Holland. She entered her chamber alone, slamming her door and crying out that they were ruining her over this business. And those who were there, her ladies-in-waiting and others, were much distressed, saying that if she did not open the door they would burst it open . . . Her grief arose from her having received news that Orange was sending her . . . Aldegonde and Count

Culemberg and another of the principal persons of his State. It is supposed they come to offer on behalf of Orange the possession of Zeeland and Holland.'[98]

A fortnight later the Earl of Shrewsbury's son, writing to his father from Court, presented much the same picture:

'Here is also Sir Henry Cobham returned out of Spain with answer of his message. Also here is come one from the Prince of Orange out of the Low Country with a couple of chief merchants of Flanders, to make offer of that country to be delivered into her Majesty's hands . . . The Council are all at the Court. They sit daily and the ambassadors come to them . . . Her Majesty is troubled with these causes which maketh her very melancholy and seemeth to be out of quiet.'[99]

We have in Burghley's own hand what he called 'The Sum of the Opinion of the Council upon the Request of the Hollanders and upon consideration had of the Messages and Negotiations of Sir Henry Cobham in Spain and Robert Corbett with the Commissioners at Antwerp'.[100]

It is not unlikely that Burghley drew up this memorandum for Elizabeth herself, and that its primary purpose was to secure her assent to the programme advocated.

In general the Council took the position that the Dutch should be restored to their ancient liberties under the government of the King of Spain as Duke of Burgundy.

They maintained that if the struggle between Philip and his rebels were allowed to proceed without interference the Dutch would be defeated, and the Spanish government, freed from all restraint upon their tyranny, would proceed to apply the wealth and resources of the Low Countries to the subjugation of England. They made no doubt of Philip's hostile purposes, arising partly out of a desire for revenge of injuries suffered, and partly out of a determination to destroy Protestantism wherever it was to be found. Once his power in the Netherlands was absolute, he would have the strongest navy in the world at his command. He would attack English commercial privileges in the Low Countries and force Elizabeth to concede free trade to Spanish merchants in England, to the ruination of English property and of Elizabeth's Customs revenue. He would make much of the cause of Mary Stuart and would inspire the English Catholics both abroad and at home to rebel. The Council even went so far as to assert that, though Elizabeth could count upon the loyal support of the great mass of her subjects, the English Catholics would be more than their equal in riches and power.

On these grounds the Council maintained that the opportunity of curbing Spanish power must be seized. But they did not advocate immediate and direct action. They thought that Elizabeth would be well advised to sound out the views of some of the leaders of the House of Commons.[101] Meanwhile, they proposed that she should send another envoy to Requescens to propose reasonable conditions for peace, and that, during the deliberations, an armistice should be agreed upon. If nothing came of that, then they advised immediate action. They suggested that, in order to make such action easy and honourable, she might procure the approbation of the French King, 'or at least of a party in France equal to the king'.

It is clear enough that the Privy Council favoured ultimate intervention; equally clear that they favoured further delay. The most surprising thing is that they made no mention of French intervention. Indeed, they hinted at French co-operation. They made no mention either of the religious issue, although everybody knew that it was the major obstacle in the way of any settlement by negotiation.

That part of the Privy Council's recommendation which advocated further efforts at mediation suited the Queen well enough and she elected to follow it. The Dutch envoys in London, awaiting her answer to their plea for immediate action, did not like it, but they were prepared to accept it, *de faute de mieux*, provided that if Requescens would not grant an armistice Elizabeth would either take them under her protection or at least grant them some reasonable secret aid.[102]

As Burghley saw the problem he envisaged an answer to them in these terms: 'Considering her Majesty meaneth to proceed orderly with the King as she would the world should understand thereof, that is to bend her actions simply and plainly to procure an accord between the King and his subjects, and that with all indifferency from both parts, and yet as much as may be to the preservation of the honour and credit of the King, she cannot without touch of her own honour, professing to deal indifferently, give any promise aforehand of aid to the King's subjects, for that would be an open prejudicing of the cause.'

He went on to point out that if she should give 'notice aforehand of her intention to aid them' she would jeopardize the property of her merchants in Spain, in Brabant and in Flanders, where they were deeply engaged in trade and had large stakes in merchandise and large credits outstanding.

He anticipated the reply of the Dutch. If they could not have the Queen's promise then they must turn to France. They had already waited three months for Elizabeth's reply. They must have immediate aid either from her or from France, or else both the Dutch and after them the English would succumb to Spanish might.

To these points Burghley then suggested what he called 'Some Kind of Answer'. 'It might', he wrote, 'be thus devised, that if indeed at their return to the Prince [of Orange] or upon signification of their negotiation here, the Prince will not, because he cannot, forbear to require aid of France. Yet in this sort the Prince might be moved to deal with France to require, but for the space of two or three months, some aid or countenance, either to be used by landing upon the frontiers of Flanders, Henault or Brabant [provinces held by the Spaniards] or otherwise to have some reasonable number of soldiers into some distinct places of Holland without putting their countries or their principal strengths into the hands of the French ... then in the meantime her Majesty might deal by treaty if it could be, and if ... she could not procure peace then she might proceed as it were, either to join with the French, or else to take the whole country into her protection; or if she would do neither, then the Prince and the Estates might further proceed to take any aid of the French King that were meet for them.'

As a kind of afterthought Burghley added: 'It were well done to consider whether it were not a better bargain for her Majesty, in respect of the uncertainty to defend all Holland and Zeeland, that they themselves might defend Holland and all the rest, saving that her Majesty might take into her charge the Isle of Walcheren where Middelburg and Flushing is [are], and to receive of the States of the Country the sum of three or four thousand florins to be dispended by her Majesty upon defence of the Isle. And if her Majesty should prove that more were dispended that then within one-half year ... the States should pay that overplus. And nevertheless that her Majesty should take the title of defence of the whole estate of the Countries until the king would make to them an assured restitution of their liberties.'

There are two other memoranda from Burghley on the subject at this juncture, neither of them dated,[103] both of them evidently relevant. In one of them he took a position favourable to giving secret aid to the Dutch while Elizabeth once more explored the possibilities of peace by mediation.

In the other, much longer, memorandum he discussed the problem from many angles. It began with a scathing denunciation of the Spanish government in the Low Countries. 'It is manifest', he wrote, 'that those oppressions, violences, burnings, drownings, murderings of them that always submitted themselves to obedience so they might have their ancient liberties saved to them ... are to be taken, reputed and adjudged not to have been by them deserved but to have proceeded by the injustice of the King's ministers.' He went on to point out that the King of Spain had no absolute authority over the Low Countries, 'as kings have in absolute monarchies, but is sworn before they take the state to observe all their liberties. These are some, that he can make no law or ordinance but with the assent of the three estates, that he can exact no subsidies nor taxes but with their consent and many such like, which the King has manifestly broken by his placards and inquisitions. And therefore it consequently followeth that to defend such people from such violence is a thing lawful and just'.

Even so, Burghley questioned the legality of foreign intervention. 'Though it be just and lawful', he wrote, 'for a man to defend another from wrong, yet, where there is a controversy betwixt a King and his subjects or a Lord and his vassals, no other body hath [the right] to intermediate therein against the will of the Lord except where there is a superior Lord and potentate that hath jurisdiction over the other ... By rule of justice there must be a judge competent from whose authority neither party, plaintiff or defendant, may decline ... It may also be said that the King doth not deny to them pardon ... neither will deny to them observation of their liberties and privileges ... only he denieth to them that, of his grant, they shall have liberty in religion contrary to the Church of Rome.'

But here Burghley interjected the observation that if the rebels surrendered their arms and their strongholds they would have no assurance that the King would keep his promise. He raised also the question as to what would happen to the Dutch Protestants if faced with the alternatives of submission or exile, for their numbers were so great that if they elected to migrate many of the towns would be virtually depopulated.

Burghley then turned to consider the English interest in the matter. 'The Queen of England', he observed, 'has more cause to procure the preservation of the Low Countries in their ancient estate in the obedience of the house of Burgundy than any other place hath . . . Now if the Low Countries should either be subdued to the Spaniards or possessed by the French, England cannot continue this manner of league. For if the Spaniard shall possess this country by conquest, as otherwise they cannot, then must they also govern it as conquerors — that is build in every country and special towns, forts and castles which must be kept and guarded with Spaniards . . . To maintain these the King must continue great taxes . . . And there will be no reason to stop him but he will set what tax he listeth upon the commodities of England and so shall England wax poor to make him rich. And then England will have no remedy. . . .

'To forbear from traffic thither it will be hard, for he will use the like imposts in Spain. To repair with our commodities eastwards, our ships must pass along the coasts of Holland where he shall have a navy lying . . . and if he shall be disposed to impeach that trade, he may easily . . . He may also make his profit of our staple of wools either by imposts or by expelling them . . . to the intent to replenish the countries with Spanish wool. . . .

'These are matters more hurtful to England than the loss of any profit, for although to hinder our traffic, to set taxes upon our commodities must diminish the Queen's customs in England, decay the revenues of all that have profit therein, desolate a multitude of people who live thereon, decay the shipping and mariners, being the necessary strength of the realm, yet the greatest danger is that when the King of Spain shall have [conquered the Low Countries] he shall be tempted, with the riches thereof to make himself potent with a navy for wars . . . (and having the towns of Holland and Zeeland at command he may more readily do . . .) in truth he shall with number of great ships and plenty of mariners, easily overpass all the forces of England. And now therefore is it worthy of consideration whether this danger, apparent and likely, ought not to be withstood by all good lawful means. . . .

'To take them into protection is to give them aid of money and men as they shall have apparent need to defend themselves . . . There is required a supply of 6000 men, 1000 pioneers and 200 light horse which cannot cost less than £100,000 . . . Besides this, the entering to defend them must needs bring a war to England with Spain and all the King's dominions, yea and, percase, with his allies. It cannot be determined how long the war will last. Maintenance of the war must proceed from the Crown and the realm, saving the allowance of 500,000 crowns to be yielded by the State of Holland. But with what assurance it shall be paid is uncertain.

'And there is no doubt but money and his [the Spaniard's] comfort may raise more lewd people [in England] than will easily be subdued, considering of what sort the number may be compounded (1) of papists, (2) of disaffected persons, (3) of needy persons that have wasted themselves, (4) of atheists, (5) of people affecting the title of the Scottish Queen, (6) of persons affected to the King of

Spain and the English rebels now outlawed, (7) of idle people, out of work by reason of stay of trade.'

He observed also that there was some danger that the Pope might induce the French King to join with the Spaniards.

In his final paragraph he dealt with mitigating circumstances. On the financial side, he pointed out that Holland was prepared to contribute 500,000 crowns and that Parliament could be counted upon for a subsidy of £100,000 or £200,000. He thought a good deal of trade might still be maintained by special licence with countries under Spanish control — and he even hinted obliquely at the possibilities of plunder. 'There will', he observed, 'be a great number of adventurers by sea to join with the Hollanders to repair to the Spanish seas.'

It is not easy to decide from this memorandum on which side of the fence Burghley stood. Whatever his personal conviction, he generally framed his memoranda in terms most likely to carry weight with his mistress. The striking thing about the memorandum just quoted was, here again, the avoidance of the religious issue. The nearest he seems to have come to a solution of that difficulty was in a memorandum of January 12th in which he suggested that all impediments to peace between Philip and his rebels might be referred 'unto the consideration of the General Estates of the Low Countries'.[104] Yet he clearly recognized its fundamental importance.

While the Dutch envoys tarried in England, Requescens, in order to counteract their efforts, dispatched an envoy to Elizabeth, Sr. de Champagny, governor of Antwerp and brother to Cardinal Granvelle, who had served earlier in the Low Countries as Margaret of Parma's chief minister. Champagny reached London on January 27th.

On the same day Burghley wrote to Walsingham: 'This evening a gentleman came with de Guaras to me from M. de Champagny to notify his arrival in the city and with compliments to require that he might come to me and also to procure for him audience as soon as it might please her Majesty. I told him that I would give knowledge of his arrival but by reason that the principal Councillors of Estate about her Majesty have required licence of 3 or 4 days to be absent as now they were, I doubted her Majesty would abear to have him at the Court until they were returned. And for his desire to speak with me, I thanked him but I thought myself very unmeet to deal with any person of estimation whilst I was a prisoner in chains of the gout, for I would be free from grief when I would speak with him ... Yet the messenger seemed not so contented, being prompted by Guaras, but that his master would come to visit me as one whom he had known in Brussels with his brother, M. de Arras, now Cardinal. I concluded that as I found myself tomorrow, after my medicine, so I would send him word. He said he would be with me tomorrow in the forenoon. And now I doubt what I shall answer, for I would gladly have you to seek her Majesty's mind herein, that if I shall not speak with him I will make my gout to answer him. If she will, I will not deny to hear him, and leave him as I can, either ignorant of anything unmeet for his appetite, or prepare him to bow to her Majesty's bendar. And yet it may be he will also purpose to deal as artfully with me, and so either of us may be as well deceived as purposed to deceive. *Sed haec fraus non est impia.* I pray you, as soon as you may, let me have your opinion or rather, her Majesty's pleasure.'[105]

The reason Champagny gave for seeking the interview was that De Guaras told him that Burghley was, in effect, king of England. Burghley received him the following day and they talked at length together.[106]

Burghley opened the conversation with an expression of pleasure at Champagny's arrival. The Queen, he said, was anxious to re-establish peace in the Low Countries. The Dutch had been forced by the oppressive rule of the Spaniards to seek outside aid. She understood that they had appealed to the French and that the French meant to occupy Holland and Zeeland. She had sent Corbett to Requescens to propose mediation and Hastings to Orange to warn him against France. So far as she could discover, all that the Dutch asked for was the restoration of their ancient franchises. She wanted no more than that.

Champagny answered that the grievances of the Dutch were altogether frivolous. He marvelled that the Queen entertained the deputies of the rebels and inquired how she would feel if Philip II took the same attitude towards her rebels. He scouted the fear of French intervention. The French King, he said, was too grateful for Spanish help against the Huguenots.

Burghley replied that the menace of French intervention was a grim reality. Champagny denied it. Then Burghley pointed out that Spain also had the Turk to reckon with, particularly in Barbary. Champagny waved it aside. The King had plenty of forces in reserve to deal with any menace from that quarter. Burghley then raised the question of Spanish financial resources and the weakening of his credit in the Italian money market in consequence of his arbitrary reduction of the rate of interest on Italian loans. Champagny pointed out that Philip had no difficulty in borrowing money in the Low Countries. He reminded Burghley that England was far from united, that Elizabeth alone stood between the country and civil war over her successor, that her life was constantly menaced and that Burghley's own position depended upon her survival.

For something like two hours they exhanged these pleasantries, in the best of temper, agreeing at the end that they would both devote themselves to the pursuit of peace.

Nothing, in short, was accomplished by the interview, but Champagny left it with the impression that the Queen meant to help the Dutch. He anticipated that positive action would be taken in their behalf in the Parliament which was just about to assemble. Burghley, he thought, supported that policy.[107] De Guaras was of the same opinion. He reported to Champagny an interview with Burghley in which Burghley had remarked: 'You people are of such sort that wherever you set foot no grass grows, and you are hated everywhere.'[108]

Champagny's conviction that the English meant to help the Dutch was strengthened by his first interview with the Queen. After keeping him waiting for almost a fortnight,[109] she received him very curtly, complained that he bore no letter from Philip and expressed surprise that no reply had been made to her

offers of mediation. She swore that she would never consent to Spanish impatroni-
zation of the Low Countries. Her father would never have suffered it and, woman
though she was, neither would she.

Having said so much, she then burst forth into a denunciation of the Dutch
Calvinists. They were trouble-breeders, they wanted to abolish monarchy and
set up some sort of an equalitarian oligarchy. Philip of Spain was an old friend.
She did not forget his kindness to her during her sister's reign. And so forth and
so on. In the end she left Champagny completely bewildered, as no doubt she
intended to do.

We need not pursue his futile mission further. At one time he seems to have
thought that Burghley was definitely hostile; at another time he took the opposite
view. He believed that the two Earls, Sussex and Leicester, were united against
Burghley. Leicester evidently made a great pretence of friendship for Spain and
so did Hatton. Champagny was a smart fellow and was not unaware of it. On
one occasion, after conference with Burghley, he claimed that he gave as good as
he got. And yet one gathers the impression that both the Queen and her councillors were playing fast and loose with him, marking time and leaving him at his
wits' end. One gets the impression also that they hoped to stimulate in him a
hatred of Spanish rule which lay just under the skin of most Netherlanders.[110]
Towards the end of his stay they began to entertain him rather sumptuously;
Hatton spread an elaborate dinner for him early in March, embellished with
music and comedies, and came to fetch him with 150 horsemen. Thomas Gresham
spread one a week later, at which the Privy Councillors were present, Burghley
among others, in a very jovial mood.

Champagny's observations on Burghley himself[111] are not particularly penetra-
ting. He described Burghley as a Puritan, devoted to the Queen's service and high
in her favour, but not too popular at Court because he encouraged the Queen's
parsimonious impulses. He thought, however, that Burghley was flexible, *facile*
he called it, and might be useful. He observed that Burghley occupied himself
much with public affairs, but except in matters religious did not get on too
well with Walsingham. Indeed, Champagny noted that Burghley, who was
getting old and was much troubled with gout and other disorders, 'was wary
of Walsingham', a much younger man, 'who began to encroach upon his
credit'.

While Champagny was still in England, Requescens, the Spanish governor of
the Low Countries, died rather suddenly on March 5th. The news reached London
about a week later, and Champagny discovered almost immediately a renewal of
the hopes of those who favoured immediate aid to the Dutch. But Elizabeth was
still resolute for mediation. She even went so far as to tell Champagny that she
did not mean to press for religious toleration. Indeed, she told him so on two
occasions, and Leicester reiterated it. But she got no response and she was very
much out of temper over the whole business. Champagny heard that she cursed
Walsingham in no uncertain terms, that she had beaten one or two of her ladies-
in-waiting, and that she was not sleeping of nights. Nevertheless, Champagny

noticed that the general attitude towards him was much less cordial than it had been.[112] To make matters worse, the cold wetness of the English spring was affecting his health. He got his congé on March 23rd, and left the following day,[113] with the understanding that negotiations for mediation would be resumed. Early in March he had been confident that he had, single-handed, diverted Elizabeth from belligerent purposes.[114] But at his parting he was not so sure.

Champagny and De Guaras both maintained that during the spring of 1576 large shipments of ammunition and supplies were going out from England to the Dutch rebels.[115] It may well have been so, though we hear nothing of them from English sources. Elizabeth professed to be quite unaware of them and probably what went was privately financed.

Meanwhile, the Dutch envoys were cooling their heels in London. Burghley was keeping in touch with them through William Herle, and through Herle he advised them from time to time. We have several of Herle's letters to Burghley on the subject in March.

Paul Buys, that member of the Dutch delegation most eager for English aid and most hopeful of it,[116] poured all his woes into Herle's ear. They had, he said, been long in England and at the beginning had good hope that they would receive English aid. The Queen had welcomed them. She had declared herself satisfied that their cause 'was just and honourable and worthy the embracing'. She would put the matter before her Council, assuring them 'on the word of a prince to deal briefly and sincerely with them'.

They had proceeded then to deal with the Council and had laid before them a complete picture of their strength, their resources, their designs and intelligence, 'leaving nothing undiscovered that might express the true confidence conceived of her Majesty'.

They had asked for a loan of £100,000, 'and she without her charge be possessed of the country either as pledge for her money or ready to be entirely hers'.

But this, being 'not well digested, they were referred over further to the Parliament ... which Parliament having continued so long and being ready to dissolve hath yet passed hitherunto without any motion at all of their case.

'And now another course is proposed unto them again ... by way of peace and reconciliation but what assurance can this peace or reconciliation have ... that cannot be contracted with any heretic?

'And yet ... they are ready to obey her Majesty in this course for peace, so she do assure them, the matter taking no place, she will receive them into her protection and that in the meantime she .... aid them with the loan of £30,000 as she did unto the prince of Condé.'

Or failing that she would endorse a loan to that amount offered by English merchants.

In the next letter, three days later, Herle reported that Buys was about to go home and wanted, for his own justification, some statement in writing of what the Queen meant to do.

Such in brief was the history of the Dutch delegation in England.

But the most pertinent part of Herle's correspondence has to do with the attitude of Burghley towards the whole situation.

'It is given out,' Herle wrote on March 14th,[117] 'very maliciously among gentlemen and soldiers and amongst those of good sort that profess the religion, that your Lordship hath been the only let and overthrow of this Holland service, dissuading her Majesty from the enterprise where otherwise the Earls of Leicester and Sussex were earnest favourers and furtherers of it ... They judge very hardly that the poor men, being sent for by the Queen's Majesty, have been by indirect dealings, contrary to her own promise and assurance, so long and many ways delayed here ... This unworthy proceeding, they say, with foreign nations doth make us the hatredest men in the world and to be condemned for mere abuses, as those that do put on religion, piety and justice for a cloak to serve humours withal and please the time.'

Burghley's answer to this letter is missing, but Herle's reply on the 16th gives a notion of its content.

'Your letter', Herle wrote, ' ... hath not a little confirmed my dulled spirits to see the honourable and religious affection that you bear so earnestly to those matters of Holland, which doth also so satisfy Paul Buys ... as he protests that your Lordship shall see good fruit very shortly ... giving your Lordship most humble thanks that it would please you to do him that honour and let him understand the inward good dispositions of your Lordship and the better sort here inclined to favour their common cause and when the same doth not so outwardly appear for other respects ... that yet the inward part doth carry the stronger meaning and force with it.'

We may presume that the burden of Burghley's letter had been that he was strong for the Dutch but that he dared not press their cause too strongly 'for other respects'. When Burghley spoke of 'other respects' he generally meant the Queen's attitude. Very likely this was, in fact, the case. As he grew older he found that he would accomplish more by not directly opposing the royal position even when he disagreed with it. That explains why he so often stated both sides of the case in his memoranda on matters at issue, even though he generally managed to produce the more impressive arguments for the side he favoured. So he got the reputation of being a dispassionate judge, to whom the Queen would always listen; to Walsingham's more blunt and direct methods she simply closed her ears. The difference in technique does not necessarily imply that Burghley and Walsingham were on different sides. Both of them knew that the final decision lay with the Queen. But Burghley preferred a half-loaf to none. He was a master of the art of the possible, and as Walsingham was irritated by what he called Burghley's 'lack of resolution', Burghley in turn too often found his subtler methods thwarted by Walsingham's impetuosity.

Burghley's one surviving letter in his correspondence with Herle was written on April 3rd, after Buys's departure.[118]

'I am glad', he wrote, 'that Paul Buys and his colleagues are departed with likelihood of speedy arrival. Of his good opinion of me towards their common cause he shall not be deceived. Indeed there have happened hindrances, but he and you have not known the whole truth therein. The cunning of worldlings is greatest in hiding their passage with contrary overt speeches, but the best trial of all men is the touchstone of their honest lives, for it is impossible to gather figs from thorns. Take heed that you do not in any conference of writing or speech enter into censure of any of us all, namely to note any hinderers of good cause, for we can better suffer our deeds to take effect than to be censured.'

Late in March, as they were about to leave, the Dutch got the Queen's answer in writing, the sum and substance of which was that she would not help them herself and would deal hardly with them if they accepted any other outside help. Buys, commenting on the answer to Herle, observed: 'It had sufficed without this aggravation that they had consumed here so much time, so many occasions and spent great sums that might have been better employed . . . yet satisfied in nothing but must depart without thanks, and yet threatened also if they do not voluntarily yield their throats to be cut at the arbitrament of others.'

Burghley had sought to mitigate the force of the blow by an explanatory letter. Once again the letter is missing, but Herle's comment upon it is revealing. 'Your Lordship's letter did greatly appease them, and I added that her Majesty's answer by writing was but a matter of conveniency which was necessary for this season . . . , which serveth them both to satisfy Champagny from the outward show very well and to help them the better in secret when the occasion were offered to her Majesty.'

With this cold comfort the Dutch delegation left for home on March 30th. Burghley was able at the last to give them a morsel of comfort. Buys had asked for permission to export 2000 pieces of cloth duty-free, and Burghley induced the Queen to grant it.[119]

CHAPTER XI

THE LOW COUNTRIES, 1576-78

THE death of Requescens left the Low Countries without a Spanish governor. The Council of State assumed control, and the King of Spain confirmed their powers for the time being. They were faced almost at once by endemic revolts of the Spanish troops, demanding their pay. Some of them had not been paid for three years and even those who fared better were twenty-one months in arrears.[1] The people in Brabant and Flanders, driven to desperation by the lawlessness of the mutineers, finally took arms against them. The English government thought the situation singularly opportune for a renewal of offers of mediation. Late in March William Davison was dispatched to the Council of State. Burghley drew up his instructions. They followed the conventional lines,[2] proposing an armistice as a preliminary to further negotiations for a settlement, pointing out the danger of French intervention and warning them that if they took no such action 'we shall be constrained for the prevention thereof [the French intervention] to put that in execution that we would not willingly do otherwise than constrained thereto of mere necessity'.

But Davison accomplished nothing. The Council of State simply replied that they lacked the power to proceed according to Elizabeth's request. It is clear enough from the words of Davison's instructions that his answer had been expected. Walsingham certainly expected no less. On April 12th he had written to Burghley:[3] 'I do not look that Mr. Davison shall have any good answer. In this case words will not help. It is too publicly known that her Majesty meaneth not to be a dealer.'

Evidently Walsingham had hoped that, notwithstanding Elizabeth's inertia, the Netherlanders would seize the opportunity. On April 23rd in his letter recalling Davison, he wrote: 'I find by your letters that there is neither courage nor judgment in the nobility there, in that they overslip so apt a time to purchase their own liberty ... whereby it is most evident that that country is in its declination and will shortly fall under the Spanish yoke to their utter undoing and our great peril, having an eye either to the Spanish malice or the corruption of our own estate.'[4]

As it turned out, Walsingham was unduly pessimistic, but the prospect looked far from hopeful, particularly in view of the increasing friction between the Dutch rebels and the Queen, arising out of the Dutch blockade of ports under Spanish control, and of the depredations of Dutch free-booters.

The situation was exacerbated by two episodes, both of which seemed to be direct affronts to Elizabeth herself. The first of these had to do with Lucretia d'Affayladi, the daughter of a rich Italian merchant in the Low Countries.[5] She was the fiancée of Giraldi, the Portuguese agent in England. At his request Elizabeth had instructed John Cobham[6] to conduct her to England. On her way, when she was within six miles of Dover, her ship, under the English flag, was intercepted by Flushingers, she was seized, her jewellery and that of her ladies taken away and the whole ship's company carried to Middelburg. Orange, when he heard of it, made haste to apologize,[7] and ordered Lucretia's release. She and her company with all their bags and baggage were released and on April 9th[8] set sail for England in a royal ship expressly sent for the purpose.

The other episode was the interception of the Earl of Oxford upon his return to England early in April by Dutch pirates, who, after stripping him to his shirt, released him.[9] We do not know the details of the affair but, coming hard upon Lucretia's adventure and shortly after some twenty English ships had been stayed at Flushing, it provoked Elizabeth to send a special envoy to Orange to protest and threaten reprisal. Robert Beale, Walsingham's brother-in-law, was selected for the mission. Burghley set forth his views about the matter in a letter to Walsingham of April 16th.[10]

'I have perused all the letters and memorials for Mr. Beale concerning his voyage into Zeeland and I do so well allow of the whole course therein taken by my Lords as I do with heart and hand sign them. And as I wrote yesterday, I find it hard to make a distinction betwixt anger and judgment for my Lord of Oxford's misusage; so surely when I look into the universal barbarism of the Prince's forces of the Flushingers, which are only a rabble of common pirates or worse, and that make no difference whom they outrage, I do mistrust of any good issue to the cause, though of itself it is to be favoured. Yet, as it is said, *bonam causam, male agendo, perisse*. I humbly thank my Lords for the regard of my L. of Oxford, in whose person surely her Majesty and the realm have taken disgrace. And if the Prince shall not yield to hang some of the principals for such a robbery, I must say, howsoever her Majesty shall bend herself for the public cause, she ought in justice otherwise to be revenged. For if justice be denied in such a notorious case, all laws betwixt mere princes do warrant a proceeding otherwise, to make an example of avenge. And surely, if Mr. Beale shall speak with the Prince, he may do well to advise him to think that such an outrage as this cannot take end without more offence to him and his than maybe the hanging of v or vj such thieves; as if he were rid of an hundred of them his cause would prosper better and his friends would increase; which, if he shall, by subterfuge in answer, delay, he will feel, shall neither prosper nor yet his friends remain obliged to him as they have. You see my anger leadeth my judgment. And yet I am not hereto moved more for particular than for the public.

'I need add nothing to your writings. Mr. Beale is wise and I pray him, if my name be of any value, to use it to the Prince, as feeling myself in the person of the Earl of Oxford interested [*sic*] with this outrage, and so also expecting the rather some honourable amends by justice in executing of the pirates.'

For some reason or other Beale did not reach the Prince until May 5th.[11] It was not until the end of that month that Orange wrote to Burghley. He professed to be shocked at the outrage and promised to do all he could to content the Earl. But Beale was far from satisfied. On June 5th he wrote to Burghley that so far as he could learn, only one arrest had been made. ' . . . I have been fed in this matter, as in the rest, with delays and, if her Majesty send not a pleasing answer to the Prince's writing, they seem to be so desperate that I think no justice, nor ought else, will be had of all my demands.'[12]

And this is the last that we hear of Oxford's misadventure. Coming as it did just at the time when Oxford broke with his wife, it is hardly likely that Burghley was disposed to press Oxford's claims to redress beyond the point of remonstrance.

The most serious matter at issue between Orange and the Queen arose out of the seizure of some twenty ships of the Merchant Adventurers at Flushing.[13] The reason for this, according to Orange, was his desire to maintain a strict blockade at the moment in order that his plans to relieve the siege of Zierecksee should not be disclosed. The arrest came early in April.[14] The primary purpose of Beale's dispatch, otherwise charged with the Oxford business, was to demand that the ships be released. Beale was to say that if the ships were not released 'she would be forced to put in execution such remedies for the redress thereof as she would be loath to do otherwise than forced of necessity'.[15] But Beale got nowhere fast. Orange refused to release the English ships until Dutch ships arrested in England were released.[16] On May 29th, Beale wrote to Walsingham: 'I see that they make no account of us but that they are turned to France.'[17] Two days later he had his answer in the form of a long list of Dutch grievances against the English. The answer is missing but it evidently proposed that the Merchant Adventurers should advance to Orange a large sum of money as a condition of the release of their ships.

This demand brought Elizabeth's temper to the boiling point. On June 19th she dispatched Sir William Winter[18] with her answer. Burghley himself drafted Winter's instructions.[19] They dealt briefly with Orange's grievances, refused to countenance the loan from her merchants and demanded restitution of the ships forthwith. If Orange would not yield except on terms, Winter was 'by practice and device to find out some way, though it be with hazard, for the stealing away of the said ships'. Failing that, he was to declare that Elizabeth meant to secure redress by force. With that eventuality in mind, Winter was to investigate the defences of the Isle of Walcheren and the landing beaches, and to prompt English captains in the Dutch service to seize upon some place and hold it for England.

Winter went and, joined with Beale, negotiated further with Orange. They came to terms: ships seized on both sides were to be released,[20] but the forced loan was passed over in silence.

Elizabeth would have none of it. She swore that she would be avenged upon Orange, ordered Dutch ships in English harbours to be seized and granted letters of reprisal right and left on Dutch commerce.[21] For a time something like a state of war existed between England and the Dutch.

An interesting memorandum in Burghley's hand, undated but evidently drawn up about the time of Winter's return,[22] reveals his thoughts about the matter. He started out by appraising the probable consequences of positive action against the Dutch rebels. They would, he said, begin at once to prey upon English shipping. And he asked himself what could be done about it.

'There are', he wrote, 'only two general ways of remedies, by force or by composition, for sufferance is a ruin to the commonwealth of this realm — except a third way might be proved by marts[23] in England to vend our commodities to strangers repairing to England.'

He indicated two ways by which force might be applied: (1) by alliance with Spain; (2) by providing naval convoy for all English merchantmen in the Narrow Seas, by arming English merchantmen and increasing their crews, by cutting off all supplies to Orange, by the arrest of all Dutch ships and merchandise and Dutchmen in England, holding the wealthy and banishing the poor ones. He estimated that the cost of providing naval protection for English shipping would come to not less than £5000 a month and that if merchant ships were armed and adequately manned the increased costs would raise the price of English merchandise.

Burghley did not think that Philip of Spain would take kindly to joint action with the English against the Dutch, particularly when he perceived that the English were forced to it by necessity, and that he would either reject it or else accept it upon terms which would oblige Elizabeth to maintain a large and expensive fleet. He thought that the defeat of the Dutch would do the English no good and the Spaniards not a little good. He anticipated that when the Spaniard had reduced the Dutch to subjection he would take immediate steps to impose heavy charges upon English traders in the Low Countries and would subsequently use the Low Countries as a base for operations against England, to re-establish Roman Catholicism there and to seat Mary Stuart first on the Scottish throne and then on the English throne. To cope with such a menace England would have to maintain a defence by land and sea, the cost of which would be prohibitive.

Reverting to settlement by composition, Burghley took the position that the Queen could not do it with honour. He thought the matter could best be arranged privately by the merchants themselves, by way of assurances (that is to say by taking out some form of insurance with the Dutch) but feared that such an arrangement would establish a precedent which the King of Spain might subsequently exploit.

'It remains to be considered', Burghley concluded, 'whether some other means might not be found to induce the Prince to be content to forbear from depredation of our subjects that shall pass generally to other countries than to Flanders and that such as shall trade in Flanders may only do it by secret bargains upon assurances.'[24]

Actually the course which Burghley outlined in this memorandum was the one which, after a month of futile belligerency, Elizabeth decided to follow.

On August 7th William Herle wrote a letter to Edward Chester, Burghley's correspondent in the Low Countries.[25] The purport of the letter is expressed in the following extract:

'If the Prince will excuse these former foul acts and spoils ... praying Her Majesty to attribute them to necessity and not to any malice or will to offend ... and that from henceforth the matter shall be redressed in such sort as the like shall not be committed again ... the Prince's friends here, that favour the course will join together to qualify Her Majesty's just displeasure and no doubt somewhat may be done by this means to reconcile the Prince again and to help him underhand with some aid to settle and confirm the strength of Holland and Zeeland together. . . .

'If', he concluded, 'the Prince do seek her Majesty's good will, the mutiny that is now in Brabant and Flanders against the Spaniards and first provoked by them will do him and the whole cause great good. But if he hearken not to so good counsel *nemo laeditur nisi a seipso.*'

But the most significant fact about this letter is set forth in another letter which Herle wrote to Burghley the following month.

'I have', he wrote, 'enclosed herewith the copy of a letter I writ unto Mr. Edward Chester in Holland *by commandment secretly of Her Majesty and Mr. Secretary* in August last, when your Lordship released a hoy upon my motion purposely to that end.'[26]

It is to be noted that nothing is said about forced loans or assurances. Presumably, as Burghley had advised, they were left to private negotiations between the merchants involved and the Dutch. In any case, along those lines friendly relations were established between Orange and the Queen.

Probably the most important consideration in the whole affair was the mutiny of the Spanish soldiers and the rising of the Netherlanders everywhere to get rid of them.

Orange was quick to take advantage of the situation. By October 1576 he had succeeded so well that a congress comprised of representatives from Holland, Zeeland and from the Estates General of the Spanish provinces had assembled at Ghent. While they were in session news reached them that the Spanish mutineers had sacked Maestrecht, and on November 7th came the much more terrible news that Antwerp itself had fallen into their bloody hands. The next day the Pacification of Ghent was signed.[27] It restored peace and free intercourse among the provinces and provided for an assembly of all the provinces to which matters still in dispute were referred. Above all, it pledged the contracting parties to do everything in their power to drive out the Spanish soldiers.

The Pacification of Ghent[28] changed the whole complexion of affairs in the Low Countries. For four years Holland and Zeeland alone under the Prince of Orange had been maintaining an unequal struggle against Spain. It was too unequal to be prolonged indefinitely and by the summer of 1576 the end seemed to be very near at hand. But in a few months something very like a miracle had been wrought. The Spanish government had become scarcely more than an idea, the Spanish army a band of murderous mutineers, and the Low Countries, north and south, Protestant and Catholic alike, were joined together to rout them out of the land. The Prince of Orange was no longer the leader of a desperate band of 'sea beggars'; he was one of the most important figures in a league which looked strong enough to dictate terms even to Philip II of Spain.

Meanwhile, on November 23rd, a new Spanish governor, Don John of Austria, had arrived at Luxemburg. He was the bastard half-brother of the Spanish King, a young soldier of great charm. At the age of twenty-four he had won against the Turk the most famous naval victory in Spanish history, the battle of Lepanto. Philip could hardly have found in his whole empire a leader of greater prestige.

The problem which faced Elizabeth was how to deal with the whole situation. Her first step, taken before Don John's arrival, but when he was on the way, was to send a resident agent to the Low Countries, one of her best men, Dr. Thomas Wilson. He had a long experience in diplomacy and was a year later to be Sir Thomas Smith's successor to the office of Principal Secretary. At the time Wilson was believed to be a Puritan and a follower of Leicester, though, as it turned out, he managed to avoid pronounced partisanship and to command Burghley's confidence. From Wilson's correspondence during the year in which he remained in the Low Countries we get one of the best pictures of the situation there.[29]

The Estates General, while the negotiations for the pacification were still in progress, had sent agents both to France and to England asking for support and assistance. From France they received sympathetic assurance both from the King and from his brother, the Duke of Alençon. Indeed, the failure of the French Crown, after four years of intermittent efforts, to arrange a marriage between Alençon and Elizabeth, tempted Henry III to exploit the struggle in the Low Countries as a way of getting rid of his rebellious younger brother.[30]

Elizabeth, well aware of the French attitude and determined to forestall it, responded to the Dutch appeal with unusual promptitude. In December she delivered to an envoy from the Estates £20,000 in ready money and the promise of a loan of £100,000. At about the same time she dispatched an envoy to Don John offering mediation. The envoy in this case was Edward Horsey, a soldier and at the moment governor of the Isle of Wight, reckoned as a Leicestrian.

Burghley drafted Horsey's instructions.[31] They are the only indications which survive of his active participation in the administration of foreign policy for over a year to come.

Horsey, in brief, was directed to offer Elizabeth's mediation in the affairs of the Low Countries and to indicate her fear of French intervention. He was to tell Don John that unless he came to terms with the Estates on the basis of their ancient privileges, she would 'aid them with all the might and power we can'. If on the other hand the Estates refused to accept reasonable terms she would join with him against them.

Horsey was directed as well to form some estimate of Don John's intentions and of his strength. And there were other matters not incorporated in his formal instructions with which he was no doubt ordered to deal. Don John himself reported that Horsey had expressed much concern on the subject of rumours widespread in England that the Spaniards would attempt a landing in England to deliver the Queen of Scots.[32]

At the second interview Horsey declared flatly that a project to remove the Spanish troops by sea was designed for the invasion of England. He referred to Don John's proposed marriage with Mary Stuart, and suggested instead that he seek the hand of Elizabeth.[33] In any case he accomplished nothing.

During the late winter of 1576-77, the issue in the Low Countries turned upon the question as to whether the Estates General would recognize Don John's leadership or would accept the leadership of the Prince of Orange. In the issue Don John won out and on February 12th came to terms with the Estates in what is known as the Perpetual Edict. Elizabeth accepted the situation and even sent Wilson to congratulate him, though she urged the Estates to make more of the Prince of Orange.

And so the matter stood for a time. And for a time Don John's charm had its effect. Men quoted scripture in the streets of Antwerp — 'There was a man sent from God and his name was John'. But Orange was steadily increasing in strength and early in June Don John, fearful for his personal safety, shut himself up in the fortress of Namur[34] and called upon the Estates to assist him in making war on Orange. The answer was not what he had hoped for. The Estates turned the other way and Don John, with his Spanish veterans on the way out, was faced once more by a united Netherlands.

All this had a marked effect upon Elizabeth's attitude. In July she dispatched William Davison, another good man, another Puritan and Leicestrian, who in his turn was to become a Principal Secretary, taking Wilson's place. De Guaras, the Spanish agent, found the whole Privy Council in favour of going to the assistance of the Dutch at once.[35] Leicester and Walsingham certainly were, and we gather from a chance survival of a memorandum of Burghley's that he was of the same mind: 'I see no way so sure for your Majesty as to keep the Prince of Orange in heart and life. For methinks his estate towards Spain and the Regent's [of Scotland] towards France stand both in one predicament, and therefore requireth both one course. The States of the Low Countries are so divided that how trust may be reposed in them when one trusteth not another I see not. Marry, if it might be brought to pass by counsel from hence that the Duke of Arschot[36] and the Estates might govern the country according to their liberties and the Prince to have the rule of their martial matters, this of all others were the surest way. Otherwise, whilst the Estates be in deliberation, it may be doubted that their overthrow may hap.'[37]

This is all we have from Burghley on the subject for some months to come. It must be accidental that so little survives to indicate the scope of his activities. He was suffering a good deal from his old enemy, and was absent from the meetings of the Privy Council during most of April. It was in that month that Wilson wrote to him from Brussels:

'I do assure your honour, your apt allegory did so well like me, in reading your letter, that, as I took pleasure in reading the same, so did I persuade myself that your Lordship was not sick at all, being so merrily disposed. But I perceive that although your heart be whole and sound yet your exterior members have been greatly vexed by your ancient enemy the gout. I do find great good by drinking Rhenish wine, which not only doth comfort my stomach but keepeth my body open and consumeth the rheum so well as I do not spit now almost at all, whereas, being at home and drinking Gascon wine, my body was filled with excessive and needless humours.'[38]

Poor Burghley! His friends never ceased to send him panaceas for his ill health. It is a pity that his merry letter is missing. Probably we must take Wilson's remarks with reservations. Burghley's humour, on the few occasions where we can sample it, leans to the elephantine.

But otherwise Burghley's attendance at Council meetings was about as regular as ever. His correspondence was apparently undiminished, though increasingly English representatives overseas addressed themselves to Walsingham and Leicester. There is virtually no mention of him either in the correspondence of foreign ambassadors and agents, and nothing in the surviving letters of Court gossip. It is to be noted that most of those who went overseas, like Amias Paulet, who succeeded Dale as English ambassador in France in 1576, and the various envoys to the Low Countries, Davison and Wilson and Horsey, were Puritans and Leicestrians. Burghley's role appears to be that of a retired elder statesman, who observed and commented but no longer took an active part. Indeed, he seems to have acted, when he did act, as advocate to the Queen for the policy which Walsingham and Leicester were promoting both in France and in the Low Countries. The opinion sometime expressed that he was opposed to active assistance of Dutch rebels and French Huguenots is without foundation, though he always preferred the method of subsidy to the method of war.

In May Elizabeth spent three days with Burghley at Theobalds.[39] In July he wrote to the Earl of Shrewsbury that he intended once more to take the waters at Buxton. 'I am now', he wrote, 'thoroughly licensed by her Majesty to come thither with as much speed as my old crazed body will suffer me.' He asked Shrewsbury to find him lodgings for himself and his son, Thomas, and Roger Manners.[40]

Shrewsbury wrote back that Burghley could have his choice of lodgings, and that other tenants if necessary would be turned out to accommodate him. Burghley replied with thanks on the 24th but would have no one dislodged 'except they were far inferior'. 'And now, my Lord,' Burghley added, 'I most heartily beseech you, when I shall once have room, leave me altogether to myself and spare yourself from any care.'[41]

Just as he was leaving Theobalds on his way north he wrote to the Earl of Sussex: 'My meaning is to be at Burghley on Wednesday and upon return of my servant whom I sent to my L. of Shrewsbury for a lodging and to Buxton for my provisions, which I trust will be about Thursday, I will the next day take my journey towards Buxton, by Darby I think and then Ashbourne in the Peak. I thank your Lordship for your wishing yourself at Buxton's, where I do wish the same, as I know no nobleman in the earth more to my heart's contentation, and thus I write, even moved with the best vein in my heart.

'My arm, my Lord, is of pain eased, but not of soreness.'[42]

Mary Stuart, Shrewsbury's royal prisoner at Sheffield, reported, on August 3rd: 'The Lord Great Treasurer is now at Buxton's, in quiet manner.'[43] And on the day following, Burghley wrote from there to Shrewsbury. He apologized for having dictated the letter. 'I have', he said, 'to use my man's hand, being not in good temper this morning.'[44]

By one of those freak accidents of survival we have two letters which Burghley wrote from Buxton to the Earl of Sussex, his old friend, one of his staunchest supporters in his long running fight with Leicester. The first of them is dated July 31st.

'As I did long to hear of you,' Burghley wrote, 'and specially of the amendment of your leg, so was I glad to hear from you, but sorry not to hear of your amendment. But I trust you will have such regard as not to hinder it with variety of medicine or plasters ... Your Lordship, I thank you, desireth to hear of my estate here, which is this: I came hither on Sunday last[45] at night, took a small solution on Monday, began on Tuesday, yesterday, to drink of the water to the quantity of 3 pints at six draughts, this day I have added 2 draughts and so drank 4 pints and tomorrow am determined to drink 5 pints and one gill. With sugar I find it potable with pleasure, even as whey. I mean not to bathe these 8 days, but will continue drinking 10 days.

'Here are in company Mr. Roger Manners, for whose company I heartily thank your Lordship; Sir William Fitzwilliam,[46] Thomas Cecil, my Lady Harrington and Mr. Edmunds, with sundry others. The weather is dry, but yet cold with winds ... From Buxton's, *in your chamber*.'[47]

The second letter was written a week later. 'I was very glad', Burghley wrote, 'to see your letter dated at the Court, both because I wish you long there and specially I feared the lack of amendment of your leg by your absence.

'Mr. Secretary hath, I thank him, advertised me of the occurrences in the Low Countries, the issue whereof I much fear, both for that I think Don John hath secretly foreseen his power to pursue his attempt and that he knoweth the weakness of the States to withstand him long, by reason of their divisions and lack of conductors. But yet, seeing he seemeth to mean evil I hope God will weaken his power and [confound][48] his Italian and Spanish practices. In the mean season God amend us in thankfulness for these divisions of our own deserved troubles.

'My L. of Shrewsbury came hither yesternight with a gouty hand and both drinketh and batheth diligently. And I think he will away tomorrow to his charge, of whom, I assure your L., neither he nor I ever had word.[49]

'P.S. Yesterday I began to be a launderer [i.e. bather] having ended my drunkenness on Monday.'

Burghley revealed in these letters the characteristic preoccupation of those engaged in cures with the details of their régime. He revealed also in the last sentence of the letter just quoted his desire to emphasize the fact that he had no dealings about Mary Queen of Scots.

We hear no more directly from him at Buxton. Sir Christopher Hatton wrote to him there on July 21st to apologize for a misunderstanding. He added: 'God speed you in your journey to Buxton's and there send you such repair of your health as your most happy and holy service to her Majesty and this realm may, with ability of your Lordship, be through many years continued.'[50] And Leicester wrote on July 23rd that the Queen wanted Burghley to send her a tun of Buxton water in hogsheads. It went off as quickly as Burghley could send it. But when it arrived at Court, Elizabeth had lost interest in it. By Leicester's account the rumour got about that she was treating a sore leg, and she scolded Leicester for sending for it. But she thanked Burghley nevertheless for his care.[51] Leicester hoped that Burghley was 'finding ease of his pain' and swore he would give 500 marks to be with him. Burghley was probably not of the same mind, though he and Leicester appear to have been at this juncture outwardly on the best of terms.

We get, however, another view of the matter from a letter which Mary Stuart wrote to the Archbishop of Glasgow, her ambassador in Paris, on July 12th.[52] Mary was writing about the visit of the Earl of Leicester to Buxton the month before Burghley's visit. According to her story, Leicester had conferred with her and had done his best to cultivate her favour. He had even gone so far as to speak sympathetically about her pretensions to the English throne. He had also sought information about the rumoured match between her and Don John. According to Mary, Burghley, having heard of Leicester's visit, moved to Burghley House with the idea of visiting Buxton and undoing what Leicester, 'son mortel ennemi', had done. But he was denied royal permission. The story is without confirmatory evidence from any other source, though the phraseology of Burghley's letter to Shrewsbury of July 19th ('I am now thoroughly licensed by her Majesty', etc.), suggests that an earlier request for licence had not been accorded. In any case, the evidence of a prisoner in Derbyshire upon backdoor intrigue at Elizabeth's Court should hardly be given much weight. There can be no doubt, however, that Leicester did speak with Mary. She herself was inclined to believe that his real objective was to break up the Don John match.[53]

Burghley left for Buxton late in August. He was certainly back at Court early in September.[54] It may have been about this time that he received an undated letter from Sussex[55] which must have warmed the cockles of his old heart.

'It pleased her Majesty', Sussex wrote, 'to have some long speech with me at Putney, of the speeches which passed between your Lo. and her at your parting, wherein she delivered such honourable speeches of your desserts to her and of her affection to you and of your sure, sound and deep judgment and council, with these words — that no prince in Europe had such a counsellor as she had of you — that if you had heard them must needs have been greatly to your contentment. And in fine her Majesty commended me that in any wise I should see you that night, thinking you had been at London, and to deliver to your Lo. such speeches as I forbear to write and will tomorrow bring to your Lo. myself. The end of her speech was that she prayed your Lo. to come to Nonesuch as soon as conveniently you might. I repaired to your house yesternight late, and, missing you there, I did intend to have been with your Lo. at Theobalds this morning. But finding myself this night so troubled as I am this morning unfit to ride, I pray your Lo. to bear with me this day and God willing I will be with you tomorrow in the morning.'

Not long after Burghley's return from Buxton he was faced once more with a problem arising out of the actions of Edmund Grindal, Archbishop of Canterbury. It will be recalled[56] that, upon Matthew Parker's death, Burghley had suggested Grindal, the Archbishop of York, as his successor, and that Elizabeth had acted accordingly. Grindal revealed from the beginning a laudable desire for reform. He was particularly concerned about the lack of competent preachers, the more so because eloquent Roman Catholic missionaries had already invaded England and were making great headway. Some steps had been taken already in particular parishes to remedy the situation, by the introduction of what were known as exercises or prophesyings. We hear of such at Norwich in 1564, and at Northampton a few years later. These exercises took the form of a public forum in which the clergy discussed scripture and the laity asked questions. The effect of them was to stimulate study among the clergy and interest among the laity. They did, however, give Puritan ministers an opportunity to disseminate obnoxious opinions. It is to be noted that Cartwright favoured them, and Cartwright's biographer remarks:[57] 'These exercises with their moderators and their mild form of disciplinary jurisdiction were really embryonic presbyteries of the modern type.'

This being the case, it is hardly surprising that Elizabeth violently opposed them. She took occasion in December 1576, when Grindal was at Court, to speak to him sharply on the subject and to direct him to suppress, as he put it, 'all learned exercises and conferences among ministers of the Church'. Instead of obeying he wrote to the Queen a long and notable letter[58] on the subject, in which he pointed out that the exercises were advocated in Holy Writ, were profitable to both the ministry and the laity participating, and that he could not consent to their suppression. 'If', he added, 'it be your Majesty's pleasure for this or any other cause to remove me out of this place, I will with all humility yield thereunto.'

Grindal says that Leicester delivered this letter to Elizabeth. In a letter to Burghley of December 17th he implied that both Burghley and Leicester had read the letter and had commented upon it. Grindal's observations on Burghley's comments (which are missing) were: 'I thank your good Lordship that you are so careful in this cause of the Church', which throws little or no light upon Burghley's attitude. Of Leicester's comment we can gather only that he raised some question about the propriety of laymen at the 'exercises'.[59] In any case, Elizabeth's response was unequivocal. In May 1577, she went over the head of Grindal and wrote direct to the various bishops, ordering them to suppress the exercises. In June she sequestered Grindal for six months from his office.[60]

Camden, the historian, blamed Leicester. 'Grindal', he wrote, 'flourished in great grace with the Queen until by cunning practices of his adversaries he quite lost her favour, as if he favoured the conventicles of the turbulent ministers and their prophesies . . . but in truth because he had condemned an unlawful marriage of Julio, an Italian physician, with another man's wife, while Leicester in vain opposed against his proceeding therein.'[61]

What little evidence we have on the subject would seem to indicate that Leicester was, in fact, not unfriendly. But one never knows about Leicester. As a recognized friend of Puritans at this juncture, we should expect him to have favoured Grindal's position. But there is no doubt about Dr. Julio's offence and that Grindal brought him to book for it. In any case, Elizabeth's attitude towards anything savouring of Presbyterianism, possibly in this case with a little prodding from Leicester, is sufficient explanation of her behaviour.[62]

Of Burghley's attitude we know no more than Grindal has told us. But throughout his career he regarded Burghley as his staunch friend, and in his will named Burghley first among his beneficiaries and besought him to supervise the administration of his estate.[63]

In June 1577 Grindal was sequestered for six months. As the end of this period drew near, Burghley bethought him of ways to restore the Archbishop to favour.

On November 29th he sent Grindal a letter on the subject. The Queen, he said, had determined that prophesyings should cease. She had instructed Grindal accordingly and he had refused to take action. Thereby 'he did show himself disobedient to her Majesty and her supreme authority ecclesiastical'. She was now intent to have his misdemeanours and his acknowledgment of his fault made plain in some public place, to wit, the Court of Star Chamber.

Burghley thought that the proceedings there would confine themselves to a justification of the Queen's position and a condemnation of Grindal's disobedience. He therefore advised Grindal as follows:

'It is meet for the Archbishop to those things to answer as may content her Majesty for so many needful respects as it is hard in few words to recite, as well for God's cause and His religion as for the satisfaction of her Majesty and pacifying her displeasure.

'And therefore it were good for the Archbishop by way of answer to the first, to allow the Queen's Majesty's proceeding, grounded upon such cases as to him it doth now appear, did move her Majesty thereto. And herein to use good speeches of her Majesty as a prince that in all her public doings hath shown her wisdom, in doing nothing without good cause to move her thereto. And therefore they were to be greatly condemned that would in any wise seek to find fault with her Majesty. And in this point the Archbishop should do well to use the more large speech, as in good reason he may do without offence of his conscience.

'To the second concerning his offence to her Majesty, if he forbear the particular recital of his fault with the circumstances, he may, with the better estimation and less burden to his conscience, use a more general speech to acknowledge his fault and to come to pardon. For which purpose His Grace may say that he is very sorry that he hath in this sort offended her Majesty as he is charged and that he requireth her Majesty to pardon him and not to interpret his doing to have been with any meaning to offend her Majesty.

'If the Archbishop would consider hereof and set down in writing his answer, or the sum thereof, that it might be seen aforehand, it is thought that thereby some good might follow and herein he is admonished to frame himself as far forth as by any good means he may to satisfy her Majesty.'[64]

It is evident that Burghley was trying to find a formula which would satisfy the Queen and not do violence to Grindal's conscience.

Exactly what followed is not clear. Grindal did not appear before Star Chamber, but sent a letter asking the councillors to intercede for him with the Queen. In any case he did not win her pardon, and there was some talk in January of deposing him. Actually he remained in a sort of twilight zone, bearing the title but seques-tered from the power of his office, until shortly before his death. Some few of his letters to Burghley survive, written during the last year of his life, when he was almost completely blind and planning for his resignation. But I have found nothing more from Burghley.

For the most part Burghley's activity in public affairs during the autumn of 1577 was directed to the problem in the Low Countries. He seems to have been more active than he had been. Mauvissière, the French ambassador, on at least three occasions, had speech with him.[65] One of them had reference to the imprisonment of De Guaras, the Spanish agent, for dealings with the Queen of Scots. De Guaras had asked Mauvissière to intercede for him with Leicester, Burghley and Walsingham. Leicester and Walsingham would have none of it. Burghley was more responsive. He observed that he had always found De Guaras an honest fellow and a good servant of his master, that he had nothing to do with his imprisonment, but that he dared not intercede for him lest he expose himself to the suspicion of being pro-Spanish.[66]

We may take this for what it is worth. On more than one occasion Burghley made a show of friendliness to Spain. It suited his purposes to be considered a dispassionate counsellor with an appreciation of the merits of both sides of the case. But there can be no doubt that at this juncture his sympathies were entirely with the Dutch and that he was doing his utmost to induce the Queen to support them promptly and vigorously.

We have, in his own hand, a long memorandum on the subject in December. It reads like a brief of his presentation of the case to the Queen.[67] The positive, immediate dangers, as he saw them, were:

First, Don John's ambitious designs, not only to subjugate the Low Countries, but also to invade England, marry the Queen of Scots and establish her claim to the English throne;

Second, the menace to English trade by the establishment of a Spanish govern-ment in the Low Countries. He pointed out that this would not only impede free English traffic there, but would also subject English traders to any taxes which the Spaniards chose to impose. In addition to that, if they secured possession of the ports of Holland and Zeeland, they could stifle English trade eastwards to Emden, Hamburg, Denmark and the Baltic. They could, moreover, exterminate the thriving English trade with Spain by the 'tortures and burnings' of the Inquisition. In short, they could rob England of all her foreign markets, cut off necessary foreign imports like ship stores for the navy, and create widespread unemployment among those in England who lived by trade. Burghley reckoned their number as over 100,000.

The Queen, he said, objected to active intervention on behalf of the Dutch on the grounds:

(1) that she would be supporting rebels against their lawful sovereign, joining with those who lacked any settled government or any responsible leaders;
(2) that she would antagonize all her Catholic neighbours;
(3) that she would be shedding the blood of Englishmen in foreign quarrels.

He undertook to meet these objections. As to the first, he pointed out that the Dutch revolt was directed by the same Council of State that the King of Spain himself had authorized to govern the country after the death of Requescens, and that they were governing in accordance with the laws of the Netherlands. They were not questioning the sovereignty of Philip II and they were ready, indeed had offered, to render him due obedience, if he governed them according to their laws.

As to the hostility of Catholic neighbours, Burghley agreed that, whether she assisted the Dutch or not, they were disposed to join in an attack on England. But, he declared, the very justice of the Queen's position 'should satisfy all reasonable people, considering that she did not seek any gain or profit for herself but simply the safety and quietness of her own country'. She was not attacking the Catholic religion. The united Netherlands, seeking her assistance, were more Catholic than Protestant; and 'in all their actions, none are more earnest in words, in deeds, in counsels, in contributions (as aids of money, men and such like) than the bishops, abbots, deans and the rest of the clergy'.

In the matter of shedding English blood for foreigners, Burghley reminded his mistress that her predecessors had sent troops into Spain and the Low Countries without her justification, that she was merely providing for her own safety.

'And', he continued, 'it may be maintained for a necessary good counsel, that her Majesty should rather send a small number out of the realm to join with a greater out of the realm, adding also that her people shall be paid without her charge, and by that means to avoid a war to be made here at home, when she shall have no aid to help her, but shall be forced, to make her forces both by sea and land, and not only to defend foreign forces to come from France, from the Low Countries, yea from Scotland by mainland, but also to be occupied in subduing rebellions at home. In which case both more of her people shall be adventured in one day than now, by aiding of the Low Countries, shall be in 40 days; and as for charges to her own coffers and to her people, the charge shall be so inestimable as no reckoning can be had therefore, neither will any treasure that she hath serve but a small time, neither shall she without offence of her people, get by subsidy that which ought to serve, for her best people shall be themselves so charged as they shall not be able to yield any help, and the discontented shall be willing to move mutinies either at the granting or levying of subsidies. And there will be no hope that selling of her Majesty's land will serve, for none will dare in such a time of doubtfulness, what shall become of her Majesty's state, to purchase lands.'

He went on to enumerate the concrete manifestations of Spanish hostility, by burning her merchants, by confiscating their goods, by rejecting her ambassadors, by aiding her rebels and fugitives, by plotting with the Scottish Queen. All the evidence pointed to the conclusion that, as soon as the opportunity offered, Philip of Spain would strike. It was her duty both to herself and to her subjects to anticipate that blow.

Since this memorandum was directed to the Queen, its arguments were those best calculated to appeal to her. It made much of considerations of trade. It left religious considerations altogether out of account — indeed emphasized the fact that the rebels were for the most part good Catholics. Elizabeth, as we have already observed, was definitely antipathetic to the Dutch brand of Protestantism. It smacked too strongly of Puritanism. Walsingham himself observed a little later, after there had been some manifestations of a spread of Protestantism in Ghent, that what the Queen 'seemeth most to mislike of . . . is the progress of religion'.[68] None knew that better than Burghley, and he shaped his arguments accordingly.

The surprising part of his memorandum is his argument for offensive as against defensive war. The validity of it rested of course upon the assumption, whether he admitted it or not, that the action of Elizabeth's neighbours would be prompted by religious considerations, that national rivalries would yield to crusading zeal and that a joint attack by the Catholic powers was inevitable unless it were fore-stalled. It sounds more like Walsingham, more like Cecil in the 1560s than Burghley in the late 'seventies. Walsingham had put the matter more bluntly when he said that Christ and Belial could hardly agree. Burghley was saying much the same thing, though in terms less likely to offend his mistress.

The immediate occasion which called forth Burghley's memorandum was the shifting position of the Queen. In September the Estates had asked for a loan of £100,000 and a force of 5000 foot and 1000 horse. Her reply had been prompt. She would lend them the money and the men.[69] But she had no sooner spoken than she began to reconsider, and when the Estates first showed some reluctance to accept her offer of troops, and at about the same time invited the Archduke Mathias, younger son of the Emperor, to act as their governor, she decided that she had been too impetuous. While she wavered, Don John sent an envoy to England suggesting mediation; she seized upon the idea. Notwithstanding that all her councillors, Leicester and Walsingham, as well as Burghley, opposed, she would have it so.[70] And she sent off an envoy to Spain and another envoy to Don John proposing an armistice and threatening military action in favour of the rebels if an armistice were refused.

It is generally assumed that Elizabeth had no policy, but that she changed her course with every shift of the wind. Her flexibility was, indeed, one of her assets. Had Philip II had more of it, the history of the Low Countries would have been far different. What Elizabeth preferred is clear enough. First of all she wanted peace rather than war. She did not want to support rebels against their lawful monarch, particularly Protestant rebels with radical ideas about the relations of Church and State. She preferred Spanish rule in the Low Countries, moderated and controlled by the maintenance of autonomous rule according to ancient privileges. If she could have achieved that end by mediation, she would have been satisfied. Burghley himself summarized her position in a brief memorandum which he drew up in February.

'Necessary for England that the State of the Low Countries should continue in their ancient government, without either subduing it to the Spanish nation or joining it to the Crown of France.

'Profitable to have the State continue as it hath done whereby England may continue both peace and intercourse.'[71]

Walsingham, speaking for his radical Protestant colleagues in the Privy Council who saw England's role as the champion of the Protestant cause, and who regarded any compromise with Spain as a concession to the powers of darkness, condemned the Queen's policy and denounced his more conservative colleagues as pro-Spanish. It is not clear which ones he had in mind. Sir James Croft, the Controller, and the old Earl of Arundel were the only two who were definitely Catholic in their sympathies, and neither of them played an important role. Of the rest, Sussex and, on occasion, Sir Christopher Hatton were suspect, but any stigma attached to them they probably owed more to Leicester's hostility than to any overt support of a pro-Spanish policy.

At all events, neither Wilkes, who went to Spain, nor Leighton, who went to Don John, to arrange for intervention, got anywhere. They had scarcely returned to England before news came that Don John had met the army of the Estates and had defeated it.[72]

This disaster threw Elizabeth back on her heels again. She forthwith dispatched Leighton once more to the Estates to reassure them of her friendship and to look into their affairs.[73]

Meanwhile, she had sent Daniel Rogers to Duke Casimir of the Palatinate to see if he could not arrange a Protestant league in Germany. On February 1st Rogers got back to England[74] and with him came Dr. Beutrich, Casimir's favourite councillor. They brought with them from Casimir expression of a desire to serve Elizabeth. This suggested to Elizabeth that she might use Casimir to fight her battles in the Low Countries as she had used him before in France. It would enable her to avoid using English troops, which would have constituted an open declaration of war on Spain. She decided to proceed that way, and so declared her intention to the agent of the Estates in England. It was not, however, until almost a month later that she made up her mind to act.

Burghley laid her decision before the Council and invited them to proceed to details. He explained that the Queen had changed her mind about sending forces, because she learned (1) that the governors of many of the provinces were opposed to the introduction of English troops; (2) that if she intervened in support of the rebels the French King would intervene in support of Don John; (3) that her expeditionary force, being infantry, could not function without the support of German cavalry.

It is evident from Burghley's note that Elizabeth still contemplated an expeditionary force to supplement Casimir's army if it alone could not achieve peace, for Burghley invited the Council to consider the organization of such a force, the cost of it and a base of operations for it on the Dutch coast.[75]

What the Council did about the matter is not recorded. The significant fact is that Burghley acted as the Queen's spokesman before the Council.

It was evidently the fear of French intervention which forced her hand. While she hesitated she learned that the Duke of Alençon had once again offered his assistance to the Dutch on most liberal terms, and evidence was accumulating that he was building up a party for himself in the French-speaking provinces of Hainault and Artois. Early in March she sent Rogers to the Estates, offering to assist them indirectly through Casimir. She was prepared to lend them £100,000 to cover the costs involved and even to send them £40,000 in cash on account, to meet Casimir's initial expenses.[76] The Estates accepted the offer somewhat reluctantly, for it meant a delay of two or three months while Casimir mustered his troops. To meet immediate needs their agent in England did succeed in getting £5000 and permission to export large quantities of munitions of war.

He might have got more had it not been for the arrival from Spain of a very clever Spanish diplomat, Bernardino de Mendoza. Of Mendoza we shall hear much in the five years which follow.[77] He was a Spanish nobleman of distinguished lineage, the last and probably the cleverest of Spanish ambassadors at the Elizabethan Court. He had served with distinction in the Low Country wars, and had published a book on the art and practice of war. This was his second visit to England, and he was already on friendly terms with Leicester and other English courtiers.[78] His letters, which have a literary quality lacking in those of his predecessors, furnish one of the best running comments extant on the English Court for the five years of his service there.

Immediately he came with messages of love and good will, which Elizabeth received rather tartly, but which had their effect. Walsingham wrote to Davison that the 'arrival of Don Bernardino . . . has put us in a vain hope of peace by her mediation. Such as are evil affected and inclined to Spain take great hold thereof, to the grief of those who are best devoted to her Majesty's service'.[79] He wrote to Burghley: 'When anatomy shall be made and the particulars of the matter looked to, I fear it will prove an offer of abuse to gain time.' From Burghley we have nothing.

In Mendoza's first conference with the Privy Council[80] (March 20th), Burghley was present, and later conferred with Mendoza at length. Mendoza thought that Burghley was trying to find out whether Mendoza was authorized to treat for peace and whether he was to remain as ordinary ambassador. He apparently evaded an answer to both questions, though it soon appeared that the answer to the first was no, to the second, yes.

Ten days after his arrival, Mendoza sent to his master an interesting appraisal of the situation in England:[81]

'During the few days I have been here and in my conversation with the Queen, I have found her much opposed to your Majesty's interests . . . and most of her ministers are quite alienated from us, particularly those who are most important, as, although there are seventeen Councillors, with the two secretaries, Hatton and the new ones, the bulk of the business depends upon the Queen, Leicester, Walsingham and Cecil, the latter of whom, although he takes part in the resolution of them by virtue of his office, absents himself on many occasions, as he is opposed to the Queen's helping the rebels so effectively and thus weakening her own position. He does not wish to break with Leicester and Walsingham on the matter, they being very much wedded to the States ... They urge the business under cloak of preserving their religion, which Cecil cannot well oppose, nor can he afford to make enemies of them as they are well supported. Some of the Councillors are well disposed towards your Majesty but Leicester, whose spirit is Walsingham, is so highly favoured by the Queen, notwithstanding his bad character, that he centres in his hands and those of his friends most of the business of the country.'

Some six weeks later Mendoza reverted to the same subject. 'I can certainly assure you', he wrote to the King's secretary,[82] 'that the Earl of Sussex is sincerely attached to his Majesty's interests, and Cecil also, although not so openly. But if he and Sussex, who is a man of much valour and understanding, are properly treated, they will both be favourable and their good disposition will be strengthened when they see it rewarded. It will be necessary, if they are to be entertained, to give them something more than jewels ... I have attempted and am attempting, by every means possible, to manage this, and the present is the best opportunity which has ever occurred, if his Majesty will be pleased to award something to Sussex, Cecil and the Controller [Croft].'

Mendoza was wrong about Sussex and wrong about Burghley. It is not recorded that either of them accepted bribes, though Croft, the Controller, was later to become a pensioner of Philip of Spain.[83]

Early in May, Alençon sent deputies to treat with the rebels and the indications were that they would come to terms. The Queen raised the question as to what should be done about it. Bacon, the Lord Keeper, advised that since the Queen herself would not send troops to assist the Dutch, and since the forces of Casimir would not be ready in time to relieve them, and since they had the choice of either accepting Alençon's aid or of driving him to support Don John against them, 'it is better for the States to receive Alençon with such conditions as they can get'. But Burghley did not agree.[84]

He had an inveterate distrust of the French, and, other things being equal, generally leaned towards the traditional English position of Burgundian alliance and French enmity. He would have preferred to settle the Dutch question by re-establishing the Spanish government there subject to the 'ancient liberties'. Whether he regarded religious toleration as a *sine qua non* or whether, like Elizabeth and Sussex, he was prepared to waive the religious issue is, at this juncture, not quite clear. He carefully avoided commitments on that point. But in general he took the position that it would be better to re-establish the Spanish government in the Netherlands on almost any terms than to see them pass to France.

A memorandum from him on the subject survives.[85] It may have been intended for the Queen. Its heading reveals its tone: 'The Way to be taken by Her Majesty for the Stay of Monsieur's intended Enterprise to make himself master of the Low Countries.' It proposed that Elizabeth should presently send over to the Estates 'personages of quality and sufficiency to dissuade them from further dealings with Monsieur'. They were to assure the Estates that, if their rejection of his offers resulted in his joining forces with Don John, she would come to their assistance with men and money. Realizing that the Dutch had lost faith in Elizabethan promises of assistance, Burghley suggested that troops should be levied out of hand and sent to points of embarkation. If the Dutch still declined then they were to be told that Elizabeth would join forces with Spain and would invite the co-operation of the Emperor and the German princes to resist the French. Burghley went on to suggest that special messengers should be dispatched at once to the Emperor, to the French King and to Alençon. They were to invite the co-operation of the Emperor in resisting the French, and they were to propose to the French Crown joint intervention in the Netherlands[86] to restore peace, threatening war if the French attempted to seize the Low Countries for themselves. Burghley even went so far as to suggest a dispatch to the King of Navarre, leader of the French Huguenots, with some comfortable message, 'as well that he may serve as a counterpoise in case the French should attempt anything in Scotland . . . as also to impeach Monsieur by way of diversion if he should join with Don John'.

Burghley seems to have been convinced at the time that Alençon's enterprise was actually supported by the French King. Walsingham's observations on the situation are pertinent.

'Presently', he wrote to Davison on May 11th, 'we are in consultation what were fit to be done in the Low Country causes, which we find subject to so many difficulties as we know not what to resolve, especially for that we are doubtful what should be Monsieur's meaning touching his late offers made to the States. Many arguments there are to induce us to think that all is but abuse, and I see a common fear in the best affected and that are of best judgment. It will behoove the Prince [of Orange] therefore to look substantially into the matter and not to forget the late accident on St. Bartholomew's day. I am greatly in doubt that those that were the authors in that banquet have their hand in the pie in this new intended matter. On the other side many reasons there are that lead me to think that a French King, being so jealous of his brother as he is . . . would be glad to set him a work abroad to live the more quietly at home in his own realm.'[87]

Burghley sketched out instructions for ambassadors to be sent to the Low Countries on June 2nd, and he drew up another memorandum on the subject three days later.[88] In both of these he emphasized the necessity for peace as follows:

'If peace', he wrote, 'cannot be had, the countries are to be conquered by Don John or usurped by the French. The Queen must of necessity give the States aid to withstand either of these two. The Queen's aid must be either wholly to the States or in some part to temper the French aid, that they usurp not the whole. The ambassadors must have authority, as they shall see cause, to offer the one or the other.'

In his memorandum of the 5th he was much preoccupied by the French menace. He even went so far as to suggest that, if the French were seeking to 'impatronize' themselves in the Low Countries, England and Casimir and Don John should join together to resist them. In that case, he observed, 'a war may grow between France and Spain, which, being maintained with some charge to her Majesty, may bring great surety to her'. He still took the position that the ambassadors should be given plenary powers, but since he recognized that 'whatever commission they have, they will not resolve or conclude of any principal matter before they have advertised her Majesty and received her resolution', so he thought it 'convenient and necessary' to hold them to her orders.

The ambassadors had already been chosen. They were Secretary Walsingham and Lord Cobham, Warden of the Cinque Ports. Leicester had wanted to go but was disappointed. Elizabeth was always reluctant to have him leave her side. There were, in any case, sound diplomatic reasons why the embassy should not be composed of two such outspoken champions of the Dutch as Walsingham and Leicester. Cobham definitely belonged to the other camp. He played little more than a nominal part in the embassy. We may perhaps regard him as Burghley's man as opposed to Walsingham, who was currently regarded as Leicester's man.

The first official draft of the instructions for the ambassadors, prepared apparently by Secretary Wilson, was chiefly concerned with the French menace.[89] But there is a striking change in the instructions as issued. All that was said in the final draft was that Walsingham and his colleague would point out to the Dutch 'because they deal with so mighty a personage [Alençon] that the aid which he is to bring unto them may be moderated in such sort as they may have help thereby and not be overruled'.[90]

Evidently Elizabeth's attitude towards Alençon's enterprise had changed in the interval. The reason for it was that Alençon had established direct contact with her, had indicated that he intended to be guided entirely by her advice and now hinted at a renewal of his suit for her hand. She dispatched Sir Edward Stafford to France in mid-May[91] to explore the situation with assuring messages of her willingness to resume the old negotiations for marriage.[92] Stafford brought back a letter from Catherine de Medicis enthusiastically endorsing the marriage project.

The choice of Stafford as envoy was significant. His mother, Dorothy, was the child of a union between the house of Stafford and the house of Pole, both of which had cherished pretensions to the English throne. She herself was Elizabeth's Mistress of the Robes. She was high in the royal favour and enjoyed a considerable amount of influence at Court. Through his father Stafford had a remote connection with Elizabeth herself. In short, he was of high lineage. In 1579 he took a second wife, Douglas Howard, the sister of Lord Admiral Howard of Armada fame and the cast-off mistress of the Earl of Leicester. Douglas, like many of the Elizabethan Howards, was secretly inclined to Roman Catholicism.[93]

Of Stafford's position when he went to France in 1578 we know little or nothing. A little later he revealed himself as a strong advocate of the Alençon match, a boon companion of some members of Alençon's rather dissolute entourage,

Victoria & Albert Museum

QUEEN ELIZABETH

a follower of Burghley and a bitter enemy of the Earl of Leicester. We may presume that Burghley, if he did not suggest, at any rate approved of his dispatch to France. Later Burghley asserted that he was unaware of the proposed revival of the Alençon courtship until late in the summer,[94] but this seems hardly probable. Burghley wrote to Walsingham late in July: 'I hear that the French ambassador here hath been the cause [of renewing the courtship] upon some conference with her Majesty to me unknown' — which may be true.[95] In any case it was probably the Queen's version of the matter. Stafford's report of the result of his mission evidently satisfied Elizabeth that she could control Alençon and keep him dangling by a resumption of her favourite game of courtship. On June 7th a letter went off to Sir Amias Paulet, her ambassador at Paris, directing him to inform Alençon 'that in some sort her Majesty would be content that he should deal in the Low Countries'.[96]

And so the embassy to the Low Countries was directed mainly to the business of inducing Don John to negotiate a peace, with intimation that if he did not do so she would have to find some other way of stopping the war. They were to appraise the strength of the Dutch and if they found that their forces, combined with those of Casimir and Alençon, were insufficient to withstand Don John they were to promise that Elizabeth would send an army from England to assist them. In that event they were to demand towns for security, preferably Sluys and Flushing.

Of Burghley's views about this volte-face we have nothing. Secretary Wilson was pessimistic. He wrote to Walsingham on the 29th that Alençon's attitude, combined with other encouraging news, 'so lull us in security that we do not fear any danger at all'. The Queen, he said, had already stopped the supply of the navy and would probably dismiss the mariners presently. 'I pray God', Wilson concluded, 'that there be never trial made within this realm, either by foreign or domestical people, either of the courage, constancy or loyal faith amongst us.'[97]

The ambassadors, when they reached the Low Countries late in June, found the military situation there better than they had expected, and reported that the Estates had a good fighting army if they could raise money to pay it. They found the Estates indisposed to treat further with Don John and would only treat upon terms which involved: (1) the withdrawal of Don John and all his forces and the delivery of all towns and fortresses which he held; (2) the recognition of the Archduke Mathias as their governor; and (3) the reference of the religious question to the Estates General.[98] These terms were obviously prohibitive and Walsingham and his colleague did their best to secure some modification of them, but to no effect. They concluded that a negotiated peace was out of the question, until at least Don John found himself faced with irresistible strength. They advocated the advancement of more money to the Dutch to enable them to secure and to reinforce their military position.

When Elizabeth received news of this situation she flew into a fine rage, and bade Burghley, in the name of the Privy Council, dispatch a peremptory letter to the ambassadors. It is to be noted, by the way, that Burghley drafted many of

G

the more important dispatches which would normally have fallen to the task of Secretary Wilson. During the summer of 1578, Burghley seems to have been constantly at Court. He even went with the Queen on Progress, a fatiguing business for an old man. Evidently her disapproval of the policy of which Leicester had been the chief advocate led her to turn definitely to Burghley. Fortunately his health was equal to the task. He seems generally to have enjoyed good health when the situation demanded it. What, in brief, the ambassadors had written was that the Estates would not offer reasonable terms to Don John and that they must have money.

What Burghley wrote in reply was that the ambassadors should come home, since the chief purpose of their going was to make peace and the terms offered by the Estates were such that she would not even submit them to Don John.[99] She had promised to underwrite loans in the aggregate of £100,000. Against this promise she had already sent them £40,000 to meet the initial expenses of Casimir's army, with the understanding that this sum should be repaid out of the first money borrowed upon her bonds. She would lend them no more, nor would she allow them to borrow against the promised £100,000 until she had better security, by the delivery to England of fortified towns. She suggested Sluys and Flushing.

Burghley commented on the Queen's attitude in a letter to Cobham of the same date.

'When', he wrote, 'she perceived that the States required more money, I will not write how greatly she misliked thereof. And as much was done by me as I could to mitigate her offence, though the same fell sharply in speech upon myself. Yesterday her Majesty ... called me before Mr. Somers [messenger to the ambassadors] and there flatly denied to lend any more money, charging me with great oversight that there was not assurance for money already lent by having of some towns in gage. I answered that for the money passed, her Majesty had the bonds of the States as was at the time thought meet.[100] And for more to be lent, if her Majesty liked not of the former assurances, I thought and perceived by Mr. Somers that her Majesty might have some towns, and so I thought best for her Majesty to proceed, whereby the common cause should be stayed from danger of ruin and also thereby her Majesty might have more hope to have repayment of her imprests. But this my advice could not content her, but that Mr. Somers should speedily depart to call you home which, though yourselves for private respects do desire, yet I would you might have stayed, so as by recovering for the States from her Majesty this much taken up by her Majesty's credit you might have seen the army in full readiness, whereby, if ever Don John would yield to terms of a peace, you might have had opportunity to have furthered the same. And now that we hear yesternight of Monsieur's arrival at Mons I wished also that her Majesty would not in this hasty sort call you away, and thereto her Majesty yieldeth that upon that occasion, if you shall see any just occasion to stay a longer time, she will that so you shall do. . . .

'Mr. Somers can tell you how sharp her Majesty hath been with some of us here as counsellors, whereof you, Mr. Secretary, was not free of some portion of her words . . . And yet we all must dutifully bear with her Majesty's offence for the time, not despairing but, howsoever she mislikketh matters at one time, yet at another time she will alter her sharpness, especially when she is persuaded that we all mean truly for her and her surety, though she sometimes will not so understand.'[101]

Burghley dated his letter at Havering,[102] 'where', he added, 'I am kept only to receive some chidings upon daily debate of these matters'.

Burghley at any rate had saved the mission, and the ambassadors in the Low Countries and the councillors at Court bombarded the Queen with arguments for a more liberal policy towards the Dutch. They had succeeded in borrowing a little money from the Italian bankers at exorbitant rates of interest on the security of the Queen's promise. But before the bankers would lend more they demanded specific security from Elizabeth. Burghley, this time from Audley End in Essex, wrote to the ambassadors on July 29th:[103]

'Since your last writing, the Queen's Majesty hath been moved to assent to the delivery of her bonds to Spinola and Horatio but no arguments can yet prevail . . . We laid before her that which I have said unto her, which cannot be answered, that if she will at this time, yea, at this instant in their most need, deal so hardly with them, they will, yea, they must, give themselves over to the French, and then her Majesty shall more repent it than the loss of £100,000; yea, she shall lose not only her money already lent but also all her good will shall be buried and unkindness raised up in the place. It is said to her also, by delay hereof, Don John receiveth comfort, for the charge of the States continueth fruitless and burdenous without profit. All this and much more, alleged with all manner of earnestness and importunity, to her displeasant. No answer will be had until she may hear what is done by you, Mr. Walsingham, with Monsieur.

'There are come to London, and shall be here tomorrow, two gentlemen from Monsieur, Sieurs Bacqueville and de Quissy, the latter zealous in religion, the other not malicious. As I hear, their errand is to break again into the matter of marriage . . . It is also said that Monsieur saith that he hath warrant from her Majesty, though to me unknown, to come thus hastily into the Low Countries as a thing that her Majesty did allow . . . We shall tomorrow understand more, but to me this course is surely strange. What other Councillors know hereof, I am not inquisitive, but I think you, Mr. Secretary, hath by this time heard the like of Monsieur, if any such thing hath passed . . . A strange thing it is to see God's goodness, so abundantly offered for her Majesty's surety, to be so daintily hearkened unto . . . I am sorry to write thus uncomfortably to you, but indeed the abundance of grief will not suffer my hand to stay. . . .

'I take leave, meaning, contrary to my other disposition, to attend here yet somewhat longer, to beat still upon the stithy, until I see some better issue of the works in hand.'

The letter strikes one as being somewhat disingenuous. In his previous letter, Burghley had denied any knowledge of the renewal of the Alençon courtship, though he must certainly have known about it. In this letter he denies any knowledge of Elizabeth's giving countenance to Alençon's expedition to the Low Countries, though Paulet had sent to him a copy of the letter to the secretaries in which the whole matter had been set forth.[104] For some reason or other Burghley, in his letters to Walsingham, was intent to demonstrate that he was in no wise responsible for the rapprochement to Alençon and that he knew nothing about it until it was well under way. His very disingenuousness invites the conclusion that he had much more to do with it than he admitted or than the known facts reveal. It may have been that he anticipated the opposition of the Leicestrians and was reluctant to cross swords with them. More likely, he hesitated to take sides until he could be surer than he was of the royal intentions. About his desire to get the Queen married to almost any eligible suitor who offered, there can be no doubt. Ever since her accession he had constantly directed his efforts to that end. In its earlier stages he had been one of the chief advocates of the Alençon match. But he had been disappointed so often that he had learned to move in matters of courtship with great caution.

On the same day that Burghley's letter just cited was written, Secretary Wilson wrote to Walsingham:

'Her Majesty and the Lords [of the Council] are in great expectation of your dealings with Monsieur and as you make report so credit will be given, for although M. Bacqueville comes tomorrow with the French ambassador to have audience and perhaps will tell a fair tale, yet her Majesty will be well advised by you before any full credit be given or resolution determined. If Monsieur would play double-hand tricks and direct his doings contrary to his protestations, I do fear greatly we should then be much to seek because of our continual security and careless dealings hitherto. The more favour offered by the States, by Casimir, by the King of Navarre and the Prince of Condé, the greater is our negligence and the less mind have we to take the benefit of occasion presented and laid open before us ... If you knew what care is used to get the bonds which are not possible as yet to be had, you would say that *fatum regit mundum*, or rather that will beareth sway instead of reason.'[105]

At this juncture a letter to Don John, unsigned, from some member of his entourage who had been twice on mission in England, throws some light upon the situation at the Elizabethan Court.[106] According to the writer, Leicester, a pompous fellow, poor and acquisitive, dominated the Queen. According to him again, Elizabeth had a way of discussing her inmost secrets with her ladies-in-waiting. He recommended that they should be cultivated, as well as the valets and ushers who knew everything that passed in the Privy Council. Among the councillors he singled out Leicester, Sussex, Burghley and Clinton, the Lord Admiral, as the most influential. Burghley, he said, was the ablest statesman of the lot. He thought well of Sussex whom he grouped with Burghley in opposition to Leicester. The two Secretaries, Walsingham and Wilson, he numbered among Leicester's adherents. Of the Council he designated Croft and Hatton as Catholic sympathizers.

The appraisal is significant not because it is sound but because it tends to reflect Spanish attitudes. It was quite mistaken about Clinton, who certainly played a minor part. And it was probably mistaken about the Catholic proclivities of Hatton, though such was his reputation at the time. In general, the Spanish assumption was that those who did not go along with the Puritans were potential recruits for the Catholic party. Both Burghley and Sussex fell within that category. It will be recalled that Mendoza had suggested a few months earlier that they should both be bribed. Croft was generally recognized as pro-Catholic in his sympathies. As to the ladies-in-waiting, we hear much of their love affairs, very little of their politics.[107] Their favour was, of course, cultivated by courtiers and statesmen alike. I cannot discover that Burghley either utilized their influence or resented it. There was no 'bed-chamber' issue under Elizabeth as there was centuries later under Queen Victoria. Certainly Burghley would never have attempted what Sir Robert Peel achieved.

After Alençon had made his final proposal and had promised to do nothing except what she would appoint and command, Elizabeth was strongly disposed to take him at his word.

Leicester wrote to Walsingham on August 1st[108] that, while she feared Alençon's appearance in the Low Countries, she believed he would obey her pleasure and return to France at her request. 'If', Leicester wrote, 'her Majesty meet that recompense for his labour that his ministers sue for here then were there some cause for her to presume of his conformity, but not perceiving any such reward like to come from hence, for ought I can see yet, I fear Monsieur will be too wise to lose an entrance of so great a fortune ... As far as I can gather she thinks that Monsieur's coming thither is rather to have the better means to step over hither than otherwise ... You know her disposition as well as I, and yet can I not use but frankness with you ... I would have you, as much as you may, avoid the suspicion of her Majesty that you doubt Monsieur's love to her too much, or that you had devotion enough in you to further her marriage, albeit I promise I think she hath little enough herself to it. But yet, what she would others think and do therein you partly have cause to know ... You have as much as I can learn, for our conference with her Majesty about affairs is but seldom and slender ... For this matter in hand for her marriage, there is no man can tell what to say. As yet she hath imparted with no man, at least not with me, nor for ought I can learn, with any other.'

Six days later Sussex wrote to Walsingham on the same subject:[109] 'Bacqueville doth here affirm that both in the causes of the Low Countries and also for Monsieur's person, her Majesty may dispose of Monsieur at her pleasure. And surely I do think, if she will make him her husband she may do as he saith. Otherwise I cannot be persuaded that she shall do anything with him that shall hinder his greatness any ways, and especially in this enterprise.'

From Burghley at the moment we get no comments on the subject. Within a week Elizabeth was reconsidering. On the 8th of the month she bade Burghley draft a letter to the ambassadors. She now directed Walsingham and his colleague to find out what Alençon's real intentions were and to suggest to him the desirability of a three-cornered conference in which he and the Estates and the ambassadors would participate; to define the number of his forces and 'with what conditions it shall seem to all parties reasonable, sufficient and honourable that the Low Countries be aided by him, as he professeth, only to be delivered of the oppression and tyranny of the Spaniards and not, under colour of receiving his aid, to become subject unto him'.[110] They were to assure Alençon that if he was indeed resolute to follow her advice this was the only course he should follow. If they discovered that he had other intentions, they should advise her with speed, 'for we have cause to be perplexed at this time, for the doubt we may have whether all these fair offers to us by his letters and messengers may prove rather an entertainment of us to win time for his particular advantage in the acquiring of those countries, which it behooveth us by all good means possibly to withstand'.

She went further than that, directing her ambassadors to inquire of the Estates whether they actually needed Alençon's services or not. If they said they did not, the ambassadors were to urge him to withdraw.

Burghley wrote to Walsingham by the same post:[111]

'About 8 o'clock this morning I finished and delivered by letter to my Lord Cobham's man who was ready to depart from hence by sea at Harwich, at which time I could not tell what her Majesty would have done with a letter which she caused me to write in all haste on Thursday[112] [August 7th] at night. And yet she seemed not to have regard thereof all yesterday. And now, being about three of the clock, she calleth for me, with some misliking that the letter was not dispatched. I answered that without her signing, it could neither go nor ride, which I spake merrily. But in earnest I told her I had no liking to the latter part of the letter, to move Monsieur to depart, as a thing dishonourable and unreasonable, without some other motion than upon bare words.

'Well, my L. of Leicester being by her, and Mr. Wilson also, was of my opinion, but I perceive Bacqueville and Mauvissière have more credit in this point. For she would not alter her purpose, and so she signed the letter ... I told her with some weight that the whole world would condemn her if the Low Countries should be joined to France which, by helping the States, she might have stayed, and yet in the end pleasured the King of Spain, against his will, with restoring of his countries.'

In conclusion Burghley referred to a pamphlet in support of the French interest which Walsingham had sent him. One gathers that the pamphlet proposed a division of the Low Countries. Burghley's comment is as follows: 'Only the title showeth what course it is likely that country will take, which, if it shall follow, I wish the Prince of Orange might retain to himself the islands and the Archduke [Mathias] Brabant or Guelders. The more the division of the Spanish coat, the better for us. But I may rather wish this than look for it.'[113]

The day after the letter went off, Elizabeth, genuinely alarmed at the reception of Alençon by the Dutch, commanded Burghley to write again to her ambassadors, expressing her fear that either Alençon would possess himself of the Low Countries or would throw his strength on the side of Spain, 'the danger of either of which our Crown and Estate cannot endure. And therefore if you should find any probable likelihood of either of those we would have you consider how the same may, though it be late, be withstood with our intermeddling[114] therein, by speedy sending over of 10 or 12,000 men or by yielding to the States the money that may be levied by the bond of £100,000.'

Burghley commented on the Queen's letter in a personal letter to the ambassadors of the same day. 'You may both,' he wrote, 'think it strange to receive a letter from her Majesty written by me in such haste as there was no leisure to rewrite it. Such was her Majesty's care to make haste therewith as upon consultation with my Lord Chamberlain [Sussex], my Lord of Leicester, myself and Mr. Vice-Chamberlain [Hatton] she concluded upon the matter of the letter. Her Majesty is greatly perplexed to think that the Low Countries may become French and, whilst she is in fear hereof, she seemeth ready to hazard any expense. It is at present determined here that if, upon your answer, necessity shall induce her Majesty to send forces, my Lord of Leicester will come over without delay and the army shall follow. Nevertheless, though this be, for the present, earnestly meant, I can assure nothing, but this only that I am uncertain of much. I pray you both pardon me, the letter from the Queen's Majesty was written in haste whilst she was making ready to horse.'[115]

Wilson's comment in a letter of the same date to Walsingham was as follows: 'I am glad to understand of this heat to do good which I pray God be not offered over late ... There was never so dangerous a time as this and temporizing will no longer serve. God grant a resolution (if any be certain) may turn now at length to the gain and profit of our country.'[116]

Francis Knollys, in one of his rare letters to Walsingham, ascribed the sudden volte-face to the gallantry of Sir John Norris, leader of the English contingent in the Dutch army, in an engagement at Rymenam on August 1st.[117]

In any case, the change came too late. Five days later the Estates reached an agreement with Alençon.

Actually he accepted from them very moderate commitments. He was to furnish them for three months with 10,000 foot and 2000 horse at his own expense and after that with 2000 foot and 500 horse until the end of the war. He was not to meddle in the government of the Low Countries, nor to treat with the provinces individually, nor to make war on their allies. In return he was to be named *Défenseur de la liberté Belgique contre la tyrannie Espagnole*, was to be preferred before all other candidates if the Estates decided to change their sovereign, was to be given three towns along the French frontier for security, and permission to keep all lands he conquered east of the Meuse, that is to say, beyond their borders.[118]

By one clause in the agreement the Estates were given until the last of August to come to terms with Don John. Walsingham and his colleague seized upon what they regarded as eighteen days of grace to confer with the Prince of Orange about ways of circumventing the French, and with Don John for peace. Orange suggested the immediate loan of £25,000 by Elizabeth and the dispatch of 5000 troops. Don John invited a conference.

After this interview with Orange, and a personal interview which Walsingham had with Alençon, they sent John Somers off to England to see what might be done, advising that the request of the Prince should be satisfied out of hand as the only way to prevent French domination.[119] At the same time they urged that the Queen release bonds in the amount of £28,000 to cover the loans of the Italian bankers. Walsingham wrote a private letter to Elizabeth recounting his interview with Alençon. But the letter is missing, though a letter which Alençon sent by him to Elizabeth contains expression of complete devotion.[120] Walsingham's impressions of the Duke are set down in a letter to Leicester.[121]

'To think', he wrote, 'that Monsieur could not be content to marry with our mistress were a vain opinion, being as she is the best marriage in her parish, but to say that he doth hope after it, considering his former trial in the attempt thereof, is very doubtful. To use the same as a means to render her Majesty more inclinable to allow of his proceedings herein standeth with good policy. The gentleman I find very wise, well spoken and not so deformed as he was. The great trouble he hath passed (which is the best whetstone) hath greatly sharpened his wit and increased his judgment. If it were not for the expectation of the Crown of France that is to light upon him, which difficulty above all others I do weigh, knowing what it is to live under a viceroy, the match were not to be misliked, seeing the necessity her Majesty and the realm hath of the same.'

Elizabeth's answer to Walsingham's call for immediate help was that she would not send troops, she would not send money, she would not even release the bonds for the promised loan of £100,000. The most that she would do was to underwrite the bankers' loan of £28,000, provided the Estates would put up plate and jewels of equal value as collateral.[122]

Burghley's comment on this message in a personal letter to Walsingham was one of resignation.[123] 'I can', he wrote, 'but wish you patience for I know that the tentation [strain] of this time in service is great, to serve so well as I am assured you do and to find so small fruits by good answers from hence. But seeing we here can get none, though we endeavour ourselves to our uttermost, you must perforce bear with that we do, that is to behold miseries coming and to be denied of remedies. This bearer [Mr. Somers] can plentifully report what we do, what we do not and what we cannot do.'

Two days later Burghley wrote again: 'We have attempted anew to make your conditions more arbitrable by you there. But though her Majesty showeth no reasons to move her to persist in her former direction, but that so (she says) she will have it, and that her pleasure cometh upon many evil conceits put into her of the state there by such as went over with you and have returned, that do sting all profession of true religion; yet I think as soon as she shall hear from you that the States cannot or will not accept the conditions she will be brought to qualify the same.'

It would be interesting to know who it was that had been in Walsingham's company and had come back to put the 'conceit' in her. The only hint we have is in Leicester's letter of August 29th:[124] 'You carried a companion over with you who hath played the right Jack since he returned — Charles Arundel. When I first heard of his going I told some of my friends to what end he would go.'

Of Charles Arundel we shall hear much later. He was in the 'seventies a courtier and one of those whom Burghley called 'lewd' friends of the Earl of Oxford. He was without any doubt Roman Catholic in his sympathies, was later mixed up in conspiracies against the Crown and died in exile a pensioner of the King of Spain.

His attachment to the Walsingham-Cobham mission meant in itself nothing. There were some 180 persons in their company, many of them courtiers for display purposes. A little later Arundel was an ardent supporter of the Duke of Alençon and he may already have been intriguing in the Duke's favour, 'stinging' the Puritans who opposed the match, as he went.

Leicester's observations upon the royal attitude at this juncture are more explicit.

'I am sorry', he wrote, 'that Mr. Somers returneth without the good satisfaction which I am sure you looked for ... It were needless to discourse at large to you what dealings here hath been on all sides to further the good cause, because there followeth so small fruit hereof. This do I most certainly find that necessity only beareth greatest sway in our arguments, which is a heavy case, as partly may appear by the letter that was sent post haste away to you from Bury written by my Lord Treasurer's hand, when, upon some hard news from you of the likelihood of the French prevailing too greatly in those parts, her Majesty was content to spend anything rather than that should take place. Now upon other dealings more calmly that way, as through the earnest semblance of Monsieur's whole direction under her Majesty's favour and none otherwise, she is both persuaded of her ability to direct all those causes without such charge as we lay down for her, and so resteth in assured hope that Monsieur will do nothing without her liking there, though she assure him of no further hope of his suit here than she hath done heretofore.'[125]

The picture we get here of the Queen standing alone and obstinate against the advice of all her councillors, Burghley as well as Leicester, is an amazing one. She was fed up by what she regarded as the pig-headed position of the Estates in the matter of coming to terms with Don John, she believed that she could control Alençon and she was evidently convinced that he did not enjoy the support of the French Crown. As it turned out, her diagnosis of the situation had more to be said for it than any of her councillors would admit.

At the moment their attention was focused upon the marriage project. Burghley wrote to Walsingham on the 29th: 'This marriage matter occupieth heads here, so as the same is the more hardly digested, because it is both earnestly followed and readily heard. The will of God be fulfilled.'[126]

Burghley with customary caution refrained from expressing his views on the subject. But Sussex was outspoken. 'What it shall please her Majesty to do', he wrote to Walsingham on the 29th,[127] 'is in the hands of God, but truly, Mr. Secretary, for my own part, I do not see any manifest surety of her Majesty but either by the marriage or by a good peace or by taking of the States to her defence, whereby she must make herself the head of the war. What likelihood there is of peace, you that be present can better judge than they that be absent. But as it seemeth to me the diffidence is so great on both sides and the demands of the Estates so far out of reason as the terms of peace be over hard. For the Queen to be the head of the war is more, I fear, than she can go through withal or the realm will maintain. And therefore if God would so put into her heart, marriage is the surest, for thereby she may give law to herself and all her neighbours and avoid all perils at home and abroad and knit herself in amity with both kings and keep them in their own bounds.'

In any case, the Alençon line was the one which the Queen elected to follow. And the hopes of those who favoured vigorous support of the Dutch rebels were blasted. Walsingham and Cobham came home late in September completely disheartened. Walsingham expressed his views of the situation in a letter to Burghley before he left.

'Besides', he wrote, 'the alienation of this country people's heart from her Majesty, which cannot but be perilous both to herself and her realm, it will render her Highness hateful to the world, many hard speeches being given out against her which we hear with grief . . . To have all the world your enemies at once, it is greatly doubted you will return Monsieur's ministers unsatisfied, which, if it so come to pass, then do I not know any Prince whose friendship you may assure yourself of. The King of Navarre and the Prince of Condé are to learn by your dealings with the Prince and the States here what they are to look for in the time of their necessity. And as for the Duke Casimir, he doth curse the time that ever he departed out of his country . . . How unpleasant it is to be employed in so unfortunate service I leave to your Lordship's good judgment.'[128]

CHAPTER XII

THE ALENÇON COURTSHIP, 1579-81

URING Walsingham's absence abroad, Burghley had carried a large part
of the duties of the Secretariat. At the same time he had been dragged by
the Queen on her summer Progress through the eastern counties which
involved short stops, generally for one night only, at some twenty different
houses.[1]

In mid-July he had escaped for a day or so to Theobalds while the Queen was
visiting her cousin, Lord Hunsdon, at Hunsdon, a few miles north of Theobalds.
But even there he got no relief from government business. On July 21st he wrote
to Thomas Randolph, an old friend, who had recently returned from a mission to
Scotland: 'I think you are advertised that her Majesty will have the ambassador
of Scotland come to Hunsdon on Thursday and to Mr. Sadler's on Friday. And
considering their highway is by my house here at Theobalds and that they must
have a retiring place for dinner time, I do pray you in my name to make the
ambassador an offer to dine here with me on Thursday, where also by that
occasion I shall be the gladder [to have you] to see my house, according as you
have said you had a desire, though there be nothing worth your desire, considering
your foreign travels; although, percase, you may see as much to content you as
in Muscovia.[2] With no other I will offer any comparison. My Lord of Hunsdon
will also here meet with you at dinner. The Queen's Majesty is privy and well
liking of this my offer.'[3]

A few days later Burghley, as Chancellor of the University of Cambridge, was
busy arranging for a delegation from the University to wait upon the Queen at
Audley End in Essex, a place which must have been filled with poignant memories
of former visits to the Duke of Norfolk. Of Burghley's participation in this
academic reception we have only a fragment or two. After the formal meeting
with the Queen, the delegates from the University distributed pairs of gloves
among the courtiers. Burghley himself received the most expensive pair, 'priced
20 shillings, together with his arms blazed out in colours, with verses annexed to
them'. He also participated in the learned discussion which followed, on two
subjects: (1) that clemency is more to be praised in a prince than severity; (2) that
the stars do not determine destiny. A moderator had been appointed to control
the debate, 'but my Lord Treasurer . . . did take upon him to moderate the whole
disputation and would not suffer any repetition or long discourses by way of
confutation'.[4] Even so it went on for more than three hours.

By October 1st Burghley, who had just passed his fifty-eighth birthday, an old
man as men reckoned age in his time, was tired out and he went home to nurse his

health.[5] He was away during most of October. On the 12th he wrote to Walsingham:

'Although I know not how my estate, for my strength, is there understood, neither yet that so small a matter requireth to hold any place amongst causes of court, yet to you, my very friend, I am bold to inform you that I find no amendment of strength, although I have in some sort kept a physical diet for 5 or 6 days and yesterday did contend with physic until I was very sick, but now am at get [*sic*], hoping that if physic will not diminish the humour that weakeneth my feet, yet time will speed it and bring me to an ebb when the flux is passed.

'If my being at the Court were either needful or required I could be brought to be a lodger there in my chamber, but to be busied much or to set abroad, surely I think I should lengthen my infirmity, and therefore I commend my case to your advice, hoping that without good cause you will rather advise me to that which might recover me than to overthrow me.

'I am in a suspense of many cogitations until I hear a further confirmation of Don John's death: I have been inquisitive to search the Queen's debts in Ireland and I find the debt greater than I hoped, by reason that there is great debt grown in this my L. Deputy's time.

'And thus, having occasion . . . somewhat to write, I do write upon my couch.'[6]

During his retirement he received a long letter from Leicester in which Leicester complained that Burghley had ignored him in some matters concerning the mint. 'I had more cause', Leicester wrote, 'to think unkindness, to be in your Lordship's company so long all this summer as I was, and so often talked of these mint matters, and would not acquaint me with your resolution, being joined as I was in commission. And blame me not my Lord therefore. For what may I think what manner of opinion you have of me that doth daily see you. Either must I think it was for want of desire to confer with me or some weak opinion conceived of my insufficiency to judge or further this cause . . . And yet to none is my care and good will for the service of her Majesty better known than to your Lordship.

'And now, my Lord, growing thus far upon occasion of your own friendly letter to me, I must the more plainly open some matter to you . . . knowing in reason what ought to have been between us more than any other I know which serve together. For we began our service with our sovereign together and have long continued hitherto together. And touching your fortune I am sure yourself cannot have a thought that ever I was enemy to it . . . How often and how far I have offered myself always in good dealing towards you — as for what friends have slipped from me and I have shaked from also, chiefly in respect of your Lordship, I know best myself . . . If I have not both long since and of late perceived your opinion, by your entire conference and dealings, better settled in others than in me, I could little perceive anything. Yet this may I say and boldly think that all them never deserved so well at your hands as myself, except in such secret friendship as the world cannot judge of. . . .

'You may suppose this to be a strange humour in me to write thus and in this sort to you, having never done the like before, although I must confess I have had

more cause of unkindness (as I have thought) than by this trifling occasion . . .
So have I withal in part enlarged it . . . because your Lordship doth upon this little
cause give such speech to me of great good will and care for my poor friendship. . . .

'Your Lordship hath been acquainted with me now almost thirty years and these
twenty years in service together. What opinion you have indeed of me I have,
for these considerations alleged, somewhat doubt, though I promise you I know
no cause in the world in myself that I have given you other than good. And
whensoever I shall find your Lordship either so to love me or to account of me
indeed, as I have been most desirous you should (as in very truth I have), then shall
your Lordship right well perceive better what my good will hath been and what
my poor assured friendship shall be. . . .

'Your Lordship is more acquainted by years with the world than I am. And
yet I, by reason we live in a worse world where more cunning and less fidelity is
used, may judge of bad and good dealing as well as an elder man, and the one
being so common and the other so scant must make the proof of the better the
more precious whensoever it is found. And surely, my Lord, where I profess,
I will be found both a faithful and a just, honest friend.'[7]

The immediate occasion of this letter was Leicester's irritation that his advice
on problems of the coinage had been ignored. He was a member of a commission
for the hearing of mint causes of which Burghley and five other councillors, including Sir Christopher Hatton, were also members. Burghley was apparently chairman of the commission. His offence seems to have been that after the commission
had made its report he neglected to get the signatures of all the commissioners to
the orders which were issued to the officers of the mint. Sir Christopher Hatton
heard of the affair and wrote to Burghley on September 28th: 'I hear you stand
troubely [sic] with my L. of Leicester, his taking of offence toward you in that
he was not made privy to this last warrant for the coining of money. Assuredly,
Sir, as I have before her Majesty answered, so must I still avow that at my Lord's
[Leicester's] return from Buxton to Havering, your Lordship declared your dealing
both to my Lord Chamberlain and his Lordship [Leicester] in my hearing. And
what advantage over and above that conclusion, by the Lords' orders set down,
you had by your most earnest travail and care won to the enriching the money,
I likewise showed her Majesty, leaving the consideration of your great desire
herein to her and my Lords, which I hope, in their wisdoms will be found far
unworthy of blame.

'But herein riseth the grief, that the bill signed was not subscribed and warranted
by the rest . . . Let not these things trouble you; they will record your memory
with high honour and singular consideration. Her Majesty greatly wisheth your
health and ease and hath commanded me yesternight to let you know that she will
pray God for it.'[8]

One wonders why Leicester made so great a fuss about so small a matter. It is
apparent from his letter that, on many grounds, he was uncertain about Burghley's
good will. Though Burghley had evidently given him the conventional assurances,
Leicester wanted something more. Certainly Burghley never trusted him and

probably never missed a convenient opportunity to discredit him with the Queen. This situation was well enough known at Court and by the foreign ambassadors. Why then did Leicester make much of it at this juncture?

Probably the reason was that Leicester had, less than a week before he wrote the letter to Burghley, taken a wife. The lady of his choice was Lettice Knollys, widow of the Earl of Essex and daughter of Sir Francis Knollys. Her father was a Privy Councillor, Treasurer of the Household and, by marriage, first cousin to Elizabeth herself. According to Camden, Leicester married Lettice twice over, 'for though it was reported that he had taken her to wife secretly, yet Sir Francis Knollys, who was father to Lettice and was acquainted with Leicester's straying loves, would not believe it (fearing lest he should delude his daughter) unless he might see the wedlock knit in his own presence with some few witnesses and a public notary'.

The marriage was concealed from Elizabeth, though it is hard to believe that she did not learn of it until nearly a year later. It is certainly hard to believe that Burghley did not learn of it and rejoice at it. The menace of a match between Leicester and Elizabeth which had plagued him for twenty years was removed at last. In any case, Leicester anticipated a royal explosion when the fact became publicly known. He realized that Burghley, if anyone, could mitigate the royal wrath. That was probably what he had in mind in his almost pathetic reaching out for Burghley's friendship.

During the four years following the futile embassy to the Low Countries in the summer of 1578, the focal point in English foreign policy was the Duke of Alençon. His enterprise in the Low Countries, his relations with his brother, the French King, and particularly his suit for the hand of Elizabeth, were the major considerations of the Queen and her Privy Council. It has been said that Alençon's courtship was a mere matter of politics, that each of the principals promoted it because each one needed the other to serve his turn — Elizabeth needed Alençon to fight her battles in the Low Countries; Alençon needed Elizabeth to strengthen his hand and to supply ways and means. If there had been no more to the matter than that, then the gestures of love-making could be examined simply as techniques and presumed to be without emotional content. But clearly that was not the case, or, if it was the case, then the wisest heads about the Queen were completely deceived.

At Court everybody believed that Elizabeth seriously contemplated marriage, and the Court circle was split in two on the subject, with Leicester leading the opposition to the match, Burghley and Sussex leading its supporters. To a considerable extent the country at large was divided, with the Puritans violently opposed, the Catholics, or crypto-Catholics, generally favourable.

Regarding the attitude of Elizabeth herself, there are two factors which call for consideration. One was her age. In September 1578 she began the forty-sixth year of her life and was approaching, if she had not already reached, what the sixteenth century would have called her climacteric, and we would call menopause. With many women this period is accompanied by great emotional instability, particularly in matters sexual. Another factor was Leicester's marriage, who for twenty years had been her perennial lover.[9] Much of Elizabeth's extraordinary behaviour during the protracted Alençon courtship is explicable in these terms. The amazing thing is that in the long run political considerations prevailed over personal considerations and the Queen once more triumphed over the woman, though her behaviour during the conflict was, to say the least, unbecoming both to the woman and to the Queen.

Burghley's position in the matter is clear enough though how far his mistress took him into her confidence is far from clear. Curiously enough the love-letters which passed between Elizabeth and her suitor and between her and the various agents whom he sent to plead his cause, and who engaged in not a little love-making on the side, are preserved among the Cecil papers at Hatfield.[10] Some of them may have been turned over to Burghley by Elizabeth, but many of them must have been secured from French sources. In any case there is no evidence that Burghley knew a priori what the Queen intended. She probably did not know herself.

It will be recalled that Alençon had made a formal proposal of marriage to Elizabeth through Bacqueville in midsummer. Elizabeth's reply, though non-committal, had been mildly provocative. She would never marry any man, she had declared, whom she did not first see. Alençon was for pushing matters. He announced his intention of sending Jean de Simier, one of his closest favourites, to England forthwith and of coming himself as soon as arrangements could be made.

Simier arrived early in January[11] with full powers to negotiate and conclude the marriage. He was, as Camden puts it, 'a most choice courtier, exquisitely skilled in love toys, pleasant conceits and court dalliance'. Elizabeth took to him at once, nicknamed him her ape (le singe) and went so far in flirtation with him as to give some colour to scandalous rumours. In matters of business she referred him to a committee of four, Burghley, Sussex, Leicester and Walsingham.[12] In their subsequent interviews with Simier they insisted that a personal interview with Alençon was a sine qua non. Simier could not budge them from this position, nor could he budge Elizabeth, though he had five different interviews with her on the subject. And so the matter rested, awaiting Alençon's reply.

The general opinion in England was that he would come, and a good many people at Court were convinced that he would not come in vain. He had made small progress in his Low Countries campaigning. By the end of the year his army was disintegrating for lack of pay and making itself unpopular by indiscriminate plundering. In December, after a treacherous attempt to seize Mons, he withdrew to France, though he lingered near the border and maintained diplomatic relations with the Estates General.

So far as Elizabeth was concerned, the effect of Alençon's discomfiture merely served to assure her that the danger of French occupation of the Low Countries was far less grave than had been feared. In a letter dated the last of February 1579 Walsingham wrote: 'The negotiation of Monsieur here taketh greater foot than was at first looked for and receives no small furtherance upon occasion of the decayed state of things in the Low Countries; for her Majesty . . . thinks this the best means to provide for her safety, in which respect it is to be thought that she will in the end consent to the match though otherwise not to her liking.' Leicester, very reluctantly, inclined to the same view. The French ambassador wrote home that nothing was lacking to the achievement of the marriage save the coming of the Duke.[13]

Alençon for his part expressed himself as keen to come, but for one reason or another he still delayed. Meanwhile, Simier, with the Queen's approval, addressed himself to the settlement of the marriage contract. Gilbert Talbot wrote to his father, the Earl of Shrewsbury, early in March:[14] 'My Lord of Leicester is now at Wanstead[15] and this day M. Simier and his company do dine there with him. He returneth again tomorrow. My Lord Treasurer was made a little affrayed with the gout, but he entreateth him [the gout] so discourteously as he [the gout] is departed from him [Burghley] till a better opportunity. Belike his Lordship is not at leisure to entertain him now so much as he [Burghley] is now on foot again and cometh abroad.'

There are two memoranda in Burghley's hand about the projected marriage dated March 27th, 1759, among his papers at Hatfield.[16] They are so revealing that they deserve to be quoted in full.

In the first one he weighs carefully the objections against the marriage:

'1. It hath always been adjudged both by private councils and by parliament that the most surety to the Queen's own estate, to the continuance of the public peace of the realm both in times present and times to come, was to have her Majesty marry with some person meet for her contentation and likely to procreate children.

'2. The choice of the person for her own contentation was always left free to her Majesty's self.

'3. The offers and suits to her Majesty for marriage have been in number very many, but yet none hath taken effect, the cause whereof may be diversely conjectured by sundry application of men's judgments, but the very true causes thereof are to be referred to God's will, without imputation to any certain known cause, in a matter ordained of God to the diminution of the worldly felicity of the realm.

'And now, if it so shall please God to incline her Majesty's heart to yield to give ear to the motion of the duke of Alençon and upon sight of him to accept his offer of marriage, it is to be allowed of all good subjects as a marriage ordained by Almighty God.

'And yet, if there shall appear any probable reasons to impugn the marriage as unmeet for her Majesty and her realm, the same ought to stay such as be called to give counsel to her Majesty in this cause to deliver their opinions thereof and not to assent thereto.

'The apparent reasons to dissuade her Majesty from this marriage:

'The first may be gathered upon consideration of her person;

'The next upon consideration of the realm.

'1. It seemeth that her Majesty's years, being about [45] years, may yield occasion to doubt either her conception or her good delivery; and if she should marry and not conceive then her Majesty would be discomfited, her realm not provided of a child to be her successor, and yet the realm charged with her husband during her life.

'2. And if God should grant her readily to conceive and not to have good delivery then the loss of her person, though the child should be living, should be no small detriment to the realm, to suffer the calamities of government under an infant. And if the child also should perish then were the loss to the realm irrecoverable.

'3. There may be also objected the uncertainty of the conditions of her husband, who may be so unpleasant to her Majesty, as both herself and all that love her might have cause to wish that she had never married such a husband, and then the repentance could bring no remedy.

'4. Finally, doubt may be made that the duke of Alençon, finding lack of issue by the Queen's Majesty, whereby he shall lack commodity to enjoy the realm after the Queen's death, [that he] will have a purpose to marry with the Q. of Scots, by whom he may hope to enjoy both England and Scotland.

'The second doubts may be gathered upon consideration of the realm.

'1. First the marriage with a stranger and especially with a prince of power, may procure misliking to the realm for that naturally this realm, as commonly all realms do, mislike not only to have strangers take commodities of the realm but chiefly to have authority to govern.

'2. Secondly, no nation can be more misliked than a prince of France for many respects:

'First, because of ancient enmities betwixt both nations continued by frequent wars.

'Secondly, because in this age it is seen that all the Kings of France, having been the children of Henry and the Q. Catherine, have governed the realm of France with great infelicity and namely have sought by all means, both bloody and otherwise, to extinct [sic] the new [or true] profession of Christ's gospel.

'Thirdly, because this duke of Alençon hath showed himself an enemy to the professors of the gospel in France and therefore most likely to attempt the change of religion in England to the tyranny of Rome.

'Again, the greatest inconvenience to the realm is, if M. d'Alençon should have a son by the Queen's Majesty, the son should, by all likelihood, considering the sickliness and lack of issue by the present king, be king of France and of England also; and thereby the realm of England should lack the continual presence and residence of a king, by reason that the superiority of the French crown would draw the king there most to reside.

'It may be also alleged that, considering her Majesty hath always deferred to assent to marriage and that when she hath yielded to give ear thereto her Majesty did declare that if it were not for the common benefit of her realm whereby, to avoid all dangers depending by reason of the uncertainty of succession after her, she would not marry; therefore, if there might be sufficient provision and assurance made for the stablishing of the succession after her Majesty's time, without her marriage, then all the difficulties depending upon her marriage might be avoided.

'And therefore, it may be thought, if her Majesty had authority by parliament to limit, in time convenient, the right of the crown to persons certain to be capable thereof and to succeed her thereby, the realm might be provided of a successor and so all quarrels might totally be removed in which' (The memo ends abruptly at this point.)

The purpose of the memorandum can only be conjectured. It may well have been the outline of the matter as Burghley presented it to the Privy Council. Or it may have been the first draft of a message to the Queen. The implication will be noted that the only justification for the marriage was the procreation of children, so that the uncertainties about the succession could be dispelled. Burghley's suggestion that an alternative to marriage might be considered in the form of parliamentary action giving the Queen power to appoint her successor, always with the proviso that she would act promptly in the matter, is reminiscent of his long struggle to achieve that solution during the first decade of the reign.

The two main objections to the marriage as Burghley stated them were that the bride was too old and the bridegroom a foreigner and a Catholic. Upon these two points subsequent discussion of the marriage largely turned.

A little later Walsingham was to base his attack upon the match on the grounds that it involved an alliance with a Catholic prince.[17] He still insisted that the only sound foundation for English foreign policy was to regard the Catholic powers as enemies and the Protestants, wherever they were, as allies. And Walsingham expressed the Puritan position. At bottom, therefore, the marriage issue was one aspect of a larger issue in which the old considerations dominant in European diplomacy, dynastic interests and balance of power, were set over against considerations primarily religious. That was the basic issue between Walsingham and Elizabeth, in which Burghley, though a much more zealous Protestant than his mistress, on the whole, and increasingly as he grew older, followed the royal lead.

In a second memorandum of the same March 27th, Burghley undertook to meet some of the objections to the marriage which he himself had raised as follows:

'Answers to the objections against a marriage with M. Alençon.

'It cannot be denied but if her Majesty, when she was younger in years [had married] it had been better for her and the realm also; but considering the proportion of her body, having no impediment of smallness in stature, of largeness in body, nor no sickness, nor lack of natural functions in those things that properly belong to the procreation of children, but contrary wise, by judgment of physicians that know her estate in those things and by the opinion of women, being most acquainted with her Majesty's body in such things as properly appertain, to show probability of her aptness to have children, even at this day. So as for anything that can be gathered from argument, all other things, saving the numbering of her years, do manifestly prove her Majesty to be very apt for procreation of children; and that it is commonly seen that women, being apt to have children, yea having no such natural good proportion in their bodies, have had, and have still, children when they are past the years her Majesty hath. Therefore in that aspect, where so many arguments serve for the purpose and nothing to the contrary but the number of her years, which are not so many but by common course of nature it is generally adjudged that not only she but all other women of her age may have children for the space of v or vi years and sometimes after the same term, it may be thought this objection is not of such weight as to dissuade her marriage which, if God shall please to favour, may be the only cause of blessing of this realm with happiness,[18] and, not being accepted but forborne, must certainly be to the realm cause of more calamities than heart can conceive or pen express.

'And besides the calamity to the realm, it may be by good reasons maintained that by forbearing from marriage her Majesty's own person shall daily be subject to such dolours and infirmities as all physicians do usually impute to womankind for lack of marriage, and specially to such women as naturally have their bodies apt to conceive and procreate children. And to this end were to be remembered the likelihood of her Majesty's pains in her cheek and face to come only of lack of the use of marriage, a thing meeter by physicians to be advertised to her Majesty than otherwise to be set down in writing.'

This is the only significant part of his answers to the objections he himself had raised. He went on to consider the objections to a childless marriage, but he had no answer to make except that if the Queen did marry, 'specially to please God . . . with a mind to have children for the weal of the realm', God should be trusted to take care of the fruitful outcome. Finally, in considering the objections to the bridegroom, he could only say that he was the best of King Henry's offspring, which he admitted was faint praise, but added that Alençon was no prosecutor, that he had zealous Protestants in his entourage, and that La Noue, the distinguished Huguenot soldier, gave good reports of him. In any case, Burghley concluded that the Queen's 'censure and liking shall be the best rule to warrant all other men's judgments that shall not be corrupted with prejudice as not allowing of her Majesty's marriage'.[19]

Burghley's discussion of Elizabeth's fruitfulness is the best thing we have on the subject. Coming from him, who was probably better informed than anyone else, and taken in connection with his persistent efforts to get her married in order that she might have children, it comes near to settling the perennial question of her ability to bear children. Certainly it should weigh heavily in the balance against Ben Jonson's idle chatter and the gossip of foreign ambassadors.[20]

It is not at all clear what the purpose of these memoranda was. They were hardly for the Queen's eye, but they may well have furnished the basis for a 'Memorial for the Queen's Marriage', endorsed and dated March 1578/9 in Burghley's hand. The copy of the memorial at Hatfield may be in Sir Edward Stafford's hand.[21]

The most significant part of what I shall call Stafford's memorial deals with the threat to the Protestant cause by the Queen's marriage to a Catholic. Stafford argued that such a marriage was more likely to benefit than to hinder the common cause of religion. It would establish a sure amity between England and France, would strengthen the position of the French Huguenots, and would present the King of Spain with such a formidable alliance that he would be glad to compose his differences with the Dutch rebels on terms which would secure Protestantism among them. At home the marriage would take away from the English Catholics all hope of promoting the cause of Elizabeth's Catholic competitor, Mary Stuart.

It may be a little rash to assume that this was Burghley's own position in the matter. Considering his rooted antipathy to France, the prospect of an alliance with France must certainly have been a hard morsel for him to swallow. But in the earlier negotiations for a French marriage[22] he had expressed the view that, while he distrusted French good faith in an alliance by treaty, he was quite prepared to endorse a French alliance by marriage. Like most of his contemporaries he attached great significance to family connections.

Simier and a committee of the Privy Council addressed themselves to the terms of the marriage contract. On March 31st, Simier submitted a draft of the proposed treaty in French. Some of his demands were admitted, some denied.[23] The better part of two months was spent on the business. Burghley took a prominent part in it, but the outcome was that practically all matters in controversy were left in suspense pending the outcome of the interview.

Early in April Elizabeth called her principal councillors together to get their views upon the problem presented if she rejected Alençon. Those present besides Burghley were Sussex, Leicester, Hunsdon, Walsingham and Wilson. Burghley spoke at length[24] though it is not quite clear whether he was spokesman for the group or whether he was delivering his personal views.

We have the record of what he said in his own hand, but it is long and tedious. According to his general practice, he addressed himself first to domestic and then to foreign dangers.

In matters domestic he presented his perennial argument which reflected his perennial fear that if Elizabeth did not marry, domestic discontent, the seed ground of rebellion, would gather around Mary Stuart and, fomented and assisted by foreign aid, could hardly be suppressed except at a prohibitive cost. He turned out to be wrong. In the case of the Alençon marriage the Puritans were sure that he was wrong and they anticipated greater danger of the triumph of Roman Catholicism by marriage with a Catholic prince than otherwise. Burghley was careful in addressing the Queen to make much of Mary Stuart and of prohibitive costs.

Regarding the foreign dangers, he argued: 'If her Majesty had issue whereby there were hope of the certainty of succession, or that there were not a known competitor, that is favoured not only by the greatest princes and potentates of Christendom but also by a great number of subjects . . . there needed no more fear of foreign perils than was in the time of Henry VIII, King Edward, yea, or in Queen Mary's time, for that there was a certainty of succession known in the three children of Henry VIII . . . which hope, because it is to end with the Queen's Majesty's refusal of marriage, the perils therefore . . . by no argument can justly be denied.

'First, it cannot be denied that the Pope, the French King, and the King of Spain do and will bear malice to her Majesty for their particular interest and for revenge of injuries, as they suppose, but specially for hurts to them done in aiding their evil subjects both secretly and openly.

'Secondly . . . they shall all for their blind zeal for the restoration of popery and, as they conceive, to suppress heresies, and principally thereby to reduce their own countries into obedience, judge it great wisdom to attempt either a common war by their own joint forces or a great rebellion in England by their support.' He went on to point out that the French Crown, 'by the instigation of the house of Guise', would begin by demanding the release of Mary Stuart which, 'whether it shall be denied or granted must needs turn to the danger of her Majesty'. The Marian faction in Scotland would stir up rebellion, and with some small French support would overthrow the King's party there. The French would also re-continue their old plot to send some small force into Ireland where '. . . with expense of 10,000 crowns they would drive her Majesty to spend 100,000'. Furthermore, if Elizabeth refused Alençon, he might well marry with Spain and 'make enmity between England and the Low Countries'.

And from Spain might grow the like dangers, by further interference in Ireland, and by cutting off English trade both with Spain and the Low Countries, without which England, 'having not otherwise sufficient vent, . . . tumults will follow in clothing countries', a danger aggravated by the development of friction with the Hansa towns.

All this again was in the conventional vein. Burghley had said it many times before and no doubt he was convinced of the truth of it. Certainly he was right in assuming that plots against the Crown, centring around the person of the captive Queen of Scots and supported by English Catholics and 'foreign potentates', would reveal themselves with alarming frequency in the years just ahead. But he miscalculated both the disposition of the English Catholics at large to rebel and the crusading zeal of the Catholic princes. In short, both English Catholics and foreign potentates were much more secularly minded than he believed. In that respect his mistress was wiser than he.

The last part of Burghley's speech dealt with the remedies to be applied, marriage being refused. His proposals in that respect conformed closely to the ideas of Walsingham and the radical Protestants.

At home he advocated: (1) 'To stablish religion sincerely, to comfort the subjects that shall orderly observe the same, to bridle and chastise the contrary by justice; (2) To govern the people with justice indifferently, to forbear to molest them with innovations, with frequent subsidies, with disordered execution of penal laws, for private men's disordered gain and not for public weal. (3) The Queen's Majesty is also to be well furnished aforehand, to maintain her navy upon the seas, to have plenty of provisions for all kind of wars, specially of provisions which must be had from foreign countries, and also to wage [to engage for wages] armies at home to withstand rebellions or foreign invasions, and in like sort there must be means to supply her treasure when it shall be spent, which must be by subsidies, fifteenths and the like, or by sale or mortage of her own lands. (4) Also an act of Parliament to disable any person pretending title to the crown from any right or claim to the same, in case by any of them, directly or indirectly, the Queen be disturbed in her government by any outward act of hostility.'

Abroad, 'there must be means used to continue the inward troubles of the French King and King of Spain, for which purpose there must be some conjunction made with the heads of these factions, and the principal must be to yield them relief of money both for themselves and strangers, namely out of Almayne, where her Majesty is also to conjoin with such princes as profess her religion, the bond of which conjunction must yearly be made by her Majesty of gold or silver, for no other means will tie them to any service.

'Her Majesty also must presently obtain the King of Scots to be at her direction, namely for marriage, which must be had by a yearly support given to himself and rewards to his nobility.

'So that, to conclude with these strangers, the verse will be verified *Querenda pecunia primum: virtus post nummos.*'

In short, Burghley held out to Elizabeth the choice of a marriage alliance with France or a commitment to belligerent Protestantism by sending her navy to the seas, by raising an army, by subsidizing the Huguenots and the Dutch and the King's party in Scotland and by retaining the service of German mercenaries. It would, he believed, cost a good deal of money and the Queen might even have to sell or mortgage some of her lands to meet the charges. Elizabeth did not like to spend money, least of all did she like to spend it in support of the Protestant cause. Burghley, with a great show of impartiality, managed to present the case for marriage in the most attractive terms and the case for the alternative in the most distasteful ones.

We have no further record of the Council meeting to which these words were addressed, no indication of any dissent, of any debate. Presumably what Burghley said was what Elizabeth wanted to hear.

Mary Stuart, the royal prisoner at Chatworth, wrote to her ambassador in Paris on July 4th: 'Leicester and Hatton are married secretly, which hath so offended this Queen that it is thought she hath been led, upon such miscontentment, to agree upon the sight of the duke of Alençon, notwithstanding she hath deferred three whole days with an extreme regret and many tears before she would subscribe the passport, being induced thereunto and almost forced by those that have led this negotiation in despite of the said Leicester.'[25] Mary was wrong about Hatton, who never married. She was right about Leicester. According to Camden,[26] Simier disclosed Leicester's marriage to Elizabeth while she was still wavering about the passport to Alençon. All this is probably true, though there is no mention of it in the dispatches of either the Spanish or the French ambassadors. In any case the passport was signed on the 6th and went off to France in a packet to Sir Amias Paulet on the 7th.[27] It was understood that if marriage did not follow the interview, the friendship of England and France should not be diminished. Walsingham wrote to Burghley early in August:[28] 'It is given out that Monsieur will be here at the time limited, yet her Majesty gives no order for receiving him, . . . it is suspected that between her Majesty and Simier (for few others are acquainted with the cause) it is concluded that he shall come over shortly in secret manner. I am of opinion that the wise men of France will never assent thereto. But matters of love and affection be not guided by wisdom. God send this cause better success than I hope after.'

Walsingham was right. When he wrote, Alençon was already on the way to England. He arrived at Greenwich on August 17th, and left again on the 29th.[29] His presence was kept secret, but both the Spanish and the French ambassadors agreed that he had made a very favourable impression. According to Mendoza, the councillors denied his presence and kept away from the Court in order not to interrupt the 'love dalliance'.[30] But the Acts of Privy Council reveal that the Council met at Greenwich every day during the first five days of Alençon's visit, indeed sat every day but two during his stay in England.[31] Burghley was present at every one of those meetings. It cannot be believed that he never saw Alençon, but there is not a word on the subject from him. Elizabeth evidently intended that the visit should not involve any official action and Burghley was clearly not the man to provide or to participate in the kind of entertainment which his mistress called for.

He had been away in Northamptonshire early in August with Sir Walter Mildmay. On August 9th he wrote from Althorp to Walsingham, partly about Irish affairs, partly about the peace conference assembled by the German Emperor to deal with the struggle in the Low[32] Countries, largely about his immediate business in Northampton.

'I pray you, sir,' he wrote, 'with my hearty commendations, tell Mr. Vice-Chamberlain [Hatton] that Mr. Chancellor [of the Exchequer] and I, on our way to Northampton, mean to survey his house at Holdenby and when we have done to fill our bellies with his meat and sleep also, as the proverb is, our bellies full, all Monday at night. And on Tuesday in the morning we will be at Northampton where, after noon, we mean to hear the babbling matters of the town for the causes of religion, wishing that we may accord them all both in mind and actions. At the least we will draw them to follow one line by the rule of the Queen's Majesty's laws or else to procure the contrariant to feel the sharpness of the same laws.'[33]

The 'babbling matters' had to do with a letter which Burghley and his colleagues received, en route, from the Privy Council, directing them to look into the behaviour of a parson in Northampton and to investigate the report 'that divers of the inhabitants of that town, refusing to conform themselves in matters of religion, do repair to Lillingstone, to Mr. Wentworth's house, and . . . there to receive after another sort'. The Council's letter further instructed them 'to send for the said Mr. Wentworth and to take such order with him for the redressing of that which shall be amiss, as by them shall be thought meet for the taking away of all occasions of dissentions amongst them, so as their Lordships be not hereafter any more troubled therewith'.[34]

Northampton was a hotbed of Puritanism and the Mr. Wentworth in question was none other than Peter Wentworth, one of the most belligerent Puritans in the House of Commons. It was a tall order to wrestle with the non-conformity of such a place and such a fighter. No doubt Burghley and Mildmay followed instructions. Unhappily we have no account of the interview with Wentworth or its consequences. Very likely Burghley was not so tough in dealing with Wentworth as he proposed in his letter to Walsingham. Years later Wentworth cherished the hope that Burghley might be won to the Puritan cause. As for Mildmay, he was a devoted, though a discreet, Puritan, and Wentworth was his brother-in-law. On these grounds we may surmise that the interview was in good temper. We may even surmise that Wentworth was persuaded to pursue a more moderate course. We hear no more of his turbulence until the Parliament of 1587.[35]

The correspondence exchanged between Hatton and Burghley on the subject of his visit to Holdenby throws interesting light upon the architectural relations of Holdenby and Theobalds,[36] two of the most pretentious private mansions in England. When Hatton learned that Burghley intended to visit Holdenby, he wrote:

'I fear me that as your Lordship shall find my house unbuilt and very far from good order, so through the newness you shall find it dampish and full of evil air ... Before God, sir, I take great comfort of your most honourable courtesy to visit your poor friend ... I humbly beseech you, my honourable Lord, for your opinion to the surveyor of such lacks and faults as shall appear to you in this rude building, for as the same is done hitherto in direct observation of your house and plot at Tyball's, so I earnestly pray your Lordship that by your good corrections at this time it may prove as like to the same as it hath ever been meant to be.'[37]

As Burghley was leaving Holdenby he wrote to Hatton:

'Sir, I may not pass out of this good house without thanks on your behalf to God, and on mine to you, nor without memory of her Majesty, to whom it appeareth this goodly, perfect, though not perfected work is consecrated; and all this I do in mind largely conceive, and in writing do mean but to touch, because I am hastened to Northampton and I will reserve matter to enlarge at my return to yourself ... Approaching to the house, being led by a large, long, straight fairway, I found a great magnificence in the front or front pieces of the house and so every part answerable to other, to allure liking. I found no one thing of greater grace than your stately ascent from your hall to your great chamber; and your chambers answerable with largeness and lightsomeness, that truly a Momus could find no fault. I visited all your rooms, high and low, and only the contentation of mine eyes made me forget the infirmity of my legs. And where you were wont to say it was a young Theobalds, truly I like Theobalds as my own, but I confess it is not so good as a model to a work, less than a pattern and no otherwise worthy in any comparison than a foil. God send us long to enjoy Her, for whom we both meant to exceed our purses in these. And so I end with my prayer for her health and thanks humbly for her Majesty's remembrance of me her weak Spirit.'[38]

Burghley's devoted interest in building, and particularly in this building which was modelled on his own house at Theobalds, is apparent here as he hobbled up and down from chamber to chamber, as it is in the three magnificent mansions he built for himself. As in Theobalds, he saw in Holdenby a house designed primarily for the Queen, with a magnificence which taxed heavily the purses of the builders, and as Burghley himself put it, 'a monument of her Majesty's bountifulness to a faithful servant'.

When Burghley got back to Court, Elizabeth was deep in 'love dalliance' with the Duke of Alençon, her frog, as she now called him. It may have been during Alençon's presence in England, certainly it was some time in August, that John Stubbs published his famous diatribe against the French marriage under the title *The Discovery of a Gaping Gulf whereunto England is like to be swallowed by another French Marriage if the Lord forbid not the bans by letting her Majesty see the sin and punishment thereof.* Probably at about the same time Sir Sidney Philip wrote a long letter to the Queen to the same effect.[39] Stubbs spoke with Puritan bluntness. The Queen, he said, was too old to think of marriage, and as for the Duke, he was rotten with debauchery — 'the old serpent himself in the form of a man come a second time to seduce the English Eve and to ruin the English paradise'.[40] Sidney was more discreet. He said nothing about the Queen's age, a little by innuendo about Alençon's personal attributes, much about his nationality, his religion and the 'unhealthiness of his whole race'. 'A Frenchman and a papist . . . The very common people know that he is the son of a Jezebel of our age, that his brother made oblation of his own sister's marriage, the easier to make massacres of our brethren in belief [St. Bartholomew's]; that he himself . . . did sack La Charité and utterly spoiled them [the Huguenots] with fire and sword.' But Sidney's main emphasis was the opposition to the marriage by the English Protestants, 'your chief, if not your sole, strength'.

Sidney, of course, spoke to the Queen's private ear. But Stubbs's pamphlet ran the length and breadth of the kingdom. What was even more disturbing, his sentiments were finding voice in the pulpits. According to the Spanish ambassador, there was talk of action by Parliament and even of popular revolution.[41]

Elizabeth was evidently disturbed, so much disturbed that she found it expedient to defend her position and the character of her suitor in a public proclamation[42] which the Privy Council brought to the attention of the Lord Mayor of London, and a few days later sent out to the bishops to be read in the churches.[43] It was quite apparent that Elizabeth, always sensitive to popular sentiment, began to waver, and many of the Privy Council with her. Burghley himself observed early in October that many councillors who had favoured the match at the beginning were taking the position that it 'could not be but dangerous to religion, unsure to her Majesty and unprofitable to the realm'.[44]

On October 22nd Elizabeth called together at Greenwich those of her Council who had been designated as commissioners in the matter, to discuss the problem. They were Burghley, Sussex, Leicester, Hunsdon, Hatton, Walsingham and Wilson. They held a second meeting on Friday, the 4th, at Westminster, and on the 6th the matter was considered, doubtless by royal direction, by what was almost a full Council. Sir Ralph Sadler and Sir Walter Mildmay were both there, and Clinton, the Lord Admiral, and Sir Francis Knollys, the Treasurer of the

Household, and Sir Thomas Bromley, the Lord Chancellor. For some reason or other, Croft and Warwick were absent. More remarkable was the absence of Walsingham. It may be that during the interval Elizabeth dismissed him from the Court 'as a protector of heretics'.[45] The Council sat again on the 7th. According to the Spanish ambassador they sat on the 7th from eight in the morning until seven at night 'without stirring from the room, having sent the clerks away'.[46] The absence of the clerks may explain the copious notes which Burghley himself took at these conferences.[47] These notes throw all the light available on the details of the debate though they are strongly coloured by Burghley's own bias in favour of the marriage. He appears to have presided. On October 2nd he laid before his colleagues the arguments against and for the marriage.

His picture of the problems which faced the Queen if she did not marry is a grim one. By and large it simply repeats what he had said many times before. In matters domestic his great fear was the continuing uncertainty about the succession, with the danger that, as the Queen grew older, Englishmen would be more and more disposed to look *potius ad orientem quam occidentem solem*, rather to the rising than the setting sun. This phrase, in Latin or in English, crops up again and again. He felt also that without an heir apparent or a recognized heir presumptive the danger that Elizabeth would be assassinated measurably increased. The English Catholics, he believed, would be encouraged to push the claims of Mary Stuart, by fair means or foul, and would enjoy the support of the Pope and the Catholic powers. He feared particularly a recurrence of the Rising of the North in her favour.

Abroad, he recited his old fears of a crusade against Elizabeth, which, he pointed out, was emphasized by the recent invasion of Ireland. He dwelt at length upon the situation in Scotland where the young King was becoming increasingly unfriendly and where the townsfolk, whose shipping had been systematically plundered by English pirates, were fighting mad.

He then asked himself what the Queen should do to deal with these dangers if she did not marry. And here he began by insisting that the laws against religious dissent should be rigidly enforced against the Catholics. He called for 'dire and upright' execution of the law in general and particularly the appointment of 'godly, learned and sufficient men, of qualities both able and devout to execute their offices without partialities by inclining to please men's extraordinary suits and commandments; for the punishment of two notable crimes that do greatly offend her people in general, that is piracies and forgers of false moneys', and 'it is more than needful that penal laws be not dispensed withal for private men's profit, a matter general misliked by all good people and a means to move men to forbear making any more penal laws'. He urged that ill-affected subjects should be kept 'within bonds of law', be deprived of 'office and credit' and generally given 'no countenance of rule in the realm . . . either by her Majesty or by any Councillor'.

He urged a closer watch on Mary Stuart and her friends and suggested that for any conspiracy in her favour 'she should be the first that should suffer for it'.

This catalogue of domestic reforms reveals what Burghley thought to be wrong in the administration — too much laxity in dealing with Catholics, too much corruption in the administration of the law, too much leniency towards pirates and counterfeiters, much too much dispensing of penal laws in favour of individuals and too much power and credit allowed to disaffected subjects. These matters can hardly be considered as relevant to the Queen's marriage. But Burghley seized upon the opportunity to emphasize a few home truths not only for the consideration of the Queen, but also for the admonition of his colleagues, many of whom were conspicuous sinners in these matters.

In dealing with the malice of Catholic powers he argued strongly for the support of Protestant rebels both in the Low Countries and in France; 'of all others [means] none hath been offered so ready and so probable as to aid such as their Kings would oppress for the same quarrel for which they would oppress her Majesty, that is, for their religion'. He suggested a league with the King of Navarre, a sovereign in his own right. He suggested the strengthening of the Queen's forces by land and sea. And, to find the money, he proposed to tap the wealth of the realm, 'which surely aboundeth in riches, as may be seen by the general excess of the people in purchasing, in building, in meat, drink and feastings, and most notably in apparel'.

In suggesting heavier taxation he made a proposal which forecasts the later practice of assigning specific portions of the revenue to specific purposes. 'And to content the people', he observed, 'to yield the greater sums only to serve the public purposes and not to be spent otherwise, it might be devised that the subsidies might be in two sorts, one to be paid to her Majesty to be kept and expended for these purposes, and the other to be in kind only a loan, and that, in every shire, to be committed to the trust of certain chosen persons, not to be spent without certain special causes that might be by law named, and otherwise, after certain years, to be restored to the lenders of other assignees. And if any lawful means could be devised how the same loan, or a portion thereof, might be yearly occupied by some merchants upon good securities, the profit thereof yearly coming might be answered notably to the lenders.'

This is an amazing proposal. The reason suggested for it was that the people would be more willing to pay if they had some guarantee that their taxes would be applied to the purpose for which they were intended. Are we to assume that already under Elizabeth there were discontent at Court extravagance and some reluctance to part with good money for lining the pockets of favourites? We hear little of it at this time. Quite possibly Burghley was speaking for himself. He was a resolute enemy of Court extravagance. His proposal of a reserve fund, created out of money popularly loaned, earmarked for a specific purpose and, if not utilized, returnable to the lenders — in the meantime lent out to merchants at interest, the interest to be distributed pro rata to the lenders — is fantastic, particularly since he had on a former occasion declined to approve legislation authorizing the lending of money on interest.[48] One wonders whether he seriously meant it. One wonders also what Elizabeth's response would have been to these restraints upon her purse.

So far as Scotland was concerned, Burghley proposed that King James should be invited to join the league with the King of Navarre and that he should be generously supported. He suggested that some of the money directed to the maintenance of Mary Queen of Scots might well be diverted to the cultivation of her son.

Burghley's catalogue of all the things which might happen to the Queen if she did not marry, and all the things she would need to do to prevent their happening, weighted the case so heavily for marriage that those who opposed it protested that he was trying to frighten his mistress into marriage.[49]

As the debate progressed, Burghley became increasingly aware that the majority of his colleagues were opposed to the match. Hunsdon and Wilson and, of course, Sussex favoured it, but all the others opposed it.[50] On the concluding day of the debate Burghley played his last card. He undertook to prove to his colleagues that the Queen herself favoured the marriage.[51] Since they all knew that she would in the end decide, and since many of them were naturally disposed to give the kind of advice she wanted, it is to their credit that they declined to make a positive commitment.[52] This was the most that Burghley could wring from them.

On the morning of October 7th, the councillors appointed a committee of four, Burghley, Lincoln, Sussex and Leicester, to deliver their findings to the Queen. Burghley himself was their spokesman. He said that they were not prepared to make any positive recommendation but would reserve judgment until they knew what course she herself wished to follow. He invited her to solicit the opinion of each councillor individually or, if that were too tedious, to direct them either to take a positive position one way or the other, or to drop the matter.

Her reply was a tempestuous one, 'not without shedding of many tears'. She had expected, she said, that they would with one accord urge her to marriage instead of giving such a dusty answer. She blamed herself for submitting the question to them at all, and dismissed them, postponing further discussion until the afternoon. When they came again in the afternoon, she scolded them sharply, particularly because, as she said, they evidently feared that Alençon, being a Catholic, might jeopardize the English religious settlement. She 'did marvel', she continued, 'that any person would think so slenderly of her as that she would not, for God's cause, for herself, her surety and her people, have so strait regard thereto as none ought to make such a doubt as, for it, to forbear marriage and to have the crown settled in her child'.

The committee thereupon reported back to the Council 'her great misliking, and conceiving her earnest disposition for this her marriage ... all the Council accorded upon a new offer to be made to her Majesty of all our assents in furtherance of this marriage if so it shall please her'.

The message was conveyed to her the following day by virtually the whole Council. She did not receive them very graciously, complained again of their critical attitude and wound up by saying that she 'thought not meet to declare to us whether she would marry with Monsieur or no'.[53]

A month later, according to the Spanish ambassador, she called her Council together, 'told them she was determined to marry and that they need say nothing more to her about it but should at once discuss what was necessary for carrying it out'.[53a]

Ten days later she appointed a small committee of the Council, from which Leicester was excluded, to arrange with Simier the terms of marriage. On the 24th they came to a hasty agreement with him, and he left for France the same day.[54]

But Elizabeth kept a door open for escape.[55] Before Simier left, he was obliged to sign a paper suspending the operation of the treaty for two months, during which she would try to win her subjects' approval of the marriage.

Elizabeth, indeed, at the end of the year, seems to have lost her enthusiasm for the match. It does not appear why. Possibly the absence of Simier had something to do with it. In January 1580, Burghley reached the conclusion that the Queen had decided not to marry.[56] He wrote a long letter to his mistress on the subject on January 18th.

It is clear from the first interminable paragraph of the letter that he was still arguing for the marriage.

'So long', he wrote, 'as it appeared to me that it pleased your Majesty to conceive that by your marriage with the duke of Alençon you might procure safety to your person and realm, by your having assured amity of a potent prince abroad and the likelihood of a successor of your own body to pacify all troubles at home; and that thereby all fear of foreign wars and troubling of your state either by open hostility of divers great powers or by the staying of the traffic of your subjects . . . and of all evil troubles either by foreign and evil maintenance of competition . . . or by secret assisting abroad and at home of papists . . . might be avoided; and therewith all such honour and surety might always grow to you . . . and that by this greatness you should rule the sterns of the ship of Europe with more fame than ever came to any Queen of the world; and that your own heart rested contented, pleased and joyed therewith — so long was I in conscience persuaded and in duty bound to advise, further and heartily desire the good and happy success of that marriage, which, in all probable reason, was to induce all those effects. But finding now, in judgment of my own heart, that your Majesty, either of your own disposition or by persuasion of others whom you trust, do not at present hold that mind, I am also even in conscience and duty persuaded to yield to that way that may best please you; not for that I do think it to be the best for you, for with my hands and heart I will defend while I live your marriage to be your only known and likely surety, at home and abroad, as a matter against the which (if it liked yourself) no sound and faithful argument hath been or can be made, nor tru Englishman can command; but because I am so faithfully addicted to your only service as I will spend my blood not only in that which I think to be best for you, but also in any other thing whatsoever yourself would have done for you which you shall take to be good, although in my own heart I be carried in a contrary opinion; and shall be in readiness to defend or bear the burden of the hurt when it cometh, which I have counselled to avoid, than any of those that have given counsel that shall bring the hurt.

'The matter then, being in those terms, that your marriage is broken and no hope left of the good that was thereby expected, it is necessary to foresee and provide, so far as man may, for the perils.'

Burghley then proceeded to outline a course of action which agrees in the main with what he had said earlier on the subject. His enumeration of internal reforms is once again interesting and, since it adds a little to what he had already written on the subject, some of it is worth quoting.

'To avoid the perils of foreign princes' wars against your Majesty and thereby the general subversion of religion, it shall be necessary that your Majesty do presently put your realm in best force for horsemen and footmen and to cause them to be duly mustered and sufficiently furnished; that your navy be presently put in full readiness; that you speedily fortify your necessary havens . . . that you do indeed pluck down presently the strength and government of all your papists and deliver all the strength and government of your realm into the hands of wise, assured and trusting protestants, who should be chosen for their worths and not for the affection of others, and of such persons as ever have depended upon yourself only and not upon the faction of others . . . That you gratify your nobility and the principal persons of your realm to bind them fast to you with such things as heretofore have been cast away upon those that in time of need can serve you to no purpose . . . and that you have some of the protestants in Germany in your pension who may be bound to serve you upon warning in England or elsewhere . . . amongst whom the Count of Emden and one of the Dukes of Brunswick do lie fittest to England and the Duke Casimir fittest for foreign places.

' . . . To avoid the stopping of traffic of your subjects it will be good to seek all vents which you may have by the Low Countries, Emden, Hamburg, all the Swedes, Denmark, Narva, Muscovy, Portugal, Italy, Barbary and Turkey, and if need be to call all strangers hither to carry away the commodities by themselves, whereby it is like that all the traffic shall not be stopped at one time, and some part being left open, the lack of the rest may be the better borne.'

He concluded as follows:

'Thus doth your Majesty see the objections of perils and shows of remedies which I do pray God not to fall out to be shows indeed. Whereas your marriage, if you had liked it, might have provided you more surety with less peril.'

The letter is actually an appeal to Elizabeth to resume the negotiations for the marriage. It reveals indignation against those who had dissuaded her, and once again discloses his feeling that his mistress was wasting on favourites resources which might better be applied to strengthening the loyalty of the nobility — that is of the principal persons of the realm. His concern for the maintenance of foreign trade, even by the encouragement of foreign carriers, becomes an increasingly conspicuous factor in all his considerations for the welfare of the realm.

Another element entered the field of Anglo-French relations at the end of January 1580, 'when God called to his mercy the old Cardinal King of Portugal'. He died of course unmarried. There were many claimants for the succession. Catherine de Medicis herself had a shadowy claim to recognition. In Portugal there were two candidates — Catherine of Braganza, the niece of the late King, and Don Antonio, Prior of Creto, his bastard nephew. Philip II of Spain had, however, the clearest title and was in the strongest position to assert it. In the spring of 1579 Elizabeth had sent Edward Wotton to Portugal[57] to survey the situation. Mendoza, the Spanish ambassador in London, reported that Wotton was carrying presents to Don Antonio and that he had commission to offer English troops. This was probably not true, but clearly enough Elizabeth realized even before the Cardinal King's death that English interests were deeply engaged. The annexation of Portugal to Spain would add the wealth of the Portuguese empire, in Brazil, in Africa and in the Far East, to Spanish strength and make Philip's position, as it appeared, overwhelmingly strong.

The French Crown was of the same way of thinking, and it is not unlikely that the Portuguese problem emphasized the necessity of joint action against Spain and stimulated interest on both sides of the Channel in the Alençon match. Not long after Alençon's brief visit to England in August 1579, Elizabeth had some words with Mendoza on the subject. She told him that she knew his master had designs upon Portugal and was raising large armies to that end.[58] Mendoza replied that, if that were indeed so, his master would merely be asserting just claims. She replied that everybody did not agree about that and that there were those at hand who would very effectively maintain the contrary.

Henry Cobham, the English ambassador at Paris, reported the death of the King of Portugal on February 23rd. A fortnight later he sent dispatches to Burghley, delivered by the Portuguese ambassador in Paris, from Catherine of Braganza to Elizabeth, seeking support in her claims to the Portuguese throne.[59]

Burghley replied on the 15th.[60] The Queen, he wrote, had confided the Portuguese dispatches to no one but himself, and she had directed him to write to Cobham 'secretly and with speed'. He was to seek an interview with the King of France and his mother and deliver a message to them from Elizabeth. He was to say that she was surprised that she had not heard from them on the Portuguese situation, 'knowing that in good reason such augmentation of riches and strength to the King of Spain ought to move all his neighbours to doubt the sequel thereof'. She had been informed that the Duchess of Braganza was 'universally taken to be the next lawful heir of the Portuguese throne'. In view of the close friendship between England and France, she ventured 'to open the secrets of her mind' to them, especially since they were both equally affected. She proposed, 'although somewhat late, yet better a little late than never', that they should give the matter serious consideration. She wanted to know how they felt about it. Though she had no concrete proposals to make, she was convinced that 'if the King of Spain shall enjoy the kingdom of Portugal he shall have power to give law both to land and sea and shall govern the navigation and trade of Christendom, and shall in time adventure to command what he will list to his neighbours'.

Cobham received Burghley's letter on March 20th, and conferrred with the French King the following day. He discovered great interest but a reluctance to make commitments. The King wanted to know what Elizabeth proposed.[61] During

April, if Mendoza is to be believed, the French ambassador pressed Elizabeth to join with France in declaring immediate war on Spain, and Burghley conferred with him at length on the subject.

But there for a season the matter rested. Elizabeth apparently did not even reply to the Duchess of Braganza's letter,[62] and Philip's armies, under the Duke of Alva, presently occupied Portugal. What little resistance was offered to Alva's Italian veterans was led by Don Antonio. He finally abandoned the struggle, took refuge in France and for some years to come tried to secure French and English assistance in the recovery of his lost kingdom.

It is conceivable, as Burghley himself hinted in his letter to Cobham, that if England and France had acted in time, they might have saved Portugal from Spain. It had been abundantly clear, when the Cardinal King had succeeded to the throne, that he had not long to live and that at his death Philip II would be the strongest claimant to the succession. Philip himself began preparations for the event at once, but his neighbours did nothing effective, nothing more than 'to view with alarm', though they had eighteen months' warning.

Probably there was nothing they could do. France at the critical juncture found herself once again plunged in civil war. The French called it 'La Guerre des Amoureux', and the issues at stake proceeded rather from Court intrigues than from religious conflict. Many Huguenots, indeed, refused to participate. The leaders were Henry of Navarre, and his brother, the Prince of Condé. At the siege of Cahors in May 1580, Navarre, then twenty-six years of age, hitherto remarkable for his wit and his wantonness at the French Court, first revealed those qualities of courage and audacity and flair for leadership which were to make him one of the great soldiers of France. Condé meanwhile had fled to Germany, intending to raise a mercenary army. On June 15th, Cobham wrote to Elizabeth that Condé intended to come to England. He arrived on the 19th. According to Mendoza, he brought an agent of Duke Casimir with him and probably was seeking financial assistance to raise German mercenaries. The Queen received him at first privately,[63] though she told the French ambassador that she had declined to see Condé except in his presence.

We have an account of the matter in a letter which Burghley wrote to Sussex:

'I came yesterday hither [from Theobalds to Nonesuch] about six of the clock, and repairing towards the privy chamber to have seen her Majesty, I found the door to the upper end of the presence chamber shut and then understood that the French ambassador had been a long time with her Majesty and the prince of Condé also, where there were none other of the Council but my Lord of Leicester and Mr. Vice-Chamberlain [Hatton], Mr. Secty. Walsingham being sick in his chamber. And so about seven of the clock, the French ambassador being ready to depart towards London, came to me and told me a great part of their proceedings, being pleased well with her Majesty for her temperate dealings but no wise contented with the prince of Condé, in whom he findeth more disposition to move troubles in France than to enjoy peace, and he addeth that he verily thinketh that those troubles in France and the prince's coming hither are provoked from hence;

wherein I know nothing of certainty, but should be sorry it should be so in truth. Nevertheless [he] augmenteth his suspicions upon the sight he hath of the great favours showed to the prince of Condé by certain Councillors here, whom he understandeth hath been many times both on Friday and Saturday with him at the banquetting house where he is lodged.

'Yesternight [June 25th] late in the evening, her Majesty told me of her dealing with the ambassador and the prince, wherein she commended the prince's modesty in declaring the cause of his coming to her ... By her Majesty I perceive his just cause of coming is for money, in this sort, that is after this rate to be borne, viz., a part by the king of Navarre and his part, another by the Duke Casimir and certain princes protestant and a third to be required from her Majesty.

'What they may prove I know not. I wish her Majesty might spent some portion to solicit from them some peace to the good of the cause of religion. But to enter into a war and therewith to break the marriage, and so to be left alone as subject to the burden of such a war, I think no good Councillor can allow.

'It is likely that the prince shall depart tomorrow by sea to Flushing ... I think he will now ... visit the Prince of Orange.

'Thus your Lordship hath all my knowledge. Her Majesty removeth on Tuesday, which day I mean to be at Westminster if I may.'[64]

Sussex replied on July 1st, from his home in Essex:[65]

'I have never heard word from my Lord of Leicester, Mr. Vice-Chamberlain or Mr. Secty. Walsingham of the coming of the prince of Condé or of his negotiations, nor to seek to know my opinion what I thought fit to do in his causes, whereby I see either they seek to keep the whole from me or else care little for my opinion, or will wrest the prince [of Condé] and the rest of that sort to think I am no friend to their cause ... By such little knowledge as I gather from some of my friends, I do find there is a hope gathered to bring the Queen to yield to the Prince's requests hastily that, having accorded with him before any answer be returned of Mr. Stafford's negotiations [with Alençon], it might be a hindrance to anything that might fall out good by that answer ... If (before she see the end of Stafford's dealings and be informed from the king what he will do for the peace) she should enter into the giving of any aid that might assist the wars, it should not only overthrow all Monsieur's intentions, but also shut up wholly all means for peace and lay the wars fully open, whereof she must be the head and in the end is not able to bear the charge — unto which I would not wish her Majesty to enter until she were driven unto it by Monsieur's refusing of the marriage and the king's refusing of the peace; which, if the matter be well handled, I think they will never do.'

It is obvious from this exchange of letters that Sussex believed and Burghley shrewdly suspected that those who opposed the marriage wished to break it off by supporting civil wars in France. In any case Condé got nothing but fair words.[66]

Two days before the letter just cited, Sussex wrote to Burghley a letter which contains one of the finest tributes ever paid to him. The occasion of the letter

H

was to express thanks for a kindly letter which Burghley had written to Lady Sussex when she was seriously ill.[67] 'I have seen a letter', Sussex wrote, 'which it pleased your Lordship most honourably and kindly to write to my wife, greatly to her comfort when she was greatly grieved, for the which I do think myself more bound to your Lordship than I can write, and so I beseech you to conceive, and therewith to make certain account that both she and I do love, honour and reverence you as a father[68] and will do you all service we can, as far as any child you have, with heart and hand, and so pray you to dispose of us both. The true fear of God which your actions have always showed to be in your heart, the great and deep care which you have always had for the honour and safety of the Queen's Majesty's most worthy person, the continual trouble which you have of long time taken for the benefitting of the commonwealth and the upright course which you have always taken, respecting the matter, and not the person, in all causes (which be the necessary fruits of him that feareth God, truly serveth his sovereign faithfully and loveth his country dearly) have tied me to your Lordship in that knot which no worldly frailty can break. And therefore I will never forbear to run any fortune that may serve you and further your honourable dealings in these your Godly actions.'[69]

Sussex was not given to flattery. He was one of the most upright men at Court and one of the most loyal friends. It will be recalled how staunchly he had stood by the Duke of Norfolk[70] ten years before. His steady support of Burghley is one of the constant factors in the shifting atmosphere of the Court and his untimely death in 1583 robbed Burghley of the one man close to the Queen who served as a counterpoise to Leicester.

No doubt Burghley and Sussex together thwarted the immediate hopes of Condé. Nevertheless, the civil wars in France had a deterrent effect upon the marriage negotiations, or at least Elizabeth used it as an excuse for further postponement. Late in July Mauvissière, the French ambassador, wrote that at dinner with good friends of the marriage Burghley and Sussex both told him that they could not advise the Queen to marry until the French Crown came to terms with the Huguenots. Burghley, whom Mauvissière designated as the first and greatest councillor of the kingdom, declared that if the French King made peace, the marriage could be taken as assured. The Queen, he said, had shown him her correspondence with the Duke and convinced him that her affections were completely engaged. But we must take this with a grain of salt. Burghley was far from certain, though he was clearly out of patience with Elizabeth's backing and filling. Mendoza reported a conversation between him and his mistress earlier. ' "My Lord," she said, "here I am between Scylla and Charybdis. Alençon has agreed to all the terms I sent him and he is asking me to tell him when I wish him to come and marry me. If I do not marry him I do not know whether he will remain friendly with me, and if I do I shall not be able to govern the country with the freedom and security that I have hitherto enjoyed" . . . Cecil replied that if it were her pleasure to marry she should do so as no harm could come to the country thereby . . . but if she did not intend to marry she ought to disabuse

Alençon at once. She replied, "That is not the opinion of the rest of the Council, but that I should keep him in correspondence." Cecil answered that he had always heard that they who tricked princes were tricked themselves.'[71] He underrated her capacity. The ticklish game of keeping her French suitor 'in correspondence' was the game which she elected to play. It is hardly likely that Alençon was deceived, but he had his own fish to fry, and the fact that the Queen of England might marry him was an asset of no mean proportions in the frying of them.

Though he had withdrawn from the Low Countries two years before, he still maintained an agent there and still cherished ambitions there. Meanwhile, the fortunes of the Dutch rebels had gone from bad to worse. The Pacification of Ghent proved to be a hollow truce and the Prince of Orange's idea of settling religious differences by mutual toleration far too broad-minded to appeal to the rank partisans for whom it was drawn.[72] The outcome was the formation in January 1579 of two unions, one of the Catholic malcontents at Arras, the other of the northern Protestant provinces at Utrecht. Five months later the Catholic confederacy was formally reconciled with Spain, and the seven northern provinces were left alone to maintain the war against Philip II.

The situation, grave as it was, was aggravated by the very conspicuous ability of the new Spanish Regent, Alexander of Parma. His vigorous campaigning in the spring and summer of 1579 revealed the fact that the Dutch rebels were not strong enough to hold their own against him. Orange therefore turned once more to foreign aid. He had abandoned hope of England. In May 1579 Elizabeth had recalled William Davison, her agent at Antwerp, and had sent no successor. The one alternative was Alençon, and in June 1579 the Estates General once more approached him. Negotiations were opened, and continued through the autumn of 1579 and the spring of 1580. In May of that year they had reached the point that deputies from the Dutch went to France to deal with Alençon in person.

Elizabeth was disturbed. On July 10th she called some members of her Council to a meeting at Nonesuch to consider the situation. Those attending were Bromley, the Lord Chancellor, Burghley, Sussex, Leicester, Hatton and Walsingham — the inner ring of the Council. Thomas Wilkes, one of the clerks of the Council, who had earlier been extensively employed in French affairs, appears to have been invited to express his views on the subject.[73]

Burghley presided and presented the problem at length.[74]

The Prince of Orange and the Estates of the Low Countries were, he pointed out, about to offer the sovereignty of the Low Countries to the Duke of Alençon. The Duke would probably accept the offer and would probably be supported by his brother, the King of France. In that event the Low Countries would inevitably, sooner or later, be annexed to the French Crown.

For England this would mean the weakening of the old Burgundian alliance. It would also mean that France, being in control of the Dutch seaports, would command the Narrow Seas and the foreign trade of England.

Alençon was in treaty for marriage with the Queen. He had made great progress and only awaited her consent to send commissioners to conclude the match. She had urged postponement but he was resolute to send the commissioners on August 15th.

There were great military preparations in France — by the King to attack the Huguenots, by the King of Navarre to defend them, by Alençon to invade the Low Countries. Since Alençon had been delegated by both sides in the civil wars to arrange a peace, it was probable that civil peace would be arranged and the military resources of France made available for Alençon's purposes.

The fighting strength of the Low Countries was divided in twain. In the south and west the malcontents had returned to the Spanish obedience, accepting the Roman religion and the sovereignty of Philip II on condition that their ancient liberties should be restored. They were very strong among the nobility, though the party of Orange commanded most of the large towns. Since the malcontents had behind them the strength of Spain, they had forced the opposition, led by the Prince of Orange, to seek French aid.

It was said that the old Duchess of Parma, Alexander of Parma's mother, who had been Spanish Regent in the Low Countries years before, would return with power to settle all differences.[75] But the Dutch thought that it was merely a device to delay the treaty with Alençon.

Burghley went on to point out that it would be fruitless to propose any settlement between the combatants except on the basis of religious toleration. Elizabeth's own disposition to ignore religious issues he ruled out in unequivocal terms. 'The prince of Orange and his party, professing their religion against the Pope, cannot and will not accept any conditions of accord with the king of Spain, nor will they submit to M. de Anjou [Alençon] save with very great assurance of continuing free for ever in their religion. For upon that point almost only stands the difficulty of peace betwixt the King and them and between the Malcontents and them.'

These as Burghley saw them were the factors in the problem. Having set them forth he turned to consider what should be done about it.

He suggested alternatives. In the first place he believed that if Elizabeth would give to the Dutch substantial assistance in men or money or both they would prefer her protection to that of France. He believed also that the English Parliament would willingly support the charges involved. He suggested that, if the Queen favoured this course, she should send an envoy to the Prince at once, with promise of 'reasonable' immediate aid. At the same time an agent should go off to Spain to point out once again the threat of French occupation, to announce that she intended to resist it, and to make clear to the Spanish King that if he would offer peace on the basis of religious toleration she was assured that they would return to their obedience. She might even offer to compel them. Finally she would send someone with all speed to Alençon, remind him of his promise to make no treaty with the Dutch without consulting her and point out that, if he did so, her subjects of all faiths would force her to abandon all thought of marriage with him. It might well be that a way would be found to reconcile his ambitions in the Low Countries with the marriage. But that would have to be worked out.

In a final paragraph, Burghley reverted once more to the policy of direct aid to the Dutch. If it were adopted, he expressed the opinion that 'the burden and sequel thereof must belong to the whole body of the realm'. Since Parliament could not be assembled before August and since time was of the essence, he suggested that Elizabeth, besides her ordinary Privy Council, should send for some special noblemen and some chief men of the House of Commons to impart the matter beforehand 'that it might not be said that so great a cause, belonging to the whole realm, is either taken in hand or left by the advice of a few'.

It is not easy to determine what course of action Burghley favoured. He emphasized direct aid but in terms which contemplated an expensive war, and preliminary consultation with the principal men of the kingdom. He can hardly have expected Elizabeth to have approved either of the war or of the referendum. Nor can he have been hopeful that Philip II would accept any settlement which involved religious toleration. Probably he still favoured the marriage, though he foresaw that England at large would oppose a marriage which would commit England to a war in the Low Countries on behalf of the heir presumptive to the French throne. One of the cardinal principles in his foreign policy was to prevent French annexation of the Low Countries. One of the cardinal principles of his domestic policy was to get the Queen married and pregnant. So far as the marriage was concerned, he must have realized that, considering the Queen's age, it had to be Alençon or no one. In short, he saw insuperable objections to any of the courses which he considered.

We hear no more of this Council meeting. There is no record of any debate or any resolution. Elizabeth's immediate response was to send Davison to the Prince of Orange,[76] and it seems not unlikely that Burghley's draft of instructions for someone to be sent to the Low Countries was intended for Davison's guidance. If so, then the sum and substance of his mission was to scold the Dutch for their ingratitude and to chide Alençon for negotiating with them without her advice and consent.[77] But Davison did not go, and no one was sent to Spain, and the Queen's procrastinating policy prevailed — to hold Alençon 'in correspondence', cultivate the good will of the French Crown, and let events in the Low Countries take their course.

As for Alençon, he went forward with his negotiations with the Dutch. In September he sent her a copy of their offers. She expressed no disapproval, and the Treaty of Plessis le Tours, by which he became sovereign of the Low Countries, passed her almost unnoticed.

The most probable explanation of her attitude was her increasing fear of Spain. The immediate danger as she saw it was the re-establishment of the Guises in France and joint action by the two powers against her. At the moment it seemed more important to involve the French Crown, through the heir presumptive, in war with Spain over the Low Countries than to guard against the ultimate menace of a union of the Low Countries with France.

Her fear of Spain was accentuated by the uprising in Ireland, assisted by a military expedition organized and dispatched by the Pope. It was accentuated also by developments in Scotland and particularly by the arrival there of Esmé Stuart, Seigneur d'Aubigny, an agent of the Duke of Guise.

While Elizabeth had been playing her cat-and-mouse game with Alençon, the situation in Scotland had rapidly deteriorated. The Regent Morton, who had held the reins of power since November 1572, ruled Scotland with a firm hand. Whatever his shortcomings, and they were many and various, he kept the peace in the north, even to the border side, and gave Scotland a measure of internal prosperity which amazed foreign observers. His disposition towards Elizabeth was friendly in the extreme, and he posed as being entirely at her command. But those who knew him best remarked that he had a fine eye for the main chance and could only be depended upon to follow English lead so long as he saw no more advantageous alternative.

Ever since he became Regent he had urged Elizabeth to enter into a defensive league with Scotland and to secure her party there by a judicious distribution of pensions. When the matter was first broached, Henry Killigrew, Burghley's brother-in-law, observed that it would cost the Queen no more than £1200 a year and would 'keep the country at her devotion'. The Privy Council at large favoured such a course of action. Walsingham in particular strongly favoured it and fought hard for it. 'For the love of God, Madam,' he wrote to Elizabeth in January 1575, 'let not the cure of your diseased estate hang any longer in deliberation ... Whatever account is made of him [Morton], there is no man of judgment that loveth your Majesty that can imagine any peril can befall upon you so great as the loss of that gentleman, either by death or alienation.'[78]

We hear almost nothing from Burghley on the subject, though one or two letters which survive from him to Walsingham indicate that he accorded with the Secretary's views. 'I did yesterday', he wrote on April 11th, 1575, 'show the Queen's Majesty the Regent's letters to you. Whereupon, Mr. Secretary Smith being present, there was great and long talk for satisfying of the Regent. But I fear there will be more smoke arise than fire. And yet I wish you would advertise her Majesty of the things contained in your letter to me.'[79]

It was in this same letter that Burghley wrote the passage already quoted in another connection: 'If my ability was, I would gladly help the plough with you either in the ridge or furrow until I had the yoke pulled off from my neck.'

But apart from this we hear little of his participation in Scottish affairs. The Scottish Regent exchanged letters with him, though we only have Morton's side of the correspondence, and on one occasion sent a present of hunting hawks. And the various English agents who went to Scotland, particularly Killigrew, his brother-in-law, wrote to him occasionally. They had found out, as everyone else in the Queen's service was to find out, that it was never safe to ignore the Lord Treasurer, even when he appeared to be a sick old man in retirement. No doubt he kept in touch with the situation, but Walsingham handled all the details. As long as peace reigned north of the border, Burghley's part, if we dare argue *ex silentio*, was a passive one. Actually his activities in external affairs seem to have been limited to periods of crises — when foreign situations became really serious the Queen called upon him. Otherwise, he tended to play the part of an interested spectator, holding a watching brief for the Queen. This was notably the case during the relatively placid period in Scotland between the capture of Edinburgh from the Castilians in 1573 and the summer of 1577.

In July of that year Robert Bowes, the Queen's Treasurer at Berwick, wrote to Burghley that the factions in Scotland opposed to Morton were joining together against him. At about the same time there were indications that the French King was beginning to interest himself in the situation.[80] Late in August, Walsingham wrote to Burghley that he found the Queen 'inclined to assure Scotland to her by pensions', though he feared that it would be too little, too late. Ten days later Bowes was dispatched to Scotland 'to break the purpose of such as seek the overthrow of his [Morton's] government'. But Bowes accomplished little or nothing, and in February of the following year Thomas Randolph, an old expert on Scottish affairs, was dispatched. 'You may make account', Walsingham wrote to him, 'that her Majesty will not stick at money considering how much it standeth her upon to assure Scotland unto her.' But by the time Randolph arrived the intrigues against Morton had gone too far to be stopped. On March 4th young James, then in his thirteenth year, announced his intention to assume the government in his own name and dismissed Morton.

Actually in little over a month Morton had recovered his position, if not as Regent at any rate as the dominant figure in the royal Council. Early in July he dispatched an ambassador, the Commendator of Dunfermline, to Elizabeth. It was in this connection that Burghley wrote the letter already quoted to Randolph who, with Dunfermline, was on his way to confer with the Queen, inviting them both to dinner.[81] Burghley added that Lord Hunsdon was to be present and that Elizabeth approved.

The presence at the dinner of Lord Hunsdon, Warden of the East Marches, Governor of Berwick and commander of the most considerable force along the Scottish border, is significant; and the fact that the Queen meant to confer with the Scottish ambassador at Standen, the magnificent residence of Sir Ralph Sadler, is also significant. Sir Ralph was the oldest and trustiest of all Elizabeth's counsellors on Scottish affairs. But the most interesting fact about the letter is that it reveals Burghley as taking an active part in the dealings with Scotland. His allusion to the Queen's consent may be taken to mean by royal command. Possibly Walsingham's absence from the Court on mission to the Low Countries had something to do with it. But it cannot be accidental that the official dispatches of English agents from Scotland, from 1577 onwards for the next four years, are addressed jointly to Burghley and Walsingham, even after Walsingham's return to court.[82]

Dunfermline did not have easy going. Burghley wrote to Walsingham on July 29th:

'We have much ado to bring her Majesty to accept such offers from the Scottish king and his nobles to commit themselves to the protection of her Majesty which all other kings of this realm hath sought by all means, both fair and foul, and never could attain the same. A strange thing it is to see God's goodness so abundantly offered from her Majesty's surety to be so daintily hearkened unto. Yet I trust her Majesty will not reject such a singular favour of God. I am sorry to write thus incompletely to you, but indeed the abundance of grief will not suffer my hand to stay.'[83]

Elizabeth did in fact, in conference with Dunfermline, acquiesce in his proposal for a league,[84] but she rejected his proposal for Scottish pensions and she declined to admit the claims of the Scottish King to the Lennox estates in England which arose by reason of the death of James's grandmother, Margaret, the Countess of Lennox.[85]

Walsingham concluded, when he heard that Dunfermline had been dismissed 'with such evil satisfaction', that the Scots, 'though the matter may be patched up for a time', would now take another course for their safety and not depend 'upon those whom they think do make little account of them'.[86]

Burghley's comment, later in August, is in the same vein. He wrote to Walsingham on the 31st: 'We of her Council are forced greatly to offend her in . . . Scottish matters, which do keep a tolerable course more by our particular fair overtures than by good matter, which, without her Majesty's royal assent, we cannot deliver to them. And so I fear they will espy our weakness and for mistrust will take some better anchor hold. God be merciful to us and direct her Majesty's heart to embrace things best for herself.'[87]

Burghley, like Walsingham, felt the need of dealing promptly and generously with the friends of England in Scotland at this juncture, but Elizabeth was for temporizing. She had no mind to spend money. She had just committed herself, much against her will, to a large loan to the Dutch rebels. Besides, she was, by tacit agreement with France, more or less committed to a neutral position in Scottish internal affairs. The parties in Scotland were so equally divided that it was no longer easy to maintain that the English party there was the nation and its opponents were a mere handful of rebels. If she intervened vigorously on behalf of Morton, the French King, with something like equal justice, might intervene in support of his opponents. She therefore preferred to keep the good will of both parties and to offer her mediation to bring them to agreement.

So the matter rested, with little apparent change in the relations between Scotland and England for almost a year. And then suddenly the danger which Burghley and Walsingham had both anticipated came from the quarter out of which it had long been expected. On September 8th, 1579, Esmé Stuart, Seigneur D'Aubigny, landed in Scotland. It may be that young James had summoned him, but he came at the instigation of the Guises in France and as their agent. He was handsome, accomplished and courtly. After a youth spent among dour Presbyterian preceptors, James more than welcomed his sprightly French cousin, and d'Aubigny had hardly been a month in Scotland before he was a force to be reckoned with in political affairs.

His steady rise to power in Scotland — his creation as Earl of Lennox,[88] his pretended conversion to Protestantism — all took place within a year. He gave countenance and support to the enemies of Morton and was largely instrumental in his imprisonment, charged with conspiracy in the murder of the King's father. Elizabeth sent agents to Scotland, sometimes Robert Bowes, sometimes Thomas Randolph, to support Morton, but he had lost faith in her promises. It seems likely that both Bowes and Randolph participated in conspiracies against d'Aubigny, though they denied it. When Elizabeth learned that he had possessed himself of Dumbarton Castle, she suggested 'the laying of violent hands upon him and his associates'.[89] And when she heard of Morton's imprisonment, she directed the Earl of Huntingdon, President of the Council of the North, to levy 2500 troops and sent Lord Hunsdon north to take command of them. Randolph opposed the use of force, but Hunsdon favoured it. Walsingham's letter to Randolph of March 18th, 1581,[90] gives us all that we know about the attitude of the Privy Council. He wrote: 'Such of her Majesty's Council as have been made acquainted with the causes, seeing no likelihood that d'Aubigny should ever be won to be at her Majesty's devotion, especially considering how her Majesty hath of late sought every manner of way to disgrace him, and finding by many probabilities that his intent is to match the king either with Spain or some other of those princes that are not the best affected to this crown, whose assistance, joined with those that are aliened from us in that realm, cannot in time to come but be most perilous to her Majesty, when the quarrel will be not for matters of border but for the right of this crown, are therefore of opinion that it were better for us to deal with them now, being weak, having neither money nor munitions, than to attend the fruit of their malice when they shall be assisted by the arm of both Spain and France, besides a party it is to be doubted will be found here.'

Presumably Burghley agreed. We have not a word from him on the subject.

But Elizabeth, always reluctant to engage in war, was more disposed to explore Randolph's peaceful alternatives. While she hesitated, a conspiracy of Morton's friends which was to furnish the *pied à terre* for Hunsdon's invasion, was discovered and the opportunity lost.

Elizabeth's opposition to armed intervention was based in large measure upon her reluctance to offend the French. The strengthening of the frontiers had called forth the protests of the French ambassador, who went to Burghley about it.[91] At this time he regarded Burghley as the best friend of France at Court. Burghley hastened to reassure him. The Queen, he said, ought not to and would not do anything in Scotland calculated to offend the French King or to hurt the young James. She loved him as a son and had no other wish than to keep him safe in Scotland. The difficulty, as he saw it, was that the Scots were neither good Frenchmen nor good Englishmen. They had become altogether Spanish, and the Spanish King himself had plans afoot to convey James to Spain, under the pretext of marrying him to one of the Spanish royal princesses. The Queen, he said, was determined at all costs to prevent this, and he made no doubt that the French King would agree that it should be prevented.

Later Mauvissière interviewed the Queen herself, and protested that the French

King would be much offended if she invaded Scotland. She replied that she would do nothing to offend him, that the strengthening of her forces on the borders was in reply to the building up of Scottish forces there. Reiterating what Burghley had said, she referred to the Spanish menace. She had heard, she said, that Philip II had plans to convey young James to Spain. She had even heard that Philip, having recently lost his wife, intended to marry Mary Stuart. If she were forced to intervene to prevent two such calamities, she would keep her French brother informed of her proceedings.

It will be remarked that both the Queen and her minister, ignoring the well-known connection of d'Aubigny and the Duke of Guise, placed the blame for Scottish troubles upon Spain. In any case, Hunsdon did not invade, his troops were reduced to 500 men, and Morton was left to his fate. Young James is reported to have said that the English might have Morton's body but he meant to keep the head. His trial and conviction followed, and in June he went to the block.

Quite possibly had Elizabeth acted in time she might have saved him. It is, however, absurd to make him out as a martyr to her interests. He had never been popular with the Scottish nobles, and he alienated the Scottish clergy by his rapacity and the young James by his forbidding ways. Even Randolph, the ablest of all English intriguers in Scotland, could not, by hook or crook, find him enough supporters to give him a fighting chance. Nevertheless, by his death Elizabeth lost a strong and useful friend. In the midsummer of 1581 this much was certain — that with Morton gone, his friends dispersed and d'Aubigny in the saddle, the postern gate of England was again wide open to the Queen's enemies.

CHAPTER XIII

THE JESUIT MENACE, 1570-83

BURGHLEY was disturbed by the developing situation in Scotland. He was even more disturbed by the revival of the Roman Catholic menace at home. During the first decade of Elizabeth's reign the fear of a Catholic rebellion had hung over him like a cloud and had been a potent factor in all his planning. His fears had been realized by the Rising of the North in 1569. But they had been at the same time allayed by its complete failure.

The publication of the bull of excommunication in 1570 and the subsequent development of the Ridolfi Plot had called forth from him in April 1572 an appraisal of the royal policy towards the Catholics.

He had complained that the Queen had been too favourable to them, too critical of those who were good Protestants; that in consequence the Catholics had increased both in the towns and in the counties. In thirteen years of government, he had declared, the strength of her supporters in religion had rather diminished than increased, that all had gone reasonably well during the first ten years of her reign, but that after the publication of the papal bull the Catholics had regained more than they had lost.[1]

Four years later, arguing in support of the Dutch rebels, he had envisaged the dangers of a Catholic uprising if Philip of Spain undertook to invade England. 'To increase the fire the greater', he had written, 'shall be ready the solicitations and offers of all English men in exile, either as rebels or discontented persons for religion or otherwise, who, having great numbers of friends and favour[er]s now secretly in England, will put out their horns boldly, when they shall find an external mighty power ready for their defence. Then shall her Majesty be driven to try the dutifulness of her good subjects, whereof she shall find a plenty of persons well willing, but in power and riches not equal to the discontented, having comfort of a foreign power.'

In another memorandum on the same subject the following year he had written:[2] 'There is no doubt but money and his [Philip II's] comfort may raise more lewd people than will easily be subdued, considering of what sorts the numbers may be compounded, as of papists, of dissatisfied persons, of needy persons that have wasted themselves, of atheists, of persons affected to the King of Spain and the English rebels now outlawed and of idle people out of work by reason of the stay of trade.'

What really disturbed Burghley was not so much the strength of Catholicism among the masses as its strength and power among the gentry and the well to do. He considered this aspect of the matter in 1579 when the Alençon marriage project was afoot and he was pointing out what Elizabeth had better do if she rejected the security offered by the French marriage.

'If', he wrote, 'Her Majesty will continue zealous of God's true honour, and maintain earnestly the laws established for religion and increase the losing [i.e. the penalty] of the same laws as by experience is found needful . . . by reason of the daily bold obstinacy of the papists in the realm, who find the laws very weak against them, then it is to be thought that the number of her devout subjects will continue and increase . . . and the contrary part shall daily diminish and either amend for fear or at the least not be able or not dare to comfort others, their friends, nor yet to relieve the rebels as now they commonly do.'[3]

He put this more succinctly in another memorandum of the same time in which he listed, in one column the 'Perils', in a parallel column the 'Remedies', as follows:

Perils	Remedies
Comfort of Obstinate Papists.	Penalties increased upon Recusants.

And again:[4] 'The keeping under the bonds of law the evil contented subjects for religion or faith is the best bridle to stay them from dangers; and as cause shall seem good, to leave them without power by offices and credit amongst the people, or by possessing of any quantity of arms offensive, and to make them bear equal burdens out of their purses with other good subjects in all causes of charge for public services for the realm and generally to give no countenance of rule in the realm to any such, either by her Majesty or by any Councillor, shall be a very good way to cut off the hope that rebels abroad or enemies shall have to gain a party here within the realm.'

In a letter which he wrote to the Queen early in the following year (1580) he touched again upon the necessity of getting the papists out of power, enumerating among other measures of security, 'that you do indeed pluck down presently the strength and government of all your papists and deliver all the strength and government of your realm into the hands of wise, assured and trusty Protestants, who shall be chosen by their worths and not for the affection of others, and of such persons as ever have depended upon yourself only and not upon the fashion of others'.[5]

Burghley was, if anyone was except the Queen, the prime factor in the definition of the official policy of the government towards the Church and its opponents. But he had to work within the frame of reference of the royal will. Generally speaking, his problem with the Queen was to temper her asperity towards the Puritans and to quicken her hostility towards the Catholics. Most of his memoranda on these subjects, since they were either addressed to her or intended for her, minimized the case against the Puritans and exaggerated the case against the Catholics. It is never safe to assume that they represented his personal views. He was certainly in the matter of Puritanism further to the right than Walsingham, further to the left than his mistress. In the matter of Roman Catholicism Walsingham and he stood together against the Queen, though he was more discreet in the matter than his colleague was and managed to create the impression that he might be won over. The same thing was true of Sussex and of Hatton. But generally speaking, after Arundel's death in 1580, all of the Privy Council except Sir James Croft were much more anti-Catholic than Elizabeth. Most of them approached the problem in political rather than religious terms. Only the Protestant left-wingers, Bedford, Knollys and above all Walsingham, were impelled primarily by religious considerations. Leicester identified himself with the Puritans. But Leicester was for Leicester. In his time he had denounced the Puritans with the same fervour with which he later denounced the Catholics. His chief objective during the first twenty years of the reign was to marry the Queen; after that to maintain the first place in her affections. As Burghley had been largely instrumental in obstructing the marriage, he was also the principal counterpoise to Leicester's continuing favour. It was the old quarrel between the woman and the Queen, with Leicester, the self-seeking courtier, even to the end of his life appealing strongly to the woman, while Burghley, the patriotic statesman, kept her constantly aware of her duties and responsibilities as Queen.

Certainly Burghley was hostile to the Catholics on political grounds and was chiefly responsible for the increasing severity towards them.

Up until 1579 he was less concerned about the priests and more concerned about the recusancy among the gentry. Until 1575 the priests were survivors of the Marian régime. They were virtually all old men and, though they ministered when they could to the religious needs of their diminishing flocks, they were not crusaders. Now and then one of them was picked up and imprisoned, but they usually got off lightly and not one of them suffered martyrdom. But the increase of recusancy among the gentry, particularly after the papal bull of excommunication, was more alarming.

The usual instruments for dealing with recusancy were the ecclesiastical courts and the courts of common law, or in practical terms the bishops in their dioceses and the Justices of the Peace in their counties. Burghley was constantly prodding the bishops to look to their flocks and the J.P.s to enforce the laws. But the laws themselves were mild ones. They enjoined attendance at the Established Church, but the penalty for non-attendance was a fine of one shilling a Sunday, which, as Burghley himself remarked on one occasion, was so small that local officials did not try to collect it.[6] But the offender was subject also to the censure of the Church, and under the law, *De excommunicato capiendo* of 1563, might, by appropriate action, be imprisoned for non-conformity.[7]

It was under the Act of Uniformity that the government, from time to time, took vigorous action against recusants, singling out those among the gentry and particularly those among the Justices of the Peace.[8] It called upon them to present themselves before the Privy Council and, if they failed to yield to this kind of pressure, imprisoned them. But the action was rather admonitory than punitive, and it accorded with Burghley's view that recusancy was dangerous only when it was associated with local prestige or local power.

A new element was introduced into the situation by the organization of an

English seminary for the instruction of missionary priests at Douai in 1568. In March 1573 a first batch of students received priests' orders,[9] and in the following year the first missionaries, three in number, left for England. By the end of 1580 the number had increased to over 110, besides 8 sent from the daughter college established in Rome in 1576, which had been taken over by the Jesuits in 1579.

The effect of the invasion of ardent young priests was to inject new life into the Roman Catholic Church in England and to arouse new hopes of a return to the old faith. Not only did it stay defections but it rapidly made new converts. It does not appear that the English government at first took this new menace seriously.[10] Certainly government action at this juncture disclosed no great apprehension. Though several of the early missionaries were captured, they were soon released after examination and short imprisonment. The first one to die for his faith was Cuthbert Mayne, who, at his second arrest, was caught with a papal bull and an *Agnus Dei* in his possession. On these grounds he was found guilty of treason in 1577 and executed. Two other executions on the same grounds followed a year later, but there were no others for three years to come.

This interval of relative toleration no doubt proceeded from the Queen herself and was provoked in her by her negotiations for marriage with the Duke of Alençon. Ostensibly, at any rate, the realization of that marriage turned upon the religious issue. Elizabeth would not formally concede to the Duke freedom to worship as a Catholic in England, and the Duke was very reluctant to agree to a marriage except on those terms. But the Queen's attitude in the matter was, to say the least, ambiguous. She hinted that Alençon could have what he wanted though she could not formally concede it to him. And she very definitely moderated hostile action against the English Catholics. The French ambassador remarked on this,[11] and even the Spanish ambassador observed that persecution was slackening.[12] Quite evidently the English Protestants were alarmed. Stubbs's *Gaping Gulf* and Philip Sidney's famous letter to the Queen furnish eloquent testimony on that point. It may have been the evidences of popular disapproval which checked Elizabeth's tolerant proclivities, though it is more likely that she rejected the match for personal reasons and used popular disapproval to justify her position to her suitor.

Another important factor in the situation was the armed intervention of the Pope in Ireland. In its first stage the enterprise centred around Thomas Stukeley, a Devonshire man who had spent most of his life in travel and adventure. For a time he pursued the career of a pirate, but later went to Ireland in the Queen's service, got into some sort of trouble there and in 1570 was summoned home.[13] He fled instead to Spain and for the following eight years was appealing now to the King of Spain, now to the Pope, to organize an expedition against Ireland. The English government through its spies was cognizant of his purposes. Philip at first promised to help him, but he finally secured papal assistance and early in 1578 set out from Civita Vecchia under the papal banner, with one ship, some 600 men and arms and ammunition for an army of 3000. According to Cardinal

Como, papal secretary, the expedition cost the Pope 'thousands and thousands of crowns'.[14] But it never got nearer to England than Portugal. There it was diverted by King Sebastian, with the reluctant consent of Cardinal Como, to the expedition against North Africa. And there Stukeley was killed at the battle of Alcazar.[15]

The English government followed Stukeley's career with interest, not to say apprehension. Within two months of his arrival in Spain a Spanish agent in London reported that the Queen and her Council 'were thrown into alarm' by his flight. In February 1571, Burghley in a letter which he drafted for the Queen[16] instructed Walsingham, her ambassador in Paris, to confer with the Spanish ambassador there about a number of things, among others about Irish refugees in Spain. 'Since', he wrote 'the first arrival of those, we know also that an Englishman, a subject of ours, namely Stukeley, not unknown, we think, for his former prodigal life both in Spain and other places, and notwithstanding great favours showed unto him divers times, upon hope of amendment and some tokens of his repentance, he did this last summer (pretending to come out of Ireland hither) suddenly turn his course into Spain, and, as we hear, hath light[ed] into the company of the aforesaid fugitives and rebels, pretending, by his superfluous expenses, which is altogether of other men's goods, to be a person of some quality and estimation and able to do some great thing in Ireland, whereas, indeed, he hath not the value of a Marmaduke in land or livelihood. He hath so solicited the King or some about him, as it is by him bruited, and otherwise with some credit reported unto us, which yet we do not believe, that the King will send a captain of his ... with a number of soldiers into Ireland to follow some vain device of those rebels, whereof we cannot but marvel that the king or any of his council, being of experience, can so lightly give any credit to such a companion as Stukeley is, which could never live long in any quiet condition at home, of whom we are not disposed to say much because we cannot say any good of him; but may so say, it shall be sufficient that his conditions may be only enquired of, and then we doubt not, whosoever shall know them, will take heed how to adventure anything with him.'

Walsingham passed on the message to the Spanish ambassador and was met with a haughty denial.[17]

Philip of Spain evidently decided, as his secretary wrote to the Spanish ambassador in England, that Stukeley's 'talent, intelligence and weight were insufficient for the purpose in hand', and sent him away.[18]

At about the same time Burghley had spoken to the Spanish ambassador in England about Stukeley, and when Henry Cobham went to Spain he had brought up the matter again there. According to a Spanish story, one of Stukeley's servants from Spain had been captured in August 1571, thrown into the Tower and tortured.[19] But we hear nothing of this from English sources and virtually nothing more of Stukeley until he left Civita Vecchia in the spring of 1578.

When news of his departure reached England sometime in February, it caused considerable alarm. Bernardino de Mendoza, on his way to England, wrote from

Paris on March 4th to the King of Spain: 'They tell me that the Queen is much alarmed by news from Florence that Stukeley has left Civita Vecchia . . . and their alarm has been increased by being told that these forces could only have been with the consent of your Majesty[20] . . . She has made great preparations all over the country.' In May the Privy Council was bidding the Lord Deputy of Ireland to be on his guard, and in June was trying to get late news of Stukeley's plans from two English merchants at Bristol just returned from Portugal.[21] What Bristol yielded is not recorded. But they had good luck in Chester. William Pillen, a merchant who got back from Lisbon in the bark *Felix* early in June[22] reported that he had met Stukeley ten years before at Vigo when Stukeley was setting out for Florida. On the basis of that acquaintance, Pillen had visited Stukeley and had subsequently dined with him. In the course of conversation, Stukeley had said that he was not going to Ireland, that he knew that country as well as the next one, that there was nothing to be got there but poverty and lice. 'They say', said he, 'that I am a traitor to her Majesty. 'Tis they are traitors who say so. I will ever accept her as my Queen. It is true that there is in England my cruel enemy, Cecil the Treasurer, who I care not for . . . I am to serve the King of Portugal in Africa against the Moors.'

Late in June the Lord Deputy of Ireland was still much concerned about Stukeley's coming and was sending frantic appeals for ships and soldiers and money. But Elizabeth herself made light of it. She would not even sanction a special meeting of the Council to deal with it. In a letter of June 21st to Secretary Walsingham, then on a mission in the Low Countries, Wilson wrote: 'I see plainly that nothing will be done till very necessity enforce us . . . I pray God that the light esteeming of so lewd a varlet be not hurtful, for though he is of no value for himself, yet he hath setters on, and the Pope, being chief, may work great mischief.'

On June 23rd Amias Paulet, Elizabeth's ambassador in France, reported that an English Grey Friar just arrived from Spain came to him with the story that Stukeley was about to leave for Africa, and Wilson wrote to Walsingham three days later that he had heard that Stukeley had quite lost his credit with the Pope.[23] A fortnight later, on July 7th, he sailed with King Sebastian to Africa.

Stukeley's diversion did not divert Pope Gregory's hostile purpose against Elizabeth. There was another rebel on the continent seeking aid for an Irish rebellion. He was James Fitzmaurice Fitzgerald, first cousin of Gerald, 15th Earl of Desmond. This is not the place to enter into discussion of the tangled affairs of Ireland. For the immediate purpose it will be sufficient to point out that the Desmonds, or Geraldines, as they were otherwise called, and the Ormonds or Butlers were the most considerable native factors in the Elizabethan history of southern Ireland, or more precisely, Munster. The rivalry between them was reflected in a rivalry at Elizabeth's Court, Leicester and his brohter-in-law, Henry Sidney, favouring the Desmonds, Sussex and Burghley the Ormonds. Elizabeth herself leaned towards the Ormonds, and there appears to have been a warm personal tie between the Earl of Ormond and the Queen. He was one of those pointed to as a possible rival to Leicester in the royal affections and one of those to whom she gave a pet name — Lucas.

It was in connection with the Desmond-Ormond conflict that she had written to Sir Henry Sidney when he was Lord Deputy in Ireland in 1565 and when he seemed to be too obviously biased towards Desmond: 'He [Desmond] hath', she wrote, 'so well performed his English vows that I warn you trust him no longer than you see one of them ... I pray God your old straying sheep (as you say) returned into fold, wore not his wooly garment upon his wolfly back.'[24]

James Fitzmaurice inevitably got involved in the rivalry. His cousin, the Earl, was proud and turbulent, but physically a cripple, mentally and morally a weakling.[25] Fitzmaurice was of sterner stuff. He was widely recognized by the Geraldines as their natural leader, a position which he actually occupied during Gerald's imprisonment in London in the 'seventies. It is probable that he early fell under the spell of David Wolf, the Jesuit, who had come to Ireland as papal legate in 1560. At one time Wolf was Fitzmaurice's chaplain. Fitzmaurice was a man of force and courage, a belligerent Roman Catholic and a bitter opponent of English rule. In 1568 for reasons partly religious but largely personal he rose in revolt, and for the next five years was engaged in a kind of sniping warfare. In this capacity his behaviour conformed to the brutality of the times.[26] He looted towns; he slaughtered garrisons; on one occasion he stripped innocent civilians, even housewives, naked, and sent them to the enemy's camp;[27] on another he sanctioned the murder of two English officials on a peaceful mission.[28] In this respect he was no better and no worse than his opponents. He finally submitted in February 1573. Two years later he fled to France, and for the next four years sought, first in France and then in Spain and then from the Pope, assistance for an Irish rebellion. At the papal Court in 1577 he came upon Stukeley and together they made their plans. After Stukeley's diversion, Fitzmaurice proceeded on his own with the papal blessing, and in June 1579 with a handful of men he set sail for Ireland. With him as papal nuncio went Nicholas Sander, the sworn enemy of Elizabeth, whose *De Visibile Monarchia Ecclesiae*, published in the summer of 1571, justified the papal bull of excommunication and the Rising of the North. And he had already begun his *De Origine ac Progressu Schismatis Anglicani*, which was to serve for years as the basis for every Catholic account[29] of the English Reformation. Sander's presence in the expedition determined its character and its purpose, to wit, a crusade under papal auspices, flying the papal banner, directed against Elizabeth's government, first in Ireland and then, it was hoped, in England. Sander had opposed the leadership of Stukeley,[30] the English swashbuckler; he enthusiastically supported Fitzmaurice. And indeed, from the English point of view, Fitzmaurice was much the more formidable of the two. His intentions were high-minded, Irish and Catholic. They were untainted by those personal considerations which had led Stukeley at the last to denounce Ireland as 'poverty-stricken and lousy'. And Fitzmaurice could command the support of one of the most powerful local families in Ireland.

On July 17th he sailed into Dingle Bay at the south-west corner of Ireland, and issued at once proclamations which left no doubt of his inspiration and his purpose. In essence he said that the Pope had deprived Elizabeth of her unjust possession of her kingdom and had appointed Fitzmaurice his captain. He was fighting not against a lawful sovereign, but against a 'tyrant which refuseth to hear Christ, speaking by his vicar'.[31]

Burghley's first recorded observations on Fitzmaurice's arrival are in a letter to Walsingham of August 9th. It reveals the fact that Walsingham had sent him late news of Irish developments, probably the encouraging news that Captain Courtenay, an English privateer, had seized and led away Fitzmaurice's little fleet.

'For the matters of Ireland', Burghley wrote, 'I am of opinion that it is still necessary that the ships should go on and that they should be double-manned, for to be able to set two or three shot [companies of soldiers] on land as occasion should serve . . . for if the enemy tarry still at the Dingle it must be the force of ships that must remove them, for, as I remember, there is no good access by land through Kerry to approach the Dingle . . . If the enemy should not now be removed from his setting on Ireland, though presently his forces be small, yet his holding and taking of footing and of a haven would be dangerous to receive from foreign parts further forces to offend her Majesty, whereof I am very jealous, if discontentation grow, betwixt France and us . . . or if the King of Spain shall be free of his troubles in the Low Countries . . . This small entry of Fitzmaurice's will be a gate for any of the two princes to offend her Majesty in Ireland in recompense of former offences offered unto them. And, besides that, the sufferance of Fitzmaurice, with his papistical forces, and offers for restoring of religion, will undoubtedly be a continual comfort to all lewd and discontented people of Ireland, whereof I think, three parts of four, or rather nine parts of ten are, for matter of religion, evil satisfied with the English government. Thus you see I cannot forbear to write my conceit, submitting it nevertheless to the better judgment of others.'[32]

Burghley supplemented this letter by another, written later on the same day, in acknowledging later news from Walsingham:

'This morning afore dinner I wrote in answer of your letters . . . And now this afternoon I have received your later letters . . . by which I see that the peril is presently greater than before appeared, but surely no greater than in time coming would prove, if the matter be not at first rooted up . . . But now no cost is to be spared or time lost for, if haste be made with the ships, I hope they shall come thither before the Pope's nuncio and Sander shall return[33] with supplies from Spain; which surely they will, with their large reports of their likelihood of success for matters of religion, procure out of Spain with connivance of the King Catholic. Therefore the more haste be used with the ships, the more sure to withstand the new supply. And the footmen from England are as necessary to withstand the inward revolts in Munster, wherein I fear more the authority and rooted malice of Sir John of Desmond than the untruth of his brother [the Earl]. The departing thither of the Earl of Ormond is worth the sending of 500 men.'

This is all we have from Burghley on the subject for some months to come.[34]

He tried to get immediate vigorous action from the Queen, but she seems to have been little concerned. And the reinforcements she doled out would have been hopelessly inadequate in the face of any real menace. Burghley himself pinned his faith on Ormond, whom the Queen had dispatched in September as Captain of Munster. It was one more feather in Burghley's cap that the Geraldines, whom the Leicestrians had supported, were quite discredited and the Butlers vindicated. Ormond indeed began to reveal himself as the great man he was.[35] In January Burghley wrote to him, alluding to the battle cry of the Desmonds — 'Papa Abo': 'Now merely', Burghley wrote, 'I must say Butleraboo against all the cry as I hear in the new language, Papeaboo, and God send you your heart's desire and vanquish those cankered Desmonds.'[36]

Walsingham handled the details of the Irish situation, but Burghley evidently played an active part. He drafted the proclamation against Fitzmaurice which the Queen issued in January, denouncing Desmond and his brethren as traitors and offering pardon to all their followers who submitted.[37] In his letter to Ormond, Burghley explained that those excepted from the pardon included 'such as have come from foreign parts, among which I mean Sander, that viper, whom of all others the Queen's Majesty is most anxious you should take hold of'.[38]

In another place Burghley denounced Sander as 'that odious, unnatural and pestiferous traitor against his native country'.[39]

Burghley's language was extravagant, but he was certainly right in believing that, of all the Irish rebels, Sander was the most dangerous. Fitzmaurice himself was killed early in the struggle as he was making off with some horses he had stolen. After that, Sander was the inspiration of the whole movement, and he alone kept the weak and wavering Earl of Desmond faithful to his engagements. His offence was the greater in Burghley's eyes because he was an Englishman and a scholar, and easily the most influential of all the Roman Catholic propagandists. But he was far from being a viper. He was indeed the most courageous and forthright of all the English Jesuits. He disdained equivocation, disdained pretending an allegiance to a Queen who he thought had no right to rule. There was no escape for him through any back door from treason. He did not ask for any. And he fought hard for what he believed as long as he lived. For two years English agents pursued him. They never caught up with him. But they wore him out, and he succumbed at last to want and cold in the wood of Claenglaise. They found him there with his breviary and his Bible under his arm. No one knows where they buried him. Of all the Roman Catholic martyrs he went to his reckoning with the cleanest hands. It was well for the England of Elizabeth that he failed. And certainly Burghley had no choice but to pursue him relentlessly. But for courage and devotion to the cause for which he fought, it would be hard to find Sander's equal, Protestant or Catholic, in Elizabethan England.

It was Nicholas Sander who defined and explained Burghley's position in the matter of the English Catholics. For Sander proclaimed that the Queen was deposed by the bull of excommunication, and Sander, under the papal banner was fighting to establish the papal position.

Under these circumstances, in June 1580, two Jesuits in disguise, Edmund Campion and Robert Parsons, arrived in England under papal instructions from Rome. Burghley learned later that the Pope had authorized them to acknowledge allegiance to Elizabeth awaiting further instructions, which he interpreted to mean that, in order to save their skins, they were to pretend loyalty until such time as military action took the place of peaceful penetration. The Pope was openly at war with England; Campion and Parsons were working hard to enlist recruits. They were Englishmen born. Were they traitors or not? Burghley thought they were and proceeded accordingly. They said their purpose was purely religious, to recall Englishmen to the true faith. But it was not easy to distinguish between what they called the true faith and treason, since the supreme spokesman for the 'true faith' had declared Elizabeth deposed and had absolved good Catholics from their allegiance. This much is clear enough, that Burghley's approach to the problem was political, not religious, though it may be assumed that, being himself a good Protestant, ideological considerations played some part in his thinking. It is also clear that he had become increasingly alarmed by the success of the Jesuit missionaries.

The arrival of Campion and Parsons late in June 1580, coming hard upon the news of papal reinforcements on the way to Ireland, alarmed the Queen. In mid-July she issued a proclamation, appealing to her subjects to stand fast. Burghley himself drafted the proclamation.[40]

It began by attributing the dangers which threatened to the machinations of English rebels and traitors overseas, and their accomplices at home, who were seeking to induce foreign princes to invade England and had already provoked a papal invasion of Ireland.

These rebels had been the one disturbing factor in twenty years of the Queen's quiet and peaceful government, unequalled 'for these thousand years either of England or any kingdom of Christendom'. Nevertheless, 'by God's goodness their attempts are likely to be frustrate'. But these same rebels are now spreading abroad a tale that the Pope, the King of Spain and other princes have agreed to invade England in force, to 'dispose of the Crown and of the possessions of the subjects of the realm at their pleasure'.

The result has been to sow discord in English minds, 'some emboldened to persist in their undutifulness, some to be afraid to continue dutiful'.

Under these circumstances the Queen feels that she ought to give thanks to God who has preserved her and her realm, and 'to maintain her honour and glory by retaining her people in the true profession of the Gospel and free from the bondage of Roman tyranny'.

She also feels that she 'ought and must use the means which God has given her and put in her hands — that is power over an infinite number of godly, dutiful, faithful, manlike and able people, her loving subjects'. With that in mind she has mustered the strength of her realm, and means to maintain that strength in readiness to withstand all hostile attempts by land or sea. 'Through God's greatness she hath such a strength as, in comparison, never any king of the realm hath had the like, to overcome all foreign malice to her and to the state of true Christian religion.

'So she thinketh it good to admonish her good people that they continue in the dutiful and true service of Almighty God ... and also to remain constant in courage with their bodies and substance to withstand any enterprise that may be offered to this realm', and that they should not be moved by false rumours 'to alter their courage', but should 'cause all such, spreading like rumours, to be apprehended'.

This was the proclamation in substance. Its purpose was clearly to discredit the rebels, Campion and Parsons among the number, to assert the strength of the Crown against all comers, to evoke the loyalty of the English and enjoin their assistance in the apprehension of all those who were seeking to sow sedition, and aid and abet traitors from overseas.

In form the proclamation ran to two folios. Its sentences were long, involved and tedious.[41] At one point it reveals uncertainty about the loyalty of some of the Justices of the Peace. As a piece of effective propaganda, by all modern standards, it leaves much to be desired. If the situation called for a royal word to the people, it ought to have taken the form of a clear trumpet call for Queen and faith. Nicholas Throgmorton might have done it, but he was dead; a young Stratford lad might have done it, but he was still in his teens; Walter Raleigh might have done it. Elizabeth herself might have made such an appeal, as she did later at Tilbury when the Armada was in the Channel.[42] But Burghley lacked the art. He believed in the power of the press, and undertook to exploit it. More than any other one of Elizabeth's advisers he directed, and to a considerable extent actually composed, official propaganda. But his style was too bookish to stir the average Englishman. It was precisely in that flair for popularity that his mistress far excelled him. But she never envisaged the Catholic danger as he envisaged it. She never believed that her people would strike for Rome against England. Here again she proved to be wiser than he.

The arrival of Campion and Parsons in June 1580 coincided roughly in point of time with the inauguration by the Privy Council of a policy of increased severity towards the recusants. The letter which they addressed to the Earl of Huntingdon, President of the Council of the North, on June 10th is symptomatic:[43]

'Upon notice given unto her Majesty of the falling away in matters of religion in sundry of her subjects of good quality and others within the County of Lancaster ... she hath thought meet at this point to grant out the Ecclesiastical Commission for the diocese of Chester ... whereby you are authorized to proceed with the parties so fallen away, for the reducing of them to conformity or to punish them according to such direction as you shall receive by the said Commission. ...

'And forasmuch as this infection, the longer it shall be suffered to reign, the more will it spread and become dangerous, therefore it behooveth that all expedition be used in the execution of the said Commission. ...

'And as this defection is principally begun by sundry principal gentlemen of that country by whom the meaner sort of people are led and seduced, so it is thought meeter that in the execution of the Commission you begin first with the best of the said recusants. For that we suppose that the inferior people will thereby the sooner be reclaimed and brought to obedience.'

In another letter addressed to the Commission some three weeks later,[44] the Privy Council defined its position further:

'The Queen's Majesty, having been often informed that divers of her subjects, not regarding the small penalty which the Statutes made in her Highness' time do lay upon them for not resorting to the church . . . hath caused the Judges and her learned Council, together with some well learned Civilians, to consider and set down in writing under their hands their opinion, how by the canon and common law a greater penalty might lawfully be set upon wilful and usual recusants that come not to the church at all. Which being done and allowed by her Majesty her Highness' pleasure is to have it executed throughout the realm. . . .

'And whereas her Majesty's pleasure is that some of the principal persons of most mark of the said recusants should be restrained from liberty and being informed that heretofore such as have been committed to your ordinary prisons have grown (by the remissness of the keepers, who suffered them too much liberty) to be more obstinate; for the remedy thereof she hath therefore thought meet that there should be certain special places appointed for the restraint of the said recusants.'

The letter ended with direction for the establishment of Halton Castle in Cheshire as a prison for recusants.

Enclosed in the letter was the 'Opinion of the Judges', the essence of which was that the Queen, by virtue of her ecclesiastical authority, might 'inflict any punishment by mulct or otherwise which the ecclesiastical laws allow of', and that the canon law conferred upon a bishop ('and no inferior judge') power to punish, 'by any pecuniary pain for any ecclesiastical crime' including that of recusancy.

These letters, signed by members of the Privy Council of whom, in every instance, Burghley was one, indicate that the Privy Council meant to proceed against the recusants by virtue of the Queen's ecclesiastical authority, intending to strike chiefly at the leaders and contemplating the segregation of these leaders in specified places under the custody 'of some apt person, so well settled in religion as there may be no doubt of his corruption'.[45]

The plan for segregating the recusants was evidently the one drafted by Walsingham and Burghley which is preserved among the Harleian manuscripts.[46] We shall probably be safe in assuming that Burghley and Walsingham between them were directing the whole procedure against the Catholics. Their elaborate plan for segregation was not broadly applied at this time. It was, indeed, never broadly applied. But it constituted an element in government planning, particularly in times of emergency. The idea, of course, was to place under surveillance the potential leaders of any Catholic rebellion. It was a sound idea but it turned out to be unnecessary. Except for a few zealous youths like Francis Throgmorton and Antony Babington, even the recusant gentry, however inconsistent it might seem, remained loyal to their sovereign.

But in 1580 Burghley was convinced that the laws against recusants and missionaries should be made more severe. And Elizabeth herself acquiesced. In 1581 she reassembled Parliament to deal with the situation.

The reason for summoning Parliament, as set forth in Sir Walter Mildmay's[47] eloquent presentation of the matter before the House of Commons, was to deal more severely with English Catholics and to provide money for defence against foreign enemies. Burghley took his seat in the House of Lords and probably was the Queen's spokesman there. But the meagre *Lords' Journal* reveals little more than his presence. He was, of course, primarily interested in the legislation about the Catholics and he evidently followed the procedure in that regard closely. So much is clear enough from his notes on pertinent documents. We have (1) a draft of the first bill passed by the House of Commons on the subject, with marginal annotations in his hand. We have (2) certain articles from the first bill passed by the House of Lords on the subject, with annotations in his hand. We have (3) a copy of a bill which resulted from a conference of the two Houses on the subject, endorsed in his hand; and we have (4) a draft in his hand of the bill which, with one important modification, finally passed.[48] But the annotations in every case reveal his own attitude towards the bills annotated. We may conclude from what we otherwise know about him that he had a good deal to do with the passage of the first bill in the Lords and with the compromise bill which emerged from the conference of the two Houses. But it is not safe to argue from the scanty evidence that these bills reflected his own views.

Both of the earlier bills in which Burghley as a member of the House of Lords actually participated — that is to say the first bill in the Lords and the compromise bill which emerged from a conference of Lords and Commons — were a good deal tougher on the Catholics than the bill which finally passed. It is probable that the Queen herself rejected the earlier bills as being too severe. Burghley's draft of the bill which finally passed suggests that he had a great deal to do with defining a position acceptable to her. But it does not necessarily follow that Burghley himself fought for the earlier bills. He may well have thought it wise to present his mistress with a convincing revelation of the strength of parliamentary sentiment against the Catholics in order to impel her to take a firm position. The evidence at hand gives little support to the assumption 'that Burghley at this time was in favour of a measure planned to eradicate Catholicism in England by making life intolerable even for its peaceful and loyal adherents'.[49] He came close to that position later but only after the Throgmorton Plot, the Parry Plot and the Babington Plot had convinced him of the necessity of greater severity.

In any case, the bill as it passed was tough enough. It increased the penalty for non-attendance at the Established Church to £20 a month. And it declared that any persons who tried to win Englishmen from their allegiance to the Queen, or, *for that intent*, to win them from the Church of England to the Church of Rome, were traitors and their proselytes with them. It imposed a penalty of 200 marks and a year's imprisonment for the saying of Mass, and one of 100 marks and a year's imprisonment for the hearing of Mass.[50]

By another Act in the same Parliament severe penalties were imposed against those who slandered the Queen, either in speech or in writing — for speaking, a fine of 200 marks, for writing, the death penalty of felony.[51]

Meanwhile, the government pursued relentlessly its hunting down of the missionary priests. Most of all, their efforts were directed to the apprehension of Edmund Campion. For over a year he succeeded in eluding capture, and he travelled all over England, winning converts wholesale by his eloquence. Campion was indeed the most formidable of all the missionaries. He was, in addition to being a good scholar, a man of great wit and charm, completely devoted to his cause. Earlier he had attracted the attention of Archbishop Parker by his *History of Ireland*,[52] and Parker had commended him to Burghley. He had not been long in England before he addressed a letter to the Privy Council. In that letter he confessed that he was a Jesuit and a priest of the Catholic Church who had been sent to England to preach the Gospel. He denied that he had any intention of dealing with matters of state and policy, declared indeed that he had been forbidden to do so. And he asked that he might appear before the Council and might be permitted to debate about matters of his faith with chosen scholars from the Universities. He even went so far as to suggest that the Queen herself should attend the debate.

The challenge was not printed until long afterwards,[53] but it was widely distributed in manuscript and it created such a stir that the government employed William Charke, a Puritan divine who had been expelled from Cambridge for nonconformity, to answer it.[54] Campion complained that the answer was no more than vituperation and about a year later published the heads of his arguments under the title, *Decem Rationes*. The pamphlet was in Latin, addressed to scholars and printed in England on a press which the Catholics had secretly set up. Some five hundred copies were distributed at Oxford Commemoration late in June 1581. Thomas Fuller, the Anglican historian, wrote later of the pamphlet that these 'Ten Reasons' were 'so purely for Latin, so plainly and pithily penned, that they were very taking and fetched many (neuter before) to his persuasion'.[55] The government indeed wheeled out its great guns, and the Regius Professors of Divinity both at Cambridge and at Oxford were drafted to answer it.[56]

Thereafter a great mass of propagandist literature poured forth from pens private and official, Catholic and Protestant. Antony Munday, at different times an actor and a playwright and one of the most prolific writers of his time, had a book off the press on the English Roman life in 1580 and another on the capture of Campion in 1581, and later five other pamphlets on the same subject, some of them running to two editions. There were at least thirty relevant pamphlets, pro and con, published before 1590, some of them in Latin, some in French, at least one in German, and one in Italian. In short, Campion and his works became a *cause célèbre*.

He was captured a few days after his 'Ten Reasons' appeared. Some four months intervened between his capture and his trial. What happened during these four months is not too clearly established. Our knowledge of it is largely derived from partisan sources. It is said that after four days in the Tower he was carried secretly by boat to Leicester's house, where he held conference with Leicester, Bedford, two secretaries and the Queen herself.[57] At his trial Campion spoke of his interview with the Queen[58] and Burghley wrote to Shrewsbury on August 6th: 'He [Campion] denieth any question of moment, being covenanted before my Lord Chancellor [Bromley] and my Lord of Leicester.'[59] Possibly it was this 'covenanting' which was later embroidered by Catholic apologists. Certainly neither of the Principal Secretaries was present — Wilson had died in June; Walsingham had probably left for France.[60] According to the story, Elizabeth made a handsome offer to Campion if he would conform, and Walsingham is said to have told the French that Campion had retracted his errors and become Protestant and was even talked of for the see of Canterbury. But there is nothing of this in Walsingham's correspondence from France. All that Campion said about it at his trial was that he had been offered his liberty if he would attend service at the Anglican Church. There was undoubtedly some effort made to win Campion to conformity late in July.

He was evidently under examination at the Tower before the 30th of the month,[61] for on that day the Privy Council issued directions for his further examination. In these directions his examinees were instructed to use the rack if he remained obstinate. Some time in the course of the examination Campion revealed the names of Catholics he had visited.[62] Burghley wrote to Walsingham on August 10th: 'We have gotten from Campion knowledge of all his peregrination in England, as in Yorkshire, Lancashire, Denbigh, Northampton, Warwick, Bedford, Buckingham. And hereof I am sure Mr. Beale will write unto you, who hath herein, with Mr. Hammond, taken great pains. We have sent for his hosts in all countries [counties].'[63]

In August it was decided to hold a public discussion in the chapel of the Tower, with Campion on the one side, the Dean of St. Paul's and the Dean of Windsor on the other. Arrangements for this discussion were made by Aylmer, Bishop of London, doubtless on orders from above. Whether these orders proceeded from the Queen or from the Privy Council does not appear. There is no direct evidence that Burghley had anything to do with the matter, though he was almost certainly involved. He corresponded with Aylmer about Campion, but unfortunately only Aylmer's side of the correspondence is preserved.[64] Nor does it appear what the objectives were. At the first conference there was a considerable audience, at later ones the audience was restricted. Aylmer himself disapproved of these conferences and Thomas Norton thought they were both fruitless and hurtful. They may have been intended to create the impression that Campion was given every opportunity to justify his position. Or they may have been a device to entrap him in treasonable utterances. After four conferences had been held, they were abandoned, and late in October the government reverted to the tactics of examination under torture. This again yielded nothing of moment. Finally, in mid-November Campion was brought to trial.[65]

It appears that the government was in some doubt about the procedure to be followed at the trial. Walsingham wrote to Burghley for his advice. Burghley replied 'that as for those lewd fellows lately sent from Rome into England', he advised 'to move her Majesty that the Lord Chancellor [Bromley] by conference with the Recorder [Fleetwood] might devise some way agreeable to the law of the realm for the punishment of them'.[66] The answer was evasive enough, though Burghley's choice of referees is interesting. Bromley was regarded as Leicester's man and Fleetwood, one of Burghley's regular correspondents,[67] was a staunch Puritan.

One wonders why he did not suggest the judges or the law officers of the Crown. Early in the reign the bench had been regarded as Catholic in its sympathies, but the same could hardly be said of Sir Christopher Wray, Chief Justice of the Queen's Bench, or Popham, the Attorney-General, or Egerton, the Solicitor-General. Possibly Burghley steered clear of those who might participate in the trial. Wray, as a matter of fact, was the presiding judge at the trial, and Popham and Egerton both participated, although Edmond Anderson, the Queen's Counsel, who became Chief Justice of the Common Pleas the year following, actually conducted the case for the Crown.

Notwithstanding the fact that the penal statute of 1581 had already become law, it was decided to proceed against Campion under the old treason law of Edward III.[68] The reason for this can only have been that the prosecution wished to avoid the religious implications of the more pertinent statute of 1581. From the first, the aim was to prove that Campion was not on trial for his religion but for his treason.

Copies of two indictments are preserved among Burghley's papers. One of them charges Campion 'with winning subjects from their allegiance', the other 'for conspiring to compass the death of the Queen and raise sedition within the realm'.[69] The latter was the one adopted. The choice was probably dictated once again by the desire to avoid the religious issue. We may have here the issue as it was joined between the Queen and Burghley, though this is mere conjecture. Burghley's views on the matter were expressed at length two years later in his *Execution of Justice in England*, and they conform much more closely to the indictment rejected than to the indictment adopted. Elizabeth was never prepared to regard her Catholic subjects as traitors, and certainly not prepared to take that position officially in her courts of justice. In the event, she turned out to be right, but so far as Campion was concerned the case against him was legally weakened. Although there were ample grounds for believing that conspiracies were being hatched against the Crown,[70] no sound evidence was produced to show that Campion had been a party to them. Under the terms of his indictment he should have been acquitted. It might have been better policy had he been acquitted. But, having gone so far, Burghley probably felt, Walsingham certainly felt, that conviction and execution as a traitor was the safest course.[71] Leaving out of account considerations of justice and mercy, the issue at stake in their eyes was the security of the Queen, the realm and the Protestant faith.

In effect they made a martyr of him and provoked a spate of Catholic pamphlets designed to emphasize that fact. We need not follow in detail the literary controversy which followed.[72] It was all anonymous and, on the government side, some of it was publishers' ventures to meet a popular demand. Some of it was issued by authority. Two of the pamphlets have been ascribed to Burghley himself:

(1) A *Declaration of Favourable Dealing by her Majesty's Commissioners Appointed for the Examination of Certain Traitors*, etc.[73]

(2) *The Execution of Justice in England, not for Religion but for Treason*.[74]

Both were published in 1583.

The only grounds for ascribing the first to Burghley seem to be that it was joined with the second in a Latin translation published in 1584.[75] It was probably written by Thomas Norton, one of the commissioners who examined Campion. But there can be no reasonable doubt that Burghley sanctioned its publication. The gist of it was that torture was legal and that its application to Campion was not so severe as to hinder his walking or writing — that it was never applied to extort answers regarding faith but simply to discover treasonable purposes — that it was never applied to wring out confessions 'at adventure' except when there were other evidences of guilt, or evasion of what came to be known as the 'bloody question', that is to say, the question as to whether the victim would remain loyal to the Queen if and when the Pope commanded otherwise.

This statement was probably true in the main, and doubtless the application of torture might have been more severe and more indiscriminate than it was. Torture, however shocking to the modern mind, was legal and was often used in cases involving treason. Yet even to the sixteenth-century Englishman it was revolting. The Catholic pamphleteers made much of it, so much that the English government felt impelled to explain and to justify its action.

In the same year Burghley published his *Execution of Justice in England*.[76] It went to a second printing almost at once,[77] and in the following year translations appeared in Latin, French and Dutch.[78] Of all that Burghley wrote for publication — and much that he wrote for publication was never published,[79] the *Execution of Justice* was the most considerable and easily the most important. It was the official justification of Elizabeth's treatment of the Catholic priests, and it is the best statement we have of Burghley's own position in the matter. If it does not succeed in vindicating the Queen's policy, at least it defines it. The government may not always have lived up to the profession, but there can be no doubt about its objective.

Burghley's approach to the problem was in political terms. He did not argue about the merits of the contending faiths. He did not attack Roman Catholicism as a form of worship or a pattern of belief. He was wholly concerned with papal claims of supremacy (over temporal rulers). He spent some time in following the history of national resistance to these claims through the long medieval struggle between Emperor and Papacy, through the English Statutes of Praemunire, down to the sack of Rome by Charles V and the siege of Rome by the Duke of Alva. He pointed out that even the Catholic Mary had forbidden the entrance of papal bulls into England and had resisted the efforts of the Pope to displace Cardinal Pole by a

Cardinal Pieto of his own choosing. 'The said pretended Cardinal Pieto, not-withstanding all the threatenings of the Pope, was forced to go up and down the streets of London like a begging friar, without his red hat.'

And Burghley called upon rulers of all Christian faiths to recognize that Eliza-beth's fight against papal supremacy was a fight in which their interests were at stake.

'Howsoever,' he wrote, 'the Christian kings, for some respects in policy, can endure the Pope to command where no harm nor disadvantage groweth to them-selves; yet sure it is, and the popes are not ignorant, but where they shall in any sort attempt to take from Christian princes any part of their dominions or shall give aid to their enemies or to any other, their rebels — in those cases, their bulls, their curses, their excommunications, their sentences and their most solemn anethe-maticals — no, nor their cross keys or double edged sword, will serve their turns to compass their intentions.'

He went on to emphasize the fact that in the whole course of Elizabeth's reign she had been singularly mild in dealing with English Catholics if they were loyal and obedient subjects. He pointed out that many prominent Marian prelates had been allowed to live out their lives and enjoy their property, with no further molestation than temporary confinement when sedition threatened. None of these were ever brought 'into danger of any capital law; no one was called to any capital or bloody question upon matters of religion'. The same was true of many promi-nent Catholic laymen.

In the main, though the plight of the Marian bishops was far from a pleasant one, Burghley was, on this point, not far wide of the mark. There was no active perse-cution of English Catholics during the first decade of Elizabeth's reign, certainly none which involved jeopardy of life or limb.

He went on to explain that the papal bull of 1570 necessitated a reappraisal of the situation. 'It cannot be denied', he said, 'that so many as should have obeyed that wicked warrant . . . should have been in their hearts and consciences secret traitors. And for to be indeed errant and open traitors there would have wanted nothing but opportunity to feel their strength and to assemble themselves with arms and weapons.'

As Burghley saw it, the papal bull excommunicating Elizabeth was a declaration of war. He regarded it as one of the important factors in provoking the Rising of the North, though it did not arrive in time to support that rising. He saw it behind the establishment of the seminaries at Douai and in Rome. He saw it most emphatically in the invasion of Ireland by a papal army under papal banners. He heard its voice in the utterances of Nicholas Sander. And he pointed out that the invasion of England by Jesuits and seminaries who came under cover, in disguise, could not but be interpreted as an effort to arouse English Catholics at large in support of the papal war.

'And thereby', he wrote, 'it may manifestly appear to all men how this bull was the ground of the rebellion both in England and Ireland and how, for maintenance thereof and for sowing of sedition by warrant and allowance of the same, those persons [Jesuits] were justly condemned and lawfully executed . . . without charging them for any other matter than for their practices and conspiracies both abroad and at home against the Queen and the realm . . . Although true it is that when they were charged and convinced of those points of conspiracies and treasons they would still in their answers colourably pretend their action to have been for religion, but indeed and in truth they were manifested to be for the procurement and maintenance of the rebellion and wars against her Majesty and her realm.'

Here Burghley was skating on thin ice. But he could hardly have denied the validity of the verdict against Campion and his followers even though active conspiracy was not proven.

He pointed out that captured documents revealed that Campion and Parsons had received dispensation from the Pope to ignore the bull of excommunication until such time as the Pope should give other orders. Burghley actually printed the salient words of this dispensation both in the original Latin and in an English translation.[80] Arnold Meyer, the eminent Catholic historian, has observed: 'No booty came more welcome to Burghley than this piece of paper.'[81] It was not found until after Campion's death. Had it been available at his trial, it would have served to cast a dark shadow over all his protestations of loyalty. It has since served Protestant historians as an excellent example of Rome's double dealing and a clear revelation of the treasonable purposes of the missionary priests.[82] Curiously enough, Burghley does not seem to have grasped these implications, or at least did not exploit them in the *Execution of Justice*.

Burghley's only comment was simply: 'Hereafter it is manifest what authority Campion had to impart the contents of the bull against the Queen's Majesty, howsoever he himself denied the same. For this was his errand.'[83]

He went on to meet a prevalent objection to the severity of the government in what is on the whole the most eloquent passage in the pamphlet:

'Yet there are certain other persons, more nicely addicted to the Pope, that will yet seem to be unsatisfied, for that, as they will term the matter, a number of silly poor wretches were put to death as traitors, being in profession scholars or priests, by the names of seminaries, Jesuits or simple schoolmasters, that came not into the realm with any armour or weapons by force to aid the rebels and traitors either in England or in Ireland . . . of which sort of wretches, the commiseration is made as though for their contrary opinions in religion, or for teaching of the people to disobey the laws of the realm, they might have been otherwise punished and corrected, but yet not with capital pain. . . .

'But for answer to the better satisfaction of these nice and scrupulous favourers of traitors, it must be with reason demanded of them . . . whether they think that when a king, being stablished in his realm, hath a rebellion, first secretly practised and afterwards openly raised in his realm by his own seditious subjects, and when by a foreign potentate or enemy the rebellion is maintained and the rebels by messages and promises comforted to continue, and their treasons against their natural prince avowed, and consequently when the same potentate and enemy, being author of the said rebellion, shall with his own proper forces invade the realm and subjects of the prince that is so lawfully and peaceably possessed; in these cases shall no subject favouring those rebels and yielding obedience to the enemy, the invader, be committed or punished as a traitor, but only such of them as shall be found openly to carry armour and weapons? Shall no subject that is a spial and explorer for the rebel or enemy against his natural prince be taken and punished as a traitor because he is not found with armour or weapon, but yet is taken in his disguised apparel, with scrolls and writings, or other manifest tokens, to prove him a spy for traitors, after he hath wandered secretly in his sovereign's camp, region, court or city? ... The answer I think must needs be yielded, if reason and experience shall here rule with these adversaries, that all these and such like are to be punished as traitors. And the principal reason is, because it cannot be denied, but that the actions of all these are necessary accessories and adherents proper to further and continue all rebellions and wars. But if they will deny that none are traitors that are not armed, they will make Judas no traitor that came to Christ without armour, colouring his treason with a kiss.'

This passage contains the gist of Burghley's argument. But the salient point which above all others he strove to drive home was that the English government was fighting that old enemy, papal supremacy, and not the Catholic faith.

'Where the factious party of the Pope, the principal author of the invasions of her Majesty's dominions, do falsely allege that a number of persons whom they term as martyrs have died for defence of the Catholic religion, the same in very truth may manifestly appear to have died (if they so will have it) as martyrs for the Pope.'

The issue was joined the following year by the publication of Allen's *Modest Defence of the English Catholics*, a tract of 250 pages[84] in response to a pamphlet of some 20 pages. A good deal of what Allen said was frankly based upon the claims for papal supremacy. In so far as this was so, he weakened his case with those peripheral English Catholics whose zeal for their faith was tempered by their strong national loyalties. He weakened it further by defending and justifying the papal invasion of Ireland.[85] The strength of his argument lay in controverting Burghley's statement that the English treatment of the priests was prompted by their treason and not by their faith. Allen was able to show, in the case of Campion particularly, that the government produced no adequate proof of treason and that in many other cases it had equated religious propaganda with political propaganda. Allen was resolute to prove what Elizabeth insistently denied, that the Catholics were being persecuted for their faith, not for their politics. The fact, of course, was that it was almost impossible to draw the line, just as it is almost impossible today to draw the line between Communism and Russian aggression. Some Jesuits and missionaries were guiltless of treason; some — a few years later both Allen and Robert Parsons among them — were definitely traitors. It was certain that every Catholic was a potential traitor and clear enough from the papal dispensation to Parsons and Campion that even professed loyalties could only be regarded as tentative and conditional. The missionaries were sworn emissaries of the Pope, and when the Pope ordered otherwise they would be in a position to direct their flocks accordingly. That was what the English government feared; that was one of Burghley's besetting fears ever since he had entered Elizabeth's service. That explains the torture of the priests, that explains their escape from torture if they agreed to accept the Elizabethan establishment. That also explains the significance of the 'bloody question'. There can be no doubt, however, that many of the agents of the government, being resolute Puritans, were prompted by purely religious considerations. The Puritans were the one group in England which could be depended upon in any dealing with English Catholics. It is interesting to note that John Stubbs, author of the *Gaping Gulf*, was employed by the government to answer Allen's pamphlet,[86] and that Thomas Norton and Thomas Cartwright were both employed in similar enterprises. Our judgment of the rights and wrongs of the matter will probably be determined by our religious affiliations. But to men like Walsingham and Burghley the potential menace of Roman Catholicism to their Queen and their faith was the impelling consideration. So far as Burghley was concerned, he had no scruples about applying torture to discover conspiracy. But he later decided that making martyrs of priests did more harm than good to the cause.

CHAPTER XIV

ALENÇON AND THE LOW COUNTRIES,
1581-84

I T was just at this juncture, when the Jesuit missionaries were weaning the English away from their allegiance, and d'Aubigny was leading the Scots into the
enemy camp, and an expedition out of Spain was landing forces to support the
Irish rebels, and Drake's exploits in the New World were adding fuel to Spanish
flames, and Philip had just added Portugal to his empire, that Elizabeth decided to
revert to the perennial Alençon courtship. On October 20th, 1580, she told the
French that if Alençon still wished it and her brother, the King, approved, she
was ready to proceed with the marriage without further delay.[1]

This started the old ball rolling again, and for the better part of two years Elizabeth's attention was once more absorbed by courtship and marriage. We may
perhaps regard the whole affair as an attempt to secure an offensive and defensive
alliance with France in the face of the increasing menace from Spain. So far as
Elizabeth was concerned there was a strong personal element in it — the last fling of
a woman in her late forties at the thrills of love-making. Whether she was as
indiscreet in her relations with the Duke and with his servant, Jean de Simier, as the
gossips reported[2] is more than doubtful. But certainly her behaviour was such
as to lend credence to such tales. In any case, she herself assumed the direction of
the whole affair, and her councillors were not consulted except when she had
involved herself in situations from which she called upon them to extricate her.
Probably she had abandoned, if she had ever entertained, the idea of marrying
Alençon. Probably her councillors were aware of that fact. And probably Burghley had given up hope that a marriage, even if it came to pass, would be fruitful
and would solve the difficult question of the succession. We have no longer any
of his long memoranda on the subject[3] nor any of long deliberations in Council.
He still favoured the marriage because he thought that Elizabeth badly needed a
French alliance and because he saw no other practicable way of relieving the
situation in the Low Countries. But he instinctively preferred the old Burgundian
connection, partly because he had an inveterate distrust of the French, partly because of the valuable commercial connections both with the Low Countries and
with Spain. He preferred to see the Low Countries in Spanish hands with their old
privileges restored to them than to see them added to France.

Of the other councillors, Sussex, so long as he lived, was of the same way of
thinking. The other influential councillors, Leicester, Hatton[4] and Walsingham,
were on the whole opposed to the marriage, though Walsingham was prepared to
accept it as a way of preventing the Spanish conquest of the Netherlands. He did

FRANÇOIS, DUC D'ALENÇON

not share Burghley's antipathy for France. All of them agreed that the worst possible course for the Queen to follow was to play fast and loose with her French suitor. But they were all ready to follow her orders, though Mendoza heard in December 1581 that a plan was on foot to provoke a revolt against the marriage in London.

Burghley was one of the most active of all the councillors in the matter. Mendoza declared him to be the most important of all the councillors, the one upon whom the Queen depended in all important matters and one of the few who held a straightforward course.[5] Mauvissière, the French ambassador, spoke of him as a Nestor in the Queen's Council[6] and observed that he was 'most exempt from all passions save for the service and honour of his mistress'. Indeed, both Mendoza and Mauvissière seem to have regarded him as their best friend at Court.

During the latter part of 1580 and all of 1581 he was very regular in his attendance at Council meetings, though he occasionally ran away for a few days to Theobalds. On one such visit he wrote to Leicester in praise of a hunting dog which Leicester had given him, 'for which,' he wrote, 'I heartily thank you as she serveth me to great purpose. For she maketh my hunting very certain and speedy. She hath never failed me, for almost every day this week but brought me in the right way to a deer. And this last week she brought me to a stag which myself had stricken with my bow, being forced to the soil[7] where, with the help of a greater water spaniel that forced him out of the water, your good brach helped to pluck him down'.[8] At sixty years of age Burghley still went stag hunting with a bow.[9]

The establishment of civil peace in France in November 1580 opened the door to an Anglo-French rapprochement. In July 1580 Burghley had told Mauvissière that once civil peace was established marriage could be assured within twenty-four hours. 'I am', he said, 'more assured of it than ever I was and the Queen, my mistress, is doing me the honour to show me and to read to me many of Alençon's letters. I have found her so resolute and full of affection that not only am I convinced that a marriage is honourable and necessary for the welfare of the two kingdoms but that the Queen herself will have it so by reason of her great love for the Duke and her great desire to live at peace with the king.'

Mauvissière asked if he could transmit these observations to the French King. Burghley replied that he could write what he would, that his great desire, before he died, was to see his mistress married and in close amity with France.[10]

A fortnight later Burghley was telling Mauvissière that the Queen 'was positively distraught (navrée) with love for the Duke'.[11]

It is not likely that Burghley believed what he said, but clear enough that he was doing what he could to revive the courtship.

In December the French King announced his intention to send commissioners to negotiate the marriage. Burghley observed to Mauvissière, early in January, that Elizabeth was eager to get on with the matter while she was still young enough to have offspring, and urged that no time be lost.

There was, however, some delay occasioned in part by Elizabeth's insistence

I

that the French commissioners should be of the highest rank. What she was thinking of was a great show. And a great show was accordingly provided. The commission, when it finally arrived in April, included François de Bourbon, the Prince
Dauphin and his brother, there for show; Pinart, the French Secretary of State,
Lansac and La Mothe Fénélon, for business. Accompanying them was a train
of some 500 gentlemen. They landed in Dover on the 16th, went to Gravesend
and then by boat up the river to Whitehall. Meanwhile, extensive preparations
had been made for their entertainment. A special banqueting hall had been
erected, '332 feet in measure about', with walls of canvas painted to look like stone,
richly ornamented within and with 92 'lights of glass'. John Stow describes it at
some length.[12] He was told by the builders that it cost £1744, nineteen shillings
and odd money.

Burghley himself seems to have worked out the programme of entertainment,[13]
including arrangements for lodgings in the Strand, Fleet Street, Chancery Lane and
Holborn. The commissioners were to be received by the Queen on Saturday,
the day following their arrival in London. On the 24th, they were to confer with
the Council, on the 25th to dine with the Queen, on the 27th with Leicester, on the
30th with Burghley, with conferences interlarded.

We have a detailed account of the Burghley dinner, which was spread at Cecil
House in Covent Garden. The English guests included all the Privy Councillors,
six of the most important peers and twenty-one others, thirty-seven all told. The
French guests are not recorded, but they must have numbered at least as many.
Provision was made for interpreters and Burghley's son, Thomas, his nephew,
Francis Bacon, and his brother-in-law, Henry Killigrew, were included in that
category along with a number of others. The kitchen bill alone came to £204 7s.,
and among other charges were enumerated in great detail carrying charges from
Burghley House at Stamford, flowers and rushes, furniture, pewter, Turkey carpets,
the Queen's picture. And there was a bill for carpenters, plasterers, glaziers, etc.,
which may have been for alterations before the banquet or for the repair of damages
after it. The total cost came to £362 19s. 12d., nearly 20 per cent of the total cost
of Burghley's household per annum.[14]

Besides dinners there were other elaborate entertainments provided. Walsingham speaks of bear-baiting on May Day,[15] but the great effort was in a 'Triumph',
originally planned for April 24th but subsequently postponed until May 15th and
16th.[16] It took place in the tilt yard adjoining the royal palace at Whitehall. Whitehall itself featured as the Castle of Perfect Beauty and the theme of the Triumph
was the attack upon the castle by four knights calling themselves the 'Four Children of Desire'. The four knights in question were Philip, Earl of Arundel, Lord
Windsor, Philip Sidney and Fulke Grenville.

The play began with the appearance of a messenger apparelled in red and white
who called upon the Queen no longer to exclude virtuous desire from perfect
beauty. If she yielded, well, but if not then they meant to attack the fortress. They
wanted the defenders of the fortress to meet them at the tilt.

These preliminaries having taken place on April 29th, on the day appointed the challengers appeared again in the tilt yard, prepared to besiege the fortress, accompanied by a float made up to represent a trench with two mock cannons mounted, an ensign flying and musicians discoursing sweet music within the trench.

Following that, the Earl of Arundel entered the tilt yard in gilt and graven armour. A contemporary description of his retinue reveals the colourfulness of the display: 'He was attended by two gentleman ushers, four pages riding spare horses and twenty gentlemen in short cloaks and Venetian hose of crimson velvet, laid with gold lace, doublets of yellow satin, hats of crimson velvet with gold bands and yellow feathers and yellow silk stocks. Then had he six trumpeters that sounded before him and thirty-one yeomen that waited after him, apparelled in cassock coats and Venetian hose of crimson velvet laid on with red silk and gold lace, doublets of yellow taffeta, hats of crimson taffeta with yellow feathers and worsted stockings.' Evidently there were some sixty followers in Arundel's company with costumes mainly in red and yellow.

Lord Windsor followed with a company of the same size in orange tawny and black with white feathers. And then Sidney with about the same company in orange and white, and finally Fulke Grenville with a somewhat smaller company in yellow and brown. Altogether something like 200 seem to have entered the tilt yard, in raiment little short of dazzling.

Once more the messenger addressed the Queen, once more called upon her to surrender. And then the float was moved up close to the royal seat and discoursed sweet music with two salutes accompanied by cornets, one urging the Queen to yield, the other calling upon the challengers to fight on to victory.

After that the two cannons were shot off, 'the one with sweet powder, the other with sweet water, very odoriferous and pleasant . . . And after that was store of pretty scaling ladders and the footmen threw flowers and such fancies against the walls'.

The defenders then entered the tilt yard, 'with every one his servants, pages and trumpeters, 24 of them all told, each one caparisoned after his own invention'.

More speeches followed. An angel spoke for the defenders, addressing herself to the assailants. 'Sir Knights,' she said, 'if in besieging the sun you understood what you had undertaken, you would not destroy a common blessing for a private benefit . . . Will you subdue the sun? Who shall rest in the shadow where the weary take breath, the disquiet rest and all, comfort? . . . We content to enjoy the light, you to eclipse it.' And so on and so on.

And then each defender in turn ran six courses against the challengers and so continued until 'night, the ordinary truce maker, wrapped all in her black and mourning weeds, . . . and therefore these knights, by the authority of darkness, very undesirously are compelled to depart from whence they came'.

The next day the challengers appeared in a brave chariot 'as men fore-wearied and half overcome'. Presently a Herald at Arms appeared and addressed the Queen, confessing that they fought without hope but that they meant to fight again, 'sooner their souls shall leave their bodies than desire shall leave their souls'.

And so the tilting was resumed and continued until evening, when the fighting ceased and the challengers made submission. 'They acknowledge this fortress to be reserved for the eye of the whole world . . . They acknowledge the least determination of Virtue, which stands for the guard of this fortress, to be too strong for the strongest desire.'

The symbolism is obvious. Desire represented Alençon, the fortress of Perfect Beauty the Queen, and the issue defined as that between making the Queen prisoner of desire or shedding her beams on all as a common blessing. It cannot have escaped the spectators that desire lost the fight. But what mattered most was the display of the great ones of France and the great ones of England making merry together. It must have been rather costly entertainment but it presented the world with a picture of Anglo-French friendship which Elizabeth probably thought was worth the price. It cannot have been without assistance from Court that the story of the Triumph was published.

What Burghley thought about it is not recorded. He was one of seven[17] whom the Queen appointed to negotiate with the French commissioners. They had their first conference on April 24th.[18] Burghley made the introductory speech, inviting the French to deliver their message. He apologized for his bad French. It had been intended that Walsingham should be their spokesman but he had a bad cold. At this meeting or at the next, three days later, they got down to business.[19] Burghley in a long speech declared that he regarded the marriage as imperative. He was answered by President Brisson of the Parlement of Paris with a speech to the same effect, who went on to produce a royal commission, empowering them to arrange a marriage, and nothing else.

According to Mendoza they continued to meet almost daily. The English commissioners suggested that whether a marriage were arranged or not they should conclude an offensive and defensive alliance. Mendoza thought that this was what the English were really after.[20]

The next we hear of them is on the 30th when they were dining with Burghley at Covent Garden. On that occasion Walsingham delivered a message from the Queen. She had, she said, sounded out the members of Parliament on the marriage and had found them doubtful, fearing that marriage with a Catholic would encourage her Catholic subjects to ignore the penal laws and that the marriage would draw her into war in the Low Countries, particularly since the French King had shown little disposition to assist his brother in the Low Countries or Don Antonio in Portugal. She had transmitted the information to Alençon and could not commit herself to any course until she had heard from him. Nevertheless, since she would not have such a distinguished company assembled to no purpose, she would issue formal instructions under the great seal for them to negotiate a treaty.

This ought to have been sufficient warning that she was herself far from committed, but the joint commissioners proceeded solemnly to the business of carving out a marriage treaty, using apparently as a basis the terms which had been drawn up hastily with Simier in November 1579.[21]

There is no point in following those tedious negotiations. Probably from Elizabeth's point of view they were mainly designed to save face and mark time.

Burghley can have had no illusions about them though he played out the role assigned to him with a straight face. It is only fair to point out that Elizabeth herself charged him to inform the Frenchmen that she would not be bound by any treaty, and that the final decision must be left to the Duke and herself. She did, however, encourage them to proceed in working out the details of a marriage agreement, if and when she decided to marry. The final results of their deliberations were recorded on June 11th.[22] But as in the case of the agreement with Simier, Elizabeth insisted that the French commissioners should in writing agree that the application of the treaty should depend upon a definite agreement to marry between the Duke and herself.[23]

Carrying that dubious answer the French commissioners went home, with matters no further forward. Mendoza says that the French left much disgruntled. 'I am assured', he wrote, 'that they are much offended at the Queen, having enticed them here on the assurance of the marriage, whereas they are going back with empty words and she has made use of their coming to magnify her own importance and diminish that of France, saying that they wished to make an alliance with her and nothing else. They resent this and with reason, as people judge that the French power must indeed be decayed if they are obliged to send so great an embassy for this purpose alone.'[24]

When the French commissioners left in June, Burghley stole away. He told Sussex that he was going to a secret place and left instructions to have his mail sent to Theobalds.[25]

Walsingham wrote to him on the 25th: 'I hope that the exercise of your body and the freedom of your mind in this little time of your absence will do you more good than all the drugs of Bucklersbury.'[26]

This time Burghley was laid up with a bad cough. His wife got in touch with Dr. Hector Nuñez, a distinguished Portuguese physician in London whom Burghley frequently consulted, and got instructions for treatment. He tried an enema, but when Burghley protested that it was too violent for hot weather, substituted oil of sweet almonds with sugar, or mixed with white wine.[27] Burghley complained about the cough and what he called rheum, that is to say, running at the nose and in the throat. Nuñez told Burghley to take the lozenges which he had previously refused to take. The treatment sounds intelligent, but Burghley was evidently not a very docile patient. We hear nothing at this juncture of his old enemy, the gout. He was back again at Court in mid-July.[28]

Not long after his return to Court he wrote to his friend, the Earl of Shrewsbury:[29]

'Your Lordship may hear of Don Antonio, entitling himself King of Portugal, who now lodgeth at Baynard's Castle [in London], as I think, by means of my L. of Leicester. I never as yet saw him, but some of my Lords of the Council that have spoken with him report him to be very wise, modest, slow but grave of speech. And he meaneth to try his fortune to be a king or nobody. He hath very rich jewels, having in France taken up great sums of money, wherewith he hireth ships and men both in France and England to repair to the isles of the Azores.'

What Burghley did not tell Shrewsbury was that there was a plan afoot, of which Walsingham seems to have been the chief promoter, to organize an expedition against the Azores under Drake's command.[30] The idea was to establish a base of operations in the Azores and there to lie in wait for the Spanish treasure fleet from the West Indies. Drake was to be commissioned by Don Antonio and sail under his flag. The expedition was to be financed by joint stock, Don Antonio himself to contribute a quarter. The plunder was to be divided among the adventurers in proportion to their investment. It was hoped that Elizabeth herself would subscribe.

With Drake in command and a convenient base of operations on the highway to the Indies, the scheme looked like an amazingly good one.

The adventurers pointed out that the realm of England was not committed. But Elizabeth was not so sure. The realm of England had not been committed to Drake's voyage of circumnavigation, but it had brought England measurably close to war with Spain. What would happen if Drake from the Azores did intercept the Spanish plate fleet could hardly be doubted. It would mean war, and Elizabeth was in no mood to invite war unless she could count upon French support.

Burghley's colleagues had evidently formed a favourable opinion of Don Antonio, but that may mean no more than that Walsingham and Leicester were predisposed in his favour. On August 21st Burghley drew up a memorandum on the subject of the Drake enterprise,[31] doubtless intended for a discussion of the matter before the Privy Council. It started out by saying that since the Azores were a possession of Don Antonio, no offence of league or treaty with Spain was involved in English assistance to him in maintaining it. 'Her Majesty', he observed, 'is not bound to take knowledge of any other rights that kings have but as their possession yieldeth knowledge.'

He went on to say that there were no treaties between Spain and England for Portugal or its possessions. He concluded that 'for a matter of league, her Majesty may permit Sir Francis Drake to serve the King Antonio to maintain that he possesseth or to recover anything taken from him whereof he was, as a King, possessed'.

That being so, he raised the question as to what was 'convenient or expedient' for the Queen to do about it. He conceded that 'it is profitable and convenient that the islands of Azores, and other territories of Portugal were rather in possession of Don Antonio than in the King of Spain for many apparent causes'.

But he pointed out that unless the French King co-operated, it would be too perilous for England alone, whatever the rights and wrongs of the matter. He said further that unless France gave very substantial aid it would not suffice to restore Don Antonio to the Portuguese throne, and that short of that, his mere possession of the Azores 'will be but a perpetual war or charge'.

Burghley observed that an expedition under Drake might provoke the King of Spain to arrest all Englishmen, English ships and English property 'within his power'.

He thought it might be well to stay merchant ships from going to Spain, to confer with the merchants as to the loss of Customs to the Queen involved, to consider whether 'in respect of the money' (that is to say Drake's plunder from his Pacific adventure), in the Queen's hands, the Spanish King would venture to seize English property. On this point Burghley may have recalled with some satisfaction Elizabeth's seizure of the Spanish pay ships in 1569, to which the King of Spain had retorted by seizing English property and had come off second best. He suggested that English merchants might get what they needed from Spain 'without conveying into Philip's dominion a greater number of ships, mariners or goods'.

On the whole, Burghley's presentation of the problem to the Council was favourable to the Drake enterprise. He then put a number of questions to the Council:

Shall Drake be allowed to proceed before the French King gives assurance that he will join with Elizabeth for defence if Philip does any violence to her subjects, by arresting their property or by invasion or by supporting her enemies in Scotland? The Council answered NO.

He then asked what assurance should be required of the French. The answer was by a letter from the French King or by his appointee.

Meanwhile, Burghley asked what was to be done about the great preparations for Drake's voyage. He pointed out that the maintenance of the ships in port was costing £20 a day or more. They might diminish the charges by discharging much of the personnel, or they might presently dispatch three ships and a bark from the fleet and keep the rest in readiness until the French answer came. Or they might abandon the whole enterprise, disposing of the victuals to merchant traders and reserving the munitions for the Queen.

Or they might carry on according to the original plan as soon as they are ready.[32]

He raised a further question as to what Drake should do if the French King joined in the action. Upon that point the memorandum is vague. Apparently there were those in the Council who favoured war upon Spain in the Canaries or in the West Indies or Peru. But there were others — Burghley himself was probably among them — who foresaw that a general war on Spanish possessions, even in Don Antonio's name, would provoke retaliation by Spain upon England, and expressed considerable doubt as to whether the game were worth the candle.[33]

Meanwhile, the French King declined to give the necessary assurance, the Queen began to balk at increased costs, and some of the adventurers withdrew. In a letter to Walsingham of August 18th, Burghley reported that Elizabeth was 'very cold in the cause of Don Antonio'. A little later in the month, he wrote again: 'Though the French King, to our ambassador there and by his own [in London], said that he would aid Don Antonio yet these be but words changeably by a Prince . . . If it please him to write a letter to her Majesty to assure her that he will join with her in aiding Don Antonio and if, for his action, the King of Spain shall offer offence to her Majesty or her subjects, he shall repute the quarrel his own, jointly with her, in defence of her and offence of the King of Spain, such a writing may animate her Majesty to that which I think otherwise she will not resolve.'[34]

He wrote again to Walsingham on September 2nd, deploring the lack of assurance from the French King. And so Drake's project was abandoned and Don Antonio left England to seek his fortune in France. Thence, the following year, he set forth on an expedition which was met and decisively defeated by the Spanish fleet. Most of Don Antonio's supporters were killed and he himself escaped with nothing but his life. The year after that the Azores fell to Spain, and Philip's possession of the Portuguese empire was complete.

Don Antonio and his claims remained a constant factor in Anglo-Spanish relations for many years to come.[35] The other constant factor was the revolt in the Low Countries. The aggressive element in the Privy Council, led by Leicester and Walsingham, favoured the exploitation of these factors for all they were worth. Elizabeth was not disposed to throw her weight in either direction unless she could count upon the full co-operation of France. Her objective at the time was an offensive and defensive alliance with France. She hoped to achieve this through the Duke of Alençon and encouraged his ambitions in the Low Countries because she thought that, as the French King's brother and the heir presumptive to the French throne, his commitment there would inevitably draw France into a conflict with Spain. It is clear enough that both Henry III and his mother, Catherine de Medicis, were very reluctant to come to blows with Spain. On the other hand, they were both very eager to get the Duke off their hands and indicated their willingness to support him in the Low Countries if Elizabeth married him. It is fairly apparent that Elizabeth had no intention of marrying him, but she found it expedient to create the impression that she would marry him. She distrusted the French King and was by no means certain that he would keep his promise of support when she had irrevocably committed herself at the altar. Henry plainly distrusted her, and evidently felt that unless she were irrevocably committed, she would leave him in the lurch after he had taken up the cudgels with Spain.[36] His position was, no marriage no league; hers, first a league and then perhaps a marriage.

In July she decided to send Walsingham to France to see what could be done.[37] It fell to Burghley's task to prepare Walsingham's instructions, and no less than seven memoranda of his on the subject survive. Two of the longest of them deal with Elizabeth's reasons for not coming to an immediate decision on marriage and the necessity for immediate joint action against Spain. Two of them envisage the possibilities of marriage.[38] It is fairly obvious that Burghley was seeking to express the royal intentions, almost equally obvious that he was groping more or less in the dark. What finally emerged, according to Walsingham's own interpretation of his orders, he summarized a little later in a letter to the Queen.

'The principal cause', he wrote, 'why I was sent over, as I conceive it . . . was to procure a straiter degree of amity between the King and you without marriage and yet to carry myself in the procuring thereof as might not altogether break off the matter of marriage.'

But he discovered presently that whatever he did was wrong. 'I would to God', he wrote to Burghley in August, 'her Majesty would resolve one way or the other touching the matter of her marriage ... When her Majesty is pressed to marry then she seemeth to affect a league and when a league is yielded to, then she liketh better of a marriage. And when thereupon she is moved to assent to marriage then she hath recourse to the league, when the motion for a league or any request is made for money, then her Majesty returneth to the marriage ... It shall therefore be most necessary for your Lordship and the rest of the Council to move her Majesty to grow to some earnest resolution in that behalf.'

He was equally bitter about her cheese-paring policy, and at the very end of his mission spoke out boldly to Elizabeth herself on the subject. 'I see it,' he wrote, 'and they stick not to say it, that the only cause that moveth them here not to weigh your Majesty's friendship is for that they see your Majesty doth fly charges otherwise than by doing somewhat underhand ... In all directions we have now received, we have special charge not to yield to anything that may be accompanied by charges. The general league must be without any certain charges, the particular league with a voluntary and no certain charge, as also that is to be attempted in favour of Don Antonio. If this sparing and improvident course be held still ... I conclude ... that no one that serveth in place of a Councillor that either weigheth his own credit or carrieth that sound affection to your Majesty as he ought to do, that would not wish himself in the farthest part of Ethiopia rather than enjoying the fairest palace in England.'[39]

Poor Walsingham was at his wits' end. He did not know what his royal mistress really wanted. Probably she did not know herself. She did not want to commit herself irrevocably to marry Alençon, even when the French King promised in that event to enter into a strait league and to bear all the burden of Alençon's Low Countries adventure. She would not contemplate open war with Spain, and she was in two minds about facilitating French conquest of the Low Countries.

Certainly Walsingham did his best, though it is open to question whether his policy of decisive action would have yielded better results than the shifty alternatives of his mistress. Actually, Burghley had the more difficult role to play, for during Walsingham's absence it fell to Burghley to direct, or at least to interpret, the royal mind. Probably he was a good deal more tolerant of Elizabeth's tergiversations than Walsingham was. He had been all through it during the first decade of the reign. In much the same terms that Walsingham used he had protested against her indecisiveness in marriage and her sparing and improvident course in general. But he had discovered that the calamities which he prophesied had not come to pass. He had watched England flourish and grow strong and rich in peace and had perhaps reached the conclusion that there was a good deal to be said for the erratic course of his erratic mistress. In any case, he had learned to accept it and be co-operative with it. He was older and wiser than he had been, less positive, more deferential. Without doubt he was the most influential of all her councillors, and he found it more to the purpose to strengthen his influence by acquiescence than to weaken it by opposition.

But with the best will in the world to see done what she wanted done, he was hard put to it to discover what her intentions were. He certainly knew what she did not want. But he could not pin her down to any positive plan of action. Probably she had no plan. By this time she seems to have realized that the great menace to her peace and security was Spain. But she had watched Philip II throw away one good opportunity after another to attack her, had heard the cry, wolf, wolf, so often when there was no wolf, that she had about concluded that her leaden-footed brother-in-law would take no aggressive action against her unless he were provoked beyond the limits of even his monumental patience. Indeed, up to the very moment when the Armada was approaching the Channel, she still thought that she might come to terms with him.

It was in such a frame of reference that Burghley had to work. On August 6th he wrote to Walsingham from the Court at Greenwich, 'where', he added, 'I am tied by your absence'.[40] He was tied indeed. From the time of Walsingham's departure until his return, Burghley did not miss a single meeting of the Privy Council.[41]

He maintained a constant correspondence with Walsingham. Copies of fifteen of his letters are preserved, though the originals, with one exception, appear to be lost.

He received Walsingham's first dispatches on August 9th, just as he was about to leave for a short vacation. 'I was on the north side of the water [the Thames],' he wrote to Walsingham from Greenwich, 'but by good fortune I had word of his [your courier's] arrival, so as I returned, being not gone from the water side.' He went on to say that the Queen had been somewhat critical of Walsingham's procedure. 'To this I answered,' Burghley wrote, 'that your order in procedure was warranted by your instructions . . . I found her touched with some fear that this league and secret treaty should be very chargeable unto her. I told her that there would be no great matter managed that was free from charge, and if she had no need of assistance to withstand her perils (which she knew and so doth all the world besides see it manifestly) otherwise she needed not to have sent you at this time. . . .

'For the greatest matter in the letter expressed by the Viscount of Turenne [a request for an immediate substantial loan to Alençon], I dealt with her Majesty earnestly therein; and having made my Lord of Leicester first acquainted with your letters, next my Lord Chamberlain [Sussex] and then Mr. Vice-Chamberlain [Hatton], I required their assistance . . . as a matter most necessary for the French cause in hand.'

Elizabeth was non-committal. Walsingham, she said, had commission to satisfy Alençon's needs. 'But presently,' Burghley added, 'upon seeking to persuade her that words were no satisfaction but that deeds must do it, and such as they could not be performed with words or thoughts, no, nor in short time, she answered me that you had warrant from her to yield to that which was required when you had found the [French] King's disposition to help his brother.' She added that the French were trying their best to lay the whole burden on her. 'This', Burghley concluded, 'is the substance of that I can wring from her.' He went on to observe that Alençon had spent a lot of time on his preparations and was still a long way from his objective. 'I fear', he added, 'the Queen Mother, finding the marriage desperate, will practice with the Duke of Parma to withdraw his siege [of Cambray] and that the town may be relieved and so Monsieur's honour saved. And thereby Monsieur may leave his general enterprise, whereunto the Spaniards ought to be contented. For thereby shall they have their wills in the Low Countries; and so also the Queen Mother may save her son from gun shot and put up all her pretences and live without offence to the King of Spain.'[42]

This letter reveals clearly the nature of Burghley's problem. It reveals also his fear that the Queen's parsimony would ruin the hope of any effective alliance with France.

Burghley evidently considered Alençon's request for an immediate loan as the most significant development in the business, and called upon the three most influential of his associates to urge it upon the Queen. It was the one positive step which the Queen a little later was willing to take. We hear little about deliberations in the Privy Council as a whole. Elizabeth was evidently playing her cards very closely to her chest, as she frequently did whenever courtship became mingled with diplomacy.

In his next letter, of the 11th, Burghley wrote that the Queen thought Walsingham had taken too positive a stand against the marriage. 'To this', Burghley wrote, 'I made answer, Madam, ... he did proceed to open your mind for forbearing to marry as you yourself did determine with us all and as he is warranted by your instructions ... I ended that I could not see that you had done anything but that I, myself, in your place, would have done the same. And I did put her Majesty in remembrance that all her resolutions with us of her Council was that you should so deal as to acquit her of the marriage; and if there might be a good amity made and by a league betwixt France and the realm to abate the King of Spain's greatness, which, I did object, required a present action and to that end you should so proceed as there might appear no hope of marriage. For as long as France could perceive any hope thereof, they would not assent to any league. To this her Majesty could not but assent, but finally she changed her opinion in saying that if she should make a league whereby a war might follow ... she had rather be at charge of a war with the marriage than without the marriage.'

Two days later she told Burghley that she would help Alençon if the French King would also help, that she would be willing to enter into a league offensive and defensive provided it did not lead directly to open war. 'In this sort', Burghley wrote to Walsingham on the 13th, 'she hath willed me expressly to write to you, not allowing any argument to the contrary whereof I made divers, ... for by these means the King of Spain's greatness shall grow to such ripeness as hereafter no open force shall withstand it ... In this sort I am commanded to write to you but in what sort you shall deal to remedy this inconvenience neither by her Majesty can I direct you nor of myself can I inform you ... I know it will greatly grieve you not to have a good answer for the loan moved by the Viscount, but surely all means are used here to help but none prevail as yet.'

Late the same day he wrote again: 'Her Majesty doubteth that the Queen Mother will withdraw Monsieur from the Low Country action, meaning thereby to obtain the marriage, which her Majesty cannot allow ... How you shall be able to order in this you must there seek the way. For aiding of Monsieur, these are her Majesty's words, that if you find the King not willing to support his brother, rather than the action shall fail, you shall say that her Majesty will not see him destitute. But the sum she will not name till she hear from you.'

Four days later, Burghley reported that she was talking about her willingness to marry. He wrote on the 17th: 'I find her Majesty in words more inclined to the marriage than at your departure.'

Walsingham had meanwhile written that reports from England indicating the Queen's disposition to marry had encouraged the French King to refuse any treaty without marriage. To this Burghley wrote on the 18th: 'She denieth that any one here hath any cause to give comfort in the marriage, but truly I think some have had such a conceit and whether they have sent it over since I know not.'

On the 24th he received dispatches from France and messages from Alençon, the gist of which was that the French King was giving no aid to his brother, who had reached the end of his resources and would be compelled to abandon his enterprise unless immediate aid were forthcoming.[43] This news seems at long last to have stirred the Queen to action. She bade Burghley write to Walsingham that she had given orders for the immediate dispatch to Alençon of £30,000. Half of it was sent at once by Lord Seymour.

It fell to Burghley as Lord Treasurer to provide the money. In a letter to Walsingham of the 27th he discussed the problem of transfer. Money, he said, was hard to come by. Leicester had discussed with Horatio Palavicino, a Genoese merchant resident in London from whom Elizabeth had borrowed money more than once, the feasibility of transferring the money by exchange to Paris, and Palavicino had undertaken to manage it. But upon inquiry Burghley had discovered that the interest charges alone would amount to about 10 per cent, that Palavicino was not certain whether he could raise that much, nor for what term. He thought he might have to deal through Antwerp, and felt that he ought to go himself to Paris. Altogether Burghley decided that the charges were too high and that long delays were almost certain. The transfer of specie involved a load which was more than two pack horses could carry. And pack horses eliminated the possibility of using the posts, the speediest form of travel. He accordingly divided the load into four parts and distributed it among four carriers, each one to ride with his portion upon a pillion. He asked Walsingham's advice about transferring the second half.[44] He himself thought it would be better to send the second half also in specie, though he feared pirates by sea and robbers by land. Walsingham agreed, and so it was subsequently arranged.[45] The correspondence on this subject presents an interesting picture of the problems involved in the speedy transfer of funds, particularly to areas which did relatively little business with England. That explains why Palavicino thought he might have to deal through Antwerp.

Elizabeth, having decided to subsidize Alençon herself, seems to have lost interest in a treaty with France. On September 2nd Burghley wrote: 'I will not write to you of the uncertainties here. As I take patience here in soliciting, so you must in the lack of what were meet for you. The letters that have been writ to you ... have been altered twice and yet scantily go with allowance.' He added, in a second note on the same day: 'What may further move her Majesty hereafter I know not, but I see it common to great and small not to think of adversity in time of prosperity and so adversity cometh with double peril'.[46]

This is the last word we have from him on the subject to Walsingham during the residue of his mission in France. He returned to England late in September with nothing to show for his pains. His failure practically marked the abandonment of any attempt to form a league with France. Elizabeth followed instead the policy of binding her fortunes with those of Alençon and keeping him in train, now by dangling the prospect of marriage before his eyes and now by lending him badly needed money.

Alençon came to England late in October and spent the next three months there. He hoped to marry the Queen, or, failing that, to secure from her large loans for his enterprises. Of his entertainment we hear very little except in Mendoza's dispatches, which are very full and, where they can be checked from other sources, not always accurate. Mendoza himself was, of course, interested in preventing an Anglo-French alliance by marriage or otherwise. He never took the marriage seriously, and on one occasion offered odds of 100 to 1 that it would never take place.[47] It is from Mendoza that we get the details of the familiar story that on one occasion, when the French ambassador demanded of Elizabeth whether she intended to marry or not, she told him to write to his master that Alençon would be her husband and kissed him on the mouth and handed him a ring in pledge.[48] It may be that the whole gesture was prearranged in order to provoke the French King to action. Elizabeth herself was presently explaining that it had no binding force.

It is hard to take seriously the cat-and-mouse tactics which followed. Leicester and Walsingham and Hatton, who opposed the marriage, evidently took them seriously. Sussex, who supported it, was non-committal. Of Burghley we hear little or nothing. In one of his diaries he records that by royal command he spoke with Alençon on November 4th. But there is no record of the conference. According to Mendoza, Burghley and Sussex and Leicester usually visited the Duke at nine in the morning, which in Burghley's case is doubtful. That was not the sort of thing which Elizabeth required of him.

We have a draft in his hand of a proposed agreement between Elizabeth and the Duke, dated November 14th, which ignored marriage altogether and was nothing more than a promise on the Queen's part to help Alençon in the Low Countries if the French King would do the like. But it can hardly be taken seriously. We have also record of Burghley's appointment to a commission of four, the others being the Lord Chancellor, Sussex and Leicester, to deal with Pinart, who came over from France late in November with assurance from the

French King that he would, after the marriage, join in league with England and would match whatever Elizabeth would contribute to support the Duke in the Low Countries.[49] According to Mendoza, the English commissioners conferred daily with Pinart, but, as was to be expected, got nowhere. Presumably they were merely marking time.

There appears to be no record of Burghley's attitude towards the match at this juncture, neither from him nor from Mendoza. Evidently Mendoza regarded him as more kindly disposed towards Spain than his colleagues and early in November found occasion to warn him that he should beware of French intrigue in Scotland and with Mary Stuart.[50] Burghley in reply pointed out that the French King was helping his brother in the Low Countries and strongly supported Don Antonio's pretensions in Portugal. Mendoza retorted that it was contrary to English interests to establish the French in the Low Countries, and that Don Antonio's cause was a hopeless one. He does not record Burghley's reply. In reporting the conversation to Philip II, Mendoza observed that Burghley was evidently interested in emphasizing Spanish need of English friendship. It is significant that it was to Burghley that Mendoza turned as a possible counter-check to the solidifying of an Anglo-French alliance.

As time went on, Elizabeth became increasingly interested in getting rid of Alençon. She called upon Burghley to get rid of him by promising him money. Leicester at a Council meeting suggested that he be given £200,000, to be raised by privy seal, and intimated that Alençon would be satisfied. But Elizabeth would not hear of it. In a burst of rage she declared that since the Duke thought fit to forget her in exchange for her money, she would neither marry him nor give him any money. And she said as much to Alençon himself. A little later she talked about being a sister to him.

At a Council meeting late in December, Burghley proposed that it would be advisable under the circumstances to mend their fences with Spain, and suggested that as a preliminary step Drake's plunder be returned. The Council at once divided on the subject, with the Admiral and the Chancellor and Sir James Croft supporting Burghley; Leicester, Walsingham, Hatton and Knollys all opposing him. No decision is recorded, but Burghley a little later found occasion to broach the subject of a rapprochement with Spain to a Spaniard who came to see him on other business. At least that was what Mendoza reported, and he went on to say that English people great and small were strong for Spanish friendship. This we may take for wishful thinking.

As December passed into January, Elizabeth's eagerness to rid herself of Alençon increased. She feared that the French King, no less anxious to get rid of his brother, would accede to all her demands. According once more to Mendoza, she asked Burghley what she could do. He advised her to increase her demands, to ask for Calais and to start civil disturbances in France.[51] She welcomed at least the first part of the suggestion, and in a subsequent interview with Alençon announced that she could not consent to the marriage unless Calais and Havre were both delivered to her and garrisoned with English troops. But she wavered once again a day or so later, and called her Council to consider. The meeting got nowhere. It seems to have ended in a brawl between Sussex, supporting the marriage, and Leicester, opposing it. Burghley had to separate them. Afterwards Elizabeth talked over the matter privately with him. We have no record of what passed between them but the outcome was that she ordered the ships to be got ready for Alençon's departure.

After several false starts he at long last set forth from London on February 1st. The Queen herself accompanied him as far as Canterbury. He took with him £10,000 and the promise of £50,000 more. At the last minute he wrote to Burghley and asked him to pay over to Palavicino the promised balance.[52] Leicester and a troop of nobles were told off to convey him to Antwerp. He embarked on February 7th, 1582, at Sandwich. Elizabeth displayed great grief at his parting, and swore she would never be happy until he came back. Her ladies-in-waiting reported that in the privacy of her chamber she danced for joy.[53]

A letter from Burghley to Walsingham written a few days after the Duke's departure[54] gives an inkling of factors in the whole affair which supplied Burghley with useful information:

'Marchemont is come to this town [Westminster] and desireth to speak with me, which I think will be for money ... Of late his lodging in Cannon Row was robbed and in a trunk his writings were also embezzled and the trunk conveyed into a yard where the persons that found it, perusing such writings, brought to me the very indented papers betwixt du Bex and you, written in your name, the discovery whereof made me ready to blush, to see by that accident such secrets made common.[55]

'As I can guess, whoredom in the house bred the theft, even as the like did to Combelles, by that infamous strumpet the Lady Hilton, a whore and a bawd to her two daughters.' Combelles, a few days earlier, had lost a gold chain in doing violence to a serving maid, and the chain turned up in the pocket of John Hilton.[56] Burghley was not only familiar with both cases, but he got possession of a whole mass of the private correspondence of Marchemont and Du Bex which is still preserved at Hatfield House.[57] One wonders whether it was all accidental or whether Burghley's channels of intelligence reached as far down as the Elizabethan underworld of bawds and strumpets.

Pari passu with the love-making at Court, Burghley had to deal with a romance of quite a different character in his own family. It concerned his second daughter, Elizabeth, the Queen's own namesake, who was just past eighteen years of age. The first inkling of it appears in a letter which Lord Wentworth wrote to Burghley on June 8th, 1581.[58]

'Truly my Lord,' he wrote, 'for his liking of my son of your daughter I never thought of it nor knew anything of it till himself opened the matter with me.' He went on to say that being conscious of his own poverty and realizing that Burghley might make a much better match for his daughter, he had hesitated to write to

Lady Burghley about it. But his son's importunity had prevailed. 'Yet,' he continued, 'I must confess unto your Lordship that I did somewhat rejoice that my son did make so honourable a choice and in so good a house and that in this wanton time he was not wantonly disposed. But I understand that he hath had this mind any time this twelve months. Wherefore, being his own choice, if God shall prosper it, he is bound to like her and love her the better.'

Thomas Wentworth, 2nd Baron Wentworth of Nettlestead (Suffolk), sprang from the Yorkshire Wentworths from which the great Earl of Strafford also traced his descent. Lord Thomas won his spurs at Pinkie, under the Protector Somerset, and later commanded Calais at the time it was lost to France. Under Elizabeth he served for a time as Lord Lieutenant of Norfolk and Suffolk, but he never held any other important office under the Crown. He was of an old and reputable family, but not comparable in rank or station or wealth with Burghley's other children-in-law.

Burghley might have aspired to a more distinguished connection for young Elizabeth. But after the sad history of his daughter Ann's marriage, he may well have concluded that kind hearts were more than coronets. In any case he favoured the match and during the summer was engaged in the business of haggling over terms. Wentworth asked that Burghley should give £2500, £2000 for himself and £500 to establish the young couple. He offered in return a jointure of £100 by the year in lands, £100 more upon his death and after the death of himself and his wife, lands to the annual value of £800. He specified that the wedding should take place in Burghley's house, and suggested that after the marriage the young couple should reside with Burghley. 'For my son,' he wrote, 'I think it much better he should remain with you both that you may see his usage and behaviour towards your daughter and also that he may learn of you to become a meet and serviceable man towards her Majesty and the Commonwealth.'

There is an intimation in this last sentence that his son, William, had been a member of Burghley's household before the question of marriage was raised. If so, that would explain the opportunity for courtship. It would also explain Burghley's evident affection for the young man.

Further haggling took the form of Burghley's trying to get more from Wentworth and trying to pay less himself. At the time Lord Wentworth was living at Mile End. He suggested (June 20th)[59] that Burghley stop off on his way to Theobalds and talk things over. All the difficulties seem to have been ironed out by August 20th.[60]

The wedding took place on the 26th of the following February, and the festivities attending it lasted for three days. The day before the ceremony Burghley wrote to Walsingham:[61]

'You know the old true saying, *ex abundantia cordis os loquitur* — and since at this present I cannot utter by mouth the fullness of my heart, by mine absence, yet my heart will not be quieted without some venting, either by speech or writing. And therefore by these few lines I am bold with you, my dear friend, to deliver unto you and so, at your commodity and in time convenient, to her Majesty, that though my conscience persuaded me, by my devout mind to her Majesty and many evidences of her Majesty's favours to me above my desert, but not above my heart, that her Majesty was my gracious sovereign and lady, yet a special argument of this day, showed to Mr. Wentworth and by him brought to me, keeping my bed, hath fast sealed up my former conceptions of her singular goodness. And as her Majesty hath used the same she hath, as it were, in one bundle overladen me and mine with a burden of benefit far beyond all our powers any wise to acquit or to lighten. For as he reporteth, her Majesty in commenting on the matching of my daughter, used so gracious speeches of me, my wife and my daughter, in such effectual sort as thereby she hath increased and stablished his liking, as could not by my purse be redeemed. And therefore her Majesty therein hath increased my daughter's value above my ability. And so I am sure the gentleman addeth this to his account more than all the money I could give with her.

'And on the other part, the gentleman, with such modesty reporteth her Majesty's good liking of himself that, though he forbeareth to utter the speeches because he will not sound out his own praise, yet, both I, my wife, and specially my daughter, esteem her Majesty's favour towards him as, in all our opinions, the same may prove for a great portion of a jointure, and so the gentleman of more value to us all by that we conceive of her Majesty's so gracious allowance of him.

'And so, good Mr. Secretary, I pray you make the best of this hasty writing, which is in my bed and therefore the worse written.'

It is characteristic of Burghley that he did not send his thanks to his sovereign direct. It is characteristic of her that she took advantage of the occasion to send him added evidence of her old affection. She did not attend the wedding. It is to be hoped that he was able to get out of bed and attend it himself. We hear nothing about it from ambassadors or courtiers, which suggests that it was a country wedding at Theobalds. In any case, it was of impressive magnificence.[62] The total expense came to £629 6s. 10d. An idea of the food and drink consumed can be gathered from a few items in the expense account, which included ten hogsheads of Gascon wine and two hogsheads of white wine, 109 pheasants, 277 partridges, 485 snipe, 840 larks, 41 turkeys, 201 capons and 135 ducks, to say nothing of incredible amounts of the old staples, beef and mutton and veal and beer. The hire of extra cooks came to £25, musicians to £10, and players to £5. We know nothing of the guests, nothing of the entertainment, though it must have approached the riotous at times if we are to judge by a bill of 37 shillings for broken glass.

After the wedding the bride and groom settled down at Theobalds, and Burghley was very happy in their company. He grew increasingly fond of his new son-in-law, and was prostrate with grief when the young man was suddenly stricken by the plague in November. Thomas Billot, his steward, wrote on the 6th that Wentworth was in the very article of death, and calling for his wife with such insistence that, notwithstanding the danger of infection, she went to him. He died the following day.[63]

Sir Christopher Hatton wrote to Burghley on the 8th:

'My singular good Lord, Her Majesty standeth so much moved with your sorrowful letters as she findeth herself more fit to accompany you in your grief than to comfort you in your incredible loss. Your Lordship, so well and holily instrumental in God's fear and so well exercised with the mutable accidents of this wretched world, will call reason to your relief, with thankfulness that God, the creator of us all, hath called this virtuous and zealous creature to the participation of His heavenly inheritance . . . My good Lord, cast off this woe, let it not touch your heart in which the wisdom of this world and state hath found her seat for so many years, to God's glory, the Realm's safety and your mortal renown.'[64]

Burghley replied the following day:

'I have great cause to thank you for your letter, full of good counsel and godly advice, which God give me grace to follow, knowing it necessary for me to obey His will in all things. But yet a hard lesson for flesh to learn and herein my case differeth from all others. For though I know I ought to thank you, yet contrariwise to all other causes that require thanks, which are given with joy from the heart, in this I cannot but sprinkle my thanks with tears and sobbings . . . I will not defend my passions, but beseech God to be my comfort, as in some part I feel thereof, by the comfortable messages sent to me and mine by His principal minister, my sovereign sweet lady, the Queen's Majesty, whom I pray God to preserve from all grief of mind and body, whereby her poor people may long enjoy her as a mother and nurse of general peace, both worldly and heavenly, by the free teaching of God's will out of His holy word . . . And truly, Mr. Vice-Chamberlain, I do not lament so much the loss of a son-in-law (which was very good) but of a virtuous gentleman, in whom I took so great delight as how my grief is the more increased.'[65]

Wentworth's father wrote to Burghley: 'I thank my God that He hath made the burden somewhat the lighter that he hath left my daughter with child, whom if it pleases His goodness to bless as my prayer is, we shall receive some comfort after this sorrow.'[66]

Burghley's grief at the death of one son-in-law was accentuated by his continued worry about his other son-in-law, the Earl of Oxford. During 1579 and 1580 Oxford had enjoyed exceptional favour at Court and with the Queen. He got into a tennis-court brawl with Sir Philip Sidney in the autumn of 1579, which might have led to a duel had not Elizabeth herself intervened. As it was, the superior rank of Oxford held the field and Sidney had to retire for a time. But the indications are that Court sympathy was with Sidney, and certainly Sidney's uncle, the Earl of Leicester, and Sir Christopher Hatton, who regarded Oxford as his rival for the royal favour, were definitely against him. Of Burghley's attitude we hear nothing, but his old affection for young Sidney, his unpleasant memories of Oxford's earlier insolences, and the fact that Oxford was still estranged from his wife, Burghley's favourite daughter, leave the matter in little doubt.

The year following, Oxford suddenly fell from royal favour. It appears that he

had secretly become a Roman Catholic, and had identified himself with some
other courtiers of the same complexion, notably with Lord Henry Howard, Charles
Arundel and Francis Southwell. For some undisclosed reason — his biographers
ascribe it to patriotism — Oxford revealed his fall from grace to the Queen and
proceeded to denounce his Catholic associates. In the royal presence he called
upon Mauvissière, the French ambassador, to substantiate his story. And
Mauvissière straightway denied any knowledge of it. The immediate consequence
was that though Howard and Arundel and Southwell were placed in restraint,
Oxford, by Mauvissière's account,[67] 'lost credit and honour and has been abandoned by all his friends and by all the ladies of the Court'.

It is not unlikely that the Queen's animosity towards him was quickened by his
love affair with Ann Vavasour, one of the Maids of Honour, a young lady of many
loves, whom Burghley described as a drab,[68] that is to say, a whore. On March
23rd, 1581, Walsingham wrote to Huntingdon:[69] 'On Tuesday at night, Ann
Vavasour was brought to bed of a son in the maiden's chamber. The E. of Oxford
is vowed to be the father, who hath withdrawn himself with intent, as it is thought,
to pass the seas. The ports are laid for him and therefore, if he have any such
determination, it is not likely that he will escape. The gentlewoman, the self same
night she was delivered, was conveyed out of the house and the next day committed
to the Tower . . . Her Majesty is greatly grieved with the accident.'

It may have been in this connection that Oxford was also committed to the
Tower, though he seems to have been released in June.

For the next two years Burghley interested himself in the restoration of Oxford
to the royal favour. But Elizabeth refused to receive him. To make matters worse,
Oxford got into a brawl, in the spring of 1582, about Ann Vavasour with Thomas
Knyvet of the Privy Chamber, in which both of them were hurt, Oxford, as it
was reported, dangerously.[70]

The affair seems to have had, momentarily, a chastening effect on Oxford. In
midsummer he was reconciled to his wife.[71] But the feud with Knyvet still
continued, spread to their followers and resulted in the murder of one of Knyvet's
servants, which Knyvet blamed on Oxford. Burghley wrote a long account of the
situation to Hatton on March 12th and undertook to vindicate Oxford.

'If', he wrote, 'his [Oxford's] own punishment past and his humble seeking of
forgiveness cannot recover her Majesty's favour, yet some, yea many, may think
that the intercession of me and my poor wife, so long and importunately continued,
might have obtained some spark of favour of her Majesty, but hereof I will in no
wise complain of too much hardness but to myself . . . Both I and she [Lady
Burghley] are determined to suffer and lament our misfortune that when our
son-in-law was in prosperity he was a cause of our adversity by his unkind usage
of us and ours. And now that he is ruined and in adversity, we only are made
partakers thereof and by no means, no, not by the bitter tears of my wife, can
obtain a spark of favour for him . . . God preserve her Majesty and grant her only
to understand the true hearts of my poor wife and me, and then I doubt not the
sequel of her gracious favours in far greater matters than we have required. We

have not many years to live, perchance not many days and the fewer, I am sure, to find lack of her favours.'

It can hardly be believed that Burghley had any personal interest in Oxford's fate. It was family pride that was in question, accentuated by the reconciliation of Oxford and his wife, and of Ann's pregnancy and hope of a son. Most of all it was Burghley's feeling that having spent his life in Elizabeth's service, and being recognized as her chief adviser, he could not at least win for his son-in-law official countenance.

It is not surprising that when he heard, a day or so after he had written in the bitterness of his spirit, that the Queen meant to visit him at Theobalds at Easter-tide, his response was something less than enthusiastic. 'My grief is', he wrote to Hatton on March 18th,[72] 'that neither my health and strength, nor my wife's presence can serve to supply the wants that will be there [at Theobalds] but they must be all covered with the serenity of her Majesty's countenance.' And he went on to speak again of Oxford's misfortunes, which 'increase my wife's grief and mine own more than I will mention'.

Actually the Queen did not visit Theobalds until late in May. Meanwhile, in April, Burghley suffered another domestic tragedy in the death of his daughter, Elizabeth, Wentworth's widow.[73] Burghley was profoundly depressed, so much depressed that Elizabeth directed Walsingham to rebuke him.

'Her Majesty hath willed me', Walsingham wrote to Burghley on April 20th, 'to signify unto your Lordship that as she hath been pleased for a time to permit you to wrestle with nature, not doubting but that wisdom and religion hath wrought in you ere this that resolution that appertaineth to a man of your place and calling; so now she thinketh that if the health of your body may so permit you, you should do better to occupy yourself in dealing in public affairs than by secluding yourself from access to give yourself over a prey to grief.

'And if you might conveniently repair hither she would be glad to have your Lordship's advice in a matter of weight concerning certain offers lately made unto her by the Scottish Queen.'[74]

And so Burghley in his sixty-third year buckled on his harness again. But he returned to Court in a depressed state of mind, sensitive to a degree and quick to take offence at any criticism. He may even have offered to resign. In any case, his mood called forth from his mistress one of her best known letters:[75]

'Sir Spirit. I doubt I do misname you. For those of your kind (they say) have no sense. But I have of late seen an *ecce signum*, that if an ass kick you, you feel it too soon. I will recant you from being my *Spirit*, if ever I perceive that you disdain not such a feeling. Serve God, fear the king, and be a good fellow to the rest. Let never care appear in you for such a rumour; but let them well know, that you rather desire the righting of such wrongs, by making known their error, than you to be so silly a soul, as to foreslow that you ought to do, or not freely deliver what you think meetest. And pass of no man so much, as not to regard her trust, who putteth it in you.

'God bless you, and long may you last, *Omnino*, E.R.'

The allusions in this letter are obscure, but the evidence of the Queen's affection undoubted. It did much to soften the blow a day or so later when he heard that his daughter, Ann, had brought forth a son and that the boy had died.[76] On May 27th the Queen visited Theobalds, spending four days there.[77]

She was attended, as usual, by a large company which included besides Leicester, Warwick, Hatton, Lincoln and Walsingham, the Ladies of the Privy Chamber and some twenty-two grooms, squires and ushers. Probably the company numbered at least fifty. We know nothing about the entertainment, but it was no doubt very costly. One remark which has been ascribed to Elizabeth on that occasion may be apocryphal but it is worth recording. 'With your head and my purse,' she said to Burghley, 'I could do anything.'

Perhaps the most fruitful result of the royal visit was to reassure Burghley of his unique place in the Queen's confidence. On the day of her departure she called Oxford to her presence, and after 'some bitter words and speeches' forgave him his sins and invited him to return to Court.[78] It is said that Walter Raleigh was largely responsible, and that Burghley was not a little put out that what had been denied to him was conceded to a young courtier. But it appears from a letter which Raleigh himself wrote to Burghley on May 13th that Burghley himself had requested his intercession. Raleigh wrote:

'I delivered to her [the Queen] your Lordship's letter, and what I said further how honourable and profitable it were for her Majesty to have regard to your Lordship's health and quiet I leave to the witness of God and good report of her Highness. And the more to witness how desirous I am of your Lordship's favour and good opinion, I am content, for your sake, to lay the serpent before the fire as much as in me lieth, that having recovered strength, myself may be most in danger of his poison and sting.'[79]

Burghley can hardly have cherished any illusions about Oxford, who was to plague him for the rest of his days. But for better or worse he had achieved his purpose. Oxford had taken back his wife and had made peace with his Queen.

CHAPTER XV

SCOTLAND, 1581-85

DURING the year following Alençon's departure for the Low Countries, Burghley took almost no active part in foreign affairs. His surviving correspondence is largely concerned with matters ecclesiastical, with Puritans and papists, with squabbles at the University of Cambridge, and with the defence of the Established Church against royal attacks from the right, Puritan attacks from the left, and from rapacious courtiers with a covetous eye upon Church property.[1] The Anglican bishops by and large regarded him as their chief friend and poured all their woes into his ears, and he did his best to secure their rights and to temper their passions. Archbishop Grindal in his sad declining years leaned heavily on Burghley. And he was chiefly instrumental in clearing the character of the other Archbishop, Sandys of York, from a conspiracy to blackmail him.

The story began in May 1581, when the Archbishop was stopping at an inn in Doncaster. An old servant of Mrs. Sandys was the innkeeper's wife. Some time during the night she entered the Archbishop's bedroom, bringing to him, according to his custom, a hot drink (caudle).[2] She straightway threw off her smock and slipped naked into bed beside him. Thereupon, by prearrangement, the innkeeper himself appeared and discovered the Archbishop, then sixty-five years of age, and the wife in bed together. He summoned Robert Stapleton who, also by prearrangement, was stopping at the inn and who at once entered the Archbishop's chamber.

Stapleton, a prominent North Country gentleman, Sheriff of Yorkshire and a member of the Court of High Commission and of the Council of the North, was the villain of the plot. He was an old friend of the Archbishop, and, posing as an old friend, pointed out that the important thing was to keep the matter quiet. Thereupon proceeded a systematic bleeding of the good prelate, first by the innkeeper, but principally by Stapleton himself, who had designs upon archiepiscopal lands. The matter dragged on for a year and a half. Finally the prelate had more than he could take. He wrote to the Queen and to Burghley, protesting against Stapleton's demands and offering to resign rather than submit to them. And finally, in January 1583, he disclosed the whole wretched business to Burghley.

'I have need', he wrote, 'of your present help, otherwise like to be oppressed with great and shameful wrong... I was upon the way fully purposed to have opened unto you their treachery and to have prayed your aid and for their condign punishment. My only fault is that I have concealed the thing so long... I am in this matter, wherewith they chiefly charge me, most innocent from all criminal fact.'

Sandys sent the letter by his chancellor, who was directed to disclose to Burghley the whole story.

When the Queen heard the story she was greatly incensed, and ordered that both Stapleton and the innkeeper be summoned to London. She apparently directed Burghley to take charge of the investigation. He had the culprits examined, then sent to the Dean of York for further information about Sysson, the innkeeper, and his wife; and by the middle of January he made his report to Hatton.[3]

'Sir,' he wrote, 'my servant shall show you why I must write so evil and so little. Sir Robert Stapleton required to come to me, and so the examiners thought good, afore whom, charging him with Sysson's confession, he protested against Sysson as a bankrupt and a beggar . . . But now coming to me he yieldeth to his offence and asked God mercy. And thus far he yieldeth, that Sysson first, and afterwards also his wife, opened to him the device to have the bishop entrapped, she pretending that the bishop had moved her to evil. The same was imparted to Mallory and Maude.[4] And Sir Robert, having conceived displeasure against the bishop, confesseth he yieldeth hereto as thereby to have the bishop under his girdle . . . He desireth pardon of her Majesty. I have quieted him, that there is no cause to doubt of his fleeing. And truly his tears do move me to have compassion of him, being myself well satisfied with the purgation of the bishop.'

Hatton replied on February 24th:[5] 'I thank God from my heart that your travail in this great case hath brought forth so blessed effects. Innocency is delivered, the truth hath prevailed to God's glory and the due commendation of your wisdom and goodness. Her Majesty rejoiceth exceedingly in it and yieldeth her most gracious thanks to your Lordship for your so great and wise proceeding in it . . . I pray God restore your health and bless your Lordship with a long and happy life.'

Burghley, in bed with the gout at his house in Covent Garden, replied on the 28th:[6]

'I pray you in my behalf to render my recognition to her Majesty of my complete acceptance of her gracious and favourable allowance of my careful proceeding to the discovery of the truth in the Archbishop's cause, which was very cunningly covered and made almost desperate to be disclosed. But, in the end, God, the father of truth, left the adversaries in fear to be otherwise convinced by the contrarieties of their own answers. For so indeed it hath fallen out by discrepancies in their own answers that if none of them had confessed their offences, the comparing of their contrarieties would have condemned them in any ordinary place of judgment.'

Burghley went on to express the hope that Stapleton, 'a man of good service in his country', would be spared 'utter ruin'. But Stapleton, instead of repentance, took on an attitude of defiance. He had been put 'under some favourable restraint', but the Queen learned that he 'suddenly seemed to change his manner of dealing' and ordered him to the Fleet in 'close prison', with further direction that if that did not tame him, the Star Chamber should deal with him as they thought fit. And in the Star Chamber the case was tried, and Stapleton and the others ordered to go down to York, and at the Assizes make public confession of their 'vile practice' and vindicate the bishop's innocency. They went through the ritual, but in such manner as to make a mockery of it. Stapleton was thereupon brought back to London, and cast first into the Tower and subsequently in the Fleet. Burghley apparently was instrumental in mitigating his punishment,[7] but he was still in the Fleet in May of 1584, begging to be spared 'the utter overthrow of his poor house and children'.[8] It was probably at this time that Burghley wrote an undated letter to Sandys, suggesting that he intercede with the Queen to secure Stapleton's release lest it be thought that his longer continuance in prison proceeded from the Archbishop's desire for personal revenge.

In foreign affairs, after Alençon's departure to the Low Countries in February 1582, the centre of interest shifted to Scotland, where the dominating influence of the King's new favourite, D'Aubigny, revived old fears of active French intervention.

Following the trial and execution of the Regent Morton in June 1581, diplomatic relations between England and Scotland were broken for almost a year. In the autumn of 1581 the Earl of Leicester established a connection with Roger Ashton, a member of the Scottish royal household, and through that channel attempted to open a breach between D'Aubigny and his right-hand man, the new Earl of Arran. Burghley was not consulted. He wrote to Walsingham on August 10th:

'By Ashton secretly I learn that he [the Scottish King] will be wholly guided by her Majesty, whereof she conceiveth hope. I pray God she be not deceived therein . . . Her Majesty uttereth not to me these Scottish matters but I learn them otherwise.'[9] He was evidently sceptical.

In October, on the lines of Ashton's reports, Elizabeth dispatched one Captain Errington to Scotland with instructions to widen the reported breach between D'Aubigny and Arran. But Errington was denied a Scottish passport, and Leicester's hopes were dashed and Burghley's scepticism justified.

In France, Walsingham learned that King James was seeking the intervention of his mother, the captive Queen of Scots, to secure recognition of his title by the King of France and that Mary was proposing instead an association of her son and herself. There were indications also of friction between D'Aubigny and Mary, and this suggested the possibility of playing the mother against the favourite. A letter from Mary to Elizabeth in October 1581, requesting permission to send an envoy to her son, opened the door, and Robert Beale, Walsingham's brother-in-law, was sent to the royal captive to explore possibilities. There is no evidence of Burghley's hand in this business, though Mary had sent a letter to him by the same post that carried her letter to the Queen, asking him to support her request.

The notion of playing mother against son was a factor in English policy for two years to come, though at the time Beale's mission yielded no more than a slight increase of Mary's freedom of action.

Another factor[10] in the Scottish situation was the extension of the efforts of the Jesuits north of the border. Watts and Holt went in the autumn of 1581, Creighton and Hay early in the year following. They do not appear to have made any considerable progress in matters religious, but they became active promoters of a plot to invade England with foreign armies from the north. This aspect of their activities was not disclosed until later, but their presence in the north and their friendly reception by King James were definitely disturbing.

Two counterbalancing factors worked strongly in Elizabeth's favour. The first of them was the attitude of the Scottish preachers, who distrusted D'Aubigny notwithstanding his pretended conversion; the second, the powerful house of Douglas, the leadership of which, after Morton's death, passed to his nephew, Alexander Douglas, Earl of Angus. Angus had attempted to organize a revolt in his uncle's favour in the spring of 1581, but had been thwarted and forced to flee to England.[11] He remained along the border until the following January and was then summoned to the English Court, where, according to Mendoza, Leicester and Hatton made much of him.[12] Of any dealings between him and Burghley we hear nothing. How much in the way of support he received in England is not revealed. In any case he probably arranged the details of Ruthven's Raid late in August 1582, which placed the young King's person in the hands of the English party and opened the door for the expulsion of D'Aubigny from Scotland in the following year.

In September Elizabeth dispatched two envoys to Scotland, Sir Robert Bowes and Sir George Carey. Carey was Lord Hunsdon's eldest son. Ostensibly Carey went as envoy extraordinary to the King, Bowes as resident ambassador. But there may have been more to the matter than that. It may have reflected a growing division in the Privy Council between those who, like Leicester and Walsingham, supported Angus and those who, like Lord Hunsdon, Carey's father, were casting about for alternatives.[13] Where Burghley stood in the matter is uncertain, but it cannot be without significance that Carey's dispatches were addressed to Burghley, Bowes's by and large to Walsingham. King James alluded to the matter later to the Queen, in which he said that he had poured into Carey's ears his inward grief in response to his request that he should speak frankly, 'promising that it should be secretly kept from all the others (albeit I used not such freedom with Mr. Bowes)'.[14]

In any case, Carey, who returned late in September, agreed with Bowes that the best way to keep Scotland in train was to grant a liberal pension to the King and to the great nobles. But Elizabeth was not responsive.

In October the French King decided to send an envoy to Scotland. He selected for the mission La Mothe Fénélon, who had been resident French ambassador in London for some seven years (1568-75). He reached London in mid-November.

Burghley had written to Walsingham on November 21st from Hertford Castle: 'My Lord Chancellor and I, considering that in 8 days the [law] term will fully end, are ignorant whether her Majesty will have us to repair to the Court, because I hear at the Court all are suspected of infection that come from hence.'

Four days later Walsingham replied, directing Burghley to repair to Court, 'for that she [the Queen] conceiveth that La Mothe [Fénélon], who upon Wednesday next is appointed to have audience, hath somewhat to propose that will require advice and consultation'.[15]

We have two accounts of Fénélon's negotiations in England, one from Walsingham in a letter to Cobham of December 12th,[16] the other from Mendoza, the Spanish ambassador.[17] According to Walsingham, everything passed off pleasantly and, although the Queen showed reluctance to give Fénélon a passport to Scotland, she finally acquiesced. Mendoza reported that Burghley and Walsingham were much alarmed by the French mission, that the Privy Council sat all day considering the situation and finally decided to dangle before Fénélon's eyes the Alençon marriage with the idea of keeping him out of Scotland. According to Mendoza, all the councillors except Leicester were opposed to giving him a passport and only yielded at the last because they learned that the King of France was sending Mayneville, a henchman of the Guises and a much less amiable character, to Scotland by sea.

This much is certain, that the Queen did try to detain Fénélon in England at least until D'Aubigny left Scotland, and that, when she finally gave him his passports, she appointed William Davison to accompany him.

Burghley wrote to Walsingham on December 19th: 'I am of the opinion that the best stay of La Mothe will fall out to be by the King's letter to him which will come as I think before he shall be half his way.[18] For from Mr. Davison I understand it will be Saturday [December 22nd] which shall be his New Year's Day[19] before he shall depart from London. And if he had come hither tomorrow or Friday he should have dined here with me. But I must depart hence on Saturday, so as I shall, I think, meet him on the way. It falleth out very happily that Mr. Bowes is in Scotland, for else *susq[ue] deq[ue]* or, . . . as they say in Ireland, our cause had been frayed.'[20]

Davison had instructions to impede Fénélon's progress northward as much as he could while Bowes at Edinburgh busied himself with getting D'Aubigny out of Scotland. Actually Fénélon on his way north encountered D'Aubigny on his way south. They exchanged words, which Davison craned his neck to hear, but mostly missed in the blustery weather.

Fénélon accomplished very little, and Mayneville, who arrived by sea some three weeks after Fénélon, still less. Meanwhile, James dispatched an envoy, John Colville, to Elizabeth early in January, to find out how much Elizabeth was prepared to do in order to secure the steady allegiance of Scotland. Elizabeth's reply[21] was that she was prepared to consider the matter favourably but wanted to know what assistance the King needed.

Walsingham wrote to Bowes in February: 'I gathered by her Majesty's speeches that she entered into some jealous conceit that the contents of your letters tended only to have drawn some treasure from her coffers, being persuaded that the information given to you of the French promises and offers of great pensions as well to the King as to others be but devices to prepare the way before Col. Steward's arrival, whereby he may the better make the market here.'[22]

Walsingham worked hard to get favourable action from the Queen, and urged her late in February 1583 to invite consideration of the Scottish problem by the Council.[23] Elizabeth sent him instead to consult with Burghley 'at London, lying there diseased of his gout'. He found there also Lord Chancellor Bromley and Sir Walter Mildmay, Chancellor of the Exchequer, and at Burghley's bedside laid before them Bowes's latest dispatches. They agreed that the Queen should spend £10,000, of which £5000 should go to the King, £3000 to the nobility and the balance for the support of an English resident ambassador. They suggested that Bowes make an effort to win the Earl of Arran to the English party, and that the noblemen around the King should increase their number so as to be more representative of the Scottish nobility at large.[24]

The striking thing about these recommendations was not the pensioning of the Scots, which Privy Councillors of all complexions seem to have favoured, but the indications that Walsingham's policy of all-out aid to Angus and his associates was looked at askance, as being based upon the temporary dominance of a small minority clique,[25] and that the feasibility of an approach to Arran was favourably regarded. It looks as though Burghley, who without much doubt dominated the conference, did not see eye to eye with Walsingham on the subject.

Meanwhile, as a result of Colville's mission, the English government expected another envoy from Scotland, in which the King should specifically define his needs. He had expressed his intention to do so on February 1st, and decided to send two envoys, Colville and Colonel Steward. But they did not get away from Scotland until late in April. Walsingham was not hopeful. He feared that Elizabeth's answer to their demands would not be favourable.

When Steward and Colville arrived late in April, Burghley was deep in grief at the death of his daughter, Elizabeth. It may have been for that reason that Elizabeth directed Walsingham and Hunsdon to deal with them. A few days later she talked with them herself. They asked for an offensive and defensive alliance, an immediate gift of £10,000, in addition to a pension for James of £5000. Mendoza has recorded Elizabeth's comment,[26] 'that her own servants and favourites professed to love her for her good parts, Alençon for her person and the Scots for her crown ... but they all ended in the same thing, namely, asking her for money'.

According to Mendoza she referred the matter to a committee of four, Leicester, Bedford, Walsingham and Burghley.[27] Mendoza declared that it was due to the first three that Elizabeth conceded something.[28] Both Mendoza and Mauvissière agreed that Burghley was opposed to granting money. Walsingham apparently inclined towards the same opinion. Before the arrival of the Scottish envoys he wrote to Bowes: 'The indisposition of some that can be most helpful doth give me just cause to doubt that answer will not be made that reason and policy requireth.'[29] This may simply refer to Burghley's absence from Court because of his daughter's death, but in the light of what follows it seems likely that Walsingham regarded him as the stumbling-block.

Mauvissière was of the opinion that Burghley did not trust the Scots. 'I will do what I can with the help of Burghley and others to block the business', Mauvissière

added in a letter to the French King. Two days later Burghley talked with Mauvissière at length on the subject.[30] In recording the interview, Mauvissière designated
Burghley as the 'principal et premier' of all the councillors. According to one of the
spies whom Walsingham had at the French embassy, Mauvissière and Burghley
were on intimate terms.[31] Burghley assured Mauvissière that the Queen intended
nothing to the prejudice of the old Franco-Scottish alliance, but insisted that she
could not be blamed for assuring herself of friends and neighbours, particularly
those who, like the Scots, were of her religion. He reminded Mauvissière of St.
Bartholomew's Eve and of the abortive attempt of Alençon to seize Antwerp, but
spoke in very kindly tones, and prayed Mauvissière to support Anglo-French amity
in the future as he had in the past, and not to write letters home calculated to sow
distrust of England, nor to be moved by the misinterpretations of the situation in
Scotland as Mayneville reported it. Mauvissière guessed that Burghley had read
some of Mayneville's letters, as indeed he had. They had been intercepted.[32]

Mauvissière complained that Scottish affairs were dominated by the preachers,
that they had forced upon the young King a Council of their choice and had sought
an English league under the pretext of religion. Burghley replied dryly that leagues
under the veil of religion were not peculiar, that the Anglo-Scottish league was
general and absolute without mention of religion and without prejudice to France.
It was not offensive but defensive. Mauvissière retorted that the league was with a
boy prince who was in fact a prisoner, or at least in the power of two or three who
might well be disavowed by all the estates of Scotland, and that, moreover, one of
the first of the Scottish demands would be money from the Queen. Burghley
replied that he would see to that, and would do nothing inconsistent with the
security of themselves and the common good of Britain and France and the French
King 'if it please him to remain their common friends'.

Evidently Burghley was seeking to cultivate Mauvissière's good will, without
making any commitments.

Sometime before the arrival of the Scottish ambassadors Elizabeth reopened
negotiations with Mary Queen of Scots. The purpose of these negotiations
apparently was to arrange for Mary's release in return for her friendship and co-
operation in establishing stable and friendly relations between England and Scotland. Elizabeth seems to have concluded that young James was altogether at his
mother's devotion and that he might be won over to the English point of view by
her intermediation. In any event every step in the negotiations with Mary was reported to James and his opinion carefully sounded. It presently became clear that
James was not nearly so devoted to his mother and not nearly so much interested in
her release as had been assumed.[33] It may well be, therefore, that the Spanish ambassador was right when he said that the negotiations with Mary were merely designed
to deceive the French.[34]

It was in this connection that Walsingham wrote to Burghley on April 20th
bidding him shake off his grief at his daughter's death and come to Court. 'If', he
wrote, 'you might conveniently repair hither she [the Queen] would be glad to

have your Lordship's advice in a matter of weight concerning certain offers lately made unto her by the Scottish Queen ... whereof I send your Lordship a copy to the end you may be better prepared to give your advice.'[35]

What advice Burghley gave is not recorded. In conversation with Mauvissière late in May he said that he had signed and given his consent to Mary's liberation, but that since James would not consent to an association of his mother and himself, it would be necessary to find some other way to relieve her confinement.[36]

This tells us nothing more than that Burghley was assuming a pose of friendliness to France. Walsingham wrote to Bowes on June 11th:[37]

'In debating of this cause of her [Mary's] liberty it fell into deliberation whether it were better to send her into that realm [Scotland] or to keep her here, where it was concluded that in no case she should be sent thither. And yet it is thought meet that you should think of such inconveniences as might ensue thereby and to foresee how the same might be prevented. For if she should be well placed in that state without working any dangerous alteration, she might be right well spared here.'

But Elizabeth decided to consult again with the Scottish King before going any further. And while she procrastinated there came a change in government in Scotland which led to a temporary abandonment of the whole plan.

Late in June 1583, James escaped from the Ruthven raiders, took refuge in the castle at St. Andrews, and presently recalled Arran. Before the end of August Arran was the right-hand man of the King.

The immediate reaction at the English Court was one of uncertainty. Walsingham favoured prompt remonstrance, but other members of the Council evidently leaned to a qualified acceptance of the new régime. Walsingham wrote to Bowes on July 27th: 'We do not proceed so effectually in our cause of great weight as were fit.' Burghley's views on the subject are nowhere clearly expressed. In a 'Memorial for Scotland' in his hand, dated August 5th,[38] he suggested that an envoy be sent to the King of Scotland to discover his intentions, to 'cherish them of the religion in Scotland', and to find out whether an English party could be had in Scotland and 'if nothing shall let their course but aid of money, to assure them therefore'. He named four candidates for the mission — Hatton or Sir Philip Sidney or Edward Wotton or Walsingham. It is to be noticed that he did not name Lord Hunsdon who, according to Walsingham, was being considered.[39] This would seem to indicate that Burghley was not at the time sympathetic with Hunsdon's policy of cultivating Arran's good will.

In another memorandum on the same subject,[40] drawn up later in the month, Burghley revealed a disposition to come to terms with Mary Stuart, 'with condition to have her person at command of her Majesty'. He also concerned himself with broader questions:

(1) 'To establish in the Church of England one uniform order according to the laws of the realm' — which was presumably directed at the Puritans.

(2) 'To put all persons serviceable and that are obedient to the laws of religion in strength' — which was directed at the prevalence of Roman Catholic sympathizers among the Justices of the Peace.

(3) To prepare the 'navy to be in readiness'.
(4) To muster and provide numbers of horsemen.[41]
(5) To look to the officers on the Scottish borders.
(6) To keep watch at the ports for suspected persons.
(7) To prepare lists of recusants of wealth and power.

Burghley evidently regarded the situation as menacing, and was still much concerned about internal disorders and about the strength of Roman Catholic sympathizers in high places.

Walsingham was dispatched to Scotland in August. Burghley drafted his instructions. The first draft was dated August 3rd. It was considerably milder in tone than the one delivered to Walsingham ten days later.[42] The news from Scotland in the interval, revealing the young King's disposition to get rid of those about him friendly to England, probably explains the change.

In the original draft no provision had been made for the event that James would not change his course in response to a promise of a substantial pension. In the final version a pension was to be offered, 'greater than ever before', and Walsingham was to take money with him for distribution where it would do most good. But specific action from James was to be required. He should pardon past offences, recall to favour all noblemen loyal to him and return all confiscated property — all to be confirmed by action in the Scottish Parliament. If the King would not agree, then Walsingham was to deal no further with him, but to cast about for some way of dealing with the opposition. He was to advise the Queen accordingly with the assurance 'that we will not neglect any means how chargeable soever it be, to further it'.[43]

Therewith Walsingham set forth, very reluctantly, with a train of some eighty persons. After all sorts of obstacles and delays James finally received him on September 9th.[44] He sent his impressions of the interview in a letter to Elizabeth two days later.

'I have sundry times,' he wrote, 'since my repair into this country, called to mind the impression I have always found that your Majesty hath of the disposition of this young King . . . for, as your Majesty hath always doubted, so I think you shall find him most ingrate and such a one as if his power may agree to his will, will be found ready to make as unthankful a requital as ever any other did that was so greatly beholding unto a prince as he hath been to your Majesty . . . Mr. Bowes and I, being careful to discover whereof the same hath risen, we found by good means that it hath grown altogether from the advice of his mother, who putteth him in comfort of a very great party within that realm [England] and that no one thing is like to add such an increase thereof as if he shall show himself to be alienated from you and to seek by degrees to alter and change the religion within this realm [Scotland].'

Walsingham, as it turned out, underestimated the craftiness of young James, who put small store by his mother's advice and though willing to toy with a Catholic connection, knew, better than he revealed, on which side his bread was buttered.

Probably had Walsingham been more flexible he might have responded to the appeal of Arran and Steward, both of whom tried to persuade him 'to run a course' with them. But he refused. And he finally left Scotland with the conviction that the only solution of the problem there was 'to throw the rascals out'. He accordingly bent his efforts towards the end[45] of his visit to 'laying some such plot as he [James] might be bridled and forced, whether he will or not, to depend upon your Majesty's favour and goodness'. But Elizabeth, notwithstanding the abundant promises of co-operation which she had made in her instructions to him, would not entertain it.

Walsingham's own explanation of the Queen's change of heart was that she began to turn to the alternate policy of coming to terms with Arran and his group. 'I hear', he wrote to Leicester on September 22nd, 'that there is a by-course in hand with Arran and the Colonel [Steward] wherein Mr. Raleigh is used for an instrument. I hope he is too wise to be used in such indiscreet dealing.' Eight days later Walsingham wrote to Bowes: 'I learn that the by-course goeth forward and is well hearkened unto, great assurances are given that the King shall be altogether at her Majesty's devotion more firmly than ever before. I am sorry that Scotland should be able to abuse us with these vain entertainments.'

Once more we are at a loss to discover Burghley's attitude. Early in October Walsingham was of the opinion that Burghley was not 'very forward to entertain the by-course'[46] but later held a different opinion. The probabilities are that Burghley, very much more open-minded than Walsingham on the subject and equally distrustful of all Scottish parties, was prepared to explore all avenues of approach.

No positive action was taken in the matter.

It was just at this juncture that Francis Throgmorton was arrested in London and his papers seized. The course of events which led up to his seizure belongs to the history of Walsingham. Burghley had no part in it.

Throgmorton under torture confessed that the Duke of Guise was preparing to invade England from the south in the Catholic cause, that he intended to liberate the Scottish Queen, that forces were in readiness, that the Pope and the King of Spain had undertaken to finance the enterprise and that nothing remained to be done except to arouse the Catholics in England. His confession made clear that the Spanish ambassador, Mendoza, had been a close confidant in the matter. He had been the chief medium for Mary's correspondence with the confederates abroad. It was through him that Guise had directed Throgmorton in his efforts to stir up rebellion within the realm.

Throgmorton paid the penalty for his treason at Tyburn. As for Mendoza, on January 9th he was invited to meet members of the Privy Council at the house of the Lord Chancellor. When he got there he found the Lord Chancellor, the Lord Chamberlain, Burghley, Leicester, Hunsdon and Walsingham assembled to meet him. Walsingham, who spoke Italian better than the rest, addressed him. The Queen, he said, was well aware of Mendoza's efforts to disturb the peace of her kingdom. She knew all about his dealings with the disaffected Catholics, with the

Scottish Queen and with those who were planning the invasion of England. She consequently preferred his room to his company and was graciously pleased to allow him fifteen days to get out of England. Mendoza stormed, denied, but ended by protesting that he would leave if the Queen wished, but that he must first inform his master. The councillors convinced him that he would do no such thing. And so he left in a great passion, closing the doors of the Spanish embassy in London for the rest of the Queen's reign.

The mad project of that madman, Somerville, to assassinate the Queen, discovered in October 1583,[47] and the revelations of the Throgmorton Plot in November, turned Burghley's mind to the inward security of the kingdom and particularly to the recusants. In October[48] he had proposed that in the case of those recusants who failed to attend church, the bishop should summon them before him and if they would not conform he should excommunicate them, and then, after forty days, procure a writ *de excommunicato capiendo* against them. In December he prepared a memorandum for the Council[49] on the ecclesiastical situation, in which he made the following recommendations:

(1) The bishops to be more diligent in reforming abuses.

(2) The parishes to be better provided with resident ministers and pluralities done away with where they are not tolerable.

(3) Beneficed clergy at universities to return to their parishes.

(4) Heads of colleges to be resident and of known conformity.

(5) The bishops to see to it that no schoolmaster, public or private, should be suffered, 'but such as are to be allowed as sound men'.

(6) Inns of Court and Chancery to be visited and recusants to be expelled from them.

(7) No lawyers, civilians or physicians to be allowed to pursue their professions who did not conform.

(8) Prominent recusants in the counties to be offered the oath of supremacy, and if they refused, to be subject to *Praemunire*, be imprisoned at the Queen's pleasure and forfeit their goods and the income from their lands.

Or, if this be not allowed, then they were to be questioned as to whether the Pope might discharge them of their allegiance, and, if they refused to answer, they were to be accounted adherents of the Queen's enemies.

(9) The Jesuits and such like to be examined upon their allegiance as against the papal supremacy, and those who took sides with the Pope against the Queen to be condemned as traitors. Of those so many to suffer death as shall be thought right, others to be banished with judgment to be hanged if they returned.

Some other sort of them to be committed to prisons specially provided, there to be taught and straitly kept from infecting others, and the charge of their diet to be maintained out of the forfeiture of recusants. Houses to be provided for this kind of person and houses also for recusants imprisoned for want of ability to pay their fines.[50]

★

The document is interesting as revealing Burghley's support of very vigorous action against both recusants and priests; but the Queen was more mercifully minded, and vigorous statutory action was deferred until 1585.

Meanwhile, attention was focused upon Scotland. Walsingham and Leicester favoured the re-establishment of Angus and the Queen's friends to power, and promoted one conspiracy after another to that end. Hunsdon proposed to come to terms with Arran. According to Walsingham most of the Privy Council favoured that course.[51] The matter was complicated by the question of the succession, particularly after the death of the Duke of Alençon at the end of August 1584. With his passing passed the last hope of the Queen's marriage.

Walsingham wrote in July: 'I find that men begin to look to the sun rising.' Of all the candidates for the English throne, the Scottish line had the best claim and was Elizabeth's preference, so far as she ever expressed a preference.[52] Burghley in his earlier years was reputed favourable to the Suffolk line, though in view of the Queen's hostility to any talk about the succession, he was careful to avoid commitments. Probably he now favoured the Scottish line — his son, Robert, certainly did. But Burghley has left no record of his preference.

In the Privy Council both Leicester and Hunsdon were personally interested. Hunsdon cherished the hope of marrying either his niece or his daughter to King James.[53] Leicester dreamed of a match between his infant son and the infant Arabella Stuart, who traced a claim to the English throne through the daughter of Margaret Tudor, Henry VIII's eldest daughter. By the letter of the law, Arabella's claim was inferior to that of James, except for the fact that she had been born in England. Possibly Leicester hoped to do for Arabella what his father had tried to do for Lady Jane Grey.[54] In any case, his aspirations were thwarted by the untimely death of his only legitimate offspring in July. Even after that Walsingham thought that Leicester was up to something in Scotland, though he could not tell what.

Burghley's connections with Hunsdon were fairly close. Hunsdon's daughter had married Sir Edward Hoby, Burghley's nephew.[55] In July Walsingham decided that Burghley was actively supporting Hunsdon's policy of coming to terms with Arran. On the 12th he wrote:

'Touching the by-course between Lord Hunsdon and the Earl of Arran, there is nothing to help it but time and trial. You know Lord Hunsdon's passion, whose propinquity in blood[56] doth somewhat prevail to enable his credit to more harm than good. And yet herein he should not greatly prevail were he not countenanced by the Lord Treasurer who dealeth strangely in the action of Scotland.'[57]

In what was apparently an earlier draft of the passage, Walsingham added: 'B. doth use H. as a counterpoise to L. [Leicester] though, God wot, he be but a weak one. B. hath always liked to entertain by-courses which groweth from lack of resolution in him which I pray God may not prove the destruction of England.'

We may take these observations for what they may be worth. Walsingham never saw but one course of action. Burghley, like his mistress, contemplated alternatives, particularly if they were less expensive. What Burghley aimed at was

K

the interest of England; what Walsingham aimed at was the interest of the reformed religion.

Walsingham wanted to coerce James, Burghley to conciliate him. This was what Walsingham called looking to the sun rising. According to Hunsdon, Walsingham was sore because he had been badly treated in Scotland, which may or may not have been so. In any case, the matter dragged its slow length along, without much progress. Resort once again was had to the King's mother. She was at first responsive. In May, after Angus and his associates took flight to England, she was disposed to stand on terms,[58] but a little later she was much more co-operative.

Mary herself seems to have regarded Burghley as her friend. In February 1584 she wrote to him in terms which suggest that she had been receiving encouraging messages from him through Shrewsbury, and she thanked him for his good counsel. Later, in instructing her secretary, Nau, before he went to Court in her behalf, she observed that Burghley was old and wise and one 'who loves the good of his country without passion or faction'.[59] She directed Nau to show himself willing to follow Burghley's advice. In the spring of 1585 she wrote several times to him asking him to support her various requests to Elizabeth.[60]

It is clear enough that Burghley was cultivating her good will; equally clear that in negotiations with her he was determined to exact the uttermost farthing. He began a long memorandum on the subject in June 1584,[61] which he left unfinished but which reveals his attitude. The first consideration was that the security of his mistress should be assured. He demanded that Mary should express regret for what she had done as Queen of France 'to the disquieting of her Majesty', should ratify the Treaty of Edinburgh and should formally renounce and disallow all her actions or practices done or attempted since that time. Mary was further to bind herself not to attempt or countenance any attempts against the government of England or its religious establishment. She was also to be bound not to publish any pretence to any title of succession to the English Crown 'but shall therein permit the same to remain in suspense, as it is, during her Majesty's life'. Besides her own assurance on this point 'by her writing and oath' she should procure the same to be ratified by Parliament in Scotland and, 'if her Majesty shall so require, also be confirmed by the French King both by writing and oath'.

Concerning Mary's liberty, 'if the same shall be granted, for her to remain in England at some place certain with some to attend on her. It were requisite that some two or three hostages, being noblemen of Scotland and France, were delivered in the custody of her Majesty'.

As to the proposed association of Mary and her son, Burghley maintained that Elizabeth could not 'allow thereof' until it had been approved by the King and the estates of Scotland.

In short he believed that Mary should be kept in England, should recognize the Queen's title, should not conspire against the state or religion, should not raise the issue of succession, should secure formal endorsement of these terms both by the Scottish Parliament and by the French King and should give hostages to abide by her agreements.

Burghley evidently did not contemplate, or at any rate did not record, what Mary was to gain in return for these concessions — presumably a greater amount of personal liberty, but within England.

Mary, for her part, by the midsummer of 1584 was prepared to concede anything in return for greater liberty, though clearly she had no intention of abiding by the terms of any agreement. Burghley after a long experience with her can have had no illusions on that score. But he thought more was to be gained by posing as her friend than as her enemy. We need not assume any ulterior motive. It was a characteristic attitude.

Mary's son, James, also appears to have been convinced of Burghley's good will. In June 1584 James wrote to Burghley that he was 'surlie informid off your ernist, cairfull and bent gudvill at all tymes quhen occatioun ves offerrit for the furtherance off our adois in theis parttis, ve haiff thocht it the smallest part off gratitud and thankfulness to thank zow hartlie yeroff heirby'.[62]

James was writing to commend Hunsdon's negotiations with Arran to Burghley's favourable consideration. Some months later in connection with the dispatch of the Master of Gray to Elizabeth, James wrote again. This time he began with a classical allusion to the remark of Alexander the Great that Achilles was not so fortunate in his wars as in 'having so willing a trumpeter to blow abroad and immortalize to all posterity and ages his worldly fame as Homer was'. James suggested a comparison between himself and Achilles, but that Burghley 'do far excel such a blind, begging fellow as Homer'. He went on to say that, like Achilles, he was fortunate in having so wise and trusty a counsellor 'about her of whose amity I have made choice above all other princes'. He announced that he had directed Gray to impart his commission to Burghley only. 'The cause', he added, 'that moves me so to do is the report I have heard how you have been the man about your sovereign these times by-gone who has had the chief and only care of the well doing of my affairs there.'[63]

James was a precocious young lad, with bitter memories of Walsingham's visit and fond hopes that, as he and Arran together had pulled wool over Hunsdon's eyes, they might beguile the Lord Treasurer. It is not likely that they succeeded. The important fact is that Burghley enjoyed at the time the good will of both James and his mother.

There was evidently a definite attempt to discredit him with James the following year. On July 29th, 1585, he wrote to Herle that he was informed that enemies of his at the English Court were telling James that Burghley was his greatest enemy. 'If', Burghley added, 'you knew how earnest a course I have held with her Majesty, both privately and openly for her to retain the King of Scots with friendship and liberality . . . you would think there could be no more shameful lies made by Satan himself than these be. And finding myself thus maliciously bitten with the tongues and pens of courtiers here, if God did not comfort me, I had cause to fear murdering hands or poisoning pricks. But God is my keeper.'[64]

Walsingham in a letter written early the following month supplies the gloss to this text. 'The Lord Treasurer', he wrote, 'findeth himself very much aggrieved for that it hath been reported . . . that he should be enemy unto the King. He supposeth this information should grow from Leicester. For my own part I can no way accuse him . . . that he should be enemy unto the King, otherwise than, *pour faire le bon valet*, he showeth himself somewhat strait touching the support. You know that Leicester is a shrewd enemy where he taketh.'[65]

In October 1584 James dispatched the Master of Gray to England. He was directed specifically to Burghley, but his dealings were all with Walsingham. It presently appeared that he was hostile to Arran, equally hostile to Mary Queen of Scots. Walsingham concluded that he might be used to displace Arran and counteract Marian influence in Scotland. Gray was a 'proper gentleman of a true and fair speech',[66] who got on well with Elizabeth. The outcome of his mission was that relations between England and Scotland definitely improved, and negotiations were presently afoot for an offensive and defensive alliance between the two countries. The matter really turned on the size of the pension to be offered to James. Elizabeth offered £4000, James required £5000. Walsingham urged generosity, not only to the King but to some of his principal councillors, notably Gray and Arran. Burghley, if Walsingham is to be believed, supported the more frugal policy.

We need not pursue the tangled situation in Scotland in detail. Burghley seems to have had little part in it. Walsingham still believed that Burghley favoured the by-course with Arran, but, if so, Burghley shifted his position a little later. The Master of Gray, a slippery fellow, decided to take up the cudgels against Arran and turned to England for support. Walsingham wrote in September that Elizabeth had referred the matter to Burghley and that they both favoured Gray's proposal. Elizabeth, however, hesitated and it took some persuading before she would allow Angus and his fellow exiles to return to the border. By the end of October they had entered Scotland, laid hands upon the young King and proclaimed Arran a traitor.

Burghley wrote to Leicester in January that the Scottish situation was very promising.[67] He thought the treaty would now go forward, but he kept his fingers crossed since he learned that the French King was doing his best to prevent it. Elizabeth added to the difficulties of the situation by declining to meet James's demands in the matter of the pension.

But difficulties were finally smoothed away, and in July 1585 a treaty was formally concluded. James became a pensioner of Elizabeth, agreed to give no aid to her enemies and to assist her with armed forces in case she were attacked.

CHAPTER XVI

PURITANS IN PARLIAMENT, 1584

WHILE matters were in negotiation with Scotland, Burghley in England was faced with three problems: the Queen's safety; the Jesuit menace; and the Puritans. The first in point of importance was doubtless the provision against further attacks upon the Queen's person and upon the realm. The impulse in this direction was quickened by the assassination of the Prince of Orange, following two former attempts upon his life, in July. The revelation of the Throgmorton Plot had made it clear that the cause of Mary Stuart was still a major factor in the machinations of those who menaced the life and the régime of the Queen. And it occurred to Elizabeth's councillors that one way to prevent assassination was to debar Mary from the throne in the event of assassination. The outcome was the so-called 'Bond of Association' which Burghley and Walsingham together drafted.[1] It took the form of a positive commitment by those who signed it to pursue to the death anyone who aspired to the Crown 'by such devilish means'. It was plainly directed against Mary, but it went further than Mary to her son, James, though neither of them was specifically mentioned. The Bond began to circulate late in October and loyal subjects by the thousands flocked to sign it.[2]

Next to Mary's pretensions, Burghley was much concerned about the developing strength of Roman Catholicism. His cogitations on that subject appear in a memorandum which he called 'On the Dangerous Estate of the Realm'.[3]

In the first part of the memorandum, Burghley considered three aspects of the matter:

(1) The diligence of the Jesuit missionaries.

(2) The lethargy of the Anglican Church in meeting their challenge.

(3) The influence of the Catholic nobles and gentry in promoting recusancy among the masses.

He dwelt at length upon the second point, taking the position that the most effective way of meeting Jesuit propaganda was the better instruction of the people by the Anglican clergy. He suggested a general survey of the Established Church from the bishops down, advocated that those bishops 'as either of their manifest insufficiency or their corrupt and covetous conversation were out of credit with the people under their charge' should be removed. He recommended also that those who 'used jurisdiction' under the bishops should be reformed. 'For certain it is', he declared, 'that the covetous execution of those officers make not only the papistical sort but the good Christian subjects to mislike of the order of the ministry.'

While he thought that the whole state of the Church should be looked to, he distrusted reform by ecclesiastical visitation 'as the bishops and archdeacons continually do use only for gain'.

He was particularly concerned about the parishes — how they were supplied with curates and how the curates were maintained. Assuming that conditions at that level were far from well, he declared that if they were not reformed, 'the people must needs be without knowledge of God, as easily led into errors or popery by any that will secretly resort to teach them'. He thought that something should be done also to make sure that school teachers, universities and law schools (Inns of Court), the bar and the medical profession were 'sound in religion'.

In the second part of the memorandum, Burghley discussed specific remedies to be applied to check the Jesuit propaganda and to punish recusancy.

As to the Jesuits, he urged first of all the efficient execution of the laws against them, the watch of the ports to prevent their coming in or going out of England, and a diligent search for them in England. In dealing with them after capture, he proposed hanging after trial, but he contemplated banishment as an alternative and so forecast statutory action taken in Parliament the year following.[4]

As to the recusants, he thought that the rich ones, in addition to the payment of the statutory fine of £20 a month, should, if they were influential men in their neighbourhoods, be removed to another place and bound to remain there, and all their offices and all their weapons taken from them. He suggested further that at the discretion of the Privy Council dangerous recusants might be tendered the Oath of Supremacy, the refusal of which involved imprisonment for life and loss of lands and goods, or even be charged with high treason. The poorer recusants he was prepared to allow to compound for their fines provided they spent one month out of three in gaol. Those recusants who could pay nothing were to be sent to a workhouse unless they could find securities for 'their good a-bearing'.

Evidently Burghley favoured a tough policy towards Jesuits and a much tougher one towards recusants than his mistress was prepared to endorse.

In his condemnation of the lethargy and corruption in the Church, he presently fell foul of the new Archbishop of Canterbury, John Whitgift. The issue turned upon the developing strength of Puritanism. Whitgift regarded this as the great menace to the Establishment. Burghley, though he did not accept the Puritan programme for the reorganization of the Church, recognized them as the strong supporters of the Queen and the most vigorous and active Protestant preachers in the campaign against the Jesuit missionaries. He was therefore disposed to wink at their deviations from the established order of worship and to utilize their zeal and eloquence at a time when zeal and eloquence were so conspicuously lacking in the clergy at large. But Whitgift would have none of it.

There ensued a running correspondence between Burghley and Whitgift of which the first surviving letter, dated July 1st, 1584, is illuminating.

'I am sorry', Burghley wrote, 'to trouble you so often as I do, but I am more troubled myself not only with many private petitions of sundry ministers, recommended from persons of credit for peaceable persons in their ministry ... but also I am now daily charged by Councillors and public persons to neglect my duty in not staying your Grace's proceedings, so vehement and so general against ministers and preachers, as the papists are thereby generally encouraged and ill-disposed subjects animated, and thereby the Queen's Majesty's safety endangered.

'Against which I answer that I think your Grace doth nothing but, being duly examined, tendeth to the maintenance of the religion established and to avoid schism in the church. . . .

'But now, my good Lord, by chance I am come to the sight of an instrument of twenty-four articles,[5] of great length and curiosity formed in a Romish style to examine all manner of ministers in this time . . . which articles are entitled *Apud Lambeth May 1584, to be executed ex officio mero*. And upon this occasion I have seen them. I did recommend unto your Grace's favour two ministers, curates of Cambridgeshire, to be favourably known. And your Grace wrote to me they were contentious, seditious and persons vagrant. Wherewith I charged them sharply. And they denied this charge and required to be tried . . . I advised them to resort to your Grace, comforting them that they should find favourable proceeding . . . But now they came to me and I, asking them how your Grace had proceeded with them, they say they are commanded to be examined by the Register at London. And I asked them whereof? They said of a great number of articles, but they could have no copy of them . . . Upon this I sent to the Register who brought me the articles, which I have read and find so curiously penned, so full of branches and circumstance, as I think the Inquisitors of Spain use not so many questions to comprehend and to trap their prey.

'I know your canonists can defend these with all their perticels [*sic*], but surely, under your Grace's correction, this judicial and canonical sifting of poor ministers is not to edify or reform. And in charity I think they ought not to answer these nice points, except they were very notorious offenders in papistry or heresy.

'Now my Lord, bear with my scribbling . . . I desire the peace of the Church, I desire concord and unity in the exercise of our religion. But I conclude that, according to my simple judgment, this kind of proceeding is too much savouring of the Roman inquisition, and is rather a device to seek for offenders than to reform any. This is not the charitable instruction that I thought was intended. . . .

'It may be, as I said, the canonists may maintain the proceeding by rules of their laws, but though *omnia licent* yet *omnia non expediunt* . . . I have willed them not to answer these articles except their conscience may suffer them.'[6]

Two days later Whitgift replied at length, defending his position. 'If', he added, 'your Lordship do keep these two from answering according to the order set down, it will be, of itself, a setting at liberty of all the rest and an ending of all which hitherto hath been done . . . Therefore I beseech your L. to leave them unto me. I will not proceed to any sentence against them until I have made your L. privy to their answers and further conferred with you thereof.'

But actually Whitgift seems to have treated the two curates in question very harshly. One of them, Ed. Brayne, wrote to Burghley: 'We fear lest our repair for relief to your Lordship hath procured us his harder opinion and dealing at his Grace's hands.'

Burghley's initial response was that Whitgift had broken faith. In his next letter to the Archbishop he wrote: 'Your Grace promised me to deal, I say, only with such as vilified order in the Church and to charge them therewith, which I allow well of. But your Grace, not charging them with such faults, seeketh by examination to urge them to accuse themselves, and then I think you will punish them. I think your Grace's proceeding is, I will not say rigorous or captious, but I think it is scant charitable. I have no leisure to write more, and therefore I will end, for writing will but increase offence. And I mean not to offend your Grace. I am content that your Grace and my Lord of London, where I hear Brayne is, use him as your wisdom shall think meet. If I had known his fault I might be blamed for writing for him, but when, by examination only, it is meant to sift him with 24 articles, I have cause to pity the poor man.'[7] Burghley signed himself, 'Your Grace's as friendly as any'.

At the same time Burghley sent Brayne's letter to the Dean of Westminster, one of the members of the Ecclesiastical Commission, with a note appended as follows:

'Mr. Dean, I cannot but receive poor men's complaints, and yet I use to suspend my opinion. If these poor men be worse used at my L. of Canterbury's hands, or his officers, I shall be sorry. The fault or lack is mine, not theirs.'[8]

Burghley's position is reasonably clear. He did not wish to break with Whitgift, particularly in view of the fact that he had the unwavering support of the Queen. Whitgift, for his part, conscious of that support, would not be intimidated or cajoled. 'For my own part,' he wrote again to Burghley on July 15th, 'I am determined to my duty and conscience without fear. Neither will I therein desire further defence of any of my friends than justice and law will yield unto me. In my private affairs I know how greatly I shall stand in need of friends, especially of your Lordship, of whom I account myself sure. But in these public actions I see no cause why I should seek friends, seeing they to whom the care of the commonwealth is committed ought therein to join with me.'[9]

And so for the moment matters came to an impasse.

In a letter to Whitgift of the 17th, Burghley wrote that the Queen intended to fill the four vacancies in the episcopate, 'whereof', he added, 'I am very mindful and desirous, for the benefit of the Church, weighing that the Church may take that good thereby that it hath need of, for here (your Grace must pardon me) I rather wish it than look or much hope for it. I see such worldliness in many that were otherwise affected before they came to Cathedral chairs that I fear the places alter the men. But herein I condemn not all. But few there be that do better, being bishops, . . . than being preachers they did.

'I am bold to utter my mind of bishops to an Archbishop. But I clear myself. I mean nothing in my conceit to your Grace. For though of late I have varied in my poor opinion from your Grace in that, by your order, certain simple men have been rather sought by inquisition to be found offenders and then upon their facts condemned, yet surely I do not for all this differ from your Grace in unity and love. But I do reverence your learning and integrity and wish that the spirit of gentleness may win rather than severity.'

Burghley was well aware that the Privy Council and particularly the Puritan sympathizers in the Council, Leicester and Walsingham and Knollys, were strongly opposed to Whitgift's dictatorial methods. It may have been at Burghley's prompting that, three days later, the Privy Council wrote a letter to Whitgift on the subject. This letter had to do primarily with conditions in Essex where many 'zealous and learned preachers had been suspended, leaving their cures without preaching or prayers and sacraments. And many had been appointed who were notoriously unfit or chargeable with great and enormous faults, as drunkenness, filthiness of life, gaming at cards, haunting of alehouses and such like.' The Council sent evidence to prove their points, but professed that they did not wish to interfere in ecclesiastical jurisdiction; they 'earnestly desired' the Archbishop 'to take some charitable consideration of these cases, that the people of the realm might not be deprived of their pastors, being diligent, learned and zealous, though in some points of ceremonial they might seem doubtful'.

The Council concluded by expressing the hope that steps be taken 'for remedy of these enormities so that they might not be troubled hereafter to hear of the like complaints to continue'.

The letter was signed by Burghley, Leicester, Warwick, Howard, Croft, Hatton and Walsingham.[10]

It came as near to a command to the Archbishop as the Council ventured to come, in view of the Queen's attitude.

Whitgift replied that he would look into the matter, but that he knew that some of the deprived ministers were 'very factious in the Church' and such as he could not suffer 'without their further conformity, to execute their ministry'.

In short, Whitgift, as he had ignored Burghley's requests, now proceeded to question the requests of the whole Council.

What looks like another issue between the Lord Treasurer and the Archbishop arose over the appointment of a master of the Temple, 'to preach and minister holy things to the society there'.

Burghley wrote to Whitgift on September 17th, 1584:[11] 'The Queen's Majesty hath asked me what I thought of Travers to be the master of the house, where I answered that at the request of Dr. Alvey [the late master] in his sickness and of a number of honest gentlemen of the Temple, I have yielded my allowance to him to the place, so as he would show himself conformable to the order of the church, wherein I was informed that he would so be. But her Majesty told me that your Grace did not so allow of him, which I said might be for some things supposed to be written by him, entitled *Disciplina Ecclesiastica*.[12] Whereupon her Majesty commanded me to write to your Grace to know your opinion, which I pray your Grace to signify unto her as God shall move you.

'Surely it were great pity that any impediment should be occasion to the contrary, for he is well learned, very honest and well allowed and loved of the generality of that house. Mr. Bond[13] told me that your Grace liked well of him [Bond] and so do I also as one well learned and honest, but, as I told him, if he come not to the place with some applause of the company, he shall weary thereof.

And yet I recommended him to her Majesty, if Travers should not. But her Majesty thinketh him not fit for that place because of his infirmity.'

Evidently Burghley favoured the appointment of Travers, which is somewhat surprising. It was no secret that some years before he had published a book on ecclesiastical discipline in which he had advocated what was virtually a Presbyterian form of Church government. Thomas Fuller says that Travers was at one time a member of Burghley's household and the tutor of his son, Robert.[14] The evidence on this point is a little vague, but certainly Travers wrote to Burghley a little later reminding him that he had used Travers's 'service for a time in the instruction of the Church in his own house'.[15]

It need hardly be added that Whitgift did not fall in with Burghley's wishes in the matter. Actually the Queen appointed Richard Hooker to the position — the same Richard Hooker who later wrote the classical defence of the Anglican position. But Travers had, at Burghley's instigation, been appointed afternoon lecturer at the Temple in 1581. He retained this office, and the Temple became a battleground for the two champions of the opposing parties. As Thomas Fuller put it: 'The pulpit spake pure Canterbury in the morning and Geneva in the afternoon.'[16] Travers was the more popular speaker. Fuller draws an engaging picture of even the greatest benchers, men like Sir Edward Coke, frantically taking notes as he talked. Whitgift silenced him later, but it may well be that he played an important role in winning over the bar to the Puritan cause.

Late in 1584 a conference was held at Lambeth on the Puritan issue, between Whitgift and the Bishop of Winchester and the Archbishop of York for the Establishment; Sparke and Travers for the opposition. Leicester and Burghley, Walsingham and Lord Grey were present as moderators.[17] Burghley's part in it seems to have been confined to questioning some of the points raised by the Puritans as logically unsound. But Walsingham was the medium through whom a compromise was achieved.[18] He seems to have induced Whitgift not to demand from incumbents of livings any subscription to the articles of faith so long as they observed the Book of Common Prayer and the laws of the Church. Thereafter he required subscription only from new incumbents, and suspended ministers were generally restored. Even Robert Beale, perhaps the sharpest thorn in Whitgift's side, seems to have vindicated himself. In an undated note among his papers he writes:

'Before my return out of the country my L. of Canterbury had made complaint of me to her Majesty and, as my Lord Treasurer said, her Highness had willed him to examine the matter. Whereupon I returned unto his L. and answered by word of mouth to such points as his L. laid unto my charge, wherewith his L. seemed to rest satisfied. And I departed with his L. good favour.'

In September Beale wrote to Walsingham: 'I have been very graciously used and hear no further of any pontifical complaints.'[19]

The year 1584 was a troubled one. Loyal Englishmen were disturbed about the progress of the Jesuits, about the state of the Church, about the Puritans; most of all about the Queen's safety. The grim revelations of the Throgmorton Plot in the autumn of 1583 were accentuated by the assassination of William of Orange in July 1584, both of which seemed to forecast a concerted effort by the Catholic powers to invade the realm and destroy the Queen. It was primarily to deal with that menace that Elizabeth called for the election of a new Parliament, which assembled late in November of 1584.[20] It represented the first parliamentary election in over twelve years, and the House of Commons was for the most part new men. Less than a quarter of its members had sat before. But it retained, indeed accentuated, the attributes of its predecessor. What it lacked in experience it made up in fervour. Its outstanding characteristics were exuberant loyalty to the Queen, intense hostility to her competitor, Mary Stuart, and a very critical attitude towards the Established Church. It was indeed definitely in accord with the Puritans in such matters. The inevitable consequence was that it clashed sharply with the Queen. Of all her Parliaments it was perhaps the one least manageable, not from any lack of loyalty, but from lack of experience in coping with the royal will.

Burghley of course sat in the Lords, and was the recognized spokesman for the Queen in that body.[21] This in itself presented no difficulties. The peers were quite prepared to follow the royal will. The problem was to utilize the docility of the Lords to temper the belligerency of the Commons. In that particular he accomplished little or nothing. His greater efforts were directed to finding an acceptable compromise between what the Commons wanted and what the Queen would accept. In this particular he met with indifferent success.

The session of Parliament was divided in two by a Christmas recess, which the Queen, for reasons best known to herself, extended from December 21st to February 4th. During the month before the recess, attention was directed in the main to bills providing for the Queen's safety and bills dealing with the Jesuits. In connection with the former, the major problem was that of reconciling legislation with the Oath of Association. This oath bound its supporters to debar from the throne and to pursue to the death any claimant to the throne by whom or for whom the assassination of the Queen should be attempted or effected. This was taken to mean not only Mary Stuart, but her son, James, King of Scotland. The first bill on the subject, prepared by a committee of the Commons, approximated the same position. It subjected the Queen of Scots to the full penalties of the Oath of Association, but gave to Elizabeth power to exempt James.

In short, it placed the supporters of the Association, bound by solemn oath, in an awkward position, caught between their oath which said one thing and the law which said another. On this discrepancy the debate upon the bill turned. At this point Elizabeth herself intervened, and sent word to the Commons that she did not want claimants to the succession to be punished without trial, and she definitely did not want penalties imposed by the bill to be extended 'to the issue of the offender unless he were himself implicated in the conspiracy', or any visitation of Mary's sins upon her offspring.

And so the further progress of the bill was stayed, and its further consideration postponed until after the Christmas recess.

In the course of the debate the question had been raised as to what would happen to the kingdom if the Queen were suddenly murdered. How was her successor to be determined and who would govern during the interregnum? Burghley wrestled with this problem during the recess. The question of an orderly succession always bothered him. He had not forgotten the uncertainties which had followed the death of Elizabeth's young brother, uncertainties so dark and dangerous that he had despaired of his life. On a previous occasion, in 1563 when Elizabeth was critically ill, he had suggested[22] that in the event of her death the Privy Council, with such additions to it as she should provide in her will, should take command until Parliament determined her successor. He proposed an analogous plan in a bill which he drew up in January, providing for a governing Council consisting of the great officers of the Crown and all the Privy Council. It would be the first business of this Council to discover and punish those guilty of the Queen's death. Meanwhile, the members of the last Parliament should be assembled and it would be their business to take control, acting through a committee of twenty, ten from each House. It would be their business also to determine the lawful successor.[23]

The plan is interesting as a revelation of Burghley's thoughts on the subject. His emphasis upon the sovereignty of Parliament is particularly significant, but it never came to anything. It was never considered in Parliament. If it ever fell under the Queen's eyes she must have frowned upon it, though Burghley in its enacting phrase inserted the words, 'upon sure hope of the assent of our sovereign lady'.

Before discussion was resumed on the bill for the Queen's safety, the necessity for action was emphasized by the discovery of the Parry Plot. It is difficult to find out the truth about William Parry. We certainly cannot depend upon what he said about himself. On the other hand, we can hardly accept at face value John Stow's scathing denunciation of him.[24] Of education he had the merest smattering; nevertheless, he claimed to be a doctor of laws. He married twice, ladies of some means, and rapidly stripped them of their substance. His connection with Elizabeth's Court dates from about 1570, and he seems to have acquired courtly graces. Certainly he was a plausible scoundrel. In the 'seventies he undertook to murder an inconvenient creditor, was tried and sentenced to death, but escaped by royal intervention. In 1580 he turned up in Paris, supplying information to Burghley about English Catholic refugees. In May 1583 he wrote to Burghley from Lyons: 'If I am not deceived, I have shaken the foundation of the English seminary at Rheims and utterly overthrown the credit of the English pensioners at Rome.'[25] He was back in London the following year, actually telling the Queen that he pretended to be plotting against her life and showing her a letter which he had received from the Pope's secretary endorsing his purpose. There can be no doubt about the letter.[26] Apparently he convinced both Elizabeth and Burghley that his pose as a Catholic sympathizer was deliberately assumed in order to discover what the Catholics were about. That explains both his speech in the Commons urging a more lenient policy towards the Catholics and the Queen's intervention in his favour when the Commons placed him in custody for his temerity.

A few weeks later, Edward Neville revealed to the government that Parry had sought his assistance in a plan to murder the Queen. Parry was forthwith imprisoned and examined. It is notable that Leicester, Hatton and Walsingham were assigned to examine him. Burghley was not included, nor was his previous connection with Parry disclosed. Parry's defence, of course, was that he was simply playing the part of *agent provocateur*, and he pointed to his previous revelations to Elizabeth as proof of the fact. In a joint letter to Burghley and Leicester he besought them to intercede for him. And up to the last he evidently hoped for the Queen's pardon. Burghley must have been not a little chagrined by the revelation of one of his agents as a traitor.[27] At a time when his relations with Walsingham were strained, Walsingham must have been not a little pleased. It is conceivable that the trial and execution of Parry were prompted in part by such considerations. It is also conceivable that the Privy Council as a whole seized upon Parry's plotting as a dramatic justification of their concern for the Queen's safety. In any case, we need not lament his death. He had earned his hanging on many accounts. But we cannot be sure of his treason.

Against the background of the Parry Plot Parliament resumed its work on the bill for the Queen's safety. The committee in charge of the matter decided to appeal to Elizabeth herself for guidance. What emerged was a new bill, possibly drafted by Burghley. It omitted all the royal objections to previous bills and came to terms with the Oath of Association by providing that the obligations arising under the Association should be interpreted according to the provisions of the bill. The bill passed the Commons and the Lords, and ultimately received the royal assent.

And presently the bill against the Jesuits, amended in the Lords to reduce the penalty of aiding priests from treason to felony, followed the same course.

With these two matters out of the way, Elizabeth pressed for action on the subsidy bill. On March 1st, Burghley wrote to Walsingham:

'My Lord Chancellor and myself, understanding by my Lord Steward how her Majesty was disposed to have the higher house to adjourn some days so as the Commons house might, in the meantime, proceed and hasten the bill of subsidy, we therewith considered how this her Majesty's purpose for hastening of her causes in the Commons house was like to be hindered, for that the Speaker was absent this day by reason of sickness and so this day lost. And if he should not speedily recover the delay would be greater. Wherefore it was thought good that her Majesty were moved, upon information hereof, to license the Commons in the lower house . . . to make choice of another meet man, being there present amongst themselves, to supply his place when he shall be absent by sickness. But who shall be meet is best known to such of her Majesty's Council as are of the said lower house. If Mr. Solicitor [Sir Thos. Egerton] were not to be employed in the causes for her Majesty as a principal member of the house, there were none in my opinion meeter.'[28]

As a matter of fact, the Speaker was back in his place the day following, and the subsidy bill proceeded.

It may be taken for granted that Elizabeth's desire to get quick action on the subsidy bill was based on her desire to dismiss Parliament and terminate its rebellious outbursts on the religious question.

The Commons made a persistent effort to secure legislation which would effectively bridle Whitgift's attack upon the Puritans. The campaign opened with a bill for the more reverent observation of the Sabbath Day. It passed the Commons and ultimately, in an amended form, passed the Lords. Burghley was a member of the committee which directed its progress through the Lords.[29] He was evidently favourable to it. But in the end Elizabeth vetoed it. She preferred, as her successor was to prefer after her, an old-fashioned Sunday.

But this was a small matter as compared with the attack upon Whitgift's position. A committee was appointed and a petition to the Lords drawn up. It contained sixteen articles. It asked for the suspension of unqualified preachers; it asked for the end of the oath of subscription by the clergy to those articles of faith not prescribed by statute; it asked for the abolition of the oath ex-officio. In short, it supported the main demands of the moderate Puritans. Two of the Queen's own councillors, Sir Walter Mildmay and Sir Francis Knollys, played an important part in its preparation. Knollys presented the petition to a committee for the Lords; Mildmay explained and justified it.

The Lords, in receiving the petition, pointed out that the Queen had forbidden all dealing with religious questions. And so the matter stood at the time of the Christmas recess. It finally came up late in February. Burghley was the spokesman. The Queen, he said, had seen the petition and she had discussed it with Whitgift and the bishops. The outcome was, in brief, that she regarded religious matters as her affair and the necessary reforms in the Church as the business of her ecclesiastics. Whitgift, who followed Burghley, spoke more at length and in general repudiated all the salient matters in the petition.

When the reply came back to the Commons, they discussed it hotly and at great length. One member even suggested that they should make the passing of the subsidy bill contingent upon the redress of their grievance. He proposed that a delegation be sent to the Queen asking her to read the petition. Good easy man! He evidently was not aware of Elizabeth's rooted antipathy towards anything which smacked of Puritanism.

On February 27th, in the presence of her principal councillors, she gave audience to Whitgift and a delegation from Convocation come to offer her the subsidy of the clergy. She seized the occasion to praise them for their spontaneous generosity which, she pointed out, was in marked contrast to the attitude of the laity who 'must be entreated and moved thereunto'.[30]

At this point Burghley interrupted with the observation that the clergy came with mites, the Parliament with pounds. She retorted to the effect that she had rather have willing mites than reluctant pounds. She went on to urge Whitgift to take vigorous action against the Puritans. But she gave Burghley another opening when she complained about the laxity of the Bishop of London.

'Truly, my Lord,' Burghley observed to Whitgift, 'her Majesty hath declared unto you a marvellous fault in that you make in this time of light so many lewd and unlearned ministers.'

Elizabeth sprang to Whitgift's defence.

'I do not', Burghley retorted, 'burden them that be here, but it is the Bishop of Lichfield and Coventry that I mean, who made seventy ministers in one day for money, some tailors, some shoemakers and others craftsmen. I am sure the greatest part of them are not worthy to keep horses.'[31]

On the whole Burghley's interjections seem inadequate. They were certainly futile. He was not prepared to cross swords with his mistress on the larger issues involved. But he did undertake to remind her that the voice of Parliament was more important than the voice of the clergy, and that, whatever she might think about Puritanism, there were major evils in the Established Church which called for attention. It is not recorded that any of the other councillors present[32] spoke at all.

Notwithstanding royal prohibition, the Commons committee on religious reform went ahead and finished its report on the same day (February 27th) that the royal conference with Whitgift took place. But the report was never submitted to the House. Two days later Elizabeth called the Speaker of the House from his sick bed to confer with her, and told him in no uncertain terms that he was to entertain no further discussion of the subject. When he reported the royal interview to the Commons, they were, as one parliamentary diarist puts it, 'deeply wounded'. Unofficially they deliberated different courses of action, every one of them in defiance of the royal command. What they did, in fact, was to launch another bill on religion together with two other bills directed specifically against the bishops. Whitgift appealed once more to the Queen. She stopped the offending bills in mid-flight, and on March 29th prorogued Parliament. Two bills on the Church had passed both Houses. She vetoed them both.

Two other bills in which Burghley was deeply interested were also considered. One of them was directed against fraudulent conveyance of real estate. It had been drafted by the Queen's lawyers and was engineered by Burghley through the Lords in November. The Commons did not like it because it provided for redress through Star Chamber. The lawyers in the House raised objections as an infringement upon the jurisdiction of the Common Law Courts. After considerable debate, and notwithstanding strong pressure from the Crown, the bill was denied commitment.

The Lords thereupon called for an immediate conference. The Commons obliged and appointed a delegation of thirty-four members to meet with a delegation from the Lords. Burghley spoke for the Lords, beginning somewhat tediously with remarks upon the three estates of Parliament, the Crown, the Lords and the Commons. He then proceeded to the business at hand. The Lords had learned that their bill to remedy fraudulent conveyances, upon a second reading in the Commons, had been 'denied to receive a committee'. The Lords, he said, regarded this as amazing and contrary to all precedents. The bill he said 'was very well favoured and liked of her Majesty, yea in so much as her Highness used to call it her own bill'. It had been prepared by the Queen's own learned counsel, carefully digested in the upper House with the assistance of the judges and especially commended to the Commons. He therefore urged the Commons to reconsider.[33]

The Commons thereupon, after some delay, replied that they did not like the Lords' bill, but that they favoured legislation on the subject and would prepare a bill of their own. This they proceeded to do and produced a bill in which appeal to Star Chamber was eliminated and redress was assigned to the Courts of Common Law. Burghley should perhaps have known better. The Lords did not relish the change, but they could do no more about it than get in a proviso that the Act as amended should not in any sort impair the jurisdiction, power or authority of the Court of Star Chamber.[34]

Two other bills in which Burghley was interested met with an analogous fate. One of these was a bill to renew the statute making Wednesday a fish day. This statute, which expired with this Parliament, was one of Burghley's own making. He had fought hard for it in the Parliament of 1563.[35] He now fought hard for its continuance. The Puritans, in the House of Commons, opposed the measure on the grounds that it was papistical; the gentry by and large for various reasons, basically gastronomical. As the bill passed the Commons it did away with what had been called 'Cecil's fast'. In the Lords Burghley tried to have it amended. He even offered a compromise which limited Wednesday fasting to regions within twenty-five miles of the sea, and scaled down the penalties.[36] This was proposed to the Commons in conference, but they would have none of it. And the Lords finally passed the bill with 'Cecil's fast' eliminated. The arguments used in the Commons against it indicate that Cecil's hopes of increasing the supply of ships and mariners by building up the fisheries had not been realized.

The other bill had to do with various devices for depriving the Queen of revenues from wardships, notably by the creation of long leases. Burghley was interested as Master of the Court of Wards. But the Commoners who regarded wardship as a burden, as indeed it was, would not be a party to any legislation preventing the alleviation of the burden. So once again in defiance of the royal wishes, the bill was dashed.

Elizabeth came down to Parliament on March 29th to end the session. Sergeant Puckering, the Speaker, had at hand two speeches for the occasion, one of them prepared by Burghley himself and still extant in his own handwriting.[37] Apparently Puckering spoke *ex tempore*, making some use of Burghley's draft, but drawing mainly upon the other version. It is worth noting that one passage of Burghley's draft was omitted in the speech as delivered. It dealt specifically with the reform of the Church, and was plainly designed to remind Elizabeth that though she had frowned upon the efforts of the Commons in that direction, she had promised to do something about it herself.

'It was well understood that your Majesty, as having by God's ordinance a supreme authority for that purpose, had straitly charged the archbishops, bishops and your whole clergy, now assembled in the Convocation, to have due regard to see to the reformation of divers abuses in the government and discipline of the church. And so our firm hope is that your Majesty will, by your strait commandment to your clergy, continue your care to see and command that such abuses as are crept into the church by the negligence of the ministers may be speedily reformed, to the honour of Almighty God and to your own immortal praise and comfort of your subjects.'

Puckering did not speak these words, or anything like them. Quite possibly he feared that Elizabeth would rebuke him on the spot if he did. But Burghley would have had them spoken. He did not wish Elizabeth's rage against the Puritans to blind her to the necessity of Church reform.

CHAPTER XVII

LEICESTER IN THE LOW COUNTRIES,
1585-87

Two things happened in the early summer of 1584 which changed radically the attitude of the English government towards the Dutch revolt in the Netherlands. One of them was the death of the Duke of Alençon in June; the other was the assassination of William of Orange in July. The loss of Alençon as a man was no great matter. He had few merits either of mind or body. But he was heir presumptive of the French Crown. More than that, since his brother, Henry III, was not only childless but without hope of children, Alençon was, in fact if not in name, heir apparent. He was the last of the Valois and with his death the French succession under the Salic law passed to Henry of Bourbon, King of Navarre, a Huguenot by birth and training. This meant that the conflict in France over religion was presently to be identified with a conflict over the succession, with the heir presumptive of the same religious complexion as the Dutch rebels in the Low Countries and the Queen of England.

Alençon had also been for at least five years the recognized suitor of the English Queen. She was twice his age and perilously close to the age when she could no longer bear children. Those of her councillors who, like Burghley, were much concerned about the succession in England if she died childless, hoped against hope that she would marry Alençon with all his shortcomings. His death put an end to all hopes for the continuation of the Tudor line. So in England as in France his death raised the question of the succession in an acute form.

Elizabeth had found Alençon a convenient instrument for coping with the Dutch revolt. He had had personal ambitions in that direction and she had encouraged them. Generally speaking, she regarded the French occupation of the Low Countries as more menacing to England than their occupation by the Spaniards. But she thought she could control Alençon and believed that as heir presumptive to the French throne he would drag France once again into a war with the Habsburgs. He proved to be a broken reed to lean upon. Yet so long as he lived, his ambition, his English connections, and his proximity to the French throne made him a menace to Spain and a potential ally of the rebellious Dutch. It is a striking fact that, notwithstanding his treachery to the Dutch cause, they continued to look to France for salvation.

William of Orange certainly looked that way. Though he always sought to cultivate English good will, his hopes of outside aid were centred in France. Meanwhile, he had to face the most competent of all the Spanish governors in the Low Countries, Alexander Farnese, Prince of Parma. In the spring of 1584, Orange was fighting a losing fight, powerless to prevent the richest cities of

Flanders from falling into Spanish hands. In July Parma was making ready to besiege Antwerp itself. At that critical juncture, Orange was murdered.

The Dutch were stricken with grief but undismayed. They appealed for help to France. In England, Elizabeth's Council took the position that without Orange the Dutch cause was lost unless France or England or both of them together came to its assistance. The Council evidently favoured joint intervention. But the initial reports from France were not promising. The French received the Dutch envoys with scant courtesy, refused their request and sent them home. This meant, if it meant anything, that Elizabeth would either have to help the Dutch herself or leave them helpless to what everyone thought was their certain fate.

Elizabeth called her Council together on October 10th to consider and advise. It seems likely that Burghley presided and that the long memorandum of that date on the subject, among his papers at Hatfield, contains the substance of the problem as he presented it to his colleagues.[1]

Burghley began by pointing out the grim alternatives, to wit, should Elizabeth intervene without French aid, and if she did not intervene, what provision should she make to face the malice of the King of Spain after he had conquered the Dutch. He elaborated on the malice of the Spanish King, his mortal antipathy to the Protestant faith everywhere, revealed nowhere more strikingly than in his long and costly wars against the Dutch, whom he might easily have recovered had he been willing to grant them freedom of worship. Burghley saw no hope that Philip's hatred would be mitigated; rather he thought that it would be accentuated now that he had acquired Portugal and all the wealth of the Portuguese Indies, now that his fear of French intervention had been quieted by the death of Alençon and the Dutch weakened by the murder of their great leader, 'who of all men living hath been the greatest stay of his conquest'.

Burghley reminded his colleagues of the long record of Spanish hostility to England, of the constant plotting of Spanish ambassadors from the days of De Quadra to the days of Mendoza, from the Ridolfi Plot to the Throgmorton Plot. He insisted that once Holland and Zeeland fell, or even the isle of Walcheren, there was nothing to stop Philip from turning his victorious army against England. In the face of these facts he concluded that Elizabeth should intervene and should make public the sound reasons for her intervention. But he bade his colleagues consider what intervention meant.

It meant war with Spain, supported by the Pope and the Empire. It meant alliance not with the Netherlands as a whole, but with the Netherlands stripped of many of their richest cities, a mere handful of what he called 'popular' states, corrupt, mutinous and without a leader, which might at any time fall apart. It was uncertain how much they would contribute in their own defence. Their promises were not to be depended upon. They had broken promises more than once before. If Elizabeth sent troops in their support, she would have to send a force strong enough not only to deal with the enemy but to deal with treachery behind the lines. And she would have to pay them. 'Common experience', he observed, 'hath taught that our nation, for lack of pay, have abidden many miseries and have been also forced to commit many disorders and thereby grown into contempt and mislike.'

He raised the question also of the effect of war upon English trade. 'If', he remarked, 'England have no other war but a stay of vent [the loss of foreign markets] then the realm would not nor could not long endure to yield either obedience or profit to her Majesty.'

Altogether, as Burghley presented it, it was a gloomy prospect. He then went on to outline a course of action in the event of intervention. She must keep her costs to a minimum. She must get solid security for her expenses by the occupation of important ports in Holland and Zeeland — he mentioned specifically Flushing, Middelburg and Brill — one of her noblemen must command the army, her officers must oversee the raising and the spending of taxes. She must make sure of the friendship of Scotland, even if it cost money. She must encourage the King of Navarre to make war on Spain for his lost provinces. She must plan attack upon the Indies. She must urge the Dutch to induce Duke Casimir to invade from the east. She must do her best to bring back into the Dutch union those provinces which had gone over to Spain.

Veering once more to the defence of England against Spanish malice, he contemplated the employment of mercenary troops to be stationed along the Scottish border and in the maritime counties, with care that they should be so distributed that they could not dominate any of the areas they occupied.

'Finally,' he concluded, 'it ought to be Alpha and Omega to cause the people to be better taught to serve God; and to see justice duly administered unto them whereby they may serve God and love her Majesty. And it may be concluded — *Si Deus nobiscum quis contra nos?*'

It was a fearful and irresolute presentation of the subject — as far as possible from a trumpet call to action. If it leaned one way or the other, it leaned against intervention.

We have virtually no account of the debate except the one Camden wrote.

'The arguments', Camden wrote, 'were very many on either side, on the one part to show the great peril and danger to her Majesty and her realm if the King of Spain should recover Holland and Zeeland as he had the other countries [provinces] for lack of succour in seasonable time, either by the French King or the Queen's Majesty. And on the other side many difficulties were remembered to depend upon the succouring of them by her Majesty.'[2]

Camden's account is mainly devoted to the argument of those opposed to intervention. 'These', he wrote, 'held it the best course if the Queen would meddle no more in matters of the Netherlands, but most strongly fortify her own kingdom, bind the good unto her daily more straitly by her innate bounty, restrain the bad, gather money, furnish her navy with all provisions, strengthen the borders towards Scotland with garrisons and maintain the ancient military discipline of England ... So would England become impregnable and she on every side most secure and dreadful to her neighbours. That this was the most commodious means for those which had ever mighty neighbours, to avoid war ... But they which were of this opinion incurred heavy displeasure amongst martial men as inclining to the Spaniards' party, degenerate and faint-hearted cowards.'

When we recall that Camden, in writing his *Annals*, leaned heavily on Burghley, and note the striking similarity between what he wrote in this connection and the arguments against intervention which Burghley himself had presented to the Council, we are perhaps justified in assuming that though the hand was the hand of Camden, the voice was Burghley's.

Most of the writers of Elizabethan history have endorsed the policy of intervention, but there is much to be said for the opposed point of view. Certainly the immediate consequences of intervention when it came did not yield the results expected by its advocates. Leicester's expedition, which we are presently to consider, was a flat failure and did as much harm as it did good to the Dutch cause. This was probably due rather to Leicester's personal defects than to the defects of the idea. It was due in large part also to the very half-hearted support he received from his mistress. But those who knew Elizabeth as Burghley knew her could scarcely have expected otherwise. The basic difference between Burghley's attitude and Walsingham's was that Burghley knew by long experience the reluctance of his mistress to support any aggressive policy. Walsingham and Leicester hoped to coerce her. Burghley knew she could not be coerced and more and more he shaped his thinking within that frame of reference. It was not what was best, but what Elizabeth could be persuaded to accept. A good deal of what looked to others like irresolution on his part was a grim realization of that fact. Nothing could be done without her, and it was only by indirect approach that much which was positive could be done with her. She cordially disliked the Dutch, both for their Calvinism and for what Burghley called their '*popularity*'. At the moment this dislike was accentuated by the impudent Puritanism of her House of Commons. The one thing which mattered to her was the peace and security of England, and she was far from identifying those objectives with the Protestant cause. But she was too shrewd a woman to ignore the fact that the radical Protestants both at home and abroad were her only certain allies. And so she was torn between her instinctive impulses and her keen political sense, going now this way and now that, as one or the other had the upper hand in her. Burghley knew that all might be lost if she were pushed too far, and that she always favoured a defensive rather than an aggressive course. And he was, of course, getting old, and the crusading spirit was drying up in him. What Walsingham was saying in the 'eighties Burghley had said in the 'sixties when the issues were much less sharply defined and when it seemed to be touch and go as to whether his mistress would not abandon the Protestant cause altogether.

The outcome of the debate in the Council on October 10th was the endorsement of the aggressive policy which Leicester and Hatton and Walsingham supported. In commenting on the debate Burghley wrote: 'In the end ... it was concluded to advise her Majesty rather to seek the avoiding and diverting of the great peril than, in respect of any difficulties, to suffer the King of Spain to grow to the full height of his design and conquests, whereby the perils to follow were so evident as if he were not, by succouring the Hollanders and their party, impeached, the Queen should not hereafter be any more able to withstand the same . . . but shall be forced to give place to his insatiable malice, which is most terrible to be thought of but most miserable to suffer.'³

The Council went on to suggest immediate action as follows:

(1) To send an envoy to Holland instructed to find out for certain whether the French King had agreed to help them; if so to approve of the same, if not to offer English assistance.

(2) To get from them a statement of the terms upon which they would accept English assistance.

(3) To inform them that she would expect the delivery to her of the ports of Flushing, Middelburg and Brill, as security for the observance of their contract.

(4) To find out how much, province by province, they were prepared to contribute to the expense of the war, and what forces they proposed to maintain both by land and by sea.

The Council also advised that the Queen come to terms with the King of Scots, assist Gebhard Truchsess, the Archbishop of Cologne, a recent convert to Protestantism, in his struggle for the possession of his see against a Habsburg competitor, urge the Dutch to invite the assistance of Casimir, persuade the French King to cut off supplies to Parma's army, induce the King of Navarre and Don Antonio to press their claims against Spain by force of arms. Finally the Council advised that Parliament should be reconvened to endorse and to finance the whole enterprise.

The Council did not raise the question of an attack upon the Spanish Indies, but in other particulars they followed the line which Burghley had suggested.

The French ambassador believed that Elizabeth would have preferred joint intervention with the French.⁴ In any case, she decided to follow her Council's advice and send a 'wise person' to the Dutch.

William Davison was chosen for the mission — an old hand in Anglo-Dutch relations, a zealous Protestant and, in the opinion of a Spanish agent in London, 'Walsingham's creature'. He reported favourably on the strength and resources of the Dutch. News from France indicated that the French King was not disposed to accept the Dutch offers of sovereignty. Elizabeth's response was encouraging. She at least went so far as to send £6000 to Truchsess at Cologne. Walsingham thought it was a bad investment and attributed it to Burghley's influence. It was at any rate a revelation of the fact that the Queen's grip upon her purse-strings was loosening a little.

At this juncture Walsingham was taken ill and the administration of affairs passed for a time into Burghley's hands. He was responsible for the dispatch which went off to Davison in January in which he was encouraged to promote joint intervention, but at the same time to prevent the French from acquiring absolute dominion. Walsingham got sight of the dispatch before it went off and protested that it was no time to discourage French intervention in any form, unless the Queen was resolute to take action herself.[5]

Elizabeth decided to explore further the French attitude. Late in January 1585 she dispatched Lord Derby to convey the Order of the Garter to Henry III but with orders to sound him out on the Dutch. While Derby was in Paris the King definitely rejected the Dutch offer, but intimated that he would join with her in assisting them.

Thereupon Elizabeth dispatched another envoy to France in March. But meanwhile Walsingham, back at Court, succeeded in persuading her of the necessity for immediate action. Davison was accordingly instructed to inform the Dutch that she was prepared to take them under her protection upon condition that she got port towns for security.[6] This message was conveyed also to Dutch agents in England,[7] and Elizabeth herself in an interview with them on March 12th confirmed it.

There are no indications that Burghley lent his support to these tentative commitments. The next we hear of him is at a meeting of the Council on March 18th at his house in Covent Garden. On that occasion he argued strongly against intervention.[8] He pointed out that Elizabeth had no claims to the Low Countries, that the justification of intervention was based upon the anticipation of a Spanish attack upon England. The case against Spain rested upon Spanish intervention in support of rebellion in England and Ireland. Burghley suggested that Spain had an equally strong case against England for intervention in support of rebels against Spain in the Low Countries, with money and with large bands of volunteers.

It was, moreover, he observed, pertinent to consider the character of the Dutch rebellion. It was directed against a lawful sovereign, its strength was of the common people, organized in what he once more called 'popular' states. These states were without a head. There were few noblemen to assume leadership and these were hopelessly divided. It was quite clear that the Dutch were reluctant to provide the sinews of war, notwithstanding their promises. Even Orange, who spent his life for them, could not win from them the money that was needed, and foreign princes who had come to their aid had been cavalierly treated. They were an incontinent, ungrateful people, much given to mutinies and corruption, divided against themselves even to 'the very bowels' of their towns. If her Majesty sent an army to their assistance the leaders of it would almost inevitably fall to loggerheads with the Dutch military leaders. He specifically mentioned Maurice of Nassau and Count Hohenlo in this connection. He did not think that they would agree to yield cautionary towns. The French King had asked for them in vain.

He reminded his colleagues that the Dutch had first offered themselves to the French, without appeal to England. They clearly preferred a French connection, and it was likely that if they accepted Elizabeth's offer of assistance it would be without enthusiasm.

Burghley also reminded his colleagues that the King of Spain was simply seeking to suppress rebellion in his own territories — 'a thing that any prince would do, and as her Majesty did upon the like occasion both in England and in Ireland'.

Intervention would mean war with Spain, the threat of invasion from Spain and the inevitable recall of all English forces overseas to defend the homeland. The costs of such a war would be very great, and the outcome doubtful. Burghley questioned whether Elizabeth's subjects would be willing to support what they would regard as an unnecessary aggressive war, directed against a neighbour at peace with England. He raised the question as to the effect of such a war upon English trade with her two best markets, Spain and the Low Countries. It would cause intolerable unemployment and would drastically reduce the 'Queen's customs which is her best revenue'.

Since the Queen had no intention of annexing the Low Countries, he thought that war would drag on until she had either established the Dutch under their own government, or had imposed some sort of compromise settlement or had abandoned the struggle, 'wearied with the trouble and charge of the war'.

He doubted whether the Dutch could govern themselves; he doubted whether any compromise peace would last any longer than any of the other analogous compromises in the Dutch or French civil wars. In short, nothing would be gained.

'Upon all which matters, thus remembered,' Burghley concluded, 'it shall be meet to consider whether it were not better to advise her Majesty to forbear this enterprise, accompanied with so many difficulties and dangers, and rather to proceed with effect in the treaty with the King and realm of Scotland, for a certain and firm peace and a perpetual league between her Majesty and them, with a perfect establishment of the cause of religion in both the realms. The assurance of which country . . . ought to be accounted of more value to withstand the enmity either of France or Spain, both because the Scots dwell with us upon one main or continent land, and because also they have cast off the Pope of Rome and so profess the same religion of the Gospel that we do, a greater bond than which cannot be between any peoples and nations in the world. This done and her Majesty's putting her own realm in that order and strength which she may and is able to do, there will be little cause to doubt any peril from the King of Spain though he should possess all the Low Countries quietly, no more than there was at such time as the Duke of Alva, his lieutenant in those parts and, having all these in peaceable possession, commanded what he liked.'

'And yet,' Burghley added, 'the King of Spain can never so keep those countries but he shall have need of the amity of England, considering the long distance of his other dominions from thence and the doubt he shall continually be in of mutinies and new revolts that may happen there, together with the necessity of the English traffic thither, without the which he shall have small revenue there.

'And finally, whether it were not better for her Majesty to shun this unnecessary war and to keep her treasure for her own defence in time of need . . . which together with the necessary preparation of all things here, whereof care is to be had, will deliver her from any peril that may come by any foreign attempt or by sedition at home.'

Burghley's argument followed in the main his argument in the preceding

October, but it was more emphatic in its opposition to intervention. His remarks about the Dutch are worth noting, because they reveal a fundamental distrust of 'popular' government, particularly if the nobility, the natural leaders of the people, were weak and divided. Striking also is his emphasis upon the importance of foreign trade. Earlier in his career[9] he had rather frowned upon it, but more and more as he grew older he came to regard it as the very life-blood of England.

There is no record of what decision was reached in this Council meeting at which Burghley spoke. Walsingham, Leicester and Hatton, the three champions of intervention, were all present. No doubt they presented opposing arguments. In any case it is not surprising that they came to regard Burghley as the leader of the opposition. Walsingham wrote to Davison: 'I find those whose judgment her Majesty most trusts so coldly affected to the cause that I have no great hope of the matter.'[10] Doubtless he had Burghley in mind. The account of the debates in the Council on the subject, written some twenty years later by John Clapham, one of Burghley's servants, is pertinent in this connection:

'Long conversations were had about the enterprise, some of the Privy Council approving and other disliking it. I have heard it reported that the Lord Burghley, the Treasurer of England, and Sir Walter Mildmay, men of great judgment and integrity, apprehending at that time some of the inconveniences that have since accompanied those wars, declared their opinion directly against it. Howbeit the earl of Leicester, being in great favour with the Prince and desirous for his own glory to have the government of those countries, urged the former considerations in the behalf of the United Provinces, so far as in the end he swayed the balance on the left side.'[11]

Spanish advices from England expressed the same opinion.[12]

Meanwhile, in France the situation was rapidly deteriorating. The Catholic opposition to the succession of Henry of Navarre took the form of a league signed on the last day of the year 1584 between the Duke of Guise and the King of Spain, for the extirpation of heresy both in France and in the Low Countries and the exclusion of Navarre from the succession. The matter was kept very secret but began to leak out in March. Before the end of April, Elizabeth was aware of it. She was convinced, though not precisely informed, that the purpose of the league included an attack upon heresy in England. After the Throgmorton Plot and the Parry Plot she could expect no less. Her immediate response was to set about the establishment of a counter-league, and she sent ambassadors to Scotland and to the German Protestant princes with that end in view. Under the circumstances her reluctance to engage in aggressive war in the Low Countries inevitably increased. That was reason enough for her coldness of which Walsingham was conscious — Burghley or no Burghley.

Early in May, Elizabeth began to talk again of aggressive action and indicated an intention to take the Dutch under her protection, provided they accepted her terms. But it now appeared that the Dutch were reluctant to concede the cautionary towns. Walsingham found it necessary to scold them in turn, and he warned the Dutch agents that they had better act quickly while the Queen was favourably disposed. There were plenty of ill-disposed people at hand, he said, to take advantage of their irresolution. Meanwhile, Elizabeth secretly called Sir John Norris, one of the best of her generals, back from Ireland to take command of an expeditionary force. Her resolution was quickened by the sudden seizure of a large fleet of English merchantmen in Spanish harbours. She forthwith sent orders to Sir Walter Raleigh to dispatch a naval force against Spanish fishermen off the Banks. And she ordered Drake to make ready to attack the Spanish West Indies.

In France the situation grew steadily darker. It became apparent that both the King and his mother, who had heretofore been inclined to support the claims of Henry of Navarre against Guise and the Leaguers, were going over to the other side. Navarre had already appealed to Elizabeth for aid in May. Towards the end of the month he sent an agent, Ségur de Pardaillan, to England to ask for a loan of 200,000 crowns. Elizabeth refused but, while Ségur still tarried, news came that the King had definitely joined with the Leaguers against Navarre and the Huguenots. This induced Elizabeth to change her tune. She now contemplated sending money to Germany to raise troops for Navarre's support.

No doubt Burghley played a major part in dealing with all these matters. Late in the summer he was urging Drake to get to sea before the Queen decided to hold him back,[13] but at the moment there is no record of his activities.

Leicester and Walsingham, having made up their minds that Burghley was the chief stumbling-block in the way of positive action, opened a covert attack upon him which began in January 1585 and apparently continued until late in August.

So far as Walsingham was concerned, Burghley evidently got wind of his ill feeling in January 1585, and wrote him a letter on the subject. The letter is missing, but we have two letters from Walsingham in reply, both dated January 30th.[14] The first of these ran as follows:

'Your honourable and plain manner of proceeding towards me giveth me just cause to hold the like course towards your Lordship.

'I cannot deny but as your Lordship hath had heretofore some reports made unto you that might work some doubtful conceit of my good will towards you, so have there the like been made unto me, that might have held like conceit.

'But when I saw some cause to suspect that the ground thereof grew of faction (that reigneth ordinarily in Courts) and that the authors thereof sought by such indirect means to draw me to be a party with them, I gave no way unto them as one that did greatly affect your Lordship's friendship and good opinion, whom in course of counsel I have always found to proceed most sincerely in the ordinary course of justice.

'But touching my late conceit had of your opposition in my suit for farming of the customs, a matter I found did greatly touch me in credit, having waded so far therein as I had done; I must needs confess I saw so many reasons, confirmed so many ways, to lead me so to think, as did not only induce me to believe that to be true but did in a sort work in me a confirmation of former reports of your L. mislike of me. And thereupon I did plainly resolve with myself that it was a more safe course for me to hold you as an enemy than as a friend . . . Now whiles I was possessed with this discontentment I confess I sought up such information as heretofore (unsought for) have been given unto me, that might any way touch your L., and meant (had I not received assurance from Sir Thomas Cecil of your Lordship's friendship towards me) to have proceeded by conference with the parties to have drawn some further light from them. . . .

'And touching the particular matter your Lordship maketh mention of in your letter, that a friend of mine should deal with an exchequer man by my order, for the search of some matter that might touch you, I do assure your Lordship I do not remember any such matter and therefore do hold myself wronged therein by the informer.

'Thus, my Lord, have I plainly let your Lordship understand my grief and the cause thereof, assuring your Lordship, if it shall please you hereafter to make account of the good will of one so far separated in quality from you, you shall find no man by effects more ready to deserve your Lordship's friendship than myself.'

It will be noted that the one specific charge which Walsingham levelled at Burghley was that he had opposed the lease of the Customs in the out-ports to Walsingham. There can be no doubt that Burghley carefully scrutinized the terms of the lease as originally drawn and suggested some amendments.[15] As the chief financial administrator of the Crown it was part of his duty to do so. It is a sad commentary on the attitude of public servants in the sixteenth century towards public funds that the watchdog of the Treasury should have been subject to the kind of persecution which Walsingham proposed simply for doing his duty.

Burghley evidently replied to Walsingham as soon as he received the letter, since he had a second letter from Walsingham the same day.

In the second letter, Walsingham professed himself satisfied. He declined to reveal the names of his informers. 'If', he wrote, 'I might do it with the credit of an honest man, I would not fail to satisfy your Lordship therein. Besides it might reach to such persons as are not to be called in question.'

One wonders whether Walsingham in the last sentence had Leicester in mind.

In any case, Walsingham seems for a time to have buried the hatchet. He did, however, resume the attack in July, using as his agent none other than William Herle, the same Herle who had served as Burghley's *agent provocateur* in the Ridolfi Plot, and who had since been active in the Queen's service.

Herle wrote to Walsingham on July 25th[16] that he had followed Walsingham's instructions and had written to Burghley telling him of a plan to help the Dutch which would yield £10,000 a month to the Queen and £1000 a month to Burghley, the whole matter to be handled secretly. Herle anticipated that Burghley would inquire further about the offer and would speak to the Queen about it. He asked Walsingham to designate someone to deal with Burghley about it.

If this means what it seems to mean, it reveals Herle as playing a double game by Walsingham's direction, dangling a bribe before Burghley's eyes. But one cannot be too sure about Herle. He was a clever scoundrel, and not above playing up to Walsingham in order to reveal his trickery to Burghley.

In any case the trick missed fire. Burghley replied to Herle's approach on July 24th:[17]

'For that which you desire to be answered, how I can be tempted with allowance of a device to gain to her Majesty £10,000 monthly and to myself one other £1000, so as her Majesty will help the States, I think I know the matter very well, having heard thereof a month past and have within these few days seen and read the project. What I think thereof I cannot but pronounce doubtfully thereof until I shall speak with the party that offereth it. In my opinion, if the matter may appear feasible, I think it allowable with some corrections of some points . . . But for any offer to myself I utterly refuse either such or a less sum, thinking it more charity to yield of mine own to the common cause than to receive a penny. I marvel that any such malicious discoursers can note me a councillor that do abuse my credit to my private gain. I may say boldly that I have neither made nor had suit from her Majesty these ten years by lease, licence, gift, loan or any other ways worth ten shillings. How others are fraught with suits the world may easily see, which I do not mislike.'

Leicester's attitude towards Burghley can generally be taken for granted, though it was sometimes concealed under a great show of friendship. In July 1584 he had written to thank Burghley 'that it pleased you so friendly and honourably to deal in the behalf of my poor wife.[18] For truly, my Lord, in all reason she is hardly dealt with. God must only help it with her Majesty . . . For which, my Lord, you shall be assured to find us most thankful, to the uttermost of our powers'. Leicester went on to describe an unannounced visit to Theobalds: 'We found both meat and drink of all sorts there, too much for such sudden guests, and most kindly used by all your servants.

'I lay in wait to have heard of your L. return before I departed . . . but so good hap came not.

'I have been bold to make some of your stags afraid, but killed none. If I had, your Lordship should have been presented with our good fortune.'[19]

Nothing could be more amiable! But Leicester's mind changed rather rapidly. The next month he lost his only son and with that loss the hope of arranging a marriage between him and Arabella Stuart. On top of that, late in the year, came the publication of the violent attack upon him in the pamphlet which came to be known as *Leicester's Commonwealth*. The picture which it gave of Burghley, in very edifying contrast to that of Leicester, probably served to quicken his animosity.[20] But his greatest grievance against Burghley was his belief that Burghley was responsible for the Queen's hesitation in going to the assistance of the Dutch.

Burghley sensed this animosity and wrote a letter to Leicester about it on August 11th, 1585. He began by observing that both his sons and his daughters were convinced of Leicester's good will, but that he had heard from reliable sources that Leicester disliked his 'doubtfulness or coldness' in supporting aid for the Dutch.

Burghley went on to say that Lady Russell, his sister-in-law, had reported to him an interview with Leicester which had served to confirm other reports of Leicester's unfriendliness. Burghley concluded:

'And therefore, knowing in the sight of God mine own innocence of any unhonest action against your L., or intention, I will quiet my hurt and arm myself against the wrong with patience, as I am sure no man of my sort has abidden more injuries this way in hearing evil when I have done well. And so I shall remain ready to do that good I can howsoever I am misused. But so will I live by God's grace. As for any man's evil will, I will not forget my duty nor stain mine honesty.

'And if the place I hold might be bestowed by her Majesty upon another without condemnation of me for mine honesty, I vow to Almighty God I would be most glad. And thereby should I be sure to be void of anyone's evil will or wrong interpretation of my poor actions. For I know my place and not my deeds procure me unfriendliness of many, which I pray God to remedy.'[21]

The letter is about as brusque as ever Burghley allowed himself to be. He accepted without question the fact of Leicester's hostility and intimated that he could hardly have avoided it without dereliction of his duties as Treasurer and councillor.

Leicester's reply[22] was a flat denial. He branded Lady Russell's tale as false.

'Your Lordship', he wrote, 'hath not found a more ready friend for you and yours than I have ever been. For if you examine all the matters wherein you have at any time employed me, when my credit was somewhat better than since it was, [ask yourself] whether I dealt not very friendly with you or no.' He alluded to the good will of Burghley's children. 'This reason ... methinks should be sufficient for to hold you from getting any new, strange opinion of me.'

He denied that he had charged Burghley with 'coldness' in the Low Countries cause. 'I have dealt, as your Lordship hath heard perhaps, more directly in those causes than a wiser man would, but I trust without any just cause given of prejudice either to you or any other Councillor. And for that many times you yourself would tell, not only among us, but to her Majesty, how you were misreported abroad for that matter, I did deal plainly with your L. even in particular, what I thought and whom I heard and most doubt of to hinder those causes.'

He rebuked Burghley for not having given him a chance to deny the charges as soon as they had been made. He took occasion once more to refer to his father's friendship to Burghley in King Edward's day.

He ended by begging Burghley to seek out proof of the tales he heard, and wound up by signing himself, 'By him that hath given you no other cause but to be his friend'.

The significant part of this letter is not Leicester's denials, but his rather pathetic reaching out for Burghley's good will. The most revealing sentence is where Leicester admits that his credit was not what it had been. It is hardly likely that Burghley took Leicester at his word. Walsingham, who was Leicester's ally, thought he was responsible for the attacks upon Burghley. And Walsingham was doubtless right.

Beginning early in July, Burghley received from Herle a series of letters setting forth what he represented to be current criticism of Burghley. The first letter from Herle is missing, but Burghley's reply reveals its purport.

'Now', he wrote, after observing that he had been long afflicted with such kind of viperous breathing, 'to this matter. I know that Ségur, the King of Navarre's ambassador, was informed by some Councillor (as he told my friend) that I was a hindrance of his negotiations even then when I did my best to further the same, being in conscience moved thereto, not only for my zeal to the cause of the King of Navarre but also in necessary consequence of the surety of the Queen's Majesty, my sovereign, and my native country ... I pray you advise the parties that make these reports either to speak with myself or Mr. Secretary Walsingham, who is best acquainted with the truth of my actions in this time. And for the action concerning the States [of the Low Countries] both he and Mr. Davison can tell in what terms and sort I have dealt with her Majesty, often to the offending of her Majesty with my earnestness. And I dare appeal to the report of any Councillor so as I may be present at the report, for I know none can be so void of grace that dare say anything of me herein that becomes not an honest, faithful and careful Councillor.'[23]

Herle's reply spoke of Ségur's leave-taking, at which he said that Burghley 'alone had dealt more honourably for his King, and yet ill handled by some even to the offending of her Majesty, but also had persisted therein more than the rest, having better passage than they altogether, which he would not only publish here, but assure his King that you were the sole personage to whom affairs ought to be addressed'. Herle went on to condemn the Queen's dilatory course: 'I have told her Majesty of late', he added, 'sundry things of great consequence proving true, but I had Cassandra's luck.'[24]

In Burghley's reply, dated the 18th, he wrote: 'I heartily thank you for your letter containing a very sensible discourse of the reasons that necessarily ought to induce or rather to hasten her Majesty to yield success to all her friends and neighbours distressed whose causes are joined with her own in respect of the common enemy, as no destruction can sever them, neither can any wit conceive their dangers to follow but ours must follow concomitant. And to say the truth the common enemy hath a more ardent malice against England than against the others; but they lie in his way and he cannot leap over them to assail us.

'Howsoever the discourses abroad do imagine of our actions, I know no one Councillor that showeth any contrary opinion, but yet some are more earnest than others. But this I dare avow without flattering of myself, no one doth use more arguments of weight than I do. It may be others may speak with greater words than I, but I am sure her Majesty thinketh my speeches to have as great force as any. And so many times she yieldeth, as overcome with argument, but yet (which is natural to her sex) hindereth resolution. I hope time will gain that which is necessary.'

Burghley then went on to defend himself against the charge that he had advised the proroguing of Parliament, which had been prorogued in March until May

20th, then to June 7th, then to June 21st and then to October. It was this last prorogation to which Burghley must have referred. Those who favoured intervention had strongly urged that Parliament be recalled to lend its support. Its prorogation until October looked to them like another device for delaying action.

Burghley wrote: 'I thank you for that you advertise that some thought me a counsellor to the proroguing of Parliament, whereof I was no more privy to the consent nor to the act than you were. I was at my house at Theobalds, preparing for her Majesty[25] both the day before it was done and when it was done. And the first time I heard of it was by my L. of Leicester's report when the Queen came to my house, who told me that her Majesty had signed the warrant the same morning and that my L. Chancellor had it of her. Whereof, as I seemed very sorry, and so was his Lordship.'[26]

On August 11th, upon news of the fall of Antwerp, Herle wrote 'that the rage of men was so great against your Lordship as it exceeded both measure and modesty'. They blamed it altogether upon his dilatory attitude. Herle went on to say that men declared England to have become *regnum Cecilianum*, that Burghley's buildings were infinite and equal to king's palaces, and that the Queen's Council, if they would obtain anything, must address themselves to him.

Herle spoke also of the favour which Burghley's son, Thomas, showed to the house of Northumberland,[27] 'even more than to his sovereign and country', and of his extravagant purchases of land, sometimes 'by plain encroachment upon the R[ealm] and the Commons'.

'To conclude,' Herle added, 'this rage or frenzy (or what shall I term it) was not among them without bitter voices of execration. But I marvel of some that I noted of this company whom I thought reason would have better bridled.'[28]

To this Burghley replied at length.[29] 'I perceive,' he began, 'that you hear the vile, false, devilish exclamations and execrations made by such as I know not.' He then went on to quote from the Psalms: 'They have sharpened their tongues like a serpent, adder's poison is under their lips.'[30]

'But I know,' he continued, 'and have proved God's goodness so many years to defend mine innocency, that I may boldly say with David: The Lord is my defence and my God is the rock of my refuge. And He shall bring upon them their own iniquity and shall cut them off in their own wickedness[31] ... If they do think me guilty thereof, they need not fear to accuse me ... Let them make [use] of any one proof wherewith to prove me guilty of falsehood, injustice, bribery; of dissimulation, of double dealing in advice, in council either with her Majesty or with the Councillors, let them charge me in any one point that I have not dealt as earnestly for the Queen's Majesty to aid the afflicted in the Low Countries, to withstand this increasing power of the King of Spain, the assurance of the King of Scots to be tied to her Majesty with reward — yea with the greatest pension that any other hath. If in any of these I may prove to have been behind, or slower than any, in a discreet manner, as becometh a servant and Councillor, I will yield myself worthy of perpetual reproach. ...

'They that say, in a rash and malicious mockery, that England is become *regnum Cecilianum* may please their cankerous humour with such a device; but if my actions be considered, if there be any cause given by me of such a nickname, there may be found in many others juster causes to attribute other names than mine.

'If my buildings mislike them, I confess my folly in the expenses because some of my houses are to come, if God so please, to them that shall not have land to make them. I mean by my house at Theobalds, which was begun by me with a mean measure but increased by occasion of her Majesty's often coming, whom to please I never would omit to strain myself to more charges than building is . . . For my house in Westminster, I think it so old it should not stir envy, many having of later times built larger, both in city and country. And yet the building thereof cost me the sale of lands worth £100 by year, in Staffordshire, that I had of good King Edward. My house of Burghley is of my mother's inheritance, who liveth and is the owner thereof and I but a farmer. And for my building there, I have set my walls upon the old foundation. Indeed I have made the rough stone walls to be of square and yet one side remaineth as my father left it me. . . .

'Now shortly for my son's adhering to Northumberland, I marvel why he should not bear favour to him that was his brother-in-law, as long as he knew no faults. For his purchases I know that he hath ventured upon more bargains than I allowed . . . And to this day I know he doth repent himself.'

To this letter Burghley added a long postscript as follows:

'After I had ended, though my leisure doth not well serve me, yet I could not omit to answer a notable, absurd, manifest lie, which is that Councillors are forced to seek at my hands means for their ends. If it were considered how and upon whom, for these late years, all manner of offices good and bad, spiritual and temporal, have been bestowed, to whom the persons beneficed do belong and whom they do follow, it will easily be judged how rare I do or have dealt therein. If great numbers be bestowed and not one upon any kinsman, servant or follower of mine, then how probable is it that I had ability to do that wherewith I am last slandered. In very truth I know my credit in such cases so mean and others I find so earnest and able to obtain anything, that I do utterly forbear to move for any. Whereupon many good friends do justly challenge me as unwise, that I seek to place neither man nor woman in the chamber, nor without, to serve her Majesty, whereby I might do my friends good. And therefore indeed I have few special friends, and so I find the want thereof. But yet I cannot remedy it, knowing my power not answerable thereto.

'True it is that her Majesty throweth upon me a burden to deal in all ungrateful actions — to give answers unpleasant to suitors that miss; where others are used to signify pleasing answers affirmatively. My burden also is this that in all suits for lands, leases or such things, her Majesty commands me to certify the state thereof from her under officers, and so I do (as it becomes) truly. And if the party obtain, I am not thanked; if not, the fault (though falsely) is imputed to me.

'If these reasons may not clear this slander, I would this only reason were weighed that is true. For myself I have not made nor obtained any suit from her

Majesty these ten years. In my whole time I have not for these twenty-six years been beneficed from her Majesty so much as I was within four years of King Edward. I have sold as much land in value as ever I had of gift of her Majesty. I am at charges by attendance at Court and by keeping of my household especially in term times; by resort of suitors, at more than any Councillor in England. My fee for the Treasurership is no more than it hath been these thirty years, whereas the Chancellor and others have been doubly augmented within these few years. And this I do affirm, that my fees of my treasurership do not answer to my charge of my stable. And in my household I do seldom find less than an hundred persons. And for that purpose I buy in London my bread, my drink, my achates, my fuel. And in the country I buy my grain, my beef, my mutton and all achates — and for my stable I buy my hay for the greatest part, my oats and straw totally. For my servants I keep none to whom I pay not wages and give liveries, which I know many do not.

'These things considered I might not thus be slandered or envied. What my pains in service are and how many [hours of] leisure or pleasure I take is too manifest. And indeed I condemn myself therein. But I cannot remedy it otherwise than I might leave my office which, in the presence of God, I could be contented to do, so as I might not be touched with note of dishonesty or displeasure of her Majesty.'

This is the last surviving of Burghley's apologetic letters. It is rather amazing to discover a man in his position writing in such terms to a man in Herle's position. The probable explanation is that Burghley was supplying Herle with ammunition to meet the charges of Burghley's vilifiers. According to Herle, these charges were some of them popular, some of them from people who ought to have known better. Burghley's replies seem to have been concerned in the main with this latter group. His reference to his lack of success in promoting the interests of his friends was aimed almost directly at Leicester. His reference to lack of personal favours from the Crown he may have hoped would reach the ears of the Queen. Herle was on reasonably familiar terms with Elizabeth.

It is therefore rather surprising to come across two letters to Herle from Burghley later in the month, protesting against the public display of his letters. The second letter runs as follows:[32]

'That I charged you with dispersing my private letters abroad I am no otherwise sure but that they which did see them, yea some that saw them also when you sent them to Court, yea to Councillors. And as their credit is with me so and in that proportion I am moved to think it true, and therefore I desire to have my letters back, with this offer notwithstanding that I do avow all to be true and much more for maintenance of mine honesty.'

Herle replied that he had never let the letters out of his hands and had only shown them to Sir John Norris.[33] In a second letter he wrote:

'I had your Lordship's own authority in answering slanders I heard and for conferring with my friends touching them which, though I say it of myself, hath been done with discretion and care.'[34]

L

At Burghley's request Herle seems to have returned the letters. But he evidently kept copies of them.[35]

Burghley's protestations must be taken with reservations. He certainly had intended what he wrote to Herle to be spread abroad, though he was naturally indignant when he learned that his own letters on the subject, in his own hand, had been displayed at the Court and in the city.

We hear no more about public attacks on Burghley. Whether indeed there had been public attacks rests on Herle's testimony. The whole business may have been a deliberate attempt to frighten Burghley into compliance with Leicester's programme. His sensitiveness to public vilification was always the weak point in his armour. Certainly his insistence upon his devotion to the cause of the Dutch in July and August was quite at variance with the position he had taken at the meeting of the Council in March. He may have yielded to pressure. He may have decided that his mistress meant to intervene and shifted his position accordingly.

At the moment he was deeply engaged with Walsingham in coming to terms with the Dutch commissioners who reached England late in June.

These commissioners had their first audience with the Queen on the 29th and there offered her the sovereignty of the Low Countries. She declined the offer but indicated that she was prepared to consider taking them under her protection. She appointed a committee of the Privy Council to negotiate with them on the subject, of which the active members were Burghley, Leicester, Hatton and Walsingham.

The negotiations which followed took place sometimes at Burghley's house in Covent Garden, sometimes at Walsingham's London house in Seething Lane. At first the Dutch pressed hard for sovereignty, but Burghley cut them off short.

'Her Highness', he declared, 'cannot be induced by any writing or harangue you can make to accept the principality or proprietorship as sovereign, and it will therefore be labour lost for you to exhibit any writing for the purpose of changing her intention. It will be better to content yourselves with her Majesty's consent to assist you and to take you under her protection.'[36]

But the Dutch would not be denied, and it was with some difficulty that Burghley, who quite evidently was acting as the spokesman for the English commissioners, brought them to face the realities of the situation.

'We have told you over and over again,' he remarked, 'that her Majesty will never think of accepting the sovereignty. She will assist you in money and men, and must be repaid to the last farthing when the war is over; and until that period must have solid pledges in the shape of a town in each province.'[37]

In short, as Motley puts it, she wanted not sovereignty but mortgages.

The discussion then turned upon ways and means, specifically upon the troops and the money to be raised and the distribution of the burden between England and the Dutch. The Dutch asked that the Queen should pay one-third of the expense. Burghley said it was too much. They estimated that an army of 13,000 foot and 2000 horse would be necessary for the field, and 23,000 foot for garrison duty. Burghley agreed about the field army but thought the assignment for garrison excessive. Other estimates seemed to him on the whole reasonable.

The next issue was over the size of the Queen's army. The Dutch demanded 5000 foot and 1000 horse, and they offered her one or two towns in each province as security. Burghley announced that the Queen could not undertake so much. But she would assume an expense of £4500 monthly if they would yield Brill and Flushing as security.[38] Meanwhile, she was prepared to send 4000 foot for the relief of besieged Antwerp.

The Dutch said it was not enough. They wanted to know who would support the garrisons in the cautionary towns. Burghley said, the Dutch. In that case, they replied, half of what the Queen advanced would have to be diverted to that purpose.

Later the Queen raised her offer a little, and would add 400 horse to the 4000 foot, provided Brill and Flushing be handed over. The Dutch replied that they had no commission to yield the towns unless the Queen granted 5000 foot and 1000 horse.

Elizabeth announced that any assistance she rendered must be underhand. Her Council was unanimously opposed. She must, if she was to survive at all, take immediate and open action.[39]

Meanwhile, alarming news came of the progress of Parma's siege operations against Antwerp. Elizabeth directed her Council to deal with that problem at once, dispatched 2000 troops and directed that 4000 more should be ready for shipment within a fortnight. A hasty preliminary treaty was arranged with the Dutch accordingly, with Sluys and Ostend as security.

The English force came too late to save Antwerp, but served to stimulate the negotiations for the general treaty. On August 12th agreement was reached.

The Queen undertook to provide and support 4000 foot and 400 horse and 700 men for garrison duty, the Dutch to yield Brill and Flushing as security until they repaid the money she spent in their behalf.

The news of the fall of Antwerp came as a considerable shock to Elizabeth. Gilbert Talbot wrote to his father, the Earl of Shrewsbury, on August 26th:[40] 'I have been at the Court. Her Majesty was greatly troubled with the rendering up of Antwerp at my coming from thence. And my L. Treasurer who was at Theobalds somewhat ill of the gout was sent for. And so my Lord of Leicester to return to the Court. And it is thought that her Majesty shall be forced of very necessity to send some great person with great forces presently for the defence of Holland and Zeeland, or else they will, out of hand, follow Antwerp.'

Davison was hurried off to the Low Countries with an offer to furnish them with 5000 foot and 1000 horse, provided they handed over to her Flushing and Brill. It is to be noted that a draft of his instructions survives, corrected in Burghley's hand — an indication of his active participation in the direction of affairs.[41]

Elizabeth had not yet made up her mind whom to put in command. The Dutch commissioners had urged her to appoint Leicester as governor-general and Sidney as governor of Flushing. But she hesitated to commit herself. Early in September Walsingham wrote to Davison:

'I see not her Majesty disposed to use the service of the Earl of Leicester. There is great offence taken in the carrying down of his lady.'[42]

A little later she bade Leicester get ready to go, but changed her mind again late in the month. On September 16th she bade him 'forbear in his preparations' until he spoke with her. But the matter was settled the following day.[43]

Walsingham thought, as he wrote to Davison in November, 'that some practices have been used to draw her Majesty to mislike of the present action and of such as advised her to enter into the same'.[44]

This would seem to point to Burghley. In September a Spanish agent in London had written to the same effect.[45] 'There is great disagreement between the earl of Leicester and the Lord Treasurer, Cecil persuading the Queen not to break with the house of Burgundy whilst Leicester uses all his great influence with the Queen to bring her to an opposite course.'

But nothing in Burghley's behaviour at this juncture supports this view. We may perhaps see indications of conflict in the selection of governors for Flushing and Brill. Walsingham wrote to Leicester on September 27th:

'I would be glad to understand whether your Lordship hath had Sir Thomas Cecil in remembrance.'[46]

It was probably in reply to that hint that Leicester wrote:

'As soon as I receive knowledge from Her Majesty of her pleasure I will write to Sir Thomas Cecil. I think a charge of horsemen will like him best, 400 or 500 . . . I will never agree to Flushing to any but my nephew [Philip Sidney]. If Sluys or Ostend may content Sir Thos. Cecil, I will be glad also.'[47]

The matter was decided some time in October. Burghley wrote to Davison on the 24th of that month: 'Sir P. Sidney to have Flushing, my son Thomas, Brill.'[48]

Burghley himself drafted the instructions for his son, which went to him from the Privy Council. One passage of them is significant, though it is doubtful if Elizabeth would have endorsed it. It was to the effect that since 'the chief cause which has moved her Majesty to give help to the poor afflicted people of these countries is the defence of those in profession of the Gospel', Sir Thomas was not to forget 'that the use of exercise of common prayer and preaching according to the laws of England be daily and publicly had and maintained in the English tongue, and to foresee that every captain with his company, not occupied otherwise . . . in necessary services do daily and orderly frequent the public exercise of prayers and preaching'.[49]

Of Burghley's activities we hear little more before the end of the year. He was, as always, much interested in the financial aspects of the enterprise, and we have at least one memorandum from him to Captain Richard Huddleston, the newly appointed Treasurer to the English forces in the Low Countries, giving him detailed directions about his accounts.[50] A letter which he wrote to Davison late in October reveals that he had already begun to worry about excessive expenditures.

'We find', he wrote, 'the charges daily to increase beyond her Majesty's good allowance, specially by the coming of my Lord of Leicester with a great company of gentlemen of value but not yet experimented in the wars, although they be such as having good hearts and reputation they will prove men quickly able to serve.'[51]

During November Burghley was much troubled by his old enemy, the gout, and was away at Theobalds.[52] Taking advantage of his enforced leisure, he drew up a 'Memorial on the State of the Queen and the Realm'.[53]

It began on an optimistic note. The Queen, he observed, was 'for her person inwardly loved and honoured of all persons that love God and profess true Christian religion. The realm, by order of justice in all outward show, obedient and disposed to peace. The people of the realm generally rich and able to endure all reasonable charges for defence of the realm. A great multitude of people, both of gentlemen and merchants and of vulgar people, specially in good towns where they be taught by discreet preachers, very zealous towards God and therefore earnestly bent to all services for her Majesty's safety.'

He then went on to indicate what he regarded as essential to the maintenance of these blessings, and as was customary with him turned first to the state of the Church.

He attacked, as he had so often attacked, the clergy. 'The bishops and clergy,' he wrote, 'that should by their teaching and devotion, and especially by hospitality and relieving of the poor, win credit amongst the people, are rather despised than respected or loved. Generally they are covetous, specially such as have wives and children. And where of late years past they made alienation of their livelihoods for use of their children, now that they be prohibited so to do by contrary laws, they do by sparing gather wealth and some make great chevances [gain] by yielding to make grant of their lands to the Queen's Majesty, not for her profit but to be granted by her Majesty to the friends of the clergy so as they partake with such as can obtain such suits of her Majesty.'

He protested against the lack of ministers, and thought that the evil might be corrected 'by dissolving of pluralities of ecclesiastical livings, whereof a few have in a manner engrossed up a great multitude'. He complained also that 'a great number of benefices are impropriated to the practice and profane use of greedy men and not sufficient livings of stipends left to the ministers that should serve the cures. In so much that many places have no service at all but are driven to resort to other churches, or else they choose someone that can read meanly. And the office lighteth upon bare conditioned men of occupation, as a tailor, a shoemaker, a smith or such like . . . All means would be used to increase the number of subjects to profess true religion and to avoid all curiosities, to the change of the orders established for uniformity in the ceremonies of the church. And in like manner all persons obstinately persuaded in popery would be either reformed by charitable teaching or corrected by ordinary justice, or made weak in credit and strength. Or else permitted to depart the realm upon some composition for a sign [i.e. as a symbol] to satisfy in some part the penalty of the law.'

He was, in short, opposed to Puritan non-conformity and resolute to stamp out Roman Catholicism.

He revealed also some concern about the administration of justice.

'Justice', he maintained, 'in all places and for all persons would be straitly observed and not violated nor altered for any respect . . . And yet no such severity is to be always observed but that may be fulfilled that is said, *fiat justicia cum misericordia*, for mercy hath her place . . . And generally no advantage would be taken by colour of law upon the people, for any private man's gain but chiefly for the benefit of her Majesty for relief of her estate.'

He dealt also with taxation. 'The people,' he asserted, 'are not to be charged but where the burden serveth to answer the service of the realm.'

'If', he concluded, 'care be seriously had for these things, the former good things afore mentioned are likely to continue for her Majesty's safety, honour and greatness.'

Burghley had said all of these things, in one form or other, more than once before. Of them all the one most radical in its implications was the sentence on taxation. It is not likely that the 'Memorial' was intended for any other eyes than his own. He liked to get his thoughts down on paper. The state papers are full of his lucubrations, often garnished as these were with quotations from St. Paul and from Solomon.

Leicester, after much backing and filling by his reluctant mistress, finally got away to the Low Countries in December. Before he left he wrote Burghley a long letter.

'Your Lordship', he wrote, 'cannot but remember the cause for which it hath pleased her Majesty to send me into the Low Countries. It was not only by your Lordship but by the whole number of Councillors agreed upon how meet and necessary it was for her Highness to yield aid and assistance for the relief of those afflicted countries . . . Albeit I have no mistrust but in so great absence and such a service I might greatly rely upon your particular good will and regard of myself. But in this case I desire no respect nor regard of me but of the cause which, I beseech you, my Lord, I may at this farewell recommend to your wisdom and great care . . . Her Majesty, I see, my Lord, often time doth fall into mislike of this cause and sundry opinions it may breed in her withal, but I trust in the Lord, seeing her Highness hath thus far resolved and grown also to this far execution as she hath and that mine and other men's poor lives and substances are adventured for her sake and by her commandment, that she will fortify and maintain her own action to the full performance of that she hath agreed on. . . .

'I beseech your Lordship have this cause even to your heart as it doth appear you have even by consenting to the adventure of your eldest son in this service. . . .

'And good my Lord, for my last, have me only this far in your care that in those things which her Majesty and you all have agreed and confirmed for me to do, that I be not made a metamorphosis, if I shall know not what to do.'[54]

All things considered it is not surprising that Leicester should have feared that Burghley would throw his weight against him in his absence. It was exactly the sort of thing which he would have done himself.

Burghley replied the following day. 'My Lord,' he wrote, 'I do assure you no less a portion of my care and travail for many respects, to the furtherance of your own honour than if I were a most near kinsman in blood. And for the advancement of the action, if I should not with all the powers of my heart continually both wish and work advancement thereunto, I were to be an accursed person in the sight of God, considering the ends of this action tend to the glory of God, to the safety of the Queen's person, to the preservation of this realm in a perpetual quietness wherein for my particular interest, both for myself and my posterity, I have as much interest as any of my degree. And thus I pray you my Lord make a perfect account of me and for my doings. . . .

'From my couch in my chamber, not yet able to rise from it. God send your Lordship a speedy good passage.'[55]

And, except when his mistress commanded otherwise, Burghley kept his word. There is, indeed, nothing to show that the three men upon whom Elizabeth chiefly depended during Leicester's absence, Burghley, Walsingham and Hatton, did not all do their uttermost to support his action, though in the case of Burghley and to a lesser degree of Hatton, they had personal reasons enough to the contrary.

Leicester left England for the Low Countries late in December 1585, returned home on leave the following November, remained in England until July and was finally recalled in November 1587. His adventure went off to a bad start by his ill-advised acceptance, contrary to the express commands of the Queen, of the governor-generalship. He himself claimed that Elizabeth had given him *carte blanche* in the matter, 'so as it might not proceed from herself but of themselves'. But she flew into a stormy rage when the news of it reached her. Her anger was aggravated by the report that Dudley's wife 'was prepared presently to come over . . . with such a train of ladies and gentlewomen and such rich coaches, litters and side saddles as her Majesty had none such'. She sternly commanded him to make public resignation. Her councillors were hard put to it to induce her to accept the arrangement. Burghley wrote on February 7th:

'To be plain with your Lordship, in a few words, I and other your Lordship's poor friends, find her Majesty so discontent with your acceptance of the government there before you had advertised and had her Majesty's opinion, that although I, for my own part, judge this action both honourable and profitable, yet her Majesty will not endure to hear any speech in defence thereof. Nevertheless, I hope a small time shall alter this hard conceit in her Majesty whereunto I have already and shall not desist to oppose myself with good and sound reasons.'

Thomas Duddeley, one of Leicester's henchmen, testified to the sincerity of Burghley's efforts.

'Truly,' he wrote to Leicester on February 11th, 'I do know by very good means that my Lord Treasurer dealt most honourably and friendly for your Lordship to her Majesty . . . He hath always besought her Majesty to keep one ear for your answer to her dislike . . . The Lord Treasurer, having been from the Court these eight days, her Majesty hath, five days agone, proposed to send Sir Thomas Heneage unto you . . . but Mr. Vice-Chamberlain and Mr. Secretary very honourably both delay his dispatch by all means they can and hopeth to put it off until

Sunday next, at which time the Lord Treasurer will be at Court, and then, by his help, they hope to qualify some part of her Majesty's intentions.'

William Davison, whom Leicester had sent over to explain his actions, gave the same report. 'My Lord Treasurer,' he wrote to Leicester on February 28th, 'I can assure your Lordship hath herein done good offices, though we have not been able to do all that he wished.'

Burghley did succeed in inducing his mistress to modify somewhat the peremptory orders which she had intended to dispatch by Sir Thomas Heneage, giving him some latitude in the delivery of it 'if he found it might hurt the common service'.

But in a letter to Leicester some three weeks later, Burghley reported that he still found her so wrathful that she would give no attention to Leicester's immediate needs.

'Since Mr. Heneage was sent from hence,' he wrote on March 6th, 'her Majesty would never be content to have any speech of the state of things needful to be known for your charge. I have not desisted to move her to give ear, but she continued her offence as in no sort I could attain to any answer meet to be given to your Lordship. And now of late, having had a mishap by a fall, whereby I have been and still am to keep my bed, I have at sundry times written to her Majesty. I have also sent my mind by Mr. Vice-Chamberlain ... but no answer to any purpose can be had. And yet I mind not so to cease but, being pushed thereto with conscience and with care of her honour, yea of her safety, I will still solicit her Majesty, hoping that God will move her to hearken to necessary motions, principally for herself.'

The fall to which Burghley alluded in his previous letter hurt his head. It was the second accident of the sort which befell him that winter. In January he had written: 'All this letter I have been forced to write in my bed, which I have kept these two days, not, as your Lordship hath known, for pain of my gout, but indeed having some days past rubbed off a good deal of skin upon my shin, I did neglect the healing of it when I should, and so am now forced to keep my bed without any hose.'[56]

His old legs were beginning to fail him. In March he was still so lame that he could not go to Court. 'Without him', one of Leicester's correspondents observed, 'I perceive she [the Queen] will conclude nothing.'[57]

On June 8th he was once more in bed, and Elizabeth went to confer with him in his chamber.[58] On the 16th he wrote to Walsingham: 'Having been all this day busy at Westminster even until evening, my son Thomas Cecil, coming hither unto me from the Court telleth me that her Majesty's pleasure is that I should attend her there tomorrow, which (although the many causes I have here might well require my presence) yet knowing them to be of no such moment as these here, I mean, if so it be her pleasure, to come thither [at Greenwich] tomorrow, which by reason of the tide must be either very early in the morning or late in the evening. I have sent this bearer of purpose to you that I might understand from you at which time her Majesty's pleasure is I should come. If I may not stay tomorrow ...

I shall hinder a great number if I be not in the Court of Wards, where I have not been but once all this week. I might wish my body or my feet were of iron or steel, for with flesh and blood I cannot long endure.'[59]

In July, the gout once more seized him by the hand, and yet he kept going. His record of attendance at the meetings of the Privy Council was second only to Walsingham's. Out of seventy meetings between the date of Leicester's departure and his return, Burghley missed only fifteen. It is abundantly clear that the burden of keeping Elizabeth loyal to her engagements to Leicester fell mainly upon Burghley's shoulders.

Walsingham wrote to Leicester on April 25th: 'I have let my Lords [of the Privy Council] understand how unkindly your Lordship taketh it that you hear so seldom from them ... They answer, as it is truth, that her Majesty, retaining the whole direction of the causes of that country to herself and such advice as she receiveth underhand, they know not what to write or to advise.' The following day Walsingham wrote again that the Queen, who had seemed to be reconciled to Leicester's generalship, had a sudden change of heart. 'I know not,' he said, 'nor can by any means imagine how the same should be wrought. There was only called into the resolution the Lord Treasurer and I. He moved her to stay the resolution until Sir Thomas Heneage's return; he showed her that there was nothing done contrary to her direction; he protested unto her that if she did go forward with the resolution it would utterly overthrow the cause. She grew so passionate in the matter as she forbid him to argue any more. Surely there is some treachery among ourselves, for I cannot think she would do this of her own head.'

But a few weeks later Walsingham had changed his mind. He wrote to Leicester on May 14th: 'Truly, my good Lord, I am now persuaded that this strange proceeding groweth from her Majesty's self.'[60] And a week after that: 'I begin now to put on an opinion that the only thwarts your Lordship receiveth groweth out of her Majesty's own disposition, whom I find daily more and more unapt to embrace any matter of weight. And whereas I did by Mr. Barker let your Lordship to understand that I thought you were crossed underhand by some great personage, I do now quit him of it and am persuaded that he dealeth honestly in the cause.'[61] Walsingham in short exonerated Burghley of any double dealing.[62]

We need not follow in detail Leicester's adventure in the Low Countries. Burghley gave him consistent support, not only in general but on particular points. Many things went wrong, partly due to Leicester's ineptitude, partly to the cheese-paring policy of the Dutch. In military affairs Leicester was no match for Parma, in civil affairs no match for the Dutch. On June 20th Burghley wrote to him:[63]

'I see still her Majesty's disposition very resolute to continue her first purpose for the defence of that action, and therein she is, with good cause, fully persuaded of your Lordship's honourable mind to prosecute the same to her honour and surety. But always I find two obstacles in her Majesty. One is, she is very careful, as a good natural prince, although in such a case as this somewhat too scrupulous, to have her people adventured in fight. The other is she will not have any more expended on her part [than] she hath yielded unto, misliking all extraordinary charges. And therefore she still calleth on us to write earnestly to your Lordship that you should now, having that general authority which you have with her good liking, press and command that the common collections of that country should answer all manner of charges to the disburdening of her Majesty otherwise than to the sums assented to.'

Elizabeth in short insisted upon a defensive war within the limits of her budgetary allowance.

It is open to question as to whether a defensive war was good strategy. Certainly Leicester with the resources at his command found it impossible to pursue any other course. As to the financial situation, it was confused and mismanaged from the start. Elizabeth put her annual commitments at £126,180 10s.[64] But before six months was out it became clear that expenditures were running considerably in excess of that amount. This was partly due to English expenditures incurred for the Dutch which were not repaid; partly due to debts contracted in the Low Countries by English captains which should have been deducted from their pay but which were in fact passed on to their mistress; largely due to the corruption in the whole system of mustering and paying the troops.

It might be presumed that the Lord Treasurer was the man ultimately responsible for the expenditure of public funds. But we get little from Burghley's extant correspondence to indicate that he did anything to set right things amiss. He wrote to Leicester on June 8th: 'At this present upon the coming of the Treasurer and the Auditor, her Majesty hath shewed some misliking of her charges there and evil content to hear how much more than needful it is to send money thither. As yet we cannot by any account find what is due either now or till any time past, though in appearance for the footmen the pay is full till the 11th of April; but how far the horsemen are behind we cannot conjecture for the lack of any certainty at which time their pay began.'

Again he wrote in July:

'I perceive that by the establishment of the Chamber of Finances your Lordship shall be more able to make necessary payments for all things requisite under your charge than heretofore you have been, the opinion of which lack hath most chiefly bred doubt in her Majesty of the good sequel of the cause.'

Again in August:

'No one thing doth more hinder her Majesty's forwardness than an old rooted opinion that she hath that all this war will be turned upon her charge, by the backwardness in payment by the States, against which I did always oppose in answering to comfort her Majesty that I was assured, so as she would continue ready payment for her numbers accorded, you would not fail but receive such sums from the States monthly as they had promised your Lordship shortly upon the committing of the government to your Lordship. And so surely I continued my hope, although in truth many private persons did advertise it very doubtful and so I am sorry to see it, as I do by your own letters, very difficult to be gotten. . . .'

Of the corruption in the army Burghley had almost nothing to say, except for a single sentence in his letter of July 21st.

'If', he wrote, 'your Lordship could bring it to pass that the poor soldiers might be paid by the poll, sometime one month's pay would do more good in that sort than two months' pay to the captain. And in like sort I see your Lordship hath care that they which shall have the disposing of the treasure may be directed so to dispose it as it may come truly and indifferently to the use of the soldier.'

Burghley's correspondence reveals great interest in matters of trade and coinage. The Dutch were very anxious to re-establish the English wool trade and the English cloth trade in the Low Countries and Leicester himself pressed for it. Burghley's observations on the subject in a letter to Leicester of March 6th reveal a firm grasp upon the basic factors involved.

'Your Lordship', he wrote, 'moveth to our merchants to trade in Holland with their cloths and also with their wools, which thing has been moved unto them heretofore. And they of the staple for wool have alleged that they have no hope to have any great vent for their wools, considering they have a good quantity of their wool lying long at Middelburgh, for which, they say, they never could have vent but to their great loss ... Nevertheless I will essay them now upon your Lordship's new motion, with the offer of the Hollanders that they will leave draping of the Spanish wools ... For the Merchant Adventurers I will also deal with them for their cloths, considering neither Hamburg nor Emden are fit places for them as the world shapeth. But I fear the greatest let will be that there will be no safe passage for their cloths to be carried up into Germany by the river Rhine, specially considering the town of Nymegen is in enemy's hands ... But if our merchants could be content to keep their marts in those Low Countries without seeking to convey them up into Germany themselves, it is likely that both Italians and Germans would come into these countries and buy them at first hand themselves.'[65]

But the merchants did not apparently take kindly to the idea, and though the Count of Emden was reputed to be Spanish in his sympathies, the Privy Council decided to encourage the Adventurers to increase their exports to Emden.[66]

Another economic problem arose in connection with an offer to pay a substantial fee to the Crown for the privilege of coining English rose-nobles in the Low Countries. It held out promise that Elizabeth would gain some 30,000 or 40,000 pounds a year. Burghley was sceptical. 'I marvel', he wrote to Leicester on March 6th, 'how much gain can be made thereof, for though for a reasonable portion to be coined there at the first utterance, the same might be uttered for great gain, yet when there should be any plenty, the greediness of them will be stayed and the true value would be known and the estimation would abate ... I was ever of that mind and shall be that new coins in any country, where knowledge is of minting, will have a higher reputation than its richness will yield ... Yet truly, it is a natural reason in all things, that *ex nihilo nihil fit*, and no great gain can ever be made to last, but where the cause and the ground of the gain shall last.'[67]

Burghley hastened to save Leicester's face in the matter, professed himself open to conviction and urged Leicester to explore further. It came to nothing in the end, for the very obvious reason that the intrinsic value of the rose-noble was far below the inflated value which for a time it enjoyed.

But Burghley in all these matters merely offered his advice. He assumed no responsibility. One gets the impression from the tone of his correspondence that he regarded the whole Low Countries adventure as Leicester's show. It is not improbable that he operated on the assumption that given enough rope Leicester would hang himself. Sir Edward Stafford, English ambassador to France, and an inveterate enemy of Leicester, wrote to Burghley a little later when Leicester was about to come home: 'If I might be bold to tell you what I think . . . if I had as much credit as your Lordship hath and he born to do me no more good than he is, I would keep him where he is and he should drink that which he had brewed. Her Majesty is not for his tarrying there bound to do more than she shall see cause. But I would keep him there to undo himself and sure enough from coming home to undo others.'[68]

But Burghley knew too well Leicester's strong hold on the Queen's affections, knew too well his own limitations, to go so far. Indeed, his acquiescence in all that Leicester advocated was so pronounced that Elizabeth rebuked him more than once for his subservience.[69]

So far as Leicester's relations with Burghley were concerned, his consistent support got him nowhere. Some time early in February, during Leicester's visit to England, he wrote a letter to Burghley.[70]

'I know not', he wrote, 'from whence my hap has it, but it hath fallen out sundry times, both contrary to my expectation . . . that I have found your Lordship more ready to thwart and cross my endeavours than any man's, especially in the presence of her Majesty . . . In these causes we have been two or three times before her Majesty, we had debated the matter before, and the course I took was no other than your Lordship did best like and advise. And to fall into contrary opinions before her Majesty caused me both to take it ill and to shew it plainly to you as I did . . . Finding myself grieved with such cross handling at this and at other times . . . I told your Lordship I saw your Lordship very ready to cross me now-a-days before her Majesty, that I liked it so ill that I would and could find way to anger you as well. . . .

Burghley replied on February 7th:

'My very good Lord,

'Your servant Mr. Blunt brought to me your L. letter at dinner time by which I perceive your Lordship hath at good length very particularly expressed sundry sentences as by me spoken in her Majesty's presence to move her Majesty to be offended with your Lordship for lack of your Lordship's procuring more certainty of the expenses and accounts of the last year's charges on the States' behalf. In brief this I note, that your L. thinketh by my means and speech her Majesty doth blame your Lordship that there is no better account made of the charges. And in brief for my defence I must say that I never did say nor mean to say that your Lordship ought to be blamed for the want of their [the accountants'] imperfections in their accounts. For I did say and do still say that their accounts are obscure, confused and without credit and so themselves do partly confess. And I find in truth that they ought to have been commanded by your L. authority to have reformed the same and made your L. more privy to their doings, for which, not doing, I condemned them and not your L. . . . and I also did affirm the same by often repetition to her Majesty that your L. could do no more but command and direct them and they, both in that as in many other things, have grossly and most rudely encountered your L.

'But, my good Lord, to return to the particular causes of your L. offence towards me, I must bear them indeed with no small grief of mind, because I protest before God I have had and always desire to have your L. favour and good liking, which if I cannot have I shall yet bear my grief with some part of consolation, that I am free in heart and mind from deserving. And the only thing in this world that I can wish is to be delivered of these ungrateful burdens of service which her Majesty commonly layeth upon me very heavily, wherein your L. hath seen and heard her tax me very sharply that, in not applauding to her censures, I do commonly flatter and I do, against my conscience, hold opinions to pleasure your L. and others — a very hard course held against me that indeed am loathe to offend her Majesty, but more loathe to offend God and my conscience. And, my good Lord, because I will neither trouble your L. nor myself any longer at this time I will end with a profession of great good will.'[71]

It may be that Burghley decided not to send this letter, but sent instead a briefer one which is less informing and more reserved. What came of this correspondence is not revealed. But it is quite evident that all he had done for Leicester was lost upon a man intent to find the explanation of his own shortcomings in the covert hostility of his most loyal supporters.

Burghley was used to it. But it hit Walsingham as well.[72] One notable consequence of Leicester's performance in the Low Countries was the opening of a breach between Walsingham and himself. If there is room for doubt about the devotion of Burghley to Leicester's cause in the Low Countries, there can be none at all about Walsingham's. He had done his best for Leicester and made himself very unpopular with the Queen in consequence. Yet Leicester maintained that he had not done enough, either in his public or his private interest. On top of that, Leicester had allowed Walsingham to bear the full burden of the debts which Philip Sidney, Leicester's nephew and Walsingham's son-in-law, had left behind him at his death. How much they amounted to is uncertain. One estimate places them at £17,000. Leicester, apparently in a position to relieve the burden by the sale of some of Sidney's lands, refused to do so. And Leicester not only declined to support Walsingham's suit for the Duchy of Lancaster, but favoured another candidate. In all of these matters, Walsingham appealed to the Queen for assistance, apparently in the form of a liberal pension. And Burghley did his best to get it from Elizabeth, reminding her of Walsingham's diligence in unravelling the Babington Plot, pointing him out, as Davison told Walsingham later, 'as one to whom under God she ought to acknowledge the preservation of her life, which she could not nor might not forget, alleging unto her the hard estate you stood in and the dishonour must fall upon herself if such a servant should be suffered to quail, to the great discomfort of herself and her friends and the discouragement of others to take the like course of hazarding their lives and fortunes hereafter for the surety of a princess so slow to consider thereof'.[73]

Elizabeth was slow to respond, and Walsingham was about to leave Court in despair. But Burghley urged him to persist, and in April Elizabeth made him a substantial grant of land.

Burghley was also largely instrumental in securing for Walsingham the Chancellorship of the Duchy of Lancaster.

The outcome was that Burghley and Walsingham grew closer together as Leicester and Walsingham drew further apart. This fact, coupled with the fact that during Leicester's absence Elizabeth appointed three new members to the Privy Council, Whitgift, Lord Cobham and Lord Buckhurst,[74] all of them opposed to Leicester, strengthened Burghley's position, but not so much as it would have, had the Privy Council as a whole played any large part in shaping royal policy. As it was, Leicester never while he lived lost his unique hold upon the affection and confidence of his mistress. When the Armada was in the Channel and she faced the greatest danger in her career, it was Leicester whom she appointed to command the forces mustered for the defence of her realm.

Simultaneously with the departure of Leicester to the Low Countries, a number of projects were set afoot for making peace with Spain. There were some five of them altogether. Three of them seem to have originated with Italian merchants, whose primary object was probably to re-establish the flourishing trade which had nearly been ruined by the Dutch wars.[75] Of these the one in which Burghley was chiefly involved was started by Carlo Lanfranchi at Antwerp, operating with Andrea de Loo, another merchant in London. Another seems to have been started by Sir James Croft, Controller of the Household, who had a kinsman 'about the Prince of Parma' named William Bodenham; a third by Walsingham, acting through a prominent Portuguese physician in London, Dr. Hector Nuñez, and Antonio de Castilio, Portuguese ambassador to England before the Spanish conquest of Portugal; a fourth by Lord Cobham through another Italian merchant in London, Agostino Grafigni; and a fifth by Sir Horatio Palavicino, whose brother had married a sister of Lazaro Grimaldi, one of the group which, with Prince Andrea Doria, governed the republic of Genoa in the Spanish interest. All of these were virtually independent one of the other, and more or less in competition. It is not unlikely that the Queen encouraged them all. The connection of Privy Councillors, Burghley, Walsingham, Cobham and Croft, reveals no more than that they realized the Queen's eagerness for peace and wanted to have a finger in the pie. Probably Cobham and Croft definitely favoured the peace movement. Walsingham certainly did not. Burghley's part calls for detailed examination.

The record begins with a letter from Lanfranchi to Andrea de Loo, dated December 14th, 1585,[76] to the effect that he had spoken with the Prince of Parma and found him desirous of peace. Lanfranchi suggested to De Loo that he open the matter with Queen Elizabeth. De Loo talked with the Master of the Rolls who prompted him to speak with Burghley.

A second letter from Lanfranchi followed on the 17th, and a third on January 25th. All of these De Loo passed on to Burghley. In the third letter Lanfranchi expressed the opinion that peace could be arranged provided that the religious issue were not raised. He thought that Elizabeth could hardly demand from Philip what she would not like him to demand from her — that is toleration for religious dissent. Lanfranchi went on to say that he had spoken to the Seigneur de Champagny, governor of Antwerp and sometime envoy to England, and Champagny had assured him that Elizabeth had some eight years before been quite willing to waive the religious issue. Champagny was the brother of Cardinal de Granvelle, one of Philip II's chief councillors. Lanfranchi suggested that a meeting be arranged between Champagny and Elizabeth.

De Loo, on forwarding this letter to Burghley, suggested that someone be sent to treat with Champagny.

We hear of the first conference between De Loo and Burghley on February 10th, and, according to De Loo, Burghley gave him some vague assurances on the religious issue.[77]

We have no record of what Burghley said on the subject. He had plenty to say on the subject later which ran directly counter to De Loo's interpretation. It seems likely that Burghley, prompted perhaps by his mistress, said little about the religious question at this juncture in order to explore further the possibilities of peace. In any case, De Loo felt justified in writing to Lanfranchi two days later: 'As to what you say of religion, you need not give yourself any uneasiness, for it will be found that her Majesty will not wish to do to others what she would not have them do to herself.'[78]

The matter seems to have drifted along for the next month, though several letters from Lanfranchi reported that all would go well if the question of religion were not dragged in. On March 16th De Loo wrote again to Burghley suggesting that Champagny would be found a perfect instrument for the business since he was a good Burgundian eager to get rid of Spanish soldiers and through his brother, the Cardinal, in a position to exert strong influence upon Philip of Spain. Once again De Loo urged Burghley to pass on the word to Elizabeth.

It may be surmised that Elizabeth, eager as she was to pursue the matter further, declined to take the first step. De Loo's letters to Lanfranchi in March and April were directed to the business of inducing Parma to assume that role. On April 2nd, De Loo wrote direct to Champagny urging him to induce Parma to write to the Queen.

Four days later he wrote to Burghley that Agostino Grafigni had spoken with Parma. A fortnight later Burghley learned that Bodenham had held two conferences with the Prince. Mediators for peace who professed to have credentials from English Privy Councillors seem indeed to have been crowding Parma's antechambers in March and April.

It has generally been assumed that all this was in strict secrecy. De Loo seems to have been particularly anxious that neither Leicester nor Walsingham should know about it.[79] But, as a matter of fact, Burghley himself wrote to Leicester on March 30th:[80]

'My Lord, where you wrote to me of that you hear about Champagny's errands, I will tell you what I know hereof. And what else is known to any other I cannot write of. There is an Italian merchant in Antwerp that pretendeth acquaintance with Champagny, and he hath written hither to another merchant to know whether her Majesty can be content to come to peace with the King of Spain. The answer is made that by the publication[81] published it is to be seen wherefore her Majesty hath sent her forces into the Low Countries, and if the King of Spain shall satisfy her Majesty in honour, according to her protestation, by restoring to those countries liberty and peace and remove all men of war from thence and restore to her own subjects their losses, she can be content to hear any reasonable offer from the King. And otherwise she mindeth to persist in defence of her neighbours and recovery of her subjects' losses. This answer is made by words only, but not from her Majesty. And whether Champagny will any further proceed I know not. But sure I am he hath no cause to make any avaunt hereof. And I trust their need shall make them sooner yield than any cause to come of this answer. It may be that there are other like motions made to her Majesty, but I think surely her Majesty mindeth not to shew any yielding.'

The statement is true in the main, though it is clear enough that Burghley's dealings with De Loo were not so forthright as he made them out to be. What he wrote about Elizabeth's steadfastness was no doubt intended to allay Leicester's fears. It does not reflect Burghley's own apprehensions. He had worked with his mistress too long not to realize that persistence in any resolute, belligerent course of action was foreign to her nature. In any case his letter disposes of the charge that he was plotting secretly to make peace.

Some time later Châteauneuf, the French ambassador in England, wrote to Mary Queen of Scots:[82] 'The Chancellor and the Treasurer seem to support the cause and favour the interests of the King of Spain, even of the English Catholics. The Earl of Leicester and Walsingham on the contrary have always shown themselves to be stout Protestants and have appeared to favour France. But in fact this is mere dissimulation, practised with the knowledge of the Queen to deceive ministers of both powers.'

The pretended secrecy in these peace manœuvres when there was in fact little secrecy may well be a case in point. It is to be observed that most of the varied efforts towards peace by the midsummer of 1586 had come under Burghley's control. The one exception seems to have been Walsingham's approach through Castilio which slowly petered out though Walsingham was still corresponding with Dr. Nuñez about it as late as February 1587.[83] Burghley advised Palavicino to abandon his approach through Grimaldi.[84] Croft's efforts through Bodenham appear to have been consolidated with De Loo's efforts. Grafigni, whom Lord Cobham dispatched in haste to Parma in May, with the idea of stealing a march on De Loo, came near to wrecking the whole enterprise.

He saw Parma, claimed to have been sent by Burghley and Croft, to have talked with the Queen, and evidently made extravagant statements about Elizabeth's will to peace. When he returned home to England in June he brought letters from Parma both to Elizabeth and to Burghley. The outcome was a letter from the Queen to Parma,[85] in which she denied that Grafigni had any warrant either from her or from any one of her councillors to express to Parma her search for peace. She supposed that her attitude towards the Low Countries had been made sufficiently plain by her public proclamation on the subject, where she had stated that her object in sending forces to the Low Countries had been to 'make safe our own state and to free our ancient neighbours from misery and from starving, . . . To these two ends we have directed our action with resolution to continue them . . . For such is our compassion for their miseries that in no manner will we allow their safety to be separated from our own, knowing how the two depend upon each other . . . Nevertheless you may be persuaded that if any reasonable conditions of peace should be offered to us which tend to the establishing of our safety and honour and to the liberty of our neighbours we shall willingly accept them.'

This letter seems to have brought negotiations to an abrupt close. Three months later De Loo wrote to Elizabeth that Parma would not even see him. A little later Parma relented a little and told De Loo that the Queen's letter had precluded the possibility of further negotiations. De Loo did his best to reopen the matter, and in a letter to Parma of December 16th sent a long account of an interview with Burghley. The words he put into Burghley's mouth were to the effect that 'the Queen wanted nothing more than to see the Low Countries in tranquillity, observing their due reverence and obedience to the King of Spain', but 'that she, being bound first to her own preservation and then to that of her subjects, would gladly see all the Low Countries again yield themselves to their due obedience to the King of Spain under the government of the born natives of those countries, removing the mistrust on both sides by the withdrawal of the strangers who were the cause thereof, and leaving the governments, forts, administrations and public commands to the said natives . . . And with this — her Majesty having also the promise of the States of the Low Countries that the King of Spain will not go to war against the realm of England, and the word of his Highness with confirmation by the King — she will be willing to restore things to their former state.'[86]

Some two months later De Loo asked Burghley to authenticate this version of his statement. To this Burghley replied, a month after that, that he had said much more besides:

'But I must require you to call to your remembrance that besides these things above recited, I did also express some other things tending to make the peace to be perpetual; whereof some are of more moment than others; but the principal was, whereof I find no mention, that some order must be taken how the people in those Low Countries that have been so christened and brought up or are so instructed in their form of religion as either they never did know any other, or that cannot without peril of damnation of their souls change their religion, might be by toleration provided for. For otherwise I then told [you] and so I do still think that there cannot be a general reduction of all the natural born subjects to their obedience to the King, which her Majesty, I am sure, doth earnestly desire; whereby the obedience to the King may be universal; and how this may be brought to pass I did remember to you the example of the Emperor Charles in Germany, and the accord also at Ghent by a pacification there made which the King did twice confirm without offence of his conscience.

'I did also remember unto you how needful it was that the King should give some order in Spain that the subjects of England, using trade of merchandise in Spain and Portugal, might not be, without some notorious action, drawn by malice to the judgment of the Inquisition; whereby great multitude of honest and quiet persons have been, without any cause given, imprisoned and famished and their ships and goods confiscate.'[87]

In another memorandum on the same subject,[88] Burghley maintained that De Loo had deliberately avoided the religious issue in his interview with Parma.

'And whereas', Burghley continued, 'de Loo maketh report of an objection made to him upon their matter of religion, which is that the Queen's Majesty doth not permit any other religion than her own in her realms . . . and therefore her Majesty ought to allow the same course to the King of Spain — which argument hath a good appearance to be allowed until it be answered with the truth and just cause of the differences betwixt the King Catholic for the Low Countries and her Majesty for her countries.

'For on her Majesty's part it may be truly maintained that she never did permit, privately or publicly, any one of her subjects for these twenty-nine years to use any exercise of religion contrary to that which is allowed by public authority, so as there is no colour for any of her subjects to require toleration in respect of former permission; whereas, contrariwise, the experience is seen in the King's Low Countries, what multitudes there are born and bred up only with the knowledge of the religion they profess. And for that also it may be that the Duke [Prince] may hear and believe such false reports as are scandalously dispersed abroad of great cruelties showed in England upon men for professing of religion, it may be avowed for truth that her Majesty did never allow that any person should be examined of his conscience and punished for the same. But when any person, being of a contrary religion, hath not been content to retain the same to himself but hath sought, not only to move a multitude to break the laws under colour of religion, but also manifestly to withdraw them from their obedience to her Majesty, to renounce their allegiance; in such cases divers have been discovered, apprehended and convicted of such capital crimes committed and for the same have been according to the laws of the realm punished. And yet, at their deaths, they would have it understood that they died for religion, where[as] they were not accused nor any process made against them for any point of religion, but only for capital crime of treason.'

The argument was not convincing, certainly not to any of the English Catholic martyrs, but it was the official answer to the Spanish demand; the same answer which Burghley had developed at length some four years earlier in the *Execution of Justice in England*.

One wonders why, after ignoring the religious issue for so long, Burghley came forward with a vigorous defence of the Protestant position. The answer must lie in the influence of other events on Burghley's whole attitude. Just a month before Burghley wrote the memorandum just cited, Mary Queen of Scots had been executed at Fotheringhay.

CHAPTER XVIII

THE END OF MARY STUART, 1586-87

WHEN Leicester returned from the Low Countries in 1586, Burghley was deep in the perennial problem of Mary Queen of Scots. After the discovery of the Throgmorton Plot in the autumn of 1583, although no evidence was forthcoming to establish her immediate implication, it became increasingly apparent that her release and the establishment of her right to the English throne were the objective, not only of disloyal Catholics in England but of the Guises in France and of the King of Spain. Some attempt was made to come to terms with her in 1584, and dragged on until the early spring of 1585, when the revelations of the Parry Plot brought them to an end.[1] Burghley observed at the time that peace negotiations with Mary were generally a prelude to another plot on her behalf and he reviewed the history of those negotiations from 1568 to 1585 to prove his point, concluding with the statement: 'It is evident that the Scottish Queen has never entered into any treaty but only of purpose to abuse the Queen of England with some treacherous attempt or other.'[2] The conclusion was hardly just to Mary, but it reflected the current attitude, both of Elizabeth and of her councillors.

Meanwhile, Mary had been removed from the custody of the Earl of Shrewsbury. This was partly a response to the reiterated requests of Shrewsbury for release, partly due to the scandals about Shrewsbury's personal relations with Mary which were being spread abroad by Shrewsbury's wife, the notorious Bess of Hardwick, who had even gone so far as to intimate that Mary had given birth to a child by Shrewsbury. There is no sound reason to suppose that Elizabeth intended at the time to impose a sterner régime, though she had on occasions criticized Shrewsbury for his leniency towards his royal prisoner,[3] and had found it necessary from time to time to remove some of his servants for conveying Mary's letters. Immediately she appointed her trusted old servant, Sir Ralph Sadler, to replace Shrewsbury until someone else could be found. Her choice fell upon Lord St. John of Bletso, a member of the same family which a century later was to produce Henry St. John, Viscount Bolingbroke, the eighteenth-century statesman. But St. John would have none of it. Burghley and Leicester both tried hard to persuade him to accept and told him flatly that the Queen would punish him for his disobedience. He replied that he would 'abide any extremity rather than to go'.[4] And so Sadler had to stay on for a season, though he complained bitterly that he was an old man (77 years old) and could not long endure 'this cold and miserable country' where he saw nothing but 'woods and mountains'. His mind reverted to his lovely home at Standen, in the much more benign landscape of Hertfordshire.

GEORGE TALBOT, 6TH EARL OF SHREWSBURY

Meanwhile, he had moved Mary from Sheffield further south to Wingfield in Derbyshire, and in the following January southward again to Tutbury in Stafford-shire.

Burghley, writing to Walsingham on March 4th, commented upon a letter received from Sadler[5] about increased expenses. 'I see', Burghley wrote, 'that her Majesty must be at a further charge with her own defrayments than she was by my Lord of Shrewsbury. The argument upon sparing and spending must consist upon her Majesty's resolution how the Scots' Queen shall be from hence kept. And therein, no extremity, in my opinion, is good, neither to keep her with over-much liberty nor with overmuch straitness. The one shall nourish her practice and increase of her party, the other will bring desperation to all her faction.'[6]

It was not indeed until Sir Amias Paulet replaced Sadler in April that the screws began to tighten. Paulet had served for three years as English ambassador to France. He was a staunch Puritan. Thomas Morgan, Mary's agent in Paris, when he heard of Paulet's appointment as Mary's keeper, wrote to his mistress:[7] 'He is a gentleman of an honourable family, a Puritan in religion and very ambitious . . . He is courteous and I hope will know his duty towards your Majesty. But he will be very curious and watchful about your Majesty and your people, and respecteth Secretary Walsingham above all the rest of the men in the service of that state. And I believe Walsingham was the procurer of him to that charge.'

Paulet was being considered as Sadler's successor as early as January 4th, 1585. On that day Burghley wrote to Walsingham that the Queen had decided not to force the matter with the reluctant St. John. 'And now,' he added, 'hearing from you of Sir Ralph Sadler's sickness she has commanded me to write . . . for Sir Amias Paulet whom I think she will send to ease Mr. Sadler until she shall be otherwise advised. Of this none knoweth but myself.'[8]

It is currently believed that Paulet was Walsingham's nominee; but a letter from John Somer, who had been sent to assist Sadler, to Walsingham, points the other way. 'Your judgment', Somer wrote, 'of the weak state of his [Paulet's] body and the distance of his dwelling I think are to be allowed for a sufficient supersedence in the matter.'[9] Burghley wrote to Sadler about the end of the month that Paulet had accepted appointment and had been created Privy Councillor.[10]

Mary, when she heard the news, was not pleased, and protested that Paulet was not a nobleman and that he had shown marked hostility to her when he was ambassador in France. But Elizabeth waved aside these objections. Paulet, she said, was of noble birth and had served her faithfully in France.

Paulet received his instructions on March 4th.[11] Walsingham himself drafted them. The emphasis was upon preventing any secret communication between Mary and the world outside, either by letter or by conference with visitors. Paulet was even directed to prevent any intercourse between Mary or her servants with any of his staff. He did not reach Tutbury until April 17th. He took over at once and proceeded forthwith to establish a more rigorous régime.

Paulet successfully accomplished Mary's isolation. The Earl of Leicester on one occasion in July expressed the opinion that 'some letters had passed'[12] but Walsingham himself denied it. The letters which Mary did dispatch were all opened and read, either by Paulet himself or by Walsingham. There was no attempt to conceal that fact from Mary or from the French ambassador, by whom almost all of her surviving correspondence during this period was transmitted. It contained little more than her complaints of ill treatment. But if one considers that she had a staff of forty-eight people about her, which included five gentlemen and six gentlewomen, two secretaries, two cooks, a physician and an apothecary, and contemplates the enormous amount of food and drink consumed, it is clear enough that Mary's ills were of the spirit rather than of the flesh. The cold and the dampness of which she chiefly complained everyone in England had to suffer, though there were large bills at Tutbury for sea coal and charcoal and firewood. She was a prisoner in the sense that she could not wander at will over the countryside and could not communicate freely with her friends. But otherwise her state was queenly.

Paulet's correspondence during the year 1585 deals almost exclusively with the details of administration. He wrote chiefly to Walsingham but often to Burghley.[13] Of Burghley's letters to him none have been found. Paulet was much the younger man and his attitude towards Burghley was always deferential, though never obsequious. A passage in his letter to Burghley of July 5th is revealing: 'My purpose and meaning is, according to your Lordship's grave and most friendly advice, to keep the broad highway in all my actions and doings.' Evidently they were on the best of terms. It was largely due to Burghley's influence that Paulet obtained the stewardship of the Paget lands which passed under royal control after Lord Paget joined the English Catholic refugees overseas.

Like Burghley, Paulet suffered much from the gout. On July 26th he wrote to Burghley: 'I must look for a fresh assault [of the gout] in the accustomed season, at which time the importance of the service will require the assistance of some honest and faithful gentleman . . . It may please your Lordship to give me leave to say plainly unto you, as to my special good Lord, that I fear there will be some cunning in the choice of my supply if he come from the Court.'[14] Paulet may have been thinking of Leicester's malignant influence. Quite possibly he had Walsingham in mind, whose spies were everywhere, even upon Burghley himself. 'I know', Paulet wrote to Burghley in July,[15] 'I have many shrewd eyes fixed upon me and that it behooveth me to eat with a long spoon.' Paulet was evidently not so entirely 'Walsingham's man' as Mary's friends believed. It is worth noting that he sent to Burghley a copy of almost every letter he wrote to Walsingham.

In December 1585, Gilbert Gifford, an English Catholic refugee and the son of John Gifford whose home was in Staffordshire, a few miles from Tutbury, landed in England. He had in his pocket a letter from Thomas Morgan to Mary, in which he commended Gifford to her favour. Morgan said that Gifford was honest and faithful, had many relatives and friends near Tutbury and through them might establish secret contacts with her.

Gifford was apprehended at Rye and conducted to Walsingham. It was probably at that meeting that Gifford agreed to betray Mary and that preliminary plans were made to open a secret channel of correspondence between the Scottish Queen and her friends, in such wise that all the letters she sent and all that she received should pass through Walsingham's office. The problem was simplified by the fact that letters to and from London and the continent could be conveyed in the official packets of the French ambassador. It was merely a matter of bridging the gap between Tutbury and London, or rather between Chartley and London, since Mary was moved, at her own request, from Tutbury to Chartley, about fifteen miles to the north, in the same month of December.

While Gifford was making himself solid at the French embassy, Walsingham sent one of his agents, a man named Thomas Phelippes, an expert in the art of decoding letters in cipher, to make arrangements at Chartley. Phelippes, of course, took Paulet into his confidence. Between them they arranged for the passage of letters by means of a water-tight box which could be slipped through the bung-hole of a beer cask. To utilize this channel, the brewer at the nearby town of Burton, who supplied beer to Mary's household, had also to be taken into the secret. All their arrangements were presumably completed when Phelippes returned to London on January 10th.

Gifford then sent word to the French ambassador that a channel of communication had been opened. Thereupon the ambassador sent a trial letter to Mary which reached her on January 16th. Gifford himself apparently carried the letter to Chartley and waited there until Mary's replies came through. They reached Paulet on February 5th who sent them off to Walsingham. They were of course in cipher and Walsingham handed them over to Phelippes to be decoded. The originals were passed on to the French ambassador. As soon as Mary and her correspondents were satisfied that their channel of communication was safe, they began to exchange ideas about ways of setting her free and organizing strength, foreign and domestic, in support of her.

The outcome was the arrangement of a conspiracy in which Antony Babington, a young Catholic gentleman of Derbyshire, played the major role. Babington came to London when he was nineteen to study law. But he presently turned to fashionable life and, since he was young, well-born, wealthy, handsome and charming, was well received at Court. But he was no mere courtier. In 1580 he was active in support of the Jesuit mission and a recognized leader of the young Catholic group. Later he travelled in France and became acquainted with Mary's supporters in Paris, notably with Thomas Morgan. When he returned to England in 1585, he carried letters of recommendation from Morgan to the Scottish Queen, whom he had previously known when he served as page in Shrewsbury's household and of whom he was a passionate admirer.[16] In May 1586 he was induced by John Ballard, a Catholic missionary priest in England, to consider seriously a project to assassinate Elizabeth.

Babington seems to have been slow in making up his mind, but by the end of June had reached his decision. Early in July he wrote to the Scottish Queen that he and six of his friends intended to murder Queen Elizabeth and asked Mary's advice about proceeding. Mary replied on July 17th.

Babington had suggested in his letter to her that her escape should first be assured before the assassins struck their blow. Mary in reply expressed her preference for the reverse order. It has been argued[17] that Mary's reply did not constitute a definite endorsement of the murder plot. What she did write, after suggesting that Catholic strength in England should be organized, was the following:

'The affairs being thus prepared and forces in readiness both within and without the realm, then shall it be time to set the six gentlemen to work, taking order, upon the accomplishing of their design, I may be suddenly transported out of this place.'[18]

If this is not an endorsement of the murder plot, bearing in mind what Babington had written to Mary about the six gentlemen and their intentions, the English language has lost its meaning. It is possible to argue that Mary never wrote anything of the sort, that the whole letter was a forgery. But if we accept the letter, and it has been accepted by one of the most competent of modern Catholic historians,[19] it establishes beyond reasonable doubt Mary's complicity in the murder plot. That fact is an important one, not because of any moral obliquity which may have been involved but because it brought Mary within the scope of the statute of 27 Elizabeth, to say nothing of the 'Bond of Association'.

Babington's letter and Mary's reply were both intercepted by Walsingham's agents. It might have been expected that as soon as Mary's letter was read the trap would have been sprung. But Walsingham decided to let Mary's letter go through to Babington, and, in the hope of implicating his confederates, added a forged postscript in which Mary asked for the names of Babington's six gentlemen and his other confederates.[20] As it turned out, Walsingham overshot his mark. Babington's suspicions were aroused and he fled. And a few anxious days followed before he was apprehended.

Up to the time of Babington's flight, Walsingham's whole counterplot was kept very secret. He sent some news of it by word of mouth to Leicester on July 9th, a day or so after Babington's letter to Mary had been intercepted. 'I dare make none of my colleagues here privy thereunto', Walsingham wrote. 'My only fear is that her Majesty will not use the matter with that secrecy that appertaineth . . . I pray your Lordship make this letter an heretic after you have read the same.'

Fortunately for the historian, Leicester did not burn the letter. He inked out the parts of it which had reference to the plot, but they can still be read.

Elizabeth evidently knew.[21] After Babington's flight and before his capture, Walsingham expressed the fear that 'she hath not used the matter with that secrecy that appertaineth'.[22] She had certainly let Burghley into the secret by August 11th, for on that day he drafted a proclamation against Babington and his fellows.[23] His first recorded comment is in a letter to Leicester of August 18th, in which he wrote:

'I doubt not but Mr. Secretary doth at large acquaint you with the discovery of the late treacherous conspiracies, the author whereof, as far forth as we do esteem, we have, saving only two . . . both of which are fled, but pursued. My Lord Chancellor and I are here continuing at London, daily occupied, first in procuring their apprehension and now in examining, etc. And so my Lord, being urged with a weak gouty right hand to leave writing, I pray your Lordship to accept these lines, so evil scribbled, in good part.'[24]

Babington was arrested on August 14th and taken to Ely House, Hatton's London residence.[25] On the 18th he was examined by Bromley, Burghley and Hatton, and wrote out his first confession.[26] On the basis of this confession he was cross-examined, and his answers recorded and signed. We have seven separate statements by him, all presumably evoked by the questioning of his three examiners. Walsingham was present at the fourth questioning, but he seems otherwise to have played a minor role in the proceedings against the conspirators. Most of the important personages involved, notably Babington himself, and John Savage and Mary's two secretaries, Nau and Curle, were handled by Bromley and his two associates.

Babington told his whole story, without reservations and without apparent attempt to protect his associates. He evidently cherished the illusion that he would win pardon by his frankness. Indeed, he seems to have been on the verge of revealing the whole conspiracy before his flight. There is no evidence to show that he was tortured. Among other things he provided a summary of Mary's long letter to him endorsing his plot, including even the forged postscript.

Burghley commented upon the examination in a letter to Leicester of September 12th: 'Your Lordship and I were very great motes in the traitors' eyes, for your Lordship there and I here should first, about one time, have been killed. Of your Lordship they thought rather of poisoning than of slaying.'

Babington had said as much,[27] but Burghley's allusion to 'poisoning', reminiscent of Leicester's *Commonwealth*, savours a little of malice.

Early in September, Burghley wrote to Hatton:

'Since your departure Dunne [one of the conspirators] that lay so long in the mire without stirring, keeping silence obstinately, hath, without any torment offered, liberally confessed as much as we conceived him guilty[28] ... The two Abingtons are taken in a sheep house in Hertfordshire. ...

'I think Nau and Curle will yield somewhat in writing to confirm their mistress' crimes, but if they were persuaded that themselves might escape and the blow fall upon their mistress betwixt her head and her shoulders, surely we should have the whole from them.

'If you shall bring any more writings from thence to touch both Nau and Curle and Pasquier it shall serve us the better and spare us from threatening them.

'I thank you most heartily for the comfort of your letter, knowing you to be the instrumental cause of her Majesty's kindness, whom God preserve long to use David's verse, *Laudans invocabo Dominum et ab inimicis salvus ero*. [I will call upon the Lord, who is worthy to be praised, so shall I be saved from mine enemies.]'[29]

Pasquier was examined on September 2nd at Bromley's house, and revealed nothing. Nau and Curle had been placed in the house of Francis Mills, one of Walsingham's trusties, where Nau seems to have passed his time discussing divinity with his Puritan host — according to Mills, not very good divinity.[30]

They were brought before Bromley and his colleagues on September 5th, and both of them seem to have made a complete confession. Both of them attested that the copy of Mary's fatal letter to Babington which was laid before them was substantially what she had written. Nau admitted that he had written it in French from a minute drawn by his mistress, Curle that he had translated it into English and put it into cipher. What induced them to betray their mistress is not too clear. According to Nau, they were led to believe that Walsingham had secured Mary's original minute and Nau's French draft from the papers seized at Chartley.[31] The indications are that neither of these incriminating documents was ever found. But the bluff worked, and Nau and Curle both hastened to clear their own skirts of any culpability. They were mere servants obeying their mistress's orders.

So the matter stood early in September. But no steps had been taken against Mary except the seizure of her papers, and Elizabeth was resolute to dispose of the conspirators before dealing with the royal prisoner. Indeed, she gave orders that no mention of Mary was to be made at their trial. On September 12th, the day before the trial, Burghley wrote to Hatton:

'Her Majesty suddenly falleth into an opinion that if anything tomorrow should be given in evidence against the Scottish Queen, whereby it might be thought that she should be touched for her life, it might be perilous to her Majesty's person, now, presently before anything should be executed upon that Queen. My answer was that I took it for a resolution always that, upon the arraignment, her writing to Babington and allowance of the attempt should orderly fall out upon charging of him and I saw no cause why, at the arraignment, it should not appear, seeing, to the common sort of all men, it is a thing notified by many means that she had consented, and it was also known that she was restrained and her secretaries detained. Besides this, I thought the indictment that must be read openly concerning Babington's offence contained this point. To this she answered that she thought it was not in the indictment and willed me to send to know with all speed, so if it were not there contained, she had a mind to have no speech thereof — a thing to me very strange ... Besides this she commanded me to write that when the judge shall give the judgment for the manner of the death, which she saith must be done according to the usual form, yet in the end of the sentence he may say that such is the form usual, but considering the manner of horrible treason against her Majesty's own person hath not been heard of in this kingdom, it is reason that the manner of their death, for more terror, be referred to her Majesty and her Council.

'I told her Majesty that if the execution shall be duly and orderly executed, by protracting the same both to the extremity of the pains in the action, and to the sight of the people to behold it, the manner of the death would be as terrible as any other new device could be. But therewith her Majesty was not satisfied but commanded me thus to write to you to declare it to the judge and others of the Council there.'[32]

It is worth noting that Burghley wrote this letter from Windsor, one of her castles to which Elizabeth rarely resorted except when she felt herself to be in grave danger.[33]

On the following day, after Burghley had handed to her a protest signed by virtually all the commissioners appointed for the trial, she changed her mind. Burghley dashed off a note to Hatton: 'In the end she is pleased that the learned council shall proceed in maintenance and proofs of the indictment as afore was meant, without exacerbation or enlargement of the Queen of Scots' crime more than shall be requisite for maintenance of the indictment.'

He had won his point, but was disturbed by the Queen's wavering attitude.

'And so,' he ended his letter, 'wishing you ready proceeding without this kind of stops that cannot but engender inconvenient opinion, although her Majesty seemeth to have no other meaning but a foresight for the surety of her own person, which God preserve above all ours.'

Burghley took no part in the trials of the conspirators. Babington, Savage and Ballard all pleaded guilty and no evidence was required to convict them. Abington and Tilney both pleaded not guilty and Babington's confession was presented as evidence against them. Father Pollen's statement that nothing was presented in evidence to implicate the Scottish Queen is somewhat misleading.[34] She was implicated in Babington's indictment and again when his confession was used to convict Abington and Tilney. So in that particular Elizabeth's wishes were not observed. The execution of the conspirators was after the barbarous manner of the times. In the case of Babington and Ballard they were hanged, cut down still alive and disembowelled. In the case of Savage, the rope broke and the executioner thereupon mutilated and disembowelled him. Burghley was right. The manner of execution by law established could be applied to impose upon the victim the ultimate human agony. All that was needed was a word to the executioner. Doubtless in this case the word was spoken.

Meanwhile, Burghley and his colleagues laboured to induce Elizabeth to take positive action against the Scottish Queen. She was still a close prisoner at Chartley. Her papers had been seized and her secretaries taken away.[35]

Late in August, Elizabeth decided to send her to Fotheringhay Castle in Northants, instructed Paulet accordingly and sent Sir Walter Mildmay to look Fotheringhay over. But she had difficulty as usual in making up her mind. Burghley wrote to Walsingham on September 8th:

'We are occupied with many offers to and fro in words but I cannot certify you what shall be determined. Yesterday the Tower was flatly refused and, instead of Fotheringhay which we thought too far off, Hertford was named and next to the Tower was thought meetest... Nevertheless I hope it will be so concluded this day.

'... The Queen hath agreed upon nine Earls besides Councillors and upon eight or nine barons to hear the cause.'[36]

On the same day he drew up a memorandum of 'Matters with the Queen of Scots to be resolved by her Majesty':

'1. To what place the Queen of Scots shall be removed;

'2. At what time the Council and noblemen shall assemble to hear the Queen of Scots' cause;

'3. At what time the judgment of the noblemen shall be affirmed by Parliament;

'Hereupon order is to be given for execution of the resolutions:

'1. Upon the first, Sir Amias Paulet is to be warned to put things in order for her removal, without giving to her or any of hers any warning longer than 2 or 3 days, not showing her to what place she shall go . . . Warning to be given to certain principal gentlemen to attend with a number of servants for that purpose, from shire to shire;

'2. To have letters sent severally to all noblemen who are about to come to London, about a day certain, or rather to the Court:

'3. According to the Queen's resolution to have a new summons [of Parliament] presently, or else to expect the 14th of November.'[37]

But the Queen's resolutions were hard to come by. Two days later Burghley wrote to Walsingham again:

'We are still in long arguments but no conclusions do last, being as variable as the weather . . . and so things are far from execution for the bringing of the Scottish Queen to some apt place where her cause and herself might be heard . . . When the Tower was rejected, we did all choose Hertford Castle, but her Majesty, after a full day's assent thereto, changed her opinion, excepting against it that it was too near London. Then Fotheringhay followed and that she thought too far from the Court, to have her Council and Lords so far from her. Then many other places were named . . . but none of these are allowed . . . And so, even with weariness by talk, her Majesty hath left all off till a time I know not. Whereupon this uncertainty, I cannot limit a day certain for the assembly of the nobility. As for any order for parliament I think there will be tomorrow a change when we shall hear from my L. of Leicester . . . This standing parliament is to be dissolved by a commission and a proclamation and writs to summon a new parliament to begin about the 10th October. And yet the hearing of the Lords to precede it, that it may end before that day. But until the Scottish Queen be removed there can be no hearing.'

Burghley then went on to speak about the military organization of the country and the appointment of Lord Lieutenants in the counties. He was apparently somewhat hurt that his appointment as Lord Lieutenant of the counties of Essex and Hertford, to which he had been nominated, was rejected by his mistress. He admitted that he was 'unmeet for such a charge'. 'And yet', he added, 'I must think myself in some small danger of discredit in that after her Majesty had, as I certainly took it, resolved thereupon, I did indeed, at my last being in Hertfordshire, confer with some of my neighbours thereupon, seeking to understand the state of the county and indeed, as it now falleth out improvidently, said that her Majesty meant to commit the care thereof to me by reason of my L. of Leicester's absence. But I shall seek for some odd salve for this sore and account it in the number of many other disgraces, though no diseases. . . .

'This case I can the better digest, being, as it may be said, *homo novus* in Hert-fordshire. But if the like chance had happened to me to have been once named in my native county of Northamptonshire and then, even at a signing, thus rejected by her Majesty that first allowed it, it would have troubled my patience. And yet I would also [have] had a plaster to have covered my sore. For in that county, where my principal house is and my name and posterity are to remain at God's will, and where I am no new planted or new feathered gentleman, I should have made a great difference from any touch in Hertfordshire.'

This is not the first instance or the last of Burghley's sensitiveness to his prestige in his home county. The interesting fact is that, though he went very rarely to Burghley House and had spoken of it only two months before as belonging to his mother and himself but a farmer, he still regarded it as his 'principal house'.

He ended the letter as follows:

'I wish your health and presence here, where your ability to attend on her Majesty at all times might greatly further causes, though by importunity, that now, for lack of following, which I cannot do by my lameness, remain unperfected.'[38]

Walsingham was laid up by an inflamed leg, which kept him from Court for a fortnight, and Burghley had to assume the lead. He ended a letter to Hatton on September 15th: 'And so, having my hands fuller than I can deliver by Mr. Secretary's infirmity, I am constrained to scribble in haste.'[39]

Some of the difficulties had been cleared up by the 15th. On that day Burghley wrote to Leicester:

'The Queen of Scots is likely to come to Fotheringhay Castle the 27th hereof and I think a number of Councillors and others of the nobility shall have commission according to the late statute 27 [Eliz. c. i.] to hear and judge her cause there, so as in the next parliament, to begin upon a new summons the 15th of October, further order may be taken according to part of her deserts.'[40]

But Burghley was not too sure that the Queen's resolution would hold. On the same day he wrote to Hatton: 'Now her Majesty misliketh of Woodstock and any other place but Fotheringhay. So as, by her commandment, I have sent both to Sir Amias Paulet and to Sir Walter Mildmay, the one to carry her away, the other to provide for her bestowing. How long this determination will last I know not, but I have set it onward. And if further time be delayed the parliament will come before the Lords can well return.'[41] [i.e. the commissioners can return their verdict.]

The best Burghley could hope for was that Mary would be at Fotheringhay by Michaelmas (September 29th). But Paulet did a little better than that and had her there on the 25th.

We hear little more from Burghley until he arrived at Fotheringhay in October. He was evidently deeply engaged in studying the evidence against Mary and in making preparations for her trial. He composed a memorandum upon the procedure to be followed and exchanged letters with the Attorney-General on the subject. He even went so far as to draw a diagram of the actual seating arrangements at the trial.[42] He gathered together the evidence against her and on occasions wrote to Walsingham for copies of letters which were missing. It was in that connection presumably that he unearthed a number of letters to and from Mary which contained references to himself in terms which indicated that both Mary and her agents regarded him as their good friend.[43]

Walsingham, when he had intercepted these letters, had thought it wise to suppress them. Without much doubt it was to them he referred in a letter to Phelippes of May 3rd: 'I have solved that point that toucheth the great person, as neither he nor the cause shall take lack.' Elizabeth evidently saw them before Burghley did.

He wrote to Sir Edward Stafford, English ambassador in France, on October 2nd:

'I must let you know that upon the interception of letters of *Morgan* and *Glasgow*, sent from thence to the *Scottish Queen*, reports have been made *of you* to bear some favour to *her* and that Lilly, your man, did pleasure *Morgan* with intelligence. Likewise the *Scottish Queen* in her letters hath signified to this French ambassador that *I also* was favourable to *the Scottish Queen*, namely for to have *her* well used by *her guardian* — which I perceive did grow upon communication heretofore had with Mauvissière who oftentimes would bemoan the *Scottish Queen* as fearing some violence to be offered. Whereupon he was answered in friendly manner always *by me*, with assurance of no such meaning either in the Queen of England or any other. *The Scottish Queen* used also means that *you* should be moved to require *me* to favour *her*. So I perceive *we both* have been sinisterly dealt withal, in that matters have been kept close, thereby breeding suspicion where I am sure none were deserved. Nevertheless, where conscience is sound, I weigh not danger of detraction.'[44]

Burghley went on to set forth tales about Stafford, of Walsingham's efforts to have him removed, of Burghley's belief in his innocence, which he nevertheless asked Stafford to substantiate.

In a postscript Burghley added: 'I was never more toiled than I have been of late and yet am, with services here that daily multiply. And whosoever scapeth, I am never spared.'[45]

It may have been his weariness which turned his thoughts to his mule upon which he rode about his garden and which figures in one of his well-known portraits. He recalled that Stafford had offered to provide another, and Burghley wrote that he wished he could match the one which Mauvissière had given him twelve years before. 'Yet now,' he added, 'both the "moyle" and her master are grown very aged and therefore, though I cannot amend, yet I would be glad to amend my old beast with a new.'

Burghley's explanation of the assumption that he was Mary's good friend is no doubt the correct one. But he was evidently disturbed. Robert Beale, Walsingham's brother-in-law, in his notes on the proceedings against the Scottish Queen, wrote:

'The Bishop of Glasgow, the Scottish Queen's ambassador in France, had written unto her how W. Cecil, son and heir to Sir Thomas Cecil, had been at Rome with the Pope, reconciled, that there is very good hope that the Lord Treasurer, his grandfather, would do her what pleasure he could. In another letter he advertised how Sir Edward Stafford, her Majesty's ambassador in France, had shown him a letter from the Lord Treasurer whereby he presumed that the said Lord Treasurer did favour her.[46] These letters came to the Queen's knowledge and the matter came to the Lord Treasurer's knowledge, who, for the purgation of himself to be nothing inclined that way, made him, as it is thought, more severe against her.'[47]

This may well be true, though there is no doubt at all that, after the discovery of the Babington Plot, Burghley's unwavering purpose was to bring Mary to her reckoning. It had indeed been his preferred course ever since the discovery of the Ridolfi Plot in 1572, but he had learned by long experience that one of the chief sources of his strength was his ability to adjust himself to the wavering attitudes of his mistress. On this particular occasion it will appear that he forced her hand. It very nearly led to his undoing.

Under the statute 27 Eliz. c. i., Elizabeth was enjoined to appoint a commission to examine and try the case against Mary, which should number at least twenty-four and include all the Privy Council.

Summons went out from the Privy Council to those appointed on September 9th.[48] As a matter of fact, when the commission actually assembled it contained (including clerks, attorneys, judges and Privy Councillors) over forty members.[49] Burghley, of course, was included, and Walsingham and Hatton, all of whom took an active part. Leicester was still overseas.

They held a preliminary meeting at Westminster in the Star Chamber[50] on September 27th and were probably briefed at that time. The incriminating evidence against Mary seems to have been laid before them. Burghley was in favour of having Nau, Mary's secretary, appear in person to confirm his testimony, but the Lord Chancellor advised against it.[51]

The indications are that Elizabeth did not like the terms of the commission. She did not like the title used to designate Mary; she thought it unnecessary to include the latest two accessions to the Council, Davison and Wooley, among the commissioners.[52] Walsingham wrote to Burghley on October 8th: 'I would to God her Majesty could be content to refer these things to them that can best judge of them as other princes do.'[53] And Davison, who had been appointed on October 1st to share with Walsingham the Secretary's office, already began to fear that 'she will keep the course as she held with the Duke of Norfolk, which is not to take her [Mary's] life without extreme fear compel her'.[54]

William Davison was destined to be the scapegoat in the tangled course of events which followed. But there is no sound reason to believe that he was selected with that role in mind. Walsingham's health was bad. He badly needed an assistant and, at a time when Scottish problems and Dutch problems were of pressing importance, Davison was the man of all available men best equipped to deal with them. He had revealed that fact in his embassies both to Scotland and to the Low Countries. He was an ardent Puritan and, though he was temporarily out of favour with Leicester, he was hand in glove with Walsingham. Burghley said of him later: 'I know not a man in England so furnished universally for the place he had, neither know I any that can come near him.'[55] And Elizabeth declared later that she had personally selected him for the office.[56]

The commissioners appointed for Mary's trial arrived at Fotheringhay on October 11th. Elizabeth had written to Mary on the 6th, giving notice of her approaching trial. On the day following she wrote to Burghley and Walsingham, authorizing them to designate two to four commissioners, including themselves, to confer privately with Mary if she so desired it; leaving to their discretion whether the trial should be public or private and whether Mary's secretaries should be called upon to testify against her in her presence. Davison repeated these orders in a letter to Burghley the following day,[57] after Burghley and Walsingham had both left for Fotheringhay. In the same letter he expressed some concern about the Queen's personal safety:

'Your Lordships may, in my poor judgment, but under your honourable correction, do a necessary deed to persuade her Majesty to be more circumspect of her person and spare to show herself publicly than she does,[58] till the brunt of the business now in hand be well over blown; which I doubt not will prevail more coming from your Lordship than from any other, for the opinion she holdeth of you.'

In the final paragraph he added: 'And so, being specially commanded by her Majesty to signify to you how greatly she doth long to hear how her Spirit and Moor do find themselves after so foul and wearisome journey I do . . . take my leave.'

Elizabeth had an adroit way of injecting a note of affectionate interest in her dealings with her councillors. Even in her formal letter of instructions to Burghley and Walsingham, her 'Spirit' and her 'Moor', she took occasion to explain that the discretionary power she extended to them was 'for special trust we repose in your fidelities and wisdoms'.

Burghley had planned to spend a day or two with Hatton at Holdenby before going to Fotheringhay,[59] though he probably had to abandon the idea. He was at Fotheringhay early in the morning of October 12th.

The proceedings opened with the delivery of Elizabeth's letter to Mary by Mildmay, Paulet and Edward Barker. Barker went along to record the proceedings. He had been appointed official *rapporteur* of the whole trial, and his report is the chief source of our information about it.[60]

Mary's initial response to Elizabeth's letter was a refusal to plead before the commission. Burghley sent off a fast message to Elizabeth reporting that fact, and declaring that the commissioners, in accordance with the terms of the commission, intended to proceed. Burghley's letter is missing, but its tenor may be gathered from Elizabeth's reply. She acquiesced in the procedure but directed him to 'stay' sentence until after he had reported to her.[61] It is evident from the tone of her letter that she regarded Burghley as director of the trial.

Since Elizabeth was at Windsor, some seventy-five miles away, and since Burghley's letter could not have been written before noon, it called for fast riding to get it into her hands the same day. We must assume a special system of posts organized to facilitate contact with her, though we have no record of it. Davison says that her reply was scribbled at midnight. It probably reached Burghley some time the following day. Davison wrote to Walsingham that he did not think it would arrive in time and hoped that it would not. But he was disappointed.[62]

The commissioners[63] spent most of Thursday trying to induce Mary to change her mind. They appointed a committee to wait on her made up of the Lord Chancellor, Lord Burghley, six Lords, two Privy Councillors, the Chief Justices of the Queen's Bench and of the Common Pleas and two civilians, Dr. Dale and Dr. Ford.[64] Bromley and Burghley acted as spokesmen. They asked Mary point-blank whether she intended to appear, and declared that they meant to proceed whether she appeared or not. Her answer was a repetition of her former objections, to wit that she was a sovereign Queen and not answerable to any English court.[65] She intimated, however, that she might answer, 'but under protestation of not subjecting herself'. She would be content, she added, to answer anything in a free Parliament, but not before a commission which she felt sure had already condemned her. She then broke forth into a recital of her grievances. At this point Burghley interrupted her. He did not, he said, speak as a commissioner but as a Councillor, well aware of the manifold favours which she had received at her arrival in England; of Elizabeth's punishment of those who had questioned her presumptive right to the English throne; of Elizabeth's intervention to protect her person after the discovery of her implication in the Ridolfi Plot when Parliament was demanding her execution.[66] In reviewing the record at this point, Burghley noted that it did his speech less than justice. 'These answers', he wrote, 'are very nakedly set down.'

Mary brushed the speech aside. She did not, she said, 'accept them for any favours'.

The immediate outcome was that she asked for a list of the commissioners and a copy of the commission. When she had studied them 'she would give her determinate answer in the afternoon'. And what she asked for was supplied.

The committee waited upon her in the afternoon. She took no exception to the commissioners, but protested against the law upon which the commission was based as directed specifically against her. She asked by what law she was to be tried, and questioned the competency of the commission to try by civil law. She was answered that proceedings would be by the Common Law of England. She then burst forth once more upon a recital of her grievances. They called her back to the point and demanded her answer. She said that she would not answer as a subject but once more implied that she might answer on other terms.

At this point Christopher Hatton made a speech which Mary said later induced her to acquiesce. He told her that royal dignity in the case of such a crime as she was charged with would not exempt her from answering, either by the Civil Law or the Common Law, nor by the Law of Nations or of nature. If, he said, you are innocent, you wrong your reputation in avoiding a trial.

She answered that she would appear before a full Parliament or before the Queen

M

and her Council, provided that her protest against their jurisdiction be admitted
and her presumptive title to the English throne acknowledged.

Bromley asked her whether she would answer before the commission if her
protest were admitted. She replied that she would never submit to the law upon
which the commission was based.

'Whereupon,' Barker records, 'the Lord Treasurer signified unto her that because she gave her direct answer . . . he was by their order to intimate and make
known unto her that tomorrow in the morning, notwithstanding her absence or
contumacy, they meant to proceed in this castle of Fotheringhay to the execution
of her Majesty's commission and according to the receiving of proofs against her;
and afterwards to the giving of sentence in the cause as upon good proofs the
matter shall appear unto them.

'Whereupon the Scottish Queen desired them to respect their honour and
conscience, and besought God that the right which the commission should do to
her should light upon them and theirs.'

On Saturday, the 14th, before the commissioners had settled down to work, a
message came from Mary requesting that a committee of the commission wait
upon her again. Another committee was selected, somewhat larger than the first,
but with the key men, Bromley and Burghley and Hatton, still among them.[67]
When they came to Mary, she asked that her formal protestation be admitted by
the commission, or that at least some public act be made and delivered to her for
testimony. Burghley asked whether she would come before the commission if her
protestation were simply received and recorded without allowance. She answered
that, though she was unwilling to prejudice her position, she was so anxious to
discharge herself of the crime alleged that she was willing to appear and answer on
those terms.

And so, on the morning of the 14th, with Mary present, the commission opened
formal proceedings.

Mary began by explaining her position. The commission was then read. She
protested against the law authorizing the commission.

'Whereunto,' Barker records, 'the Lord Treasurer replied that every person
within the realm is bound by the laws thereof, though never so newly made, and
that she might not speak against the laws; saying that their commission was to hear
the matter and to proceed at that time and place. And therefore if the Scottish
Queen would hear and answer anything, she might, or otherwise, if she list not to
do so, yet they were to proceed to the execution of their charge for this was the
time appointed.

'Whereupon she said that under her protestation aforesaid she would be
contented both to hear anything that could be said against her concerning
any act against the Queen of England's person, and to answer as occasion would
serve.'

The Queen's Sergeant [Gawdy] thereupon laid the case before the commission,
describing the Babington conspiracy and concluding that she knew of it, approved
of it, assented unto it, promised her assistance and showed the ways and means.

Her answer was a flat denial. She did not know Babington, she had never heard of his enterprise, her implication in it would have to be proved either by her own words or in her own hands.

Her correspondence with Babington was then read out.

She denied having written the incriminating letter, said that it could easily have been forged with the help of a copy of her cipher. She feared that Walsingham had done it. She had never plotted against Elizabeth's life, though she would do what she could to deliver the English Catholics from their oppression.

At this point, Burghley again intervened.

'No man', he said, 'who hath shown himself a good subject was ever put to death for religion, but some have been for treason, when they maintained the Pope's bull against the Queen.'

'Yet I', said she, 'have heard otherwise, and have read it also in books, set forth in print.'

'The authors', said he, 'of such books do write also that the Queen had forfeited her royal dignity.'

Burghley's marginal note on this passage in the record was as follows: 'This answer was of more length, with necessary circumstances.'

After him, Walsingham arose and protested that his mind was free of all malice. 'I call God', said he, 'to record that as a private person I have done nothing unbeseeming an honest man, nor, as I bear the place of a public person, have I done anything unworthy of my place.'[68]

At that point the commission rose for dinner. It reassembled at two and sat until six.

The afternoon was devoted largely to the confessions of Nau and Curle. Burghley told Mary that they had both confessed that they had tried to dissuade her from dealings with Babington and that she had resented it. He also pointed out, in confirmation of her suggestions to Babington, that there had been stirs in Scotland and disturbances in Ireland. He charged her with an intent to deliver her son to Spain and to transfer her title to the English Crown to Philip II if her son did not become a Catholic. He also referred to her letters to Glasgow and Mendoza and the Pagets about her contact with Babington. She answered that those who wrote the letters might put in what they would. He referred to her pension to Morgan after she knew that he had prompted Parry to kill Elizabeth. She replied that Morgan was her faithful servant. She disapproved of some of his efforts in her behalf but was in no way responsible for them.

The last session of the commission was on Saturday morning, the 15th, from eight until eleven, largely devoted to a restatement of her grievances and her complaints about the dragging of irrelevant matter into the procedure. She had been inveigled to appear before the commission by the plea that it would give her an opportunity to clear herself and declare her innocence. Instead of that, she found herself in a situation in which her judges had already found her guilty. She had been denied counsel, her papers had been taken away from her. She demanded another trial before another, unbiased, assembly.

Burghley replied: 'Whereas I bear a double person, one of a Commissioner, another of a Councillor, receive first a few words from me as a Commissioner. Your protestation is recorded, and a copy thereof shall be delivered unto you. To us our authority is granted under the Queen's hand and the great seal of England, from which there is no appeal; neither do we come with prejudice, but to judge according to the role of justice. The Queen's learned Counsel do level at nothing else but that the truth may come to light, how far you have offended against the Queen's person. To us full power is given to hear and examine the matter, even in your absence; yet were we desirous you should be present, lest we might seem to have derogated from your honour. We purposed not to object anything unto you, but what you were privy to or have attempted against the Queen's person. The letters have been read to no other purpose but to discover your offence against the Queen's person, and the matters to it belonging, which are so interlaced with other matters that they cannot be severed. The whole letters therefore, and not parcels picked out here and there, have been openly read, for that the circumstances do give assurance what matters you dealt with Babington about.

'She, interrupting him, said, "The circumstances may be proved, but never the fact." Her integrity depended not upon the credit and memory of her secretaries, though she knew them to be honest and sincere men. Yet if they have confessed anything out of fear of torments, or hope of reward and immunity, it was not to be admitted, for just causes, which she would allege elsewhere. Men's minds, said she, are diversely carried about with affections, and they would never have confessed such matters against her but for their own advantage and hope. Letters may be directed to others than those to whom they are written, and many things have been often inserted, which she never dictated. If her papers had not been taken away, and she had her secretary, she could better confute the things objected against her.'

' "But nothing," said the Lord Treasurer, "shall be objected, but since the 19th day of June; neither will your papers avail you, seeing your secretaries and Babington himself, being never put to the rack, have affirmed that you sent those letters to Babington; which though you deny, yet whether more credit is to be given to an affirmation than to a negation, let the Commissioners judge. But to return to the matter, this which followeth I tell you as a Councillor; many things you have propounded time after time, concerning your liberty; that they have failed of success, it is long of you, or of the Scots, and not of the Queen. For the Lords of Scotland flatly refused to deliver the King in hostage. And when the last treaty was holden concerning your liberty, Parry was sent privily by Morgan, a dependent of yours, to murder the Queen."'

' "Ah (said she) you are my adversary." "Yea (said he) I am adversary to Queen Elizabeth's adversaries. But hereof enough, let us now proceed to proofs." Which, when she refused to hear; "Yet we (said he) will hear them." "And I also (said she) will hear them in another place and defend myself."'

Thereupon the evidence in the case was once again reviewed, with emphasis upon Mary's letter to Mendoza in which she had offered to transfer her presumptive right to the English Crown to Philip II, a letter which, as Mary herself had observed, would, if revealed, 'be in France the loss of my dower, in Scotland a clear breach with my son and in this country [England] my total ruin and destruction'.[69] No doubt it was with these objects in mind that the passage was read aloud and spread verbatim on the record. Mary's answer was simply that since she had lost all hope of England she was fully resolved to seek foreign aid.

Burghley thought it necessary to observe that no one could convey the right to the succession in England but that it went according to the law. He then asked Mary if she had any more to say.

In reply she asked that she might be heard in a full Parliament or that she might confer with Elizabeth in person and with her Council. 'Whereupon she rose up with great confidence of countenance', and so terminated the session. It was prorogued to meet again at the Star Chamber on October 25th.

According to the official record, Mary at the last had some private conference with Burghley, Hatton, Walsingham and the Earl of Warwick. But we do not know what passed between them; probably nothing more than a last-minute effort on Mary's part to bring her charm to bear upon the four men (Leicester being absent, she aimed at him through his brother, the Earl of Warwick) in whose hands, she realized, her fate really rested.

Mary was probably right in asserting that the commission had already made up its mind about her guilt before the trial began. The trial itself followed the usual pattern of English trials for treason in the sixteenth century. Obviously it does not conform to modern ideas of justice. Its object was not to establish Mary's guilt, but to display the evidence upon which the judgment was based. On the evidence presented she was, without much doubt, guilty. Her letter to Babington, confirmed by Babington's confession and by the confession of Mary's secretaries and by the implications of other letters which she wrote at the time, leaves little doubt about the matter. Mary's demand that her guilt must be determined by her own words or her own writing could not be met. She dictated what she would have written to Nau in French and Curle wrote out the letter in English and then put it into cipher. The best that could be hoped for was Nau's notes and many of them were recovered when his papers were seized, though not, unfortunately, his notes on her fatal letter to Babington. The trial was imposed by the provisions of the law 27 Eliz. c. i. Even so it is probable that Elizabeth would never have consented to it unless she herself had concluded that the evidence itself was decisive. From the actual course of the trial, which seems to have been under Burghley's general guidance, we may conclude that its main objectives were: (1) to convince Mary's English supporters — notably Lord Lumley and Viscount Montacute, those two members of the commission whose Catholic sympathies were notorious — of her guilt; and (2) to disclose the fact that Mary was quite prepared to sacrifice the interests of her son and of her French connections and to offer all that she had for Spanish support. It is worth noting that before the commission had terminated its sittings an envoy was already on the way to France with copies of her letter to Mendoza offering to Philip II her presumptive right to the English throne.[70]

Burghley left Fotheringhay on the afternoon of the 15th and went to Burghley

House, only a few miles away. From there he wrote to Davison on the 15th:[71]

'Mr. Secretary, yesternight, upon receipt of your letter dated on Thursday, I wrote what was thought would be this day's work. The Queen of the Castle was content to appear again afore us in public to be heard, but in truth not to be heard for her defence, for she could say nothing but negatively — that the points of the letters that concerned the practice against the Queen's person was never by her written, nor of her knowledge. The rest, for invasion, for scaping by force, she said she would neither deny nor affirm. But her intention was, by long artificial speeches, to move pity, to lay all blame upon the Queen's Majesty, or rather upon the Council, that all the troubles past did ensue; avowing her reasonable offers and our refusals. And in this her speeches I did so encounter her with reasons out of my knowledge and experience as she had not the advantage she looked for. As I am assured, the auditory did find her case not pitiable, her allegations untrue. By which means great debate fell yesternight very long and this day renewed with great stomaching.

'But we had great reason to prorogue our session which is run till the 15th and so we of the Council will be at the Court the 22nd.

'And we find all persons here in commission fully satisfied as, by her Majesty's order, judgment will be given at our next meeting. But the record will not be perfected in 5 or 6 days and that was one cause why, if we should have proceeded to judgment, we should have tarried 5 or 6 days more. And surely the country could not bear it by the waste of bread specially, our company being there and within six miles 2000 horsemen. But by reason of her Majesty's letter we of her Council, that is the Lord Chancellor, Mr. Vice[72] [Chamberlain], Mr. Secretary and myself only did procure this prorogation for the other 2 causes.'

The last clause reveals the fact that Burghley and his colleagues thought it wise not to reveal the fact that sentence had been stayed by royal command. Walsingham's letter written on the same day to Leicester is illuminating on this point. 'We had proceeded presently', he wrote, 'to sentence, but that we had a secret countermand and were forced, under some other colour, to adjourn our meeting until the 15th of the month at Westminster. I see this wicked creature ordained of God to punish us for our sins and unthankfulness. For her Majesty hath no power to proceed against her as her own safety requireth.'

Walsingham, like Burghley, made much of the fact that Mary had failed to impress the commission. 'In the opinion of her best friends,' he observed to Leicester, 'that were appointed commissioners, she is held guilty.'[73]

On the 15th Davison wrote to Walsingham: 'For the course of your doings there I find her Highness to accept very well thereof and namely in the choice both of the number of persons selected to repair unto that queen upon her refusal to appear publicly before you, as also of the answers made unto her by the Lord Treasurer to the reasons she pretended for the same . . . Her Majesty doth observe that in these last letters both from yourself and my Lord Treasurer no mention made of your proceeding to sentence which I find doth a little affect her, notwithstanding her pleasure signified to the Lord Treasurer of a few words in her own hand . . . which her Majesty now conceiveth may have wrought some hindrance to the rest of that course in proceeding to the verdict.'[74]

Elizabeth in short was beginning to waver again. On the same day she wrote to Burghley[75] (and Hatton and Walsingham), directing them to call the commission together again as soon as possible and to proceed to the sentence.

Burghley's response to this letter is missing, but in a letter to Walsingham of the 16th he revealed the gist of it:

'I have showed', he wrote, 'how impossible it is to convene us together afore the 25th, ... almost in fact impossible to come sooner than our day appointed. I have given hope that the matter will take a good end, and honourable for such a cause, which would not, upon only two days, or rather but upon a day and a half hearing be also judged. For so we might verify the Scottish Queen's allegation that we came hither with a prejudgment. . . .

'I take my leave of Mr. Vice-Chamberlain and yourself, wishing myself [with you] seeing I could have neither [of] you with me.'[76]

Burghley's letter was dated at Burghley House. Three days later he was on his way south. On the 19th he wrote to Walsingham: 'I mean to be at Theobalds tomorrow at night and at Westminster on Friday [the 20th] at night.'[77]

The commission reassembled in the Star Chamber on the 25th.[78] On that occasion the evidence against Mary was reviewed at length and Nau and Curle were present to confirm their written testimony by word of mouth.[79] Walsingham observed in a letter to Stafford describing the trial that the testimony of Mary's secretaries 'brought a great satisfaction to all the commissioners, insomuch that albeit some of them, as you know, stood well affected to her, yet, considering the plainness and evidence of the proofs, every one of them after this gave his sentence against her, finding her not only accessory and privy to the conspiracy but also an imaginer and compasser of her Majesty's destruction'.[80]

It is significant to note that the commissioners took advantage of the occasion to declare that the verdict against Mary in no wise prejudiced the claims of James of Scotland to the English succession, and that their statement, made over the hands and seals of the commissioners, was confirmed by the judges present over their hands and seals.[81]

The only statement we have from Burghley on the proceedings in Star Chamber is in a letter which he wrote to the Earl of Shrewsbury, who was absent on account of illness, the day following.

'Yesterday in the Star Chamber, when all the Commission, among which no one of them wanted, only your Lordship and my L. of Warwick, both upon one cause, was assembled and pronounced their sentence all in one manner, to charge the Queen of Scots with privity of the conspiracy and with the compassing and imagining also of divers things tending to the hurt and destruction of her Majesty's person . . . And then it was ordered that against Monday next, the process with this sentence would be put in writing in form of a record, to the which it is meant that we all should put our names and seals.'[82]

Burghley wrote to Davison on the 30th: 'Tomorrow in the afternoon, the

Commissioners must meet in Star Chamber, so as the cause, being of great length, to hear and conclude upon the whole process in form of a record, it will be late before I can come thither, specially seeing I shall bring the gout with me in my foot, which nobody either here or there will accept from me I am sure. But I thank God my heart is free.'[83]

All that remained to be done with Mary Stuart was to proceed to her execution. But that turned out to be the hardest task of all. Even the verdict was not proclaimed until after confirmatory action by Parliament.[84]

Meanwhile, both the French and the Scottish ambassadors were interesting themselves on Mary's behalf. Two days before the verdict was reached in Star Chamber, the French ambassador, being denied audience, wrote a letter to Elizabeth for the stay of proceedings against Mary. 'But it was answered', Walsingham wrote to Stafford, 'by her Majesty, that it was not convenient to stay the proceedings and [she] hoped that the King, his master, would not be an intercessor in that behalf, and if he should, she could not but take it unkindly at his hands.'[85]

James of Scotland had sent a special envoy to intercede for his mother. But both Elizabeth and her councillors were convinced that the Scottish King was chiefly concerned about his presumptive rights to the English succession. That accounts for the explicit statement on the subject by the commissioners and the judges at Westminster.

Burghley undoubtedly took an active part in dealing with the Scottish and the French delegations, of which a few fragments are recorded. We hear of him wining and dining Archibald Douglas, James's quasi-ambassador in London, sometime parson of Glasgow, who had played some part in the murder of the King's father and was at the moment playing some part in betraying the King's mother, but who temporarily enjoyed the King's favour. We hear also of a long debate between Burghley and Pomponne de Bellièvre, one of the French King's ablest councillors, who had been sent to intervene for Mary on points of law involved, interlarded with quotations from Cicero and the *Corpus Juris* and historical precedents from Lars Porsena of Clusium[86] to Robert of Sicily.

Bellièvre, after his return to Paris, made come complimentary remarks about Burghley to the English ambassador there. He knew nobody, he said, of the Council of England so impassionate as Burghley, saving only the Queen herself.[87] He complained, however, that Burghley seemed to be counting upon an early peace with Spain, an indication that Burghley seized upon the occasion to play upon the old rivalry of Habsburg and Valois.

It cannot be doubted that Elizabeth herself was somewhat concerned about both the Scottish and the French attitudes — though mainly because she herself was more than doubtful about the expediency of the final step and therefore disposed to over-emphasize all objections to it. Davison reported to Walsingham on October 29th that he had long arguments with her on the subject. 'She laid before me the same objections she had used before to yourself, which I did repel with all the reason I had and in the end, as I conceive, left her satisfied. The most material point she urged was the danger she stood in of the son, after the mother should be taken away, to whom all her [Mary's] friends would be ready to offer themselves. I let her see the fear to be utterly vain if she list to take such a course, as in honour and surety and good policy she ought, that her [Mary's] friends consisted of our enemies in religion, which could have no hope in him, remaining as he is ... Another scruple was that yet the King of Spain, having a title, might affect the kingdom for himself. The affecting of it I granted, but the likelihood of attaining it I impugned ... This and a great deal more passed between her and me yesternight.'[88]

Burghley and his colleagues all felt that the best way to strengthen Elizabeth's resolution was by Parliament. As early as September 8th he had written to Walsingham:[89] 'We stick upon parliament which her Majesty misliketh, but we do all persist to make the burden better borne and the world abroad better satisfied.'

The Parliament called in 1584 was still in being, and by its last prorogation was to meet again on November 15th. The Privy Council held that this was too late and persuaded the Queen to dissolve it on September 19th and to summon a new Parliament. In order, however, that the personnel of the Parliament in being should be preserved as far as might be, the Privy Council sent off letters to the constituencies urging them to favour the sitting members.[90] The new Parliament was summoned for October 15th, but the delays attending upon Mary Stuart's trial led Burghley to the conclusion that October 15th was too early. He dug up a precedent from Elizabeth's first Parliament which justified a postponement of the day of assembling and instructed Walsingham to prepare a warrant accordingly. Burghley suggested that October 22nd would be a good day.[91] Elizabeth thought this hardly allowed time enough, and actually Parliament did not meet until a week later.[92] Obviously a verdict had to be reached on Mary before Parliament could be asked to consider her further fate, the sole reason for its summoning.

The Parliament of 1586-87[93] was a momentous one. At this point we are only concerned with its first session which adjourned on December 2nd and did not reassemble until Mary had gone to her reckoning.

On October 16th, Burghley wrote to Shrewsbury: 'Tomorrow the parliament shall be prorogued until Saturday, at which time her Majesty will come from Lambeth to Westminster, return to Lambeth until Monday forenoon and then, having allowed of the Speaker, return to Richmond.'[94] Evidently Elizabeth's original intention was to open Parliament in the usual fashion. But she changed her mind between Wednesday and Saturday.

As it turned out, she absented herself from the opening ceremonies, and remained at Richmond, not wishing, as she herself said later, to participate in the proceedings against her kinswoman. Instead she appointed a committee of three, Whitgift and Burghley and the Earl of Derby, to act for her.

Up until the adjournment on December 2nd, Parliament devoted its attention almost exclusively to the Queen of Scots. There were eloquent denunciations of her in the Commons, the best of them by Sir Christopher Hatton; analogous denunciations in the Lords with Bromley and Burghley the principal speakers. Of Burghley's we know no more than the brief entry of it in the *Lords Journals*:[95] 'The which, by Wm., Lord Burghley, Lord Treasurer of England, as one unto whom the said Queen of Scots' whole proceedings were better known by reason of his long service done unto our most gracious sovereign Lady, since the beginning of her reign, were more fully dilated.'

The burden of all the speeches was that Mary should 'suffer the due execution of justice according to her deserts'.

Both Houses then proceeded to prepare a petition to the Queen. Burghley evidently played an important part in the drafting of the petition.[96] The gist of it is as follows:

'We beseech your Majesty that declaration of the said sentence [against the Scottish Queen] and judgment be made and published by proclamation and thereupon direction be given for further proceeding against the said Scottish Queen according to the effect and true meaning of the Statute of 1584-5.'

It was presented to the Queen at Richmond on the 12th. She was evidently restless to receive it, asked Burghley if he could get it to her on the 11th. He had to point out to her that it could not be arranged.[97] Nothing which was done seemed to suit her. Burghley wrote to Davison on the 11th:

'Yesterday in the parliament chamber grew a question whether it were convenient for the two archbishops and four other bishops to accompany the Lords temporal in the petition to her Majesty for the execution of the Scottish Queen. Some scruple I had whether her Majesty would like it because in former times the bishops in parliament were wont to absent themselves. But yet I do not think [it] unlawful for them to be present and persuaders in such causes as the execution of the sentence tends to the state of the church as it does.'[98] He bade Davison consult the Queen's pleasure.

He wrote to Shrewsbury on the 12th[99] that the petition was to be presented the same day at Richmond 'by 21 Lords temporal, 6 Lords spiritual and 40 of the Commons'. But at the last moment again Elizabeth decided otherwise,[100] and the clergy did not appear. Burghley needed all his sang-froid to adjust himself to these royal whims. 'I still find by experience', he wrote to Walsingham 'that such direction must be taken as princes shall give, after counsel given.'[101]

The petition was presented on the 12th with speeches by the Lord Chancellor and the Speaker of the House. The Queen's reply is among the more notable of her public utterances.

She began with an expression of her gratitude to God for his mercies. She rejoiced in the good will of her subjects, 'which, if haply I should want, well might I breath but never think I lived'. In this connection she referred to the Bond of Association as eloquent testimony of their devotion. She declared that she was not unwilling to die if she might serve her people that way. She swore that she was without malice to Mary and would gladly have pardoned her if she had confessed her faults. And finally she asked for time to consider — to seek divine guidance. But she promised a speedy answer.[102]

Burghley described the speech 'as princely wise and grave . . . not only to the admiration of all that heard it but to the drawing out of the tears out of many eyes'.

In reporting Elizabeth's answer to the Commons on the following Monday (November 14th), Hatton mentioned something which the Queen had forgot and which she had charged him to declare to them. It was to the effect that she would be glad to spare the 'taking of her [Mary's] blood, if by any other means to be devised by her Highness' Great Council of this realm, the safety of her Majesty's own person and of the state might be preserved'.

This suggestion was debated during the ensuing week in both Houses and the answer was unanimous — Mary must die.

The parliamentary committee was called again to wait upon the Queen on November 24th, to give their answer and to receive hers. Elizabeth's speech on this occasion followed very much the same lines as her earlier one. She had hoped they would find another way out. She complained that having winked at so many treasons she should now be forced to take action and spill the blood of her own kinswoman. She was not so much concerned to prolong her own life as to save both their lives. She spoke of her accession, of the religion in which she was born, of her determination to maintain it. She claimed that she had been a just ruler. She appreciated their advice which she took to be wise and honest and conscionable. But she was still in doubt.

'Therefore,' she concluded, 'if I should say I would not do as you require it might peradventure be more than I thought — and to say I would do it might perhaps breed peril of that you do labour to preserve.'

It was, as she herself described it, an answer answerless.

What she did intend at this juncture is past finding out. Her immediate intention was clearly to disclaim all desire to bring Mary to her reckoning, and at the same time to make manifest her devotion to her subjects, to their faith and to their interests. It is not improbable that she hoped that someone of those who had signed and sealed the Bond of Association would take the law into his own hands. In that connection her effort to have the Bond mentioned in the petition and her own emphasis upon it in her speech are significant. In any case, she proceeded to rid herself of further parliamentary pressure by a sudden decision to prorogue Parliament.

Elizabeth's speeches were rushed into print. They appeared in pamphlet form before the end of the year.[103] John Stow set them forth in what was virtually the last item in the second edition of Holinshed which came out early in January 1587. A French version was published in the same year.[104] There is sound reason to believe that the editor was Robert Cecil, Burghley's youngest son, who sat in the Parliament of 1586. Robert was only twenty-three years old at the time, but precocious beyond his years. Accepting his authorship, it may be conjectured that Burghley prompted the publication. He was a firm believer in propaganda of that sort. Certainly Elizabeth herself approved. She even went so far as to correct the copy in her own hand before it went to press.[105]

But Burghley was far from happy at Elizabeth's non-committal attitude. He wrote Davison on November 24th, the same day upon which Elizabeth delivered her 'answer answerless':

'I pray you remember her Majesty to send in writing the manner of the speech that my Lord Chancellor shall use tomorrow at the prorogation of the parliament. I know her Majesty meaneth to thank them for their pains, and especially for their care and continuance therein for her safety, but if they have not some comfort also to see the fruits of their cares by some demonstration to proceed from her Majesty, the thanks will be of small weight to carry into the countries [i.e. counties]. And then the realm may call this a vain parliament or otherwise nickname it a parliament of words. For there is no law made for the realm and if also there be no publication presently of so solemn a sentence, the sentence against the Queen of Scots will be termed a dumb sentence, whereof the nobility that have given it and all the parliament that have affirmed it may repent themselves of their time spent.

'The sentence is already more than a full month and four days old.

'If her Majesty will sign it this day both the ambassador of Scotland may be prevented this day in that point, as done to satisfy the importunity of all the noblemen [of] the Commission and of all the States in the parliament. And tomorrow also my Lord Chancellor may declare the same, to the liking of parliament.

'And for hope of the last part for execution, if her Majesty shall be content that it be said that therein she will prefer no other men's advice, being strangers, afore her own people, she shall leave hope of execution. And to that hope I beseech God give full perfection.

'Thus you see I cannot but utter my opinion, long afore daylight, for I have been up since five.'[106]

Burghley's reference to the Scottish ambassador is explained by a letter which he wrote to Shrewsbury on the 12th, in which he referred to a request by Mr. Keith, the Scottish envoy, for 'a stay of proceedings against the Queen of Scots, and that nothing be done to the prejudice of any title of the King'. 'The latter', Burghley wrote, 'is granted; the former can hardly be granted without her Majesty's peril and discontentation of all the parliament, wherein the sentence against her is already confirmed.'[107]

Elizabeth, at the last moment, postponed prorogation for a week and, in deference to Burghley's objections, shortened the period of recess to February 15th.[108]

But she could not be persuaded to proclaim the sentence against Mary until after Parliament had risen.

Burghley got word of this latest royal volte-face at nine o'clock in the morning when the Lords were already assembled and the Commons on their way to join them for the prorogation. It arrived at the last possible moment in the Queen's own illegible hand — so illegible that Burghley had to write it out for the Lord Chancellor's perusal. He observed in a letter to Davison that Bromley 'also misliked such a sudden warning'. He added: 'These hard accidents happen by her Majesty being so far from hence'[109] — a shrewd thrust at Elizabeth's deliberate retreat to Richmond.

Instead of prorogation, Elizabeth ordered that the Parliament be adjourned for a week. She was evidently sparring for time, uncertain about her next step.

Meanwhile, Burghley pressed forward. On the 29th the commissioners of the trial assembled at Star Chamber to subscribe the sentence against Mary. The following day Burghley wrote to Shrewsbury, apologizing for not writing sooner. 'Truly,' he added, 'the impediment is lack of leisure, being of late time and yet still more toiled with a care of her Majesty's affairs than I was these many years . . . The sentence was subscribed yesterday by all the Commissioners . . . I left a place for your name. The session shall be prorogued on Friday next [December 2nd]⁴ as I think, but I must ride tomorrow to Richmond and thereupon her Majesty will conclude.'

The following morning he wrote to Walsingham: 'I passed through the city and Southwark afore daylight, which served me to small purpose, for though I came [to Richmond] about 8 yet her Majesty did not stir before ten.'

He had with him his draft of the proclamation.

'I had good hap to please her fully to all respects, as she affirmed before my L. of Leicester and Mr. Secty. Davison, with that which I brought to be proclaimed. And so having caused it to be engrossed, which could not be before three . . . Whereby I could not have time to bring the warrant signed, as I desired, that it might have been proclaimed tomorrow. But she will not have it published before Saturday.'¹¹⁰

'What will follow,' Burghley wrote to Shrewsbury, 'a few days will declare. Her Majesty is greatly pressed by the French and Scottish [ambassadors] to stay from the action. God must direct her therein which I most desire to be for her honour and her safety.'¹¹¹

The sentence was proclaimed on Sunday, December 4th, two days after Parliament was prorogued. Burghley had worked hard to have it announced in Parliament, but Elizabeth would not have it so. She evidently felt that its publication in Parliament would unduly intensify her commitments. Possibly one reason why she released it for publication at all was the opportune return of Leicester from the Low Countries on November 24th, who for over a month had been urging upon her the necessity of disposing of Mary.¹¹²

Burghley hoped that the proclamation of the sentence would be followed at once by an order for Mary's execution. He and Walsingham together drew up an order accordingly, with the idea that it should be dispatched the day after the sentence was proclaimed. On the 10th, Burghley, in Elizabeth's name, drafted orders to Paulet to proceed to the execution.¹¹³ But once again she declined to act.

It was probably with the idea of prodding her to action that a conspiracy was hatched early in January, in which Des Trappes, one of the servants of the French ambassador, was named as the *agent provocateur*, and William Stafford, renegade brother of the English ambassador in France, the assassin. The objective was twofold, first to frighten the Queen into action, second to cut off the communications of the French ambassador and so prevent further French intervention until action with Mary was taken. We have a long account in Burghley's hand of a conference with Châteauneuf at his house, at which Leicester and Hatton and Davison were all present. Châteauneuf admitted that Stafford had come to him with a plot to murder the Queen but that he had refused to have any part in it. Burghley observed that, if that were so, Châteauneuf should have felt morally obligated to reveal the conspiracy. He refused to admit the obligation. And so the conference ended.[114]

On January 11th, Burghley wrote to Sir Edward Stafford: 'I am right sorry of an unhappy accident . . . whereof the ambassador will complain, though we have cause to complain of him. But hereof you shall hear more very shortly. I am commanded not to write to you at this time, although I think the messenger will give you some taste, which, though it may seem somewhat sour at the first, yet you shall have no cause for yourself to doubt any sinister opinion, either by her Majesty or any impassionate Councillor.'[115] The final sentence here of course refers to Stafford's renegade brother.

Shortly afterwards William Waad was dispatched to the French King with an official account of the plot. We need not pursue the matter further. Châteauneuf was denied audience until after Mary's execution. He was then by degrees received back into favour. Des Trappes was released and in March Walsingham told Châteauneuf that he was convinced that the whole business amounted to nothing more than an effort on William Stafford's part to extort money from the French ambassador.[116] Walsingham blamed Davison, by this time the established scapegoat for all the sins of the English government. In any case the conspiracy served its turn.

Of Elizabeth's attitude towards Mary we hear little or nothing after the proclamation of the sentence against her on December 4th. Months later Burghley wrote that she was being constantly urged by her Privy Council to proceed to the execution of the sentence,[117] 'but [they] were dismissed unsatisfied with no other reason but that it was a natural disposition in her, utterly repugnant to her mind'. This probably was true, though, when Burghley wrote it, his purpose was to convince the King of Scotland that Elizabeth had nothing to do with Mary's execution.

The events which followed, Davison set forth at length in a long letter to Walsingham. By his account Elizabeth had ordered Burghley[118] to draw up a warrant for Mary's execution shortly after the sentence against her had been proclaimed. This warrant Burghley left with Davison with directions to have the Queen sign it. After some delay, occasioned by the intervention of Scotland and France, she decided to sign it, and on February 1st she directed Lord Admiral Howard to order Davison to bring her the warrant. He did so. She called for pen and ink, signed it and told Davison to take it to the Lord Chancellor to receive the Great Seal, charging Davison to keep the matter secret, but suggesting that he show it to Walsingham, who was sick in bed in his London house. ' "The grief thereof", she merrily said, "would go near to killing him outright." ' She then went on to speak of the execution. It should be as secret as possible and be done in the hall at Fotheringhay. At the same time she complained that others might have eased her of the burden and suggested that a letter be written to Paulet and Sir Drue Drury sounding out their disposition to take the law into their own hands and, in accordance with the Bond of Association, dispose of Mary without warrant. Davison argued strongly against such a course. But Elizabeth retorted that it had been suggested to her by wiser persons than himself. Beale said later that Leicester had inspired the idea,[119] which seems not improbable. In any case Elizabeth would have it so.

Davison went at once to Burghley and related what had passed, thence to Walsingham to whom he passed on Elizabeth's instructions about the letter to Paulet and Drury, and so to the Lord Chancellor who had the Great Seal attached to the warrant.

Next day early Elizabeth sent Henry Killigrew to him with orders not to have the warrant sealed until she had spoken to him. He went to her and explained. She protested against his haste, declared that it might have been done in some other way and finally dismissed Davison impatiently with the remark that she wanted to hear no more of it until it was done.

Davison then went to Hatton, the Vice-Chamberlain, told the whole story, disclosed the Queen's wavering attitude and said he could do no more. He and Hatton together then went to confer with Burghley, and the three of them decided to lay the problem before the Council. Burghley read to Hatton the instructions which he had drafted for the execution, which Hatton thought went into too much detail. Burghley undertook to rewrite them and, when the Council assembled later in Burghley's chambers, Burghley submitted the revised copy.

Davison went on to say that Burghley then addressed the Council.[120] The Queen, he said, had done everything she could do. He was aware of the fact that she was wavering in her decision, but he called to mind that she had told Davison that she wanted to hear no more of it until it was done. For his part he was prepared to bear his share of the burden without troubling her further. The Council agreed, and they selected Robert Beale to carry the orders to Fotheringhay.

The following morning Elizabeth spoke to Davison again, told him of a bad dream she had, a bad dream about Mary. Davison asked her whether she was resolute to go through with the execution of the warrant. 'Her answer was yes, confirmed with a solemn oath in some vehemency.' But she once more raised the question of disposing of Mary some other way, and in the afternoon she asked whether he had heard anything from Paulet. He told her no. But he heard from Paulet a little later in the day, and took his reply to the Queen the following morning.

It is a well-known letter. The essence of it is contained in two sentences: 'My good livings and life are at her Majesty's disposition and I am ready to so leave them this next morrow if it shall so please her ... But God forbid that I should make so foul a shipwreck of my conscience or leave so great a blot to my poor posterity to shed blood without law or warrant.'[121]

It was a noble letter from a noble man, but Elizabeth did not find it to her liking. She complained of his daintiness, of his disregard of the Bond of Association which he had signed, stormed against 'the niceness of those precise fellows (as she termed them) who in words would do great things but indeed perform nothing'.

And she went on to name 'one Wingfield' who with some others would undertake it. Finally she grew weary of the debate and retired.

It is only fair to Elizabeth to point out that her preferred alternative was later endorsed both in Scotland and in France.[122] But it was not English, not even six-teenth-century English. Most of Paulet's countrymen would have shuddered, as Paulet shuddered, at the idea of assassination. To this day it is a foul blot upon the memory of the Virgin Queen.

The next morning she had another change of heart, and declared to Davison that 'it were time this matter were dispatched', swearing a great oath that it was a shame that it was not already done, considering that she had for her part 'done all that law or reason could require of her'.

This, according to Davison, was his last speech with her. The next day news came of Mary's execution.

Years later, Robert Cecil, in describing the perils of the Secretary's office observed: 'Only a Secretary hath no warrant or commission in matters of his own greatest peril but the virtue and word of his sovereign.'[123] Davison has given us his report of his interviews with Elizabeth, but it depended upon her virtue and word to validate them. It does not appear that she directly contradicted him. All she remembered, or chose to remember, of what passed between her and Davison was that she had told him to keep the matter secret and he had disobeyed. His answer was that the Lord Chamberlain knew, the Lord Chancellor knew, and she had herself told him to tell Walsingham. Under these circumstances he interpreted her injunction as not including her most intimate councillors.[124] But the Queen insisted that he had broken faith with her, and on those grounds he was sentenced to a fine of 10,000 marks and thrust into the Tower. He was released after eighteen months, his fine apparently was remitted and he continued to receive his Secretary's salary until his death twenty years later.[125] But he never recovered the Queen's favour.

Robert Beale's account of his part in the business took up the story where Davison left it.[126] Beale was Walsingham's brother-in-law, the same Beale who was one of the stoutest defenders of the Puritan position both in the Court and in the Commons. We need not follow his narrative in detail. He told how Davison called upon him at eleven o'clock on the night of February 2nd, met him the next morning at Walsingham's house and notified him that the Privy Council had selected him to carry the death warrant to Fotheringhay.

Beale went to Greenwich the next morning and appeared before a meeting of the Privy Council in Burghley's chambers. Eleven councillors were there, including Burghley, Leicester, Howard, Hatton and Davison. Walsingham was too sick to attend.[127] Burghley presided. He explained the situation to Beale, impressed upon him the need for great speed and secrecy, the danger to the Queen if his errand were known, and gave him detailed instructions as to his procedure. In order to cover Beale's real mission, he was provided with a commission to investigate hues and cries in Hertfordshire and thereabouts.[128] He was also provided with letters to Shrewsbury and to Paulet, which Burghley drafted, Davison wrote,[129] and all the councillors signed. Walsingham's signature was even obtained in his sick bed.

These instructions given, the councillors then promised among themselves not to reveal to the Queen the sending down of the warrant 'before the execution were past'.[130]

Some time before Beale left for Fotheringhay, Burghley and Walsingham together seem to have given some thought to the ritual of the execution. We have a memorandum in their two hands on the subject. Opposite Walsingham's note, 'To consider what speeches were fit for the two Earls to use at the time of the execution' Burghley has written: 'To express her many attempts both for the destruction of the Queen's person and the invasion of this realm, that the hope and comforts she hath given to the principal traitors of this realm, both abroad and here at home, are the very occasions of all the attempts that have been against her Majesty's person, and so confessed, and yet do continue, so as sure by the laws of God and man she is justly condemned to die. The whole realm hath often time vehemently required that justice might be done, which her Majesty cannot longer delay.'

Opposite Walsingham's note, 'To direct the Earls what to do in case she shall desire any private speech' Burghley has written: 'Not to refuse it so it be to three or two at the least.' Other details had to do with her servants, her jewels, her burial. Burghley noted that she should be buried in the parish church in an *uppermost* place. One interesting question was raised by Walsingham as to what should be done if the Sheriff of Northants, in direct charge of the execution 'by some great impediment cannot attend'. Burghley answered: 'The Lords at the Court to give out that there will be no execution.' A strange query and a strange answer.[131]

Beale carried out his orders, and the execution proceeded as arranged. It has been well said that nothing in Mary's life became her so well as the leaving of it.[132] When it was all over, Beale sent an account of it[133] to the Privy Council. Preserved among Burghley's papers at Hatfield is a résumé of this account in his own hand.[134] It may have been made for the Queen's perusal. That may explain why, though Burghley followed the text of the report fairly closely, he left out altogether the following passage: 'She demanded to speak with her priest, which was denied unto her, the rather for that she came with a superstitious pair of beads and a crucifix.'

This brutal intolerance smacked of Puritanism. Elizabeth would not have liked its flavour.

Reviewing the events of the momentous week which lay between Elizabeth's signing of the death warrant and Mary's execution — and there can be little doubt about the facts — it appears that the immediate responsibility for Mary's execution lay squarely on Burghley's shoulders. He must have concluded that Elizabeth favoured Mary's death but disliked to assume the responsibility for it. Long experience must have taught him that, so far as Mary was concerned, she would never take the straightforward course. And he decided to act for her. It was a calculated risk and he took it, though he made sure that all the essential orders bore the signatures of the Privy Council. It is tempting to assume that the whole procedure was by prearrangement with his mistress and that even her indignation was feigned. But the subsequent course of events does not bear out that interpretation. In any case, his decision was one of the most heroic events in his career, and it seems to have come as close as anything he ever did to accomplishing his downfall. At least he seems to have thought so. This much at least is fairly certain; had he not acted as he did, Mary would have been spared to plague Protestant England as long as she lived.

CHAPTER XIX

HENRY OF NAVARRE AND THE FRENCH SUCCESSION

O N February 11th, 1587, Secretary Wooley wrote to the Earl of Leicester:[1] 'It pleased her Majesty yesternight to call the Lords and others of her Council before her into her withdrawing chamber where she rebuked us all exceedingly for our concealing from her the proceedings in the Queen of Scots' case. But her indignation particularly lighteth most upon my Lord Treasurer and Mr. Davison ... She hath taken order for the committing of Mr. Secretary Davison to the Tower, if she continue this morning in the mood she was yesternight, albeit we all knelt upon our knees to pray the contrary. I think your Lordship happy to be absent from these broils.'

Burghley was away at the time, laid up with a bad leg got by a fall from his horse. On the day following he drafted two different[2] letters from the Council to the Queen. One was a dignified defence of their action, the other a plea that she would not allow her grief to affect her health. 'We beseech your Majesty, in your great wisdom, though you will yet continue offended against us, yet cease to grieve yourself with thinking of that which never can be revoked and let us bear your offence to our griefs until it please your Majesty either to hear us for our defence or to change your mind when you shall plainly see with your eyes and hear with your ears of all your faithful subjects that there was never any worldly act that could bring more surety to your own life, more strength to all your good subjects at home and your friends abroad, nor, contrarywise, more grieve and discomfort your enemies in seeing the anchor of their hold lost and the foundation of all their intended machinations dissolved.'

If either of these letters went off, it was probably the second one. The draft of the first one, as it survives, is torn down the middle.

The next day Burghley wrote a letter to his mistress, begging her to hear him in his own defence.[3] He could not, he wrote, speak as a Councillor because she would not hear him. He had not been able to defend himself because of his bad leg. He asked to be heard. He offered to resign from all his offices. He was ready, he said, to abide her censure, 'and to wear out the short and weak thread of my old, painful and irksome days as your Majesty shall limit them, being glad that the night of my age is so near by service and sickness as I shall not long wake to see the miseries that I fear others shall see that are like to overwatch me'. It was a pathetic letter, the letter of a sick and weary old man.

The ending of it makes clear that the charge against him of sheltering himself behind Davison was, at the outset, quite unfounded.

'And having ended what concerneth myself, I cannot in duty forbear to put your

Majesty in mind that if Mr. Davison shall be committed to the Tower, who best knoweth his own case, the example will be sorrowful to all your faithful servants and joyful to your enemies. And as I can remember many examples in your father's and your brother's and your sister's, yea in your own time, of committing Councillors either to other men's houses or to their own, so can I not remember any other example of a Councillor committed to the Tower but where they were attainted afterwards of high treason and never served afterwards. And what your Majesty intendeth towards this your servant I know not, but sure I am, and I presume to have some judgment therein, I know not a man in England so furnished vaydfully [sic] for the place he had, neither know I any that can come near him.'⁴

Burghley sent the letter to Hatton for delivery. Probably Hatton tried to deliver it and probably Elizabeth refused to receive it. Burghley wrote again four days later, asking her at least to give him a hearing:

'Finding my mind continually oppressed with grief for your displeasure and mine old body and lame limbs by night and day vexed with pain and that thereof I can imagine no remedy but by continuance of my humble intercession to your Majesty either to receive my submission or rather first to hear me answer to anything wherewith your Majesty shall charge me . . . My case alone is most miserable. For though for this late fact, for which your Majesty is deeply offended, I am no more to be charged than others, yet I find and hear by report that your Majesty doth with more bitter terms of displeasure condemn me than others. And this, I suppose, increaseth by reason your Majesty hath not heard me as you have others whom your Majesty hath admitted to your presence, which I through my lameness and infirmity, being not able of myself to come unto your presence is my principal let and stay. And yet such is my earnest desire to appear before your gracious presence as I am most willing to endure any pain, to be carried to some place, if to be laid on the floor near your Majesty's feet, there to receive your gracious censure.'

The letter is endorsed 'not received'.

It was probably at this time that Burghley sought consolation in jotting down passages from the Bible and from classical authors bearing upon his afflictions, mostly in Latin, once in Greek, setting forth such comforting phrases as 'It is better to do well and suffer than to do evil'; 'Whom the Lord loveth He chasteneth'; 'Charity is nowhere more becoming than in a prince'. He drew heavily on Job and the Proverbs, and wound up with the lugubrious cliché, 'Death brings an end to all woes'.⁵

The Queen relented a little late in February, and told Sir Thomas Cecil that, though she was not yet prepared to receive his father, she would read what he had to write. Upon that hint Burghley wrote a third letter on February 23rd.⁶ He said he found it difficult to write. He quoted a verse from the Psalms which ran: 'There is no soundness in my flesh because of thine anger.'⁷ He could not understand why she would not hear him, remembering her natural clemency and compassion, in comparison 'with this late accidental quality of your mind by only one act miscontented'. He begged again that she would receive him.

The letter is submissive to a fault, but it is to be observed that he did not admit any wrongdoing. He simply asked for a fair hearing. There was nothing cringing about his attitude.

He seems to have made no headway in the royal favour. Indeed he wrote a letter in the week following which reveals that he was genuinely alarmed.[8] The letter is a copy without signature or address. It was evidently to a close and trusted friend, well acquainted with affairs of state and in easy contact with the judges. The man who fulfils all these requirements is Sir Walter Mildmay, Privy Councillor, Chancellor of the Exchequer and second in command, under the Lord Treasurer, in the Court of Exchequer.

In the first part of the letter, Burghley alluded to the Queen's anger, particularly against Davison and himself. He went on to say that he was forbidden, or at least not licensed, to go to Court and justify his action which he was prepared to 'defend both in *foro conscientii* and in *foro humano*', adding one of the clichés which he had set down a few days earlier.[9]

The surprising part of the letter ran as follows:

'Her Majesty, I know not how, is informed that by her prerogative she may cause Mr. Davison to be hanged and that we may all be so convicted as we shall require pardon.[10]

'Hereupon yesterday, she, having Mr. J[ustice] An[derson][11] with her, and demanding whether her prerogatives were not absolute, he answered, as I hear, yea. And so, charging my Lord of Buckhurst with his assertion that she could not hang the S[ecretary] against the laws, she rebuked him bitterly and avouched Mr. J. An. answer for the same. . . .[12]

'She since hath declared the judgment of Mr. Anderson to serve her purpose and as I think, she, being led by this fearful or ill-advised judge, will have the minds of the rest of the judges understood. I have a reverent opinion of them all, but if they be not well advised to answer these questions, where the goods of men may be lost by their answers, without form and order of law, I would be loathe to live to see a woman of such wisdom as she is to be wrongly advised, from fear or other infirmity. And I think it a hard time if men for doing well before God and man shall be otherwise punished than law may warrant, with an opinion that her prerogative is above her law — nay, as the case is intended, it may be extended against the laws.

'I know surely, sir, this proceeding will seem strange and I am only fearful of the harm may grow to her reputation if it should be known.

'I pray you retain it to yourself. But yet my meaning is that you should secretly admonish the Chief Justice of [the Queen's Bench], the Chief Baron [of the Exchequer], Justice Pe[ryam][13] and [the] Chan[cellor] for of these I have good opinion for their consciences, that if they be dealt withal upon the question, to be well advised what answer they give, that no ill success follow, to be repented for want of foresight. I mind not to express what I think they should answer, but if they follow Justice Anderson's weak answer they may percase hereafter, either in themselves or their posterities, find cause of repentence.

'Now I have revealed my mind, which I protest before God is for love and duty

I bear to her Majesty, I will leave my motion to your own discretion without any mind to press you further than yourself shall think good. And when you have considered of my letter I pray you return it to me, either now or in a day hence by some trusty messenger. *Tribulatio patientiam operatur.*[14]

'My chief sickness is grounded upon ingratitude, which is worse than a continual fever.'

The letter is significant from many angles. It reveals the fact that Burghley was fearful that the Queen's irrational anger would take a form menacing to the whole reign of law. It recalls to mind that Burghley was himself a prominent member of the judiciary, both in the Court of Wards and in the Court of Exchequer. It fore-shadows the issue between prerogative and common law, which was to plague Elizabeth's successor, with Anderson in the role of a 'lion under the throne' and Burghley as Sir Edward Coke. And it was, in its concluding sentence, a *cri de cœur*. When Burghley wrote of ingratitude he must have had in mind that he had assumed the responsibility which Elizabeth had shirked. He had delivered her from the greatest single menace to her security. And all he got for his courage and his pains was her disdain and her insults.

It appears that she summoned him to Court a few days later to discuss the problem of the Low Countries. On March 15th he drafted a letter to Sir Christopher Hatton.[15]

'I am so wounded by the late sharp and most heavy speech of her Majesty to myself in the hearing of my Lord of Leicester and Mr. Secretary Walsingham, expressing therein her indignation at such time as I was called to her presence for matters of the Low Countries, myself giving no occasion by any speech of the matters of the Queen of Scots until her Majesty did charge me therewith; as since, regarding with myself the weight and nature of her Majesty's displeasure so settled and increased, and mine own humility, not able without my heart bleeding to abide the countenance of such her displeasure, I am most careful how by any means to me possible, I may shun all increase of this her Majesty's so weighty offence, knowing it very true that was said by the wise king, *Indignatio principis mors est.* And though my conscience doth witness me in the sight of God, to whose everlasting indignation and loss of my body and soul I commit myself if I say an untruth, I never had thought, nor did ever any act with thought to offend her Majesty. But now, finding this bitter burden of her Majesty's displeasure rather increased than diminished, since her Majesty, of her princely compassion, admitted me first to her service upon her late displeasure, I have cause to fear that this in-crease groweth more by means of some secret enemies than of any hard influence of her own princely nature.

'And therefore, though I cannot imagine that any person is my enemy for any private offences committed . . . but only in respect of my service to her Majesty, wherein I know I have procured of long time many mislikings for doing my duty.

'Yet, being so publicly known as I find it to be, that her Majesty is grievously offended against me, as my enemies presume her ears to be open to any calumnia-tion to be devised against me.

'Seeing I cannot devise any remedy against the malice of men that may be devised for things past, but only hope upon her Majesty's gracious interpretation by experience of my service past, yet now, in this time of her Majesty's disfavour, whereof evil disposed persons may take advantage, for any thing to be done by me presently, I think it needful for myself to live warily, and of duty to her Majesty to withdraw myself from all voluntary public actions of state whereunto I am not expressly by her Majesty commanded, until I may be relieved with such comfort to come to her presence as others have. . . .

'And having a desire to notify this much to her Majesty I do, notwithstanding, remain free and ready to do and to serve without respect of pain or peril as I understand shall best content her Majesty.'[16]

It seems probable that this letter was not sent. In any case, it reveals Burghley's state of mind in mid-March. On his draft of it he records that another letter was sent by Henry Killigrew on March 20th, but was not answered.[17]

As to Burghley's suspicion that secret enemies were working against him with the Queen, it will not be forgotten[18] that Leicester early in February had charged Burghley with double-dealing towards him in matters concerning his enterprise in the Low Countries and had threatened reprisal, and that Burghley in a letter written the very day before Mary Stuart's execution had denied the charge. A week later, when Burghley was temporarily in disgrace, he may well have thought that Leicester was feeding the Queen's wrath. It was the sort of malice to be expected of Leicester. Robert Beale declared later that Leicester had, in fact, inspired Elizabeth's attitude, that he had even suggested the imprisonment of Burghley in the Tower, but that Elizabeth would not go that far, fearing that it would be the death of him.[19] But there is at least one witness to the contrary. An anonymous letter written on March 24th to the Earl of Warwick,[20] devoted in the main to an account of proceedings in Star Chamber against Davison, ends as follows: 'Your brother [Leicester] hath merited in this, eternal memory and obligation, being the only mean from God to qualify the Queen's bitter humour and to stay the ruinous course provoked at home and abroad, which likewise concerned her Majesty's authority and credit . . . and the alienation of the greatest members of the Court and the realm.'

Evidently the writer was one of Leicester's henchmen. His appraisal of Leicester's contribution to the situation is directly at variance with Beale's, and with what we otherwise know of Leicester and his ways. There is a constant temptation to single out Leicester as the invariable villain in the piece. Burghley himself always regarded him as such. But in this case the evidence, though it establishes a presumption, is too scant to justify a verdict.[21]

Whether this be true or not, there seems to have been no immediate amelioration of the situation. On March 27th,[22] acting under orders from the Queen, the Lord Chancellor, the Archbishop of Canterbury and the two Chief Justices, called before them at the Lord Chancellor's house the Privy Councillors who had sanctioned the execution. They were challenged to justify their procedure. In reply they explained that they had been guided by Davison's report of the Queen's resolute intention to proceed to the execution and that they had proceeded swiftly and secretly, being fearful of the Queen's safety, to send down the warrant to Fotheringhay. What they did not say was that they had exchanged a promise among themselves not to reveal their action to the Queen until it was consummated.

Burghley was then questioned as to why the Council had met in his chambers. He replied that he had hurt his leg, could not move about and that Davison had assembled the Council there, without specific instructions, but as had been done several times before when Burghley was incapacitated.

Burghley was further questioned about Davison's report to him of the Queen's intention. He answered that he had asked Davison 'whether he found the Queen to continue in her mind for proceeding therein', and that Davison had answered yes.[23]

A memorandum dated April 1st, in the hand of Henry Maynard, Burghley's secretary, reveals that Burghley was questioned a second time about the matter. Maynard quotes Burghley's answers as follows:[24]

'I was not, neither do I know that any of us was commanded by her Majesty herself to write or cause the execution to be done. But how we did write and what else we did appeareth in the former answers, *without directing any point for the execution*. . . .

'To the second, there were many things which moved me and as I think the rest to write at that time as we did, wherein *we did only signify* to the two earls of Shrewsbury and Kent that the bearers of our letters did bring the Commission to them, being the two principal persons named in the same, without any other direction therein expressed for them. And where it is demanded by whose information it came to pass, it appeareth how the same came by Mr. Davison, then her Majesty's secretary. And if I should set down the particular causes with the circumstances that moved me, and as I think the rest to write at that time, my answer would be longer than as I perceive by Mr. Fortesque is required.'

We do not know whether Burghley appeared in person to answer these questions. Probably not. His answers are straightforward and in accord with the facts as we otherwise know them. He admitted that he got what he knew about the situation from Davison, but he showed no disposition to censure Davison on that account. Indeed, in his first letter to the Queen he had been outspoken in Davison's defence. Not the least amazing part of the whole amazing story is that Elizabeth in her days of indecision apparently never took counsel with Burghley nor with Hatton, nor with Walsingham nor with Leicester, the four councillors upon whom she most depended. It almost looks as though she had from the outset singled out Davison as the scapegoat.

Robert Beale, in some notes on Davison's trial, recorded that Burghley 'had set his hand to a writing whereby he confessed that he had been abused by Mr. Davison, which was produced as evidence against him'. No such writing survives. All that does survive indicates that both the Council and Burghley, as was undoubtedly the case, were content to accept Davison's statement of Elizabeth's attitude without further inquiry. It can hardly be doubted that they were well aware of the waverings of the royal mind. That explains why they pledged themselves not to reveal either their deliberations or their decision to their mistress. It is absurd to imagine that Burghley was 'abused by Davison'. If he said so, he lied. The phrase rests upon Beale's testimony, and Beale was clearly a prejudiced witness. In any case, Burghley probably said that he had gathered Elizabeth's attitude from Davison's report.[25] This was true in part. What he does not seem to have said was that both he and his colleagues in the Council were so doubtful about Elizabeth's resolution that they decided to go ahead with the warrant and say nothing to her about it until Mary was dead and gone. No one at Davison's trial inquired why neither Burghley nor Hatton sought confirmation from Elizabeth herself[26] of Davison's report. Probably they did not dare risk it. It is to be observed that neither Hatton nor Burghley was present at Davison's trial; nor were any of the other Privy Councillors who had been involved in the action. Burghley's testimony was submitted in writing.

The trial itself never brought out all the facts. Davison never revealed Elizabeth's preferred course of action by assassination. He never revealed the secret resolution of the Council to conceal their action from her. Burghley's testimony, even if it did not go so far as to maintain that Davison had 'abused' him, certainly did not disclose the basic reason for action. His inquisitors were careful not to raise the question. So was he. He could hardly have done so without charging Elizabeth with her own procrastinating tactics. Davison inevitably bore the brunt of the burden. Burghley could hardly have saved him without assuming the full burden himself, and so far he was not prepared to go. He had probably hoped that Elizabeth's indignation was largely assumed and would pass after she had satisfied herself that Mary's execution would, after appropriate gestures of protest, be accepted by Scotland and France. But when Burghley discovered that with the passing of time her disfavour towards him rather increased than diminished, he was too much concerned about himself to think of Davison. He may indeed have mistaken the royal purpose and have done what he presumed Elizabeth wanted him to do. But he never said so.[27]

On April 3rd,[28] Walsingham wrote to Leicester: 'Our sharp humours continue here still which doth greatly disquiet her Majesty and discomfort her poor servants that attend her.[29] The Lord Treasurer remaineth still in disgrace and behind my back her Majesty giveth out very hard speeches of myself, which I the easier credit for that I find in dealing with her I am nothing gracious. And if her Majesty could be otherwise served I know I should not be used.'

On April 12th Burghley wrote to Walsingham: 'I do imagine that her Majesty hath some further intention to my misliking than for my grief you will utter to me. But herein you may be bold to let me know the worst, for I am, thank God, provided of an armour of proof to defend my conscience from all assaults. And I hope in God to make profit of any adversity. For I see no cause to return to any love of court, saving always my reverence to her Majesty for whom I can do no better service than by my hearty prayer to recommend her to the favour of God by whom she reigneth.'[30]

On the 16th he wrote to Leicester: 'Why her Majesty useth me thus sharply I

know not. To some she saith that she meant not that I should have gone from the
Court, to some she saith she may not admit me nor give me audience. I shall
dispose myself to enjoy God's favour and shall do nothing to deserve her disfavour.
And if I be suffered to be a stranger to her affairs, I shall live a quiet life.'

He ended by asking Leicester to 'purchase me leave to come to the baths [at
Bath] to succeed my Lord of Warwick with my lame legs to be recovered as I hear
[his] are'.[31]

As late as June 1st one of Walsingham's intelligencers reported: 'Not many days
past, her Majesty entered into marvellous cruel speeches with the Lord Treasurer,
calling him traitor, false dissembler and wicked wretch, commending him to avoid
her presence, and all about the death of the Scottish Queen.'[32]

But evidently Elizabeth's attitude changed as June progressed. The Earl of
Derby, one of Burghley's colleagues in the Privy Council, wrote to him on June
12th: '[I am] sorry to understand that you have been so much pained of late that
you have not been able to stir out of your house. And yet I perceive you have been
often sent to by her Majesty, the messengers being her greatest Councillors to
consult of her cause, which favourable usage of her Majesty argueth the great good
will she carrieth towards you and the great account her Majesty maketh of you,
the which, even as I perceive by your letters, is to you great comfort.'[33]

An undated letter from Burghley to Walsingham was probably written not long
after the letter just cited.[34]

'My hand', Burghley wrote, 'refuseth to serve me now when I have need, but I
must not correct it but favourably bear with it as with an old servant. You see I
can be merry with you even in the midst of grief.

'I send only to inquire of her Majesty's good health for I never desire to inquire
of the contrary. Evils will come unsought for. And herewith, by my Lord
Stafford, I am bold to send my many most humble thanks for the tokens of her
Majesty's compassion of my torments by her often sending to know of my state
which I am sorry is not answerable for her service.'

Evidently the skies were brightening. On June 19th Burghley wrote to the
Earl of Shrewsbury from the royal palace at Greenwich:[35]

'I might be ashamed to have foreborne from writing to your Lordship if my
lameness of both my hands had not been the stay. And therefore, good my Lord, I
pray you make more account of my heart than of my hands, for whilst I shall live
I can make you good assurance of my heart, in sickness or in health, but of my
hands or my feet I cannot make any firm promise.

'Of her Majesty's health, of her intention to come to Theobalds the 27th hereof
and to abide there, as she saith, a fortnight or three weeks . . . your son can advise
you.'

There is no obvious explanation of the royal change of heart. The return of
Leicester to the Low Countries was probably a factor. The increasing friendliness of
James of Scotland was probably a factor. But the vagaries of the royal temperament
defy analysis. Elizabeth had a way of going berserk on occasions, but invariably
in the long run, particularly as she perceived that national sentiment ran strong

against her, she returned to sanity. It was that amazing perceptivity and resilience in her which made her the great queen that she was.

Of the royal visit to Theobalds we have no other record than a brief sentence in Burghley's diary.[36] She went late in June and was still there on July 16th.[37] But it marked — doubtless Elizabeth designed it to mark — the end of four months' estrangement, the longest in Burghley's forty years in her service. Thereafter and for the rest of his days he resumed his place beside her as her most trusted counsellor.

Though Burghley was for some four months exiled from the Court and the Queen, he continued to exercise his ordinary duties in the Privy Council,[38] the Court of Exchequer and the Court of Wards. In the session of Parliament which began on February 14th and was terminated by dissolution on March 29th, he played no part at all. On February 10th he had made some notes in preparation for the session which included a query from the Queen as to who should act for the Lord Chancellor, at the time critically ill. Burghley suggested that sometimes the Chief Justice had served in that capacity, sometimes the Lord Treasurer.[39] Elizabeth named the Chief Justice of Common Pleas. When she decided not to be present at the closing ceremonies she named a commission to act for her. Burghley had been one of the commissioners who served in that capacity at the opening of the Parliament. He was not included in the commission which dissolved it. This we may take to be another manifestation of the royal disfavour.

The disgrace of Davison imposed once again on Walsingham the whole burden of administration. He was a sick man, perennially troubled by a disorder of the kidneys which forced him to withdraw periodically from public service. Whenever that happened, Burghley, notwithstanding his own physical ills, had to take over. Between the two of them, they saw England through the critical year 1587 and made ready for the supreme test of 1588.

Before Burghley's return to Court, he was called upon to deal with a trade depression of formidable dimensions.[40] He wrote of it at length in a letter to Sir Christopher Hatton of May 12th:[41]

'My Lord, I am sorry that my pains are such as I cannot attend on you today in the Star Chamber, having yesterday, by more zeal of service in the Exchequer Chamber than of regard to my harms, so weakened and pained my leg, as I cannot stir it out of my bed; but this my declaration of my state is to no purpose to occupy your Lordship withal. This great matter of the lack of vent not only of cloths, which presently is the greatest, but of all other English commodities which are restrained from Spain, Portugal, Barbary, France, Flanders, Hamburgh and the States, cannot but in process of time work a great change and dangerous issue to the people of the realm, who, heretofore, in time of outward peace, lived thereby, and without it must either perish for want, or fall into violence to feed and fill their lewd appetites with open spoils of others, which is the fruit of rebellion; but it is in vain to remember this to your Lordship, that is so notorious as there need no repetition thereof.

'The evil being seen and like daily to increase beyond all good remedies, it is our duties that are Councillors to think of some remedies in time, before the same become remediless; and briefly the best means of remedy must follow the consideration of this evil, and so *"contrariis contraria curare"*. The original cause is apparently the contentions and enmities betwixt the King of Spain and his countries, and her Majesty and her countries. The reduction hereof to amity betwixt the Princes, and to open traffic according to the ancient treaties or intercourse, would be the sovereign remedy. . . .

'But to insist upon this remedy is as yet in vain, and therefore such other poor helps are to be thought of as may somewhat mitigate the accidents present, and stay the increase thereof, whereof when I do bethink myself, I find no one simple remedy, but rather compounded of divers simples, and to say truly they are but simple remedies, until peace may ensue, which is the sovereign sole medicine of all. To have vent increase, there must be more buyers and shippers than there are, and seeing our merchants say that they cannot have sales sufficient,

1. 'It were good that the Steelyard men were licensed to trade as they were wont to do, with condition upon good bonds that our merchant adventurers shall have their former liberties in Hamburgh.

2. 'These Steelyard merchants must also have a dispensation to carry a competent number of unwrought cloths that are coarse, which are the cloths whereof the great stay is in the Realm.

3. 'Beside this, the merchant strangers might have a like dispensation for the buying and shipping of a competent number of like white coarse cloths.

4. 'And if her Majesty, for some reasonable time, would abate only 2s. upon a cloth, I think there would grow no loss to her Majesty, having respect to the multitude of the cloths that should be carried, whereas now the strangers carry few, but upon licences, for which her Majesty hath no strangers' customs but English.

5. 'The strangers also must have liberty to buy in Blackwell Hall, or else there may be a staple set up in Westminster, out of the liberties of the City of London, which, rather than London would suffer, I think they will grant liberty to strangers in respect of the hallage money which they shall leese [lose]. Notwithstanding all these shows of remedies, I could wish that our merchant adventurers were made acquainted herewith, and to be warned, that if they shall not amend the prices to clothiers for their coarse cloths, whereby the clothiers may be reasonably apparent gainers, and that to be put in practice this next week, that then her Majesty will give authority to put the former helps in practice. Thus, my good Lord, because I understand you are to go to Court this afternoon, I have thought good to scribble, as I do (lying in pain), these few cogitations, submitting them to a more mature disquisition.'

What Burghley suggested was the opening of the export trade in cloth to those ports in Europe which were still open to English traders, heretofore a virtual monopoly in the hands of the Merchant Adventurers, to traders at large, including the Hansa merchants. He did not regard this as the best answer. Two days later he wrote to Walsingham that he thought the Queen had a better opinion of his suggestions than they deserved.

'Many of the clothiers', he wrote, 'do deserve little favour and in this time are more comforted, as I perceive, by some gentlemen of the country even for faction against the Merchant Adventurers, to whom, if her Majesty had lent some reasonable sums of money, there should need no innovation, to have notified to the world of our lacks which now to be done by proclamation will give too great triumph to the enemy.'[42]

Walsingham was of the same opinion. Burghley's letter just cited crossed one from Walsingham to him.[43]

'It is to be feared,' Walsingham wrote, 'that both the Steelyard (Hansa merchants) and other Merchant Strangers will not, in this dead time for vent, be easily drawn to enter into the trade for transporting of cloths in such numbers and at such prices as is looked for . . . It is also to be feared that the Merchant Adventurers, having so many cloths beyond the seas in their hands, will supply the foreign wants in such plentiful sort as the stranger that followeth him shall find but a cold market which, the said stranger foreseeing, will not easily enter into trade.'

Within a very few days, Burghley himself verified the soundness of Walsingham's prognostications. On May 26th he wrote to Walsingham:[44] 'I am ashamed to write it as I understand it most certainly, that notwithstanding that good quantities of cloth have been brought both to Blackwell Hall and the place at Westminster,[45] a very fit and convenient place, yet is not yet one cloth bought. And having herein had some speech with Webb, the clothier, I find in him little hope of better success, for that it is now alleged by the merchants, both English and stranger, that before they can deal with the buying of any they must understand how they may carry and vend the same in Germany . . . I perceive very well that there is no hope of relief to the clothiers by the Merchant Adventurers.'

Finally, after a year's trial, Burghley's experiment in free trade was abandoned, and the monopoly of the Merchant Adventurers was re-established.

The temptation is to ascribe his attitude in part to an antipathy towards the Merchant Adventurers, of which he had given some indication in the first decade of Elizabeth's reign.[46] But he clearly regarded freedom of trade as a *pis aller*. Like Walsingham he would have preferred the solution of the problem proposed by the Merchant Adventurers. In a discussion of the matter before the Privy Council in December, they had offered to make their customary purchases of cloth even if they had no market, provided the Queen would make them a substantial loan to finance the operation.[47] This would have relieved the unemployment among the weavers which was the government's chief concern, and which bore with particular hardship because 1586 had been a year of poor harvests and the price of corn was inordinately high. Had this policy been followed, the inevitable result would have been a further accumulation of cloths unsold. Such devices for defying the laws of supply and demand are familiar enough nowadays, and government carries the bag. That was probably what the Merchant Adventurers had in mind when they asked Elizabeth to finance the venture. She may have been shrewd enough to realize it. In any case, she would not sanction it.

And so the experiment in free trade was a failure. The enemies of the Merchant

Adventurers liked to attribute all commercial evils to their monopoly, but in fact the fault was not theirs but with market conditions. Relief came with the establishment of an outlet at Stade on the Elbe and with the opening up of the Rhine passages consequent upon the withdrawal of the Spanish from Guelderland. On top of that was an abundant harvest in 1587 and a consequent drop in the cost of foodstuffs.

During the period between the execution of Mary Stuart in February 1587 and the coming of the Spanish Armada in July 1588, foreign affairs were the most important concern of the Queen and her Council; notably those with the Low Countries and Spain, but to a lesser degree with France and Scotland.

France was deep in civil war, the so-called War of the Three Henrys — Henry III of Valois, the King; Henry Duke of Guise, the leader of the Catholic party; and Henry of Navarre, the leader of the Huguenots. The issue was primarily religious, but out of the religious issue had developed the issue of the royal succession. Henry of Navarre was not only the leader of the Huguenots but he was also the heir presumptive to the French throne. Henry III had no children and it was clear that he would have none. Failing them, Navarre was next in line. But the Catholic leaders revolted at the idea of a heretic king. Already Henry of Guise had formed a secret league with Spain to extirpate heresy. Already the Pope, Sextus V, had excommunicated Navarre and declared him unfit to rule. An alternative was found in Navarre's uncle, the decrepit Cardinal of Bourbon. So Henry of Navarre was fighting not only for his faith but for his birthright. His reply to the bull of excommunication was characteristic: 'To Sextus, who calls himself Pope — if you say that I am a heretic, by God you have lied.' And he offered to prove it. He raised again the question of the Gallican liberties. He pointed out that the leader of the Catholic party was a Lorrainer, not an authentic Frenchman. What was even more to the point, he turned out to be, notwithstanding his dissolute youth, a born leader of men, the bravest of the brave on the battlefield.

Elizabeth was well aware that Henry of Guise was her sworn enemy. She was aware of his league with Spain. The position of Henry of Navarre was equally clear. What was in doubt was the position of Henry of Valois. He had submitted to the control of Henry of Guise and had given formal sanction to his attack upon the Huguenots. But Henry of Valois feared Guise even more than he feared Navarre and was disposed to leave the one and join with the other if Navarre could be persuaded to abandon his heresy.

Such was the situation which faced Elizabeth in France. Her most influential councillors strongly urged her to support Navarre by providing money to subsidize German mercenaries. Burghley had been accused of opposing such a policy and had indignantly denied it. All that we know about his attitude in the years following indicates that he and Walsingham did their best to enlist the support of the German Protestant princes in Navarre's behalf. But the Queen as usual was reluctant to spend money. Buzenvals, Navarre's representative in London, wrote to Burghley on July 14th, 1586, that the King of Spain had offered Navarre

50,000 crowns a month if he would change his religion, and plainly implied that if help were not forthcoming Navarre might be forced to accept it.

Burghley seems to have held a long conference with Buzenvals a few days later. At any rate he drew up a memorandum on the subject[48] which was plainly designed to meet Navarre's threatened defection. It is headed 'Considerations to be had of the cause of the King of Navarre as it now seemeth to stand very dangerously both for himself, for the common cause of the Christian religion and consequently for her Majesty and state'.

'The said King, being solicited by the house of Guise and by likelihood of all his friends, servants and followers . . . who are Catholics, to yield to a peace and to a friendship with the house of Guise, it cannot be imagined but that therewith he must of consequence make profession to change his religion and to become for himself a Catholic.

'Herewith must follow these inconveniences: First, a manifest offence to Almighty God, to make a profession in religion contrary both to his own conscience and against the word of Almighty God — the horror whereof cannot be by words expressed, for that the King shall never feel quietness in his mind but shall be continually afflicted in his heart as with a worm perpetually biting the same;

'Secondly, hereby he shall endanger all his friends both in France and elsewhere in Christendom that have ventured their lives and all their worldly goods for his defence;

'Thirdly, he shall never have like assurance of friendship of the Catholics as he now hath of the Protestants, for that the Protestants do love him with a bond of conscience, the Catholics shall love him but so far forth as he may be profitable to them, and they will also always doubt him for changing of religion, or for revenge. . . .

'For staying of him from these dangerous courses he may be informed that the Queen's Majesty hath yielded to as much in money to be delivered in Germany as was at the first desired, which is 100,000 crowns,[49] so that, with such help as others his servants shall procure with the help of Casimir and the other princes and also with the help that is certainly accorded by the Swiss, there remaineth good hope that the army may be ready to enter into France by November. Likewise it is to be remembered how her Majesty hath ready such a sum of money in France, even in Paris, as was required by the princesses of Bourbon to enterprise great actions in his favour when the army should enter. And that purpose of those princesses doth still continue firm and to very great purpose. And if the King shall not persist in his action but shall alter the same, those princesses, being of the blood, shall be in great hazard for their friendship towards him.

'Lastly, if the King shall find his peril so great as, before the army can come, he shall be in danger to be besieged in La Rochelle, the Queen may offer that, for safety of his person, she will spare no charge, by the strength of her navy to bring him safe into England, maugre all the forces of France on the seas.

'And so his person, being here, free, all his friends, all his forces, shall be as ready to restore him as if he were still in France. And no doubt but the French

King, by the end of this year [will] be so exhausted as he shall not be able to begin any such wars in France as he hath done this year.

'And when the King shall be here, the right of his title in succession shall not be impaired, considering it is not to take place but by the French King's death. And during his life the King of Navarre's right cannot be impeached by any present possessor.'[50]

The support of Navarre which Burghley had outlined in the memorandum was produced, and Navarre's agent in Germany wrote to Burghley in September that he was the chief instrument in producing it.[51]

But what Elizabeth furnished was not enough, and the expected financial aid from German Protestant princes was not forthcoming. Nevertheless, Duke Casimir proceeded to muster his forces, though the invasion which Burghley had expected was delayed until August of the following year. The money deposited in Paris to which Burghley refers seems to have amounted to 18,000 crowns,[52] and was intended to bribe the Counts of Soissons and Montpensier, two Catholic princes of Bourbon, to support Navarre.

The delay in the German invasion was largely due to lack of funds. Walsingham wrote to Leicester on April 11th, 1587: 'By the gentleman from Duke Casimir, you will learn in what hard terms the preparations there for supporting the King of Navarre are in because of the coldness of certain princes there who promised to contribute. If this gentleman speak truth, without some further contribution from her Majesty, the money already advanced will be lost and the poor King of Navarre, from want of assistance, overthrown. And unless it shall please God to dispose her Highness' heart otherwise . . . so far off is she from any inclination to yield any further supply as she seemeth altogether bent to have the said preparation stayed.'[53]

However, the German army, nothing like so large as had been promised and already grumbling for lack of pay, got under way in August.[54] In September it came to a halt in Lorraine, the soldiers refusing to advance further until they were paid. On the 7th of the month, John Wooley, Elizabeth's Latin Secretary, who seems to have been serving as her personal secretary during Walsingham's illness, wrote to Burghley that the Queen was much disturbed by the news and wanted Burghley's advice. He wrote at once, sending a copy to Walsingham who was home sick.

Walsingham acknowledged it in a brief note as follows: 'Your letter to Mr. Wooley I have perused. It was not possible for your Lordship to write more earnestly or more effectually than you have done.'[55]

But Burghley was not hopeful. In answer to Walsingham's note he wrote: 'I see nothing likely to work her Majesty danger but seeking to spare that which shall never save her if she lose her opportunities of her parties in France and the Low Countries. But hereof I can say nothing more than I did in my letter to Mr. Wooley which it pleaseth you to allow. I fear nothing more than that her Majesty by her own coldness and temporizing shall be forced to sing *haud putaram*. And yet she will throw it upon some of us. But therein I will have afore God a clear conscience. And yet this mischief will go onward. . . .

SIR CHRISTOPHER HATTON

'As you write, it is likely I shall be sent for shortly and then I will be ready, having no mind otherwise, for in very truth I have no hope to have my advices allowed.

'And so, resting this night in a mammering[56] whether to go unsent for or no, I think tomorrow to determine further, whereof you shall know, whether I have time to come by you or no as I promised. From my house at Theobalds.'

This letter can leave little doubt about Burghley's position, and no doubt at all that he and Walsingham were in complete accord.

Three days later Burghley wrote to Walsingham from Court: 'I was entreating with her Majesty about the matters of the King of Navarre for relief of the reiters and with much argument her Majesty yielded to have Palavicino to be sent for, to understand in what time he could provide by exchange a portion of 50,000 crowns in Germany . . . So as I thought the matters should proceed in good sort. And as I was rising to go from her Majesty with intent to send for Palavicino and to advise you, one of your grooms brought your packet towards me, which, her Majesty seeing, took into her hands and would needs see all the writing, and upon reading of the French letter sent to Mr. Stafford[57] she took great hold to alter her by reading the sentence . . . alleging that the Swiss were well contented, desirous of nothing but of bread and not to be naked and the others contented also with their pay of a half month, looking by promise for no more until they should meet with the King of Navarre. So as she framed a conclusion that there was no need of money, and to confirm this she said that Palavicino had reported to her the like. To which I answered that I thought the compact very absurd and not to be believed that they should be content to lack pay until they should meet with the K. of Navarre . . . Well, her Majesty stood upon her conceit adding that Palavicino had affirmed the like, and I stood as fast in my opinion to the contrary.

'Afterwards I went to Council and in the meantime her Majesty . . . sent for him [Palavicino] and spake with him without my knowledge. And afterwards I, finding of him, he told me that her Majesty had questioned with him, moving him to remember such a speech, but he answered her that in part it was true . . . but this he added, that if the same [meeting with Navarre] should not happen within 40 days after their first entry, then they should, at the end of the 40 days, have their full days. But yet her Majesty, as he said, would gladly conclude that they should not need to have her money. And yet I mind to follow my first course . . . What may follow tomorrow I know not, but I hope well, for I see she seeth the danger. And so I take my leave, being almost asleep.'

This letter gives us a clear picture of the Virgin Queen in action — trying to save money, seizing upon a packet of letters not intended for her, pitching upon a clause which sustained her position in a letter which Stafford had sent, getting hold of Palavicino, the banker who was handling the transfer of funds to Germany, behind Burghley's back, insisting that Palavicino also sustained her position, ignoring his qualifying clauses. It was no easy matter to deal with such a lady. But Burghley persisted.

The next day he wrote to Walsingham again: 'For relief of the army in France

N

Mr. Palavicino will report to you how we have gone in and out but no final conclusion.'

Six days later he wrote: 'At my coming to the Court afore six I understood that her Majesty looked earnestly for my coming. And so, nevertheless, when she understood that I was come and offered to wait on her, she sent me word that I should stay until this morning. And within a while after, Mr. Wooley came and told me that he had written by her Majesty's commandment that I should deliver out no money for Palavicino, for, he added, that by Sir Edward Stafford's last letter she saw no need thereof. Hereupon I have written to Palavicino that he should stay in his hands all that he had received, for I had given order for £2000 to be paid him and meant within two days to pay more. Thus you see how her Majesty can find means at small holes to stop her own light. And so must I tell her today what danger she seeketh to spare.'[58]

Already Elizabeth had advanced 100,000 crowns, or something over £30,000. Burghley and Walsingham between them were asking for more. At the time Casimir's army, decimated by disease, savage from hunger and embittered by lack of pay, was wandering about in eastern France, without much guidance or much discipline, chiefly engaged in pillaging. Possibly if money had been forthcoming for their pay, they might have been shaped into an effective fighting force. As it was, they rapidly disintegrated and finally straggled back to Germany, having accomplished practically nothing except the diversion of the Guisan armies from Navarre. It was hardly Elizabeth's fault. Had Casimir's other supporters contributed as she had contributed, what they had promised, the result might have been different. Burghley and Walsingham both felt that their mistress would have done well to supply what was lacking. But she did not see it that way.

In the following year another German expedition was contemplated, and Elizabeth was for a time prepared to advance £4000, but she changed her mind before the money was paid, and the expedition was abandoned.

One complicating factor in Anglo-French relations was the strange behaviour of Sir Edward Stafford, English ambassador at Paris since 1583.[59] Stafford's political career and his political and religious convictions were largely determined by his family connections. On his father's side he was closely connected with Queen Elizabeth herself. His father's first wife was Mary Boleyn, Elizabeth's aunt. This connection, though Sir Edward was the child of a later marriage, gave him a special claim upon the Queen's attention. His mother, Dorothy Stafford, was the child of a union between the house of Stafford and the house of Pole, both of which had cherished pretensions to the English throne. Her paternal grandfather, the Duke of Buckingham, had lost his head on that score in 1521, and her brother, Sir Thomas Stafford, had lost his for the same reason in 1557. It is not unlikely that this tremendous birthright had a definite effect upon Stafford's fortunes. The consciousness that he had royal blood in his veins may account for his restlessness and his impatience and his condescending attitude towards such parvenus as Leicester and Walsingham. His mother was Elizabeth's Mistress of the Robes and one of the Queen's favourite ladies-in-waiting. She enjoyed a considerable influence at Court and was in an excellent position to promote her son's interests.

Sir Edward's second wife contributed another significant factor in the shaping of his public career. She was Douglas Howard, granddaughter of Thomas Howard, the hero of Flodden Field and sister of Lord Admiral Howard of Armada fame. She was the cast-off mistress of the Earl of Leicester, cherished a passionate hatred of him and, like almost all the Elizabethan Howards, was secretly inclined to Roman Catholicism. Her influence on Stafford, whom she married in 1578, was great. She certainly stimulated, if she did not create, his hostility to Leicester, and was no doubt partly responsible for his leanings towards the Roman Catholic party.

In the year of his marriage he entered the royal service as special envoy to France in connection with the Alençon courtship, and during the next four years was chiefly occupied with that business. He established close contacts in France, particularly among Alençon's followers; with Simier and Marchemont he was especially intimate. They seem to have encouraged his naturally extravagant habits, particularly his love of gaming. He admitted later that he had lost some six or seven thousand crowns in play with them.

From the very beginning of his public career, Stafford enrolled himself under Burghley's banner and professed to be Burghley's man. He was almost equally frank in proclaiming his hostility to Leicester. As a natural consequence, he provoked the antagonism of both Leicester and Walsingham.

He went to France as ambassador in the autumn of 1583. From the first the English Catholic refugees in France and the agents of Mary Stuart there had hopes of Stafford. Not long after his arrival, Charles Paget came to see him. 'I mean to use them all well,' he wrote to Walsingham, 'if they come to me.'

Stafford's professed intention was to pretend to favour the Roman Catholic cause in order to get information serviceable to the Queen. He therefore entertained the advances of Lord Paget and of Charles Arundel, who had fled from England to France in the autumn of 1583 after the discovery of the Throgmorton Plot, in which they were both implicated. Walsingham warned him to be careful. 'Her Majesty', Walsingham wrote, 'hath willed me to signify to you that she is assured that the alliance that my lady your wife hath with them shall not make you to be more remiss to perform your duty towards her.'

Stafford at once took offence, and from this time forward appears to have been convinced of Walsingham's hostility towards him. Of Walsingham's attitude towards Stafford, nothing more is to be gathered up to the end of 1584 than that he shrewdly suspected that two of Stafford's servants, Lilly and Moody, were dealing secretly with Catholic refugees. Stafford did not deny it. It was an old trick, to use pretended Catholics to ensnare Catholics, which Burghley and Walsingham had often used. Indeed, Stafford even suggested that his undercover operation might be regarded at Court with some distrust as a way of removing Catholic suspicion of double dealing. At least as late as the end of the year 1584 the integrity of Stafford himself does not seem to have been questioned.

Indeed it was not until a year later that evidence against him began to accumulate. In January 1586 Walsingham completed his arrangements for intercepting the captive Mary Stuart's correspondence, and late in February he caught a large bundle of letters to her which had been accumulating at the French embassy, among them one dated in January 1585 from the Archbishop of Glasgow, Mary's ambassador at Paris, describing an interview with Stafford at which he had professed to be Mary's very affectionate servant, one from Thomas Morgan to the same effect and another from Glasgow in March 1586, reporting that Stafford had promised to intercede with Burghley on Mary's behalf.

With this evidence at hand, Walsingham addressed an inquiry about Stafford to Thomas Rogers, one of his secret agents who had been spying upon English Catholic refugees in France and who returned to England early in 1586. In reply, Rogers charged Stafford with revealing state secrets to Charles Arundel and with providing facilities for Catholic refugees to dispatch letters and messages to their friends in England. The gravest of the charges was that Stafford was being successfully bribed by the Duke of Guise to show him English dispatches.

We might dismiss these charges as proceeding from a tainted source if it were not for a dispatch on the same subject written at about the same time by Bernardino de Mendoza, sometime Spanish ambassador to England but in 1586 resident Spanish ambassador in Paris, to Philip II, which ran as follows: 'Charles Arundel, an English gentleman to whom your Majesty granted eighty crowns pension a month in respect of the Queen of Scots, was constantly in the house of the English ambassador ... which Muzio [the Duke of Guise] assures me was at his instructions, as the English ambassador was needy and he, Muzio, had given him 3000 crowns. In return for this the ambassador gave him certain information through this Charles Arundel.'

By the end of the year 1586 these facts about Stafford can fairly be said to be well substantiated: First, that Walsingham suspected him of treachery; second, that Mary Stuart's most active agents in France believed that Stafford might be serviceable in Mary's cause; thirdly, that one of Walsingham's agents in France directly accused Stafford of selling information to the Duke of Guise; and fourthly, that this accusation is confirmed from Spanish sources. None of these charges[60] absolutely proves that Stafford had treacherous intentions towards his sovereign. He himself maintained that he was merely posing as a traitor in order to learn more completely the plans and purposes of Elizabeth's enemies. But Walsingham at any rate was convinced that he was not a safe man to have in France. In October 1586 he was urging the Queen to recall him.[61]

Burghley's position is hard to appraise because, with the exception of one important letter on the subject, none of his letters in his long and intimate correspondence with Stafford has been found. He was deluged with letters from Stafford, largely given over to defence of his own questionable behaviour and to violent attack upon Walsingham, Leicester and the agents of the King of Navarre. We know from Stafford's acknowledgments that Burghley wrote frequently to him, but the acknowledgments give no inkling of the contents of his letters. This fact in itself is suspicious. It suggests that Burghley ordered his letters to be destroyed or returned, as he had on many occasions in the past. His one surviving letter, of

October 1586,[62] dealt with the indications of a favourable attitude towards Mary Stuart revealed by her intercepted correspondence. Burghley exonerated Stafford from the charge and said that he would oppose his recall. But it is to be noticed that he called upon Stafford to explain other charges against him. Not much can be argued from this one letter, except that Burghley defended Stafford at a time when they were both under attack.

It can hardly be supposed that Stafford would have attacked both Walsingham and Leicester in his letters to Burghley unless he was convinced of a sympathetic response. With respect to Leicester, Stafford's conviction was sound enough. But Burghley made his peace with Walsingham early in the following year, and during the critical years following, indeed until Walsingham's death in the spring of 1590, was on the best of terms with him. So that Stafford's efforts to discredit Walsingham and what he took to be Walsingham's policies missed fire.

It is not surprising that Burghley accepted the role of Stafford's best friend at Court. The man was of the blood royal and his mother was one of the most influential of Elizabeth's ladies-in-waiting. In both these capacities he offered a counterpoise to the Court influence of Leicester. But Burghley's policy is not to be identified with Stafford's; certainly not to be identified with Stafford's treachery. The really indefensible part of Stafford's performance — his betrayal of state secrets to the King of Spain, of which more presently — Burghley never discovered. It even eluded the argus eyes of Francis Walsingham.

Stafford's policy in France ran directly counter to that of both Burghley and Walsingham. While he distrusted the King of Navarre, he did his best to lure the King of France from his alliance with the Guises and the League. He believed that Henry III was eager to escape from his bondage to the League and would join forces with Henry of Navarre if Navarre would abandon his inconvenient religious scruples and return to the Catholic faith. He sought to induce Elizabeth to promote that policy, and on two occasions seems to have tried to prevent financial aid to Casimir.[63]

In April of 1587 Stafford had an interview with Mendoza, received 2000 crowns and undertook to devote himself to whatever service the King of Spain required.[64] From that time forward he was supplying information to Mendoza and his conduct of French affairs was coloured by that fact.[65] A case in point occurred the following month. Stafford had sent word to Walsingham early in May that a group of Frenchmen had offered to furnish the Queen with a *pied à terre* on the French coast near Calais, presumably at Gravelines, if she would finance the venture in the amount of 50,000 crowns. The proposal evidently appealed to Burghley. He wrote to Walsingham in June: 'My principal cause of writing is to pray you not to let the opportunity of Gravelines pass for a small sum of money. The glory shall be great to her Majesty many ways to have the old fox La Motte [governor of Gravelines] overreached in his own den, to have a neighbourhood to Calais which will in the sight of the world [be] a subject of many deep judgments. Surely I am with child with this more than with any other offer.'

As it turned out, Elizabeth rejected the offer.[66]

This is all that we have on the subject from English sources. But the Spanish dispatches reveal the fact that Stafford had passed on the news of the proposal to Mendoza early in May, and what little we know about it comes from Mendoza's dispatch to Philip II. When Stafford heard from Walsingham that Elizabeth had rejected the offer, he transmitted that information to Mendoza forthwith.

From that time forward, every important move which Stafford made in his official capacity Mendoza knew about, even the fact that Stafford had appropriated to his personal use the funds sent to Paris for winning over the Count of Sessions. Charles Arundel served as go-between. After his death in December 1587, Mendoza established direct contact with Stafford, going to his house at night. On one occasion Stafford showed him the latest official dispatches from England.

Most of what Mendoza got had to do with the movements of Sir Francis Drake and the English fleet. But one can get a fairly complete picture of Anglo-French relations in 1587 and 1588 from what he told the Spanish ambassador. On one occasion, having news that Elizabeth was planning to support another German invasion of France, he asked Mendoza whether it would be in the Spanish interest for him to try to prevent this or not — boasting that he was able to arrange the matter as the King of Spain would direct.[67]

Under these circumstances it is not surprising to discover that Stafford's account of his secret interview with the French King on February 24th, 1588, which Stafford had promised to reveal to no one but Elizabeth herself,[68] was in Mendoza's hands, probably even before the Queen herself received it.

All that Stafford reported to England about the French situation must be looked at askance. It does appear that, in the spring of 1588, Elizabeth made a definite effort to induce Henry III to take a stand against the Guises and to reconcile himself with the King of Navarre. But since she would not urge Navarre to change his religion and since Henry would not consider the matter on any other terms, her efforts were fruitless. What she had in mind, of course, was the imminence of the Spanish Armada and the fear that French ports along the Channel would be open to the Spanish fleet. But Henry III, failing the support of Navarre, was forced to yield to the pressure of the League. On July 15th, when the Armada was well on its way, a peace was signed between the King and Henry of Guise, and the old league between France and England declared broken. So the situation in France was as unfavourable as it might be when the Armada sailed up the Channel.

CHAPTER XX

PEACE OVERTURES, 1587-88

FRANCE in 1587 and 1588 was in too disordered a state to constitute a serious threat to the security of England. The real menace came from Spain. In the face of this menace, English policy was directed (1) to the support of the Low Countries; (2) to the efforts to make peace; (3) to military and naval preparations to meet an impending Spanish attack. These three aspects of English policy developed simultaneously, but it will make for clarity if we pursue them separately.

The problem of the Low Countries focused on the person of the Earl of Leicester, his relations to the Queen, to his colleagues in the Privy Council, to other Englishmen engaged in Low Country affairs and to the government of the Low Countries. Elizabeth, though she did not give Leicester the support he asked for, gave him a large measure of personal affection. His position in the royal favour was never higher than it was during the interval between the spring of 1587 and his death in the early autumn of 1588. Neither Burghley nor Walsingham cherished any illusions on that score. They both worked against him underhand, but they both professed complete accord with him in their personal relations. Very little of the running correspondence between Burghley and Leicester during the period survives, and what little does survive is for the most part from Leicester to Burghley. The Walsingham-Leicester correspondence is much more voluminous,[1] and much more revealing, but evidently both Burghley and Walsingham in their relations to Leicester were playing the same double game.

The reports of Walsingham's agents make it clear that what he learned from them was directly at variance with what he said to Leicester, and those whom Leicester singled out for attack looked largely to Burghley for their defence. But this was all *sub rosa*. Everybody knew what a vindictive fellow Leicester was and everybody knew that he could almost certainly count upon royal support. Thomas Wilkes, John Norris and Lord Buckhurst all discovered this to their sorrow, though Norris's mother was one of Elizabeth's favourite ladies-in-waiting and Buckhurst a Privy Councillor.

The period between the execution of Mary Stuart early in February 1587 and the following June was a period in which Elizabeth seems to have been chiefly concerned with clearing her own skirts of any responsibility for Mary's death. Burghley was away in disgrace, Walsingham in great disfavour. He wrote to Leicester on April 10th: 'The present discord between her Majesty and her Council hindereth the necessary consultation that were desired for the prevention of the manifold perils that hang over the realm.' And again, a week later: 'I never found her

391

Majesty less disposed to take a course of prevention of the approaching mischief towards this realm than at the present. And to be plain with your Lordship there is none here that hath either credit or courage to deal efficiently with her in any of her great causes. Mr. Vice-Chamberlain [Hatton] who returned to this court on Saturday last hath dealt very plainly and dutifully with her, which hath been accepted in so evil part as he is resolved to retire for a time. I assure your Lordship I find every man weary of attendance here.'[2]

Both Burghley[3] and Walsingham strongly urged that Leicester be sent back to the Low Countries. The reasons for this had little to do with his fitness for the service. He had already revealed his incapacity to get on with the Dutch, had antagonized their leaders, Barnevelt and Maurice of Nassau, and had done his best to sow dissension among them by supporting hare-brained democrats like Colonel Sonoy in north Holland and Deventer in Utrecht. He had quarrelled with his best soldier, John Norris, and with his wisest counsellor, Thomas Wilkes. He had revealed no skill either as a soldier or an administrator. His great asset, indeed his only asset, was his favour with the Queen. Despite all his shortcomings, his presence in the Low Countries was more likely to keep Elizabeth faithful to her engagements there than that of any other commander.

That was probably what weighed most with Burghley and Walsingham, since both of them believed that the support of the Dutch rebels was essential to the safety of England. Mixed with this motive was a strong urge to get Leicester out of England and out of Court. He was coming to be regarded as Elizabeth's evil genius. Certainly she was more manageable and more reasonable in his absence than in his presence.

Her own hesitation in consenting to his return to the Low Countries proceeded partly from a desire to keep him at her side, partly from her inveterate reluctance to spend money, partly from a hope of peace with Spain.[4]

Early in March she went so far as to send Lord Buckhurst, one of her Privy Councillors, to the Low Countries to investigate the situation. He reported that two things were necessary: one was money to pay the Queen's soldiers and the other was the return of the Earl of Leicester. Buckhurst remained in the Low Countries until Leicester's arrival in June. Before he left he had incurred the enmity of Leicester and, through Leicester's misrepresentations, of the Queen. Burghley[5] and Walsingham both befriended him as much as they dared, but without success. When he got home he was banished from the Court and confined to his own house. He was not restored to royal favour until after Leicester's death.

One or two of his observations on Leicester are worth recording.

'How lamentable a thing it is,' he wrote to Walsingham in July,[6] 'and how doth *Leicester abuse her Majesty*, making her authority the means to justify and under her name to defend and maintain all his intolerable errors which, I thank God for, that neither his might nor his malice shall deter me in the laying open of all things which my conscience knoweth.' On another occasion he wrote: 'It [the command] had been better bestowed upon a meaner man of more skill.'[7]

At one time Leicester charged Buckhurst with an ambition to take over the government of the Low Countries; at another with responsibility for the loss of Sluys to the enemy. Buckhurst commented on this latter charge in a letter to Walsingham: 'I account his accusation of the loss of Sluys to be so ridiculous as, except he will also charge me with taking the Tower of London, I mean not to answer it.'[8]

Leicester was quite prepared to return to the Low Countries, but only upon condition that the Queen would send money to pay the soldiers and lend him £10,000 to meet his personal expenses.

Walsingham worked hard to secure the Queen's assent; as usual she wavered. On April 10th she would have none of it.[9] On the 14th she agreed to the £10,000 loan provided it was repaid within a year. On May 2nd the matter was still doubtful.[10] As late as May 23rd Walsingham wrote to Burghley:

'Yesterday at the earnest request of the Earl of Leicester I did press her Majesty to grow to some present resolution touching his employment, letting her understand that the same could abide no delay, the harvest approaching so fast as it doth. But after long argument I could draw no conclusion from her. I found some disposition in her rather to use my cousin [John] Norris than the earl. I did humbly pray her (the matter importing her as it doth), that it might be considered of by certain of her choice Councillors, which motion was also rejected.'

Burghley, of course, was still in exile and could do nothing, though Walsingham wrote him again on the 26th: 'I wish your Lordship here so as it might stand with your health, to the end there might be some resolution taken in the great causes.'[11] Evidently Burghley was well on his way back to the royal favour. It may have been due to him that Elizabeth finally dispatched Leicester late in June. Burghley, with Walsingham's assistance, drafted his instructions.[12]

They dealt with the re-establishment of his authority and the promotion of the peace negotiations. So far as his authority was concerned, Elizabeth was even prepared to sanction the original offer of the Estates which had driven her to a fine frenzy in 1586. So far as the peace was concerned, Leicester was charged to approach the leaders of the people, even before he raised the question with the Estates General. The order of procedure was important because it seemed to ratify his cultivation of the democratic faction which both Wilkes and Buckhurst held to be disastrous.[13] In fact Leicester got in his instructions what Leicester wanted. The important thing was to get him away.

One of the impelling motives which induced Elizabeth to dispatch Leicester was Parma's progress in the siege of Sluys, the possession of which would give him a good port on the Channel from which to launch an attack on England. Leicester's first business after his arrival was to organize forces for the relief of Sluys. His efforts proved inadequate. If the Dutch had co-operated with their navy, the campaign might have succeeded. But they refused. One reason for their refusal was their distrust of Leicester and their increasing fear that the English were trying to get towns in order to improve their bargaining power with Parma.[14] In any case, Sluys fell (July 29th)[15] though Sir Roger Williams, in command of the defence, put up a gallant fight, which provoked Parma's admiration and Leicester's jealousy.

Walsingham wrote to Leicester on August 2nd: 'The ill success of Sluys, though your Lordship hath done your uttermost for the relief thereof, hath wrought some alteration in her Majesty's favour towards you and causeth her to pick some quarrels to your L.'s proceedings in that action . . . I find there is some dealing underhand against your L. which proceedeth from the younger sort of our courtiers that take upon them to censure the greatest causes . . . a disease I do not look to be cured in my time.'[16]

If we are to believe William Herle, Walter Raleigh was the leader of the opposition. The young Earl of Essex, Leicester's step-son, sprang to his defence.[17]

Walsingham referred to the matter again in a letter to Leicester of August 7th. 'The loss of Sluys', he wrote, 'hath wrought some alteration of her favour towards you and also towards the cause itself; in such sort as she seemed bent and resolved to abandon those countries and to have revoked your Lordship presently. But now this overture of peace, whereof before she seemed, upon the loss of Sluys, to be in despair, hath calmed these sharp humours . . . The Lord Admiral stood very friendly for you to her Majesty, being very well backed by the Lord Chancellor and my Lord Treasurer, who did let her Majesty very roundly and plainly understand how greatly this hard course towards you would not only discourage you but all others that should be employed in public service, to be charged in that sort your L. is with other men's errors. And further that if the States learn of it all could go upside down and make you unfit to deal either for war or peace. She promised that she would forbear to give out any speeches of dislike, denying that she had delivered any but to one or two of her Council, though the Court is full of it.'[18]

Leicester was alarmed. He found himself *persona non grata* among the Dutch and rapidly growing out of favour with his mistress.

Most of his surviving letters home are directed in the main to attacks upon those whom he chose to regard as his enemies and to requests to be recalled.

Of Burghley we hear nothing. He evidently carried on an active correspondence with Leicester, but none of his letters seems to have survived. From Leicester's surviving letters to him it is clear that they were on friendly terms.

It may be presumed that Burghley, like Walsingham, had reached the conclusion that Leicester's policy in the Low Countries was so damaging to the cause that he had better be got home. Elizabeth told Essex in September that no lady in England could more desire Leicester's presence than she did, but that she feared any sudden recall would create the impression that she was abandoning the Dutch.[19]

Her real reason was that she was looking to Leicester to persuade the Dutch to participate in the negotiations for peace. Leicester for his part was loath to do so. His failure to do so irritated Elizabeth not a little. Late in September, when Walsingham was away ill, she directed Burghley to draft a letter to the Estates General, in which she set forth her intentions regarding peace and censured Leicester for not having taken up the question with them earlier.[20] The letter seems to have been sent, but Leicester postponed its delivery and wrote to the Queen a long letter in his own defence, protesting that the letter if delivered would ruin his credit and dishonour him. She apparently acquiesced, but charged Leicester to deliver the substance of her message to the Estates. After that Leicester's one idea was to get home, expending his energies in the meanwhile in sowing dissension and in trying to get more towns into his hands. He wrote to Burghley in November that the cause was lost.[21] In the same month Elizabeth recalled him and he got away early in December.[22]

He reached England on the 9th. According to a Spanish intelligencer, he was well received by his mistress but badly by the people.[23] Unlike Essex, his successor in the royal favour, Leicester, notwithstanding his Puritan connections and his democratic professions, was never a popular figure.

Camden tells the story,[24] which lacks confirmation from other sources, that 'Buckhurst and others' intended, upon Leicester's return, to summon him before the Council and call him to account for his mismanagement in the Low Countries. According to Camden, Leicester appealed to Elizabeth, 'cast himself down privately at the Queen's feet with tears', and begged her protection; and she intervened and saved him. Camden can hardly have made up the story though he may have elaborated it in the telling. In any case, Leicester stepped back at once into the royal favour.

When he left the Low Countries, he did not relinquish his authority but placed the Council of State in general charge and Peregrine Bertie, Lord Willoughby, in command of the English forces. Willoughby's mother, Katherine of Suffolk, had been one of Burghley's oldest friends.[25] At the same time Henry Killigrew, Burghley's brother-in-law, was the English representative on the Dutch Council of State. Burghley was therefore in a strong position to follow the development of affairs in the Low Countries. Most of what we know about his connections comes from the voluminous correspondence he carried on with Willoughby. Unfortunately, here again we have only the incoming letters; Burghley's end of the correspondence is missing. It is clear that he had a good deal to do with Low Countries affairs even at the administrative level. He and Walsingham together seem to have been responsible for the definition of the Queen's programme of assistance to the Dutch, which she sent to Willoughby on March 1st, fixing the annual charge at £125,389 13s. 4d. And Burghley drafted many of the Queen's letters.

Up until Leicester's formal resignation in March 1588, Elizabeth continued to support the policy he had pursued. He had undertaken to build up a party in the Low Countries out of those elements in a confused situation which opposed Barneveldt and Maurice of Nassau and the oligarchy and sought to establish what Burghley had once called scornfully 'a popular government'. The party received strong support from the militant left-wing Calvinist members of the Dutch clergy. In short, Leicester's programme in the Low Countries was analogous to the programme of the left-wing Puritans in England.

It is absurd to assume that Queen Elizabeth, a resolute opponent of Puritanism and 'popularity' if ever there was one, consciously endorsed such a programme. Infatuated as she appears to have been, she simply accepted Leicester's friends as her friends. But she never went further than to advocate their cause to the Dutch.

She never sent them money or troops. There is no record of any discussion of the matter in the Privy Council, nor of any dissenting voice from Burghley or Walsingham or Hatton. In the Low Countries, Willoughby and Killigrew apparently concurred. Willoughby even went so far as to advocate armed intervention in behalf of the Leicestrians.

After Leicester's resignation, he apparently lost interest in the Low Countries,[26] and the royal policy became increasingly conciliatory to Barneveldt and his associates.[27] Thanks largely to Willoughby's efforts, the popular leaders in north Holland, Utrecht and elsewhere were brought to terms. And when the Armada came up the Channel in July, the Dutch governors and the Queen were on relatively friendly terms.

During the period from midsummer 1587 until the arrival of the Armada in July 1588, Burghley's services appear to have been divided between seeking for peace and preparing for war.

The actual peace manœuvres seem to have been mainly under his control. Most of the surviving material on the subject takes the form of a running correspondence between him and Andrea de Loo, chiefly of letters from him to Burghley.

De Loo's position was a rather ambiguous one. He was an Italian merchant, primarily interested in the re-establishment of trade. It does not appear that he had official credentials either from Elizabeth or from Parma. He wrote in Italian, but he seems to have been an accomplished linguist and something of a classical scholar. On more than one occasion in his letters to Burghley he quoted from Virgil's *Eclogues*. He appears to have received some compensation from Elizabeth, and though his enemies declared that he was highly paid by both parties he swore that he never had a penny from Parma and that after two years' effort he was on the verge of financial ruin. Financial ruin was a chronic complaint of all those in public service.

His technique was to persuade Parma that Elizabeth was eager for peace and to persuade Elizabeth that Parma was eager for peace, discounting or minimizing the objections raised by both sides. He went so far as to tell Parma that Elizabeth would raise no difficulties over religious issues and to tell Elizabeth that Parma had plenary powers to treat and would arrange for a cessation of arms not only in the Low Countries but also in Spain as soon as English commissioners arrived to negotiate a peace — neither of which was true.

Actually he was encouraged by both parties to persist.

From the beginning Parma had no powers and no intentions to agree to a peace on any terms likely to be acceptable to England. His objective was to stimulate English hopes of peace in order to slacken English preparations to resist Spanish invasion.

In England the Privy Council, almost to a man, was opposed to peace. The one exception was Sir James Croft, the Controller, who had been removed from the command of Berwick early in the reign[28] for treasonable correspondence with the enemy and who had been for some years a pensioner of Spain. Elizabeth's attach-

ment to Croft is something of a mystery. It may stem from the time before she
was queen when he was implicated in Wyatt's rebellion. He may even have been
in the Tower when she was. And she never forgot her friends of those dark days.
In any case, she appointed him to the Privy Council in 1570. In that capacity he
was steadily pro-Spanish. He had been one of the chief instigators of the peace
movement in its initial stages but, no doubt at the Queen's bidding, Burghley
himself took over. In 1587 Croft was past seventy years of age. Parma, in a letter
to Philip II, described him as a 'weak old man of seventy with very little sagacity',[29]
and Lord Admiral Howard referred to him as 'a long grey beard with a white head
witless'.[30] But he was the one staunch advocate of peace among Elizabeth's advisers. And she encouraged and applauded him. He above all others was responsible for the peace efforts. Indeed, they were referred to at Court as 'Mr.
Controller's Peace'.[31]

The great opponents in the Council to any form of peace-making were Leicester
and Walsingham. Walsingham's views are set forth at length in his correspondence with Leicester during the summer and autumn of 1587 when Leicester was in
the Netherlands. Walsingham believed that Parma was simply seeking to gain
time, but he feared that the Queen's desire for peace would lead her to throw
caution to the winds and ignore the fact that preparations were well advanced for
a Spanish invasion of England. Walsingham was opposed to peace-making, but
he may have exaggerated, even deliberately, Elizabeth's pacifistic impulses in order
to stir Leicester to action. Quite possibly his urgent desire to hasten Leicester's
return to England proceeded from the conviction that Leicester was the one man
to whose influence the Queen was most likely to respond.

Elizabeth's own attitude is harder to appraise. She wanted peace. It is probable
that she appointed Croft to the commission to negotiate peace because she was
certain that he would do his best to achieve it. But she wanted peace on her own
terms, and though she may easily have been willing to sacrifice the religious freedom of the Dutch in the interests of peace, she was not prepared to pull her forces
out of the Netherlands and to surrender the towns which she held there as security
for her large loans to the Dutch. She may have thought she could secure peace on
terms which would at least compensate her for the money and men she had poured
into the Low Countries. None of her other advisers, except Croft, thought she
could. They did not fear that peace would be achieved. What they feared was that
the hope of peace would lead her to slacken her preparations for defence.

Unfortunately we have very little upon which to base a judgment of her attitude.
The French ambassador's dispatches, those few of them which survive, yield
practically nothing, and there was no longer a resident Spanish ambassador. We
miss Mendoza's colourful dispatches. He was Spanish ambassador to France at the
time and retained his interest in English affairs, but he had no competent agent in
England and what he learned from the treachery of Stafford reveals little about the
Queen herself. What there is from Spanish sources displays Elizabeth at her worst
— at one time prepared to accept peace at any price; at another storming at Burghley and Croft for promoting peace.[32] A Portuguese agent in London wrote in

November 1587: 'She told the Treasurer that he was old and doting, to which he replied that he was old and would gladly therefore retire to a church where he might pray for her.' Which may or may not have been true, but which was eminently characteristic.

Burghley's behaviour in the whole matter calls for a more detailed examination. It is to be noted, in the first place, that he made no secret of the peace manœuvres. He kept Walsingham in touch with every step in the proceedings.

Even before the fall of Sluys he had directed De Loo to urge Parma to abandon the siege as a token of good faith. On July 16th he wrote to Walsingham:[33] 'I am greatly encumbered with such directions as her Majesty will have prosecuted upon Mr. Controller's report to her Majesty of his man's mouth — Morris. He saith that the Duke of Parma is willing to make a cessation of arms by treaty with my Lord of Leicester before the commissioners [to be sent from England to negotiate peace] shall come. And this she will have proceed with speed. And yet by the very word of Andrea de Loo's letter to the controller,[34] wherewith I send you herewith an extract in the Italian words, it manifestly appeareth that the cessation of arms to be made with the E. of Leicester should be during the communication of the Commission. And so I have showed her Majesty the very words. But yet she will be persuaded by Mr. Controller to the contrary, upon his man's report. And so in all haste she will have the controller's man to return with the answer, that the commissioners shall come without fail if he will assent to cease arms.

'I objected to this that it were necessary to know of my L. of Leicester whether the state of his affairs and the public cause will accord with this manner of proceeding and whether it shall profit or endanger his actions. To which her Majesty answereth that she will undertake that my L. of Leicester shall do herein what she will command. But I do reply to this that yet it is not thereby resolved whether it be meet so to be commanded or a thing good for her Majesty. But I am answered peremptorily that so it shall be. And she will that I shall send back for Needham your servant to receive letters to my L. of Leicester for this purpose.[35] And so I pray you send him hither with speed, for so her Majesty commandeth.

'I am unfit to be an executor of these sudden directions, especially where the effects are so large and dangerous. But lords and ladies command and servants obey.

'From my garden at Theobalds where her Majesty is and chargeth me to write in haste.'

But apparently Burghley persuaded his mistress to take a more cautious course. It must have been with her knowledge and approval that he wrote to De Loo two days later that if Parma would raise the siege of Sluys, the English commissioners to treat for peace would come forthwith.

He took occasion, however, to call to De Loo's attention that he had shed no light upon the issue of religious freedom, 'a matter whereof I did always warn you that without the same I never could hope of any sound conclusion or effect of peace'.

The fall of Sluys on July 16th, news of which had reached England by August

1st, provided a temporary revulsion of feeling in the Queen towards Leicester and the Dutch. She talked of recalling him and leaving them to their own devices,[36] but within a week she had reverted to the peace-making. On August 9th she directed Leicester to inform the Estates that she had decided to negotiate with Parma and to request them to appoint commissioners to participate in the negotiations.[37]

Meanwhile, a safe-conduct from Parma for the English commissioners had reached England.

Burghley wrote to De Loo on the last of August[38] that the Queen was delighted to hear that Parma expected the coming of the commissioners, acknowledging that the safe-conduct had arrived but that it needed revision. He went on to say that his mistress had directed Leicester to inform the Dutch of her offer to treat and to request them to select commissioners to participate in the negotiations, and would defer action until she had their answer.

At the same time Burghley raised the question as to whether Parma was acting under the King of Spain's commission; if not, then it would be a great hindrance to negotiations. He named the Earl of Derby, Lord Cobham and Sir James Croft as members of the English commission, but subject to change.

Burghley's letter is more remarkable for the difficulties it raised than for the promotion of the peace-making.

He wrote to Walsingham on September 5th:

'Of late Andrea de Loo wrote to me that the Duke still expecteth the coming of the commissioners and that he would not cease arms until their meeting and that he looketh [expecteth] at the end of the month . . . from all parts, 40,000 men. Mr. Controller first delivered this letter to her Majesty, but how she was moved in it I know not. He sent it to me and I returned it with an answer of my opinion how dangerous her Majesty's paradings are, to run a contrary course in sight of her enemy. I think my sharp writing will offend, but I am indeed so chafed as I cannot hold my peace where peace will be lost. I have increased the project of the instructions though I never hope for any good thereof, and have sent them to Mr. Controller because he saith he must be a principal actor therein. And I wished him to send them to you.'[39]

It is clear that Burghley was not in favour of peace-making at that juncture; clear also from his last sentence that he had already set about preparing instructions for the English peace commissioners.[40]

Six days later he wrote to Walsingham again with reference to the offer of the King of Denmark to participate in the peace negotiations. The Queen, he wrote, had decided to send Rogers (clerk of the Privy Council) to speak with the King and to explain to him the delay in opening negotiations.[41]

Burghley drafted Elizabeth's instructions to Rogers on September 20th.[42] He was to inform the King of Denmark that she foresaw that the great obstacle to peace would be the Dutch insistence 'upon freedom of religion, without which there could be no fruit of peace', and to urge the King to press that point strongly in the negotiations. If the Spaniards should prove obdurate, Rogers was to urge

Denmark to join with her in assisting the Dutch and to do his best to persuade the princes of Germany to concur in the action.

The implications of this message were that unless Philip conceded religious freedom to the Dutch, Elizabeth would support joint action by England and Denmark, assisted, if possible, by the German Protestant princes in support of the Dutch position. There is no other evidence that Elizabeth was prepared to go so far in support of religious freedom. And it may very well be that she emphasized the point in dealing with Frederick of Denmark because she had reason to believe that he was pro-Spanish in his sympathies[43] and was even acting at Spanish prompting. In any case, Frederick sent no representative to the peace conference, though up to the last moment one was expected.

On September 13th, Burghley wrote again to Walsingham: 'I am to return [to Court] as soon as any news come from my Lord of Leicester of his negotiations with the State for the matter of peace, which I fear will not be gotten to our contentment unless the King of Navarre prosper, whereupon dependeth *cordem totius nostrae felicitatis*. 13 September at night, 1587, being my birthday, whereby I am warned to ask God forgiveness for my years past and to preserve me from dwelling in sin.'[44]

An interesting revelation of the good will between Burghley and Walsingham at this juncture is set forth in a letter from Walsingham to Burghley of September 18th:

'My very good Lord; This bearer, my servant, having made a very rare coach for ease, strength and lightness, whereof I made this day a trial upon London stones, I am bold to present the same to your Lordship. And in case your Lordship shall not find it large enough, or shall like to have a new coach made with some further addition, if it may please you to acquaint the said bearer with your mind therein I will undertake he shall see it performed to your L. contentment.

'The said coach hath many artificial points in it that without his demonstration will not easily be discovered and therefore I have appointed the said bearer to attend your Lordship's leisure to acquaint you with the same.'[45]

A week later on September 26th, Burghley wrote again to Walsingham from Theobalds, acknowledging the receipt of letters from De Loo. ' . . . Of the Court causes,' he added, 'I hear nothing to move me to stir from hence. I wish there were no accident to hasten me.'

It was between term times in the courts and he was on vacation.[46]

Meanwhile, the negotiations for peace dragged along. Burghley in his letter of August 31st had indicated the Queen's intention to send her commissioners to treat for peace before Michaelmas. That was the one phrase in an otherwise rather sceptical letter upon which De Loo seized. In his reply to Burghley of September 15th he waived aside all objections and looked forward to the speedy consummation of all his hopes.

But September passed without further progress and early in October De Loo wrote to Burghley that he had abandoned hope and was about to return home. But this did not suit the Queen's fancy. Acting upon her instructions, Burghley,

Walsingham and Croft sent off a joint letter to De Loo on the 15th. The Queen, they wrote, was greatly displeased with the delay in the dispatch of the commissioners, which they attributed to the reluctance of the Dutch to 'hearken to any treaty of peace'. But she was also disturbed by De Loo's announcement of Parma's intention 'to go to the field'. Had it not been for that she would have sent her commissioners without waiting for the Dutch answer. 'As it is she is reluctant [to send commissioners] fearing that Parma had lost interest in peace negotiations.' They bade De Loo return to Parma and get his response to her doubts, if possible in writing. If his answer was favourable the commissioners would depart forthwith. They ended by testifying to Elizabeth's earnest desire for peace.[47] Parma answered in a personal letter to Elizabeth protesting that it would not be his fault if the negotiations for peace did not go forward.[48]

Walsingham referred to this letter in writing to Leicester on November 12th: 'A letter from the Duke of Parma to her Majesty hath bred in her such dangerous security as all advertisements of perils and dangers are neglected and great expedition used in dispatching of commissioners.'[49]

But the one thing Elizabeth did not favour was expedition. Burghley wrote to De Loo on the 11th that the Queen accepted the Duke's assurances in good part. But she did not find them consistent with his warlike preparations by land and sea of which she was well aware. She wanted further assurances.[50]

De Loo kept bombarding Burghley with letters giving all sorts of promises and assurances. A cessation of arms would be arranged as soon as the commissioners met, and this would include belligerent action both in the Low Countries and in Spain. Elizabeth meanwhile was being bombarded by reports both from Spain and from the Low Countries that preparations were well advanced for an attack upon England. One gets the impression, despite Walsingham's pessimism, that neither side really hoped for peace and that each was trying to throw the other off guard.

Early in December Leicester came back to England, and it cannot have been without significance that the problem of peace was discussed at the first session of the Privy Council after he resumed his seat.[51] It is the first indication we have that the Queen was laying the whole problem before her Council, and we may fairly presume that this was one of the immediate consequences of Leicester's return.[52] We have two memoranda in Burghley's hand[53] associated with this meeting, and we have a memorandum in Walsingham's hand of the Privy Council resolutions.[54] It seems likely that Burghley's memorandum of the 14th was in fact an outline of his presentation of the problem to the Council. It may at any rate be taken to reflect his position.

He began by asserting the need for peace, went on to say that peace could only be secured by treaty, and then proceeded to deal with the conditions of peacemaking. The commissioners should meet in a secure place. There should be a cessation of arms during the negotiations as well in Spain as in the Low Countries. The Dutch should either appoint commissioners to represent them at the conference or else authorize the Queen to represent them. The terms of peace should be such as to give real assurance of peace, eliminating such causes of friction as, for example, the subjection of Englishmen to the Spanish Inquisition. The Dutch should not be penalized for anything they had done and should enjoy their liberties and freedom and have the use of their religion openly now professed in their churches. Her Majesty should be paid such sums of money as she had advanced to the Dutch. The peace should be secured as heretofore by binding the towns both in England and in the Low Countries to observe it.

He went on to argue in favour of holding the negotiations in England. He thought it more difficult to arrange for a cessation of arms in Spain than in the Low Countries, but he maintained that if the Duke [i.e. Parma] were empowered 'to covenant for it' it might be hoped for. He suggested that if the Dutch refused to participate in the negotiations, the Queen might treat for herself, hoping that the Dutch would come in later.

On the thorny question of religion he proposed that the Queen might find out what protection the Dutch would require. If this could not be obtained, then the Queen might declare to the world a just cause for breaking off negotiations and strengthen the Dutch and secure Scotland and cast about for further means to support her war.

The significant points in the memorandum are (1) that Elizabeth should get her money back, (2) that the Dutch should get freedom of religion. The second point Burghley plainly regarded as a *sine qua non*.

According to Walsingham's memorandum, all that positively emerged from the Council meeting was that the English commissioners for peace might be detained until the Dutch sent answer to the Queen's demand for their participation.   It was recommended that Mr. Herbert, who had been sent to negotiate with them about the matter, should fix a certain day for their answer and if it did not come by that day he was to return home, the implication being that the Queen would then go ahead without them.

Instructions went off to Herbert in accordance with the Council's recommendations on December 10th.[55] Whether by accident or design they did not reach him until nearly a month later.[56] He came home in January with nothing to show for his pains.

Meanwhile, at the royal command, Burghley drafted the instructions for the English commissioners.[57] They followed in the main the outline as he had defined it at the Council meeting. After fixing upon a place of meeting and examining credentials they were to demand a cessation of arms. It was only after this had been granted that they were to proceed to the peace-making. The issue between the King of Spain and the Low Countries was to be considered first, and the English commissioners were directed to get from the Dutch a statement of their demands and to urge them strongly. The instructions in this particular did not go quite so far as Burghley wanted. Religious toleration was not definitely stated as a *sine qua non*. Upon the point of the repayment of the Queen's loans, the instructions were adamant. If the Spaniard would not agree to that, no full accord should be made. Other points of difference were touched upon. The commissioners could, at a pinch, agree that no more English aid should go to Don Antonio. They could agree to prohibit trade with the Spanish West Indies and the Portuguese East Indies provided that these terms applied only to territory actually occupied. They were to demand freedom from the Inquisition for Englishmen in Spain.

Burghley had indicated to De Loo in August that the Earl of Derby, Lord Cobham and Sir James Croft were to be the English commissioners but subject to change. Dr. Valentine Dale, a civilian, was named later. Sir Amias Paulet, sometime keeper of Mary Queen of Scots, was also named, but for some reason or other, possibly because of ill health, more probably because of his outspoken opposition to the peace-making, he did not go. At one time Walsingham had feared that he himself might be appointed, and had sworn that come what might he would not serve. At another time Leicester had the same fear. Ultimately Dr. John Rogers, son of the Marian martyr and brother of Dr. Daniel Rogers, clerk of the Council, took the fifth place. He lacked both the religious devotion of his father and the ability of his brother. His outstanding qualification appears to have been his knowledge of Italian which he seems to have tried to exploit but without success. The group was a conservative one. Derby and Cobham and Croft were Privy Councillors. Derby's mother was a Howard, but he seems to have been free of any taint of Catholicism. Cobham was one of Burghley's old friends who had been in trouble twenty years earlier for concealing evidence in the Ridolfi Plot. After Paulet was dropped, the war party lacked representation. Leicester had earlier been of the opinion that it should have been represented, and repudiated the suggestion that only those 'not too hot, but temperate in religion' should be chosen. But as it turned out, the religious zealots were all left out. This was probably Elizabeth's own doing. Leicester and Walsingham seem to have acquiesced,[58] probably because they had decided that nothing would come of the peace-making. They may even have concluded that it might serve to stave off the Spanish attack. Actually Croft proved to be the only enthusiastic pacifist in the group. Derby was little more than a figurehead, but Cobham and Dale both counterchecked Croft at every turn.[59]

The English commissioners set forth in mid-February, but were detained ten days at Dover by contrary winds and did not reach Ostend until early in March.

They spent two months wrangling about the place of meeting and the presentation of credentials, and really never got down to the heart of the business. Croft undertook to seize the bull by the horns, defied his colleagues and went off in April to confer with Parma personally.

Elizabeth rebuked him for his temerity, but was evidently willing to explore that line of approach. Croft's initial report of his interview indicated that Parma had shown him his commission from the King and had virtually conceded everything asked for except religious freedom. He had even granted a 'surcease of arms'. Actually Parma had made no such concessions.

Croft understood no language but English. De Loo had served as interpreter at the interview. He may have misrepresented what Parma said, or Croft may have taken polite answers for complete assurance. Or the messenger, John Croft, who carried the report of the interview to Burghley, may have misinterpreted it. He delivered it to Burghley at Theobalds where he was on leave nursing his health. He returned to Court at once and delivered the report to the Queen. She was pleased, but sceptical, observing that a message of such importance should not have been sent, unsigned, in an open letter by a man of no better reputation than John Croft. Burghley cross-examined John Croft with reference to the surcease of arms, and Croft declared that it would be extended to Spain as well as to the Low Countries, and that Parma had sent off a courier to Spain for the purpose.

In any case, Elizabeth instructed her commissioners to check on Croft's report, and if they found it accurate to proceed with the peace-making without further delay.

As it turned out, Sir James Croft had completely misrepresented Parma's response. The official answer to Croft's requirements was produced before a meeting of the English commissioners a few days later,[60] and it was quite non-committal upon all the points at issue. The outcome was that Elizabeth ordered Croft to return to England forthwith. The poor old man begged to be spared that indignity, and Burghley and Walsingham induced the Queen to let him stay on.[61] But when he got home in August he was sent to the Tower and kept there for over a year.[62] His son blamed Leicester for all these misfortunes, and after Leicester's death was charged with employing a conjurer to do away with him.[63] Croft père was not involved. He was released from the Tower late in 1589, recovered the Queen's favour and died the following year.

This diversion did not interrupt the course of the negotiations. They were transferred to Burborough late in May, and were not definitely abandoned until the Armada was actually off the English coast. Towards the end the English commissioners became fearful of their personal safety, and at their request Elizabeth sent two pinnaces to cruise off the coast and take them off if the situation demanded it. Up to the end, both Croft and De Loo still took an optimistic view of the prospect for peace. As late as August 8th, De Loo still thought a peace was possible.[64]

During the winter and spring of 1588 Burghley was far from well, and he spent much of his time at Theobalds. Most of what we know about his attitude towards peace we gather from his correspondence with Walsingham. Quite evidently they were growing closer and closer together. The old reserve, the old distrust seem to have melted quite away. Walsingham was still deferential, but Burghley was definitely more expansive. It is quite clear that Burghley was more disposed to peace-making than Walsingham, but equally clear that he insisted upon the establishment of freedom of religion in the Low Countries as an indispensable condition. We have one memorandum in his hand early in January in which he mustered the arguments likely to induce Philip of Spain to make peace: his resources had been put to a heavy drain by the wars in the Low Countries; his indebtedness was greater than ever it was; he might hesitate to adventure all his naval forces in an attack upon England and so expose Portugal to a sudden invasion by Don Antonio, the Portuguese pretender. And Philip was old, and his son young, and he might be thinking of his latter end. Under such circumstances it might be expected that he would be more disposed to set his house in order than to indulge in quixotic crusades.[65]

But Burghley was never sanguine about peace. On February 6th he wrote to Walsingham:

'The more I think about this matter of war and peace betwixt her Majesty and the King of Spain, though I might say betwixt her Majesty and the most part of her neighbours, the further off I am to imagine how there might be some good end. *Opus est aliquo Dedale*[66] to direct the maze.'

Burghley went on to express his fear lest Elizabeth's cavalier treatment of the Dutch would induce them to seek a separate peace with Spain, either as a whole or province by province. He advised that the Dutch deputies in England be assured that whatever peace she made she would not suffer them to perish, and be urged to preserve their union and maintain their forces in the field. 'I pray you', Burghley concluded, 'use this my projection as you see cause. I mean it earnestly.'[67]

Apparently this advice was taken, and in a royal message to the Dutch deputies later in the month the assurances were given.[68]

Burghley wrote again to Walsingham on April 10th.[69]

'I cannot express my pain newly increased in my left arm. My spirits are even now so entenuated [attenuated] as I have no mind towards anything but to groan with my pain. Therefore pardon me for not answering to you.

'I am sorry to see [in the negotiations for peace] more respects had to accidents than to substance. Surely, Sir, as God will be best pleased with peace, so in nothing can her Majesty content her realm better than in procuring of peace, which, if it cannot be had, yet is she excused afore God and the world. I have received many letters from the L. Cobham requiring my furtherance for resolution of things but I can only answer his expectation with my prayers.

'I am bold to send you two letters from Robert Cecil when you have leisure to read them. I refer the longest to your consideration,[70] only I would not thereby we should be made slower in our preparations.'

In short, seek peace but prepare for war.

We have a memorandum in Burghley's hand dated June 10th and endorsed, 'The Best Conditions for Peace'. In this he enumerated the restoration to the Low Countries of their ancient liberties including freedom of conscience, the repayment of the money expended by the Queen in assisting the Duke, and the withdrawal of all foreign troops from the Low Countries.

If the King of Spain would not yield to these conditions, then the Queen should continue in a joint defence with the provinces whom she had contracted to aid.[71]

Burghley went on to estimate the probabilities that those conditions would be met, and concluded that they were far from promising. But he did not contemplate any compromise in what he considered essential to a satisfactory peace. His position, in short, remained unchanged.

Two days later he received from his brother-in-law, Sir Henry Killigrew, a copy of Cardinal Allen's vicious attack upon Elizabeth with its appeal to English Catholics to rise up and depose her;[72] and on June 24th, a copy of a 'roaring hellish bull' excommunicating her.[73] Taken together, these two manifestoes constituted a virtual declaration of war and had immediate repercussions upon the peace negotiations, particularly since Parma was named in the bull as its principal executor. Burghley drew up a memorandum on the subject, which served as the basis for a letter which he himself drafted and which went off from the Queen to her peace commissioners on June 29th.[74] It directed them to send Dr. Dale off to Parma, call his attention to the Cardinal's book and the Pope's bull and inquire if he had any part in them. If he admitted as much, Dale was to ask for passports. If Parma pleaded ignorance, Dale was to demand that the book should be burned and its printers punished, and that Parma in his own name should denounce it. If he refused, Dale was to declare that his mistress was not satisfied and was once again to demand passports.

Parma's response was not satisfactory. It was discussed at a Council meeting on July 15th and Burghley was charged with the business of drafting an answer. He wrote to Walsingham on July 16th:[75]

'Sir, Having had a very painful and restless night against my expectation and thereby forced to keep my bed, I could not but be mindful of the matters passed in speeches yesterday and so do deliver my conceits into this paper for your sight. For the message to the Duke of Parma, I think the argument would be pressed, to be well answered.' He went on to point out that Allen had written his book and the Pope prepared his bull long before the King had commissioned Parma to treat for peace, that the King of Spain 'had taken upon him' to execute the papal bull and that Parma himself had been designated in the bull as its 'principal executor'.

'And therefore,' Burghley concluded, 'joining hereto the King's refusal to accord a cessation of arms during the treaty and his haste of so great preparations as he maketh to come with his power to the seas, her Majesty cannot interpret these actions otherwise than that there is no meaning to make any peace but by treaty to win time to have both the forces of Spain and those Low Countries join for the execution of the said bull, the success whereof her Majesty doubteth not but by God's special goodness, who is the Lord of all hosts, she shall make void and frustrate.

'And yet, because it shall appear to the world that her Majesty hath not a mind to continue any wars to the shedding of Christian blood, she will be contented, when those great forces shall have done their worst, and by God's goodness not prevailed, to renew the treaty of peace, so as the like pains be taken on the King's part to send his commissioners into England as her Majesty have done for the space of [blank] months.'

But even with Burghley's concluding paragraph, designed no doubt to soften the blow and to reconcile his reluctant mistress with the prospect of immediate war, his advice was not followed. Walsingham wrote to Burghley two days later[76] that the Queen 'had resolved that the treaty should be continued as a thing proceeding from the commissioners themselves and that her former project for the recharging of the Duke should be stayed, lest it might breed a present breach before things be put in a readiness for defence'.

Elizabeth, always procrastinating, cherished the delusion that the Spanish attack still waited upon the outcome of the peace negotiations. This is the first intimation we have from the English side that the negotiations were designed to delay attack. It was not until July 24th, when the Spanish Armada was actually in the Channel, that Elizabeth called her commissioners home.[77]

An appraisal of the profit and loss of the peace negotiations reveals little on either side of the ledger. The peace effort certainly antagonized the Dutch and did nothing to improve Anglo-Spanish relations. Philip and Parma went ahead with their plans. It was the preparation for invasion and not the promise of peace which forced Parma to postpone active operations against the Dutch at a time when they were particularly vulnerable. What Elizabeth did gain by the presence of her commissioners was an opportunity to observe Parma's military preparations at close quarters. But he made no secret of them, and she had plenty of information about them from other sources. It is doubtful if the cake was worth the penny. The evidence at hand makes it clear that Burghley, though an advocate of peace, was far from favouring peace at any price.

The early months of 1588 were momentous ones in Burghley's private life. In March he lost his old mother in her eighty-eighth year. The place she had filled in his life is revealed in a letter he wrote to the Earl of Shrewsbury on March 15th:[78]

'Upon knowledge of God's pleasure to call to his mercy out of this world and from my comfort the surest, the eldest, yea, the first friend that ever I had, I could not endure the affairs of the Court nor of City, nor of my own family. But by permission of her Majesty I have been here at my house, or rather in my chamber at Theobalds and so mind to continue for a season . . . And though I cannot myself travel to the funeral at Burghley,[79] yet I am a little, both with comfort and discomfort, occupied to perform the duties of such a son as old Tobias[80] had, whom he commanded [to bury] his mother by his father, and so hath my mother required me, who hath two years [ago] made her will and then did actually dispose [of] what she had, saving her little apparel necessary for her life. So as now, a good time before her death, she had no care to dispose anything. And therefore, varying from the form of all other wills, she hath said, I have given, not I do give, which example, God sending me grace, I mind to follow as my degree will suffer me.'

Elizabeth, though she was sympathetic, thought that his grief was excessive. She sent a message to him by John Wooley, her Latin secretary: 'She was old, as her Majesty saith, and you wise. And therefore, her death, happening according to natural course, is to be taken moderately of you. To withdraw therefore your troubled mind from private grief to public cogitations, she prayeth your Lordship to think upon the speedy dispatch of commissioners for Munster with all the haste you can.'[81]

In June, Burghley lost Ann, Countess of Oxford, his favourite daughter. She had been formally reconciled to her husband in 1582 and had borne him a son who had died in infancy, and two more daughters, one in 1584, the other in 1587.[82] The father apparently would have none of them and Ann's three daughters were raised in Burghley's household.[83]

Of Ann's death we have only one recorded comment from her father's pen, dated June 24th: 'And so I end *in crepusculo* . . . a dark night afore a black morning for me and mine.'[84] On the 25th Ann was buried in Westminster Abbey with all pomp and circumstance. It is not recorded that her husband was among those present. A eulogy on Ann at Hatfield singles out for praise her modesty, patience, Christian zeal, loyalty to the Queen, reverence to her father, fidelity to her husband. Of more lively virtues we hear nothing. Perhaps that was why Oxford, who had neither modesty nor patience nor Christian zeal nor fidelity, preferred the company of one of the notorious harlots at Court.

Ann's death was not without its compensations. It relieved her father of her constant nagging on her husband's behalf. As long as he lived, Oxford continued to exploit his connection with the Cecils for all he thought it might be worth. He even went so far on one occasion as to contemplate the assumption of some part of the expense of his own daughters' maintenance. But Burghley assumed full responsibility for their upbringing. Elizabeth, the eldest, married the Earl of Derby; the other two were married after Burghley's death, Bridget to James Norris, later Lord Norris of Rycote, Susan to Philip Herbert, later Earl of Pembroke. All three made what were currently regarded as good matches. In Elizabeth's case the choice was plainly hers, after she had rejected a more distinguished alternative. As for Bridget and Susan, both married courtiers, men of violent tempers, notorious loose livers, notoriously unfaithful to their marriage vows. It is hardly likely that Ann's daughters were much better off as wives than she had been. Poor Burghley! He did his best for his offspring, but much of what he did turned out to be wrong.

The one conspicuous exception, was his son, Robert. Unlike his half-brother, Thomas, Robert was a frail boy, deformed by a fall when he was a baby. Bacon had him in mind when he wrote in his *Essay on Deformity*: 'Certainly there is a consent between the body and the mind and when nature erreth in the one she adventureth in the other.' Like his father, Robert was a lover of books, and he followed his father's footsteps to St. John's College, Cambridge, and then to Gray's Inn. When he was twenty, Burghley sent him to Paris where he spent the autumn of 1584 in the household of Sir Edward Stafford, the English ambassador. His behaviour in Paris is in edifying contrast to that of Thomas some twenty years before. Thomas got in trouble with a girl; Robert attended disputations at the Sorbonne and wrote long treatises on French noble families.[85]

He had taken his seat in the House of Commons before he was twenty, and before he was thirty could boast that he had sat in five Parliaments.

But we may date his début into the executive branch of the government in the early spring of 1588, when Burghley sent him to the Low Countries with the English peace commissioners. His letters thence are good reading. They have an ease and grace which his father's letters rarely if ever attained. Virtually all of them were to Burghley, but one to his father's secretary, Michael Hicks, is particularly engaging, revealing as it does that we have here a normal, humorous young man, not the prig which he is sometimes made out to have been. 'My health', he wrote, 'was never so good, I praise God . . . Many things I could be merry with in my letter to you both but *literae scriptae manet*; and *vivat* the good Earl of Derby whose muttons die, his hens starve and we are fain nevertheless to eat them . . . Your nose would drop in faith, don Michael, if you were cold as we have been. Not a fair woman nor an honest.'[86]

He gave pictures of hunting partridges with a setting dog and a net. He sent affectionate regards to his sister, Ann. He took his hardships easily and with a jest. He travelled at large to Ghent, to Bruges, to Antwerp. At Bruges he came upon his father's name written on the chimney — a reminiscence of William Cecil's visit there over thirty years before.[87] At Antwerp he lodged with Carlo Lanfranchi, who had played his part in initiating the peace negotiations. They seemed to have let him go anywhere. He scrutinized the preparation of shipping and wrote to his father: 'It will be but a scarecrow.' This letter Burghley sent to Walsingham.

None of Robert's letters is of great importance, except as an early revelation of his wit, his wisdom, his power of acute observation, his obvious affection and reverence for his father, his father's increasing affection and respect and trust in him. Thomas had failed him, but Robert was to be the guide and stay of William's old age. It was to Robert at the last that with failing hands he was to throw the torch.

From this time forward their relations became increasingly close. Indeed, the working partnership between Burghley and his son is one of the most remarkable of its kind in English history. Unostentatiously, without friction and without jealousy, Robert gradually took the burden from his father's shoulders, always offering advice tentatively, always seeking it deferentially. It was a great tribute to both men. To Burghley, growing very old and very tired, it was a God-send.

CHAPTER XXI

THE COMING OF THE ARMADA, 1588

D
URING 1587 and until the Spanish Armada actually appeared in the Channel, all other considerations of English policy were dominated by the approaching shadow of an attack from Spain by the sea. The part which Burghley played in the preparations to meet that attack now calls for consideration.

Though the nominal minister of marine was the Lord High Admiral, the ultimate responsibility for providing and maintaining the royal navy fell actually upon Burghley's shoulders and had rested there since the beginning of the reign. At the time of Elizabeth's accession, England was still at war, had recently suffered the loss of Calais and was frantically busy strengthening her naval defences. Burghley (then Sir William Cecil, of course) addressed his attention to the problem. He was busy with it in the early spring of 1559, reorganizing the Admiralty office[1] and seeking information and advice from important officials of the Admiralty, all of whom had carried over from the previous reign. The so-called *Book of Sea Causes* was in his hands in March 1559.[2]

It included a summary of the actual state of the navy. The effective fighting force it reported as 22 sail of all classes, besides 45 merchant ships, easily convertible, and 20 ships fit for supply, calling for personnel of 10,600 men, the whole force of which might be mobilized in two months. The report went on to recommend a naval programme proposing that in five years the royal fleet should be increased to 30 vessels of which 24 should be ships of 200 tons or larger. It is to be noticed that emphasis is laid upon ships of 400 to 500 tons. The experts were already getting away from the larger, more unwieldy vessels, useful in a form of naval warfare which consisted of hand-to-hand fighting by boarding the ships of the enemy, in favour of ships of greater manœuvrability and heavier gun-fire designed to destroy the enemy at long range.[3]

It does not appear that the advice was immediately taken, and of the ships constructed during the first fifteen years of the reign, the proportion of oversized ships was still large.[4]

Burghley from the start brought some order and some economy into naval construction, but during his first twenty years in service he does not appear to have increased the size of the royal fleet or made any notable contribution to its fighting power. In the 1560s he was disturbed at the decay of English shipping, and sponsored legislation to improve the situation,[5] notably by building up the English market for fish. And he took a definite interest in maritime enterprise, was one of the early subscribers to the Russian Company, participated in the slave-trading adventures of John Hawkins, encouraged Sir Humphrey Gilbert and gave Martin Frobisher substantial support.[6]

Outside of Europe he did not recognize sovereign rights when unsupported by effective occupation. But he looked askance at Hawkins's exploitation of the slave market in Spanish America as an invasion of legitimate Spanish rights and definitely opposed Drake's plundering expeditions, disguised as reprisals for Spanish treachery, as quite illegal and not far removed from pure piracy.

There are no substantial grounds for the charge that he tried to sabotage Drake's expedition to the Pacific in 1577, though he was among those who thought that Drake's booty should be restored. He never endorsed the position of 'No peace beyond the line', nor identified the pursuit of plunder with religious zeal. He was, in short, legally minded and he had a decent respect for property rights, whoever possessed them and wheresoever they were possessed.

But he had to cope with a difficult mistress, who did not want war but had a covetous eye upon all sources of wealth, licit or illicit. She disclaimed all responsibility for Drake's enterprises but claimed a lion's share of his spoils. When, upon his return from his famous voyage of circumnavigation, she knighted him on his own quarter-deck, she gave official sanction to one of the most outrageous and most profitable piratical enterprises in the annals of the century.

The fact was, of course, that maritime adventure, licit or illicit, was an admirable training school for English mariners, both in coping with the high seas and, in so far as it involved conflict with Spanish ships and Spanish mariners, in coping with the potential enemy. In that school Hawkins and Drake learned the lessons which enabled them to build up the Queen's navy and to lead it to victory when the supreme test came. But it was provocative of open war and, when Burghley compared the fighting strength of England and Spain, open war was what he wanted to avoid.

By the books Philip II of Spain was easily the mightiest monarch of the west. And Burghley was a bookish man. Being a devout Protestant, he expected the Lord of Hosts to fight on his side. But he was also a man of business, and found it safer to assume that the Lord would favour the side with the heavier artillery. Acutely conscious of English weakness, he could find no strength in the English nation commensurate with Spanish strength. War for him was a matter of soldiers. Sea power he recognized as an important instrument of defence but not as a decisive factor. He never thought of it as Drake thought of it, as the instrument for striking at the very vitals of Spain's power, her 'soft under-belly', in the Caribbean and the Pacific.

This does not mean that Burghley was for peace at any price, certainly not at the price of Protestant survival. Throughout the abortive negotiations for peace he insisted that religious freedom for the Dutch was a *sine qua non*, even though he was well aware that Philip of Spain could never be brought to concede it. Upon that point he stood firm.

He favoured peace but constantly urged preparation for war, both by land and sea. Probably his most important single contribution to defence was the appointment of John Hawkins to be Treasurer of the Navy in 1578. Hawkins was not only the first of the great Elizabethan seafarers, but he was also a good business man and turned out to be an excellent administrator. His predecessor in the office, his father-in-law, Benjamin Gonson, had retired from active duty. We know relatively little about the details of Hawkins's appointment. It may have been the outcome of a long memorandum on naval administration which he submitted to Burghley at about this time.[7] The essence of it was that naval maintenance costs could be cut by the elimination of corruption. This was a form of argument well calculated to commend him to Elizabeth, and it may have been drawn with her in mind. Hawkins subsequently proved that he was right. But his economies struck a shrewd blow at the perquisites enjoyed by other officials of the Admiralty, notably by Sir William Winter, the Surveyor, who held office for thirty years. They banded together against Hawkins and did their best to drive him from office. In the autumn of 1587 their attacks were particularly virulent, and went so far as to inform Burghley that the ships of the royal navy were in a deplorable condition.[8] He was plainly disturbed. In September he wrote to Walsingham: 'I hear every day that the Queen's ships are in such decay as they are not serviceable until great cost may be done upon them.'[9] Burghley appointed a committee of two to investigate, both of them old Admiralty men, one of them Sir William Winter himself. The outcome was Hawkins's complete vindication.[10] This put an end to the efforts to remove him. He remained in charge until his death. To him if to any single man belongs the chief credit for the first-rate fighting fleet which Elizabeth was able to launch against the Armada. And he was Burghley's man.

The military strength of the kingdom was something else again. It was derived in the main from the county levies, based upon the obligation of all males between the ages of sixteen and sixty to render military service. The institution had been regularized by legislation under Edward VI and Mary. It found concrete expression in the annual summer musters, in which the military strength of the county was assembled, appraised and in part trained.[11]

The musters supplied the infantry. The horse and the armour were levied upon the gentry in proportion to their means. The nobility might be called upon in an emergency to make a special contribution. Elizabeth called upon them in June 1588 to attend upon her 'with such a convenient number of lances and light horse' as might stand with their ability. Burghley on that occasion responded with fifty lances and fifty light horse, though it does not appear that he led them in person to the Queen, or that he contemplated, as Walsingham did, attiring himself in battle array.[12]

The musters were managed differently at different times and in different places. But increasingly they became the business of the Lord Lieutenant, originally regarded as a temporary expedient but by the mid-eighties virtually universal throughout England except in London and the far north. Many of them were Privy Councillors, and so brought local administration under direct royal supervision. They were selected with an eye to their local affiliations and came to be regarded, or at least regarded themselves, as the natural leaders of the county gentry.

In September 1586, Burghley wrote to Walsingham:[13] 'Her Majesty hath been earnest to have the counties committed to Lieutenants and to have the musters put in order for a strength about herself.' He went on to complain that though she had virtually promised to appoint him to the Lieutenancy in Hertfordshire and Essex, during Leicester's absence in the Low Countries, she had declined to sign his commission. He found some consolation in the fact that he was a *homo novus* in Hertford, but observed that had Northampton, his 'native county', been in question he would have felt much more strongly about it. As a matter of fact, two days later, Elizabeth appointed Sir Christopher Hatton to Northampton.[14]

It cannot be supposed that the royal slight was deliberate. Elizabeth probably regarded the office as a military one, and certainly the Lord Treasurer, whatever his other attainments, was no soldier.

The matter came up again in May of 1587, when the appointment of a Lieutenant for Lincolnshire was in question. Burghley wrote to Walsingham on the 22nd:[15]

'Some ones of my county of Lincolnshire have sent to me to prevent that my Lord of Lincoln[16] be not their lieutenant. They all fear his government. If there be a lieutenant thought meet I hope that neither Herts, where my standing[17] house is [Theobalds], nor Northants, where my principal house [is], have been thought to be committed to me, in respect of others that were partly greater and partly in more favour, yet in Lincolnshire, my native county, where also my livelihood resteth, shall not be thrust upon some others with whom, for government and for country liking, I dare compare. But if I were not by my countrymen earnestly admonished hereof and that I knew not my Lord of Lincoln's cunning to work underhand for his appetite, I would not write a word hereof ... But so none others be appointed I am content to lack it.'

Walsingham replied the day following:[18] 'I will stay the course of the earl of Lincoln's suit for the lieutenancy. It were a great wrong unto your Lordship, having your chief house in that country, that either he or any other should be preferred before your Lordship.'

These letters need no comment. The interesting thing about them is Burghley's emphasis upon local prestige. Elizabeth hastened to make amends. He was presently commissioned for Lincolnshire, and, after Leicester's appointment as commander-in-chief the following year, for Essex and Hertford as well.

The basic defects of these military arrangements were that they depended entirely upon local financing and that they provided no adequate system of training for the raw recruits. The weapons and the armour, during the period between musters, were stored and apparently no opportunity afforded during the interval for target practice. In the old days the archers had had their own long bows and got their skill from shooting 'at the butts'. But muskets had to come from the common store, and ammunition was expensive and hard to come by. During the musters there was a short period, generally less than a week, for more or less intensive training. But it was rudimentary in character. Add to that the local corruption, about which Sir John Falstaff made merry and which too often resulted in the selection of the worst for active service, and you get a picture of military preparedness which inspired no confidence at all.

The fact of the matter was that Elizabethan England had to pay for years of peace by having no adequate army to defend her in war. Except for the handful of soldiers in Ireland, who could not be moved in the face of threatened Spanish invasion, the only Englishmen who had military experience against trained troops were those who had gone with Leicester to the Low Countries in 1585 or had been sent to reinforce him there in subsequent years. Actually some thousand of them were brought back to England in the crisis of 1588. More could not safely have been withdrawn, since they constituted a first line of defence against the menace of Parma's descent from the Low Countries.

In the navy, officers and men had been engaged in running warfare with the Spaniards for twenty years and more. Man for man and ship for ship, they were easily better than the Spaniards. But the army was in a bad way.

Burghley had long taken an interest in the development of an effective soldiery. In 1569, for example, faced with the threat of a rising in the North, he had drawn up a memorandum designed to increase the numbers and the skill of the arquebusiers, which provided, among other things, for target shooting twice a month. But the idea never developed, probably because it was to be financed locally. Evidently Burghley belonged to the school of thought which preferred the arquebus before the long bow, though in the shooting matches he contemplated he did suggest that bowmen might compete for a second prize.[19]

He faced the problem again in February 1584[20] when there was a general fear of invasion following the discovery of the Throgmorton Plot. On that occasion he confined his attention to the maritime counties, and the essence of his proposal was a periodical inspection of county musters by royal experts.

'One sufficient gentleman,' he observed, 'well chosen, with entertainment of 10 shillings a day for his journey and 13/4 while he is in the county would do more good, being sent from her Majesty, than the work of all the commissioners [of array] for double the fine.'

He evidently had in mind no more than a temporary expedient to meet an emergency. The danger passed and nothing was done, but an analogous arrangement was applied some four years later to the local levies, mustered to meet the Spaniards in 1588.

In general the Lord Lieutenants were competent, discreet and faithful. It is probably safe to assume that Burghley had much to do with the choice of them,[21] not so easy a task when one considers that local prestige, royal favour and freedom from any taint of Roman Catholicism were basic requirements.

Those who, like Burghley, were Privy Councillors, functioned through Deputy Lieutenants. We have, in at least two instances, Burghley's instructions to his deputies, one for Lincolnshire in December 1587, and one for Essex and Hertford in March 1590.[22] Both of them reveal careful and intelligent discussion of the problems involved and, in the case of the latter one, some profit from the experience of 1588. Burghley evidently selected his own deputies for Lincolnshire though two of the four had held office under his predecessor.[23] Of the other two, one was his son, Thomas, the other a local magnate, Lord Willoughby of Parham.

Thomas had sat for Lincolnshire in the Parliament of 1585, and had afterwards served for a time as governor of Brill in the Low Countries. There he had seen active service, and was the only one of his father's four deputies who had faced the enemy in the field. But it is doubtful if he remained in Lincolnshire for long. He turns up in April 1588 as Deputy Lieutenant in Northants.[24] In July of the same year he was appointed one of the colonels in Lord Hunsdon's army to defend the Queen's person. Camden says that both he and his half-brother, Robert, as well as their brother-in-law, the Earl of Oxford, served as volunteers in Howard's fleet, and Burghley himself, in a pamphlet published anonymously after the Armada fight, confirmed the story.[25]

In the early 'eighties increasing interest was taken in the training of the better men in the musters, notably those equipped with fire-arms and currently known as 'shot'. This interest was intensified in the early spring of 1587, on the basis of reports from Walsingham's excellent spies in Spain that the Armada would attack that summer. Such indeed was Philip's intention, had not Drake 'singed his beard' and upset his arrangements. In February Burghley drafted orders to the maritime counties which throw considerable light upon the progress of military preparations in the counties.

'Whereas', Burghley wrote,[26] 'there have been general musters at sundry times made and thereupon numbers of footmen, with armour and weapons of sundry kinds, have been put in array and sorted into bands under captains and leaders and have been also trained and instructed by muster masters and others, partly from the lieutenants of the shire or their deputies and partly by commissioners of musters; now, considering how this present time, and that without any delay, requireth to have not only the foresaid numbers of men arrayed for the war to be put in readiness with their armour and weapons, but also the whole strength of the shire prepared, to their utmost power, for defence; . . . therefore her Majesty doth will and command that with all speed there be commandments for mustering of all such numbers as have been heretofore chosen and appointed for soldiers.'

From the last sentence it is evident that Burghley had in mind the muster of the trained bands. He drafted other orders 'for putting in strength the power of the realm, as well in maritime counties as in the inland' a fortnight later.

These drafts formed the basis of orders which went out from the Privy Council to the counties early in March, together with instructions for drill and directions for the levy of horsemen.[27]

We hear nothing more from Burghley on the subject until October. He fell out of the royal favour in March by reason of his part in the execution of Mary Queen of Scots. He was exiled from Court, though he sat regularly with the Privy Council and participated in its defence measures.

Actually, during the late spring and summer, if we may judge from the entries in the Acts of Privy Council, it was much more active in sending recruits to

Leicester in the Low Countries than in providing for defence at home. We hear in August of a sudden muster of men in the maritime counties when 220 ships were reported off the Scilly Islands and, later in the same month, we hear of munitions dispatched to the maritime counties.[28] But otherwise, nothing. Nor, except for the fortification of Portsmouth and an occasional letter from Lieutenants, protesting that they were unable to furnish the levies required,[29] do we hear of activities from any other source. It may be that the government was satisfied that Drake's expedition to the Spanish coast in the spring had effectively prevented any Spanish effort that summer.

But early in October fears of an immediate attack ran high. Walsingham had retired from Court in September to wrestle with his health[30] and the burden of administration once more fell upon Burghley's shoulders.

In a memorandum, evidently drawn up for consideration by the Privy Council in October,[31] he proposed that the navy be alerted, that the ports be closed and that the Lord Lieutenants be directed to assemble their fighting men. The Council took action on the 9th.[32] Burghley himself drafted their letter which went out to the Lieutenants, to the effect 'that you should presently, without any delay, use all good and speedy means ... for the putting of the forces under your charge in strength and thereupon to cause all persons heretofore mustered to be in readiness so as they may, with their captains and leaders, upon all sudden warning or occasion speedily repair to such place as by former instructions they ought to be ... Her Majesty willeth that no delay of time be used herein, but that all forces under your charge may be ready to march upon an hour's warning.'[33]

In November he wrote to Walsingham that the Queen was inquiring about an army to guard her person. She insisted that he should be constantly at the Court. 'When I am absent,' he added, 'she complaineth thereof, but when I come I find her Majesty otherwise occupied.'[34]

Later in the month he wrote to his old friend, the Earl of Shrewsbury,[35] apologizing for not writing more frequently. 'True it is,' he wrote, 'I have of late been so oppressed with business, now by Mr. Secretary's absence and by the heaps of affairs that this busy time breedeth, and therewith joining my late extreme anguish in my whole body, as I assure your Lordship on my faith I have not once dealt with friend or servant in any particular cause of mine own these ij months ... And for these fourteen days I have not without pain subscribed any letter. And yet have I indicted all matters of weight that be passed from her Majesty or the Council. And even now the whole burden is forced upon me, that I assure your Lordship I am weary to live.

'P.S. I need not certify your Lordship of my infirmity for I am ashamed that all London knoweth it to be notorious ... and Westminster Hall can witness the like, where I have been forced to be absent most of this long while.'

Evidently he was troubled by the neglect of his judicial duties in the Court of Wards and the Court of Exchequer.

The government had some difficulty in getting from the Lieutenants an accurate statement of the forces at their disposal and in December sent trained officers to the counties to review the situation at first hand, an arrangement which had been suggested by Burghley some three years before.

Leicester got back from the Low Countries in December 1587. It may be that he was responsible for the charge lodged against Burghley and Walsingham that they had neglected the business of strengthening England at home and abroad. In any case, on December 2nd, Walsingham on his sick bed drew up a defence of their actions which gives a fair picture of their achievements.[36]

He pointed out that by their efforts an army of 26,000 foot and [blank] horse had been organized and trained, 'a thing never put in execution in any of her Majesty's predecessors' times', and had been provided with ammunition. Besides that, they had organized and trained a second army of 24,000 foot and [blank] horse 'for a guard of her Majesty's person'.

He went on to describe their joint efforts to secure the friendship and support of the King of Scots, to strengthen the forces opposed to Parma in the Low Countries and to reinforce Henry of Navarre and the Huguenots in France.

He finally pointed out that they both had urged the Queen to dispatch Drake with a strong fleet a second time in the summer of 1587, to intercept the Spanish plate fleet from the West Indies, 'whereby the present storms that now hang over this realm might be closed and prevented'.

The claim was a just one. Between the two of them they had done their uttermost to strengthen England at home and secure the support of her allies abroad. Unfortunately all this cost money which the Queen doled out with such a sparing hand that they succeeded in achieving less than half of what they undertook to do. Scotland was still uncertain, Parma was master of the field in the Low Countries, and the best that could be said about France was that Navarre had at least not capitulated.

As for the army — strangely enough Walsingham said nothing about the navy — it consisted, as he pointed out, of some 50,000 foot and perhaps 10,000 horse, inexperienced to be sure, and very inadequately trained, but ready to defend their Queen and their country.[37]

But the actual mobilization in July fell far short of that figure. Leicester's army at Tilbury was only 11,500 strong and Hunsdon's army to guard the Queen's person could show only 1200 foot and 87 horse during the critical first week of August.[38] It seems likely that, beside these two armies, large forces were stationed in the maritime counties along the channel. One list puts the figure at 21,272 fighting men.[39]

Walsingham returned to work in December and resumed the detailed tasks of administration. He and Burghley worked closely together upon the problems of final preparations. Of Leicester we hear very little until he was appointed to command the army at Tilbury in July 1588, though he attended the meetings of the Council regularly and on one occasion at least served on a small committee of the Council to consider naval problems.[40] Much of what we do hear has to do with Walsingham's efforts, apparently successful, to make peace between Leicester and Sir Roger Williams and the Norrisses, who were among the best of Elizabeth's

o

trained officers and indispensable for the business of beating the raw levies into some kind of fighting shape. They were among Leicester's staff officers at Tilbury. He himself claimed credit for this, but one suspects royal pressure.

The problem of preparing the army was that of making a fighting force out of raw levies. The success remains problematical. It was never brought to the test. The navy, thanks to John Hawkins, was well equipped, well manned and ready for action on short notice. Burghley's part in this was the appointment of Hawkins in the first place, the support of him against attacks from many quarters, and the finding of money to finance the work of building new ships and maintaining old ones. There is no evidence to indicate that Burghley took any more immediate interest in the details of naval administration. He did, however, as early as February 1584, when the discovery of the Throgmorton Plot aroused a lively fear of invasion from Spain, outline a pattern of naval action[41] which to some extent anticipated that actually applied against the Armada.

'The Queen's navy', he wrote, 'would be put in readiness and the great ships of the realm would also be stayed from their voyages to join with her Majesty's navy.

'And the whole navy would be divided into 3 companies whereof the one would lie about the isles of Scilly, the second about the Isle of Wight, the third near Harwich or in the Downs.

'It is to be supposed that the adversary's forces must come from the west and if any of the same will attempt in force, the force of Scilly shall follow them and, upon knowledge had by land from Cornwall, so may that of the Isle of Wight resort thither, and if any force shall be ready on the land in Wales, the adversary will not hastily land, knowing what forces are in his tail. The English navy shall always have the English ports for their succour to avoid danger. . . .

'If the adversary will come eastward, that of Scilly is to follow and that of the Isle of Wight also, and if the adversary will greatly proceed all the three companies shall fall into one consort about the Downs.'

He reckoned the naval personnel at 12,000 men and costs at £40,000 for three months' service. It is not clear whether he included in these figures the auxiliary merchant ships or not.

Burghley contemplated a purely defensive operation. The idea of striking at the enemy in his home waters he did not in 1584 even consider. He evidently expected the decisive engagement to take place east of the straits of Dover, assuming probably that the enemy fleet would aim at the port of London.

Four years later, in February 1588, a group made up of Hatton, Leicester, Walsingham, Wooley and Burghley met together to consider the problems of defence, and Burghley laid before it a long memorandum on the subject.[42]

He first examined the strength of Spain and painted a grim picture of Spanish resources, both naval and military, adding to the strength of Spain that of Portugal and the Spanish dependencies in Italy and in the Low Countries. He thought Philip II might count also upon the support of the Holy Roman Empire, both for religious and for dynastic reasons. 'He is', Burghley concluded, 'the mightiest enemy that England ever had, mightier than his father, the emperor Charles, or any other monarch of Christendom was these many years.'

Burghley anticipated that the Spaniards would attempt to invade England and Ireland simultaneously and might also send to Scotland trained captains and some soldiers and enough money to induce the Scots to invade England from the north. He pointed out that there was a large party in Scotland of 'devoted papists and sworn enemies of England'.

Burghley went on to appraise England's opposing strength. He put first of all, as always, the Lord of Hosts. But after expressing the firm hope of divine assistance, he went on to enumerate other sources of strength. Invasion, he observed, could only come by sea and could only be resisted at sea.

'Her Majesty's special and most proper defence must be by ships. For ships of England, her Majesty is of her own proper ships so strong as the enemy shall not be able to land any power where her Majesty's navy shall be near to the enemy's navy. The ships of her subjects are also at this day both in number, in strength, in all captains and mariners, stronger than ever they were in the memory of man.'

He added to these the ships of Holland and Zeeland, which they were by treaty bound to supply. He envisaged other ships from Denmark or at least a Danish blockade of the Baltic and the cutting off of naval supplies to Spain from that quarter. He even suggested the possibility of ships from Scotland, 'small vessels, to empeach landing'.

France he thought could be counted upon at least for benevolent neutrality and the restraint of exports of foodstuffs and mariners to Parma in Flanders.

Burghley then turned to naval strategy, proposing that the English navy should be divided into two fleets, one to guard the narrow seas, the other 'towards Ireland and Spain, by which means the Spanish navy shall not be able to come to the Low Countries . . . for the English western [fleet] shall follow them if they come to the east and they shall be intercepted by the English east navy'. In this particular he once again anticipated the strategy which Howard and Drake actually followed.

He went on to advocate a naval expedition to Portugal which might inspire confidence in the Portuguese when the Spanish fleet was away, and suggested that if the King, Don Antonio, were enabled to land in Portugal, 'the King of Spain should hazard the crown which he now possesseth, whilst he seeketh for another that neither he hath nor ought to have'.

Burghley went further than that, and suggested that another fleet be prepared to intercept the Spanish ships at the Azores, 'the execution thereof will be very profitable for the maintenance of the charges of the wars, and the report of the intention to put such a navy in readiness, in the name of Sir Francis Drake, may be an occasion to diminish the number of the King's shipping against England or percase a diversion of his purpose against England'.[43]

Clearly Burghley had no mean idea both of the defensive and the offensive potentialities of the English navy. But he recognized the immediate necessity of providing naval stores, 'powder, sails, masts, cordage'. He called for a stay of all ships in English ports, a listing of them and an enrolment of all their mariners. He advocated also the interception of all ships carrying naval stores to Spanish ports.

He then turned to the army, referred to the system of training already inaugurated, suggested that troops available be sent to the sea coasts and that steps be taken to stimulate the work of the Lord Lieutenants in the counties and to meet the needs of both horse and foot without delay. He called for a report from all the counties of the forces they had mustered, including an account of what the gentry could furnish independently, which he reckoned at one-half the mustered forces.

Finally he considered the thorny question of financing this vast programme.

The strength of the royal navy he put at 36 ships and pinnaces, with some 6000 mariners, the cost of which for three months in wages and victuals he estimated at £34,000.

In addition to these he envisaged the maintenance of 30 other 'ships of merchants meet for war' with 4200 mariners, the cost of which he put at £17,000. To these he added 20 other ships with 2000 mariners, at £9000 or £10,000.

These figures covered simply victuals and wages, though in the case of the auxiliary ships it probably included ship hire. He estimated that 'powder and other munitions, with cordage and other apparelle' would cost another £5000.

In short, for the navy alone, taking no account apparently of the fleets to be dispatched to Portugal and the Azores, £66,000.

At the same time he did not forget that the Queen would have to maintain her forces in the Low Countries at an annual cost of £130,000, would have to increase her forces in Ireland, at a cost for six months of £7000, in addition to the current cost of £25,000. And he thought that, in view of the doubtful attitude of Scotland, a force of at least 3000 men should be stationed on the borders, which for four months would cost £13,000.

He suggested that the forces in Kent and in Portsmouth should be reinforced at a further cost of £4000.

He contemplated two armies, one to defend the coasts, one to defend the Queen, the first of which should number at least 10,000 at a cost of not less than £12,000, the cost to be doubled if the enemy actually effected a landing. The army to defend the Queen should, he believed, number not less than 20,000, the cost of which for two months he estimated at £40,000.

Altogether, on the assumption that mobilization would be for three months, the bill, by Burghley's reckoning, would come to something over a quarter of a million pounds. He made no suggestion for finding this sum of money.

There were a number of problems which Burghley was quite aware of but which he did not cover. He said nothing of his fear that the Dutch might make a separate peace with Spain and withdraw from the fight.[44] He hinted at, but did not elaborate, his concern about an uprising of the English Catholics.

For some reason or other, Burghley was the one member of the Privy Council who took the most lively interest in the Catholic recusants. He was the one, above all others, who seems to have been most fearful of their disloyalty. He could never see, what his royal mistress saw clearly, that, in spite of papal bulls, the great majority of English Catholics were basically loyal to their country and their Queen. His impulse invariably was, when danger threatened England from without, to be on guard against danger from within.

Up until the mid-'seventies when the Roman Catholic missionaries began to arrive in England in increasing numbers, the treatment of the recusants had been singularly mild. But the success of the Jesuits provoked a much more rigorous policy. In 1581 the fine for non-attendance at church services was suddenly increased from a shilling a Sunday to £20 a month, and the punishment of recusants who sheltered priests made very severe. In 1584 Burghley sent instructions to various counties to call upon the recusants to furnish horsemen for service in Ireland, and they were exploited in the same way the following year to supply Leicester's army in the Low Countries.[45] Their response to these demands was so satisfactory that early in 1586 offer was made to the recusants to reduce their fines from £20 a month to a smaller sum commensurate with their resources.[46] It may well be that the government found it impossible to collect the full fine and was willing to settle for a half or a third, or, in the case of the less well-to-do, a quarter. In any case, the recusants were somewhat better off, though at some time during the year they were called upon to surrender their armour and weapons.[47]

But the following year their plight deteriorated. In February 1587, when the impending execution of the Scottish Queen seemed likely to provoke a Catholic uprising in her behalf, Burghley advocated the imprisonment of all recusants of wealth and station.[48] Later in the same year he sought from the Anglican bishops a confidential report of the religious proclivities of the Justices of the Peace in their dioceses, raising the following questions:

(1) Are any of them recusants?
(2) Do any of them favour recusants?

About the same time he proposed that all Justices of the Peace should take the Oath of Supremacy and should forbear to exercise their office until they had done so.[49]

In October 1587 he directed Walsingham to have a list made of well-to-do recusants in every shire, 'that there be such order taken with them as they may do no harm nor be any comfort to the enemy'.[50] In December he sent out orders that all recusants who had returned from overseas should be tendered the Oath of Supremacy and, upon refusal, be certified to the Privy Council.[51]

All of this led up to an order issued in January 1588 by the Privy Council to the Lord Lieutenants in the counties, ordering them to apprehend all 'popish' recusants, to commit the most obdurate to the common prisons and the more moderate to the custody of ecclesiastical persons.[52]

In April the weapons which had been taken for the two years before were sold or distributed to mustered men in need of them.[53]

After the Armada had come and gone, Burghley declared that the recusants were not restrained out of any doubt about their loyalty but to discourage the renegade English refugees in France and Flanders. He even observed that the Privy Council was of two minds about setting them at liberty. But this was in a pamphlet designed to conciliate the recusants and must be discounted.

Scotland was another source of anxiety. In July 1585 James had agreed to an English alliance in return for a pension of £4000 and an assurance that his right to the succession would be protected. For the next year relations with Scotland were friendly, but James took umbrage at the execution of his mother early in 1587, particularly since he was having difficulty in collecting the promised pension. The consequence was that the Spanish Catholic party in Scotland increased steadily in favour and the threat of the Armada quickened James's natural disposition to fish in troubled waters. Walsingham feared the worst. He was as usual pessimistic, Burghley hardly less so. In November he wrote to Walsingham:

'As one sick man to another I write uncertainly, understanding that her Majesty is with you and that I am sure she will speak with you of Scottish matters, from which all evil or good is shortly to come. I thought good to send you a copy of a writing that Archibald Douglas gave me four days past. He also declared to me yesternight an accident of a combination of a great part of the nobility for favour of papist religion and Spanish favours. He said that he had declared the same to her Majesty. Many things concur therewith, as your advertisements out of Spain by way of France. . . .

'I send you also a letter from my Lord of Hunsdon by whose last clause of his letter, written with his own hand, . . . we have no cause to hope well of the Scottish King. Yet I am sure he would do any office to reclaim him. Absence of conference engendereth stratagems and so in the end disdain. In this matter is to be considered whether her Majesty may do the King of Scots more harm or he her. Because her Majesty, as I perceive, will come to me from you, I have thought to present you with these lines, of a hand lame.'[54]

The following April Burghley wrote to Wooley, the Latin secretary: 'If this fire be presently quenched in Scotland, her Majesty need fear no offence to be yielded by Spain or Flanders. Otherwise, the danger by foreign war will speedily come from thence, where with surety they may make wars without any resistance by sea, but herein I cannot nor dare not give advice to her Majesty because I know not how her Majesty hath dealt with the Master of Gray and with Wemyss.'[55]

Burghley never could be sure what his mistress was up to behind his back. He was in close touch with Scottish affairs and in constant correspondence with Archibald Douglas, the King's representative in England. He evidently felt reasonably secure against an attack by sea, far from secure against an attack by land, particularly through the north where the English Catholics were strong and of doubtful loyalty. He could depend upon a well-equipped, well-trained navy as he could not depend upon an improvised army. His policy towards Scotland coincided with that of Walsingham and they worked together upon Elizabeth to persuade her to be more generous and upon James to convince him that he had more to gain from an English connection than from any alternative. But the Scottish situation was still 'tickle' at the time when the Armada arrived in the Channel. William Ashley, who was dispatched to Scotland in July, wrote to Burghley on August 6th.[56]

'The necessity of the time and the imminent danger of a revolt in this country by the approach of the Spaniard into the narrow seas has made me make such offers as follow, to satisfy his Majesty for the time and to qualify the minds of the nobility to keep all in quiet whilst her Majesty and her Council resolve what is to be done.'

He admitted that he had exceeded his instructions, but pleaded the force of circumstance. In short he offered to James an English duchy with reasonable revenues attached, a yearly pension of £5000, the maintenance of a bodyguard of 50 gentlemen about his person, and so forth.

Needless to say, these offers were repudiated when the danger was past. But the fact that they were made reveals a sense of the immediacy of the danger. When James discovered that he had been tricked, he threatened to take advantage of Spanish offers. But it was too late.[57] Elizabeth, flushed with victory, was no longer to be intimidated.

When the English navy took its position in the early spring of 1588, it was divided into three — a small fleet under Seymour in the narrow seas to watch Parma, the main fleet under Howard at Portsmouth and a third fleet under Drake at Plymouth. Later Howard joined with Drake at Plymouth preliminary to a projected attack upon the Armada in Spanish waters. This was Drake's idea and it was endorsed by Howard himself and by his other naval councillors, Hawkins, Frobisher and Fenner. That it was not executed was due to the Queen's reluctance to take the offensive while she was negotiating for peace. It was not until June that she withdrew her objections, and Howard was for getting to sea at once, and would have gone with only three days' supply of victuals. But the wind, which blew steadily from the south-west, not only prevented his supplies from reaching him, but made it very difficult to get his fleet out of Plymouth harbour, and virtually impossible to reach the Spanish coast.

It has too often been assumed that Burghley was opposed to such bold tactics, but the evidence in support of this view is unreliable. It comes from Spanish sources. The Spanish ambassador in Paris got it from Stafford, the English ambassador there. Burghley always posed as a friend of Spain, even when his intentions were quite otherwise. He may, by this time, have come to share Walsingham's distrust of Stafford and made use of him to mislead Mendoza in turn. What evidence there is to the contrary is mainly negative. Nothing in Burghley's correspondence with Howard or with Hawkins (there is virtually none with Drake) indicates that he was not in complete harmony with the war party. There is one morsel of direct evidence. On April 13th, 1588, writing to Thomas Bodley in the Low Countries, Burghley closed his letter: 'And so because I will not stay the messenger, the wind serving him better than it doth, to our great grief, our navy in Plymouth to go to Spain.'[58]

Probably Burghley's most positive contribution to the preparations for war was in providing funds for the pay of mariners, the building and repair of ships, the supply of munitions and of victuals. These were the topics which figure most prominently in his correspondence with Howard, with Hawkins and with James Quarles, the surveyor of victuals for the navy. Like all treasurers, Burghley was always casting about to reduce expenditures. On the basis of one surviving memorandum[59] in which he made suggestions for saving money on victuals, it has been intimated that he was more interested in saving money than in defence. The intimation does him a grave injustice. No one knew better than he the amount of extravagance and corruption that permeated all branches of public expenditure, both in peace and war. No one worked harder than he to eliminate it. That was about all he could do. The fact was, of course, that the whole service of supply was hopelessly inadequate to meet the demand. It had been devised for a small fleet and a short war. James Quarles was new to the business. He had been in office less than a year. When he came to it there were virtually no reserve stores of provisions on hand. The Queen, preoccupied with the pursuit of peace, was of no mind to spend money in preparation for war. She mobilized her navy in December, but reduced Howard's crews to half strength in January.

Burghley had outlined a plan of belligerent action in February, and had compiled rough figures of its probable cost. In the same month Elizabeth sent off her peace commissioners to Parma. When the peace negotiations were finally abandoned, the Spanish Armada was at the mouth of the Channel with no time left for an adequate reorganization of the service of supply. The amazing thing is that it did not break down altogether.

No wonder Walsingham wrote to Burghley in June: 'I am sorry to see so great danger hanging over this realm so slightly regarded and so carelessly provided for . . . Seeing we have neither recourse to pray nor to such effectual preparations as the danger importeth, I cannot but conclude (according to man's judgment) *"Salus ipsa non servare hanc rempublicam"*.'[60]

When Elizabeth named Charles Howard as commander of the fleet in December, she appointed Burghley a deputy Lord High Admiral.[61] But there is no evidence of his functioning in that capacity, though it must have increased the burden on his old shoulders during the spring of 1588. It was probably at his suggestion that the Queen called for a loan from her better-to-do subjects in January.[62] It yielded some £75,000, and she borrowed £30,000 from the city of London in March.[63] In April she decided to shift the expense of furnishing and equipping the auxiliary fleet to the port towns — a device which developed into ship money and became a major grievance fifty years later. It is impossible, on the basis of what evidence we have on the subject, to discover who was the author of this device. Probably it was not Burghley. His estimate of expenses in February makes no mention of it.[64]

In July Walsingham wrote to him: 'For the defraying of the charges, her [Majesty's] pleasure is your Lordship shall consider what course may be held for the taking up of a convenient sum of money. Her Majesty named £40,000 or £50,000. I had some speech with Mr. Horatio [Palavicino] about the matter . . . He thinketh that upon the Merchant Adventurers' bonds, there will be money found. There be divers rich Flemings residing at Cologne, Hamburg and Frankfurt that can furnish great sums.'[65]

Burghley replied the following day: 'I have had conference with Palavicino and with Saltonstall [governor of the Merchant Adventurers] how £40 or £50,000 might be had for 10% but I find no probability how to get money here in specie, which is our lack, but by exchange to have it out of the parts beyond sea, which will not be done but in a long time. Yet there is some likelihood that our merchants of Stade might practice for £20 or £30,000 for which there shall be some proof very secretly.'[66]

In the same letter Burghley wrote that Howard and Hawkins were both crying for money for wages and victuals, that the Admiralty needed £7000 to discharge an old debt and £6000 to meet current needs. He managed to induce them to pay off their debt by instalments.

The ordinance department was calling for £8000 for equipment for the levies.

And so forth — including money to pay 5000 foot and 1000 horse for defence against the enemy landings in Essex. 'A man could wish,' he added, 'if peace cannot be had, that the enemy would not longer delay but prove (as I trust) his evil fortune. For as these expectations do consume us so I would hope by God's goodness, upon their defeat, we might have one half year's time to provide for money.'

In August he was negotiating for a loan with the London livery companies, and interviewed the heads of companies — the Grocers and Drapers at one o'clock, the Skinners, Goldsmiths, Fishmongers and Haberdashers at three, the Mercers at four,[67] etc. He managed to raise an additional £25,970 that way,[68] though most of it was not paid over until after the crisis was past.

He was much concerned about the popular reaction to the heavy financial burden. On July 18th he wrote to Walsingham: 'The reports which I hear out of sundry counties of the reiteration of unsupportable charges towards musters[69] do trouble me as much as the expenses of the Queen's treasure. I assure you I know that whole towns pay as much as four subsidies,[70] so as it will be very unreasonable to demand new subsidies, specially even now, when within 1 or 2 months a second assessment is to be paid.[71] If these demandings for musters, for powder and new weapons were not demanded of the poor in towns, the matter were of less moment, for the rich may well bear greater. I see a general murmur of people and malcontented people will increase it to the comfort of the enemy. I pray you bear with my earnestness herein though I cannot prescribe a remedy in certainty.'

So Burghley wrote less than a fortnight before the Armada arrived. Less than a fortnight after it had left he published a pamphlet which set forth in glowing terms the response of the English people to the call to defend 'their religion and their liberties'.

'I forgot', he wrote, 'to report unto you the great numbers of ships of the subjects of the realm, or of London and other port towns and cities that voluntarily this year were armed, all to make a full navy . . . and all at the proper costs of the burghesses . . . with men, victuals and munitions, which did join the Queen's own navy . . . a thing never in any former age heard of otherwise than that such ships

were always hired, waged and victualled by the kings of the realm, which argued
. . . a most vehement and unaccustomed affection and devotion in the cities and the
port towns, such as they showed themselves therein ready to fight, as it had been,
pro aris and focis.'[72]

The facts, of course, were that the contribution of ships was not voluntary but
by order of the Privy Council, and was greeted by a storm of protest, particularly
from the smaller towns.[73] But everything looked different in mid-August than it
had in mid-July. It was Burghley's business to make it look different. His letter
in July was a confidential letter to a friend and colleague; his pamphlet in August
was addressed to the world at large.

Burghley was in his sixty-eighth year, and a very old man by contemporary
reckoning. During the spring and summer of 1588 he was almost always in pain.
In mid-July he wrote to Walsingham: 'I hope to get out of my bed this day but not
without great pain. As soon as I may be well carried I will endeavour to be brought
to Court.'[74]

The one thing he never contemplated was quitting.

Too often when he got to Court he found his mistress preoccupied with other
things. 'I see many times', he wrote to Walsingham in June, 'that we who do
employ ourselves both forenoons and afternoons at Westminster, when we are
called to Court in manner of alarm . . . the greater part of our time at Court is not
spent in service causes. Yet I hope this time will amend those courtly errors. I
pray you let me know if on Wednesday the rest of the Council shall come and I
will not be behind any.'[75]

On June 12th he received from his brother-in-law, Killigrew, a copy of Cardinal Allen's vicious attack upon the Queen. In sending the book to Walsingham,
he wrote: 'Good consideration would be had how both to suppress it from being
public here and to have some answer made to the reproof and remedy. Surely I
could wish it forbidden as the time requireth, upon pain of treason to any that shall
come to have it and not destroy it, without communicating it to any but a Councillor. For answer I could wish some expert learned man would feign an answer
as from a number of Catholics that notwithstanding their evil contentment . . .
should profess their obedience and service with their lives and power against all
strange forces offering to land in this realm, and to advertise the Cardinal that he is
deceived in his opinion to think that any nobleman in this land or any gentleman
of possessions will favour the invasion of the realm.'[76]

Ten days later he received a copy of the papal bull deposing Elizabeth and calling
upon her subjects to rise against her. 'Surely,' he wrote to Walsingham on June
24th,[77] 'the publication hereof would be impeached, though all men of judgment,
not corrupted with Romish poison, will be rather stirred to defend the Queen's
person and their country than to offend. I have perused Mr. Solicitor's draft of a
proclamation which I like very well and allow the manner of prohibition of the
same better than in my writing was contained. And yet my desire in that point may
in some sort be added to his, for the destroying or bringing of the same to the Lieutenants, who are meeter men than the *custos brevium* named by him.'[78]

In the same letter, Burghley enclosed a copy of a proposed declaration. 'When you shall read it,' he wrote, 'you shall find a purpose to notify the people both all her [Majesty's] former actions in dealing in Scotland and France and now in the Low Countries, and her present preparations to defend the country, for that her actions are by the enemies abroad published as original causes of the civil troubles in all foreign countries.'

It does not appear to have been published. One wonders how Burghley managed to write it in the midst of so much other business and so much bodily pain. It is one more amazing revelation of his vitality.[79]

Early in July at the end of Trinity term the Lord Chancellor, following the customary practice, called together in Star Chamber the Justices of Assize and addressed them on current problems.[80] On one or two previous occasions Burghley had substituted for the Chancellor. On this occasion he spoke after him. The bare bones of his speech are preserved among Robert Beale's papers.[81]

Burghley spoke on three subjects — Allen's book, the preparations for war and the negotiations for peace. He referred to Allen as a 'base companion', a Cardinal of the Roman Church, but not at all the sort of fellow usually selected for that office. Ignoring Allen's virulent attack upon the Queen, Burghley emphasized what he called Allen's 'Luciferian authority', his claim to have been appointed to set the royal crown of England upon the head of any person whom the Pope and the King of Spain should select. This, Burghley evidently felt, was what would hit the average Englishman hardest — not criticism of the Queen, but assumption of power by a fellow who was not even a gentleman to hand over the English crown to a foreigner.

He left Allen at that, and turned to the threatened invasion, boasting that the Queen's navy was stronger than that of any sovereign before her. He expressed his conviction that with God's grace she would win. His colleagues on the Council, he said, were eager to see her fleet join in battle with the enemy. But he personally did not think that the Spaniards would risk an engagement, pointing out that the Queen's Channel fleet had challenged Parma to come out and fight, a challenge which Parma himself was disposed to accept, but his mariners would have none of it. This was Burghley's version of Parma's refusal to attempt invasion before the Spanish fleet arrived to defend his passage.

Burghley left his audience with the impression that the Spaniards might not fight at all, but if they did the English navy was more than a match for them.

Burghley then had something to say about the peace negotiations. He had heard them criticized. The truth was, he declared, that Parma had initiated the peace movement, which the Queen at first was wary of, 'but being further pressed, her highness, knowing that peace was the gift of God, was very loath that the world should imagine that she had refused any honourable means to come by the same'. She had sent her commissioners to negotiate on terms which were both reasonable and honourable, and she had encountered nothing but trifling. Under these circumstances he saw little hope of peace.

It must have been hard for Hatton, the Lord Chancellor, to suppress a wry smile at this version of Elizabeth's eagerness for peace, and hard for Burghley to keep a straight face as he told it. But such was the official version. The fact that Burghley felt called upon to state it suggests that there was a considerable amount of adverse criticism in the air about her peace manœuvring.

Burghley concluded 'with a great exhortation that every man should provide to serve his Queen and his country, men of peace with looking to the peace, men of arms with addressing themselves to arms'.

No doubt Burghley spoke at much greater length than this. Brevity, either in speech or in writing, was not among his virtues. And yet he was currently regarded as a great orator and some of the most important pamphlets issued by the government in defence of its policy came from his pen. The best of the Catholic pamphleteers, Thomas Morgan, for example, or Allen himself, did a much better job of it; and the Puritan, Martin Marprelate, whoever he was, was presently to demonstrate how it really might be done.

One aspect of the war preparations should not be ignored — the resort to prayer. Burghley himself always put the help of God first of all. One prayer, composed by a gentleman of the Household[82] for use in the Queen's chapel, but widely used in other places, was of singular beauty:

'O Lord God, heavenly Father, the *Lord of Hosts*, without whose providence nothing proceedeth, and without whose mercy nothing is saved: in whose power lie the hearts of princes, and the end of all their actions; have mercy upon thine afflicted church; and especially regard thy servant Elizabeth, our most excellent queen, to whom thy dispersed flock do fly, in the anguish of their souls, and in the zeal of thy truth. Behold! how the princes of the nations do band themselves against her, because she laboureth to purge thy sanctuary, and that thy holy church may live in security.

'Consider, O Lord, how long thy servant hath laboured to them for peace: but how proudly they prepare themselves unto battle. Arise therefore, maintain thine own cause, and judge thou between her and her enemies. She seeketh not her own honour, but thine; not the dominions of others, but a just defence of herself; not the shedding of Christian blood, but the saving of poor afflicted souls. Come down therefore, come down, and deliver thy people by her. To vanquish is all one with thee, by few or by many, by want or by wealth, by weakness or by strength. O! possess the hearts of our enemies with a fear of thy servants. The cause is thine, the enemies thine, the afflicted thine; the honour, victory and triumph shall be thine.

'Consider, Lord, the end of our enterprises. Be present with us in our armies. Terrify the hearts of our enemies; and make a joyful peace for thy Christians.

'And now, since in this extreme necessity thou has put into the heart of thy servant Deborah to provide strength to withstand the pride of Sisera and his adherents, bless thou all her forces by sea and land. Grant all her people one heart, one mind, and one strength, to defend her person, her kingdom, and thy true religion. Give unto all her council and captains wisdom, wariness, and courage; that they may speedily prevent the devices, and valiantly withstand the forces of all our enemies: that the fame of the gospel may be spread unto the ends of the world.

We crave this in thy mercy, O heavenly Father, for the precious death of thy dear Son Jesus Christ. *Amen*.'

The Spanish Armada under Medina Sidonia reached the mouth of the Channel on July 19th. Contact between the two fleets was established on the 21st and for the next nine days there was a running fight up the Channel. On the 30th the Spaniards, badly battered, reached the North Sea and were flying northward with Howard and Drake at their heels. Drake wrote to Walsingham on the 31st: 'We have the army of Spain before us and mind with the grace of God to wrestle a pull with him. There was never anything pleased me better than the seeing the enemy flying with a southerly wind northward. I doubt not, ere it be long, so to handle the matter with the Duke of Sidonia as he shall wish himself at St. Mary Port among his orange trees.'

Drake was denied the opportunity of striking the *coup de grâce*. But what he failed to do the storms in the far north largely accomplished. It was, however, some weeks before the English were satisfied that the danger had passed.

Between July 20th and August 10th the Council sat daily at Richmond until July 30th and after that at St. James's in Westminster. Burghley attended virtually every session. A few of his memoranda survive which reveal that he was active in such divers matters as naval supply, the price of armour and the examination of Spanish prisoners.[83] Probably, with his eye always on the expense account, he was largely responsible for the rapid demobilization of the army, county by county, as the threat of land attack from the Armada receded with its eastward course. He had his eye also on the ripening grain, and the imperative need of turning spears into reaping hooks for the harvesting. As early as August 5th, three days before the Queen's famous visit to Tilbury, Leicester was ordered to discharge one-third of his infantry, selecting those from near-by counties so that if the need arose they could be called back quickly.[84]

Burghley did not accompany Elizabeth to Tilbury, but he visited the camp a few days later. Leicester wrote to Shrewsbury on August 15th: 'The gentleman [the bearer] hath seen our camp and a fair show I made my Lord Treasurer, who came from London to visit us.'[85]

Unfortunately for the historian, Burghley's daily association with Walsingham at the council board precluded the necessity of correspondence between them, our chief source of information at this juncture about his thoughts and his doings. His first letter to Walsingham, in August, on the 9th, was provoked by the absence of Walsingham with the Queen at Tilbury. One would have expected it to be aglow with victory. But it began with a fear that the Armada might have taken refuge either in Denmark or in the Firth of Forth, and went on to say that he had £8000 or £9000 on hand for payment of Howard's mariners which he hesitated to deliver until he knew the Queen's pleasure. And then he turned to the question of naval demobilization.

'The Lord Admiral', he wrote, 'I think will discharge all sick men and the refuse of the small vessels. But being here alone I dare not direct anything to him, presuming that with her Majesty's liking you there will advise him how to keep his strength only of ships of value, considering there are in the Narrow Seas with my Lord Harry [Seymour] so many small vessels.

'I am not of opinion that the Spanish fleet will return from the North or the East, being weakened as they are and knowing that our navy is returned to our coasts where they may repair their losses and be as strong as they were afore. And without a north or east wind the Spanish fleet cannot come back to England.

'I wish, if they pass about Ireland, that four good ships, well manned and conducted, might follow them to their ports, where they might distress a great number of them, being well beaten and where the number of gallants will not continue on ship board.

'It is in vain to write any more . . . until by my Lord Cobham we may learn some things of the Duke of Parma who now resteth the enemy to be withstood.'

Walsingham replied from Tilbury the same day. He had arranged, he wrote, to call a council meeting the following Sunday at St. James's for conference with Howard and Leicester about demobilization. The Queen, he added, had word that the Spanish fleet planned to return and to assist Parma in his plans for invasion.[86] Her disposition at first had been to remain with the army, 'a conceit her Majesty had that in honour she could not return [to Court] in case there were any likelihood that the enemy would attempt anything. But she presently changed her mind. Thus your Lordship seeth that this place breedeth courage. I fear now more the hand of God in respect of unseasonableness of the weather than the enemy.'

In another letter of the same date he explained his reference to the weather. 'The Flushingers were forced to retire from Dunkirk the last storm, the gap left open being not yet retrieved. But I hope that through the Lord Admiral's care they will be stopped in their passage.'

Drake had also paused in his triumphant pursuit of the Spaniards to insert a note of warning about Parma. None of them seem to have grasped the fact that with the English navy in command of the Narrow Seas it would have been sheer suicide for Parma to attempt a crossing. No one knew that better than Parma himself. But neither Burghley nor Walsingham was disposed to take any chances. They feared that the cheese-paring attitude of their mistress would insist too soon on demobilization. 'It were not wisdom,' Walsingham wrote to Burghley on August 9th, 'until we see what will become of the Spanish fleet, to disarm too fast.'[87]

But the Lord Treasurer began to count the cost. On the 12th he drew up a memorandum of the expenses of maintaining Howard's and Seymour's fleets and arrived at the rather staggering figure of £13,033 16s. per month. His comment is revealing:

'To spend in time convenient is wisdom.

'To continue charges without needful cause bringeth repentance.

'To hold on charges without knowledge of the certainty thereof and the means to support them is lack of wisdom.'[88]

This stated the problem but did not supply the answer. If the spending was necessary, where was the money to come from? That was what he was asking himself.

Actually demobilization of the navy began late in August, and by September 4th out of 197 ships with crews aggregating 15,925 men which represented the strength of Elizabeth's navy on August 1st, only 34 ships with crews aggregating 4453 remained at the Queen's charge.[89] The problem of discharging the others, which involved paying them off, fell for the most part upon Sir John Hawkins's shoulders as Treasurer of the Navy. Between the demands of the mariners and the shortage of money he had a bitterly hard time of it. He went as fast as he could, but not fast enough to suit Burghley, who was anxious to save every penny he could in a rapidly diminishing treasury.

'I would to God', Hawkins wrote to Walsingham early in September, 'I were delivered of the dealing for money and then I doubt not but I should as well deserve and continue my Lord's [Burghley's] good liking as any man of my sort. But now I know I shall never please his Lordship two months together, for which I am very sorry, for I am sure no man living hath taken more pain, nor been more careful to obtain and continue his Lordship's good liking and favour towards me ... God I trust will deliver me of it ere long, for there is no other hell. I devise to ease charge and shorten what I can for which I am in a general misliking, but my Lord Treasurer thinketh I do little.'[90]

Somehow or other Burghley found time during August to write for the press. In the early autumn a pamphlet was published in London, entitled *The Copy of a Letter sent out of England to Don Bernardino de Mendoza, Ambassador in France for the King of Spain, declaring the State of England.* It was written as though from a devoted Catholic whose hopes of deliverance had been blasted by the defeat of the Armada. There can be no reasonable doubt that Burghley was the author.

Among his papers in the Lansdowne MSS.[91] is a complete draft of the pamphlet in his own hand; a revision of this draft in the hand of his secretary, Henry Maynard, with copious interlineations and marginal additions in Burghley's hand; and finally a revision of the introductory paragraph in Burghley's hand.

The pamphlet as printed follows fairly closely the revision of Burghley's manuscript text. There are some interesting variations between the first draft and the revisions, and some between the revisions and the printed text, but no essential changes.

We should perhaps regard this pamphlet as the logical outcome of Burghley's own suggestion in June that Allen's virulent attack upon Elizabeth should be answered by some 'expert learned man, pretending to speak for English Catholics and professing their obedience and service with their lives ... against all strange forces offering to land in this realm'. After the Armada, Burghley took on the job himself. The title page of the pamphlet declared that it had been found among the papers of Richard Leigh, a seminary priest who had been executed at Tyburn on August 30th. Leigh was therefore in no position to contradict. Burghley in his text sustained his assumed role well, so well that to this day his pamphlet is ascribed in the *Short Title Catalogue* to Leigh.[92] Actually Burghley never pretended to be Leigh, never attempted to play the part of a seminary priest. He wrote as a Catholic layman, lamenting the failure of the Armada, which he attributed to faulty appraisal of English strength both by land and sea and to an unjustified expectation that the English Catholics would rally to the support of the invader.

He then proceeded to paint a picture of English military and naval strength which, although somewhat exaggerated, was not too much at variance with the facts. In this connection he asserted that the English fighting ships had proved themselves more than a match for the Spanish ships, that not a single English ship had been sunk and that plans were already on foot to add to English naval strength, so much so that it was futile to suppose that a second attempt would be more successful than the first. He made much of the fact that many of the English ships had been contributed gratis by Englishmen and had been fitted out and victualled at their expense — a somewhat distorted account of the forced levy by the Privy Council.

In his estimate of military strength he tended to confuse potential man-power with trained soldiers; for example, he placed the strength of Hunsdon's army at 40,000 foot and 6000 horse though it actually hardly mustered one-tenth of that number. Here again he emphasized the voluntary efforts of the nobility, particularly of those held to be Catholic sympathizers. And this led him off into an enumeration of the greater nobility and their contributions, an elaboration which does not appear in his original draft. He made no mention of the naval exploits of his son, Thomas, at first, but Thomas crept into the revision. He made no mention of his son, Robert, or of his grandson, William, either in the first or the revised draft. They both appear in the printed version. He wound up with the statement that all of the nobility without exception played their part or wanted to play their part in the defence of their Queen and country, speaking at length of Lord Montague, a recognized Catholic sympathizer, who marched to the Queen with his son and his grandson and a goodly retinue, all in battle array; and of the Earl of Arundel, a Catholic pensioner in the Tower, who begged that he might be allowed to serve.

A large part of the pamphlet was devoted to the demonstrated loyalty of the English Catholics. In that connection he called attention to the fact that good Catholics who remained loyal to their faith and loyal also to their Queen were in no jeopardy of life and limb, though they had to pay heavy fines for refusal to attend the Established Church, contrasting their position with that of the Protestants under Mary and the English victims of the Inquisition in Spain. Speaking as an English Catholic he deplored the techniques of those who, professing themselves to be priests, many of them being both very young and of light behaviour, came secretly into the realm to preach treason. It had been better, he suggested, for the cause if 'discreet, holy and learned men were sent', who, 'without intermeddling in matters of state', by teaching strengthened those of the faith and won over others that are not rooted in heresy. He suggested that the Pope might alleviate the lot of the recusants if he granted them dispensation to attend the Established Church occasionally, 'so they might then avoid heavy fines and enjoy their livings and liberty'. For so, he concluded, 'did all Christian religion at the first begin and spread itself over the world, not by force but only by teaching and example of holiness in the teachers against all human force'.

Of all Burghley's contributions to the literature of propaganda, this letter to Mendoza was the best thing he ever did. His touch was never a light one, but he nevertheless contrived to present a plausible picture of an English Catholic, loyal to his faith, paying tribute by indirection to the English war effort, to the English nobility, to the gallant Queen, and most of all to the national loyalty of English Catholics; and at the same time denouncing papal policy and making mock of Mendoza's omniscience and of Spanish invincibility.

During the early autumn Burghley kept busy with his pen. Not long after he had finished his *Letter to Mendoza*,[93] but before it had gone to press, Burghley received a letter from Sir Henry Wallop, Lord Justice in Ireland, enclosing examinations of several mariners from the Spanish fleet who had been taken prisoner on the Irish west coast. Taken together they presented a harrowing revelation of the destruction suffered by the Armada in Irish waters. Burghley, and it was probably he, at once seized upon the idea of publishing these examinations, translated of course, but otherwise unchanged,[94] as a kind of supplement to the *Letter to Mendoza*. He had to work fast,[95] and perhaps on that account refrained from transmuting the actual words of the prisoners into his own ponderous prose. Certainly as propaganda the material was much more effective as it stood. Burghley did not even comment on the examinations, though he did add at the end a summary of the losses which the Armada had suffered in men and ships during the engagements in the Channel and through September shipwrecks in Ireland. He put the loss in ships at 32 and in mariners at 10,185. Later researches reveal that the Spaniards lost 63 ships, almost twice his estimate, and approximately half of the entire Armada.

In both editions of the *Letter to Mendoza*, published in October, the so-called *Certain Advertisements out of Ireland* were issued under the same cover. Taken together they constituted a very convincing picture of the fate of the Invincible Armada.

But Burghley did not stop at that. On December 30th, 1588, he wrote to Walsingham:

'At this present I am not free of pain in this right hand but free from any other pain, though weak and sore in my legs. I send you, translated out of the Spanish, lies which I have termed a Pack of Spanish Lies ... with the discovery of the same pack in English. I mean to have the same printed in Spanish for the comforting of Don B. Mendoza.'[96]

This letter leaves little doubt that Burghley composed this pamphlet, though it is not clear whether he sent it to Walsingham in manuscript or in print. The date of actual publication, 1588, may mean any date as early as March 25th, 1588, or as late as March 25th, 1589.[97]

The full title of the pamphlet explains its contents:

A Pack of Spanish Lies sent abroad in the world, first printed in the Spanish tongue, and translated out of the original. Now ripped up, unfolded and by just examination condemned, as containing false, corrupt and detestable wares worthy to be damned and burned.[98]

No doubt the Spaniards were liars and no doubt they were ripped up. The technique applied was to state in parallel columns first the Spanish lie and then the truth.

The best passage deals with a report dated September 2nd from the governor of Rouen to the effect that he held Drake's chief pilot, who reported that the English had been overthrown, 22 ships sunk, 40 captured, Drake himself a prisoner. Answered as follows:

'The governors of Boulogne and Calais can inform the governor of Rouen that the English army fought with the Spanish, chased the Spanish as a brace of grey hounds would a herd of deer. The Spanish ships were beaten, spoiled, burnt, sunk, some in the main seas afore Dunkirk, some afore Flushing and the rest chased away; so as they fled continually afore the English navy ... without daring to abide a fight. Yea some of the English ships fought with three of their galleons, the Spaniards never attempting to board any English, but as many of them as could sail away fled with all their sails until they were chased out of all the English seas, and forced then to run a violent course about Scotland and Ireland ... Why durst any report that twenty-two English ships were sunk and forty taken when in truth there was not one sunk or taken.'

The rest was of like character, written with a vigour of style which hardly suggests Burghley's handiwork. He may merely have conceived the idea and furnished the facts. But certainly he if anyone should be accredited with the pamphlet.

In view of his letter to Walsingham of December 30th, it cannot have been published before the end of the calendar year. It was certainly translated into Dutch and Spanish, and probably, following the usual practice, into Italian and French. Doubtless it was intended chiefly for overseas consumption. So far as the English were concerned they needed no further revelation of the complete defeat of the Spaniards. Quite possibly, as the last phrase in Burghley's letter to Walsingham suggests, one objective was to discredit Mendoza, who was in Paris working hard to strengthen the Catholic league and the Spanish alliance. He was at the time almost blind, but indefatigable. Throughout Burghley's writings at this juncture he made much of what he called 'Mendoza's mendacities'.

About a year later Burghley received a letter of intelligence from an English agent overseas, recounting interviews which the agent had had with one John Dutche, an Englishman in the service of Cardinal Allen. Dutche talked about Philip's intentions regarding Elizabeth when she was defeated, he talked about portraits of her secretly cherished by good Catholics in Rome. And he talked about Burghley, as follows:

'He said', the agent wrote, 'he could not more aptly compare the Lord Treasurer of England to any man than to a waterman of the Thames, whose affair is to look one way and row another. When he is to work or to compass any matter of importance he will give out matters carrying great show of reason. And while eye is had upon the same and means working to cross as much, then he putteth in execution a contrary determination . . . by which course of policy, with his expedition in all his actions, together with his long time of continuance in place of government, and having wit at will, he is so experienced and grounded, with so deep a judgment, as his piercing eye foresees and looks into all accidents and sequences that may prejudice or further his purposes and intentions in any matter he takes in hand, or is to be handled in government of the realm, and practised and followed against any other state.'[99]

The statement is interesting because it reflects a growing sentiment abroad that Burghley was the wittiest, the craftiest and the wisest statesman in Europe. In the last decade of his life he gradually acquired almost legendary proportions.

Leicester left Tilbury in bad health and set off to Buxton to recuperate. On the way thither, on August 29th, he wrote to Elizabeth inquiring in affectionate terms about her welfare. A week later he was dead. His letter still survives among the state papers,[100] and across it, in the Queen's own hand, 'His last letter'.

Camden asserts that Elizabeth at the end contemplated his appointment as Lieutenant under her in the government of England and that letters patent had actually been drawn, 'had not Burghley and Hatton prevented it and the Queen in time foreseen the danger of too great a power in one man'.[101] The story lacks confirmation from other sources, but it is not improbable. In 1562, when she was desperately ill with the smallpox, she had begged her Council to make Leicester Lord Protector of England.[102] One of the most amazing things about this amazing woman was her blind faith in Leicester. This is more understandable when she was not yet thirty and he was an ardent suitor and an eligible widower than it was when she was in her middle fifties and he a rather paunchy married man. But so it was. It seems to have been stimulated by his personal presence and weakened in his absence. It can hardly have been a rational judgment. It must have been a primitive, emotional attraction — in sixteenth-century language, a malignant spell cast upon her.

There were few tears to grace his obsequies; none from the Puritans, who must have realized that they had lost a powerful friend at Court; virtually none from the scholars and poets who had lost a generous patron. Edmund Spenser, sometime his secretary, wrote about a year later:

> He now is dead and all his glories gone
> And all his greatness vapourèd to naught
> That as a glass upon the water shone
> Which vanished quite, as soon as it was sought
> His name is worn already out of thought.
> Ne any poet seeks him to revive
> Yet many poets honoured him alive.[103]

He had antagonized the soldiers like Norris and Williams. He had antagonized the statesmen. If either Burghley or Walsingham expressed any sorrow at his passing, it has not been preserved. Even Elizabeth, though she nursed her grief for a few days,[104] was presently investigating Leicester's financial affairs with an eye to collecting money he owed her from his estate.

England, indeed, was well rid of him. He had no successor. It was said in London that Hatton's position was strengthened by Leicester's death. Doubtless it was, but Hatton never took Leicester's place, and Hatton's influence was steadily in support of his two colleagues, Burghley and Walsingham.

CHAPTER XXII

THE YEAR AFTER THE ARMADA, 1589

O F Burghley we hear relatively little during the remainder of the year 1588. The Queen still leaned heavily upon him. One letter to Walsingham in November reveals the fact that he was not having too easy a time with his temperamental mistress.

'I pray you,' he wrote, 'remember my message by Mr. Beale. All irresolutions and lacks are thrown upon us two. The wrong is intolerable.'

And yet, early in the following year, she proposed to elevate him in rank and station. On January 18th Burghley wrote to his old friend Shrewsbury:

'Her Majesty, finding a great want of noblemen for parliament is minded to create some earls and barons. . . .'[1]

'Her Majesty hath some speech with me to call me to some other degree, but I have showed her Majesty just cause to leave me as I am, having cause to diminish my livelihood by providing for my younger son. And beside that I am meeter to be let down into my grave than to be set up any higher. And with these and many other reasons I hope I have satisfied her Majesty.'[2]

The title she had in mind for him was the earldom of Northampton.

Burghley's reply, in short, was that he could not afford the honour. Possibly had Elizabeth offered lands to sustain the position he would have accepted. He attached great importance to such distinctions. But his plea of poverty has substance in it. It is clear from such household accounts of his as survive from the last decade of his life that he was living more frugally as he grew older. His average annual housekeeping expenditures for the four years, 1592-95, were scarcely one-third of what they had been twenty years before.[3]

As a matter of fact, Elizabeth made none of the promotions contemplated at the time, though Charles Howard, the Lord Admiral, got his earldom in 1596. Hunsdon, Hatton, Cobham and Buckhurst, all of them contemplated, were none of them elevated, though Hunsdon was made K.G. in 1588 and Hatton K.G. the following year. Quite possibly they all rejected the honour for Burghley's reasons.[4]

The Armada had not yet completed her disastrous homeward voyage before Elizabeth turned her thoughts to retaliation. Walsingham wrote to Howard in mid-August that she was thinking about an expedition to intercept the plate fleet from the Indies.[5] Howard talked it over with Drake, and the result of their deliberations was that the ships of the navy were in no condition for immediate action and could not be got ready in time to intercept the Spanish flota, which

usually arrived in August or early September.[6] Drake came up to Court to
discuss the matter with Elizabeth. The outcome of their conversations was a
projected expedition against the Spanish coast. The expedition was to be financed
by private subscription, with royal assistance and Dutch co-operation.

Its exponents had three objects in view: (1) To attack and destroy the remnants
of the Spanish Armada which had taken shelter in the Biscayan ports of Santander
and St. Sebastian. (2) To attack the Azores and intercept the Spanish treasure
ships from America. (3) To attack Portugal, and place Don Antonio, the pretender, on the throne.

It is pretty clear that from the start Norris and Drake put the Portuguese part
of the adventure first.

The Queen's original idea was to capture the treasure fleets, but when she
learned that a substantial fragment of the Armada had got safe home, she decided
that the first step must be against the Spanish ships, as insurance against any
counter-attack. She emphasized that fact in the instructions drawn up for the
adventurers in February, and later pointed out that they had sworn to follow
her directions. She even sent with them, when they finally got away, one of the
clerks of the Privy Council, Antony Ashley, to keep a watchful eye on their
doings.

It does not appear what part Burghley played in defining the royal attitude.
In a brief memorandum dated September 20th, he recorded the plan submitted by
Sir John Norris on the 19th, but without comment. All that we can gather from
it is that from the start he took an active part in the deliberations.

We hear nothing further from him on the subject until December.

Meanwhile, Norris had gone off to the Low Countries early in October, to enlist
Dutch support. At the time Parma was laying siege to Bergen-op-Zoom in
Brabant, a vital point in the Dutch line of defence. Norris took with him 2000
English troops to assist in its defence. Before they arrived, the crisis had passed
and Bergen was saved. Norris then addressed himself to the business of winning
Dutch support for the Portuguese expedition. What he asked for was some two or
three thousand shot, transports and heavy artillery.[7] What he got was the firm
promise of 1500 troops, to be shipped as soon as might be.

Shortly after his return, Burghley wrote to Walsingham. He did not yet know,
he wrote, how successful Norris had been, 'but if it be as I hear it by report out of
Holland, that the substance of the footmen and horsemen which he shall have
shall be out of the Queen's army there, . . . I doubt, whilst we attempt an uncertainty, we shall lose a certainty, and so seek for a bird in a bush and lose what
we have in a cage'.[8]

The letter is a reflection of a long letter from Lord Willoughby to Burghley
written ten days before.[9]

Willoughby was the son of Burghley's old friend, Katherine of Suffolk. He
was in command of the English forces in the Low Countries. In October he had,
by a miracle of good luck and good management, raised the siege of Bergen. It
was a brilliant achievement, but Willoughby was plainly discouraged. His field

army was so small that he advised that it be disbanded altogether and English effort be confined to the garrisoning of the towns in English hands. From his letter to Burghley it is clear that he resented the intrusion of Norris into the picture and the plundering of his meagre forces to stage a show in Portugal. He particularly resented the fact that, while he had to dip into his private purse to pay his troops, Norris was talking glibly about the good pay, to say nothing of the good plunder, to be had from the Portuguese enterprise.

It is against that background that Burghley's letter to Walsingham, cited above, must be placed. From the reports of his brother-in-law, Henry Killigrew, the English representative on the Dutch Council of State, and from Willoughby, he found good reason to fear that the English position in the Low Countries was in grave jeopardy. That was the bird in the cage which he did not want to lose in pursuit of the Portuguese bird in the bush.

It does not follow that he was opposed to the Portuguese expedition. What he knew was that the English treasury was dangerously low, its reserves practically exhausted and anticipated income much less than inevitable outgo. England indeed,[10] from a normal pre-war annual expenditure of about £150,000, had spent in 1587, £367,000 and in 1588, £420,000. To meet this additional burden Elizabeth had been forced to expend £245,000 from her savings.

In December the Privy Council had to resort to another forced loan, which was strongly resisted and yielded comparatively little.[11] The following February an agent was sent to borrow £100,000 in Germany. He spent the summer in futile flitting from German fair to German fair, and got nothing. No wonder that the Lord Treasurer scrutinized expenses with an anxious eye.

And yet, when the subscriptions from the private adventurers to the Portuguese expedition came in too slowly to meet current expenses and Drake and Norris pressed the Queen to increase the payments on her share, Burghley supported their request, fearing, as he wrote to Walsingham, that otherwise the whole enterprise would be overthrown.[12]

But they pressed for more. They pressed, indeed, for the payment of Elizabeth's cash commitments in full, though it had been agreed that she should pay no more than £5000 until the other subscribers had paid up.

This time Burghley hesitated, and thought the matter ought to be carefully considered before the Queen put up more money. On December 30th he wrote as much to Walsingham. 'These doubts,' he added, 'I mean not as unwilling to further the voyages, but before I would myself subscribe such a warrant I have thought it good to show my doubts ... submitting myself to that which shall be further thought meet to the contentation of her Majesty.'[13]

But he was careful not to broadcast his doubts.

'I have taken some pain', he added, 'in writing hereof with a sore hand, because I would not make any other acquainted with the matter.'

That is all that can be said with certainty about his attitude towards the whole adventure. There is no evidence that the difficulties and disappointments which beset the preparations were of his making or indeed of his mistress's[14] and no indication in the letters which he received both from Norris and from Drake that they were in any doubt about his support.

With Leicester gone, Burghley and Hatton and Walsingham dominated the Privy Council. They stood together and presumably approved the course of action outlined in the formal instructions to Norris and Drake.[15] They in turn accepted these instructions and, if Elizabeth's own word is to be trusted, swore to abide by them.

But Drake was used to ignoring instructions. It may almost be said that he had achieved his brilliant results by ignoring them. The one thing that Elizabeth had learned to expect from him was success, the kind of success which would increase her prestige and make large contributions to her treasury. And so he and Norris together went their own way. And they failed. In the efforts put forth, the ships engaged, the forces employed, the expeditionary force compared favourably in strength and striking power with the Spanish Armada itself. And it was commanded by the Queen's best general and best mariner. And Spain could offer no resistance by sea, nor even any formidable resistance by land. Yet the results achieved were pitiably small. The enfeebled Spanish navy was not destroyed, Portugal was not occupied, the flota from America was not intercepted. And when Drake and Norris came limping home in July they had nothing but 80 hulks laden with grain to show for their pains.

It was the end of Drake, and the end of his dreams of a smashing victory. Had he been satisfied with the more limited objectives imposed by his instructions, he might have achieved substantial results. He might at least have struck a fatal blow at Spanish naval power and opened wide the door to the cutting off of Spanish resources in the new world. In his case, if nothing succeeded like success, nothing failed like failure. Leicester, had he lived, might have saved him. Walsingham perhaps might have saved him, but Walsingham was a very sick man and his days were numbered. The result of Drake's disgrace was inevitably the increasing strength of the more conservative leaders, with more limited objectives.

Parliament was summoned to meet in November 1588, though it did not meet until the following February. On September 19th, Burghley wrote to the High Sheriff of Hertfordshire: 'Considering the parliament is rumoured to begin about the 13th of November next, for which purpose there is choice to be made of 2 knights of the shire, and therefore I know that you, as being of credit with the freeholders of the shire to whom the election belongeth, should have opportunity to further any of your friends to those places. If so it be that you have not made any earnest determination to grant your good will to some others, then I could be content to have your favourable allowance to favour my son, Robert Cecil, being already a Justice of the Peace in that shire and one that after me shall have a reasonable freehold in the same, that he might have the voices of your friends, to be one of the said two knights of the shire for the parliament to come.'[16]

Robert Cecil was somewhat young for the part, though he had sat in the two previous Parliaments for Westminster. The knights of the shire were a cut above the burgesses and were the choice plums of the county families. Burghley, already after Leicester's death Lord Lieutenant of Hertfordshire, now strengthened his grip upon local prestige by putting forward his son for the county seat recently vacated by Sir Ralph Sadler's death. The request was tantamount to a command. Young Cecil got the seat and held on to it until his elevation to the peerage when James of Soctland succeeded to the English throne.

Parliament opened on February 4th with an oration from the new Lord Chancellor, Christopher Hatton, who had already distinguished himself as a leader for the Crown in the Commons. It seems likely that he consulted Burghley before preparing the speech. In any event, Burghley prepared a long note for the occasion[17] which apparently Hatton did not find to his taste. As a matter of fact, though Burghley had some reputation as an orator, Hatton far outshone him. It does not appear, however, that Hatton displaced or ever tried to displace Burghley as leader for the Crown in the Lords.[18]

Of Burghley's activity in the Lords at this Parliament there is almost no record in the *Journals* of the Lords, though he appears to have been the chairman of such committees as were appointed to deal with bills. The record as usual is scant in the extreme.

It is rather surprising that we hear very little of him in connection with a bill to reform procedure in the Court of Exchequer, since he was the head of that Court. Sir Edward Hoby, who introduced the bill in the Commons, complained that he had been sharply rebuked 'by some great personage' for his introductory speech. It has been surmised that this 'great personage' was his uncle, Lord Burghley, though it is hard to believe that Burghley opposed the substance of the bill. It was supported in the Commons by two of the most important members of the Exchequer Court, Sir Walter Mildmay, the Chancellor of the Exchequer, and Peter Osborne, the Treasurer's Remembrancer. In any case, the bill passed the Commons and went up to the Lords.

Another bill introduced in the Commons reflected popular dissatisfaction with royal purveyance, the prerogative right of the Crown to compel subjects to sell provisions for the royal household under the market price.[19] It had been attacked in the Commons, in the second and third Parliaments of the reign and again in 1587, every time without success. The bill introduced in February 1589[20] passed two readings in the Commons and was referred to a committee of which apparently Sir Thomas Heneage, the Vice-Chamberlain, was the chairman. The committee was authorized to consult with officers of the Crown on the subject. It may be that at this point Burghley intervened, hoping to save the bill by moderating it.[21] It is hardly likely that he conferred with the committee, but he may very well have passed his suggestions on to Heneage. The bill was amended, though it does not appear[22] that the amendments were those that Burghley proposed. It passed in its amended form and was sent up to the Lords on the 22nd. On February 25th both the Exchequer bill and the Purveyors bill were in the Lords. Two days later the Commons received a message from the Lords desiring them to send a delegation to hear a message from the Queen. They did so the same afternoon, meeting with a delegation from the Lords in a room adjacent to the Lords' Chamber. There Burghley himself addressed them.[23]

'He showed then that the message from her Majesty . . . was concerning two bills lately passed the house, . . . the one concerning purveyors and the other touching proofs and pleadings in the Court of Exchequer, a thing misliked of her Majesty in both cases, the one tending to the officers and ministers of her own household and the other to the officers and ministers of her own court of her own revenue, in both of which, if any should demean themselves any way unlawfully or untruly, her Majesty was of herself both able and willing to see due reformation' with more to the same effect.

The sum and substance of his speech was that reforms in administration were the Queen's affair — rather more graciously put than usual, but to that effect.

The response of the Commons was a request that they might send a delegation to confer with the Queen about the matter.

We have in outline at least the arguments which the delegation presented to the Queen,[24] and at least one memorandum in Burghley's hand in which he complained that hitherto the Commons had proceeded in such matters by petition, not by bill, and that they had charged the Queen with knowledge of abuses which she would not reform. The Commons replied to the first that there were many laws on the statute books against purveyors, and to the second that they had not charged the Queen with foreknowledge of abuses but had simply undertaken to inform her of them.[25]

It is a little hard to fit Burghley's observations into the procedure on the bill. Possibly they were intended for the Queen's guidance in dealing with the Commons delegation. It is worth noting that his objections were rather to the form than to the substance of the bill. And Elizabeth in her reply to the Commons did not herself directly question the right of the Commons to deal with the matter. She said that she had plans under way for investigating the misdemeanours of the purveyors and would at once take steps for reform. As for the Exchequer, she would look into that also. She may even have invited the Commons to appoint a consultant committee on the subject.[26] But she made it quite clear that those matters which touched her prerogative lay outside the sphere of parliamentary action.

Burghley's share in the whole business indicates that he was not unsympathetic with the demands of the Commons, but that he felt bound to support the Queen's position.

He played an active part also in a bill introduced in the Lords on February 10th, 'a bill concerning Captains and Soldiers'. It was probably sponsored by the government, was apparently read twice and was then referred to a committee of which Burghley was chairman.[27] In committee, so many defects were discovered in the bill that the committee proposed a new bill, which had its first reading on the 14th. It passed its second and third reading without difficulty, and on February 22nd went down for action in the Commons.

There it had its first reading on the 26th, which was followed by an animated debate,[28] and encountered so much opposition that it was said, but officially denied, that one speaker suggested that the bill should be rejected and cast out of the House.

Unfortunately there is no record of the debate, nor does there seem to be any exact copy of the bill in question. The title suggests that it dealt with much the same matters as were covered in the statute enacted in Edward's reign[29] entitled *'An Act for the Reformation of Captains and Soldiers Serving in the Wars'*.[30] That statute provided penalties for soldiers who stole their equipment, for captains who took from the Crown for soldiers' wages more than was justified or who released one soldier and hired another for personal profit.[31]

We gather from the memorandum of Burghley that the Commons objected to the new bill, that it was imperfect, defective and more punitive than the old bill, that the definition of a soldier's equipment was vague, that the term used 'to defraud the service' was ill-defined. They wished to make it explicit that noblemen who offended should not be exempted from punishment, but should rather be punished for example — and such like, none of them very weighty.

The bill had its second reading in the Commons on March 19th and, upon a motion to commit, the vote was close.[32] It was referred back from committee on March 29th in terms which made its rejection almost certain. At this juncture the Lords, prompted no doubt by Burghley, fighting to save the bill, asked for a conference. The Commons appointed a committee to meet with a committee from the Lords the same afternoon in the Council Chamber. Burghley presided and we have notes, corrected in his hand,[33] of the Commons' objections and his answers. Burghley's notes are too brief to be very illuminating. His answers were designed to show that the new law was substantially the same as the one on the Statute books. The Commons committee, following their instructions, engaged in no discussion. There is no record of any further action on the bill in the Commons. It was presumably dropped. Burghley's efforts failed.

It is hard to understand the opposition of the Commons to this bill, except on the grounds that the country gentry were fearful that their military perquisites might be jeopardized. So far as their objections to the bill are recorded, they seem trivial. It is worth noting that James Morice, one of the belligerent Puritans in the Commons, was nominated as spokesman of their delegation at the conference. Evidently they were in no mood for compromise. Possibly they were reluctant to reject a government bill, did not wish to pass it and decided that with Parliament on the verge of dissolution they could delay action, avoid commitments and let the bill die as unfinished business. We may have here an early example of what became known later in the United States as filibustering.

The Parliament of 1589 was in session during the time when the Puritans were conducting a vigorous literary campaign against the personnel and the government of the Church and particularly against Archbishop Whitgift's severity in dealing with ministers and preachers of doubtful orthodoxy. This was as it had been; the difference was in the manner, not the substance. Beginning in October 1588 a

Puritan, writing under the name of Martin Marprelate, put forth a series of tracts which are masterpieces of effective propaganda, among the choicest bits of Elizabethan satire. Dr. Bridge's and Bishop Cooper's dull droning efforts to reply to them did no more than set these prelates up as targets for Martin's further raillery. He came back with 'Oh read over Dr. John Bridge for it is a worthy work', and 'Hay any work for Cooper'. Right or wrong, the Establishment was made to look ridiculous. The Elizabethans, who always revelled in an attack on the clergy, rushed to buy the tracts. Courtiers, who gave not a fig for the issues involved, were vastly taken by Martin's wit. Essex, the royal favourite, is said to have carried one of the tracts about in his pocket. Elizabeth was furious, so much so that she issued a proclamation[34] denouncing the writer and printers of 'schismatical books, defamatory libels and other fantastical writings', and bidding them desist 'as they will answer to the contrary at their utmost peril'. She did not stop Martin but she made clear her own position.

It was in such an atmosphere that the Parliament of 1589 assembled. Hatton dwelt upon the matter in his opening speech and strictly charged the members 'not so much as once meddle with any such matters or causes of religion'.[35]

But Puritanism was too strong in the Commons to be silenced even by royal command, though it was subdued to a point that only one mild measure of Church reform actually reached the floor of the House as a bill. It was offered on February 27th and was aimed at clergymen with cure of souls who held more than one benefice. Even so it contravened the Queen's orders. But the Commons would not be denied. A second reading followed on March 1st, and a few days later the bill passed the Commons and went up to the Lords.

Burghley saw it on March 10th and made a summary of it in his own hand.[36]

The surprising thing is that the bill was not only received by the Lords, but three days later had its first reading.[37] This must have been Burghley's doing. One wonders whether he consulted the Queen about it or went ahead in defiance of her general prohibition. It seems hardly likely that Whitgift would have participated in the proceedings as he did without at least royal acquiescence. In any case, the first reading was followed by debate and Burghley himself spoke in support of the bill. We have the rough notes of his speech,[38] not full enough to enable us to reconstruct it, but enough to reveal his argument. He began by explaining his temerity in speaking at all. He was, he said, impelled by his conscience and by his love for his country. He praised the preamble of the bill, its provision for regular services, for the preaching of the sacred word, for the care of the poor, for the advancement of learning.

It is worth noting that he did not attack existing conditions, except in the case of private chaplains. For the most part he was concerned with the historical background of the fight against pluralities and non-residence, going back as far as the *articuli cleri* of Edward II and forward through Henry VIII's legislation on the subject,[39] to the canons inspired by Archbishop Parker in 1571. He praised the work of Grindal and of Whitgift — a strange conjunction which Whitgift probably did not relish — in seeking to reform the abuses under consideration. And he ended with the suggestion that a little more leniency should be allowed to learned men in the Church, perhaps by permitting them to hold two benefices so long as they were not too far apart.

It was a discreet speech, rather heavy on the whole, though he undertook to lighten it with a merry tale which unhappily was not recorded. We need not assume that it was unedifying;[40] Burghley was not given to droll stories. In any case, he managed to present the case without treading on anyone's toes.

Whitgift apparently replied. His speech has not been preserved. Lord Grey de Wilton who followed, speaking for the bill, said flatly that after listening to Whitgift he favoured Burghley's position more than ever. Grey was definitely belligerent. He went so far as to suggest that the bishops might be dealt with by *Praemunire* as in good King Henry's day, and lamented the fact that the Queen conferred only with those who opposed reform. He thought lay peers should be joined with the bishops to confer about the matter. At this point Burghley intervened. 'The Bishops,' he said, 'if they were wise, would themselves be humble suitors to her Majesty to have some of the temporal Lords joined with them.'

This is the last we hear of the bill. Probably Elizabeth learned of the debate from Whitgift and imposed the royal veto. The price which Martin and his followers paid for their wit was to stifle even moderate reform.

Parliament held its closing session on March 29th,[41] and Hatton delivered the final speech. The speech itself is lost, though we have a brief report of it.[42] Evidently Hatton submitted his valedictory before he delivered it to Burghley. Two days earlier Burghley, in his own hand, wrote to him: 'I have perused the method of your intended speech ... and so meant to have returned it with my very good liking, as untouched with any tittle. But, to demonstrate that I have read it, I have interposed to put my pen, though unneedfully, to some places, assuring myself that upon those articles your Lordship's facility in utterance and perfection in knowledge will make the speech both plausible and perfect. And so I end, not well able to use my hand or any member, for my grief in my holy bone.'[43]

On the morning of the 29th the Lords asked for a conference of delegates of both Houses and proposed that they should all join in petition to the Queen, asking her to declare open war on Spain. The action was probably prompted by Burghley. A memo in his hand,[44] dated March 29th, runs as follows:

'The heads of the declaration and offer to be made by the Lords spiritual and temporal to her Majesty of their readiness to serve her Majesty in this sort following. To be delivered by speech of the Lord Chancellor.

'Although upon great consideration appearing to them of the mighty and resolute determination of the King of Spain in making of open wars against her Majesty and the realm, for God's cause, and to extirp the Christian religion in others, and specially upon the sight [of] his last years open invasion attempted against this realm with intent to have conquered the same, the Lords and the Commons of the realm have most willingly yielded to a kind of subsidy, though in their opinions not so sufficient to answer her Majesty's charges to be sustained as were requisite, yet for a fresh manifestation and declaration of their most bounded duties, both towards the defence of her Majesty and the realm against so mighty attempts and also to offend her said enemy, they do offer with all manner of duty and willingness to her Majesty that whensoever she shall find it meet and profitable to denounce an open war against the said King and his adherents they shall be rea[dy] with all their powers, their bodies and their lives, lands and goods to serve her Majesty therewith, as well by offensive wars abroad as defensive at home against the said King and all his adherents.'

This is a rather stirring pledge of loyalty. It may have been presented for action by Burghley at the joint conference on the morning of the 29th. The sentiments expressed in it were certainly endorsed by the conference. Knollys, who headed the delegation of the Commons, reported back to the House that Burghley had revealed to them the views of the Lords regarding war with Spain, had asked that the Commons join with them in the matter and had proposed that the Speaker of the House, in his formal speech, present a petition to the Queen in the name of both Lords and Commons.[45]

And so it came to pass. Burghley's idea of having Hatton deal with it was not carried out. One wonders why. It would have come with more force from the Lord Chancellor, the one official who could speak for both Houses.

Less than a week after Parliament rose, Burghley lost his wife, to whom he had been married for over forty years. She was the last to go of the three women who meant most to him. His mother died in 1587, his favourite daughter, Ann, in the spring of 1588, and now Mildred — all within two years.

We hear little of Mildred[46] during the last twenty years of her life. She went regularly to Court, but after Elizabeth's marked favour to Oxford, the renegade son-in-law, Mildred evidently found Court life increasingly distasteful. In any case, she was not the type of woman who appealed to the Queen. If we may judge from her portrait she lacked feminine charm.[47] She was, moreover, a resolute Puritan. During the first decade of the reign she had taken an active part in the Puritan crusade. After that we hear no more of her in that connection. Burghley may have whispered in her ear that she was doing more harm than good.

Unfortunately, during the last thirty years of their life together, not a single letter between husband and wife appears to have survived. We have no other gauge of their conjugal relations than what Burghley wrote of her after her death.[48] Fortunately for the historian, he always seems to have had an irresistible impulse to get his thoughts down on paper, even when he had no other purpose than to discharge an emotion.

'There is', he wrote,[49] 'no cogitation to be used with an intent to recover that which never can be had again; that is to have my dear wife to live again in her mortal body, which is separated from the soul and resteth in the earth dead, and the soul taken up to heaven, and there to remain in the fruition of blessedness unspeakable until the general resurrection of all flesh; when, by the almighty power of God (who made all things out of nothing) her body shall be raised up and joined with her soul in an everlasting, unspeakable joy, such as no tongue can express nor heart can conceive.

'Therefore my cogitation ought to be occupied in these things following:

'To thank Almighty God for his favour, in permitting her to live so many years together with me, and to have given her grace to have had the true knowledge of her salvation by the death of his son, Jesus, opened to her by the knowledge of the gospel, whereof she was a professor from her youth.

'I ought to comfort myself with the remembrance of her many virtues and godly actions wherein she continued all her life. And specially in that she did of late years sundry charitable deeds whereof she determined to have no outward knowledge while she lived. In so much as when I had some little understanding thereof, and asked her wherein she had disposed any charitable gifts (according to her often wishing that she were able to do some special act for maintenance of learning and relief of the poor), she would always only show herself rather desirous so to do than ever confess any such act. As since her death is manifestly known to me and confessed by sundry good men (whose names and ministries she secretly used) that she did charge them most strictly that while she lived they should never declare the same to me nor to any other.

'And so now have I seen her earnest writings to that purpose of her own hand. The particulars of many of these hereafter do follow, which I do with mine own handwriting recite for my own comfort in the memory thereof, with assurance that God hath accepted the same in such favourable sort as she findeth now the fruits thereof in heaven.'

He then proceeded to enumerate Mildred's benefactions: an exhibition [scholarship] at St. John's, Cambridge, for two scholars, endowed in perpetuity; a loan fund to the Haberdashers Company for helping six poor artisans, 'smiths, carpenters and such like', in Romford, Essex, every other year to an aggregate of £120; another in Cheshunt and Waltham, to the aggregate of £80; a fund to provide twenty poor people in Cheshunt with a good meal on the first Sunday of every month; the endowment of four sermons at St. John's, Cambridge, quarterly, and money quarterly to all the prisons in London to buy bread, cheese and drink for four hundred persons, and shirts and smocks for the poor in Cheshunt and London, and money to the master of St. John's for fires in the hall on Sundays and holy days, from All Saints' Day to Candlemas (November 1st to February 2nd), and books in Hebrew to Cambridge University and books in Greek, etc., to St. John's, and also to Christ Church, Oxford, and to the college at Westminster.

And wool and flax for poor women in Cheshunt, to be wrought into cloth and given to the poor.

And money for wheat and rye to be dispersed among the poor in time of dearth.

It is an impressive tribute, to a wise good woman, devoted to learning of which she was herself a great exponent, devoted to the welfare of scholars (note the fires in the hall at St. John's during the bleak season between Michaelmas and Candlemas), devoted to the relief of the poor, particularly the deserving poor, as in the loan to artisans or the jobs for poor women in spinning and weaving.

One could wish that Burghley had said something about Mildred as a wife and a mother. The document is a little too much like an *oraison funèbre*, not quite enough like a *cri de cœur*. The letter Burghley wrote after his mother's death to the Earl of Shrewsbury two years before had a more intimate personal significance. One wonders whether Burghley's conjugal relations lacked warmth. On Burghley's part they certainly did not lack respect and admiration.

Mildred's funeral was on April 21st.[50] Burghley instructed the Dean of St. Paul's who was to preach at the funeral:

'I am desirous to have it declared, for the satisfaction of the Godly, that I do not celebrate this funeral in this sort with any intention thereby, as the corrupt abuse hath been in the church, to procure of God the relief or the amender of the state of her soul, who is dead in body only. For that I am fully persuaded by many certain arguments of God's grace bestowed upon her in this life and of her continual virtuous life and godly death, that God of his infinite goodness hath received her soul into a place of blessedness, where it shall remain with the souls of the faithful until the general day of judgment when it shall be joined with her body. And with that persuasion I do humbly thank Almighty God, by his son Christ, for his unspeakable goodness towards the salvation of her soul, so as I know no action on earth can amend the same.

'But yet I do otherwise most willingly celebrate this funeral as a testimony of my hearty[51] love which I did bear her, with whom I lived in the state of matrimony forty and two years continually.[52]

'Further than that is here done for the assembly of our friends, is to testify to the world what estimation, love and reverence God bears to the stock whereof she did come both by her father and her mother, as manifestly may be seen about her hearse, by the sundry coats of noble houses joined by blood with her, which is not done for any vain pomp of the world, but for civil duty towards her body, that is to be with honour regarded for the assured hope of the resurrection thereof at the last day.'[53]

It has seemed worth while to quote both of these writings in full because they reveal not only Burghley's devotion to his wife[54] but a good deal also of his views about eternal life, the resurrection of the body and the last judgment. They conform to the Articles of Religion and the creed of the Anglican Church. Burghley evidently accepted them and fervently endorsed them.

During the closing months of Mildred's life, Burghley had been making arrangements for the marriage of his son, Robert, to Elizabeth Brooke, the daughter of his old friend, Lord Cobham. On June 1st he created a trust, to which his older son, Thomas, and Lord Cobham were parties, conveying Theobalds and other properties in Hertfordshire, together with some properties in London, after his death, to the use of Robert and his heirs, or, failing heirs, to the use of his three granddaughters, Elizabeth, Bridget and Susan Vere.[55]

Walsingham became desperately ill early in March and withdrew from Court for three months.[56] There was no one but Burghley to take his place and, though far from well himself, he bent his old shoulders to the burden. Fortunately, with Leicester's death, the dissensions in the Council faded away. Sir Christopher Hatton, who next after Burghley and Walsingham was the most influential of the Privy Councillors, was in general accord with the other two. He attended Council meetings regularly, but was too much absorbed in legal affairs to give much attention to other public business. Heneage, the Vice-Chamberlain, and John Wooley, the Latin Secretary, served as immediate attendants on the Queen and, during Walsingham's illness, as intermediaries between her and Burghley, but neither of them played a more important role. Actually Elizabeth felt so strongly the need for Burghley's guiding hand that only a week after his wife's death, while he was still at Theobalds in mourning, she bade him return to Court.

Wooley wrote to him on April 11th:

'I could not before this time fully acquaint her Majesty with the letters your Lordship sent me both yesterday and this day, but even now it hath pleased her to peruse them well either with her own eyes or by having me read them to her. The matters being of high consequence both for the troubles in Scotland and for affairs round about us, her Majesty prayeth your Lordship, though I told her of your weak estate, to return hither to your house again tomorrow in the morning to the end she may the better use your advice in those matters that so deeply concern her estate and so hopeth your Lordship will be hither at your house in the morning by ten of the clock.'[57]

He was there, of course, and for the next three months was the managing director of public policy, in addition to his particular tasks at the Court of Exchequer and the Court of Wards. After a month of it he wrote to Sir Thomas Bodley: 'Mr. Secretary's absence breedeth me more work than at this time I am meet for.'[58] The number of dispatches he drafted or dictated is incredible for one of his years. Unfortunately very few of them survive.

They dealt mainly with foreign affairs, and one way or the other with Spain, Scotland, the Low Countries and France.

There seems to have been little fear of a renewal of Spanish attack. In May musters were ordered, but they were perfunctory, rather in the nature of a check-up of able-bodied men available for service. The necessity of training was apparently left to the discretion of the Lord Lieutenants.

Spanish matters for the most part centred upon the counter-Armada under Drake and Norris which was to put forth in April. They went and came back with no more plunder than 80 'hulks', most of them Hansa ships, laden with corn and naval stores. This raised an interesting question — were these neutral ships lawful prize or not?[59]

We get no direct word from Burghley on the subject, but Walsingham wrote to him in July: 'I find her Majesty most backward in following the advice given touching the restoring of the Easterlings [Hansa merchants] to their ships and such goods as are not comprehended within the title of munitions. The only reason that moveth her to be stiff therein is the profit, which I showed her that

P

I feared the same would be purchased at too dear a price . . . It is of so great weight
as it will behoove us all to press her effectually therein.'[60]

The pressure was applied successfully. On July 27th the Privy Council issued
an order in which they set down at length their reasons for confiscating munitions
of war in the hulks and discharging the ships themselves and their other merchandise. They pointed out, as was undoubtedly true, that the Hansa merchants had
contributed substantially to the Spanish Armada in 1588, and that the representative of the Hansa towns in London had been informed that Elizabeth regarded
this as an unfriendly act and warned that if it were done again she would confiscate
both the ships and the cargoes. An interesting part of this order was its definition
of munitions of war, which included naval stores, weapons, powder and bullets,
copper, lead and match, and, under the head of victuals, wheat and other cereals
and bacon.[61]

Burghley thought the Queen should justify her action by a public declaration,
and Walsingham passed on the suggestion to Robert Beale, his brother-in-law,
advising him to consult with two well-known civilians. Beale forthwith addressed
himself to the task and produced both a Latin and an English version of a declaration, which was published under the title *A Declaration of the causes which moved
the chief commander to take and arrest in the mouth of the river of Lisbon certain
ships* . . . , etc.[62] It was largely an attack upon the King of Spain, partly a rebuke of
German Protestant traders for supporting the arch-enemy of their faith, partly a
definition of contraband of war.

Some time later Burghley decided to write something himself on the subject.
Once more his itching pen got the better of him.

What he wrote he apparently never published — he never even finished. But
his manuscript in his own hand is preserved among his papers,[63] and it reveals
what he thought needed to be said to the world at large in justification of the
Queen's action.

It began with a rather tedious prologue, on truth and the necessity of making
the truth manifest. 'Upon these considerations,' he continued, 'at this time the
Queen of England, a lady, even as the handmaiden of God, that hath now most
happily reigned and governed in great happiness her kingdom, countries and
peoples very near thirty-three years, perceiving that though Almighty God, her
only protector, hath preserved her above many others in this lamentable age,
wherein no kingdom almost of Christendom, but hers, hath had continual greatness, yet her actions . . . have been in some parts by ignorance but in great part
by malice and envy depraved and falsely reported . . . There is of late spread
abroad some new slanders . . . that her Majesty's forces and navy, which she is
forced to keep upon the seas for her defence against the mighty power of the King
of Spain and to withstand his threatening invasion, do manifestly impeach the
lawful trade in the seas of merchandise of her neighbours and most specially of
the maritime towns of the east parts, wherein her Majesty findeth that her actions
are wrested and misreported and the rather credited because it cannot be denied
but of late some Eastland ships were stayed on the coast of Spain when they were

ready to have entered into the havens of Spain and Portugal with their full lading of victuals and munitions to have fortified and armed the Spanish navy, then prepared purposely to have invaded England a second time, so as the stay and arrest at that time is not denied, neither, when the cause is more largely showed, can it be justly misliked. And it is not also denied but that there hath been some others of like condition stayed upon like cause in some other parts of the narrow seas. . . .

'Her Majesty thinketh and knoweth it by the rules of law, as well of nature as of men, yea specially by the law civil, that wheresoever any doth directly help her enemy with succours of men, victuals, armour or any kind of munitions, to enable them to make invasion of her realm, she may lawfully intercept the same even though the aid come from her friend, and this agreeth with the law of God, the law of nature, the law of nations, and hath so been in all times practised and in all countries. . . .

'The ships that were arrested were ships of the East, laden with corn and other victuals, with masts, cables and all kind of cordage, and very many other things proper to serve the King of Spain for his ships and his army then in preparation to have made a second invasion of England and without which he could not renew his rent and spoiled navy which was the year before overthrown by God's goodness and the force of her Majesty's navy . . . And it is to be specially noted that these ships came from those towns in the east country called Hansa towns, to the which request had been made to forbear to give to the King of Spain . . . any such aid . . . yea, knowledge also given to them that if they should do so her Majesty might not willingly suffer the same, but her power would stay and impeach the same. And this information was 2 or 3 years together renewed . . . And so her Majesty had a firm hope to have had the effect of this her request observed . . . But as it was after proved . . . the said Esterlings had covertly, in their great hulks, outwardly with peaceable merchandise, during the space of two years carried into Spain the greatest part of all the masts, cables, cordage, sails, copper, saltpetre and powder that served to furnish the same navy, that without these provisions had never been able to come out of the ports of Spain . . . In the said navy . . . there was no greater nor stronger ships . . . than was a great number of the Hansa towns . . . Of this unfriendly, nay rather hostile, action of the Hansa ships her Majesty had great cause to mislike and so complaint being made thereof to such merchants . . . they for some excuse alleged that the King of Spain constrained them to serve him with the said hulks. But he could not have constrained them if they had not come thither furnished as ships for the war . . . And it is notably known to all persons that haunt the maritime coasts of Spain that without having of masts, boards, cables, cordage, pitch, tar, copper out of the Eastland, all Spain is not able to make a navy ready to carry the meanest army that can be imagined. And if his money brought out of the Indies should not tempt the Hansa to bring him these provisions, Spain would not offer to make war by sea with England. . . .

'The reports spread abroad that she doth with her navy impeach and disturb all usual traffic of the Hansa towns by sea, whereas in very truth she never minded to abridge them of their usual trade with merchandise through the narrow seas into Spain, Portugal or in other parts of the west, so as they would use the same as in former times they were accustomed. . . .

'And as it may be objected that merchants must and will, as times do change, to yield gain so to pursue their trade without any respect of loss or gain to any other, to make profit to themselves; so also they are to understand that if any person shall find themselves damnified and endangered by such trade, reason warranteth them to require them to forbear.'

Burghley went on to discuss at some length the precedents for Elizabeth's action, laying particular emphasis upon examples 'at their own doors, yea within their own havens' in the wars between Denmark and Sweden and Sweden and Russia.

He evidently intended to consider some other aspects of the subject, but after one sentence to that effect he ended abruptly.

The discourse, though rather wordy and repetitious, was a good discussion of the case for contraband and a good answer to the more obvious objections. It might, of course, have been used with equal cogency against England. But the Hansa, lacking any strong national backing, was in no position to do so. What was right or wrong on the high seas depended upon sea power. The nation with sovereignty of the seas could impose its own rules. And that was in fact the position of England during the residue of Elizabeth's reign. But it is not immaterial that Burghley should have sought to justify it in terms of precedent, the civil law and the law of nations.

With Scotland, as usual, friendly relations ebbed and flowed. After the defeat of the Armada, James the King was furious when he discovered that Elizabeth repudiated the large promises which her ambassador, William Ashley, had made during the critical days when the Armada was in the Channel. And he talked bravely of entertaining counter-offers from Spain. In point of fact, although he was a resolute Protestant, he had a strong personal affection for the Earl of Huntly, the leader of the Scottish Catholics. In February 1589 a Scotsman had been intercepted in England carrying letters from Huntly and some of his Catholic confederates to the Prince of Parma. The letters, when deciphered, revealed that the Catholic group were looking forward hopefully to a second Spanish Armada, were receiving money from Spain and were even undertaking to master King James. The English Privy Council forwarded copies of the letters to Ashley with instructions to show them to the Scottish King. The letter-carrier was also sent to confirm the validity of the letters.

The King's initial response was favourable. He called his Council together and by their advice imprisoned Huntly in Edinburgh Castle. But the day following James went to the castle and took dinner with Huntly, 'Yea he kissed him at times to the amazement of many'.[64]

Burghley was naturally somewhat disturbed. He urged Elizabeth to send a special envoy to the Scottish Court. On March 10th he wrote to Walsingham:

'Her Majesty yesterday was well disposed to send some special man to the King, and I named Sir Henry Cobham and she Mr. Dyer. But I find Mr. Dyer unwilling, for lack [of means]. This evening she is still earnest, wishing to have your opinion. I do insist not so much upon a man as upon special comfort for the King and for the Chancellor. But she will in no sort yield thereunto but persisteth in reprehension of the King for childishness, folly and cowardliness. I fear the evil succession of this error in her Majesty is grounded upon sparing ... I care not who goes so he carry matter of comfort in deeds.'

In English eyes the sovereign remedy for all Scottish ills was money.

Ten days later Burghley wrote to William Fowler, an English agent at the Scottish Court, expressing the Queen's appreciation of Fowler's service but warning him to subdue his English proclivities 'lest you be there precluded from inward causes.' 'I know', he added, 'the manner of that nation.'

'Her Majesty', he continued, 'hath conceived a great misliking of the contrarious proceedings of the King, but yet I do require her to hope better of the end, considering the King's devotion in religion and the diversity of government there, that he hath not so absolute authority as she hath and the nobility there are not acquainted with absolute government, but rather are themselves in a manner absolute.'[65]

Burghley ended the letter with an apology for its brevity, 'lacking leisure by Mr. Secretary's long absence and a busy parliament'.[66]

As it turned out, James, under some pressure from his Council, had already decided to remove Huntly from his command of the royal guard and to send him home. Huntly tried to persuade James to go with him, but failed and withdrew to the north with his fellow conspirators. Presently James, enraged, was organizing his forces to pursue them. Walsingham succeeded in inducing Elizabeth to send him £3000 to finance the adventure.[67] At the Brig o' Dee the two armies met but there was no engagement. Huntly, finding the King in earnest, fled to the north and by May 1st peace was restored.

Meanwhile, James had been turning his thoughts towards matrimony. Fowler ascribed this to the pressure of his councillors, and believed that James was indifferent to women. He wrote to Walsingham to that effect in December 1588: '[The King] never regards the company of any woman, not so much as in any dalliance.'[68] But James had a romantic streak in him which presently revealed itself. Two ladies were under consideration — Ann, the daughter of the King of Denmark, and Catherine de Bourbon, the sister of Henry, King of Navarre. The Scottish townsmen, both for religious and for commercial reasons, favoured Denmark. Ann had the advantage of age; she was not quite fifteen, eight years younger than the King. Catherine was thirty-one, eight years older.

Elizabeth favoured the French match. So did Burghley and Walsingham, probably because they wanted to strengthen Navarre's position in France and to destroy the old ties between the Scottish Crown and the Guises.[69] But they do not seem to have regarded it as a matter of vital importance. Elizabeth herself declined an invitation from James to advise him on the subject, pleading that since she had forborne marriage herself she was not qualified to advise in matters matrimonial.[70]

Lord Wemys, the Scottish envoy in England, to whom she made this observation, got back to Edinburgh in May saturated apparently with English opposition to the Danish match. There was some talk of sending Sir George Cary to urge the English view, or Burghley's son, Sir Robert Cecil. But Elizabeth decided instead to use the services of the Master of Gray, in banishment at the time but expecting momentarily to be restored to James's favour. Burghley favoured Gray and considered him a 'very sufficient gentleman'.[71] He returned to Scotland at the end of May and later in the year resumed his seat on the Privy Council. So far as the marriage was concerned, he got nowhere. By the end of May, James had become emotionally involved. He even went so far as to apply the £3000 which Elizabeth had sent him for paying the army to the equipment of a splendid mission to Denmark. At the start he made large demands of the Danish King. Burghley remarked when he heard them: 'Either the scope of them is to have no marriage . . . or it will prove like the old speech — he that demandeth 100 oaks will be content with twenty.'[72]

As it turned out, when the Danes rejected the terms, James waved them aside, remarking that he 'would not be thought a merchant for his wife'. So all obstacles were removed and James began to make arrangements for Ann's coming. He had no decent house in which to receive her, no adequate plate to furnish forth her table.

As late as the end of July Burghley was not without hope that the match might be stayed. He wrote to Ashley on the 30th: 'I hope the accident of France will hold the King in some suspense for his marriage.' Burghley referred to the murder of the Duke of Guise, Navarre's chief opponent. But James by that time was beyond the reach of argument.

Walsingham wrote to Ashley on August 20th that Elizabeth was ready to give the Danish match her allowance. But he went on to say that if the King expected 'any great supply' of money for his nuptials he would almost certainly be disappointed. Elizabeth did, however, send him £1000 in cash and promised £2000 to purchase plate in England.[73]

Burghley got involved in the purchase of the plate. He apparently gave his personal security to the silversmiths. The Queen was slow to honour his commitment and Burghley wrote to Ashley asking him to get the King to write and thank his mistress for £3000, hoping evidently to put Elizabeth to shame. If this did not work, he added, he would have to pay the money, 'though I leave not myself a spoon of silver'.

In the end Burghley got his money and James his plate. The marriage was celebrated by proxy in Copenhagen on August 20th, and ten days later Ann set sail for Scotland. But after three attempts against adverse winds she put back to Oslo in Norway and there she stuck. James did not even hear of her plight until October 10th, and he then decided to go in person and fetch his bride. He married her in Oslo in November but remained away until the following April.

Maitland, the Chancellor, was with him and the arrangements which James had made for the government of Scotland in his absence were not of the best. Lennox, a youth of fifteen, was to be President of the Council, with the Earl of Bothwell, a man of wild and unstable temper, as his assistant. Lord John Hamilton was placed in charge of the Borders. Burghley was somewhat anxious. On December 1st, not long after James's departure, he drew up a memorandum[74] on the situation which formed the basis of the instructions to Robert Bowes, a veteran in Scottish affairs, who was sent to replace Ashley a few days later. Bowes was directed to address himself to Lord John Hamilton, and to be guided by his advice in dealing with Bothwell and others. Bowes was further to promise Hamilton that the Queen's border forces would be sent to his assistance if he needed them, and that the Queen was organizing a further force of horse and foot, under the Earl of Huntingdon, which would be ready to march if the situation demanded it.

No intervention was called for, and the arrangements in Scotland during James's absence worked unexpectedly well. At the beginning of the year 1590 the postern gate was reasonably secure.

In France, Henry III, when the Spanish Armada was in the Channel, appeared to be bound hand and foot to the pro-Spanish policy of the League led by Henry of Guise. He had pledged himself never to lay down his arms until he had destroyed the Huguenots, and had appointed Guise as commander-in-chief of the royal army. At this inopportune moment Buzenvals, the agent of Navarre in London, appealed to Burghley for assistance in support of his master.[75] There is no record of Burghley's response. He was too deeply engaged in making preparations to meet the Spaniard to take much thought of French affairs. Indeed we hear nothing from him on the subject before the end of the year.

Both he and Walsingham were apparently in accord with the policy of cultivating the good will of the French King. They were well aware that he was restive under the Guisan yoke and casting about for means to free himself. They were therefore careful not to embarrass him by pressing him harder in the right direction than he was prepared to go, or taking sides against him by open support of Navarre, though Walsingham had little faith in Henry's ability to take any independent action, more especially since his mother, Catherine de Medicis, was using her influence to line him up in support of the Guisan programme.

It was characteristic of Henry III's distorted mind that he thought in terms of assassination as the road to deliverance. In December he had Henry of Guise and his brother, the Cardinal of Guise, who was the brains, as Henry was the brawn, of the family, murdered. Less than a fortnight later the King's mother, Catherine de Medicis, died.

Elizabeth welcomed the news. 'She is minded', Walsingham wrote on December 24th, to Stafford, the English ambassador at Paris,[76] 'to send a gentleman over to comfort and encourage the King to proceed thoroughly, as well to a severe correction of his corrupt subjects as also to persecute his enemies abroad.' Walsingham envisaged an alliance of France and England against Spain. 'If', he continued, 'you find them there as well disposed to embrace such a course as they are here, then it is a match.'

We have nothing from Burghley on the subject; presumably he agreed. But before any action was taken, it became clear that Henry III was in no mood for an English connection. He seems rather to have contemplated placing himself at the head of the Holy League and carrying forward its policy.

Elizabeth changed her course of action accordingly. In her instructions to Stafford of December 29th she directed him to confine his dealings with Henry III to a general offer of assistance.

As time went on, Henry discovered that the Catholic party would have none of him. Quite the contrary, they were mustering their forces to oppose him, and by the beginning of February had not only taken possession of most of the Channel ports but had raised an army as strong as the King's own, among them 1200 horse from the Prince of Parma.[77]

Henry accordingly began to cultivate his English connection. In March he conferred with Stafford and asked for Elizabeth's good offices in assisting him to raise troops in Germany. He seems to have gone so far as to request a loan of 150,000 crowns. Stafford carried this message to England in person, and on his way thither conferred at length with Henry of Navarre. What part Stafford played in arranging an agreement between the two Henrys does not appear. But on the 24th the French King and the heir presumptive agreed to turn their joint forces against the Catholic League.

This is the bare outline of what happened. We have nothing from the English side, nothing from Walsingham who was away on sick leave, nothing from Burghley who was acting in his place.

He observed in a letter to Shrewsbury of May 27th:[78]

'My Lord, the state of the world is marvellously changed when we true Englishmen have cause, for our own quietness, to wish good success to a French King and a King of Scots; and yet they both differ, one from the other, in profession of religion. But seeing both are enemies to our enemies we have cause to join with them in their actions against our enemies. And this is the work of God for our good; for which the Queen and us all are most deeply bound to acknowledge his miraculous goodness, for no wit of man could otherwise have wrought it.'

It was a changed world indeed for Burghley, brought up in the tradition of the Burgundian alliance and the Hundred Years War against France. He cannot altogether have welcomed the change, remembering the days when Spain had been one of England's best markets and the Spanish Netherlands the very core of her commercial prosperity. But he had no choice. For the rest of his life he had to accept France and Scotland as England's chief allies, Spain and the Spanish Netherlands as her chief enemies. The Dutch rebels were of course something else again, but except as a canker in Spain's side, they were rather a liability than an asset in English foreign policy.

Meanwhile the tide was turning fast, and in June the combined armies of the two Henrys were moving upon Paris. The French King late in May sent an envoy, Pierre de Mornay, seigneur de Buhy, the older brother of Philippe de Mornay, the famous Huguenot publicist, to seek aid from Elizabeth. De Buhy asked for a loan of 250,000 crowns, about £45,000. The Privy Council told him that the Queen was much too deeply committed elsewhere to consider such a sum. But she would assist the King in borrowing 150,000 crowns in Germany and would bind herself jointly with him for its repayment. De Buhy rejected the offer. Elizabeth found his manner offensive and said so in a letter to the French King.[79] Nevertheless she raised her offer a little, undertaking to borrow the whole sum required on her own credit. De Buhy seems to have left England in a huff early in July. But upon his arrival in France he thought better of it and wrote a letter to Burghley, beseeching him 'as father of the state', for a cash loan of 100,000 crowns to pay the mustering charges of a German army. Burghley himself seems to have favoured the suggestion and so did Walsingham.[80]

In a memorandum dated July 13th he defined his own position in the matter as follows:

'(a) The Queen should procure and place at the French King's disposal at Stade in Germany within a period of — months, £20,000.

'(b) She should try to induce the Princes of Germany to contribute further sums.

'(c) She should join with the French King in underwriting a loan of 250,000 crowns, or if the French bonds were not acceptable to the money-lenders, she should underwrite the whole sum herself, provided the French King delivered to her his bonds for the repayment of principal, interest and costs involved in procuring the loan, with a special pledge, under the Great Seal of France, to repay the £20,000 cash loan.'

She should expect in return from the French King some assurance, 'though it be privately in writing, signed with his hand, that he would in time of need assist Elizabeth against attack by the King of Spain and the Pope's forces'.

She would also expect that he would prohibit the carriage of any grain or other victuals into Spain or Portugal or the Spanish Netherlands or the use by Spain of any mariners out of France.

Burghley went on to propose 'a strait league, both defensive and offensive' between France and England against Spain, to include also those princes in Germany 'that have cause to doubt the King of Spain's overgreatness'. He thought that the young King of Denmark might also be induced to join and the King of Scots and probably Venice and Florence and other Italian states, fearful of Spanish domination in Italy.

'The scope of this confederacy', as he defined it, 'may be ordered to be only to withstand the injurious, forcible attempts of the King of Spain and his associates, so as he may be restrained to use any forces against his neighbours, and may also be thereby induced to accord with his peoples in the Low Countries that they may live in peace with their liberties and so his external forces of men of war may be removed out of the Low Countries.

'And such may be the fruits of this confederacy as all Christendom may enjoy a universal peace and be the more able to withstand the forces of the common enemy [the Turk?]. And by this means all the seas may be free from the forces of war and piracy. And by this means the free trade of merchandise may be restored to France, England, to Scotland, Denmark and Eastland.

'And the Pope's . . .' At this point the manuscript ends abruptly.[81]

The document is an interesting revelation of Burghley's dream of a peaceful Christendom, free to go about its normal business. As it stands it ignores the religious issue. Burghley evidently meant to deal with it. Maybe the difficulties which it presented made him, in despair, drop his pen in the middle of an unfinished sentence. It ignores all the traditional national and dynastic rivalries. To some extent it foreshadowed the offensive and defensive alliance of England, France and the Low Countries some seven years later. It came to nothing at the time. There is no indication that it was even considered.[82]

Indeed, before any action of any sort was taken to implement the French King's appeal, less than a fortnight after Burghley had written his memorandum, Henry III was assassinated.

Anglo-French relations during the period immediately following his death are somewhat obscure. Henry of Navarre was his lawful successor, and was accepted as such by those about him. But the Catholic party under the leadership of the Duke of Mayenne, Henry of Guise's uncle, rejected Navarre's claim, and chose instead his uncle, the Cardinal of Bourbon.

Henry of Navarre abandoned the siege of Paris, moved into Normandy and presently took up a defensive position on the north coast, between Arques and Dieppe. His army had dwindled to a force of about 9000. Mayenne brought against him a force of some 30,000.

Henry appealed at once to Elizabeth for aid. On August 9th he sent a special envoy to England and wrote urgently of his needs to both Burghley and Walsingham. He asked immediately for money and munitions. He suggested an offensive and defensive alliance to which other Protestant powers should be invited to join — something like what Burghley's memorandum a month before had envisaged. We have no record of the negotiations which followed, or any indication of the position which either Burghley or Walsingham took. Burghley was certainly worried about money. He wrote to Walsingham on August 27th:[83] 'God help us, for we shall lack money to do necessary things unless the residue of the loans [Privy Seals] will come in.' Walsingham replied on the 29th:[84] 'When your Lordship alleges the great lack of money, I see no other way but that the city of London must be dealt withal to furnish her Majesty's lacks until she shall be able to make some money by the sale of some land[85] and shall receive the loan money, wherein I do understand they will be found willing. The loan money, I do doubt, will arise to no great sum.'

The efforts to borrow money in Germany had proved fruitless and, as Walsingham prophesied, the Privy Seals yielded little. There was, of course, an instalment of the parliamentary grant due in October, and of the grant from the clergy. Altogether some £90,000 was collected from that source, but it was far from adequate to meet current needs.

Some attempt was made in June and July to correct abuses in the assessment of the subsidy. Burghley had apparently made reference to them in the debates on the subsidy in Parliament.[86] The Queen herself, looking over the subsidy rolls, was amazed at the discrepancy between the obvious and the assessed wealth of knights and squires she knew.[87] Very likely Burghley brought them to her attention. He had himself as Lord Lieutenant of Hertfordshire written to his Deputy Lieutenants in June, pointing out that many rich Londoners had acquired land in the county and claimed exemption from them on the ground that they were already taxed in London. He ordered that all of them who had more than a garden, an orchard and ten acres of ground, whether they resided in the county or not, should be taxed according to the annual value of their lands.[88]

In July the Privy Council at the Queen's prompting sent out a letter to the assessors of the subsidy in the counties, directing them to reassess the richer men and to see to it that they, the assessors themselves, were adequately taxed; indeed, commanded them to send their personal assessments to the Privy Council for scrutiny.[89] This was not the first nor was it the last time that an effort was made to adjust taxes to the developing wealth of England. Burghley made a more determined effort at reform four years later. But he accomplished little or nothing, largely because the assessment was in the hands of the country gentry who persisted in looking after their own interests.

Generally speaking, efforts at tax reform coincided with periods in which the government found itself financially embarrassed. On this occasion it may be taken as one more testimony to the fact that Elizabeth's financial resources were strained to a point where she naturally hesitated to advance money to Henry of Navarre.

It is therefore remarkable, indeed almost unprecedented, that in less than a month after the dispatch of Henry's envoy the Queen had not only agreed to lend Navarre £20,000 and a quantity of munitions, but that Burghley had actually paid over the money at his house in Covent Garden.[90] When he received it, Henry is said to have remarked that he had never before seen so much money in one place. Within a year she had increased the loan to over £60,000.

More than that, she agreed to send over to France a force of 4000 men and ordered that £6000 be drawn from the depleted treasury for their pay and equipment.

Two days after the payment of the money, the Privy Council summoned Lord Willoughby to take command of the expeditionary force and within a week they had begun to assemble the troops.[91] Before the end of September, the English army was in Dieppe, paid for one month.[92] If he wanted them longer, Henry would have to pay them himself.

In point of fact they were in France for three months, the last two of them without pay, without shoes, almost without food. Henry simply did not have the money. But they made a gallant showing, so gallant that even Elizabeth was loud in their praises. 'My good Peregrine,' she wrote in one of her best known letters, 'I bless God that your old prosperous success followeth your valiant acts, and joy not a little that safety accompanyeth your luck. Your loving sovereign, El. R.'

But we hear little from Burghley, except complaints that he did not hear from Willoughby and had no accounts for the payments. On December 6th he wrote to Willoughby:

'My Lord, our lack in hearing from you hath been truly to me, your good friend, very grievous, for we might hear more frequently from Venice than we have done from your Lordship. But I cannot excuse Thomas Flud that never did advertise any jot of his service as your paymaster.'[93]

No wonder! Willoughby was dashing about France at too furious a pace to have time for dispatches. When he did write, it was to report the needs of his troops. Burghley managed to divert a few hundred pounds from a second loan to Navarre for the purchase of apparel for the half-naked soldiers. We need not follow further Willoughby's exploits in France. He brought his depleted army, reduced to a quarter of its original strength, back to England in January, leaving Navarre considerably strengthened and for the time being at least able to carry on alone.

Most of what we know about Burghley during the second half of the year 1589 has reference to the Low Countries.

The relations of England and the Dutch rebels had suffered considerably by the efforts of the Earl of Leicester, when he was commander of the Queen's army in the Low Countries, to develop a party among the radicals, who in turn tried to use English power to overthrow the Dutch oligarchy headed by John of Barneveldt and Maurice of Nassau. Leicester failed, and he left the Low Countries in December 1587, disappointed and humiliated. So long, however, as he lived, he prompted his mistress to lend support to the radicals. By a curious paradox the same woman who violently opposed Puritanism in England gave a certain measure of countenance to the Dutch equivalent of Puritanism, in its most extreme, militant form, among the Dutch.

Leicester's successor as Lieutenant-General of the English forces in the Low Countries, Lord Willoughby, was a much more competent soldier and a much more amiable man. Along with Leicester's office he inherited Leicester's unpopularity. At home he enjoyed the royal favour, but he lacked Leicester's unique influence over Elizabeth. It was his business to re-establish friendly relations between the two countries and at the start he was reasonably successful. In this particular he reaped a fair harvest by the defeat of the Armada in midsummer and by a brilliant defence of Bergen-op-Zoom which Parma, with the best army and the best leader in Europe, attempted to capture as soon as his hope of invading England melted away.

The defeat of the Armada, indeed, shifted the whole balance of power in the north and, though the contribution of the Dutch to that defeat was small, it did strengthen the ties between the two countries and relieved Dutch fears that Elizabeth meant to come to terms with the enemy. To some extent, since England was now irrevocably committed to war with Spain, the Dutch turned from fear to over-confidence. Elizabeth now was bound to support them and they might stiffen their own terms.

They were not altogether wrong. Elizabeth recognized that the Dutch wars were a vital element in her actions against Spain. At the same time she was resolute to keep her assistance within the bounds dictated by the increased strain on her resources. She would abide by the terms of her treaty with them, maintain a force of 5000 foot and 1000 horse in the field and English garrisons at Flushing and Brill. Thanks largely to Burghley's efforts in eliminating corruption, her annual expenses had been reduced to a little over £100,000. She would do no more.[94]

And she insisted that the Dutch should also abide by the treaty, should accept the military leadership of her Lieutenant-General, should recognize the wide executive power of the Council of State, on which she had two representatives, and should by degrees pay back the money which she was expending in their behalf. But she would not assume sovereign powers. She would assist, but she would not control.

For the year following the Armada, Anglo-Dutch relations were mainly concerned with the interpretation of the treaty, each party charging the other with a breach of its terms.

The Dutch were increasingly intent to keep all substantial power in their own hands. They encroached more and more upon Willoughby's position and more and more shoved aside the Council of State. Their government, as they proceeded to develop it, was dominated by the province of Holland, dominated in turn by John of Barneveldt, and their army was led by Maurice of Nassau, William the Silent's son. They declined to participate in any reckoning of what they owed the Queen; they complained that she did not maintain the forces she had agreed to furnish, and they blamed her for the one major loss they suffered in 1589, the defection of Gertrudenberg.

Willoughby[95] gave up in despair and returned to England late in March. Burghley tried to induce him to return, but without success. No one was appointed in his place and the English forces were without a recognized leader until the following August, when Sir Francis Vere took over with the more modest title of Sergeant-major-General. Henry Killigrew, the senior English representative on the Council of State, had been recalled the previous December, and Thomas Bodley, who was later to found the great library which bears his name, was appointed in his place. In the subsequent process of devolution by which Elizabeth gradually divested herself of major responsibility for the affairs in the Low Countries, it was probably just as well that the two foremost exponents of the older order of things should be removed. Killigrew, though Burghley's brother-in-law, had actually promoted Leicester's policy, and Willoughby, though by no means a Leicestrian, had inherited Leicester's conception of the position of Lieutenant-General.

In England the direction of English policy in the Low Countries remained in the hands of Burghley and Walsingham. During the spring of 1589, when Walsingham was away on sick leave, Burghley was in sole charge. But the two men worked so closely together that the policy either one directed was the policy which both supported. Nor does there seem to have been any problem of managing Elizabeth. She seems to have been willing to do anything which her two most trusted councillors advised. All three of them — Hatton was the third — were aware that with English resources strained to the limit no more could be done than had been agreed upon in the treaty of 1585. Indeed, the English position was the treaty, the whole treaty, and nothing but the treaty.

In the negotiations on the subject during the spring, which were carried out in part by Bodley in the Low Countries and in part by Joachim Ortell, the agent of the Provinces in England, both parties professed to take their stand on the treaty. It is not necessary to follow them in detail. They came to nothing, though it was clear enough that the English had not lived up to their engagements in the matter of maintaining the agreed quota of troops and that the Dutch were busily engaged in reducing or circumventing the powers of the English Lieutenant-General and the partially English Council of State.

A few of Burghley's letters to Bodley survive,[96] but they are concerned rather with details than with general policy. In his one extant memorandum[97] he was evidently wrestling with the problem of corruption in the English expeditionary force. Bodley thought that the actual withdrawal of the English forces would be the one effective way of bringing the Dutch to terms. The Dutch would apparently have been glad to see the English depart bag and baggage if the Queen would contribute money instead of men. But that would have meant the surrender of the cautionary towns, Elizabeth's one security for the repayment of her moneys, and she would not hear of it.

The one step she did take, and it worried the Dutch not a little, was her restraint of trade with Spain. Commerce was the life blood of Holland and the sale of licences to trade with the enemy one of her chief sources of revenue. Bodley[98] warned the Dutch in January that the Queen meant to prohibit trade with Spain and that any Dutch vessels caught at it would be treated as lawful prize. And the English government proceeded to enforce this ruling, not only with ships of the navy but with swarms of privateers. Had Elizabeth been disposed to push the blockade, she might have starved the Dutch into submission on those terms. But nobody dreamed of that. The Dutch tried to buy her off by suggesting that she establish a system of tolls in the Narrow Seas after the pattern of the Danish tolls at the entrance to the Baltic. It would yield, they estimated, some £200,000 a year. But the Privy Council thought not, and there is no indication that Elizabeth, avaricious as she was, entertained the suggestion.

There is some reason to believe that after Drake and Norris had returned from the Portuguese expedition some move was made to mitigate the prohibition. Walsingham wrote to Burghley in August 1589,[99] recalling a conference at which it was proposed that the Dutch would be permitted to trade with Spain if they carried neither victuals nor munitions and used only smaller vessels. Walsingham added that the matter 'was never set down in writing'. This is indeed all that we hear of it.

In any case, Dutch trade with the enemy continued in spite of English efforts to check it. Over a year later, on December 30th, 1590, Burghley wrote to Bodley:

'I have perused the answers of the States and see nothing to content us, but rather to wish we were rid of them; for thereto they tempt us by their continual furnishing of the Spaniards with all kinds of munitions ... No enemy can more displeasure [us] than they do by their daily trade to Spain. In very truth her Majesty is herewith tempted greatly both to repent herself of aiding them and to attempt how to be quit of them. I pray you think thereof.'[100]

Such was the attitude both of the Queen and of her chief ministers towards the Dutch after five years of fighting and the expenditure of over half a million pounds in their behalf.

The Dutch were no more kindly disposed towards the English. Each regarded the other as a necessary evil, not to be dispensed with but certainly not to be embraced.

The picture was no longer that of a thin line of Dutch Protestants standing out on a sand dune against the serried powers of a Catholic fanatic. It was of a band of shrewd merchants, getting rich by trade and trying to drive a hard bargain, encroaching upon the English fisheries, driving the British traders out of the Baltic and underselling them in the European markets.[101]

CHAPTER XXIII

THE RISE OF ESSEX, 1590-93

SIR FRANCIS WALSINGHAM died early in April 1590. We have only one notice from Burghley on the subject, in a letter which he wrote to one of Walsingham's friends in Florence.

'I cannot', he wrote, 'otherwise think, but you have afore this time heard, or else I am sure shall hear before this letter can come to your hands, of the death of Mr. Secretary Walsingham who left this world the 6th of April as we account by ancient custom; whereby, though he hath gained a better estate, as I am fully persuaded, for his soul in heaven, yet the Queen's Majesty and her realm and I and others, his particular friends, have had a great loss, both for the public use of his good and painful long services and for the private comfort I had by his mutual friendship.'[1]

Burghley might well lament, for in the seventieth year of his age he had to take over once again the laborious tasks of the Secretariat.

His first impulse was evidently to distribute responsibility among members of the Privy Council. Three days after Walsingham's death he drew up a memorandum to that effect. It began as follows:

'It is very meet that public affairs which are of importance should be made known to some principal persons of the Council whereby her Majesty might be informed of the state thereof and so by her order the same Councillors, with one of the secretaries or both, might either by themselves or with assistance of the rest of the Council put things in execution.' And he proceeded to enumerate the problems domestic and foreign which he had in mind.[2]

'To have care that all papists and recusants which by their wealth and credit may seem dangerous, be restrained and punished according to the laws ... also is the care to be taken to suppress all the turbulent Precisians who do violently seek to change the external government of the church.'

It was characteristic of him that he placed religious problems first and interesting that he bracketed papist and Puritan together for suppression.

He went on to enumerate: the navy, the ordnance, the borders of Scotland, the musters, Ireland, France, the Low Countries, Spain, the Hansa, Denmark, trade with Russia and the Ottoman Empire, and relations with Venice and other Italian merchants, and the secret service in Spain, the Low Countries and Italy.

He had always complained that too much of the burden of government fell upon too few shoulders, and he wanted to divide the burden and the responsibility. His reference to two Secretaries is surprising. There was at the moment, following Walsingham's death, but one — John Wooley, Latin Secretary. We may perhaps presume that he expected Elizabeth to proceed at once to the appointment of Walsingham's successor.

But his advice was not taken. There were, indeed, very few members of the Privy Council qualified. Of those of Burghley's own generation, except for Croft who did not matter, there were only two left, Hunsdon and Knollys, both of them closely related to the Queen, Hunsdon her first cousin by descent, Knollys her first cousin by marriage. Hunsdon was a bluff, honest soldier, who spent most of his active life on the Scottish border — the one man who had fought and won the only pitched battle in the Rising of the North. Elizabeth selected him to lead the army organized to defend her person in the crisis of 1588. At one time Walsingham thought Burghley was trying to groom him as a competing favourite to Leicester. But Hunsdon was no courtier and not much of a statesman. There was, however, a certain military aura about him which endeared him to the aspiring young soldiers at Court. As for Knollys, he was first, last and all the time a belligerent Puritan, six years Burghley's senior and virtually in his dotage. What we hear of him in the last five years of his life (he died in 1596) takes the form of letters, devoted to the defence of Puritanism or directed against the Anglican bishops and their claims of divine right.

Otherwise the Council had lost most of its competent and influential members. Leicester died in 1588, Walter Mildmay in 1589, Walsingham in 1590. Hatton was to die in 1591. Only one new councillor had been added — to replace Mildmay as Chancellor of the Exchequer — John Fortescue.

During the Elizabethan wars which, in one form or other, filled the period between 1588 and the end of the reign, the councillors were in the main men of the robe. Until Essex joined it in 1593 there were only two men of the sword — Hunsdon and Lord Charles Howard, the hero of the Armada, both of them dear to the Queen but neither of them comparable to Burghley either in political competency or in influence. In 1591 and 1592, two other councillors were added, Robert Cecil and John Puckering, appointed to fill Hatton's place, but with the less exalted title of Lord Keeper of the Great Seal. Certainly one of them, probably both of them, may be accounted Cecilians. It was not until 1596 that two soldiers, Sir William Knollys and Sir Roger North, were added to redress the balance; plus Sir Thomas Egerton, an Essex partisan at the outset, who became Lord Keeper when Sir John Puckering died in 1596, and minus Hunsdon who died the same year.

Burghley evidently expected Elizabeth to appoint Walsingham's successor as soon as might be. Under him, as indeed under Cecil before him, the Principal Secretary had become the chief of administration, particularly in foreign affairs. He began to press his mistress about it in July.

On July 15th, Hatton wrote to him:

'My very good Lord, We have received your honourable letters and can well witness your endless travail which, in her Majesty's princely consideration, she would relieve you of. But it is true that affairs are in a good hand, as we all know, and thereby her Majesty is the more sure and we her poor servants the better satisfied. God send you help and happiness to your better contentment.'[3]

All of which, though very flattering, was not very helpful.

Again in October he had a letter from Thomas Windebank, Clerk of the Signet and sometime tutor to Burghley's son, Thomas.[4] At the time Windebank was acting as personal secretary to the Queen. He acknowledged various letters from Burghley which he had read to Elizabeth. 'I took occasion', he added, 'thereby to tell her Majesty how greatly her favour should be extended to your Lordship by easing your burden she layeth upon you through want of a secretary, wherein, according to my poor means, I dealt more earnestly and largely than I will trouble your Lordship with the writing thereof.

'She confessed as much, and took very well your Lordship's words of your vow to such a saint.'[5]

But still Elizabeth delayed action. Very likely she found it more comfortable to work with Burghley, her oldest and most trusted councillor, whose ideas on State and Church were more in accord with her own than Walsingham's. And Burghley, for his part, though he urged immediate action, very likely had his son, Robert, in mind and was not unwilling to act as *locum tenens* for the time being.[6] There may have been other factors in the situation as well. The young Earl of Essex was pressing hard for William Davison, the scapegoat of Mary Queen of Scots' execution, who had been released from captivity in 1588 and still drew his pay as royal Secretary though he had not recovered the royal favour.[7] And, if we can believe Essex, Hatton favoured Davison as well. But Elizabeth would not hear of it.

In May 1591 Elizabeth visited Burghley at Theobalds. It was a formal state visit, and included not only the royal person but also prominent members of her Court, including the ladies-in-waiting, the Lord Chancellor, the Lord Admiral, the Earl of Derby, the Earl of Essex, Sir Walter Raleigh, and others.[8] According to Burghley's diary[9] the Queen arrived on the 10th and left on the 20th. The Privy Council met at Theobalds three times during her presence there.[10] So the atmosphere at Theobalds could not have differed greatly from that of the Court elsewhere. But no doubt Burghley had more opportunity to discuss problems with his mistress. What passed between them can only be conjectured. It may be presumed that they considered together the question of the Secretariat and that she saw something of Burghley's son, Robert. In any case, what actually eventuated was that she knighted Robert before she left, and some three months later appointed him to her Privy Council.[11] It was generally assumed that he would presently be made Secretary.[12] But nothing followed, and nothing was to follow in that direction for five years to come.

The explanation of the situation remains pure conjecture. Most probably Burghley insisted that he could no longer carry the burden of the Secretariat unaided and proposed that Robert be appointed. Most probably the Queen insisted that Robert was too young and too inexperienced for the post. It may be that Burghley then suggested that Robert be appointed to the Privy Council and be in a position to prepare himself for the Secretariat while his father continued to assume responsibility for the office.[13] That certainly is what happened, and in the five years intervening between Robert's entrance into the Council and his entrance into the Secretariat the burden of the office was gradually shifted from father to son.

Among others who accompanied the Queen on her visit to Theobalds was Robert, second Earl of Essex, not yet of the Council but very much of the Court. He was at that time twenty-six years old, but had already begun to play a major part in English political life. For the seven years following (the seven remaining years of Burghley's life) he was to play an increasingly important part.

He was the son of Walter, the first Earl, who had died in Ireland in 1576. During his absence in Ireland, the Earl of Leicester had interested himself in Lady Essex, and it was currently rumoured, though without justification, that he had hastened Walter's latter end. In any case, two years later Leicester married the widow who was, by the way, the daughter of Sir Francis Knollys and, through her mother, second cousin to the Queen.

Walter, in a letter written the day before his death to Burghley,[14] asked that his son, Robert, not yet ten years old, should be brought up in Burghley's house-hold, and since Robert was a royal ward, Burghley as Master of the Court of Wards acted as guardian.[15] We hear of Robert in residence at the Burghley home during the two months in the spring of 1577 before he entered Trinity College, Cambridge, and very likely he spent considerable time there during his adolescence. The important fact is that he not only knew Burghley as a foster father, but he knew well the whole Burghley household, notably those two children who were still at home — Robert, and Ann, Oxford's cast-off wife.

Young Essex was three years younger than Robert Cecil, but Robert was a frail, emaciated hunchback and Essex a handsome, vigorous, athletic young fellow. We can only surmise what effect this striking physical contrast had upon their attitudes, one towards the other. There is no evidence of boyhood companion-ship, but certainly they knew each other well, from early youth up.[16] Probably Robert Essex developed early towards Robert Cecil a superiority complex which led him later to discount Cecil's strength and ability. It can hardly be doubted that towards Burghley himself the young Earl entertained a filial regard which must not be ignored in considering their later relationship.

The career of Robert of Essex was a meteoric one. His mother's marriage to Leicester brought him under Leicester's eye, and in 1584 he entered Court, more or less under Leicester's auspices. The following year he went with Leicester to the Low Countries. Before he left, Leicester named him (being then nineteen years old) General of the Horse.

During the two years following, Essex was Leicester's henchman, identifying himself with Leicester's quarrels and with Leicester's friends. Evidently Leicester was grooming him for the position of royal favourite, and in December 1587 finally induced Elizabeth to accept his resignation as Master of the Horse and to appoint Essex in his place.[17] It was a position involving close attendance upon the Queen. Leicester had exploited it for all it was worth in the early days of the reign when he still aspired to the royal hand.

This connection of Essex with Leicester is important because, upon Leicester's death the following year, Essex was accepted as the leader of the Leicestrians. What he actually came by was Leicester's military attachments, which drew around him the aspiring young soldiers at Court. He did not inherit, or at least he did not vigorously cultivate, Leicester's Puritan connections.[18] His followers were recruited from those of all religious complexions — Puritans, Catholics, Anglicans alike. Like his royal mistress, his approach to politics was basically secular. He was much more interested in immediate power than in ultimate salvation.

It was characteristic of Burghley that, in defining the functions of the Secretariat immediately following Walsingham's death, he should have dealt first with the religious problem.

Some time early in 1590, about the time when Burghley took over the Secretariat, he drew up a memorandum in which he advocated that the well-to-do recusants, who had been constrained in 1588 and then released again, should be once more restrained, and that others of the same category, who had escaped restraint before, should be restrained, particularly those in remote parts and in the maritime counties. In the maritime counties he advocated that even 'the mean sort of recusants . . . of bodily ability to do hurt' should be committed to the custody of the sheriffs and that no noble recusant 'should be suffered to continue near the sea side'. All this reveals a lively fear of a Spanish invasion and of a consequent Catholic uprising. For the same reason he proposed that all the weapons of the recusants should be sequestered. In a final item he dealt with recusant wives of Anglican husbands — an issue which provoked much debate in Parliament three years later. In his view they should be indicted and condemned, and either imprisoned or their husbands made liable for the fine imposed by law.[19]

It does not appear that Burghley's recommendations were followed in all particulars, but the restraint and the disarming of recusants went on throughout the year.[20]

In the year following, more stringent measures were taken, provoked partly by Philip II's all-out attack upon France, but mainly by the policy of Pope Gregory XIV, elected in December 1590, a man completely Spanish in his sympathies, who threw all the weight of his office in support of Philip's efforts both against France and against England. It was understood that he was planning to send missionaries to England in large numbers.[21] The Queen's answer took the form of a proclamation issued in October, directed primarily to the purpose of catching missionaries by a careful check upon recusants who gave them shelter and support. Commissioners were appointed for this purpose in every county.

This proclamation in its application served to establish an inquisition into the lives and habits of the recusants which made their condition almost unendurable. It was confirmed and intensified by statutory action in the Parliament of 1593.

Catholic leaders blamed this policy on Burghley. One of them alluded to it as 'the new Cecilian Inquisition'.[22] Camden says that they attributed the proclamation itself to his authorship.[23] Robert Parsons in his reply[24] directed his fire

ROBERT DEVEREUX, 2ND EARL OF ESSEX

specifically at Burghley. There is no more direct evidence that he wrote the proclamation, though the probabilities are that he did. Most of the important royal proclamations came from his pen. The sentiments expressed, particularly the denigration of the missionary priests, smack strongly of his famous pamphlet, published eight years earlier, on the *Execution of Justice in England.*[25]

The savagery of this attack upon the recusants was certainly not inspired by religious considerations. It probably can be explained by the analogy of the recusants' position to that of the French or Italian 'underground' in World War II. They were giving the agents of the enemy aid and comfort, and offering a network of shelters through which these agents could move from place to place. They inevitably provided at least the nucleus of any domestic uprising. Actually they were politically weaker than ever they had been. Mary Queen of Scots was gone; their national leaders were either dead or in exile. The hopes of a successful intervention by Spain in their favour had been blasted by the fate of the Armada. It presently appeared that a substantial majority of them, loyal to the Queen, definitely opposed the political activities of the missionaries. Nevertheless, the recusants were always a potential menace and the revealed intentions of both Philip II and of Gregory XIV whom, the proclamation declared, 'he now hath hanging in the girdle', called for action to reduce the menace to a minimum.[26]

In the same agenda in which Burghley called for action against the recusants, he went on to say: 'Care is to be taken to suppress all the turbulent Precisians who do violently seek to change the external government of the church.'[27] By 'Precisians' he of course meant Puritans. Actually the word 'violently' robs the statement of most of its meaning. None of the responsible Puritans, even the radical separatists, advocated reform by violence. Nevertheless this was a new note from Burghley.

Up to this time he had been a Puritan sympathizer, though a discreet one. More than once he had broken a lance with Whitgift on behalf of Puritan preachers. He had condemned the use of the *ex officio* oath in the procedure of the Court of High Commission.

He had befriended Thomas Cartwright, the recognized leader of the Presbyterian movement, and would befriend him again. Morice and Beale, the two leaders of the fight against the *ex officio* oath, both looked to him. So did Peter Wentworth. So did the separatists, Barrow and Greenwood and John Penry. Robert Brown, who touched off the separatist movement in 1582 with his Middelburgh manifesto — *Reformation without tarrying for any* — was a Stamford man and a distant kinsman of Burghley, enjoyed his protection and, largely through his favour and influence, was reconciled with the Anglican Church and spent the last forty years of his life as a rector of a parish in Northants.

But as Burghley grew older he became increasingly irritated with the Puritans as trouble-makers. Disputes and dissensions weakened the Elizabethan position and supplied the enemy with telling arguments against the Establishment. This was particularly true when these disputes and dissensions were led out of the field of academic disputations into the market place. Puritan propagandists in the 'eighties aimed at the man in the street and reached him not with learned quotations from the early fathers but with catch-words and slogans, satire and abuse. The Martin Marprelate tracts, for example, were in everybody's hands. They owed their popularity to their spicy, witty style, above all to the fact that they made the royal Church ridiculous. But though they made the unskilful laugh, they made the judicious grieve. Burghley was shocked by their flippant irreverence.

It is interesting to note how a man like Cartwright and a man like Robert Beale in their letters to Burghley made a point of insisting that they were completely out of sympathy with Martin and his ways. So, for that matter, did John Penry, the Welsh martyr. Very likely Martin finally convinced Burghley that something had to be done about Puritanism.

This should not be taken to mean that he fell in with Whitgift's policy of ruthless repression. Quite the contrary. In 1593 he rebuked Whitgift publicly for his violent courses. He did what he could to save Barrow and Greenwood and John Penry from execution,[28] and was chiefly instrumental in securing the release of James Morice from imprisonment because of his attack in the House of Commons upon the *ex officio* oath. The circumstances of that release are illuminating. Puckering, the Lord Keeper, and Burghley summoned Morice, who, as attorney of the Court of Wards was of the Queen's Council, to Burghley's house in Covent Garden, where he was in bed with the gout. There, as Morice himself tells the tale,[29] Burghley announced to him his release.

' "Her Majesty's pleasure was, I should be delivered, thinking me, notwithstanding anything past, to be both an honest man and good subject. Nevertheless, her Majesty would have me to be admonished of two things; the first was that if aught were amiss in the Church or Commonwealth, I should not straightway make it known to the common sort, but declare it to her Majesty or some of her Privy Council." [Burghley reinforced the admonition by reminding Morice that he, like they, was of the Queen's council. It was their duty to complain only to the Queen.] "If it please her to reform it, it was well: if not, we were to pray to God to move her heart thereunto, and so to leave the matter to God and her Majesty." '

This was Burghley to the life. He accepted the Acts of Supremacy and Uniformity in all their implications. In matters of public worship the decision lay with the Queen. She might be influenced, she certainly might not be coerced. Burghley's quarrel with the Puritans, particularly with the separatists, was that their position implied coercion, 'Reformation without tarrying for any', as he read it, was a slogan of rebellion against constituted authority.[30]

He may have been influenced by the fantastic behaviour of one William Hacket in the summer of 1591. Hacket claimed to be Jesus Christ. With two other followers he staged a public performance in London in July, addressing the crowd from a cart in Cheapside, where he attacked the Queen, the Lord Chancellor and the Archbishop of Canterbury. Great crowds turned out to listen to him.[31]

The Privy Council took cognizance of the affair and ordered Hacket's arrest. His behaviour at his trial made it clear that he was quite crazy. It even appeared that he had been puncturing Elizabeth's picture in vital parts. He was condemned and executed in Cheapside, uttering 'execrable blasphemies' until the last.

The attention which he attracted, the crowds which hurried out to listen to him, seem to have alarmed the government and even the Queen.[32] The Privy Council evidently thought that there was more in Hacket's performance than met the eye, and in the course of his imprisonment had him put to torture to disclose his confederates. Actually they got nothing, but they thought the matter serious enough to call for a public explanation and the following year put forth a pamphlet describing the whole affair,[33] written by a member of the Ecclesiastical Commission and entitled *Conspiracy for Pretended Reformation.*

Evidently, in the general tension, the doings of a crazy fanatic attracted more attention than they merited. The general disposition was to classify Hacket with the 'sectaries', following hard as he did upon the seditious pamphlets of Barrow and Greenwood. No wonder that Burghley, like his mistress, was disturbed.

Martin's blasphemies and the defiant attitude of the separatists robbed the Puritans of Burghley's support at a time when they particularly needed it. Within two years they had lost their three most valiant supporters in high places, Leicester in 1588, Mildmay in 1589, Walsingham in 1590. No one, unless it were Burghley, was left to do battle for them in the Council. His estrangement explains his acquiescence in the measures taken two years later against Puritanism in Parliament — explains perhaps why these measures were taken at all.

During the eight years which remained of Burghley's life after 1590, relations with France occupied the first place in Elizabeth's foreign relations. Even the war with Spain was, to a considerable extent, fought on French battlefields. As for the Low Countries, her war there, maintained reluctantly and on a strictly limited basis, played its part rather as a training school for English soldiers, and a source of supply for seasoned troops to be used elsewhere, than as a resolute military operation.

Early in 1591, the Emperor Rudolph made an attempt to arrange a peace between Spain and the Dutch, which created some alarm in England and called forth from Burghley one of his discourses[34] in which he set forth at length reasons why the Dutch should reject the imperial approach. He sent it to the Queen and she approved of it. In a letter of February 20th Windebank wrote about it to Burghley:[35] 'The Queen, having read herself a good part of the writing, being your Lordship's labour, and caused [me] to read the other part, hath willed me to send you word of her great liking thereof; and perceiveth that howsoever your want of health is, your care wanteth not. Only her Majesty seeth not how it may be justified to charge the King of Spain with seeking or procuring directly her death, and therefore would have that allegation altered or someway mitigated, or else left out.'[36]

Two days later Burghley wrote to Thomas Bodley in the Low Countries that he had dashed off ('suddenly made') an answer to the imperial peace approach, 'wherewith her Majesty, being acquainted, she doth so well allow thereof as she hath commanded me with all diligence to send it unto you with intention that you should impart the same to such of the general estates or of the Council as you should think capable of such a matter'.[37] Burghley even went so far as to suggest that the Dutch might use it as a reply to the imperial commissioners. He further suggested that the substance of his discourse might be published both in Dutch and in French and 'in sundry other languages'.

Bodley did not agree. The Dutch, he wrote, had heard no more of the imperial envoys. When they came they would need a passport, which he was well assured they would never get.[38]

But Burghley was not to be denied. He wrote again on March 21st that the Queen would be glad to see the 'Project' printed.

To this Bodley replied on April 3rd that no Dutch printer would print the 'Project' without consultation with the Dutch government, which would be certain to attribute it to Elizabeth. He thought that since the peace project 'is wholly quailed of itself', it would be unwise to revive it and stir up controversy which might do more harm than good. Burghley seems to have acquiesced.

We need not follow the matter further, though Burghley and Bodley corresponded about it for over a year. The imperial commission did get as far as Brussels under guard provided by the Duke of Parma. There they spent the rest of the year trying to establish contact with the Dutch Estates General. It was not until the following April that they received a categorical refusal from the Dutch to negotiate.[39]

Elizabeth was at first alarmed, but she was always ready to entertain peace projects, and at one point in the correspondence she suggested to Bodley that he might perhaps arrange for an imperial mission to England.

As to Burghley's 'Project', which ran to six folio pages, it constituted an impressive indictment of Philip II's government of the Low Countries, of his malevolence towards England and his aggressive actions in Europe at large. It pointed out that Philip's objective was clearly to separate the Dutch from their two staunch allies, England and France, and that any promises he might make of religious toleration were obviously insincere and untrustworthy. All of these points Burghley had made more than once before. The interest of the 'Project' lies chiefly in its revelation of his disposition once more to try his hand at pamphleteering and once more to apply the power of the press, not this time in England, but in Europe at large. I find no evidence that it was ever published in any language.

During 1590 there were no English forces in France, but Burghley and his sovereign were both concerned about the increasing activity of Spain against France, through Parma from the Low Countries, the Duke of Lorraine from the east, the Duke of Savoy from the south-east, from Spain itself through Guyenne and, most serious of all, by the landing of 3000 Spanish troops in Brittany in October. Henry IV was trying to raise an army of German mercenaries to meet these threats, but he lacked the necessary funds and appealed urgently to Elizabeth for help. Camden asserts that 'there were those' who advised Elizabeth to have nothing to do with the French, and this has been interpreted to mean that her Council was divided on the subject. But there is no indication elsewhere of any such dissension.[40]

In November 1590, Burghley drew up a brief statement of the French situation.[41] He pointed out that without German assistance Henry could hardly hope to survive the next summer's campaigning. Burghley estimated the cost of an adequate German army at £60,000 a month, suggested that Elizabeth might contribute £10,000 and expressed the opinion that the Merchant Adventurers at Stade might advance the money on the security of their merchandise 'laden thither lately'.

Elizabeth assented with considerable reluctance. During a long reign she had had more than her fill of German mercenaries. The best that could be said for them was that they created a diversion. Besides that, her finances were in desperate straits, notwithstanding the large parliamentary grants of 1589[42] and the sale of Crown lands the year following which yielded something over £125,000.[43] In addition to this she had been forced, very reluctantly, to resort to another issue of Privy Seals,[44] collected first in London and later in the country at large, which brought in another £75,000.

Under these circumstances parsimony was not only understandable, it was virtually obligatory. And yet she continued to feed both money and troops to the French King. Before the end of the year 1590 she had loaned him some £60,000 without taking account of the cost of Willoughby's expedition to France in 1589. Curiously enough, Burghley, generally charged with prompting her thriftiness, seems to have supported wholeheartedly both her loans and her military contributions.

The news of Parma's invasion of France in August 1590 and of the landing of Spanish forces in Brittany in October stirred Elizabeth to action. In September she had been contemplating the dispatch of 3000 men to support an enterprise for the seizure of Dunkirk. But the demands from France gave her pause.[45] For over a month she seems to have wavered between Dunkirk and France. As late as October 10th[46] Burghley wrote to Bodley that Elizabeth was resolute to proceed with her plans against Dunkirk; in November she had definitely decided to send an expeditionary force into Brittany under the command of Sir John Norris. Late in that month Burghley was making arrangements[47] for transporting English troops from the Low Countries to Plymouth. In January 1591 he wrote to Bodley that Norris was on his way to the Low Countries to see if he could induce the Dutch to release 3000 English troops for French service.[48] Burghley's letter reveals the fact that Norris was very unpopular with English officers in the Low Countries and that they were reluctant to serve under him. Burghley did indeed, on the same day, draft a long letter to Norris,[49] to the effect that the Queen was aware of the hostility of the officers towards him, 'specially such as have served with Sir Francis Vere', and had charged Bodley to compose their differences. Norris was directed to enlist captains not hostile to him and in no case to discharge the bands of hostile captains. Elizabeth, having read this letter before its dispatch, not only approved of it but commanded the Lord Admiral to sign it. One gets a hint here of factions in the Council — Howard being recognized as Norris's staunch supporter, Burghley as his critic.

As was expected, the Dutch were strongly opposed to the withdrawal of 3000 seasoned troops even though Elizabeth agreed to replace them with troops levied in England. A compromise was finally arranged,[50] by which 1500 men were drawn from the Low Countries (under promise of replacement from England) and the other 1500 levied in England.

On May 3rd the army assembled at the Isle of Jersey and on the following night reached Paimpol on the Breton coast. Meanwhile, a commission of three — Burghley, Howard and Hunsdon — had come to terms with the French ambassador regarding the financing of the expedition, and the King of France had obligated himself not only to meet all the expenses of the levy and transportation of the troops, but to pay them their wages week by week in France.[51] He promised further to maintain in Brittany French forces twice as large as the English forces.[52]

We need not follow Norris's course in France. From the very start it was apparent that King Henry was not living up to his engagement to maintain the agreed quota of French troops. Burghley's letters to Sir Henry Unton, who went over to France in July as English ambassador, were filled with complaints on this score and threats to withdraw Norris altogether.[53] But no such drastic step was taken. Norris lacked the strength to engage the forces of the enemy and Elizabeth refused his requests for reinforcements. He himself returned to England the following January and his little army, now dwindled to some 1200 men, was left inactive in eastern Brittany.

We hear nothing from Burghley, except what he wrote at the Queen's command about Norris's abortive campaign in Brittany, which was overshadowed in August by another English expedition into Normandy under Essex.

In May Burghley's interest was diverted to quite another quarter. It had to do with Dr. John Dee, whom Burghley had met earlier in connection with the Frobisher expedition in 1578 and again in 1583 when he had invoked Dee's assistance in his abortive efforts to reform the English calendar in accordance with the new Gregorian usage in Roman Catholic Europe.[54] Dee was that curious combination of mathematician, astrologer, alchemist and necromancer, which was not uncommon in a century when magic was gradually and reluctantly yielding to science. Late in 1583 a Polish nobleman visiting England became much interested in Dee's experiments and induced him and his collaborator, Edward Kelly, to go with him on his return to Bohemia. Dee's correspondent in England was Edward Dyer, courtier and poet, who had for many years been playing about with alchemy. Dyer heard, early in the year 1588, that Kelly had at last discovered the secret of transmuting base metals into gold. Dyer was so much interested that he left England in June, when the Spanish Armada was on its way, and set out for Bohemia. It seems not unlikely that he had a private commission, either from Elizabeth or from Burghley, though there is nothing to prove it. When Dyer reached Prague he learned that Dee and Kelly had fallen out, but he established contact with Kelly and presently, to his surprise and delight, Kelly demonstrated, at least to Dyer's satisfaction, that he could do the trick.

Dyer hastened back to England and revealed his discovery both to the Queen and to Burghley. Royal letters at once went forth to both Dee and Kelly inviting them to return to England. Dee went back the spring following. Kelly, unresponsive, remained at Prague.

Dee was cordially received, but he did not possess the great secret.

The next we hear of Kelly is from an English agent who wrote to Burghley in March 1590 that he had seen Kelly at Prague, who had treated him courteously and handed him a box of ore and powder from the silver mines to deliver to Burghley himself.[55]

Dyer went to Prague again in January but accomplished nothing. Meanwhile Kelly had aroused the interest of Rudolph II, the Emperor, and was created a 'Golden Knight', handsomely endowed with landed estates and even promised the office of Privy Councillor. All this increased English interest, and an active correspondence between Burghley and Kelly ensued, in which Kelly indicated his willingness to return to England if Elizabeth would match the favours he had received from the Emperor.

In March 1591, Burghley wrote to Sir Horatio Palavicino, who was at the time on official business in Germany: 'I pray you learn what you can how Mr. Edward Kelly's profession may be credited.'[56] Palavicino's reply was not encouraging. 'There is good reason to believe', he wrote to Burghley, 'that his [Kelly's] knowledge of how to make gold is pure fraud.' In May Burghley wrote two letters to Kelly which are preserved. One of them dealt mainly with Burghley's health:

'I hope to hear from you to have something of your approbation to strengthen me afore the next winter against my old enemy, the gout, which is rather fed by a cold humour than a hot, and principally by a rheumatic head, which I also think receiveth the imperfection from a stomach not fully digesting the food received. But to affirm, what I take to be the most direct cause, is oppression with affairs and lack of liberty against the which no medical receipt can serve. And yet I will be glad to make use of any you will send me, with your assurance that it shall do me no harm.'[57]

Evidently Burghley, in his own mind, had added magic medicine to Kelly's other magical attributes.

In another letter undated,[58] Burghley once more urged Kelly to return, pointing out that, though Kelly was widely regarded an impostor, he was of a different opinion.

'Such', Burghley wrote, 'is my allowance of your royal profession, such opinion I do firmly conceive of your wisdom and learning . . . such also is my persuasion of your ability to perform that which Mr. Dyer hath reported . . . as I rest only unsatisfied in your delay of coming, and again [am] expressly commanded of her Majesty to require you to have regard to her honour, and according to the tenor of her former letters to assure yourself to be singularly favoured. . . .

'Good Knight, therefore let me end my letter with God's holy name, by which

I do conjure you not to keep God's gifts from your natural country, but rather to help to make her Majesty a glorious and victorious prince against the malice of her and God's enemies ... Let no other country bereave us of this felicity, that only, yea only, by you, I say, is to be expected.'

What Burghley expected is revealed in a letter, also undated but of about the same date [May 1591] to Dyer,[59] in which he expressed some scepticism. 'If', he concluded, 'you cannot obtain Sir Ed. Kelly's return personally, yet you would, for maintenance of your credit, procure some small, though very small portion of the powder to make demonstration in her Majesty's own sight of the perfection of his knowledge ... I wish he would, in some secret box, send to her Majesty for a token some such portion as might be to her a sum reasonable to defray her charges for this summer for her navy which is now preparing to the sea.'

Burghley wrote the letter at Theobalds during a royal visit which had cost him over £1000. He added in a postscript: 'I would be contented [the Queen's short visit] might have been tripled, so I had but one corn of Sir E. Kelly's powder.'

But before Burghley's letter got to Prague, Kelly was a prisoner and Dyer under restraint. When news of this reached England, Elizabeth dispatched a messenger to secure Dyer's release,[60] and Dyer got back early in July. As for Kelly, he remained for two years a prisoner, subjected to torture to disclose his secrets. After his release he resumed his correspondence with Dyer, in the hope that he might be brought to England. In 1595 he was again imprisoned and, in an attempt to escape by jumping from a window, was fatally injured.

The whole story is an incredible one. If we are to judge from Burghley's letters, he was as much Kelly's dupe as Dyer was, or the Emperor Rudolph. But it is clear enough that his main objective was to win Kelly's confidence and lure him back to England. He was careful in his letters not to discredit Kelly, but he wanted to be shown. Faced with an empty treasury, he envisaged the possibility that Kelly might easily send in a 'secret box' enough of the gold-making powder to finance the cost of mobilizing the English navy. In short, Burghley was a creature of his time, sceptical of magic, but ready to exploit it for all that it might be worth.

Early in July 1591, notwithstanding the fact that the English force under Norris in Brittany was making no progress, a second English expeditionary force was dispatched to Normandy. It was under the command of the Earl of Essex. He had been disappointed not to have commanded the Breton army[61] and, when King Henry in October sent the Viscount of Turenne to appeal for further aid, he instructed Turenne to make much of Essex and to solicit his assistance.[62] Indeed, Henry sent Essex a private letter to that effect. Essex needed no urging and he was incessant in his appeals to Elizabeth to let him go; on one occasion he spent two hours on his knees in supplication. In the end he secured her consent.[63] Later, when his campaign in France was going badly and he himself was in disfavour, Burghley wrote to Unton:[64] 'I assure you, Sir, at this present her Majesty is so deeply offended as I am perplexed what advice to give, for I am strongly charged to have been the principal furtherer in this voyage and I cannot deny nor do I repent me of my counsel, though I now wish I had not so done.'

We must of course make allowance for the fact that Unton was Essex's man and that Burghley felt sure that what he wrote to Unton would be revealed to Essex.

In any case, it is a little difficult to reconcile Burghley's professed support of the enterprise with his concern about increasing expenses. It may well be that he was alarmed at the steady growth of Essex in the royal favour. He had had a long experience with royal favourites in the case of Essex's stepfather, the Earl of Leicester, and had learned that the best way to diminish their influence was to send them overseas. It cannot have been altogether accidental that in less than a week after Essex set sail Robert Cecil was sworn to the Privy Council.[65] Thomas Wilkes, a clerk of the Privy Council and a shrewd observer, wrote to Sir Henry Sidney: 'Sir Robert Cecil, as you may have heard, is sworn to the Council, though not secretary, whose election will be a bar to the choice of any secretary during the life of his father.'[66] Wilkes was substantially correct. No Secretary was in fact appointed until the increasing feebleness of Burghley in 1596 made it impossible for him even to pretend to perform the functions of the office. Years before that Robert was doing substantially all the work.

Indeed, Burghley's incapacity was becoming increasingly apparent towards the end of the year 1591. On October 31st, his secretary, Henry Maynard, wrote to Robert Cecil: 'My Lord hath had but bad rest this last night and now this enemy of his, the gout, hath possessed both his hands, whereby of necessity the ploughshare must stand for a time.'[67]

In January 1592, when Essex finally returned to England, with almost nothing to show for his efforts, his prestige was somewhat tarnished and he was out of favour with his mistress. During his campaigning it had been part of Burghley's business to transmit royal rebukes. He did his best to mitigate them in transmission and, so far as he dared, to make light of them. In October 1591, for example, he wrote to Essex: 'Your Lordship's so liberal bestowing of knighthoods is here commonly evil censured, and when her Majesty shall know of it, which yet she doth not, I fear she will be highly offended, considering she would have had that authority left out of your commission if I had not supplied it with [i.e. substituted for it] a cautelous instruction. But *quod factum est, infectum esse non potest*, and hereby you have increased the state of ladies, present and future.'[68]

But Essex was not amused. His disposition was to attribute his failure to Burghley's machinations.[69] This is not surprising. It was customary for those in the field to blame their misfortunes on those at the Court. There is no evidence at all to justify his distrust, though one never knows how much of royal policy was due to Burghley's prompting. In any case, we may date from Essex's return to England his efforts to countercheck the Cecil influence. Up to that date he had been content with his role of courtier and soldier. After that he began to play politics.

Even before that date there are some inklings of rivalry. Essex's efforts to block

Robert Cecil's appointment as Secretary by restoring Davison to the position are a case in point. Thomas Lake, Clerk of the Signet, wrote to Sir Robert Sidney in October 1591: 'Mr. Bodley doubtfully and Sir E. Norris hath fallen into the high indignation of my Lord Treasurer . . . in effect for nourishing or depending upon others besides his Lordship.' Lake advised Sidney to hitch his wagon to Burghley's star. 'Old Saturnus', he observed, 'is a melancholy and wayward planet but yet predominant here . . . Whatsoever hope you have of any other, believe it not.'[70]

At this juncture Essex became involved in the fortunes of Burghley's two nephews, Anthony Bacon and his famous younger brother, Francis. Anthony had just returned from a sojourn of more than twenty years in France, where he had played some part in Walsingham's secret service. Francis meanwhile had pursued his career at the bar. By the time he was twenty-five years old he had passed through all the stages of progress which qualified him to plead before the Courts at Westminster Hall. But there is no evidence that he engaged actively in the practice of the law. He sat in every Elizabethan House of Commons which met from 1584 onwards. And before he was thirty he wrote at least three discourses on public affairs, one of them certainly at the prompting of the government, one of them frequently ascribed to Burghley, all of them revealing political wisdom far beyond his years. From the meagre record of his earlier life, it may be gathered that he looked to his uncle, Burghley, for favour and advancement. In an undated letter written to Burghley either in 1591 or early in 1592 he wrote: 'The greatest part of my thoughts are to deserve well of my friends, and namely of your Lordship, who, being the Atlas of the commonwealth, the honour of my house and the second founder of my poor estate, I am tied by all duties, both of a good patriot and of an unworthy kinsman and of an obliged servant, to employ whatsoever I am to do you service.'[71]

Later in the same year he wrote a response to a libellous pamphlet by the Jesuit, Father Parsons. Parsons's attack was mainly levelled against Burghley and was, as we have seen, the Catholic answer to the vicious proclamation against them of October 1591. Bacon's reply, which was not published until much later but which circulated widely in manuscript,[72] was largely Burghley's vindication. It is too long to be quoted at length, but the following extract constitutes what is in fact the greatest tribute ever paid to Burghley.

' . . . let men call to mind that his Lordship was never no violent and transported man in matters of state, but ever respective and moderate; that he was never no vindictive man in his particular, no breaker of necks, no heavy enemy, but ever placable and mild; that he was never no brewer of holy water in court, no dallier, no abuser, but ever real and certain; that he was never no bearing man nor carrier of causes, but ever gave way to justice and course of law; that he was never no glorious, wilful, proud man, but ever civil and familiar and good withal; that in the course of his service he hath rather sustained the burthen than sought the fruition of honour and profit, scarcely sparing any time from his cares and travels to the sustentation of his health; that he never had nor sought to have for himself or his children any pennyworth of land or goods that appertained to any person that was attainted of any treason, felony, or otherwise; that he never had or sought any kind of benefit by any forfeiture to her Majesty; that he was never a factious commender of men to her Majesty, as he that intended any ways to besiege her by bringing in men at his devotion, but was ever a true reporter unto her Majesty of every man's deserts and abilities; that he never took the course to unquiet or offend, no nor exasperate her Majesty, but to content her mind and mitigate her displeasure; that he ever bare himself reverently and without scandal in matters of religion, and without blemish in his private course of life; let me, I say, without passionate malice call to mind these things, and they will think it reason that though he be not canonized for a saint in Rome, yet he is worthily celebrated as *pater patriae* in England; and though he be libelled against by fugitives, yet he is prayed for by a multitude of good subjects; and lastly, though he somewhat be envied without just cause whilst he liveth, yet he shall be deeply wanted when he is gone. And assuredly many princes have had many servants of trust, name, and sufficiency; but where there have been great parts, there have often wanted temper of affection; where there have been both ability and moderation, there have wanted diligence and love of travail; where all three have been, there have sometimes wanted faith and sincerity; where some few have had all these four, yet they have wanted time and experience; but where there is a concurrence of all these, there it is no marvel though a prince of judgment be constant in the employment and trust of such a person; of whose faithfulness, as she hath had proof so many years in her own time as it were very hard but, if he had gone about to abuse her, at some time she should have espied it; so to begin withal, he brought with him such a notable evidence of his constant loyalty as a greater could not have been.'

It would be rash to assume that Bacon meant all that he said. Already he had begun to look towards Essex. Some fifteen years later, in his 'Apology', Bacon recalled his attitude towards Essex in 1590 or thereabouts. 'I held at that time', he wrote, 'My Lord [of Essex] to be the fittest instrument to do good to the state and therefore I applied myself to him in a manner which I think happeneth rarely among men for I did not only labour carefully and industriously in that he set me about whether it were matter of advice or otherwise, but neglecting the Queen's service, mine own fortune and in a sort my vocation I did nothing but advise and ruminate with myself . . . of anything that might concern his Lordship's honour, fortune or service.'[73]

Here again we must take Bacon's testimony *cum grano salis*. It might be nearer the mark if we decided that Bacon turned to Essex because he was not getting ahead fast enough under Burghley's patronage.

In February 1592, Francis's brother, Anthony, reached England. Some years later he wrote to Essex: 'On the one side, coming over I found nothing but fair words, which makes fools fain, and yet even in those no offer or hopeful assurance of real kindness which I thought I might justly expect at the Lord Treasurer's hands who had inned my ten years' harvest into his own barn, without any halfpenny charge. And on the other side, having understood the earl of Essex' rare virtues and perfections and the interest he had worthily in my sovereign's favour, together with his special noble kindness to my germain brother . . . I did extremely long to meet with some opportunity to make the honourable earl know . . . how earnestly I desired to deserve his good opinion and love . . . presuming always that my Lord Treasurer would not only not dislike but commend and further this my honest desire and purpose.'[74]

We may dismiss Anthony's presumptions as plainly disingenuous. Francis claimed that he was responsible for drawing his brother into Essex's service.[75] In any case, Anthony was a valuable asset. His wide acquaintance abroad enabled him presently to organize an intelligence service for Essex which supplied him with information which he in turn passed on to the Queen before it had reached her through Cecilian channels.

The year 1592 reveals a marked reduction of Burghley's activities. Throughout the year what he called the gout troubled him a good deal, particularly in his hands, which made it difficult for him to write. He was desperately ill in January.[76] In February Henry Unton wrote to Robert Cecil that he was much grieved by the illness of his father, 'whose lack I beseech the Almighty we may never feel, for he will not leave his like behind him'.[77] In March Burghley himself wrote to Unton that he was far behind in his correspondence by reason of his infirmities.

Early in June he was in Bath taking the waters. There, on the 3rd of the month, he received important dispatches from France. He wrote to the Queen that he was in the midst of his cure and reluctant to interrupt it, but that if the Queen needed him he would come at once.[78] Two days later he was in conference with her at Greenwich. Later in the summer, when he was accompanying Elizabeth on her summer Progress, he wrote from Cirencester:[79] 'Her Majesty continueth this her progress in health, although many were cast behind by sickness . . . I myself would fain be cast behind . . . not by sickness but to recover some strength, having but a scant portion to carry me onwards.'

He was dangerously ill again at the end of the year. One correspondent wrote in January 1593: 'The Lord Treasurer has been dangerously ill but is well recovered, thanks be to God, for the whole state of the realm depends on him. *If he go, there is not one about the Queen able to wield this state as it stands.*'[80]

Nevertheless, he still continued to function as Secretary, sat regularly with the Privy Council, and in the Courts of Exchequer and Wards. He apparently spent little time at Court, and his contacts with the Queen were maintained for the most part through his son, Robert. Almost all the incoming official correspondence was directed to him. But little survives of his replies. The Scottish correspondence, for example, was very bulky. It occupies over two hundred pages in the condensed version of it. Yet only two of Burghley's letters appear to have survived, and those two of little importance. His side of the correspondence with Thomas Bodley in the Low Countries diminishes, though more complete than any other.[81] What there is has chiefly to do with the withdrawal of English troops for service in France.

French affairs were still the dominating factor in Elizabeth's foreign relations. Burghley's part in them is chiefly revealed in those dispatches of his which survive, to Sir Henry Unton, the English ambassador in France, and after his recall in the middle of the year to Thomas Edmondes, his secretary. One or two memoranda in Burghley's hand reveal little more than his concern about finance, and about the increasing 'weariness of the people' with the expenditure of men and money in foreign service.[82]

There can be little doubt that Burghley gave strong support to the English wars in France, and particularly in Brittany, where the Spanish invasion constituted a major threat to English Channel ports and to English control of the Channel itself. 'I had rather', he wrote to Unton in May, 'both Paris and Rouen were left unrecovered, than have Brittany lost.'[83] The French King felt differently, and a good deal of what passed between the two powers took the form of insistent urging by the Queen to induce the King to greater efforts in that quarter.

After Essex left France in January 1592, Elizabeth was increasingly reluctant to add to her commitments in France. King Henry was constantly calling for reinforcements. In January he asked for 3000 men. Finding that out of the question, he reduced his figure to 1500. Burghley wrote to Unton in February that he thought Elizabeth would go that far and had prepared the necessary documents for her signature. But she declined to risk further losses in a campaign which appeared to be making no headway. He then suggested that she withdraw 2000 English troops from the Low Countries for French service.[84] But she thought it too risky to exhaust her small reserves of seasoned troops when she had good reason to believe that the King of Spain was making plans to dispatch another Armada against her. It was not until news reached her in May of the disastrous defeat of the small Anglo-French army in Brittany that she was forced to reconsider.[85] When the French King called for further assistance, she appointed a committee consisting of Burghley, Howard, Hunsdon and Buckhurst to negotiate with the French ambassadors on the subject. The outcome was an agreement, signed on June 30th, by which Elizabeth agreed to send another 4000 men to France, of which 2500 were to be drawn from the Low Countries and the balance levied in England, and with Sir John Norris in command.[86] She later agreed to increase the number to 5000, but presently, against the advice of her Privy Council, changed her mind, though they did induce her to allow an additional 500 to fill up incomplete English companies. It was not until the following January that these reinforcements finally reached Brittany.

Perhaps the most interesting of Burghley's surviving letters on French affairs is one which he wrote on October 2nd to the Duc de Bouillon,[87] in answer to one from him. Bouillon was Marshal of France, and one of the ablest of the Huguenot followers of the French King. He had been closely associated with Essex when Essex was in France, and they remained on affectionate terms, so much so that Bouillon told Sir Henry Unton on one occasion that he was as much Essex's as he was the King's.[88]

During the summer Bouillon had been participating in negotiations for peace between Henry and his rebels. Actually his letter reached Burghley by the same post that brought reports that Henry was prepared to accept conversion to the

Q

Roman Catholic faith.[89] Bouillon in his letter sought Burghley's advice on the French religious situation.[90]

Burghley replied as follows:

'I am sorry that I am not able to make recompense, but with my good will, which shall be always ready to accompany your actions there in that realm for the service of God, as long as it pleaseth God to use the most Christian King as his minister to maintain his gospel. And though I see that it pleaseth not God, for some respects best known to his providence, to increase his church there in France, as I am sure both the King and your excellency do most desire, yet I know it shall best please that same God if the King shall show his zeal to the furtherance of the gospel by favouring all such his subjects as profess that gospel from oppression of their contraries and by continuing himself in constancy of his own Christian profession. And so far forth as God shall give him means to dilate his church, so far to use his diligence . . . No reasonable man can require further of him. For the building up of God's church is not to be wrought by man's will without God do give the means, which, when God shall offer to man, then he is bound to follow with all diligence. And in the meantime patience must be exercised, holding this for certain: *Nisi dominus aedificaverit civitatem, in vanum laboraverint qui aedificavent eam.*[91]

'But I am bold to imagine that you will take all this my writing to be very apt for a theologian and that you are not ignorant thereof, but you would be more desirous to hear of some politique counsel how the King may attain to a peace in his realm by subduing his evil subjects and vanquishing his foreign enemies; wherein, though I have no such wisdom as to show the ready means thereof, yet considering, besides the means that Almighty God may give him, which be gotten by prayer and pleasure of God, and worldly strength also both to defend and offend, wherein it seemeth the King hath lack and his enemies abound by God's sufferance, yet to retain his subjects that love him as their King and not for religion, I am bold to show for my opinion that either they be tolerated in their religion or gentle means used to win them to the King's religion. And considering the greater part of his subjects are of a contrary religion both to the truth and to the King — part being well devoted to his service, part being rebellious and favouring his outward enemy, it is not to be reprehended in the King, if, when God does not give him means by outward strength, to be a party without his own Catholics, nor to be able to vanquish his rebels with main force, that he do permit them both to use their own religion, though it have some errors in it, and thereby with patience to overcome, if he can, their obstinacy or find means, by the good example of his own party or profession and manners, to allure them to allow of his religion, for in no Christian history can it be found that Christian religion was established with the sword.'

Evidently Burghley avoided the question which must have been uppermost in Bouillon's mind, the question of Henry of Navarre's impending apostasy. The furthest Burghley was prepared to go was to concede the necessity of toleration for the French Roman Catholics.[92]

When Henry of Navarre finally decided, in the spring following, that Paris was worth a Mass, we have no comment from Burghley about the matter at the time,[93] though later he spoke of Henry's perfidy to God and man. Elizabeth wrote a letter of pained surprise to the French King[94] and ordered her troops to get ready to return home. Eight companies under Sir Roger Williams were withdrawn the following November for service in the Low Countries. But Norris and his troops, though they withdrew to the seaside, remained in Brittany.[95]

We have one letter from Burghley to his son late in May 1593 when the French King's position on the religious situation was still swaying in the balance. It had to do with a discussion in the Council about sending troops to succour Boulogne. Those councillors directly involved were Burghley, Essex, Howard, Cobham and Robert Cecil.[96] Essex had been made a councillor in February,[97] was diligent in attendance and probably almost from the start was the recognized leader of the military group which certainly included Howard and Hunsdon.

Burghley wrote: 'The great haste that the Lords made yesterday in the morning showed a great difference between their humours and mine. For although they were quick, as martial men are most commonly, and I slow, as men in their years are, yet I used no delay [except] for the purpose to understand the cause of the peril and so to provide remedy. In this, I find by your letter that her Majesty misliked not my slowness, whereby I am the better confirmed in my opinion.'[98]

Too much weight should not be given to this letter. It does not justify the assumption that the Council was sharply divided. All that Burghley said was that he had checked the impetuosity of his colleagues and that the Queen had approved. It sounds as though she had herself sat in on the discussion. And it may be that the need to succour Boulogne was based upon very imperfect information, the fruit perhaps of Essex's new intelligence service. We hear nothing of it otherwise.

A little later, after Henry IV's 'great apostasy', when Elizabeth, irritated beyond measure by Henry's refusal to provide her with any adequate base of operations on the French coast, insisted that the English troops should be withdrawn from France, Burghley came forward with a compromise measure. In a letter to the Queen early in December,[99] he suggested that Norris retire with his forces to the Channel Islands, and that, as soon as he got there, dispatches should go off to Henry to the effect that, if he showed himself more amenable to her requirements, Norris and his forces would return again. Burghley suggested that the transports should linger in the islands, either to convey Norris back to Brittany or to bring him back to England as the situation developed.[100] The idea pleased the Queen and instructions went out to Sir John Hawkins to make ready the transports, and to the governors of Jersey and Guernsey to prepare to receive the troops.

But Norris objected so strenuously that the plan was dropped, and his forces remained in Brittany during the winter.

Meanwhile, Burghley's health was failing. In February 1593 he wrote to Bodley apologizing for not writing. 'I did use', he wrote, 'to send your letters to the Queen's Majesty by my son Sir Robert Cecil to the Court from whence I think you have received some directions.'[101] Thereafter this was the customary procedure, though Burghley wrote an occasional letter to Bodley when he felt up to it. He followed the same course in the correspondence with Edmondes in France,[102] and with Bowes in Scotland. Sometimes in transmitting these letters to his son he commented on their contents.

One interesting example of this is a letter to Robert of May 21st, 1593. It had to do with the Scottish situation, where the affair of the Spanish blanks, to which Burghley had referred in his speech in the Lords in March,[103] revealed an active conspiracy among the Catholics in Scotland to invite a Spanish invasion. The Scottish King was well aware of the conspiracy, but to English thinking very dilatory in dealing with it. Henry Locke, an Englishman and a poet in a small way, turned up in Scotland about 1590 and found favour with the King and the Queen.[104] In May 1591 the King dispatched Locke to England on official business and apparently he was serving as an agent for the transfer of messages between James and Elizabeth for the next year or more.[105]

In the course of his wanderings he got in touch with Earl Bothwell, and Bothwell sent messages by him to Elizabeth offering his services if she would assist him to regain the King's favour. Elizabeth, and probably Burghley, thought Bothwell, though an unprincipled scoundrel if there ever was one, might be used to quicken the King's action against the Catholic conspirators. Locke was dispatched in February 1593 with instructions, drafted by Burghley himself, to inquire more particularly as to the nature of the services which Bothwell was prepared to render.[106] There is no record of Bothwell's answer. But Burghley drafted a message to him in April,[107] the gist of which was that Bothwell should attempt nothing against the Catholic conspirators until the middle of May, by which time, if the King continued to dally in the matter, then Bothwell might proceed with his plans.

It is clear enough that Burghley was playing fast and loose with the decencies of intercourse with a friendly neighbour. His observations on the subject in his letter to Robert of May 21st, reveal some twinges of conscience.

'The matter you wrote of concerning the answer to be made by Locke is very piquant[108] for difficulties on both sides, wherein the rule of Christian philosophy consisteth in difference between *utile* and *honestum*, and yet *utile incertum* and yet *honestum certum*. But if *honestum* were reciproche, it were to be preferred with more constancy. In private men's causes *cretizare cum cretenses* is allowable.

'Thus you see how I begin to wander before I dare affirm anything. If my hand were free from pain I would not commit this much to any other man's hand. And yet you may impart my words to her Majesty without offence.'[109]

After some philosophizing, Burghley ends up with the position, *cretizare cum cretenses* — in a word, in Scotland do as the Scots do. It was not exactly the message one would expect from Burghley, always careful of the moral welfare of his son.

The following day he wrote again in his own hand: 'I have entered into the consideration of the earl of Bothwell's cause and I have uttered the state thereof into some writing with my own hand which I dare not commit to be better written by any others here with me. Therefore if you may have leisure to come hither I would more boldly impart the same to you to be showed to her Majesty.

'And yet I find the matter as in a labyrinth, easier to enter into it than to go out.'[110]

Evidently he was in no condition to confer with Elizabeth in person. Three days later he wrote again to his son: 'I find myself so decayed in strength as I find it more needful for me to be occupied about my last will and other establishments for my children.'[111]

Two days later, on May 28th, he wrote to Robert again: 'I have received your letter of this 28th. Hereupon, though I am weak and uncertain how I shall come to the Court, with opinion that after one or two days her Majesty will license me to return to seek my amendment or to take my journey to follow *universam viam carnis* [the way of all flesh]. And to this latter journey I am most disposed with persuasion that if souls have sense of earthly things, I shall be in God's sight an intercessor for the prosperity of His church here and for her Majesty as His governor thereof to His glory. You must allow me to be in this humour, for I find no other taste of any other thing. If I shall be able by coach or litter (for I provide both) I will be with you tomorrow.'[112]

He sat with the Privy Council at the Star Chamber the following day, and again at Nonesuch two days later. He was still at Court on June 8th.[113] But for the next fortnight he was laid by the heels again.

On June 18th he wrote to the Lord Keeper: 'I perceive you had some hope I would have come to London sometime this term.[114] But truly, my Lord, I have been so backward for my health as I have not been able to come to the Court, much less to London.'

We hear little of his health until December. He returned to Court at the end of June and attended virtually every meeting of the Privy Council in July and August.[115]

On December 1st, he wrote to Robert: 'I pray you give my most humble thanks to her Majesty for her often sending to know of my head and neck which on Saturday seemed to be made of lead and yesterday somewhat lighter, as of iron. I hope to have them in weight bone and flesh. I have not without some pain written this. Therefore it is not legible for her Majesty.'[116]

On the 7th he wrote from Theobalds:[117] 'I dare not write to you of my wooing [of health] until I hear how her Majesty alloweth of my absence to follow it. But, in the meantime you may assure her Majesty that I find no great hope of speedy success. I find the lady [health] somewhat strange to give ear to my request, for that she useth not to give audience in cloudy and foul weather, and thereof is here too great plenty, but betwixt showers I do attend and follow her train.'

The same day, later at night, he wrote a longer letter to Robert, in which he discussed various problems, Irish, French and Dutch.[118] His remark on the coming of deputies from the Low Countries is worth recording: 'I see the intention of the sending of the deputies is (as I at the first did conjecture) to borrow money of her Majesty which, in a paraphrase, is to carry away money. And to leave writings under seals, whereof her Majesty hath great plenty.'

He referred also to 'my former allegorical letter written to you, in which I perceive her Majesty discovered the literal sense thereof before the midst of it seen.

I must confess that my cunning therein was not sufficient to hide the sense from her Majesty, though I think never a lady besides her, nor a decipherer in the Court, would have dissolved the figure to have found the sense as her Majesty hath done. And where her Majesty alloweth of me that I made myself merry, in very truth I did it rather to make her some sport, myself therein not altered, no otherwise than her Majesty's lute is in her hand, that maketh others merry and continueth itself as it was.'

It was obviously one of Burghley's better days. Unfortunately his allegorical letter is missing.

CHAPTER XXIV

THE ATTACK ON PURITANISM,
BURGHLEY'S SWAN SONG, 1593-95

WRITS went out for a Parliament early in 1593, and the Parliament assembled on February 19th. It was called primarily, as most Elizabethan Parliaments were, for money. The final instalment of the subsidies granted in 1589 was due in February 1593, and the Queen with an army in France and another army in the Low Countries needed money badly.

Burghley, of course, sat in the Lords, along with several other Privy Councillors — Howard, Hunsdon, Buckhurst, Cobham, Archibshop Whitgift and Robert, Earl of Essex, who was admitted to the Council on February 25th.[1] There were indeed more councillors in the Upper than in the Lower Chamber. Hatton, the Lord Chancellor, had died late in 1591, and his place was taken by Sir John Puckering, with the lesser title of Lord Keeper.

Puckering opened the session with a speech for which Burghley had provided a brief outline.[2] This was the second time Puckering had called for Burghley's advice in speech-making, and even Hatton had invoked his aid on one occasion.[3] We may regard this as tribute to Burghley's oratorical powers, though perhaps it was simply a measure of precaution to avoid giving offence to Elizabeth, for whom Burghley so often acted as spokesman.

The speech dealt with the dangers facing England and the need for money to prevent them. In the closing paragraph, definitely at Burghley's prompting and for the first time, I think, in Elizabeth's relations with her Parliament, Puckering raised the question of tax assessments. Since we are here less interested in Puckering's phraseology than in Burghley's, we may quote his exact words:

'Her Majesty cannot overpass to let this assembly understand that though they have heretofore, for lesser dangers than these are, offered some relief to her Majesty towards her charges, yet the same hath been so abused generally through the realm in the taxation of men of wealth that should have given most, and if it should be by some examples specified . . . how little the men of greatest livelihood in counties have yielded, it would seem an absurd thing for her Majesty to receive that with thanks. And except such abuses can be remedied her Majesty will account her gift to be in words, not in deeds, and so herself abused in her expectation and the realm frustrate in their intentions.'

There was a great deal of hammering on the question of the iniquities of tax assessment both in this Parliament and the next. But nothing was done about it.

In Burghley's outline he said nothing about religious problems, though Puckering referred to them casually in his speech, and Elizabeth herself made much of them in an interview with Sir Edward Coke, the Speaker, during the session.[4]

As it turned out, it was a religious subject that got its first hearing in the House of Commons, though it came near to being the old question of the succession, which Peter Wentworth, elected to this Parliament, had intended to present. He had written a pamphlet on the necessity of settling the question of the Queen's successor some five years previously and had hoped, through Burghley's good offices, to arouse Elizabeth's interest. Burghley was polite, and no doubt sympathetic, but he knew too well how the Queen felt about it to have any part in it. Wentworth then turned to Essex, but in the process of getting a fair copy prepared for Essex's perusal, it came to the attention of the Privy Council, and Wentworth was sent to gaol. This was in August 1591. He was released the following February, and began at once to make arrangements for discussing the matter in Parliament. Five days after Parliament assembled he delivered a petition to the Lord Keeper asking that the two Houses should join to petition the Queen to take action in the matter of the succession. The following day he was called before the Lord Treasurer, Lord Buckhurst and Sir Thomas Heneage. They took a friendly attitude, but the Queen was so offended that they had no choice but to commit him to the Tower. And there, after further examination, he remained to the end of his life.[5]

Burghley's role in the Parliament of 1593 was played, of course, in the House of Lords. Once again the *Lords Journals* are so very brief that we get no inkling of his activity. Indeed, the only mention of him is in the list of attendance. He had been the government leader in the Lords ever since his elevation to the peerage in 1572, and all the evidence at hand supports the view that he still occupied that position. We may therefore fairly assume that he was responsible for the engineering of government measures through the Lords. It may also be assumed that he was the mouthpiece of the Queen. What is difficult to believe is that he was personally sympathetic with the measures which he sponsored.

The main question at issue in both Houses was that of dealing with the recusants and the seminary priests. The government introduced two bills dealing with this question, one in the Commons, the other in the Lords.

The bill in the Commons was designed to increase the punishment of recusants. The fines to be imposed upon them involved the surrender of all their goods and chattels and two-thirds of the income from their lands. They were to be excluded from all public office and from the learned professions. Their wives were to lose their dowers. Their children were to be taken away and reared at their expense under government supervision. It amounted to virtual extermination.

The bill had been prepared by the judges. It can hardly be doubted that Burghley had much to do with the drafting of it, though his health was so bad that he was reducing his work to a minimum. As for the Queen, she must certainly have known what was going on.[6] Both of her spokesmen in the Commons, Heneage and Robert Cecil, supported the bill. Notwithstanding her traditional leniency towards the Catholics, she may in this instance have been impelled by the same fears which impelled Burghley.

The bill had rough going in the Commons, particularly when its ambiguous phraseology invited the question as to whether it was applicable to Protestant as well as Catholic dissenters. The Puritan interest, still strong though lacking its old belligerency, secured an amendment defining recusant as popish recusant. At that point the government seems to have lost interest in the bill. Discussion of it was finally abandoned on March 17th.

A fortnight later at a conference between the two Houses, Burghley remarked that the bill against the recusants was making no progress. He went on to say[7] that there had been some thought of a bill to the same purpose in the Lords, 'including generally all such as refused to come to church'. The Lords, he said, had not agreed upon any bill. They wanted to know how the Commons felt about it. The Commons, with some reluctance, agreed to consider any bill the Lords sent down.

And so the initiative passed to the Lords. We know nothing of the progress of their bill in the Upper House, except that the bishops were solidly behind it. It passed rapidly through all its stages and was in the Commons on the last day of March. The text of it is missing. According to its title it was simply explanatory of obscurities in the Act of 1581. The sum and substance of it was to apply to 'seditious sectaries' the penalties imposed in that bill upon Catholic recusants. The wording was sufficiently vague to include all Puritans within its scope. In the Commons it was chewed over word by word and amended out of recognition, but it finally passed and went back to the Lords. The Lords found it hard to digest the amendments, but Whitgift and Burghley between them insisted. And so they pushed it through.

Briefly it punished Protestant recusants who refused to go to the Established Church, or who attended some other form of worship, with imprisonment for a term of three months, at the end of which, if they had not submitted to the law, they were to be banished, with the death penalty for any who returned. Actually no more were put to death in Elizabeth's reign. But many migrated to establish themselves in the Low Countries. It was from these, in the next reign, that the 'Pilgrim fathers' set forth to America.

The original intention of the government in 1593 was to deal with Catholic and Protestant recusants in one bill. This was the case in the original bill introduced into the Commons and the substitute bill provided by the Lords. But the substitute bill in its stormy passage through the Commons emerged as a bill dealing solely with the Protestant recusants, the bill we have just discussed.

The Catholic recusants were dealt with in another bill which originated in the Lords. We know nothing about its history in the Lords except that it passed two readings in four days and was apparently committed. In committee it underwent such extensive changes that it was discarded and a new bill substituted. The second bill was in some particulars more lenient than the first, the Lords being evidently more kindly disposed towards the Catholics than were the judges and Privy Councillors. The bill passed through both Houses without substantial change. It did not change the penalties imposed upon recusants in 1581, but it did impose restraints upon their movements. They might not, except by special permission, go more than five miles from their place of abode, under penalty, if they did, of the forfeiture of all their goods and chattels, and the loss of all their lands and rents during their life time.

We have no record of Burghley's connection with this bill, but must presume, in view of his position, that he played a large part in the drafting of it.

Parliament had also been called to meet the need for money. The problem was approached early in the session in the Commons, and had proceeded on the assumption that the Queen would be satisfied with the extraordinary grant of two subsidies made in the previous Parliament. Even Robert Cecil, who made the opening speech and who was presumed to be the Queen's spokesman, seems to have proceeded on that assumption. After two days' debate it looked very much as though the grant of two subsidies would pass the Commons. But on March 1st they received a message from the Lords asking for a conference.

Meanwhile the matter had apparently been approached in the House of Lords. Burghley had made a speech. We have the text of that speech in his own hand.[8] It is undated, but Burghley must have delivered it at about the time his son, Robert, was introducing the matter of the subsidy in the Commons.

The obvious purpose of Burghley's speech was to impress upon his audience the necessity of extraordinary efforts to meet extraordinary dangers.

It is too long to quote in full, but deserves to be quoted at some length.

After an introduction on the changed nature of European warfare, and a general reference to the menace from Spain, he continued:

'Wherefore, in discharge of my duty, with your patience in suffering an old man, beside his years, decayed in his spirits with sickness, to declare some part of his knowledge of the dangers and peril imminent. . . .

'First, the King of Spain since he hath usurped upon the Kingdom of Portugal, hath thereby grown mighty by gaining the East Indies. He is . . . now greater than any Christian prince hath been. He hath lately joined with his intended purpose to invade this realm, . . . the invasion of France, by sundry ways, not as in former times when the emperor Charles and the French Kings . . . made their greatest wars . . . For in those wars none of them intended more but to be revenged of supposed injuries by burning or winning of some frontier town . . . Wherein neither party had any special advantage, they fell to truces and in the end to peace, with knots sometime of intermarriages. And by these kinds of wars none of them did increase in greatness to be dangers to their enemies . . . But now the case is altered, the King of Spain maketh these his mighty wars, not purposely to burn a town . . . but to conquer all France, all England and Ireland.

'And for proof hereof, first for France, he hath invaded Brittany, taken the ports, builded his fortresses . . . waged [i.e. paid wages to] a great number of the subjects as rebels to France. And there he keepeth a navy to impeach all trade of merchandise from England to Gascony and Guyenne, which he attempted this last vintage and so he had had his purpose if, to the great charges of the merchants and by countenance of her Majesty's navy, . . . the shipping of England had not been much stronger than his.

'Besides this his possessing of a great part of Brittany towards Spain, he hath at his commandment all the best parts of Brittany towards England, so as he is become as a frontier enemy to all the west parts of England, and by his commandment of Newhaven [Havre], he hath enlarged his frontiers now against all the south parts of England as Sussex, Hampshire, the Isle of Wight.

'... If he had attempted nothing at all in Normandy and France, yet the dangers hereof might appear so great as ought to induce England to spare no cost to withstand it. But herewith he is not content to seek this dukedom [of Brittany] but he destineth all his forces to conquer the kingdom of France, the principal kingdom of Christendom. And to achieve this enterprise he hath, these two years day[9] and more, corrupted with great sums of money and large pensions certain factious noblemen, not of the blood royal of France nor great officers of the crown, and ... with these rebels and by waging of their soldiers in some of the principal towns of France, he hath procured a rebellion against the King ... but, finding these rebels not strong enough of themselves, he hath at his great charge levied and sent into France ... armies collected of Walloons, Lorrainers, Italians, Spaniards, Alemains and Switzers, wherewith he hath twice entered France, though God gave him no good success and but great loss and reproach. Besides these foreign armies sent from the Low Countries, he hath caused his son-in-law, the Duke of Savoy, to invade France by Provence ... and the Duke of Lorraine, by Burgundy ... and to environ France further, he hath set armies by sea out of Spain to environ Languedoc. And even now at this present, all these foreign forces are newly made ready to re-enter into all parts of France ... He hath also the pope so addicted to him as he, that never was wont to send to any parts out of Italy but bulls with lead and parchment, did now levy and send an army into France. And though he coloureth it with matter of defence of the Catholic religion yet both he and the King of Spain maketh war against all the princes of the blood and officers of the realm, being sound Catholics. ...

'These are the dangers in France and must of consequence draw England to like peril, without God's special goodness and their speedy support to be given to her Majesty for protection thereof.

'Now to manifest the King of Spain's attempt to invade England, whereof I think no good Englishman is so want of feeling to think otherwise, yet I will remember to you divers manifest arguments.

'First, none ought to think, because he was disappointed of his intention for the conquest of England by his huge navy, therefore he will put that disgrace up and leave with that loss. It is certain he hath the last two years ... made a number of ships of war, as near as he can to the mould and quantity of the English navy, finding by experience his monstrous great ships not mete for the Narrow Seas. He hath lately armed a number of galleys on the coast of Brittany, which he intendeth to send this summer to Newhaven [Havre]. He hath also, these two years days,[9] both bought and built great ships in Eastland. He hath both from thence and by corruption of our faint and covetous neighbours in Holland and Zeeland recovered, with silver hooks, both mariners, ships, cordage, powder and all provisions, these being now on the point of readiness to serve on the seas. . . .

'How he and the pope ply themselves to win a party in England to be ready and second his invasion, I am sorry and loathe to relate, and how far they have prevailed herein to gain so great a multitude of vulgar people, yea of some that are of wealth and contenance, to adhere to these invaders at their entry, with vain hope to attain to the place, honours and livelihoods of such as are now known true, natural Englishmen and good subjects.

'But to such as these arguments will not suffice . . . this that followeth shall fully suffice any man, yea of any that useth to believe nothing until he shall see it.'

Burghley went on to describe the discovery of a Spanish conspiracy in Scotland, the so-called Spanish blanks, news of which had reached the English government early in February. He had saved it to the last. It can hardly have been widely known and it must have fallen upon Burghley's audience like a bomb shell.

'There are taken in Scotland and imprisoned certain that came first out of Spain near afore Christmas from the King [of Spain] . . . These messengers brought assurance to certain noblemen of the greatest calling in Scotland that, if they would send their bonds under their hands and seals to serve the King of Spain for the invasion of England by land the next summer, the King would send an army of 25,000 to the west of Scotland[10] and would give the noblemen wages for 10,000 Scots, to join with 20,000 of his to invade England, and would keep 5000 of his in Scotland to aid them to overrule the King of Scots and to change the religion. This accord was pledged by three noblemen, the earls Arroll, Huntley and Angus, promising their own assistance.

'Now for proof hereof the messenger that was sent and on shipboard, was taken with the bonds of the noblemen . . . the messenger hath confessed the whole. . . .

'Thus far have I followed my purpose to show the dangers and to give counsel for the remedy. *Hoc opus, hic labor est.*'

It was an effective speech. In conclusion Burghley expressed the wish 'to have some company of whom I might have some light', which suggests that a committee of the Lords was presently appointed to discuss ways and means. Probably from some such committee the invitation proceeded for a conference with the Commons.

The conference took place on March 1st, with Burghley as the spokesman.

He began by explaining that the conference was called 'to consider of our dangers and to consult of remedies'. He then pointed out that the proposal of two subsidies by the Commons was quite inadequate. A similar grant in the last Parliament had yielded but £280,000, since which grant the Queen had spent in defence of the realm £1,040,000. For want of adequate funds she had been forced to sell Crown lands. On these grounds Burghley declared flatly that the Upper House would not consent to less than a triple subsidy. And he went on to say that the method of assessing the subsidy would have to be revised. The wealthy were paying only a fraction of their just share. He cited London as a case in point, which in movable property was easily the richest part of the kingdom. No one there, he said, was assessed at more than £200 in goods, and only eight above £100. He insisted upon further consultation.[11]

It was a tactless speech, if only because it seemed to arrogate to the Lords the initiative in taxation which had long belonged to the Commons. There was bad management somewhere. Normally the whole question of the subsidy would have been fought out in the Commons under the guiding hand of the royal spokesman there. It may have been that Sir Thomas Heneage who occupied that place was laid by the heels with the gout and that Robert Cecil, at the last minute and inadequately instructed, had to take his place.[12] Quite possibly it is another indication of Burghley's failing health.[13] Or Elizabeth herself may have changed her mind and, having acquiesced in the plans for a double subsidy, suddenly realized that it was not enough.

In any case, the Commons took umbrage, and some days were spent quarrelling over precedents. But the matter was finally straightened out by Sir Walter Raleigh, who pointed out that the Lords simply wanted to confer, not initiate.

A second conference followed accordingly on March 6th, at which Burghley dwelt at length on the dangers confronting the country, and amicable relations between the two Houses were resumed. We hear no more of Burghley in the matter.

There is preserved among his papers[14] the outline of a speech which he delivered on a bill to limit new building in London and thereabouts. The bill originated in the Lords, passed there and came down to the Commons on March 31st,[15] and passed virtually unopposed. It now stands on the statutes as 35 Eliz. c. 6.

The bill was little more than the statutory confirmation of a proclamation on the subject put forth by the Queen on July 7th, 1580.[16] Burghley's speech, with which the bill was evidently introduced, explained the reasons for it. The overcrowding of London, he pointed out, had led to the increase of 'idle, vagrant and wicked' persons, with the consequent danger of disorder and a threat to the safety of the Queen. Here we may perhaps detect a repercussion of the Hacket affair. He went on to point out the difficulties of victualling such a mass of people and, with vivid recollections of the mortality attending the outbreak of the plague in London the previous year, the danger of the plague. All these arguments were no doubt designed to reconcile Londoners to the restrictions on their growth.

At the same time he called attention to another problem which was rapidly developing — antipathy towards London in English towns at large. The increasing population of the metropolis was taking place at the expense of other urban communities, which were being stripped of their artisans. He said something also about the lack of fresh air brought about by congestion, the lack of space for recreation, such as walking and archery.

Actually what he said was largely repeated in the preamble to the bill. What it did was to prohibit further building in London, Westminster and three miles beyond them, except for the habitation of the better-to-do.[17] It further forbade breaking up of large houses into apartments.

Evidently Burghley was still a good mercantilist, still like King Canute trying to stem the flood tide of economic change by royal command.

From the Queen's point of view, the Parliament of 1593 was an unusually satisfactory one. In her concluding speech she was loud in its praises. She assented to every bill it passed except one, and that one of little moment. Burghley got all he fought for, the housing bill, the triple subsidy and the bills dealing with recusants and Puritans. Probably he would have preferred more rigorous action against the recusants, and it is hard to believe that he was in sympathy with the action against the Puritans. In that particular, in his support of it, he spoke rather for his mistress than for himself.

In February 1593 Essex was sworn to the Privy Council and began to interest himself actively in political affairs. Having been thwarted in his effort to control the royal Secretariat, he undertook to develop what was a secretariat of his own, established direct contacts with the English ambassadors overseas and organized a secret service which kept five secretaries busy. In this connection, as we have seen, he made use of Anthony Bacon, Francis Bacon's older brother, and got involved in the political aspirations of Francis himself.

On February 4th, 1593, Sir Gilbert Gerrard, Master of the Rolls, died. There was in consequence a great fluttering at the Court about his successor. The office was an important one, just below the Chancellor himself in the Court of Chancery, with attractive perquisites. It seems to have been anticipated at Court that the Attorney-General, Sir Thomas Egerton, would be appointed. The real issue, therefore, was as to the successor to his office. Bacon was a candidate. As early as April 16th he was writing to Robert Cecil soliciting his support and asking him to use his influence with Lord Burghley, his father.[18] At the same time he was making the same appeal to Robert's half-brother, Sir Thomas Cecil. It was probably in response to this request that Thomas wrote to his father[19] as follows:

'It may please your Lordship. The title of being your son, as it is a cause that many do use me as their mediator with your Lordship in their private suits, an office which often through importunity I am thrust into against my will, yet at this time I must confess I am importuned with my will to be a motioner unto your Lordship for one nearly allied to your house and whose gifts and qualities of mind I know your Lordship will not think unfit [for] the place he seeketh. It is Mr. Francis Bacon who, hearing of late that the Attorney is likened for the Master of the Rolls, his desire is to be remembered by me unto your Lordship's good acceptance and conceit of him for that place which Mr. Attorney shall leave and thereby to be recommended by your Lordship to her Majesty . . . I know none that is likely to be called to the place that is and ought to be more assured to your Lordship than he, and an honour to your Lordship to prefer them that are assuredly tied to your Lordship in blood as well as in benefit, if their worth be fit for the place.

'Thus, my Lord, I have discharged both my promise and desire to do the gentleman good, and he doth rest to know by me how your Lordship doth accept of this motion, which I humbly beseech your Lordship to signify unto me by your letter, or to himself in my absence.'

Burghley's reply, if he made one, is missing. The substance of it may perhaps be read in a letter which Robert Cecil wrote to Bacon in May.[20]

'Of the matter of which you speak of I do assure you there passeth not so much as any bruit by mine ears. And therefore in mine opinion the vacation[21] may happily pass over before the places be altered.'

He went on to recommend that as a first step Bacon should gain access to the Court again, and suggested that the best way to obtain that would be through the good offices of the Earl of Essex.

Essex had already spoken twice with Elizabeth and kept hammering at her. By the middle of June it seemed likely that Bacon, who had offended Elizabeth by a speech on the subsidy in Parliament, would be restored to favour again. But nothing happened.

Early in June, Essex wrote to Sir Henry Unton, who had returned from his embassage in Paris in 1592 and was cultivating Essex's favour:[22] 'They here do remain in the same state they did. They who are most in appetite are not yet satisfied, whereof there is great discontentment. If it stand at the stay a while longer they will despair, for their chief hour glass hath little sand left in it and doth run out still.'

It can hardly be doubted that Essex referred to Robert Cecil's aspirations to the Secretariat and Burghley's failing health.

The developing antipathy of Essex to Burghley came out again in connection with the request of Anthony Standen for an audience with the Queen. Standen had been a Catholic refugee and had been drawn by Walsingham at Anthony Bacon's suggestion into the secret service. He was, indeed, under the name of Pompeo Pellegrini, Walsingham's chief source of information in Spain about the preparations of the Spanish Armada.

At Anthony Bacon's instigation, Standen had returned to England. He remained a loyal Catholic, but hoped that, in view of his signal services, Elizabeth would allow him to resume his place among the English gentry. Essex espoused his cause and even tried to get Standen's brother reinstated as Justice of the Peace. According to Essex, Burghley blocked the way — 'The man', he wrote, 'that is most against him is my Lord Treasurer, the cause pretended is he and his wife's backwardness in religion, I mean their not conforming to the law on that point . . . What else is in my Lord's heart I know not.'

As a matter of fact, Burghley persuaded Elizabeth to receive Standen, which led Essex to write to Standen: 'I see . . . my Lord is wise enough, when he sees a thing will come to pass, to have the thanks of it himself . . . only this caution I will send that your affection to me breed not too much jealousy in the other parties, or affection against you.'[23]

All that we get about the developing rivalry between Essex and the Cecils comes from Essex or his followers. We hear nothing on the subject at this juncture either from Burghley or from his son.

During the late summer Burghley did take an active interest in Bacon's suit for the Attorney-Generalship. He wrote a letter to Lady Bacon, his sister-in-law, on August 29th:

'I thank you for your kind letter and for your sons I think your care of them is no less than they both deserve, being so qualified in learning and virtue, as if they had a supply of more health they wanted nothing . . . For my good will to them, though I am of less power to do my friends good than the world thinketh, yet they shall not want the intention to do them good.'[24]

This was friendly but non-committal. A month later he wrote to Bacon that he had 'attempted to place' him but that the Queen had a list of others from the Lord Keeper, one or two of whom he preferred before Bacon. 'I will', he concluded, 'continue in the remembrance of you to her Majesty and implore my Lord of Essex' help.[25] Robert Cecil wrote on the same day to much the same effect.

But Bacon himself was sceptical. He wrote to Essex that he had his suspicions of 'the lately recovered man that is so much at your Lordship's devotion'. He may have meant Burghley, just out of bed from a long illness; he may have meant Cecil. His description of 'the lately recovered man' might have been either one. 'He is a man likely to trust so much to his art and finesse (as he that is an excellent wherryman, who, you know, looketh toward the bridge when he pulleth towards Westminster) that he will hope to serve his turn and yet preserve your Lordship's good opinion.'

We can forgive Bacon much for his mastery of his mother tongue. What he lacked and what he failed to see in Burghley was devotion to the Queen and to the public service as opposed to his particular interest.

We need not follow Bacon's fortunes further. Burghley clearly did not think he was the best man for an important position like the Attorney-Generalship,[26] though endorsing him without equivocation for the position of Solicitor-General when Sir Edward Coke got the Attorneyship. There is no evidence that Bacon's suspicion that Burghley secretly favoured Coke was in fact the case. Indeed, the Queen herself was the stumbling-block. Perhaps she was shrewd enough to perceive that while Essex and Bacon were for Essex and Bacon, Burghley and Coke were at heart loyal and devoted public servants.

Essex made clear his own attitude in a conversation, reported by Standen, with Robert Cecil.[27] Essex and Cecil were riding in a coach together when Cecil turned the conversation to the Attorney-Generalship. ' "My Lord," Cecil said, "the Queen has resolved ere five days pass to make an attorney general. I pray your Lordship to let me know whom you will favour." The Earl answered that he wondered that Sir Robert should ask him that question, seeing it could not be unknown to him that resolutely against all whomsoever he stood for Francis Bacon. "Good Lord," replied Sir Robert, "I wonder your Lordship should go about to spend your strength in so unlikely or impossible a matter", desiring his Lordship to allege to him but one only precedent of so raw a youth to that place of such moment. The earl, very cunningly working upon him, said that for the attorney-ship, which was but an ordinary office other than the prince's favour, he could produce no pattern . . . but that a younger than Francis Bacon, of less learning and of no greater experience, was suing and shoving with all force for an office of far greater importance, greater charge and greater weight than the attorneyship. Such an one, the earl said, he could name to him. Sir Robert's answer was that he well knew that his Lordship meant him, and that admitting that both his years and experience were small, yet weighing the school which he had studied in, and the great wisdom and learning of his schoolmaster, and the pains and observations he daily passed in that school, he thought his forces and wisdom to be sufficient to sway that machine, alleging withal his father's deserts in these his long and painful travails of so long an administration, to merit a mark of gratitude from her Majesty in the person of his son. And with regard to the affair of Mr. Francis Bacon he desired his Lordship to consider of it. "If at least," said he, "your Lordship had spoken of the solicitorship, that might be easier of digestion to her Majesty." The earl, upon this answered, "Digest me no digestions, for the attorneyship for Francis is that I must have, and in that will I spend all my power, weight, authority and amity and with tooth and nail defend and procure the same for him against whomsoever, and that whosoever getteth the office out of my hands for any other before he have it, it shall cost him the coming by. And this be you assured of, Sir Robert, for now do I fully declare myself. And for your own part, Sir Robert, I think strange both of my Lord Treasurer and you that can have the mind to seek the preference of a stranger before so near a kinsman. For if you weigh in a balance the parts every way of his competitor and him, only excepting five poor years of admitting to a house [i.e. inn] of court before Francis, you shall find in all other respects whatsoever no comparison between them." '

Though we have the story at second hand in a letter from Standen to Anthony Bacon, it is probably true in the main. Both of the performers were well aware that Elizabeth had decided to appoint Coke to the coveted position. Essex, at his swaggering best, insisted that Bacon should get the position at all costs, and threatened dire consequences to any who opposed him. Cecil pointed out the futility of such an attitude, and met Essex's thrust at himself by a modest disclaimer, attributing his qualifications for the Secretariat to the virtues of his father's teaching. It is plain enough that Cecil was trying to save Essex from himself and that Essex would have none of it, certainly not from an emaciated little hunchback not half his size and with nothing like his charm. We get a fair picture of the two men and their techniques. We get also a plain intimation of Essex's belligerent attitude towards the Cecilians, father and son.

The interview took place as Essex and Robert Cecil were returning together from the Tower, where they had been examining Dr. Roderigo Lopez.

The so-called Lopez Plot has been represented as having been discovered by Essex's secret service, scoffed at by the Cecils at the outset but finally demonstrated to be true. The story of the scoffing comes again from Standen's pen. According to him, Robert Cecil, after his first hearing of Lopez, posted to London before the Earl and told the Queen that there was nothing in it. When Essex in turn reported, Elizabeth 'took him up, calling him rash and temerarious youth to enter into a matter which displeased her much and whose innocence she knew well enough'.[28]

Reduced to its lowest terms, and taking account of the bias of the story-teller, we may assume that Cecil's report to the Queen was simply to the effect that nothing incriminating had been found among Lopez's papers.[29]

The story of the plot has been told too often to need repetition.[30] Like the Parry Plot in 1585, it turned upon the question as to whether Lopez, who, like Parry, pretended to be in the secret service of the enemy in order to facilitate his secret services for the Queen, at the last turned traitor. Lopez had been used by Walsingham and, after Walsingham's death, by Burghley. It may be that Essex exploited the whole affair with the idea of discrediting the official secret service and exalting his own. The weakness of the case against Lopez is exposed by the lack of any confirmatory evidence from Spanish sources, and most scholars now agree that Lopez's guilt was more than doubtful. But in the end Essex had his way.

In the examination of the conspirators Robert Cecil took an active part. From a letter which Essex wrote to him on February 26th,[31] it appears that they were in close co-operation. Lopez was adjudged guilty by a large commission appointed by the Queen to try him, composed of the Lord Mayor of London, the Chief Justice of the Queen's Bench, Essex, Robert Cecil, most of the other members of the Privy Council, and several others. Burghley was not named to the commission, doubtless because of his ill health.

Cecil was in complete accord with the verdict.[32] Burghley, as usual, took charge of the publicity. Immediately after the trial he asked William Waad, the Clerk of the Council, to prepare a narrative of the Lopez treason. Waad sent him a manuscript of eleven folios on March 4th. Two weeks later Burghley himself drew up a shorter report on the case, evidently designed for publication. For some reason or other it was not published.[33] Quite possibly Elizabeth herself, still unconvinced, held it up for the same reason that she held up the warrant for Lopez's execution. He was not, in fact, executed until June 7th.

Later in the year[34] Burghley wrote and published *A True Report of Sundry Horrible Conspiracies of late time detected to have (by barbarous murders) taken away the Life of the Queen's most excellent Majesty. . . .*[35]

Burghley incorporated with his account of the Lopez Plot an account also of the plot of Yorke and Williams. The emphasis throughout in both accounts was upon the complicity of the King of Spain. Obviously they were designed to arouse popular anger against Philip. The pamphlet ended:

'It is to be avowed for a most manifest truth that there hath been never any subject of the Queen's Majesty of England, or any other person of what nation soever, that hath or could be challenged by any of the King of Spain's party or by any other person to have, with the privity of the Queen of England, or of any minister of hers, ever attempted, yea or offered to have endangered or harmed the King of Spain's person, although it need not be doubted, but if her Majesty either would or had so base a mind as to practise so vile a matter, she could not have wanted instruments.'

Philip in short was labelled a murderer. In a previous pamphlet Burghley had applied the same label and Elizabeth had bade him remove the offending passage.[36] But she did not raise the issue in this case. Though she was not quite convinced of Lopez's guilt, the facts brought out in his trial presumably satisfied her of Philip's murderous intentions.

Sir Edward Coke's comment on Burghley's pamphlet, written on a copy of it in the British Museum,[37] is worth noting: 'The Lord Treasurer Burghley thought best to rely principally upon the confessions of the delinquents without any inferences or arguments. This book was never answered to my knowledge, and this is the best kind of publication.' It is the only contemporary appraisal we have of Burghley as a pamphleteer and helps to explain why Burghley's style of writing, which certainly lacked the qualities usually associated with effective propaganda, commended itself to the Queen and her legally minded councillors.

The year 1594, which opened with the disclosure of the so-called Lopez Plot, brought other fantastic plots to light which never got beyond the wishful thinking of young Roman Catholic refugees. One of the suspects under examination in August revealed an interview in which he observed that 'it were foolish to think of killing the Queen who is continually mewed up in a chamber and that it were better service to kill the Lord Treasurer's horse, for he would take it so grievously if the old jade were dead that he would die also'.[38] The only part which Burghley played in these matters, as we have seen, was to write and publish the official account of them.

Otherwise the year was a relatively quiet one for England and for Burghley.[39] Early in January he was taking an active interest in the trained bands,[40] but on the 23rd he wrote to his son, Robert: 'I am not in tune to write myself, being forced with very faintness to keep my couch.'[41] In February he was contemplating the levy of 3000 men to be financed by a special tax on bishops and office-holders.[42] About the same time, probably because of the revelation of the Lopez Plot, he was drafting instructions for the apprehension of suspicious persons coming from overseas and increasing the restrictions upon access to the Court. Early in March he was formulating plans for the more rigorous treatment of the recusants.[43] But late in the month he was in the doctors' hands.

In April he thought of going to Buxton for the treatment. 'My continuance of pain without remission', he wrote to Robert on the 25th, 'maketh me to hearken to all means of remedy or ease ... I have had also now this evening by report the sundry opinions of physicians concerning the baths, but therein more reasons of dissuasion than of provocation – and that which is worst, from none any direct advice for my cure. Only exercise of body and idleness of mind is prescribed. For these two I have none to further me but her Majesty. If I might have a receipt [recipe] thereof from her Majesty's cabinet I would make proof to be able to be her Majesty's porter at Theobalds upon her second journey.'[44]

But four days later he wrote again: 'This day I have been in the Court of Wards with small ease and much pain. The afternoon I have appointed divers of her Majesty's causes to be heard. And tomorrow I am to be in the Exchequer Chamber about writs of error which, without my presence, can hardly be ended. And upon Wednesday is the Star Chamber, which I think I may be spared.

'These things being let known to her Majesty, I shall be careless to put them under and to come when she shall command, whereof I pray you send me word forthwith. I live in pain and yet spare not to occupy myself for her Majesty's causes . . . I am forced to spare my hand, having notwithstanding, more need to save my head.'[45]

We have no record of his attendance at either the Court of Wards or of the Exchequer, over both of which he presided. Nor have we any record of his attendance at Privy Council, the register of which for this year and most of the next is missing. But if we may judge from his attendance in 1595, when his physical condition was worse, he did not miss many meetings.

In June Elizabeth visited him at Theobalds and spent a week there.[46] All that survives of her visit is a speech delivered to her by Robert Cecil in his old role of the Hermit. The one pertinent passage is in his reference to his father:[47]

'Only this', he said, 'perplexeth my soul and causeth cold blood in every vein to see the life of my founder so often in peril; nay, his desire, as hasty as his age, to inherit his tomb. . . .

'But this I hear (which is his greatest comfort and none of your least virtues) that when his body, being laden with years, oppressed with sickness, having spent his strength for public service, desireth to be rid of worldly cares, by ending his days, your Majesty, with a bond of princely kindness, even when he is most grievously sick, holds him back and ransometh him.'

Some time during the late spring or summer the Cecils, father and son, and the Earl of Essex were reconciled. Robert wrote to his half-brother, Thomas, about it in August,[48] but there is evidence of it in the tone of the letters exchanged between Robert Cecil and the Earl as early as May.[49] We may ascribe it in part to the ending of the issue over the Attorney-Generalship by the Queen's appointment of Coke in April, and the whole-hearted support both by Burghley and by Robert Cecil of Bacon's suit for the Solicitor-Generalship. Hereafter, as long as Burghley lived, there was no open breach between them. From the crowd who surrounded Anthony Bacon there was occasional sniping at the 'old man' as they called Burghley, and *le bossu* as they called Robert. There was also some revelation of irritation on Burghley's part towards those who having sought his favour turned to Essex as the better bet,[50] and some irritation also at the fact that news from foreign parts was reaching Essex before it arrived through official channels. But there were no major issues between them.

In October Burghley supported Essex's plea to the Queen for an extensive grant of royal parks. 'I am sorry', he wrote to his son, Robert, on October 19th, 'that her Majesty is not more inclinable to relieve the Earl [of Essex] with some grant of parks, in such sort as may be no diminution to her Majesty's revenue and yet relieve him in a sort very reasonable. I move not these things for the earl *pro merito* but *pro condigno* for her Majesty.'[51] The cryptic last sentence may perhaps be interpreted to mean that the Queen had made some commitment to Essex which she was bound to honour, irrrespective of his deserts.

Burghley seems to have supported the operations in Brittany with as much vigour as Essex did. When the Spaniards established themselves in the spring of 1594 in the harbour of Brest and threatened complete occupation of the best port in Brittany, and Elizabeth was in two minds about sending reinforcements to prevent them, Burghley argued that the effort should be made. 'Something', he wrote to Robert on July 19th, 'must always be attempted in great matters, for with no attempt no profit can follow, but sometime great loss.'[52] He advised Robert, however, to present these views 'temperately, so that they may not be taken offensively'. Essex wanted to lead the reinforcements, but the Queen would not hear of it. On that point Burghley was discreetly silent.

His health failed him again in midsummer. On July 21st he wrote to Robert:[53] 'I can affirm nothing of my amendment but if hereafter my attendance shall be earnestly required I shall be content to wear out my time at the Court as I do here ... I pray you in all your letters certify me of the Queen Majesty's health, for she being well, my sickness will not discomfort me.'

Early in September he got reports of a proposed peace conference between Spain and France, 'whereto', he observed to his son, 'though the King [of France] pretendeth a mislike, yet surely the Catholic counsellors, with the disposition also of the people, will work some further operation therein and so both England and the Protestants in France shall feel the smart thereof. But I am bold to hope of the favour of the King of Kings that can abridge the King of Spain's life and show some notable avenge upon the French King for his perfidy towards God and man'.[54] Evidently he had completely lost faith in Henry of Navarre. He ended: 'My hand is so weak as I am unable to write any more.'

Later in the same month Michael Hicks, his secretary, wrote to Robert Cecil: 'Methinks he [Burghley] is nothing sprighted but, lying upon his couch, he museth or slumbereth. And being a little before supper at the fire, I offered him some letters and other papers and he was soon weary of them and told me he was unfit to hear suits. But I hope a good night's rest will make him better tomorrow.'

The day following Hicks wrote again: 'My Lord hath had but ill rest tonight, is now abed and I know not whether he will rise or no.'[55]

But a few days later Burghley was in conference with the French ambassador.

Early in October he reminded Robert that the Archbishopric of York was vacant and that steps should be taken to fill the position. 'It is likely', he wrote, 'many will gape after it. And I wish the choice were rather in her Majesty's own judgment than in the ambitious desire of them which seek *quae sua sunt, non quae Dei et ecclesiae.*'[56]

Again on the 13th he wrote to Robert: 'I see by your letter how desirous her Majesty is to have me there. Now I have a mind to come thither tomorrow, but you shall not be known thereof until I shall come. Cause my chamber to be made ready. Herein I shall venture percase my life, but I remit all to God. *Fiat voluntas sua.*'

He went to the Court at Nonesuch the day following, returned to Westminster two days later and, though sick at the time, sat at the Exchequer on the 17th.

We hear no more of him until December. He wrote to Robert on the 2nd, complimenting the Queen on her able letter to the King of France, and reminding him that she should send money to Ireland; and again on the 27th with further reference to Irish needs.[57] But at the end of the year he was very desperate about his health. As a postscript to the letter just cited, he added: 'I have no hope to amend towards the world.'

During December, Burghley was making plans for the marriage of his grand-daughter, Elizabeth, the oldest offspring of the ill-fated marriage of his daughter, Ann, with the Earl of Oxford. Elizabeth's bridegroom was William Stanley who, by the sudden death of his brother, Ferdinando, fifth Earl of Derby, without male heirs, became sixth Earl of Derby in April 1594. He had remote claims to the English throne through his mother, Margaret Clifford, grand-daughter of Henry VIII's younger sister. And he was, besides, probably the richest peer in England.[58]

For all these reasons, added to the fact that the bride was the Queen's namesake and one of her maids of honour, Elizabeth decided to have the wedding ceremony at Greenwich Palace. She sent word to Burghley that she expected him to dance at the wedding. He wrote about it to Robert on December 2nd: 'For her hope to have me dance, I must have a longer time to learn to go, but I will be ready in mind to dance with my heart when I shall behold her favourable disposition to do such honours to her maid for the old man's sake.'

He wrote again on January 2nd, 1595: 'Though my hand is unable to fight and my right eye unable to take a level, yet they both do stoop to return my humble thanks for continuance of her favour at this time when I am more fitter for an hospital than to be a party for a marriage. I will be a precise keeper of myself from all cold until Friday on which day I will venture to come thither. If you should hear that this night I have played at post and pare you will guess that I shall recover, for I have lost all I played for.'[59]

The marriage took place on January 26th. Curiously enough, we hear nothing of it from Burghley, not even in his diaries. John Stow in his *Annals*[60] notes it among the events of the year, but gives no details except that 'the marriage feast was there most royally kept'. It is probable, though not certain, that Shakespeare's *Midsummer Night's Dream* was written for the occasion, and presented as part of the festivities. We can fancy if we like the ageing Queen with her old servant in rapt attention and with mingled feelings as Oberon spoke those winged words:

> Cupid all armed, a certain aim he took
> At a fair vestal thronèd by the west,
> And loosed his love-shaft smartly from his bow
> As it should pierce a hundred thousand hearts.

But I might see young Cupid's fiery shaft
Quenched in the chaste beams of the watery moon
And the imperial votaress passed on
In maiden meditation, fancy free.

True or not, it was the way Elizabeth liked to think of herself, and the way Burghley, though he knew the long story of her courtships all too well, liked to think of her.

Some time before the marriage Burghley had been directed by the Queen to adjudicate on an issue between the new Earl of Derby, who had succeeded to the title by the death of his brother in April 1594, and the brother's wife. The issue was a complicated one, involving substantial property rights,[61] and even as early as May 1594 the Dowager Countess had expressed some fear that Burghley's decision might be influenced by the fact that the wedding of his grand-daughter and the new Earl was already being talked about.[62] Burghley must have rendered his decision at about the time of the marriage. He wrote to Robert on February 1st, 1595:

'I perceive by your letters that my Lord Chamberlain hath made a report to her Majesty of my upright and favourable dealing in the hearing of the cause betwixt my Lord of Derby and the Countess his sister [-in-law] . . . But when her Majesty hath pronounced her gracious sentence of me as of her spirit and hath commended you, as you write, to give me a million of thanks, I am most glad of her favourable censure for which I most humbly thank her as not meriting so much. But for her million of thanks you may merrily say from me that she may be noted somewhat over liberal, for to give a million of thanks where she oweth none, but may challenge all I can do to be as a debt not able to free me from bondage to her, both by God's ordinance and by her royal and princely favours.

'And to write seriously, I have done nothing in this case but that my conscience did prescribe me, and if the earl shall think otherwise of me as I doubt he may be thereto led, yet he shall understand that I gave my child to him but not my conscience nor my honour which no blood [ties] shall ever gain of me.' He ended the letter: 'I find no ease of pains nor increase of strength. And yet I assure you I expedite more suitors than I think any judge or minister of law doth in this term.'[63]

He was indeed quite busy with public affairs in January and February. He prepared a memorandum on the affairs of the Low Countries in which he justified out of the civil law the Queen's demands for some repayment of her loan to the Dutch.[64] He wrote to Edmondes a long explanation of the Queen's action in withdrawing her troops from France.[65] He reminded Robert to remind the Queen that in nominating bishops for Winchester and Durham she should not forget that they owed her money. At the same time he called attention to the fact that the position of Solicitor-General was still vacant and that there was only one Sergeant-at-Law. She nominated Yelverton to be Sergeant-at-Law. 'As for any Solicitor,' he added, 'I will not presume to name any for some respects.'[66] This was the position that Essex was trying so hard to get for Francis Bacon.

At the same time he had to cope with a local brawl in Stamford, where his son, Thomas, was at odds with Lord Willoughby, and which developed to a point at which Thomas challenged Willoughby to a duel.[67] And during the summer he had to read urgent appeals from his renegade son-in-law, the Earl of Oxford, who was trying to induce the Queen to grant him the pre-emption of tin in Cornwall.[68]

We hear nothing of him in March. In April he was at Theobalds whence he wrote to Robert on the 29th:[69]

'I thank you for your letter which I cannot answer with mine own hand in any sort. I allow your discretion in concealing from the Queen my last night's pain and though I had yesterday a painful journey with my hand and have had this night a continuance thereof with some new pain in my foot, whereby I am forced to keep my bed this forenoon, yet you shall do well not to be known hereof to any. If I had come well hither and the weather fair I might have tarried here but now I know not how long I shall be forced to tarry here.'

He was back at his house in Covent Garden on May 6th,[70] but on the 11th not able to write or get out of bed.[71] He managed to scribble a few lines to Robert a day or so later, in which he suggested that Thomas Bodley, who had come back from the Low Countries for conference, be directed to press the Dutch for some repayment of her loan to them.

'If', he wrote, 'they [the Dutch] shall be content to pay her Majesty's people [forces in the Low Countries] and grant a good yearly sum towards the discharge of their debt, her Majesty remaining their protector and they continuing their defence against the King of Spain, I could be content.'

On the 20th he wrote again to Robert: 'I am willinger than able to come [to the Court] on Monday[72] and yet Mr. Chancellor and I have appointed a special meeting here that afternoon with the officer of the Custom House and so must my Lord Keeper and I with other judges meet tomorrow about difficult business, so as I am not idle in my afternoon though far unable to bear such burdens. I cannot say that I will come on Monday, but I must say I must be carried there very painfully and unmeet to be seen to her Majesty's presence.'[73]

But some time during the month he found time and energy to outline, in his own hand, a programme for dealing with the shortage of corn in London.[74]

In June he was somewhat better — 'but tired with London stones'.[75] Even in a coach it was fatiguing business bouncing over rough pavements.

In July he was in good health and working hard.[76] On the 14th he wrote to Robert that he was well weaned from Theobalds and 'without desire to see it for any contentment' but only to be free from suitors. He went on to say that he had been fully occupied with the other officers of the Exchequer in dealing with debts to the Queen from customers, receivers, surveyors, tax collectors, etc., so that by Friday he hoped to have a store of money. He added that he would go with the Lord Keeper to the London Guildhall on the morrow to deal for the subsidy in London. After that he hoped to take some air abroad, he cared not whither, to be free from suitors.

In August he was off on a holiday with his old friend, Lord Cobham. He wrote to Robert on the 20th that his messenger had found them on horseback: 'My Lord and I have been hunting of a stag, but with a great shower of rain we turned back.'[77]

At the time he was deeply involved in the projected voyage of Drake and Hawkins to Panama. It was a private venture but substantially supported by a royal contingent of seven first-rate fighting ships. Elizabeth gave her consent to the expedition late in January. But it was not yet ready in May. Drake was still busy with it in July when a sudden attack by a small squadron of Spanish men-of-war upon the Cornish coast changed the whole picture. The Queen in alarm ordered Drake to send soldiers to Cornwall. A little later news reached her that a Spanish fleet was on the way to Ireland. She therefore sent fresh instructions to Drake — diverting him from his intended objective — to sail round the Irish coast and thence to the Spanish coast, where they were to cruise about for a month in hope of intercepting the West Indies plate fleet. After that they might proceed to the West Indies, on the grim condition that they would be back in time to deal with any Spanish Armada the following summer.

It seems probable that these instructions were inspired by Lord Admiral Howard. Drake and his fellow commanders protested. They were not equipped for such a voyage. If she insisted, then they thought the private venture should be abandoned and Elizabeth assume the expense of the new arrangements.

At this point Elizabeth called Burghley into the picture. He and Robert between them drafted further instructions on the 9th, but they were apparently not sent, and more temperate ones were drafted on the 11th. Burghley himself probably drafted the revised version.[78] It modified the original instructions, limiting the Irish and Spanish parts of it to a preliminary reconnaissance to the coast of Spain and then a course westward to Panama, with the idea of intercepting the Spanish plate fleet from Havana. The one thing the Queen insisted on was that they should be back within six months.

These conditions were accepted by Drake and his colleagues. On August 20th Burghley wrote to Robert that he was glad to hear that the Queen was contented with their answer.[79]

Two days before, Drake and Hawkins wrote to Burghley: 'We humbly thank your Lordship for your manifold favours which we have always found never variable but with all love and constancy, for which we can never be sufficiently thankful but with our prayers to God, long to bless your good Lordship with honour and health. . . .

'So, looking daily for a good wind, we humbly take our leave from Plymouth.'[80]

This letter can leave little doubt about Burghley's position. From a well-informed source we have a hint that Essex would gladly have diverted the fleet to an attack upon Spain, 'but checked from above, or crossed underhand not without a great distemper of humours on both sides, for a few days; yet in most men's judgments the likeliest way to divert our present fears'.[81]

We hear nothing of this from other sources, but it may well be true. Evidently the conflict suggested was between him and the Cecils, and evidently both the writer and the recipient of the letter were Essex sympathizers; hence the term 'underhand'.

In September, Burghley was worse again. The Queen and Council sat in his chamber on the 2nd.[82] On the 5th Maynard wrote to Robert Cecil that he still kept his bed, though he was somewhat better and able to write a few words.[83] The day following he wrote a long memorandum on military preparations, chiefly about supplies of powder and weapons and the fortification of south-west ports.[84] Much of what we hear from him during the rest of the year had to do with an anticipated invasion from Spain the year following.[85]

He was better on the 9th. The Queen heard that he had gone to Theobalds and sent a messenger there to inquire about his health. But he was still in London, having his good days and his bad days. On the 13th he wrote at length to Robert in comment on dispatches out of the Low Countries, Russia and Scotland. But he ended on a dismal note:

'If I shall not recover my health at this time wherein the sun is departing, I shall despair to continue the next winter alive or out of misery.'[86]

Four days later he was back again at Theobalds, writing to Robert about Northamptonshire affairs, but ending with a postscript: 'I can find no amendment as yet in my head and neck, using nothing but warm clothes.'[87]

But he had a short respite. On the 22nd he was called back to Court, this time to deal with Irish affairs.[88] We have a memorandum from him on the subject two days later.[89]

He sat at every meeting of the Council during October, but was absent almost all of November.[90]

On October 3rd he dictated a letter to Robert, being himself unable to write, reporting that he had spent the day at the Exchequer with the Lord Keeper nominating sheriffs, 'finding great lack of material men though otherwise able for wealth and knowledge.

'And so, returning forthwith to my house I am laid down with great pain, not being able to sit up.'[91]

On the 8th it was reported that he had taken physic 'which doth not work and disquiets him'.[92] On the 10th he wrote:

'I am both sorry and sore grieved that I cannot endure the pains to come thither to Court which maketh me thus to will you to inform her Majesty thereof.' He reminded Robert that steps should be taken to fortify Milford Haven, 'considering all common reports from Spain make mention of the haven'. And he pointed out that nothing had been done to provide powder, saltpetre and match, 'all which are to be brought beyond seas where I hear that prices arise . . . There also her Majesty is to disburse a great sum of money, wherein I cannot be so forward as others'.[93]

On the 14th he received in his chamber De Loménie, an envoy from France to seek further support, who reports him as indisposed.[94]

On the same day he wrote to Robert to urge the Queen to look well to Ireland. But he observed: 'My aching pains so increase that I am all night sleepless. If this continue I cannot ... I can hardly read what I have written not being able to bow my head to the paper.'[95]

Yet the next day he sat in Star Chamber, and on the day following conferred again with the French envoy.

On the 18th he sent Robert a letter from Bodley and observed: 'Hereby is to be seen what harm the French King's reconcilement [to Rome] with such servile conditions is like to work in the world. But I most fear the intent of the princes of the Empire that are purposed to propound conditions of peace to a people wearied of war, will work a revolt, specially the time being now taken when the enemy doth prosper and the States [of the Low Countries] with their forces have decayed all this year.'[96]

But Burghley's chief concern at the time seems to have been to meet the expected Spanish invasion, which, as Rowland White observed, 'doth breed incredible fears in the minds of most men'.[97]

We have three memoranda from him on the subject, one dated October 21st, one the 30th and one November 14th.[98] They had chiefly to do with the supply of guns and munitions, with the musters, with the raising of forces by the clergy and the nobility, with the recusants and such like, reminiscent of the preparations to meet the Armada in 1588. The 'Memorial' of October 30th dealt specifically with dangerous places for the landing of the enemy, from Wales and along the south and east coasts from Cornwall to Norfolk; indicating, county by county, the danger spots and the number of armed men presumed available, and outlining specific measures to be taken to repel the enemy. It ended with letters of instructions to be sent to the Lord Lieutenants, directing them to have their horsemen in readiness for immediate action upon news of invasion, and stores of food and munitions to be established with provision for immediate transport to the fighting front.

It was a considerable performance for an old man, and one more illustration of the fact that, even to the very end, Burghley's energies were always vitalized by a national emergency.

The activities of the Privy Council during the winter and spring which followed were largely directed to the objectives as he had defined them. But the enemy never arrived after all, though he set forth for England with a fleet of ninety vessels the following October. 'God blew with His wind and they were scattered.'

During November, Burghley was at Covent Garden ill most of the time. On December 2nd he wrote to Robert: 'I have read your letter whereby I perceive you have showed my letter of my handwriting to her Majesty who saith that she will have a battle with my fingers and then, aforehand, I know who shall have the victory by the battle. For I have no warrant for my fingers, but her Majesty is allowed to say as King David said in the 114th Psalm: "Blessed be the Lord my strength which teacheth my hands to war and my fingers to fight." And in his next verse he addeth that which properly belongeth to her Majesty: "My goodness and my fortress, my high tower and my deliverer, my shield and he in whom I trust, who subdueth my people under me." And if her Majesty's hands or fingers were to fight, I durst match her with King Philip and overmatch him. Thus you see that I cannot spare my fingers where my heart is fully contented to utter my opinion of her estate and value.'[99]

We have news of him during December in Rowland White's letters to Sidney. White wrote on the 8th that the Queen had directed Burghley to remain at his house in Covent Garden, to stay there until milder weather, and added that the Privy Council was meeting that afternoon in Burghley's house. On the 13th, White wrote that Sir Walter Raleigh was making ready a second expedition to Guiana, and that Burghley had ventured £500 with him, and his son 'a new ship bravely furnished, the very hull of which cost £800'.[100] We hear very little about Burghley's relations with Raleigh at the time, though Robert was on familiar terms with him. It is surprising to hear that Burghley advanced so much money, particularly since his household accounts reveal that he was cutting his living expenses drastically during the last five years of his life. Probably the glowing accounts which Raleigh was sending to Robert[101] of the great wealth revealed by his first voyage thither, from which he had just returned, had something to do with it.

Burghley wrote to Bodley in the Low Countries on the 15th to the effect that the Queen had decided not to press her demands for the payment of the Dutch debt to her, 'but will forbear to do anything which might serve for colour of any disorder or confusion at this time when there are so many devices used to gain the popular with fraudulent offers of peace'.[102] He wrote to Edmondes in France three days later with reference to the return of Unton as ambassador to France.[103] But these two letters are virtually the last of his surviving dispatches overseas. On the 27th he was in bed with a cold;[104] on the 29th he was too sick to write but sent a message to Robert Cecil in Maynard's hand, asking Robert to come and see him.[105] And so the year ended.

Some time in 1595[106] Burghley was busy composing a treatise called 'Meditations on the State of England'.[107] It runs to 38 folio pages and is unfinished.[108] We may judge from the style that it was intended for publication, probably for publication overseas. In its essence it is a hymn of praise of Elizabeth's reign and a defence of her against her detractors. In form it suggests dictation from memory. Some of his facts are wrong, some of them deliberately misrepresentations, as for instance when he describes the election of bishops by the Cathedral chapters with never a word about the royal *congé d'élire*. It was the last of all his extant works designed for publication, and like all the rest of them was definitely propagandistic in character.

It is a pity that it was so. No man knew more about the reign of Elizabeth than he did and no man could have contributed more to our knowledge of it than he could. In the late afternoon of his life, when he had nothing to gain or lose, he might have told us the inside story. But it would not have been true to character had he done so. We must look for his criticisms to his confidential memoranda for his mistress or for the Privy Council. Publicly he was all for the Queen and for her government.

The document is, therefore, more valuable as a revelation of Burghley than of his time. It is much too long to be quoted in full. For the most part it deals with foreign affairs, in which he emphasized the fact that Elizabeth's wars both in the Low Countries and in France were not wars of aggression but were fought simply to help her neighbours — to return to the Dutch their ancient liberties and to help the French King to win his throne. There is no talk here of 'building fires in neighbours' houses'. He wrote at length about Mary Queen of Scots, but simply restated the official case against her. Though he went into the Ridolfi Plot and its ramifications in great detail he added nothing to what we know of it from other sources. In general he had little or nothing to say about military operations except to declare that they were uniformly successful. Even in dealing with English intervention in the French civil wars in 1563, which was a dismal failure ending in the surrender of Havre, Burghley takes the position that Elizabeth voluntarily withdrew her forces because of sickness. He makes much of Elizabeth's re-organization of her military strength, through the Lord Lieutenants, the musters and the establishment of stores of munitions in the towns. His account of the Armada is brief and uninspired, and except for Drake's voyage round the world he virtually ignores the exploits of Elizabethan seamen. He dilates, however, on Elizabeth's development of her navy.

In matters religious his chief concern is with the papists and their evil ways, and with the justification of the Anglican Establishment. He labours at some length to prove that Elizabeth never claimed to be head of the Church, but simply governor of the kingdom in matters ecclesiastical as well as civil. In accordance with the prevalent sentiment of the time, he gloried in the fact that she alone among the Christian powers successfully 'maintained one profession of Christian religion, according to the Gospel, the doctrines of the Apostles and the decrees of the first general Council, condemning all other sects of papists, anabaptists and fond Puritans'.

About Puritanism he had little to say. 'Some others', he writes, 'there are that secretly impugn the orders established in the church both for external government and for the form of ceremonies who, upon nice conceits would have a change of government, of which number some, by show of liming, do secretly entice the vulgar sort to be vehement in desiring such a change, who do practise the same by their leaders in sundry secret places. [Some], discovered by the bishops and governors of the church, have been apprehended and partly reformed by correction. So as at this day, though the papists do slander the church, with these kind of people commonly called Puritans, yet the church and state is not disturbed thereat.'

In such wise Burghley dismissed the whole religious issue which was to plague England for a hundred years to come.

Probably the most interesting and valuable of these meditations are those which deal with the government and with matters economic. Of the general pattern of government he wrote as follows:

'Her Majesty's Councils consist upon parliament, upon assemblies of judges in courts of justice, in Councils attending upon her person for affairs either foreign or for government within the realm, and other council for the revenues of her crown and good order of her tenants [Exchequer], besides sundry others.'[109]

He has little to say about Parliament except to boast that, in comparison with Henry VIII, Elizabeth called hardly half as many.[110] 'In these that have been held there have been always ordinances established for their [her subjects'] benefit partly in expounding or reforming of the difficulties or extremities of the laws, or for the public weal at the earnest requests of the Commons and the other two estates.' He proceeded to enumerate examples — relief of the poor, corrections of vagabonds, increase of fishermen, increase of tillage, good laws against fraudulent conveyance and abuses in common informers, and for learning; measures for particular towns and boroughs, repair of highways and bridges.

At this point he leaves Parliament with no mention of the issues between the Commons and the Crown which fill two stout volumes in Sir John Neale's latest work.[111] Burghley turned then to the judiciary and enumerates what the Queen has done in that department, to wit, increase of the fees of judges and a liberal allowance for their diet and riding charges when on circuit, increase of circuit judges in Wales, support of the Councils of Wales and of the North for those seeking justice in those remote parts, 'so as no corner of the realm is void of aid by justice as the cause may require'.

Regarding the Privy Council, he wrote: 'Her Majesty, like a provident prince, at her first coming to the Crown, made a choice of about twenty Councillors.' He proceeded to enumerate them, emphasizing the fact that many of them had been carried over from Mary's reign. In this connection he named first Archbishop Heath, Mary's Lord Chancellor, who had been invited but declined, a fact which Burghley either forgot or suppressed.

He also emphasized the prevalence of the nobility on the Council. He spoke of ten commoners, of whom 'two had served as principal officers and councillors' to Elizabeth before her accession. He did not include himself in this group though he had been Elizabeth's surveyor in those days, but he did speak of her Secretary without naming him, 'that had served King Edward as his Councillor and secretary'. The reference of course was to himself. He went on to say that of the original Council only two survived, one the Vice-Chamberlain [Knollys], 'the other that was her Councillor and secretary, who also by continual travail in service and by age and infirmities, is not able to attend as he hath done, but yet, for his long experience and his fidelity, is by her Majesty in all great causes of consideration usually called to give his advice as a counsellor — which cannot long endure'.

He then proceeded to consider the Council as it was when he wrote, lamenting the fact that the proportion of noblemen had been reduced by death, so that only five were left [Essex, Howard, Hunsdon, Cobham and Buckhurst]. He did not include himself in this number. His description of Essex is worth noting, he being the only one selected for comment: 'Who is indeed of very noble stocks divers ways and a personable, valiant and wise gentleman, and very well given, learned and addicted both to warlike actions and to knowledge of all foreign affairs.'

Finally he mentioned Sir Robert Cecil, 'one who is the son of the aforesaid and past Councillor and in nature of a secretary without any special entertainment other than her favour, which she yieldeth to him the rather for his father's worthiness'.

Burghley found it necessary to apologize for the shortage of noblemen in the Council in 1593. 'Her Majesty', he added, 'will not long defer choice to supply the said number with persons of like degree.'

Towards the end of his 'meditations' he undertook to explain how it was that the Queen was able to meet the heavy charges at home and to lend substantial financial help to her neighbours, out of her own resources, 'a power not granted to any king or prince her neighbour'. This led him to consider the sources of her wealth.

He regarded her 'thriftiness', her parsimony as he called it, as the chief cause of her riches. To this he added her reforms in the collection of the Customs, by the elimination of carelessness and corruption, which greatly increased her revenues.

He spoke of her careful conservation of Crown lands, in contrast to the extravagant alienation of them by her immediate predecessor. She had, he admitted, made sundry grants for services rendered, but not in perpetuity, only to the beneficiaries and their heirs male.

And at this point he referred to the composition for purveyance, for which he himself had been largely responsible. 'Her Majesty', he wrote, 'hath of late attempted [to free] the people [of] her realm of purveyors for the household by means the most part of the counties in the realm have agreed to yield certain proportions of victuals upon reasonable prices and to be free from purveyors, whereby the counties are already generally comforted.'

His comments on parliamentary grants are confined to a few disjointed sentences which implied that such grants were only justifiable and, as he put it, only made in an emergency 'when the enemy prepared great forces'. He admitted that they were larger on paper than they had been. But he pointed out that they really did not yield much more because the Queen had done away with the old assessment under oath and accepted the taxpayer's estimate of his taxable wealth. Nevertheless, he concluded, the subsidies 'as they were collected did also increase her power'.

We may gather from this that he still held the old view, that under normal circumstances the Queen should live upon her own, and that he regarded voluntary assessment, though he phrased it in terms of royal magnanimity, as a poor idea from the point of view of royal revenue. Probably he slipped over the whole subject hastily because he realized that his mistress had done nothing at all to reform the obvious defects in the levy and collection of taxes.

The meditations ended abruptly in the middle of a justification of the Queen's right to the throne.

Evidently Burghley's main purpose was to glorify his Queen and his country. We may almost take it as his final work, his *nunc dimittis*. When he was young he was constantly trying to make things better, but now that he was very old, very helpless, he sat back and contemplated the structure which he had played a large part in erecting, and found it good. But he made no public claim for any credit. That all belonged to his mistress and his Queen.

CHAPTER XXV

1596

DURING 1596 Burghley's activities oscillated with his health. Except for Scotland he practically abandoned his correspondence with ambassadors abroad.[1] At least, almost none of it seems to have survived. The ambassadors in turn, once again with the exception of Scotland, were more and more directing their dispatches to Sir Robert Cecil. No doubt Burghley was reading the incoming foreign dispatches, and was often helping his son in drafting the outgoing ones. At long last Sir Robert got the name of Secretary in July — once again when Essex was overseas. Thomas Bodley said later that both Burghley and Essex wanted him to accept the Secretariat, but that he declined. This may mean no more than that he was to be one of two. Burghley certainly intended the office for his son and, according to Bodley's report, turned against his candidacy when he discovered that Essex was for it.[2]

In January he was busy with Irish affairs,[3] with the Low Countries[4] and with the unlawful export of French ordnance from St. Malo. His letter to Robert Cecil on the last subject is revealing. He wrote that he and the Lord Keeper got the report, but had not seen the proof. A writ of error had been lawfully granted. But, he added, to delay the matter, 'My Lord Keeper and I have accorded that where we both should be in the Exchequer Chamber, both for other writs and for that also, one of us shall be absent and so the writ shall be delayed, wherewith the Frenchmen will storm, exclaiming already of injustice done them'.[5] Burghley, well aware that Elizabeth needed all the ordnance she could lay hands on, did not hesitate to exploit the law's delays in her service.

On the same day he forwarded to Robert a dispatch from Sir Henry Unton, the newly appointed English ambassador to France.

The immediate occasion for Unton's appointment is set forth in a letter from Sir Thomas Lake at Court to Sir Robert Sidney, on December 13th. Lake wrote:

'We are dispatching Sir Henry Unton unto the French King to divert him from a course [of peace-making with Spain] which, by his own answers to Mr. Edmondes, and by other conjecture, he is like to enter into, the pope working earnestly to bring it to pass and all his council discovering no good concept of our amity. I know not yet what will be the success of his journey, but . . . I do not know what we are able to offer or perform that may encourage him to renew the war.'[6]

Unton's reception was not promising.[7] He was convinced that unless Elizabeth sent speedy aid, peace between France and Spain was inevitable. It was his dispatch on the subject to Burghley that Burghley sent on to Robert on January 16th, enclosed in the following letter:

R

'I do send Sir H. Unton's dispatch, wherein I see a most dangerous course intended by the most ungrateful king that liveth. I will not comment hereupon but I am sure her Majesty will deeply consider of this indignity and intend some course to meet herewith in time . . . We have need to crave and expect the favour and protection of Almighty God, whereof I cannot doubt for the goodness of our cause, though I cannot devise the means.' He signed himself, 'Your loving father bitten with a cold'.[8]

Burghley never trusted Navarre, and in this case did him something less than justice. His position was a desperate one and the pressure for peace even from his own Council almost irresistible. But Burghley could see nothing but ingratitude. All the information at hand made it clear enough that the Queen must either send immediate aid or face the consequences of peace between France and Spain. And yet Burghley refused to give advice, represented Henry's attitude as an indignity to his mistress and commended her to the Almighty.

At this point the matter rested for some weeks to come. There must have been much debate about it in the Privy Council, and Burghley did not miss a meeting between November 27th, 1595, and February 8th, 1596,[9] but we have nothing from him. He received many more letters from Unton, but, if he answered any one of them, his answers do not survive.

He seems to have fallen ill again some time after February 8th, for he missed Council meetings for a fortnight. On February 14th Maynard wrote to Robert sending a message from his father about Irish affairs. On the 20th Burghley dictated to Maynard a letter to Robert, which he signed in a very shaky hand: 'Although I cannot come to Court as my desire is, finding my infirmity rather to grow upon me than to diminish, yet I cannot be careless of such her Majesty's service as I doubt is not remembered by others.' He then bade Robert remind the Queen that there was neither a President nor a Vice-President of the Council of the North, and they could not meet without one.

Two days later he wrote again with reference to Irish affairs. Disorders, he wrote, were reported, 'without advice how to reform them, because the feet dare not reform the head. And so you may say of me that neither have a good head, nor feet, but yet nobody is pained herewith but my poor self alone'.

The following day he wrote again: 'I will not have you come hither to me for by God's leave I will venture to be there [at Richmond] tomorrow by water in the afternoon, where I pray you to send but two horses to accompany me with my coach from Mortlake. If this night shall not make me unable, I will in the morning send you word.'[10]

He sat with the Council at Richmond on the 25th, and so to the end of the month. His son reported him still ill on March 4th.[11] We hear from him again on the 16th:[12] 'I am here all this day, bed rid by reason of a sore sick night past and yet in my head and stomach tormented, so as I write this with pain of head, heart and hand. And therefore I do desire of her Majesty's pardon, if I shall not have satisfied her expectation, which is the mark I shoot at.'

The body of the letter had to do with the Queen's commission to Essex and

Howard for their expedition against the Spanish coast. It is a little short of amazing that there is no record of Burghley's connection with this enterprise in its formative stages. It was under consideration in November 1595. Early in that month Burghley had told Caron, the Dutch ambassador in England,[13] that if the Dutch would supply some thirty ships to meet the Spaniards, the Queen would cease pressing them for repayment of their loans. At that time it was not made clear whether this assistance was to meet a Spanish attack or to support aggressive operations. Quite probably the Queen had not made up her mind. We must envisage long conferences about the relative merits of defensive and offensive operations, complicated by the urgent necessity of sending assistance to the French King if only to prevent him from coming to terms with the enemy. But we hear nothing of them, certainly nothing of Burghley's part in them. *A priori* we might have expected him to favour a defensive policy, and yet he had vigorously supported the expedition of Drake and Hawkins earlier in 1595, and made a large contribution to Raleigh's second Guiana expedition in November of that year. What little evidence we have of his attitude at this time reveals him to be acquiescent to, if not in complete sympathy with, aggressive tactics. There is nothing even in his surviving letters to Robert at this juncture to the contrary, though to be sure he burned at least one of Robert's letters as soon as he had read it. His letter to Robert of March 23rd[14] is very revealing not only of his support of the expedition but also of his position in general when he found himself at odds with his mistress:

'I am sorry', he wrote, 'to see the uncertainty for resolution, considering the delays doth harm both wise [both ways] as well for loss in the continuance of the matter [preparations] if it should dissolve, as for hindrance to the expedition by the staggering. I do hold, and will always, this course in such matters as I differ in opinion from her Majesty, as long as I may be allowed to give advice. I will not change my opinion by affirming the contrary, for that were to offend God, to whom I am sworn first. But as a servant I will obey her Majesty's commandment, and no wise contrary the same, presuming that, she being God's chief minister here, it shall be God's will to have her commandments obeyed, after that I have performed my duty as a counsellor, and shall in my heart wish her commandments to have such good successes as I am sure she intendeth.

'You see I am in a mixture of divinity and policy, preferring, in policy, her Majesty afore all others on the earth and in divinity the King of Heaven above all betwixt Alpha and Omega.'[15]

In any case we do not hear that he played any part in the Essex expedition until he received from his son on March 16th a draft of the commission for Essex and Howard.

Robert Cecil had drawn up the commission and sent it to the Queen on the morning of the 16th. She had apparently read it and sent it to Burghley with instructions, as Burghley put it,[16] to insert in it 'some caution to restrain the general from offending of such as are not her Majesty's enemies but are in amity with the King of Spain, wherein her Majesty's princely care and foresight is

highly to be commended. And therefore, though these two lords, being Councillors and knowing what complaints remain unsatisfied to Denmark and sundry
free cities in Germany for spoils made, will carefully have regard from [sic] all
such offences. Yet, *ad majorem cautelam*, by interlining in certain places, added
such special words as in my poor concept will manifestly direct them whom justly
to invade and offend, and observing these words, no friends of her Majesty shall
have cause to complain except they shall openly show enmity to her Majesty.'

On the same day he drew up a series of notes on the proposed expedition,
addressed 'To the Queen Majesty's only most fair hands from a weak head'.[17]

The essence of his memorandum was to the effect that the Queen should get
an exact statement from Essex and Howard as to how many of the Queen's ships
they meant to use, with their names, the number of their crews, their captains,
the monthly charge, the course they intended to take, the port of Spain or Portugal
they intended to seize, how their force should be organized, and what sort of an
advisory council should be provided. When he spoke of an advisory council he
evidently had in mind some sort of instrument of control whose approval should
be a *sine qua non* for all actions both on sea and land, a self-perpetuating body,
empowered to fill vacancies in its own numbers. It was plainly designed to keep
the wild young Earl of Essex within the confines of his instructions.

Somewhat later Burghley himself drafted the instructions,[18] which required the
commanders first to destroy warships and naval stores in Spanish harbours,
second to capture and destroy towns on the coast, third to secure booty and to
intercept fleets from the Indies if there was any news of their coming.[19] A council
of ten was appointed, and the commanders were obligated to accept their advice.
The councillors themselves were directed to avoid partisanship and to determine
their advice by majority vote. The commanders were enjoined to avoid unnecessary risks either for profit or glory, saving their men for the defence of their
country. A number of humane provisions prohibited the slaughter of women,
children and old men.

The preparations were suddenly interrupted by news late in March of the
siege of Calais by Spanish forces. Maynard wrote to Robert Cecil on the last of
the month:

'My Lord hath willed me to write to you, himself not being well able, without
pain of removing to be set up, that he is much troubled in his mind with the
alarm of Calais ... And therefore, for the quiet of his mind he prayeth you as
soon as you shall understand the certainty thereof, to let him know the same.
And in case it should fall out to be true, his opinion is that my Lord of Essex and
Lord Admiral cannot with more honour employ themselves and her Majesty's
forces than to the succouring thereof, and their whole pay to be answered by her
Majesty. But this, his opinion, his Lordship would have you as yet to keep to
yourself. Now, towards evening my Lord's pain beginneth to hold him in his
head and neck, as it did yesterday, but I hope with less grief.'[20]

On the following morning[21] Burghley himself wrote: 'The alarm of Calais
hath kept me waking all night and hath stirred up in me many cogitations.' He

then went on to suggest that six thousand men be levied in the south-eastern counties, 'for England may not endure this town to be Spanish, and the Queen hath also promised him [the French King] aid'.

Three days later, on Palm Sunday, the Queen gave orders to levy a relief expedition.[22] On the same day Burghley notified Robert that he was raising money to finance it.[23]

But the Queen had a change of heart. Burghley wrote to Robert on April 10th:

'I am heartily sorry to perceive her Majesty's resolution to stay this voyage, being so far forward as it is. I am of opinion that the citadel [of Calais] being relieved, the town will be regained. And if for want of her Majesty's succour it shall be lost, by judgment of the world the blame will be imputed to her, and seeing that Soucy [an envoy from France] will be here so shortly, her Majesty might defer the matter until his message be heard.'[24]

But it was already too late. Four days later the citadel fell, and Calais, which commanded the Narrow Seas, was in the hands of the enemy.

Notwithstanding the loss of Calais, Henry decided not to make peace with Spain but to negotiate with England. He sent delegates to England in mid-April, among them the Duc de Bouillon, with whom Burghley had been in correspondence earlier. Elizabeth appointed five of her councillors to treat with them. Burghley led the group. The others were Hunsdon, Fortescue, Cobham and Sir Robert Cecil. They held the first session on April 20th, and spent the better part of a month battling to and fro.[25]

Burghley did almost all the talking for the English, mostly in French, a language in which he had at long last acquired some fluency. Sieur William du Vair, one of the French delegates, to whom we owe most of what we know about the deliberations, remarked that Burghley was '*fort consommé*' in political affairs, full of ideas but very tired. His manner, Du Vair thought, was rude and ungracious.

Burghley indeed took a tough attitude. He started out by asking the French what they wanted. They replied that they wanted a league offensive and defensive. Burghley inquired what they were prepared to offer in exchange. They pointed out that since Spain was the common enemy both parties would profit by an alliance. Burghley answered that his mistress could do no more with a league than she was already doing without a league. He pointed out that she had already loaned the French King a million and a half crowns[26] and had maintained armies against Spain both in France and in the Low Countries. The French, he said, ought rather to thank her for what she had done than to ask her for more. Her resources were almost exhausted, she had lost both Drake and Hawkins, her best mariners, and she had to finance wars in Ireland and pensions in Scotland.

The French argued that in any case England was far better off than France. When they referred to the advantages of hospitable French harbours for English maritime operations, Burghley murmured, *sotto voce*, in English, that they were trying to sell the skin before they had killed the bear. Soucy, the resident French ambassador, heard him and retorted that they were not trying to sell the skin, but to overcome the bear.

And so it went. The French, impatient, finally declared that if the English were unable to do anything they might as well go home.

Burghley then produced from his pocket a concrete offer. The Queen would furnish 3000 troops if the King would provide money to cover the cost of the levy and one month's pay before they left England. The French retorted that if they had that much money at hand they could easily raise troops in Switzerland and Germany. They then made a serious gesture of departure. But the Queen bade them stay, gave to them £6000 for the defence of two towns in Picardy and undertook to send troops and lend money to pay them. The terms of treaty were finally agreed upon in mid-May. They provided for an offensive and defensive alliance and the dispatch of 4000 troops to France as soon as might be, to serve for six months and to be paid by her, though this was presently modified by a secret agreement reducing the number to 2000 men and the service to four months.[27]

Burghley's technique was an orthodox one, designed to throw the burden of proof on the other party and to keep concessions in France down to a minimum. The remarkable thing is that, notwithstanding the general state of his health, he was able to carry the negotiations through to a finish virtually unaided. But that also was characteristic. Throughout his life, the harder he worked the healthier he appeared to be.

When it was all over he went home exhausted. Elizabeth had been loud in praise of his performance. He wrote to Robert on May 26th:[28]

'You have filled my heart so full with your large reports of her Majesty's allowance of my insufficiencies as sufficient, and of her superabundant care and desire of my amendment, as I cannot contain, in the flowing of my heart, without sending to you, to be presented to her Majesty,[29] some portion of the comfort of my heart by way of most humble thankfulness to her Majesty; with a portion also of my sacrifice to Almighty God by my hearty prayers for the continuance of her happiness, wherein she exceedeth all her equals in body and government.

'My heart hath forced my weak hand thus far.'

A week later he wrote to Robert again: 'God send me some good hours, for I have no good days.'[30]

Meanwhile, the Queen's interest in the Essex-Howard enterprise was cooling. Burghley himself, as he turned matters over in his mind, began to question its wisdom. We have a memorandum[31] of his, written probably some time in May, which may simply have been designed to clarify his own thinking or may have been passed on to his son for the Queen's perusal.

The disturbing factors to his mind were the fall of Calais, which provided the Spaniards with an excellent port on the Narrow Seas, the death of Drake and Hawkins, certain news of which reached England in mid-May, and the continuing news of a new Spanish fleet making ready to invade. With these in mind, Burghley questioned the advisability of stripping the realm of its ships and its mariners for a doubtful adventure against the Spanish coast. If it accomplished its objectives, it might intercept the Spanish fleet or destroy it in Spanish ports. Burghley was not too fearful of what the Spanish fleet, even if it invaded England in the west, might do. He thought that the military preparations already provided were adequate to deal with that. And until the Spanish position in Calais was solidified he did not look for immediate danger in that quarter, though he expected it in the summer of 1597. As to the destruction of the Spanish fleet in Spanish ports, he was doubtful whether, in view of the increase in Spanish strength, enough would be accomplished to make the game worth the candle.

On the other hand he raised the question as to how the commanders would be reimbursed for the money they had expended, and how the soldiers and sailors would be paid, and what the Queen's friends would think if she abandoned the enterprise.

He considered the possibility of sending the expedition away with other commanders in diminished strength,[32] but rejected it. The consideration of this possibility may have been provoked by Burghley's suspicion that the Queen's reluctance was prompted in large measure by a desire to keep Essex by her side.

Burghley's analysis of the situation was sound enough, and in general accord with his cautious policy. But there is no evidence at all that he was trying underhand to thwart Essex's plans. Even Anthony Bacon, who seized every chance to malign 'the omnipotent couple' as he called them, apparently never raised the question.

Essex himself blamed it upon the Queen. Reynolds, his secretary, ascribed her attitude to the influence of the French treaty commissioners in London who were trying their best to divert English strength to their own needs. But Essex thought not. He wrote to Reynolds on May 10th: 'The Queen wrangles with our action for no cause but because it is in hand. If the force were going to France she would then fear as much the issue there as she does our intended journey.'[33]

Essex was always on the alert for Cecilian opposition. But later, flushed with victory, he wrote to Sir Robert: 'I desire to give you all satisfaction, since by your industry and assistance we have had the means to do her Majesty and our country service.'[34]

And in his 'Apology' to Anthony Bacon, for what it may be worth, Essex protested that he had no more part [in the expedition] than the Lord Treasurer, Lord Admiral, and Sir Robert Cecil, who were all privy to it from the beginning and assented to it as much as himself.[35]

Burghley's final contribution to the enterprise took the form of a *Declaration of the Causes moving the Queen's Majesty to prepare and send a navy to the seas for defence of her realm against the King of Spain's forces.*[36]

It justified the enterprise as a defence measure on the grounds that the King of Spain was preparing an armada against her. Its purpose was to notify all persons, except Spanish subjects or such neutrals as aided the Spaniards, that she intended no hostility towards them. It warned all those who had given aid to the King of Spain with ships, victuals and munitions, to withdraw such ships and provisions out of the harbours of Spain and Portugal, and either to take them home or to join the Queen's navy, promising them protection both for their persons and goods. If they refused, then they would be regarded as lawful prize.

The *Declaration* was signed by Essex and Howard, was printed in French, Italian, Dutch and Spanish,[37] and was ordered distributed, as 'conveniently might be' in the ports of Spain and Portugal and other ports under the King of Spain's subjection.

No doubt this declaration was prompted by the difficulties encountered, particularly with the towns of the Hansa League, over the capture of their ships bound for Spain and seized in Spanish waters in the period following the Armada of 1588. It announced once again the English position regarding contraband of war, and, though it did not undertake to define the term as precisely as had been done earlier, it listed men, ships, victuals and provisions — categories broad enough to include virtually everything.

We hear nothing else of Burghley during June. Meanwhile, Essex had accomplished great things on the Spanish coast. On June 20th he had cast anchor off the city of Cadiz and two days later had captured the city. The news of his victory was delayed by contrary winds. But Burghley certainly knew of it on July 3rd. On that day he composed a prayer of thanksgiving.[38] It was subsequently printed and probably was designed for publication. That will explain certain passages in it, setting forth facts of which the Almighty, to whom the prayer was addressed, was presumably well aware.

'Thou hast', he wrote, 'this present summer so favourably conducted the royal navy and army sent to the seas by our gracious Queen (not for any other worldly respect, but for the defence of this realm and us, thy people, against the mighty preparations of our enemies, threatening our ruin) by safely directing them to the places appointed and by strengthening the governors and leaders of the same with counsel and resolution and blessing them with notable victories both by sea and land. . . .

'And direct our armies by providence and favourable support to finish these late victories, to the honour of our sovereign and safety of our realm . . . so as the noblemen and all others, serving in the same navy and army in their charge, may with much honour, triumph and safety, return home to their countries, and to give thee due thanks for thy special favours marvellously showed unto them, all this summer time from all contagion and mortality by sword or sickness, notwithstanding their force and violence most manfully exercised against their enemies to the vanquishing [of] great numbers . . . and to the destruction of their most mighty ships, that heretofore have attempted to invade this realm, and of their forts and castles, and waste of their notable substances of their churches, without hurting any person that did yield, or any women or children or religious persons.'

Burghley himself must have offered up this prayer with great fervour. He had not expected such a great triumph. But there was more to the matter than his private devotions. The fact that the prayer was published meant that it was distributed for use in the parish churches. At a time when newspapers and other modern vehicles for conveying messages from the Queen to her people were lacking, the church furnished a convenient medium for enlisting popular support for government action. It might be from the pulpit as it had been in the middle ages.

It might be from the official books of homilies. But the pulpit was hard to control and the book of homilies had become so stereotyped that it remained virtually unchanged though some ten different editions were published during Elizabeth's reign.[39]

More and more as the reign progressed the government resorted to special prayers for special occasions. Burghley seems to have inaugurated the practice in matters political by a long prayer of thanksgiving for the Queen's deliverance from the Parry Plot. It was employed again in 1586 after the Babington Plot, and again in 1588 before the coming of the Armada, and increasingly in the last decade of the reign in connection with military and naval enterprises. Burghley himself was a prolific prayer-writer. Drafts of many prayers for public use are preserved among his papers. None of them seems to have been printed or, if they were, no copies have survived.

News of the fall of Cadiz reached Burghley early in July. But after that there was a long silence. He began to fear that his thanksgiving was premature. On the 26th he wrote to Essex and Howard that no report had been received from them since their departure. One of the unofficial tales which reached him had spoken of the loss of 1200 Englishmen. 'This report', he wrote, 'is not here published nor imparted to her Majesty. But yet for my own part I am much perplexed therewith, fearing that, if the same loss should be true, it might light upon some capital persons unmeet to be spared for the realm of England.'[40]

As it turned out, all was well and Essex and Howard were back in England early in August.

Early in July, with Essex out of the way, Burghley realized at last the objective for which he had been striving ceaselessly since Walsingham's death in 1590. On July 5th, in the Privy Council, 'by her Majesty's express commandment', Sir Robert Cecil was sworn Principal Secretary to her Majesty.[41] Burghley himself was present. Immediately afterwards, tired out, he withdrew to Theobalds. Anthony Bacon remarked, when he heard the news: 'Now the old man may say with the rich man in the Gospel, "requiescat mea anima".'[42]

Burghley wrote to Robert from Theobalds on the 8th:[43] 'I came hither rather to satisfy my mind by change of place, to be less pressed with suitors, than with hope of ease or relief, for I have brought with me a new pain in my knees and feet ... I found the ways so foul as I never found them worse in mid-winter. And therefore I hope by tarrying here some time to find them better at my return.'

But he went on to say that he was not writing to report on his health but to remind Robert of things to be attended to, such as an escort for the Duc de Bouillon back to France, the preparation of a mission to France to carry the Order of the Garter to the French King, the dispatch of a new resident ambassador to France, and so forth. Though he was relieved by Robert's appointment of responsibility for the duties of Secretary, he still had his mind on the details of administration.

Four days later he wrote again[44] with reference to a 'renegade' priest who had been captured, and who refused information: 'It were convenient that the Council would take order to cause him to be pinched with manacles, or some such like thing, without danger of any member of his body, and thereby compel him to answer more directly.'[45]

He went on to consider a letter from Caron, the resident Dutch ambassador, and expressed the opinion that further troops should be sent to Flushing as had been promised.

'And though', he concluded, 'I find myself nothing amended of my grief, yet upon this occasion I will, with God's leave, if I shall be able to lie in my coach, be there on Saturday or Sunday.'

He sat with the Privy Council at the Court at Greenwich on Sunday the 18th.[46]

Thereafter he sat at practically every session of the Council until the middle of October. He was away sick during most of the rest of the year.

Meanwhile, three members of the Privy Council had died — Puckering, the Lord Keeper, in April; Knollys and Hunsdon, two of Burghley's oldest friends, in July. Puckering was succeeded almost at once by Sir Thomas Egerton, generally regarded as an Essex supporter;[47] Hunsdon by his son the next year.

Stephen Powle, Deputy Clerk of the Crown, records in his 'Common Place Book' an episode in connection with Egerton's appointment. After Egerton had received the seals of office, he attended Elizabeth in the Privy Chamber. She said to him: 'I began first with a Lord Keeper, and he was a wise man I tell you, and I will end with a Lord Keeper.' Burghley, who was present, remonstrated: 'God forbid, madam, I hope you shall bury four or five more.' 'No,' Elizabeth replied, 'this is the last.' With that she burst into tears. Egerton, himself much moved, observed that the first Lord Keeper had been indeed a wise man. This remark intensified rather than assuaged her grief. She turned to go. 'None of the Lord Treasurer's men', she said, 'will come to fetch him away so long as I am here. And therefore I will be gone.' As she left, she called out: 'He will never be an honest man till he be sworn. Swear him! Swear him!'

It is an engaging picture of an embarrassed Queen, overwhelmed by poignant memories, whose first thought was of her gallant, crippled old Treasurer, and her next, to cover her own confusion by shouting out an order.[48]

Reynolds, Essex's secretary, wrote to his master upon his return early in August that his 'more speedy return than some expected had much crossed their designs, for their meaning was to have holden him much longer in this employment, because they would have more time to work and effect their purposes for officers and Councillors. Their malice', he continued, 'worketh still and her Majesty is much incensed'.[49] Evidently Reynolds was shooting at the Cecils. There is no independent evidence to support his diagnosis except the fact that two new councillors, Sir William Knollys and Roger, Lord North, were sworn to the Council on August 30th, both of them soldiers and followers of Essex. 'It is hoped', Anthony Bacon wrote, 'that their preferment will serve for some counterbalance and bring forth honourable effects for her Majesty's service.'

Thomas Lake, a shrewd observer, wrote to Sir Robert Sidney in November: 'The factions never more malicious, yet well smoothed outward. She whom it most concerneth doth rather use her wisdom in balancing the weight than in drawing them all to one assize.' On the same subject Sir Robert Sidney wrote early in September: 'I am glad that our new Councillors were brought in by the Earl. Those which are lukewarm will trust more in him and such as be assured unto him will be glad to see he hath power to do his friends good.'

All this seems to suggest that the conflict between the Cecilians and the Earl was becoming tense again and that he was using the prestige acquired by his victory to increase his power at their expense. Essex himself makes reference to it in a letter to Anthony Bacon of September 8th, in which he speaks of a conference before the Queen of the two Cecils and himself, on the question of spoils from the Cadiz expedition. 'I was more braved', he wrote, 'by your little cousin than ever I was by any man in my life. But I am not nor was not angry, which is all the advantage I have of him.'

Later in the month Burghley and Essex exchanged letters on this subject of the spoils.

Burghley wrote to Essex on the 22nd from Theobalds:[50] 'My Lord, My hand is weak, my mind troubled. And therefore my letter must be shorter than the subject offered me and a few lines be interpreted with favour until I may by speech add a commentary in a paraphrase.

'I came from Court with the burden of her Majesty's displeasure expressed, as my Lord Buckhurst and Sir John Fortescue did hear, with words of indignity, reproach, rejecting me as a miscreant and a coward for that I would not assent unto her opinion that your Lordship ought [not] to have the profit of the prisoners [ransom], wishing her to hear you both with what conditions your Lordship received them ... But herewith her Majesty increased her ireful speeches that I, either through fear or favour, regarded you more than herself, which she said she did otherwise observe in me. But hereof I have no comfort to write much now, being come thence laden with grief for her so implacable displeasure, only for this your cause.

'I am further laden with report of your displeasure also whereof my Lady Russell [Burghley's sister-in-law] hath advertised me largely by her letter ... so as I am in a worse case than the sense of the old verse, *Incidit in Scyllam qui vult vitare Charybdim* ... Her Majesty chargeth and condemneth me for favouring of you against her. Your Lordship, contrarywise, misliketh me for pleasing of her Majesty to offend you. My case is miserable if against you both I had not comfort by God through a good conscience, and therein I will rest ... Otherwise I see no possibility ... to shun both these dangers but by obtaining of license to live an anchorite, or some such private life whereunto I am meetest, for my age, my infirmity and my daily decaying estate.'

Essex replied the following day. Some passages in his letter are obscure because it refers to the letter from Lady Russell which is missing. Apparently she had referred to a speech of Burghley's to Essex in her presence. In any case, Essex wrote: 'Whether I did receive prejudice by your Lordship's speech or no I will make yourself judge when next I wait on you. In the meantime I pray your Lordship believe that I have no ambition but her Majesty's gracious favour and the reputation of well serving of her. And if your Lordship shall hear or apprehend anything that may make you think I deserve them not, if you make me know it, I will either be cleared by making my just apology, or reformed, when once my fault is proved to me, and by your Lordship sooner than by any man. For I have ever desired, and so do, that your Lordship were well edified of me.'

This was Essex at his best and his most gracious, the engaging young man who had grown up in Burghley's household. Burghley replied in the same spirit, on the 24th:

'As at my last writing to your Lordship, I had two impediments to give liking to my letter, the one which was lesser, my rude and weak-handed writing, the other the unquietness of my mind. So now you may evidently see that the first continueth without likelihood of amendment; the other, I trust your Lordship will by my present words, see changed to the better with likelihood of amendment.

'Your Lordship's letter sent me by my Lady Russell in answer of mine, giveth me full contentation, with more respect of me than I am worthy of, save in honest desire to deserve your Lordship's favourable censure of me, only I challenging good will for good will, which I perceive your Lordship well disposed to yield to me.

'And if I shall not be able with deeds to show so much good will, as in measure you shall exceed mine, I will be a debtor to your Lordship until I shall be able to make equation.

'The prejudice which your Lordship noteth to have received by my speeches I know not. But I shall be content, I hope to satisfy you, or otherwise, if I can, to make amends.'[51]

It is evident that Burghley was resolute to keep on good terms with the young Earl and that Essex on his part, however he might feel about Sir Robert, cherished a real reverence for his father. That probably explains why the Essex-Cecilian rivalry kept within bounds so long as Burghley lived.

We hear almost nothing else of Burghley during the summer and early autumn of 1596.

Late in September and early in October he was appointed to treat with a delegation from the Low Countries. Rowland White wrote to Sidney on September 22nd: 'The States have audience upon Friday (24th) in the afternoon and my Lord Treasurer is sent for. If they mean to do any good here they must . . . gain the furtherance of my L. Treasurer and Mr. Secretary. I hear that they will hardly prevail in having of any men.'[52] They were, in any case, graciously received by the Queen.

They came with a request for more men and with an offer to assume the charge of all English companies in the Low Countries, not in the garrisons of the cautionary towns, and to pay annually in discharge of their heavy indebtedness to the Queen, £20,000, the same offer which they had sent over by Sir Thomas Bodley earlier.[53]

The Queen appointed a committee of the Privy Council, of Burghley, Buckhurst, Lord North and Sir John Fortescue, to negotiate with them.

We know little about the negotiations from English sources. Burghley seems to have been the spokesman for the English and to have taken an unfriendly attitude.

He wrote to Robert on the 15th: 'I send the answer made to the States deputies, of which only a short abstract was given to them, with their reply in French. I see no cause to answer further till the Queen has been made acquainted withal. I have sent for Mr. Bodley and required him to deliver them the Queen's message.'[54]

He wrote again a month later:[55] 'I know not what determination her Majesty hath for any further proceeding in the cause for which the Deputies of the States came hither. But for your information I have thought good to set down the state of the cause as I do take it now to rest; being moved thereto because by the suspense hereof her Majesty is charged with the continuance of her auxiliary [army] which at the least is above £50,000 yearly. And if the numbers of them that are, contrary to the contract, brought into the cautionary towns, might be paid by the States, her Majesty might thereby be eased of a greater sum. But as these ij towns [Flushing and Brill] have drawn in from the auxiliary great numbers, the charge of the auxiliary now cometh but to £23,783, which is the sum that the States pretend to discharge. And so her Majesty for her cautionary [towns] shall stand charged with £43,000 yearly.'

Burghley in short pointed out that, though the Dutch had offered to discharge the Queen of the costs of maintaining her army in the field, she would be relieved not of £50,000 but of less than half that sum. But Elizabeth took no action and no agreement was reached regarding the discharge of the Dutch indebtedness to her until two years later.

Meanwhile, Burghley had left the Court and was away for the better part of a month. On October 10th he had already begun to feel the double strain of judicial work at Westminster and political work at Court, and in what was probably a memorandum for his son he wrote:

'I myself am also desirous to know her Majesty's pleasure whether I shall in the term time attend on her both at Court and in her service at Westminster, which will be very hard for me in regard to my weakness, which I am sure will increase towards winter. But yet I shall willingly strain myself to my uttermost to obey her commandments herein.'[56]

We do not have Elizabeth's answer unless it be in a letter from Michael Stanhope to Sir Robert Cecil conveying messages from the Queen. 'She willed me further to tell you that she was angry with my Lord your father that he would jog his body now, being in that case he is, and was angry with me that I did not stay him.'[57]

Stanhope also reported that he had heard Essex say that he and Howard were on the way to see Burghley and would arrange to have the Council meeting at his house.

Early the following month Essex reported that the Queen had appointed a committee on martial affairs, Lord Willoughby, Lord Burrow [Burgh?], Lord North, Sir William Knollys, Sir Francis Vere and Sir Conyers Clifford, to which he proposed to add Raleigh and Carew, and that they would meet at Burghley's house and have him preside.[58]

This action was provoked by news that the threatened Spanish attack was about to be made. What happened at the meeting is not revealed. Doutbless Burghley presided and probably, in preparation for it, he drew up a long memorandum of measures to be taken for the defence of the realm.[59]

This memorandum contains nothing new. The Lord Lieutenants are to hold the county levies in readiness; as many ships of the navy as can be manned and supplied are to be sent to the west; provision is to be made for grain from Holland and all foreign shipping laden with corn is to be seized, that destined for Spain confiscated, the rest paid for; two armies are to be organized, one in the west, the other in the south-east; a Lieutenant-General and his chief subordinates appointed. County bands are to be left in charge of the country gentry, their accustomed leaders. Noblemen and gentry are to supply their own bands of horse and foot, and the bishops and clergy as well. Recusants are to be imprisoned or placed in charge of loyal subjects. Mobile horse-drawn artillery is to be provided to repel landing parties; horses, cattle and victuals to be removed if the enemy does land, and mill-stones and the cross sails from windmills.

All of this is as it had been and much of it had already been anticipated by action in the Privy Council. Some parts of it the Privy Council asked Burghley himself to attend to.[60] Sick as he was, he was still functioning.

Actually before these measures were even considered, the threatening Spanish fleet had virtually been destroyed by storms at sea. But the news of this did not reach England for some time to come and the country remained on the alert until the end of the year.

CHAPTER XXVI

LAST DAYS, 1597-98

OUR sources of information about Burghley in 1597 become increasingly sparse. His diary ends in January; his surviving correspondence is limited in the main to his letters to his son,[1] with a few notable letters to the Earl of Essex. Foreign dispatches were flowing almost entirely to his son. And yet one gets the impression that he was better than he had been in the preceding year — not better physically perhaps, but less prepossessed by his failing vigour and his approaching end. His attendance at Privy Council was amazingly regular. So far as the records show, and they are far from perfect, he missed only one meeting in January, was absent most of February and about half of March. Early in March he lost two more old friends, Lord Cobham, who was Robert Cecil's father-in-law, and Sir William Hatton. One who saw him remarked[2] that he was much depressed, as an old man is apt to be when he sees his contemporaries dying all about him. But he was back at work late in March, and after that he attended virtually every session of the Privy Council during the spring and summer. In August he missed the first half of the month, and was away during most of October. But he attended regularly during September, November and December. On at least four occasions the Council sat in his own chamber at Court, once with the Queen herself present.[3]

It was in this year that he completed his long task of arranging with the counties to compound with the Queen for her rights of purveyance. In July he submitted to the Queen 'A Report of the Lords of the Privy Council in Commission for Household causes' in which he revealed the fact that many of the counties which had compounded earlier had agreed to increase their charges and the eighteen counties which had not yet compounded agreed to compound. As Dr. Woodworth observes: 'Without being obliged to resort to illegal forms of taxation to meet mounting expenses, . . . Lord Burghley was able to tap what amounted to vast sources of additional revenue. He did it without having to face a struggle in parliament. In fact he caused the shires to assume of their own free will the additional costs of running the household.'[4]

In his *Meditations* written two years before, he had emphasized the fact that his mistress had arranged to free the counties of 'cruel purveyors'. The report which he handed to the Queen in July stressed the increase in revenue by compositions enlarged and new compositions arranged. It pointed out that the result meant an annual increase of revenues of £19,000.

We have numerous memoranda of Burghley's on public business,[5] designed perhaps for consideration by the Privy Council or perhaps as suggestions to his son, which cover almost the entire range of administrative problems — defence against Spain, preparations for the Island Voyage, the pay of soldiers in France, Irish affairs, supply of corn to meet the current dearth and so forth. One dated November 29th, for the most part in his own hand, is divided into three columns headed 'Matters for the Queen and Council', 'Matters of the Exchequer' and 'Mixed Matters', which is particularly interesting because it reveals the fact that he was still taking an active interest in the administration of the Court of Exchequer.

He was busy with the financing of the English contingents in the Low Countries, and in May was wrestling with the problem of clothing for the soldiers there. The matter was delayed by competition between contractors for the business.

He wrote to Robert some time in May: 'The lack of a resolute answer from her Majesty driveth to the wall. I pray you once again move her Majesty, for her people suffer great extremities for want of relief of money and clothes . . . I weigh not who shall have the offer.'[6]

In October he exchanged letters with Sir Thomas Egerton, Lord Keeper, regarding the corn supply of London. Burghley wrote on October 15th, acknowledging the receipt of two letters on this subject: 'I was beginning to write my conceit thereof, agreeable to my message sent you yesternight by my servant Maynard, and though now by your servant I understand you allowed my opinion and wished me to draw some form of letters for execution thereof, I have thought good in writing at some length to send my opinion, but do forbear to indite any letters thereupon until the rest of the Council shall determine hereupon, considering this late opinion is contrary to the resolution of them all and of myself also before time. But now by mere necessity I do alter my former resolution.'[7]

The fact was that the sale of corn out of the markets had been prohibited both by public proclamation and by order of Council, and the current supply was not adequate to take care of the needs of the population, particularly since there had been a great influx of noblemen and others by reason of the beginning of the law term and the assembling of Parliament. It is interesting to note that the Privy Council in accordance with Burghley's advice reversed their earlier position. But Burghley was careful not to anticipate their decision. He became increasingly careful to take no positive action or even to express an opinion about matters *sub judice* except by order of the Queen or of the Council.[8]

Occasionally he drafted documents for the Queen, such as directions to the counties regarding the musters and the training, or instructions for finishing the fortifications of the Isle of Wight, or instructions for the paymaster in the Low Countries. One memorandum on the problems of financing overseas forces bears marginal notes by the Queen herself.[9]

Occasionally he expressed himself privately in his letters to Robert about matters upon which he took no official stand. For example, he refused to endorse a suit for Thomas Wilkes, possibly in connection with his patent for the monopoly of salt-making,[10] holding it to be an absolute monopoly. It was one of those which were swept away by proclamation in 1601.

In a letter to Robert in July he referred to a proclamation issued by the Queen[11] restricting the elaborations of apparel, one of her many attempts of the sort. 'I doubt much', he wrote, 'that the length of all these commandments and provisions will hardly be executed abroad until there be some good example in the Court and the city.'

Late in July an ambassador arrived from Poland to complain about the interception or confiscation of Polish grain ships bound for Spain. He appeared before the Queen on July 25th, and in the presence of the whole court delivered an elaborate though somewhat tactless speech in Latin. Elizabeth replied in Latin *ex tempore* with a speech of her own. Robert Cecil sent a description of the whole affair to Essex three days later. 'I swear by the living God', he wrote, 'her Majesty made one of the best answers *ex tempore* in Latin that ever I heard.'[12]

It was on this occasion that the Queen, after she had spoken, turning to her Court, exclaimed: 'God's death, my Lords, I have been enforced this day to scour up my old Latin that hath been long a-rusting.'

Burghley thereupon prepared a speech for further dealing with the Pole and forwarded it to his mistress. Elizabeth sent for John Stanhope, Treasurer of her Chamber, at ten o'clock at night on the 27th and commanded him to write to Sir Robert 'that as she liked your father's speech which he had drawn in answer to the ambassador of Poland above anything else she had ever heard in that nature, and that she said I would have left [off] admiring that little she had spoken to have wondered at the great learning expressed in his Lordship's speech, with the eloquence of words and deepness of judgment'. She thought, however, that since the next move should come from the ambassador, it would be better to let the answer 'stand a while', etc.[13]

It was one of her gracious gestures to her old servant, discounting her own speech with which the whole Court was ringing, in comparison with his.

Burghley was busy for the next fortnight with Polish matters. His secretary, Henry Maynard, wrote to his other secretary, Michael Hicks, on August 10th:

'The Polak hath troubled us here as no day hath stopped my Lord from writing something for his dispatch, and this evening it is engrossed to be signed, whereby I hope my Lord may take some ease, to get him out of his chamber, and for the most part in his bed this whole fortnight that he hath been here.'[14]

For most of the year Burghley was at his house in Covent Garden, with bad intervals, but not enough to keep him from Court. He went away for about a fortnight early in July. On the 8th he wrote a letter to his son which he ended:

'From my house at Theobalds, the rooms whereof I have not seen, more than my bed chamber, my dining place and my chapel, so lame I am on one leg, as Sir Edward Hoby I think can show you, by whom I returned my most humble thanks to her Majesty, notifying her that where I spent at Court the substance of my poor wit I find no measures here to restore it, being forced daily to feed on an ass's milk and so subject to be as dull as an ass.'[15]

But he was in better spirits on the day following. Michael Hicks wrote to Sir Robert on the 9th: 'Here dined today Sir Jerome Bowes, Mr. Fr. Bacon and Mr. Hare, clerk of the Court of Wards. Their errands were nothing else but to do their duties. They be all gone since dinner and now we be alone, my Lord under a tree in the walks with a book in his hand to keep him from sleeping, and we ready to take bowls into our hands but that the weather is somewhat too warm yet.'[16]

He was back again at Court later in the month,[17] but returned to Theobalds in August. On August 25th he wrote to Robert that he had had a family dinner, fourteen of them, old and young, 'descended of my body'.

He returned to the Court at Greenwich the next day,[18] but went back to Theobalds before the end of the month. It was probably from there that he wrote to Robert on September 13th:[19]

'Since my last writing to you I am more unable to write than then I was, and therefore am forced to use another man's hand . . . By your letter I understand that her Majesty would have me with my presence to advise how to answer the Danish embassage for which purpose she would have me come to London where she hath appointed my Lord Keeper, my Lord Buckhurst and Sir John Fortescue to join with me and to consider what were fit to be said to them in answer and thereof, her Majesty being first advised, so her Majesty to allow or disallow as shall please her and thereupon consequently to give them an answer at my house. I have considered of their demands propounded, whereof the principal matter, tending to a mediation for peace, requireth many circumstances of weight beyond my ability to resolve thereon. The other matter, being a demand of free traffic and navigation upon the sea, I think cannot be more reasonably answered than was answered to the Polish ambassador, although I see by the Danish ambassador, they temper their request with a modification. Thus you see how doubtful I am in these two great matters. But yet her Majesty, joining me with other great Councillors, it may be by their advice I may have some clearer understanding. Though my body be this very day at the period of three score and seventeen years[20] and therefore far unable to travail either with my body or with lively spirits, yet I find myself so bound with the superabundant kindness of her Majesty in dispensing with my disabilities as, God permitting me, I will be at Westminster tomorrow in the afternoon to attend the Lords.'

He went, conferred and returned to Theobalds in time to welcome Elizabeth herself. She was there on the 20th, with Sir Robert, Lord Buckhurst, Sir John Fortescue and Lord Admiral Howard.[21] Egerton apparently did not come.

The Danish envoys there had audience[22] and received her answer to their requests. In the matter of mediation for peace between England and Spain, she said that since she did not break the peace at the outset she never would sue for it. 'The Queen of England', she remarked, 'hath no need to crave peace. For I assure you', said she, 'that I never endured one hour of fear since my first coming to my kingdom and subjects.' In the matter of freedom for trade, she said that if the Danes had any just complaint, they had but to present their case to the Council for redress.[23]

The business finished, Elizabeth went on her way. Early the next week she appointed Sir Robert Cecil Chancellor of the Duchy of Lancaster,[24] which had passed to Sir Thomas Heneage after Walsingham's death in 1590 and since Heneage's death in 1595 had been in commission.[25] It was an office of considerable dignity and large perquisites. Cecil had been seeking it since Heneage's death, but Essex blocked the way. It was no accident that the Queen made the appointment when Essex was abroad on his Island Voyage.

Burghley wrote a letter of thanks to his mistress. Lord Admiral Howard was with her when she received it and she read it to him. On October 10th Howard wrote to Burghley: 'Her Majesty commanded me to write this to your Lordship, that you do not give her so many thanks for that she did to your son, as she giveth herself for the doing that which may any way comfort you. And also to give your Lordship thanks from her for your kind and most thankful letter — and saying, although you have brought up your son as near as may be like unto yourself for her service, yet are you to her in all things and shall be Alpha and Omega. Her Majesty also prayeth your Lordship that you will forbear the travail of your hand, though she is sure you will not of your head for her service.

'Her Majesty giveth your son great thanks that he was the cause of your stay, for, she saith, wheresoever your Lordship is, your service to her giveth hourly thanks; and prayeth your Lordship to use all the rest possible you may, that you may be able to serve her at the time that cometh.

'My honourable Lord, let me crave pardon that for want of memory cannot so fully write her Majesty's gracious words . . . It sufficeth that your Lordship knoweth her excellency and my weakness to express it: but I protest my heart was so filled with her kind speeches as I watered my eyes.'[26]

The letter needs no comment. The very writing of it brought tears to the eyes of the man who nine years before had smashed the Armada in the Narrow Seas.

By the same post Howard sent a letter to Sir Robert, telling him the news. 'Well,' he added, 'father and son are blessed of God for her love to you and the Lord continue it to the end.'[27]

Four hundred years later the Queen's gracious letter would have been interpreted as a polite invitation to retire. But Elizabeth did not mean it so, and Burghley certainly did not take it so. Quite the contrary. He summoned up his strength for renewed effort. During November and December he did not miss a single meeting of the Privy Council.[28] In addition to that, and to what he was able to do at the Exchequer and the Court of Wards, he was summoned to attend Parliament, which assembled on October 24th. Indeed he was expected to form part of the procession, two and two with the Lord Keeper, which conducted the Queen from Whitehall to Westminster to open Parliament. Whether he was actually up to even that short walk does not appear.[29] He certainly sat in the Lords that day.[30]

We have little record of his activities in the Upper House. He still was, as he had been, the spokesman for the Crown there. He sat in all the important committees[31] and probably presided over their deliberations.

Almost all that we know of Burghley's activities in this Parliament comes from the *Lords Journals*. That they are more adequate and complete than in any previous Parliament was largely due to Burghley himself. He was well aware of their shortcomings and early in the session moved that hereafter the journals for each Parliament should be viewed and perused by a committee of the Lords appointed for the purpose. The motion was approved, and its effect upon the official record became immediately apparent.

A little later Burghley offered another motion to the effect that peers who were absent and had not sent proxies might be admonished. The motion passed. One wonders whether it was aimed at Essex, who was sulking in his tent over a matter of precedence.

Of all the bills considered, the ones in which he was most active were not the ones for which this Parliament is chiefly remembered, notably the bill reviving the old legislation against enclosures and the bill for the relief of the poor. He is not revealed as having anything to do with them either in debate or in committee. We get therefore no light upon his attitudes. In the debate on the enclosure bill speakers came forward, Sir Walter Raleigh among them, against the whole policy of economic regimentation — early advocates of *laissez-faire*. Burghley was certainly not of that company. To the end he was a staunch mercantilist. As to the poor law, which reorganized poor relief on a national rather than a local basis and which definitely committed the government to responsibility for looking after the poor, though he served on the committee to which it was referred, we know nothing of his position. Neither the Enclosure Act nor the poor law were government measures, so Burghley had no particular responsibility for them.

Burghley was most active in connection with the Bill for Tellers and Receivers[32] — a government bill, designed to authorize the seizure and sale of lands belonging to officers connected with royal finance if they defaulted in their obligations to the Queen. It was largely in explanation of an Act to the same effect passed in 1570.[33] It had a stormy passage. The original bill, after a second reading in the Lords on November 7th, went to committee where it was found so full of doubts and difficulties that the committee asked Sir Edward Coke, the Attorney-General, to draw a new bill. The new bill had its second reading on November 19th and went to committee. Burghley reported that in committee it encountered much criticism and that the committee was to meet again for further consideration. This again produced a new bill, which finally passed its third reading on the 28th and went to the Commons.[34]

In the Commons it met with further objections. Two conferences were held with the Lords after which the Commons produced a new bill, which passed and went up to the Lords to be met with still further objections. These in turn produced another bill from the Commons, which had its second reading in the Lords on February 6th, three days before the Queen dissolved the Parliament. We hear no more of the bill until it appeared in the Statute books. Presumably the Lords accepted the final effort of the Commons without amendment.

Such is the tangled history of the bill on its progress through Parliament. But what all the wrangling was about is not disclosed. We have a few vague notes in Burghley's hand on the subject,[35] probably for use in one of the conferences with the Commons and seeming to indicate that the Commons were seeking to mitigate the rigours of the bill. But nothing much else can be gathered from them. What is abundantly clear is that the various committee meetings and conferences at which he presided on this one bill alone must have made heavy demands upon his failing strength.

One episode in the story of the relations between the two Houses is worth noting because of Burghley's part in it. The question at issue was as to the proper ritual to be observed by the Lords in the reception of a delegation from the Commons.

The Lords 'consulted precedent as it had been observed and particularly noted and remembered by some of them that were the most ancient and of longest continuance in parliaments, and especially by the Lord Burghley, Lord Treasurer, the most ancient parliament man of any that were at that time present either of the Upper House or House of Commons'.[36] Burghley and the rest of them found an answer which satisfied both Houses. He knew if anybody knew. He had sat either as a commoner or a peer in every Elizabethan Parliament, and in his time had been the spokesman of the Crown in both Houses. This was to be his last performance and it was a very creditable one. Almost all of the legislation he wanted he got, and in the changed temper of the time he was not called upon to deal with any of the thorny questions which had marred the relations of Crown and Parliament in earlier times, questions of the succession, questions of religion, questions of finance. The succession had not even been mentioned, the criticism of the Church had been met by prompt measures for reform in the Church itself. And the Commons had passed without a murmur the largest appropriation of money in the annals of the reign.

In 1597 Burghley made a definite effort to reconcile differences between his son and the Earl of Essex. As early as March we hear of Sir Walter Raleigh acting as mediator.[37] In April Essex and Cecil and Raleigh dined together and, as one of Essex's partisans remarked, confirmed the treaty of peace among them.[38] In May it was observed at Court: 'Here is all love and kindness between Essex and Burghley with the rest of that tribe and furtherance given to his desires.'[39]

Burghley had at the very beginning of the year been a strong advocate of a further attack on the Spanish coast to prevent a Spanish expedition to Ireland. In a memorandum dated January 20th he considered two propositions, one from the Earl of Cumberland, one from Essex. That of Essex was the more ambitious and would have involved ten or twelve ships of the navy besides twelve from London and twenty from Holland, and 5000 men. Burghley was in two minds about the expediency of such an operation, fearing that if it were defeated the loss would seriously weaken England, and pointed out that Cumberland's alternative was much less expensive. It is difficult to judge from his memoranda which plan he favoured. But he declared that if it was to be Essex's the preparations should begin at once.

We hear little more of the matter until April, when the Privy Council was engaged in active preparations. In May Essex was definitely appointed to lead the expedition and his instructions were drawn on June 15th, directing him to attack the Spanish fleet and destroy it in harbour,[40] or, if it was at sea, to pursue it and destroy it. After that he was to intercept and capture Spanish treasure ships, either at the Azores or elsewhere.

Burghley wrote to Robert on July 5th: 'I do send you a letter written to my Lord of Essex, to whom I did not write since his departure [to Plymouth], nor until now that God hath showed him favour from heaven with the new moon to send him a prosperous wind. I could not write comfortably, neither for myself nor for him; and now I do write unto him with my weak hand only to congratulate with him for this favour of God, and do exhort him, as a Christian soldier, to acknowledge the same beyond all man's power and wit. I have also written unto him, that I am sure you will frequently advertise him of things convenient . . . I pray you by the next safe messenger send this my letter to his Lordship, letting him know that I am here licensed for a while to be at my house [Theobalds] where, I assure you, I continue in such pain of my foot as I am not able to stir abroad but in my coach.'

Three days later Burghley wrote to Robert again:[41] 'I have, with your letter written yesterday, received two letters to you, one from my Lord of Essex written on Wednesday;[42] since which time I have gladly observed every day a most favourable wind to set him forward.'

On the following day he wrote to Robert that he had received a letter from Essex asking for supplies but not indicating specifically what he wanted. 'But herein,' he added, 'I trouble myself too much, finding the uncertainties of their requests.'[43]

Essex and his expedition started off on July 10th from Plymouth, but ran against such bad weather that he had to put back again.

Burghley wrote to him on July 23rd: 'It is not right to condole with you for your late torment on the seas, for I am sure that should be but an increase of your sorrow and no relief to me. I am but as a monoculus by reason of a flux falling into my left eye and you may see my impediment by my evil writing and short letter. I trust you and your company will refer all your accidents to God's will, thanking him for all favourable accidents and acknowledging the contrary as a punishment to you and us all that have an interest in your actions.

'In the time of this disaster I did, in common usage of my morning prayer on the 22nd of this month, in the 107th Psalm, read these nine verses which are very proper for you to repeat and particularly six of them of which I enclose a copy.'[44]

The copy he referred to was in Latin. He seems always to have preferred the Latin Bible before any English version. It was neither by accident nor by deliberate choice that he had chosen the 107th Psalm for his morning prayer of the 22nd. That Psalm was assigned to that day in the Elizabethan Prayer Book. It still is. But the appropriateness of it to the occasion, Burghley found irresistible.

The verses are familiar enough, particularly those to which Burghley undoubtedly referred. In the King James version they begin as follows:

'Those that go down to the sea in ships, that do business in great waters, they see the works of the Lord and his wonders in the deep. For he commandeth and raiseth the stormy wind which lifteth up the waves thereof . . . They reel to and fro and stagger like a drunken man and are at their wits end. Then they cry upon the Lord in their trouble and he bringeth them out of their distresses.'

Burghley as he grew older became more and more fond of the Psalms. He quoted from them more than from any other book. After all, he was well soaked in them. At the morning and evening service which he attended regularly in his private chapel, he read them through every month.

But the most striking thing about this letter is the patriarchal attitude which Burghley is assuming towards Essex. It is almost as though he were harking back to the time when the boy Essex was a ward living in his household.

Essex replied in the same spirit.[45] 'This is to acknowledge', he wrote, 'how much I hold myself to be bound to you for your honourable and kind letter and in it for your Lordship's grave and sound advice. I hope your Lordship shall find that I will be in such disasters as these no more grieved than the interest of my dear sovereign and my country should make me. . . .

'I do also acknowledge your Lordship's excellent choice of a psalm, fit for the time and the occasion. And, I assure your Lordship, I had it at sea both read and read upon.

'If it please your Lordship to continue me still in your good favour and bestow on me your good direction you shall never find any that by his services would more strive to inworthy himself towards you.'

It was Essex at his best, writing as a son to an honoured father. Whether he meant it or not, it reveals a responsiveness and a perceptivity which go far to explain the affection with which all those with whom he came in contact regarded him.

There is no sound reason to believe that he did not mean it, at least for the time being.

Burghley at any rate took him at his word. No more of his side of the correspondence survives until Essex, who got away from Plymouth on August 17th, returned home late in October with virtually nothing accomplished.

Burghley wrote to him as soon as the news of his return reached the Court, two letters on successive days,[46] rejoicing that he had returned safely, regretting that he had failed to capture the Spanish treasure fleet, 'which would have been a perfect cordial to all our infirmities here'. 'But yet', he added, 'you and all your friends may well vaunt that you have the victory of your enemies, both at their own doors and far off, only you have been overcome with contrary winds against which no creature can contend but with loss.'

There were no congratulations from the Queen, who received Essex coldly and criticized him for his failure either to destroy the Spanish fleet or to capture Spanish treasure. Essex left the Court and returned to the country, his bitterness accentuated by the fact that during his absence she had given the Chancellorship of the Duchy of Lancaster to Cecil and had elevated the Lord Admiral to the rank of Earl of Nottingham, which would give him precedence both at the Court and in Parliament. On the latter grounds Essex refused to come to Court and refused to take his seat below Howard's in the House of Lords.

It was on this last subject that Burghley wrote to him on November 9th.

'I need not by words', he wrote, 'to show my weak hand which my writing doth manifest. Since I did not see your Lordship I have diversely heard of the cause of your absence, by some of your own, that you are sick. And therefore I do send the bearer my servant only to understand the state of your health. As to some other cause of your absence, I wish it were in my power to remedy. But thereof I can do no good by reciting the same in this my letter. But it requireth another manner of remedying it, where your Lordship may command my service both for that and any other thing for your Lordship's contentation.'[47]

Two days later he wrote to Essex again: 'For that contrary to my hope that you would have come to the Court, especially at the festivity of her Majesty's coming to the crown [November 17th], yet by report I hear that your Lordship is indeed very sick, though I trust recoverable with warm diet. I do send my servant, this bearer, who at his last being [with you] you used too courteously, to bring me word from your Lordship, both of your state of health and what hope you will give us of the time of your return, where you shall find a harvest of business needful for many heads, wits and hands.'[48]

And he wrote a third letter on the last of the month:

'I know not how to write to your Lordship, for my satisfaction with your contentation. Sorry I am to see your absence from hence, whereby her Majesty hath want of her service and yourself subject to diversity of censures. I find her Majesty sharp to such as advise to that which were meet for her to do and for you to receive.

'Good my Lord, overcome her with yielding, without disparagement of your honour, and plead your own cause with your presence, whereto I will be as serviceable as any friend you have to my power, which is not to run, for lack of good feet, nor to fight for lack of sound hands, but able and ready with my heart to command my tongue to do you due honour.'[49]

It can hardly be doubted, in view of these letters, that Burghley was working hard to heal the breach between Essex and the Queen. The disposition of Essex's followers was to blame it all on the Cecils, and one of them wrote late in December that the Queen herself blamed it on them.[50] Lord Henry Howard wrote to Essex in November: 'If you could once be so fortunate in dragging old leviathan and his cub, *tortuosum colubrum* [coiled serpent] as the prophet termeth them, out of this den of mischievous device, the better part of the world would prefer your virtue before that of Hercules.'[51] Less than a month before Howard had written to Burghley: 'I am of your Lordship's making and it lieth in you to fashion me. My trust is that as you began with me with your most honourable and fatherly care, whereby I have been brought to that good I have, so by that which is now in your power I shall be so honourably friended as ever I must and will acknowledge myself most deepliest bound to your Lordship and ever rest.'[52]

As a 'coiled serpent' Lord Henry Howard was second to none.

It seems not unlikely that Burghley found a way out of the impasse by suggesting that the Queen revive the office of Earl Marshal, which had been in abeyance since the death of the Earl of Shrewsbury in 1590, and confer it upon Essex. Elizabeth accepted the suggestion somewhat grudgingly,[53] but she made the appointment in December. It gave precedence over the Lord Admiral, and Essex presently was himself again.

On the last day of November, André Hurault de Maisse, ambassador extraordinary from Henry of France, landed in England. The object of his mission was to find out whether Elizabeth was willing to join in peace negotiations with Spain or whether she preferred to continue the war.

Throughout the year there had been a constant fear in England that Henry would come to terms with Philip and leave Elizabeth in the lurch. The English ambassador at the French Court gave warning of the danger as early as February.[54] He kept on writing about it. Early in July Sir Robert sent a French dispatch to Burghley when he was at Theobalds, which called forth the following comment in Burghley's letter to his son of July 8th:[55]

'I see no likelihood for the French King to seek peace at this present when by all advertisement the Cardinal [Albert of Austria, Spanish governor in Flanders] as yet hath no money to wage [pay] his men to come to the relief of Amiens, nor his new levies as yet come out of Italy . . . But yet it may be that the Pope and his legate and the Cordelier[56] may tempt him thereto and the King's discontented state may move him to forget his honour. On the other side it may be suspected that this chanting of peace is a song, only to allure the Queen's Majesty to yield him still aid of more men and money, or both, wherein I can yield no other opinion than that her Majesty should yield no more than good reason may warrant with conservation of her own estate. And though it may be feared that by the French King's peace her enemy the Spaniard may become more to be feared, yet in God's goodness, whose cause her Majesty defendeth, she may say with David, "I will extoll thee, oh Lord, for thou hath lifted me up and hath not made my foes to rejoice over me."[57] But you may say my conceits are spiritual. And so ought all human actions to be governed.'

But certainly neither Burghley nor his mistress contemplated with any satisfaction the possibility of facing Spain alone.

The mission of De Maisse came at the end of the year when peace negotiations between Spain and France were far advanced.[58] De Maisse himself presented the problem to Elizabeth in terms of alternatives, either an effective war or a peace. He was himself a keen observer and in the journal which he kept of his English mission he presents an interesting picture of England as he saw it: Elizabeth in her extravagant attire, with bosom often bare and the front open as low as the navel; Essex and his petulant behaviour; the rivalry between him and the Cecils; along with a description of the English government and the English Church. He made some attempt to analyse English attitudes towards peace and war: reached the conclusion that both Elizabeth and Burghley favoured peace though they would not entertain it unless the Dutch were included; that Essex opposed it.[59]

His observations on Burghley are worth quoting.

'The Lord Treasurer', he wrote, 'is the principal man in her Council, he is the first man in her household; he is baron of Burghley. The Queen trusts greatly in him even in her most urgent affairs. He has always been kindly disposed to the house of Burgundy and it seems to him that he would make a great stroke if, before his death, he could bring back peace between the crown of Spain and England. He is very proud and presuming in his words, as they say, even to those who have business with him. His son is secretary of state. . . .

'He seems envious of the fortune of the earl of Essex who has won a great reputation amongst the nobility and amongst the people and wins it daily; the admiral is of their [the Cecil] party . . . Formerly there was always great jealousy between them in everything, one against the other, and a man who was of the Lord Treasurer's party was sure to be among the enemies of the Earl, and it was a thing notorious to all the Court.'

It will be observed that De Maisse speaks of the Cecil-Essex rivalry as though it were a thing of the past. In other passages he speaks of it as still current.[60] Always, in reading his account, we must remember that he leaned towards Essex, who was an old friend of his master and much of what he says about Court factions he probably got from Essex supporters. Nevertheless, just as he was leaving, he observed that Burghley and Essex had great respect for each other.

Again he wrote: 'The nobility and the people are dissatisfied with the govern-ment of the Lord Treasurer and hate him strangely.'

This was certainly not true in general. It was probably true of the young soldiers among the nobility.

Again: 'The Court is ordinarily full of discontents and factions and the Queen is well pleased to maintain it so: and the Lord Treasurer, old as he is, is exceedingly ambitious and finds nothing but amusement in these Court broils. And his son is altogether immersed in them.'

In speaking of an audience with the Queen, De Maisse wrote: 'In this chamber called the Privy Chamber, which resembles somewhat a closet, in which there is no bed, there were several ladies . . . The chief men of her Council also were there, that is to say, the Lord Treasurer, who is carried in a chair and is very old and white', etc.

Again: 'The treasurer is very old and is aged eighty-two; he is very deaf and I have to shout quite loud. The admiral often helps by interpreting in English.'

The facts that Burghley had to be carried in a chair and that he was quite deaf are definite contributions to our knowledge of him otherwise. This is the first mention I have seen of his deafness. It may account for a certain brusqueness of manner which French envoys complained of more than once. Those who do not hear find it difficult to follow remarks, particularly in a language of which they have an imperfect knowledge, and incline to a domineering tone, if only to forestall the difficulties of listening. De Maisse was, of course, wrong about Burghley's age. He was a few months over seventy-seven.

Again: 'Two things they say are faults, the one of the English, the other of the French. That of the French is never to have well understood how to treat with the Lord Treasurer, and to know that it is he who can accomplish everything in England with the Queen, being her principal Councillor.'

This is a cogent observation and probably true, though Burghley probably made things difficult by his innate distrust of the French, partly traditional, partly due to a distaste of their courtly manners which jarred the essential Puritan in him.

Again: 'The same day M. de la Fontaine went on my behalf to speak to the Lord Treasurer to learn from him if I should have audience with the Queen's Council. He told me that he knew nothing of the two audiences which the Queen had given me, that he had not been there, particularly as he was ill of the gout.'

For nearly a month after the first audience De Maisse's formal contacts were limited to audiences with the Queen. She seemed to be reluctant to have him confer with her Council and it was not until January 6th that a meeting was finally arranged. At that meeting only four councillors were present — Burghley, Buckhurst, Howard and Sir Robert Cecil — all of them of the peace party. The discussion turned upon the position of the Low Countries in regard to peace. Burghley proposed that the three allies should first meet in England and decide upon a common policy before meeting the Spanish commissioners. De Maisse objected that it would take too much time and pointed out that commissioners from the Low Countries were already in France. Burghley and his colleagues wanted De Maisse to wait in England until they had sent to the Low Countries. He said it was impossible. He had to be back in France by January 15th. They replied that they would communicate with the Queen. 'And so', De Maisse concluded, 'we accomplished nothing.' Burghley, in the course of the conference, inquired whether Spain had offered to make peace on the terms of Cateau-Cambrésis in 1559. De Maisse said it was so. Burghley then wanted to know what disposition they intended to make of Calais. De Maisse answered that the King of France should decide. He noticed that the English still had a strong desire to recover Calais.

Another meeting with the Council was held four days later, Elizabeth herself being present. Burghley arrived first and chit-chatted with De Maisse about the reformation of the calendar. When the rest had gathered, six of them this time, including Essex and Hunsdon, the Lord Chamberlain, appointed in his father's place in April 1597, Burghley took the floor and declared that the Queen had commanded them to convey her resolution. He then proceeded to say that there were three parties at interest, the French King, the Queen and the Dutch. The Queen had determined to send commissioners to France to confer with the King. She had sent, she said, to the Dutch to advise them to give their commissioners power to treat. Later De Maisse saw the Queen who told him that she thought peace might wait until after the death of the King of Spain, 'which', she added, 'could not much longer be delayed'. But she referred the whole question to her commissioners who were to go to France.

After dinner that same night, De Maisse went to take leave of Burghley. Burghley told him that the Queen was about to send commissioners to France and, speaking of peace, said that he wished for nothing else before his death; getting that, he could sing his *nunc dimittis*. But he reminded De Maisse of large sums of money owed by the French King to his mistress, some of it overdue. De Maisse observed: 'He desires peace, thinking that if he is the author of peace, that will be a firm assurance for his family in future time.'

And so the mission ended. Its total achievement was that Elizabeth agreed to send commissioners to France to talk of peace and intimated that the Low Countries must be a party to any treaty with Spain. All this from French sources. From English sources we have little more than a dispatch from Sir Robert Cecil to Edmondes, the English agent in France.[61] He informed Edmondes that the Dutch would not treat and had sent commissioners to France to dissuade the French from peace. The Queen, wishing to know how the King 'digesteth this their refusal', would send over commissioners with a proposal that either in peace or war the three allies should work together.

From Burghley's pen we have one memorandum, entitled 'Reflections', which shows the way his mind was working.[62]

He thought that peace, on the basis of the *status quo ante bellum* would be profitable to France but he feared that such a peace would destroy the hope of recovering Calais for England and the probability of collecting large sums of money which the Queen had loaned to the French King.

From England's point of view he saw much to be gained by peace in enabling the Queen to re-establish order in Ireland without Spanish interference and to effect great economies in the expenditure both of money and man power. He made much of the re-establishment by peace of English trade with Spain, Portugal, the Levant, Barbary and the Baltic (curiously enough he said nothing of the East or West Indies), and proceeded to enumerate the port towns which had decayed from the stoppage of trade — Newcastle, Hull, Southampton, Bristol, indeed practically all of them except London.

And then he turned to the thorny problem of the Dutch Republic, evidently with the thought in mind that any treaty between Spain and England would have to include them. It would be almost impossible, he thought, to re-establish the *status quo ante bellum* in the Netherlands, since it would involve the restoration of Church lands, the stripping of Dutch towns of their garrisons, and toleration for Roman Catholics in the Dutch Republic — in short rob the Dutch of all their safeguards against a revival of Spanish aggression. He came to no conclusion but it is clear from the instructions which he subsequently prepared for the English commissioners going to France that he regarded a settlement satisfactory to the Dutch as a *sine qua non* in any treaty making.

Burghley's health seems to have been good in the first two months of 1598. He sat in every meeting of the Privy Council during January and February. On the night of February 24th he had a sudden attack, but the following morning, as Rowland White wrote in a letter to Sir Robert Sidney of the 25th: 'it pleased God, for the good of his country, to ease him of his pain and to give him some rest which, God willing, will restore him to his former health'. With the departure of his son on a mission to France in February, though Essex assumed the routine duties of the Secretariat, Burghley's load was perceptibly increased. From Dover on his way out Robert wrote to his father: 'I do find that it pleased God to direct your Lordship to strain your body in my absence to do what I should do if I were there, besides your own great dispatches. I am thus driven between comfort in your [well being] and fear of overthrowing your Lordship's health. Yet I do quiet my heart with hope in God's providence, that he will set back your aged body and by degrees, as it is overgrown, the vigour and strength of your mind, out of whose treasure many younger wits may daily be fed and instructed.'[63]

In another letter from Robert in April he sent his father 'humble and affectionate thanks for your care and goodness, beseeching God to send me the happiness to see you as I left you, if no better'.

We have only three letters from Burghley to Robert while he was in France, none of them very illuminating except to show that Burghley was still taking a keen interest in the problems of state.[64] The last sentence in the second letter is not without significance:

'By your letter you should thank Lord Essex for the pains he takes in your absence about matters that you should supply.'

In March Burghley was not so well. He missed most of the Council meetings. Writing to Robert on the 1st, he said: 'The bearer will report to you my great weakness. Do not take conceit thereby to hinder your service ... God bless you on earth and me in heaven, the place of my present pilgrimage.'

He was not much better in April though he attended a few meetings. On the 27th of the month the Council sat at his house in Covent Garden. He got special permission to be absent from the annual meeting of the Knights of the Garter on St. George's Day (April 23rd), 'by reason of your want of health and weak estate of body yet remaining through your late great sickness'.[65]

In May he seems to have been in better shape. Robert got back from France on the last day of April, and that indefatigable letter-writer, John Chamberlin, wrote on May 4th: 'Master Secretary returned the first of this month, somewhat crazed with his posting journey. The report of his father's desperate estate gave him wings, but for ought I can learn the old man's case is not so desperate, but he may hold out another year well enough.'[66]

It really looked in June as though he might. He was present at most of the Council meetings between the 7th and the 18th, and again on the 29th and 30th. He wrote frequently to Robert in June.

On the 9th he wrote: 'I see you continue in your care for me ... I took not your house for that it was too near the breathing of Westminster; nor Wimbledon [Sir Thomas Cecil's residence] because of the discommodities in passing the river. But came hither [to Theobalds] to my familiar place, although forced to seek a resting place, but want rest.

'As yet I cannot recover my appetite, only I supped yesternight with 4 or 5 leaves of an artichoke. But this morning I have eaten a small panado ... I will prove all good means, either to amend, or to make a good end.'

On the 10th he wrote again, having heard that the Queen was angry at the delay of sending men and victuals to Ireland, 'whereunto I have thought it preposterous counsel to send men into Ireland before the victuals were ready, or at least some part of them'. As for the men, he said he had no warrant to deliver any money for their pay. And he called to witness various people. Quite evidently he was much disturbed by Elizabeth's displeasure. 'I pray you,' he wrote, 'as you find the Queen not satisfied with me, to pray her to hear this my letter.'[67]

In concluding the letter he wrote: 'And so I end, with an ill stomach to write of these matters as I have torment, which is hitherto fitter for fasting than for feasting. And the weather so cold as I am fitter for a fire than for a garden.'

In his next letter of the 11th he was less depressed, and went into details of supplying victuals for Ireland. The postscript ran as follows: 'I pray you present my humble thanks for her Majesty's frequent messages, for which I acknowledge my debt greater than I am able to acquit. But yet I will gage my heart to be thankful with prayer.'[68]

Notwithstanding all of which he sat with the Council on the 11th and again on the 13th, probably at Greenwich.

Henry Maynard, his secretary, wrote to Michael Hicks, his other secretary, on the 15th:

'A more melancholy time was never spent by any other than this hath been, here by my Lord, without any comfort. What will become of it God knoweth. He sleepeth well but eateth very little. He neither hath disposition to go to the Court or to London and, for ought I see, well may stay here, I know not how long.'[69]

But Maynard reckoned without his amazing vitality. Three days later he sat again with the Council and he seems to have returned to his house in Covent Garden at the end of the month. He sat twice in the Council in July, the last time on the 15th, and he was doing business at the Exchequer as late as July 4th,[70] and hearing cases in the Court of Wards as late as June.[71]

During the last months of his life he was bending much of his thought to peace with Spain. Robert Cecil had accomplished nothing by his mission to France. Two days after his return, Spain and France signed the Treaty of Vervins. A loop-hole was left in this treaty for English participation, and the Spaniards agreed that they were prepared to negotiate with England at any time within the six months following. The Dutch commissioners under John of Barneveldt had been in France trying desperately to prevent the French King from breaking with the Triple Alliance. They followed Robert Cecil to England. Arriving on May 11th they had audience with Elizabeth on the 16th.[72] Their objective was to keep Elizabeth true to her alliance with them. They were not well received. She began by denouncing the perfidy of the French King and went on to denounce the Dutch for not participating in the peace negotiations. She swore that she could not and would not assist them any longer. Barneveldt endeavoured to pacify her without success. Why, she inquired, could they not carry on as they were, with a guarantee from England and France to protect them from aggression? She wanted her men back and her loans repaid. In short, they got little or no encouragement from her.

After they had taken their leave of her they went to talk with Burghley and found him sitting in an arm-chair wrestling with the gout. He was more polite but no more encouraging than Elizabeth. He was, he said, a strong advocate of peace, and thought the French King had acted wisely and hoped that his mistress would seize the same opportunity. The Dutch urged the validity of the Triple Alliance and the agreement to make no separate peace. The interview went no further. Burghley's position was clear.

When the Dutch had gone, Burghley wrote out a memorandum[73] which he called 'Considerations of the motion for a treaty of Peace with the King of Spain'. It is the last surviving memorandum which he wrote with his own hand. The writing is shaky, but there is no trace of mental deterioration. As it stands the manuscript has relatively few corrections or interlineations.

He began with a statement that if it was certain that the Queen could not gain by treaty adequate assurance for the Dutch that they could continue without evident danger of being, within a short time, subdued to Spain's absolute power, then it was futile for England to negotiate a peace since England could not be assured of peace unless the Dutch were freed from danger of conquest. In that case he thought the French King should be advised accordingly.

But he cast about for a more hopeful alternative — what he called a second course.

He suggested that the Queen should consent to treat if only to find out what the Spanish had to offer. She might inform the French King that she was prepared to treat if he was quite satisfied that the Spanish commissioners had definite authorization from the King of Spain, and if no representative of the Pope participated in the negotiations, and if the meeting were held somewhere in Picardy as near the sea coast as might be.

On the assumption that this course was followed, he proceeded to outline instructions for English commissioners.

As a preliminary, there must be an exchange of commissions, the King of Spain's commission to his envoys, the Queen of England's to hers.

Burghley then suggested that old quarrels should not be rehashed, but that the English commissioners should demand sufficient assurances that the United Provinces be allowed to retain their present status, their ancient liberties and their right to practise their own religion. They should be admitted to trade with Spain. They should be permitted to remain in arms and even to hire English troops provided they did not engage in aggressive warfare against territories actually in the King of Spain's possession. Foreign soldiers were to be sent away from all those parts of the Netherlands under Spanish control. England was to hold Flushing and Brill.

Burghley's concluding paragraph runs as follows:

'But, for conclusion, if reasonable conditions may not be had for the Estates' security, nor that we may fastly retain our two towns, we think the particular peace [i.e. without the Dutch] will not be profitable for us and therefore will rather reject and stand to our defence with some large aid from the States, considering reasonable conditions shall be refused, wherein we doubt not but all persons that are indifferent, that shall understand that we desire but our security, will allow our action.'

Burghley's position in short was that the Queen should negotiate with the Spaniards whether the Dutch participated or not, but should see to it that the Dutch were allowed to keep their present government, their present army, their ancient liberties, their religion with the added right 'to resort to any of the King of Spain's countries, without restraint, either for their religion or any other cause'. He ignored the question of sovereignty but clearly had in mind a kind of 'dominion status' within a Spanish empire.

Burghley was for peace, but not for peace at any price. The terms which he suggested he could hardly have expected the Spaniards to accept. Yet, in his cautious way, he left the door open even if the Spanish refused to pay the price, reserving to the Queen herself the decision to terminate the negotiations.

The memorandum is undated, but it certainly was not written until after the departure of Barneveldt and his colleagues on May 21st.

Camden, the historian, relates that the question of war and peace was furiously debated in England, with Burghley the spokesman for the peace party and Essex the spokesman for the war party. There can be little doubt about the discussion. Even John Chamberlin was aware of it. Before Barneveldt's departure he wrote to his friend Dudley Carleton: 'Barneveldt . . . is here and has had audience these two days together but I fear we are deaf on that side and no music will please us unless it be to the tune of peace. One of the chiefest reasons I can hear for it is a kind of disdain and envy at our neighbour's [the Dutch] well doing, in that we, for their sake and defence entering into the war and being barred from all commerce and intercourse of merchandize, they in the meantime thrust us out of all traffic to our utter undoing (if in time it be not looked into) and their own advancement.'[74]

Camden in his account of the discussion also alluded to the fact that the Dutch 'by the war grow rich whereas all other nations are impoverished'. And certainly this economic factor was in the background of Burghley's thinking. He had alluded to it more than once before. Probably Camden was not far wide of the mark when he defined Burghley's position as chiefly determined by 'the benefits of peace, which are certain, present and necessary . . . knowing the chance of war to be uncertain, the charge infinite, the treasure of England exhausted . . . and (as he said) no good could come to England by this war, but an aversion of evil, which amongst all good things is the least'.[75]

Essex's position was clear.[76] He took his stand upon the obligations of the contract, upon the defence of Protestantism, upon the distrust of any commitments from Spaniards, who acknowledged 'no faith with heretics'. But he was out of favour with his mistress and the peace party apparently dominated the situation. And yet peace was not made, not so long as Elizabeth lived.

According to Camden, in one of the last debates in the Council, Burghley turned on Essex and said that he breathed nothing but war, slaughter and blood; and, reaching out a Psalter, pointed silently to the 23rd verse of the 55th Psalm: 'The bloody and deceitful men shall not live out half their days.' Which, though certainly unfair, was, as Camden observes, prophetic and gave the old statesman the comfortable assurance that his position was supported by Holy Writ.

Burghley was certainly not for peace at any price, but it can hardly be imagined that in the summer of 1598 he put up a vigorous fight either for peace or for any-thing else. In July he began to fail rapidly. On the 10th he wrote to Robert the last letter he was to write in his own hand:[77]

'Though I know you count it your duty in nature so continually to show you careful of my state of health, yet were I also unnatural if I should not take comfort thereby, and to beseech God to bless you with supply of such blessings as I cannot in this infirmity yield you.

'Only I pray you diligently and effectually let her Majesty understand how her singular kindness doth overcome my power to acquit it who, though she will not be a mother, yet she showed herself by feeding me, with her own princely hand, as a careful nurse. And if I may be weaned to feed myself I shall be more ready to serve her on the earth. If not, I hope to be in heaven a servitor for her and God's church.

'And so I thank you for your partridges.'

He added in a postscript:

'Serve God by serving of the Queen, for all other service is indeed bondage to the devil.'

In the same month in which Elizabeth boxed the ears of Essex and bade him go and be hanged, she sat by Burghley's bedside and fed him with a spoon. Such were the wonderful ways of Good Queen Bess!

Nevertheless, Burghley was sitting in Council five days later. And in the last of all his surviving letters he is concerned not about his health but to comment on the stupidity of arrangements which sent Lincolnshire troops to Plymouth and Cornish troops to Bristol for embarkation.[78]

To the very end his primary concern was with the Queen's service.

There are two accounts of his last days, both of them written by members of his household.[79]

Towards the end he seems to have been much troubled by discontentment and grief of mind, 'which caused him oftentimes with tears to wish for death'. His anonymous biographer writes: 'His mind was troubled that he could not work on peace for his country which he earnestly laboured and most desired of anything, seeking to leave it as he had long kept it.' Camden and Clapham both say that towards the end he offered to resign all his offices, but the Queen would not hear of it.

Late in July he took to his bed, troubled with twinges of the gout but otherwise without continual pain.

On the evening of August 3rd he called his children (and his grandchildren) about him, he blessed them and took leave of them, commanding them to serve

s

and fear God and to love one another. He prayed for the Queen that she might yet live long and at last die in peace. He called Thomas Billott, his steward, to his bedside, and handed to him his Will, saying: 'I have ever found thee true to me and I now trust you with all.'

The chaplain bade him to remember his Saviour, to whom he replied that it was done already. For he was assured that God had forgiven him his sins and would save his soul. He repeated the Lord's Prayer in Latin.

At midnight his speech began to fail, but later he occasionally called for death: 'Oh, what a heart have I that will not die!' When he was almost gone, the physicians 'by infusion of hot waters into his mouth, temporarily revived him'. He rebuked them for calling him back. His last remembered words were 'The Lord have mercy upon me'. About seven in the morning, 'he mildly yielded up the ghost'.[80]

William Camden, who was a friend of Burghley's, years later wrote the most satisfying of all the shorter obituaries:[81]

'Certainly he was a most excellent man who, to say nothing of his reverend presence and undistempered countenance, was fashioned by nature and advanced with learning, a singular man for honesty, gravity, temperance, industry and justice. Hereunto was added a fluent and elegant speech, and that not affected but plain and easy, wisdom strengthened by experience and seasoned with exceeding moderation and most approved fidelity; but above all singular piety towards God. To speak in a word, the Queen was most happy in so great a Councillor and to his wholesome counsels the state of England for ever shall be beholden.'

BURGHLEY'S LAST AUTOGRAPH LETTER

NOTES

Titles to books referred to are abbreviated. The full title will be found in Read, *Bibliography of Tudor History*, 2nd ed. 1959, under the number indicated after R in parentheses. P.R.O. precedes documents located at the Public Record Office; B.M., documents in the British Museum.

Contemporary pamphlets are referred to by their number in the *Short Title Catalogue* (*S.T.C.*).

CHAPTER I

[1] *Cal. S.P. Scottish, 1569-71* (R 4924), 180.

[2] Ibid., 95.

[3] HAYNES, *Burghley Papers* (R 185), 575-6.

[4] *Cal. S.P. Scottish, 1569-71*, 99.

[5] Ibid., 101.

[6] LA MOTHE FÉNÉLON, *Correspondence* (R 813), iii, 100.

[7] According to Leicester, Cecil had the two Hertford boys in his own house. I have found no other evidence of this.

[8] *Cal. S.P. Spanish, 1568-79* (R 868), 262. He repeats the old story that Cecil had been accumulating money for years in Germany to provide for himself there.

[9] Ibid., 265.

[10] FÉNÉLON, iii, 123.

[11] LODGE, *Illustrations* (R 264), i, 505.

[12] FÉNÉLON, iii, 144ff.

[13] B.M., Cotton MSS., Caligula C ii, ff. 63-5.

[14] Cecil supplies a list of the councillors present at the meeting. They were Bacon, Northampton, Bedford, Clinton, Knollys, Cecil, Arundel, Leicester, Howard, Croft and Sadler.

[15] *Cal. S.P. Scottish, 1569-71*, 162.

[16] Ibid., 162-3.

[17] FÉNÉLON, iii, 169.

[18] Froude gives the date May 15th (x. 59) and the same date is given in *D.N.B.* art. Felton. But it was ten days later. Cf. POLLEN, *English Catholics* (R 2366), 153. There is a copy of the bull at Hatfield (*Cal. Salisbury MSS.* (R 185). De Spes sent a copy to Alva on May 10th (LETTENHOVE, *Relations Politiques* (R 923), v, 653).

[19] P.R.O., S.P. xii-75-58 with corrections in Cecil's hand. A fragment of it, entirely in his hand, is in B.M., Cotton MSS., Caligula B iv, ff. 235ff.

[20] FÉNÉLON, iii, 199, ibid., 187.

[21] Ibid., 188-9.

[22] *Cabala*, ed. 1691 (R 274), 165.

[23] *Cal. S.P. Scottish, 1569-71*, 183.

[24] One impelling factor was the termination of the Third Civil War in France. Early in August FÉNÉLON observed that the leaders of the Council feared that the King of France would now take a more aggressive position in Mary's behalf (iii, 295).

[25] *Cal. S.P. Scottish, 1569-71*, 244.

[26] FÉNÉLON, iii, 283.

[27] *Cal. S.P. Scottish, 1569-71*, 244, 282.

[28] Ibid., 328.

[29] Ibid., 330.

[30] FÉNÉLON, iii, 335. Lady Lennox also mentioned this admonition in a letter to Cecil of October 5th (*Cal. S.P. Scottish, 1569-71*, 372).

[31] On his sickness, cf. *Cal. S.P. Domestic, Addenda, 1566-79* (R 86), 319; FÉNÉLON, iii, 309, 314; *Cal. S.P. Scottish, 1569-71*, 351.

[32] *Cal. S.P. Spanish, 1568-79*, 280.

[33] *Cabala*, 167.

[34] *Cal. S.P. Scottish, 1568-71*, 302, 309, 351, 355.

[35] MURDIN, *Burghley Papers* (R 185), 770; cf. also CAMDEN, *Annals*, ed. 1635 (R 302), 128, who speaks of the journey as dangerous. The weather continued bad. On October 2nd Cecil wrote: 'We mean to prolong no time for, this morning, unlooked for, some winter entered into these freakish mountains, having a large snow fallen around us.' B.M., Additional MSS., 48049, f. 165v.

[36] HAYNES, 608-21. French versions are in LABANOFF, *Lettres* (R 5181), iii, 106; TEULET, *Relations Politiques* (R 4929), ii, 406.

[37] Copies of two letters, signed by Cecil and Mildmay, dated October 1st-2nd and October 5th are preserved in B.M., Additional MSS., 48049, 164ff. NARES, in his *Life of Burghley* (R 739), iii, 536ff., has printed extracts from them. The originals are missing.

[38] *Cal. S.P. Scottish, 1569-71*, 386.

[39] B.M., Additional MSS., 48049, f. 166; *Cal. S.P. Scottish, 1569-71*, 371.

[40] MURDIN, 770.

[41] *Cal. S.P. Scottish, 1569-71*, 387.

[42] On Mary's objections, cf. Leicester to Sussex, *Cal. S.P. Scottish, 1569-71*, 374.

[43] FÉNÉLON's comment (iii, 362) on their return was that Elizabeth was well satisfied with his mission.

[44] Cecil to Walsingham, April 7th, 1571, in DIGGES, *Compleat Ambassador* (R 803), 78.

CHAPTER II

[1] FÉNÉLON (iii, 275) describes him as *'très confidant du Secrétaire Cecil'*.

[2] DIGGES, I. FÉNÉLON (iii, 281) believed that Walsingham was to give more positive assurances to the Huguenots and to threaten the King that she and the Germans would help them if they were attacked.

[3] DIGGES, 8.

[4] READ, *Walsingham* (R 759), i, 99; cf. Sir T. Smith's discussion of the Anjou match in STRYPE, *Smith* (R 570), 184ff.

[5] FÉNÉLON, vii, 146.

[6] Cecil had indeed a remote connection with the Greys. His wife's brother had married Catherine Grey's cousin, *v.s.*, i, 278.

[7] FÉNÉLON, iii, 358.

[8] Ibid., iii, 417.

[9] MURDIN, 771.

[10] FÉNÉLON, iii, 462.

[11] Ibid., iv, 12.

[12] Ibid., iv, 45.

[13] DIGGES, 53.

[14] It is endorsed 1570, which might be any time in 1571 up to March 25th. *Cal. S.P. Foreign, 1569-71*, 383. The discourse ascribed to Bacon, printed in extenso in *Egerton Papers* (R 610) follows closely Cecil's line of reasoning and may be another version of his memorandum.

[15] As quoted in FROUDE, x, 128-9.

[16] The *Letters Patent* is in P.R.O., S.P. xii-77-17; cf. CAMDEN, ed. 1635, 132.

[17] P.R.O., S.P. xiv, 89, f. 7. Another copy is in the Bodleian Library, Rawlinson MSS., C404/169.

[18] DIGGES, 51.

[19] Ibid., 54.

[20] STRYPE, *Smith*, 72, says June 24th, *D.N.B.* art. Smith, July 13th.

[21] *Cal. S.P. Spanish, 1568-79*, 295.

[22] B.M., Lansdowne MSS., 102/84.

[23] Howard and Winchester were the other members, *Cal. S.P. Scottish, 1569-71*, 488.

[24] B.M., Cotton MSS., Caligula C ii, f. 88, 93.

[25] FÉNÉLON, iv, 20, 50.

[26] P.R.O., S.P. xii-66-42.

[27] FÉNÉLON, iv, 103.

[28] D'EWES, *Journals* (R 1037), 146.

[29] DIGGES, 94, undated but probably May 5th.

[30] A memorandum in his hand (P.R.O., S.P. xii-78-35) reveals that he was interested in a bill for developing arquebusiers and for strengthening fish-day regulations.

CHAPTER III

[1] P.R.O., S.P. xii-85-11. For intended publication, cf. LETTENHOVE, vi, 187. In 1595, in a discourse on the state of England (S.P. xii-255-84) Burghley wrote another account of the plot which adds nothing.

[2] Cf. correspondence of Fitzwilliam and Lee in LETTENHOVE, vi, *passim* and in *Cal. S.P. Domestic, Addenda, 1566-79*.

[3] Cf. *Cal. S.P. Foreign, 1581-82*, 574; LETTENHOVE, x, 702. Burghley himself testified that Herle was very well born, 'a gentleman of very good quality, wise, learned, of great experience . . . He has her Majesty's favour and is well known of her'. B.M., Lansdowne MSS., 21/15.

[4] LODGE, i, 526.

[5] MURDIN, 14.

[6] LODGE, i, 521.

[7] Burghley gave Fénélon a detailed account of Ridolfi's plans late in the month (*Correspondence*, iv, 160). Elizabeth in an interview with Fénélon in June revealed complete knowledge of Ridolfi's movements (ibid., iv, 144). On this occasion she quoted Machiavelli to him: 'The friendship of princes is adapted to their convenience.'

[8] Audley End — today one of the finest survivals of Elizabethan architecture.

[9] FROUDE, x, 291. Cf. Corbett to Leicester and Burghley, *Cal. Salisbury MSS.*, i, 521.

[10] MURDIN, 67. Among other papers a cipher between Leicester and Norfolk was found (*Cal. S.P. Domestic, Addenda, 1566-79*, 366).

[11] Probably the one in LABANOFF, *Lettres de Marie Stuart*, iii, 180.

[12] MURDIN, 148. The Catholic refugees abroad blamed Burghley for Norfolk's arrest (*Cal. S.P. Domestic, Addenda, 1566-79*, 358). Both FÉNÉLON (iv, 235) and De Spes (*Cal. S.P. Spanish, 1569-78*, 335) reported that the people of London flocked to acclaim Norfolk on his way to the Tower. Foot cloth was an ornamented cloth laid over the back of a horse and hanging down to the ground on either side.

[13] MURDIN, 152.

[14] LABANOFF, iii, 180ff.

[15] *Cal. S.P. Scottish, 1569-71*, 691, 701. FÉNÉLON reports that she was very angry at Norfolk (iv, 138).

[16] MURDIN, 99, 110.

[17] LETTENHOVE, vi, 187.

[18] Under the title *Salutem in Christo*, S.T.C., 11504.

[19] MURDIN, 158ff.

[20] FÉNÉLON, iv, 111.

[21] Cf. MURDIN, 18; cf. Ross's account of this in MURDIN, 54.

[22] Cf. MURDIN, 20-54.

[23] Ibid., 57.

[24] FÉNÉLON, iv, 292.

[25] *Cal. S.P. Spanish, 1568-79*, 348, 354.

[26] Cf. also his letters to Shrewsbury in LODGE, i, 521ff.

[27] MURDIN, 185. The letter, as dispatched in French, is in LETTENHOVE, v, 230.

[28] *Cal. S.P. Spanish, 1568-79*, 356. De Spes sent an account of the affair to Alva on December 14th.

[29] DIGGES, 161-2. Burghley gives a hint here of the Hawkins pretended conspiracy, which is set forth in full in WILLIAMSON, *Hawkins* (R 3190), 243ff. I have not dwelt upon it since Burghley took no active part in it.

[30] *Cal. S.P. Spanish, 1568-79*, 364.

[31] FROUDE, x, 311ff.

[32] The confessions of Mather and Berney are in MURDIN, 194-210. On the arrest of Borghese cf. LETTENHOVE, vi, 288.

[33] So CAMDEN says (*Annals*, 152), and so Burghley says in his diary (MURDIN, 772). Herle's letter is among Beale's papers, in B.M., Additional MSS. 48023.

[34] DIGGES, 164.

[35] Ibid., 166.

[36] *Cal. S.P. Spanish, 1568-79*, 375.

[37] A very full account of his trial is in HOWELL, *State Trials* (R 1645), i, 957ff.

[38] FÉNÉLON, iv, 346.

[39] HOWELL, i, 974ff.

[40] FÉNÉLON, iv, 350, 359.

[41] DIGGES, 164, 166.

[42] FÉNÉLON, iv, 391.

[43] By one account this attack came on the night of the 21st (LETTENHOVE, vi, 350), but Burghley wrote to Smith about it on the 20th (DIGGES, 199); FÉNÉLON, iv, 411-12. Sweveghem wrote to Alva, April 11th, that Elizabeth after her illness showed

more affection for Leicester than ever and contemplated marrying him (LETTENHOVE, vi, 373).

[44] This is puzzling since the attack seems to have lasted many days. Elizabeth told Fénélon she had been for five days in expectation of death.

[45] DIGGES, 199. Smith's quotation is an old Italian proverb: When the danger is past, the promises made to the saint for help are forgotten.

[46] Cf. NEALE, *Elizabeth I and her Parliaments* (R 1067), i, 242.

[47] Sweveghem wrote that rumour had it that Parliament was called to confirm Elizabeth's marriage to Leicester and to establish James of Scotland as successor (LETTENHOVE, vi, 373).

[48] HOWELL, i, 1035.

[49] MURDIN, 773.

[50] Ibid., 167, 169.

[51] But cf. FÉNÉLON, iv, 103, on his speech in the Lords (May 13th, 1571).

[52] NEALE, op. cit., i, 263.

[53] Ibid., i, 290.

[54] On May 23rd, NEALE, i, 263. Doubtless Burghley knew of it when he wrote on the 21st.

[55] B.M., Cotton MSS., Vespasian F vi, 64. The version in DIGGES, 203, is very faulty.

[56] DIGGES, 212, original missing.

[57] DIGGES, 219, undated but probably July 2nd.

[58] DIGGES, 203.

CHAPTER IV

[1] DIGGES, 58, cipher passages in italics. Arbitrary symbols are used in the cipher for proper names. The key to the cipher may be worked out from original dispatches in the P.R.O. and the Cotton MSS. (Vespasian F vi) but in a good many cases the only copy of the letter preserved is that printed in DIGGES, and his printing of passages in cipher is hopelessly inaccurate, as can be discovered by comparing cipher passages in Digges with the same passages in originals when they are preserved. When the originals are lacking, cipher passages in Digges are generally undecipherable.

[2] Ibid., 62, 66, 70, 72.

[3] READ, *Walsingham*, i, 27.

[4] FÉNÉLON seems to have had a hand in his selection and said that Burghley was well disposed to C. (*Correspondence*, iv, 5).

[5] DIGGES, 78, misdated March 7th, since the letter mentions the capture of Dumbarton (April 4th, 1571).

[6] FÉNÉLON, iv, 58.

[7] DIGGES, 87.

[8] READ, op. cit., i, 127-8.

[9] DIGGES, 87-8.

[10] READ, op. cit., i, 130.

[11] Cf. Leicester's interview with FÉNÉLON of May 2nd, *Correspondence*, iv, 85.

[12] DIGGES, 94, 100, 104. The original of p. 100 is missing. The text in Digges is obviously faulty, and in spots unintelligible.

[13] FÉNÉLON, vii, 233. According to the instruc-

tions which accompanied him, the French King had received a letter from Leicester to the effect that Elizabeth would allow Anjou the private use of his religion (ibid., vii, 228).

[14] DIGGES, 114-15.

[15] READ, op. cit., i, 141-2.

[16] DIGGES, 129.

[17] P.R.O., S.P., xii-80-17.

[18] READ, op. cit., i, 137, 143.

[19] DIGGES, 54.

[20] Ibid., 81.

[21] READ, op. cit., i, 152-3.

[22] DIGGES, 123; original in P.R.O., S.P. Foreign, Eliz. cxix.

[23] Ibid., 125, 129, 136.

[24] *Cal. S.P. Foreign, 1569-71*, 313. In Trinity College, Dublin (MG. 3.2.26; E. 1.34) are two copies in a seventeenth-century hand of a manuscript entitled 'Certain replies and objections answered by Wm. L. B. at the Council table' which contains a vigorous defence of the policy of assisting Louis of Nassau. It is so at variance with Burghley's attitude in the memorandum quoted that I cannot think the ascription of it to Burghley is correct. Another copy is in the B.M., Additional MSS., 12511, and in ibid. 48023, f. 18.

[25] FÉNÉLON, iv, 215.

[26] DIGGES, 133-4.

[27] P.R.O., S.P. 70-119, August 31st.

[28] FÉNÉLON, iv, 226.

[29] *Cal. S.P. Spanish, 1568-79*, 331.

[30] DIGGES, 134.

[31] P.R.O., S.P. 70-120, W. to B. October 8th, 1571, in cipher. The letters from B. to which W. alludes in this dispatch are missing.

[32] DIGGES, 138; the crucial word is in cipher, undeciphered, but the meaning seems plain.

[33] Ibid., 139, 146, 148.

[34] *Cal. S.P. Foreign, 1569-71*, 575.

[35] DIGGES, 152; the passages in italics are in cipher, undeciphered.

[36] . . . passage in cipher, undecipherable.

[37] DIGGES, 153.

[38] Fénélon said he tried in vain to get a copy, that they had been drafted by Burghley himself in conference with the Queen and Leicester, and that no one else had seen them.

[39] *Cal. S.P. Foreign, 1572-74*, 3, 11-13 FÉNÉLON asked for the suppression of Buchanan's book in December (*Correspondence*, iv, 301) and Elizabeth declared that it had been published in Scotland and in Germany but not in England (ibid., 305). A French translation was printed in Edinburgh in 1572 (*S.T.C.*, 3979).

[40] *Cal. S.P. Foreign, 1572-74*, 14.

[41] DIGGES, 164.

[42] FÉNÉLON, iv, 354.

[43] DIGGES, 165.

[44] FÉNÉLON, iv, 370.

[45] *Cal. S.P. Foreign, 1572-74*, 36, 39, 50, 65.

[46] FÉNÉLON, iv, 396, 407.

[47] *Cal. S.P. Foreign, 1572-74*, 65.

CHAPTER V

[1] READ, *Walsingham*, i, 177ff.

[2] *Cal. S.P. Scottish, 1571-74*, 1.

[3] So Burghley names them (DIGGES, 157). FÉNÉLON names seven, those named by Burghley plus Bedford and Howard (*Correspondence*, iv, 372).

[4] *Cal. S.P. Scottish, 1571-74*, 61.

[5] *Cal. S.P. Scottish, 1571-74*, 93, 100, 103.

[6] DIGGES, 154, 157.

[7] READ, *Walsingham*, i, 186.

[8] FÉNÉLON, vii, 288; iv, 392, 397.

[9] Ibid., iv, 401-2.

[10] LETTENHOVE, vi, 352. He wrote at the same time to Philip of Spain (*Cal. S.P. Spanish, 1568-79*, 376). Sweveghem suspected Burghley's sincerity. He wrote to Alva, April 11th, that the 'third person' of the De Guaras correspondence was William Meric, but that he believed that Burghley's approaches were 'a lie and a mockery'. (LETTENHOVE, vi, 372).

[11] LETTENHOVE, vi, 362.

[12] *Cal. S.P. Spanish, 1568-79*, 383, 379-80.

[13] FÉNÉLON, iv, 410, 415, 424.

[14] Cf. READ, *Walsingham*, i, 194.

[15] DIGGES, 203.

[16] B.M., Cotton MSS., Vespasian F vi, no. 19; DIGGES, 189.

[17] *Cal. S.P. Spanish, 1568-79*, 376.

[18] On the whole matter cf. J. B. BLACK, *Queen Elizabeth and the Sea Beggars* (R 931).

[19] B.M., Cotton MSS., Vespasian F vi, no. 19.

[20] Walsingham's letter is doubtless that of March 29th in DIGGES, 184. Walsingham's comment on La Marck is worth noting: 'I attended the dispatch of Count Louis' man, thinking to have sent by him, but after that he understood her Majesty had banished these lewd sea robbers, caused him to stay. And yet he meaneth to send you a gentleman to thank her Majesty for that undeserved favour she had showed to these lewd ministers.'

[21] FÉNÉLON, iv, 454, 461.

[22] B.M., Cotton MSS., Vespasian F vi, f. 64. The printed version in DIGGES, 203, is very defective.

[23] DIGGES, 202-4.

[24] LETTENHOVE, vi, 420. The Memorial bears no positive evidence of Burghley's authorship, but I agree with LETTENHOVE (vi, 420 n. 1) and with STÄHLIN (*Walsingham* (R 774), 478) in ascribing it to him.

[25] DIGGES, 212.

[26] Ibid., 216.

[27] LETTENHOVE, vi, 425. According to De Guaras he had recruited 300 men in May (*Cal. S.P. Spanish, 1568-79*, 391).

[28] LETTENHOVE, vi, 454n. FÉNÉLON, v, 43, reports his departure with 1000 soldiers on July 8th. Another report ascribes to him 1200 men (LETTENHOVE, vi, 458).

[29] *Cal. S.P. Spanish, 1568-79*, 397.

[30] FÉNÉLON, v, 43.

[31] LETTENHOVE, vi, 460.

[32] B.M., Cotton MSS., Vespasian F vi, 131.

[33] I accept this ascription of this letter in the *Cal. S.P. Domestic, 1547-80*, 449. The original (P.R.O., S.P. xii-89-3) is not signed or addressed in Burghley's hand.

[34] LETTENHOVE, vi, 486.

[35] Cf. J. B. BLACK, op. cit.

[36] Who went to France to receive the French King's formal signature to the treaty.

[37] DIGGES, 218. FÉNÉLON dwells long and lovingly upon the Queen's entertainment (*Correspondence*, v, 18, 20, 29).

[38] Doubtless the one printed in DIGGES, 214-15. Burghley's letter is undated in Digges, but can be fixed by Walsingham's acknowledgment. Cf. DIGGES, 219.

[39] B.M., Cotton MSS., Vespasian F vi, f. 111, 114. The version of these letters in DIGGES, 219-21, is very faulty. Digges for instance prints the French phrase, '*du plomb en son cerveau*' as '*de la plume en son cerveau*' which means just the opposite. Cf. STÄHLIN's note on this in *Walsingham*, 495 n. 3.

[40] FÉNÉLON, v, 45, 52, 53, 74. It appears later that the doctor was sent and the remedies were applied with some success (ibid., 159).

[41] DIGGES, 226-30.

[42] B.M., Harleian MSS., 6991, f. 4. The version presented in DIGGES, 225, is inaccurate.

[43] Cf. FÉNÉLON, vii, 303, 314.

CHAPTER VI

[1] FÉNÉLON, iv, 410.

[2] Ibid., 437. Some years later Leicester confirmed his refusal of the Lord Treasurership in an interview with the Earl of Northumberland, claiming that he had refused the Treasurership in Burghley's interest (B.M., Lansdowne MSS., 20, no. 38).

[3] P.R.O., S.P. xii-88-20, written by William Penson, Lancaster Herald. There is another copy of this document with some variation in B.M., Sloane MSS., 1786, f. 92b.

[4] MURDIN, 745, gives the date as July 13th, but the original in Cecil Papers, vol. 229, reveals that this is a misprint for 15. Cf. also MURDIN, 773. Holinshed (ed. 1586), iii, 1238, gives the date July 13th. Francis Thin, one of the authors of Holinshed, at this point inserts a history of the Lord Treasurer and follows it with a pedigree of William Cecil. In the letters patent creating Burghley Lord Treasurer (P.R.O., C.66/1090, memb. 14[28]) it is stated that his tenure of office dated from July 1st. The patent conferred upon him all rights, commodities, privileges, etc., of the office as they were in the terms of the four previous Treasurers, Dynham, Norfolk, Somerset and Winchester. In the patent the position is described as Treasurer of the Exchequer (*Thesaurarius Sccaij nostri*). The patent itself is dated at Woodstock September 15th.

[5] By procedure known as English Bill.

[6] HOLDSWORTH, *History of English Law* (R 1544), iv, 255.

[7] Ibid. It ought to be remarked, however, that there was a commensurate increase in the rolls of Common Pleas.

[8] Burghley's correspondence with Fanshaw on Exchequer matters is to be found in the Fanshaw Papers in the P.R.O., S.P. 46/18-20, 29-41, much of it in Burghley's own hand; after 1590 generally in the hand of Henry Maynard, Burghley's secretary. A few of his letters to Petrie, the Lord Treasurer's Remembrancer, are in P.R.O., E407/126, 129. Cf. also Decrees and Orders of the Exchequer, P.R.O., E123.

[9] B.M., Lansdowne MSS., 171, ff. 431r ff. At the end of this manuscript is the following note: 'Thus have I set out unto your good L. my own experience and observations both *magno scaccario* and *recept. scac.*, wherein I may perhaps have overscaped or mistaken some special matters. Yet most humbly I beseech your L. to accept my poor travail [so far as myself... have learned], conceived as your Lord. required by your letter. Ivy Lane, 9 Oct. 1572.'

[10] Cf. Burghley to Fanshaw, January 1st, 1595/6, P.R.O., S.P. 46/40.

[11] PECK, ii, 2.

[12] Bribes were offered, cf. Poddon to Burghley (P.R.O., S.P. xii-202-65) in which Poddon first promised Burghley £200 and raised the offer to £300 (July 28th, 1587).

[13] WOODWORTH, *Purveyance ... in the reign of Elizabeth* (R 1253), 3-5.

[14] Ibid., 13ff., 83.

[15] Cf. NEALE, *The Elizabethan Scene* (R 742).

[16] B.M., Cotton MSS., Vespasian F vi, f. 131.

[17] MURDIN, 773. The elaborate arrangements for this visit are set forth in *Cal. Salisbury MSS.*, xiii, 110. DIGGES, 231.

[18] B.M., Cotton MSS., Vespasian F vi, f. 131.

[19] *Cal. S.P. Spanish, 1568-79*, 403.

[20] FÉNÉLON, v, 78. There is nothing in the Spanish calendar to support Hume's statement (*Courtships of Queen Elizabeth* [R 709], 162) that Burghley gave a dinner for Le Mole. Fénélon mentions a dinner given by the Treasurer of the Household (*trésorier de la maison*, Sir Francis Knollys (FÉNÉLON, v, 97).

[21] Ibid., v, 88, 97.

[22] *Cal. Salisbury MSS.*, ii, 21; *Cal. S.P. Foreign, 1571-74*, 163.

[23] FÉNÉLON, v, 111.

[24] B.M., Cotton MSS., Vespasian F vi, f. 142. The version of this letter in DIGGES, 237, is full of blunders, the most obvious of which is the rendering of 'visage' as 'usage'.

[25] FÉNÉLON, v, 121.

[26] WRIGHT, i, 438; cf. also Archbishop Parker, in *Correspondence* (R 1737), 398.

[27] *Cal. S.P. Spanish, 1568-79*, 413.

[28] LODGE, i, 547.

[29] MURDIN, 224, dated September 10th, which must be too late since Killigrew left on the 7th. Robert Beale in some miscellaneous notes (B.M., Additional MSS., 48027, 707) said that Killigrew's instructions 'was written all with the hand of the Lord Treasurer in a Roman hand on one sheet of paper and signed with her Majesty's hand'. Beale also noted later (Additional MSS., 48027, f. 638): 'Mr. Henry Killigrew told me, R. B., that he being in Scotland and commissioned for her Majesty to deal with the Earl Morton, Regent, to receive her [Mary] home to execute her, but he would not.'

[30] This from Killigrew's dispatch of November 23rd, 1572, printed in TYTLER, *History of Scotland* vii, 467.

[31] B.M., Cotton MSS., Caligula C iii, f. 408.

[32] For FÉNÉLON's letters cf. *Correspondence*, v, 120-33; for Burghley's cf. DIGGES, 246, a letter signed by five members of the Council but composed by Burghley, as he himself admitted in his private letter to Walsingham of September 11th (B.M., Cotton MSS., Vespasian F vi, f. 148, printed very imperfectly in DIGGES, 246).

[33] FROUDE, x, 420.

[34] FÉNÉLON, v, 132.

[35] B.M., Cotton MSS., Vespasian F vi, 148.

[36] B.M., Cotton MSS., Vespasian F vi, 157 (in DIGGES, 246). Five councillors signed the letter, Burghley, Leicester, Knollys, Smith and Croft.

[37] In the Council's letter Burghley had written: 'It is her Majesty's desire that you were here from that place, and so her meaning is to devise for your revocation, but presently it cannot, without some breach of amity, be done.' Both Smith and Leicester wrote to Walsingham by the same post. Anent the massacre, Leicester wrote that Fénélon had assured him privately 'that this matter is not

the King's and that he doth detest it so much as he will make revenge upon it', which Leicester took with many grains of salt. Smith wrote that the English wine merchants were afraid to go to France. Both letters are in DIGGES, 251-2.

[38] B.M., Cotton MSS., Vespasian F vi, f. 150 (in DIGGES, 251, very imperfectly).

[39] DIGGES, 264.

[40] He went further than he was warranted. The most Catherine would offer was an interview at sea or in the Channel Islands, and Fénélon had to make his apologies to her later.

[41] FÉNÉLON, v, 137.

[42] B.M., Cotton MSS., Vespasian F vi, f. 205.

[43] FÉNÉLON, v, 155, 175, 202, 256.

[44] Cf. *Cal. S.P. Foreign, 1572-74,* 219. He appears to have applied some pressure to raise subscriptions for Montgomery (PARKER, *Correspondence,* 420).

[45] Ibid., 292, 310, 345.

[46] The original of the last half of this letter is preserved in B.M., Cotton MSS., Vespasian F vi, f. 9. Both halves are printed in DIGGES, not without many inaccuracies.

[47] Vespasian F vi, f. 185. The words in italics are in cipher; blank spaces indicate symbols which I have not been able to decipher. Cf. STÄHLIN'S note on this in his *Walsingham,* i, 599 n. 2. La Torrey is probably to be identified with the Count de Thoré, the youngest of the Montmorenci brothers.

[48] READ, *Walsingham,* i, 246.

[49] B.M., Cotton MSS., Vespasian F vi, f. 205.

[50] Ibid., f. 207.

[51] B.M., Cotton MSS., Vespasian F vi, f. 222, 255, 261.

[52] WRIGHT, i, 451.

[53] *Cal. S.P. Foreign, 1572-74,* 234.

[54] B.M., Cotton MSS., Vespasian F vi, f. 327, in cipher. Cipher passages in italics. Walsingham's letter of the 20th appears to be missing.

[55] DIGGES, 306.

[56] B.M., Cotton MSS., Vespasian F vi, f. 259. Cf. also Vespasian F vi, f. 271 (DIGGES, 327). Cf. Walsingham's reply in *Cal. S.P. Foreign, 1572-74,* 232, 253, 264.

[57] B.M., Cotton MSS., Vespasian F vi, f. 271.

[58] I find no mention of the matter in Fénélon's dispatches.

[59] *S.T.C.,* 7601. The author has never been identified. He speaks of himself in the preface of the English edition as having intended originally to publish it in another tongue, and as a foreigner who had lived thirty years in England and as having been present at Elizabeth's coronation. But it would be unsafe to take him at his word. For two Scottish suspects, cf. *Cal. Salisbury MSS.,* ii, 46; *Cal. S.P. Foreign, 1571-74,* 484, 492, 505, 513, 535. On Sir Thomas Wilson's search for the author in the Low Countries, cf. LETTEN-HOVE, vii, 386, 397, 433. Elizabeth issued a proclamation against the book in September 1573 (STEELE, *Proclamations* (R 1017), i, 74) which Burghley himself drafted (*Cal. S.P. Scottish, 1574-81,* 553). Evidently Burghley at one time contemplated

a reply; cf. his copious notes on the subject in *Cal. S.P. Scottish, 1574-81,* 554-61. WARD (*Oxford* (R 786)) asserts that the author was Henry Howard and promised to prove it from B.M. G5443, 2 and P.R.O., S.P. xii-147-4, 6. The references he cites furnish no proof.

[60] FÉNÉLON, vi, 163.

[61] Sweveghem had returned to the Low Countries in May 1572.

[62] The French ambassador speaks of a San Victor (FÉNÉLON, v, 163) probably the Baptista Vitores who had served De Spes. Cf. *Cal. S.P. Spanish, 1568-79,* 249, 351n.

[63] *Cal. S.P. Spanish, 1568-79,* 417; LETTEN-HOVE, vi, 525.

[64] In the same letter De Guaras observed that the Queen had 8000 men and ships ready in case Orange should prevail. He added that they had already sent Orange £20,000.

The question of whether Elizabeth actually loaned money to Orange at this time is difficult to answer. Fogaza wrote in September that she had sent £30,000 to Orange and planned to send another £36,000 (*Cal. S.P. Spanish, 1568-79,* 415). Again in October he wrote that Killigrew was taking 200,000 crowns to Orange, though Killigrew was certainly in Scotland at the time (ibid., 428). FÉNÉLON wrote on November 9th (*Correspondence,* v, 196-7) that the Queen had given orders to send 66,000 crowns to Orange, but that she changed her mind after his collapse. There is nothing on the subject in English sources. If we may judge from a long report which William Herle, one of Burghley's agents (the same who had helped unravel the Ridolfi Plot), made of a conference with Orange (LETTENHOVE, vi, 764), Orange had been hopeful of receiving assistance in the autumn of 1572 but had been disappointed, which conforms in the main to Fénélon's appraisal of the situation.

[65] *Cal. S.P. Spanish, 1568-79,* 422.

[66] *Cal. S.P. Spanish, 1568-79,* 423-4.

[67] Printed in full in LETTENHOVE, vi, 613, where it is conjecturally dated January 1573. It is obviously the memorandum to which De Guaras referred in his letter of October 12th.

[68] LETTENHOVE, vi, 642.

[69] Burghley set forth his position in a long memorandum which is printed in full in LETTEN-HOVE, vi, 642, where it is conjecturally dated February 1573, though in the course of the discourse Burghley himself dates it at the beginning of October 1572 (ibid., 644).

[70] LETTENHOVE, vi, 646-7.

[71] *Cal. S.P. Spanish, 1568-79,* 525.

[72] Ibid., 427, 434.

[73] DIGGES, 268-9.

[74] *Cal. S.P. Spanish, 1568-79,* 428.

[75] Ibid., 435-7.

[76] Ibid., 437. From Alva's acknowledgment of the receipt of this draft (LETTENHOVE, vi, 615), it is quite clear that the memorandum is that one misdated March 1573 and printed in LETTENHOVE, vi, 675. Making allowance for the different language, Alva quotes virtually verbatim passages from Burghley's memo.

[77] Alva's deliberations with his Council on the subject may be followed in LETTENHOVE, vi, 600, 601n., 618. Evidently his Council took a tough stand at first and it was Alva himself who decided to accept Burghley's terms.

[78] Cal. S.P. Spanish, 1568-79, 444, 448, 451.

[79] It is to be noted that nine letters of De Guaras in December, January and February, published in Lettenhove are not included in the Spanish Calendar. Some thirty-six of De Guaras's letters dispatched during the rest of the year 1573, given in Lettenhove, are also omitted. On the final discussion and difficulties cf. LETTENHOVE, vi, 692.

[80] The final form of the agreement, in Latin, is in S.P. 70-126, ff. 182-4v.

[81] WRIGHT, ii, 444; B.M., Harleian MSS., 6991, f. 15.

CHAPTER VII

[1] Quoted in FROUDE, x, 442.

[2] Reference to the proposal to make him Bishop of Rochester under Edward VI.

[3] ELLIS, Original Letters, 3rd series, iii, 375n.

[4] Froude's account of Knox's final days is Froude at his best. Cf. x, 454ff.

[5] Cal. S.P. Scottish, 1571-74, 272.

[6] B.M., Cotton MSS., Vespasian F vi, f. 205; a faulty version in DIGGES, 283.

[7] There was, as usual, talk of poisoning, but Burghley was probably right.

[8] Cal. S.P. Scottish, 1571-74, 440.

[9] MURDIN, 230-4.

[10] DIGGES, 289, 293, 296.

[11] Cal. S.P. Scottish, 1571-74, 478, 486.

[12] WRIGHT, i, 456.

[13] DIGGES, 315, 334; Cal. S.P. Scottish, 1571-74, 485.

[14] Cf. Cal. S.P. Scottish, 1571-74, 460, 487, 495, 512, 514, 520.

[15] FÉNÉLON, v, 308-10.

[16] Cf. Cal. S.P. Scottish, 1571-74, 499.

[17] Cal. S.P. Scottish, 1571-74, 562, 565, 569. Killigrew says he was well liked and Drury says he was well behaved. The Regent made much of him.

[18] Cal. S.P. Scottish, 1571-74, 573.

[19] RUSSELL, Maitland (R 5266), 501, gives date as 11th or 12th; D.N.B., art. Maitland, gives it as the 9th, which is more probable, since Burghley had heard of it on the 14th.

[20] LODGE, ii, 26.

CHAPTER VIII

[1] In Parker's correspondence relatively few letters from Burghley seem to have survived, either among Parker's papers in Corpus Christi College, Cambridge, or elsewhere.

[2] B.M., Cotton MSS., Caligula C iii, f. 234, in Burghley's hand. I have used the condensed version in Cal. S.P. Scottish, 1572-74, 273-4. Words in brackets are conjectural.

[3] POLLEN, English Catholics in the Reign of Elizabeth (R 2366), iii, and MEYER, England und die k. Kirche (R 2356), (trans. McKee), 65.

[4] v.s., p. 316; cf. NEALE, Elizabeth I and her Parliaments, i, 192ff.

[5] PARKER, Correspondence (R 1737), 478. DR. H. C. PORTER in his recent book, Reformation and Reaction in Tudor Cambridge, throws much light upon Burghley's attitude towards Puritanism at Cambridge University.

[6] PARKER, Correspondence, 246, 263.

[7] Cf. KNAPPEN, Tudor Puritanism (R 2433), 208.

[8] Cecil was not yet Burghley, but to avoid confusion I have called him so.

[9] Cf. PEARSON, Cartwright (R 2437), 25ff.

[10] P.R.O., S.P. xii-73-4.

[11] September 25th, 1570.

[12] The letter is printed in PEARSON, appendix vii.

[13] So PARKER designated him (Correspondence, 410).

[14] D.N.B. art. Dering. Dering's letter is in B.M., Lansdowne MSS., 12, 86. It is printed in STRYPE's Parker, iii, 219-20.

[15] v.s. i, 137.

[16] P.R.O., S.P. xii-85-75.

[17] STRYPE, Annals, iv, 483.

[18] 1 Timothy, v, 1.

[19] Romans, xii, 16.

[20] STRYPE, Annals, iv, 487.

[21] NEALE, op. cit., i, 295-6.

[22] STRYPE, Parker, ii, 102.

[23] NEALE, op. cit., i, 354.

[24] PARKER, Correspondence, 397.

[25] Ibid., 418, 437.

[26] STEELE, i, 687, 689.

[27] B. M., Cotton MSS., Titus B ii, f. 249. Printed with a few minor inaccuracies in STRYPE, Parker, ii, 350 ff.

[28] READ, Walsingham, ii, 265.

[29] PARKER, Correspondence, 479.

[30] v.s., i, 271.

[31] NEALE, op. cit., i, 99.

[32] Cf. DIXON, Church of England (R 1780), v, 390.

[33] HAYNES, 582ff.

[34] B.M., Lansdowne MSS., 104, nos. 11 and 12. Both of them are in Burghley's hand, undated. STRYPE dates the first in October, the second in September 1572. He prints the first in Annals, iii, 305, and the second in Parker, ii, 205. I have accepted Strype's dating, but have found no positive evidence to justify it.

[1] The best account of his work on Burghley House, by Christopher Hussey, is in *Country Life*, December 3rd, 1953, pp. 1828ff.; December 10th, pp. 1962ff. These two sections, of an article in five parts, cover the history of Burghley House in William Cecil's time. Its subsequent history is followed in three sections (*Country Life*, December 17th, 24th, 31st, 1953), bringing the story down to the present. All the articles are magnificently illustrated.

[2] STOW's *London*, ed. Kingsford, ii, 98.

[3] Cited by GOTCH, *Houses of the Cecils*, 55. There is some account of Cecil House in CUNNINGHAM, *Handbook of London*, i, 171.

[4] MURDIN, 752.

[5] He purchased land for enlarging his garden from the Earl of Bedford in 1566. Cf. *v.s.* i, 352. Cecil House was burned in 1627. The Lyceum Theatre stands upon part of its site.

[6] Cf. Salisbury MSS., i, 274; *Victoria County History, Herts.* iii, 447; MURDIN, 369. An interesting account, preserved in Cecil Papers, vol. 143, records his land purchases in Herts., in connection with Theobalds, beginning with the fee farm of Theobalds and ending in 1583. The total spent comes to £12,295 18s. 3d.

[7] Virtually everything I say about Theobalds I have learned from John Summerson, Curator of the Soane Museum, particularly from the paper which he read before the Society of Antiquaries in December 1954 and of which he was good enough to present me with a manuscript copy before it was published. He has also given me a drawing of what he thinks Theobalds looked like which was published in the *Listener*, March 31st, 1955.

[8] We can trace in Burghley's household books, preserved at Hatfield, from 1566 to 1578, his mounting expenditures. In 1566-67 it is a mere £120. During the four succeeding years it rises from £1200 to £1500. Altogether, including the land, Theobalds cost him about £25,000.

[9] Cf. Burghley's diary, in MURDIN, 747ff.

[10] PECK, *Desiderata Curiosa*, 33. Accounts are preserved at Hatfield (Box G 16) of the royal visits for fourteen days from May 24th to June 6th, 1575, and for three days from May 15th to 18th, 1578. These accounts include kitchen and cellar and woodyard charges (i.e. meat, drink and fuel), rewards to the Queen's officers and the hire of extra help and extra equipment. In 1575 the total bill was £340 17s. 4d.; in 1578, £337 7s. 5d. I find no figures to justify the costs estimated by the anonymous biographer. We have a fairly full account of the Queen's entertainment for ten days at Theobalds, May 10th to 20th, 1591, which totals £998 13s. 4d., to which must be added, as Burghley himself added it in the endorsement, 'For a gown for the Queen, £100' (P.R.O., S.P. xii-238-157).

[11] Summerson MSS., 15. On Hawthorn *v.* Summerson, ibid.

[12] PECK, 34.

[13] SINGLETON, *The Shakespeare Garden*, 27.

[14] Cf. Summerson plan.

[15] On his household expenses cf. PECK, 28; READ, *Household Accounts* (R 4090).

[16] PECK, 32.

[17] HURSTFIELD, *The Queen's Wards*, 249.

[18] *v.s.*, i, 426.

[19] Edward Manners, 3rd Earl; cf. *D.N.B.*; born 1549.

[20] At Queen's College, Cambridge, when he was nine years old. Subsequently he transferred to St. John's, Cambridge.

[21] Cf. *Cambridge Bibliography of English Literature*, i, 546. The most pretentious of the various advocates of Oxford in this connection is *This Star of England* by CHARLTON and DOROTHY OGBURN, New York, 1952. They do not hesitate to quote Shakespeare as evidence on obscure points of Oxford's career. Their idea of what constitutes valid historical evidence is widely at variance with my own.

[22] Cited in WARD (R 786), 20.

[23] WARD, 32-3.

[24] MURDIN, 764.

[25] Cecil Papers, ix, f. 92, undated.

[26] WARD, 40.

[27] He was born April 12th, 1550, and took part in the procession to Parliament, as hereditary Great Chamberlain, April 2nd, 1571, not quite twenty-one; but there was no requirement before 1685 that a peer must have reached his majority before he took his seat (PIKE, *House of Lords* (R 1093), 275.

[28] Cited in WARD, 56; cf. FÉNÉLON, iv, 89, 156, 312. DIGGES, 152.

[29] Cf. Hatton's letter, cited in WARD, 75.

[30] Cited in WARD, 61.

[31] Cf. her epitaph, printed in WARD, 286. Apparently no portrait of her survives.

[32] *v.s.*, i, 436-8.

[33] Ann was born December 5th, 1556 (*Cal. Salisbury MSS.*, v, 69).

[34] *Cal. Rutland MSS.*, i, 95.

[35] Cf. for example Rutland's letters to Burghley from the north in 1569, in *Cal. S.P. Domestic, Addenda, 1566-79, passim*. It is worth noting that when Rutland, having reached his majority, set forth for France in 1571, he turned to Burghley for counsel, and Burghley wrote him a long letter of advice which is preserved in P.R.O., S.P. xii-77-6.

[36] FÉNÉLON, iv, 315, 319. It was rumoured by one letter writer that the marriage was originally planned for September (WARD, 63). On the basis of this rumour the Ogburns argue that Oxford ran away and had to be fetched back. Their supporting evidence is from *All's Well that Ends Well*. Op. cit., 161ff.

[37] DIGGES, 164.

[38] Frances Vere married Henry Howard. Frances Vere was Oxford's paternal aunt; Howard was Norfolk's father.

[39] P.R.O., S.P. Domestic, Addenda, xxi, 23.

[40] P.R.O., S.P. xii-95-92, cited in WARD, 66.

[41] FÉNÉLON, iv, 312; cited in WARD, 66.

[42] WARD, 67, citing S.P., xii-151-46-9.

[43] WARD, 76, citing B.M., Lansdowne MSS., 14, no. 85.

[44] Cecil Papers, ix, f. 92.

[45] S.P. xii-151-45. Cf. also Henry Howard's letter to Elizabeth in B.M., Cotton MSS., Titus C v, f. 6v, ff.

[46] LODGE, *Illustrations*, ii, 16.

[47] There is, however, no sound proof that he was Elizabeth's paramour and that the Earl of Southampton was their illegitimate son, as the Ogburns in *This Star of England* maintain.

[48] The story can be followed in LETTENHOVE, vi, in the correspondence of De Guaras and Alva. Cf. also Ralph Lane to Burghley in *Cal. Salisbury MSS.*, ii, 68. Sir Edward Seymour, son of the Protector, was also involved.

[49] *Cal. S.P. Foreign, 1571-74*, 532.

[50] B.M., Harleian MSS., 6991, f. 82.

[51] WARD, 94.

[52] *Cal. S.P. Domestic, Addenda, 1566-79*, 469.

[53] WRIGHT, i, 507.

[54] B.M., Harleian MSS., 6991, f. 100 — misquoted in WARD.

[55] P.R.O., S.P. xii-98-2.

[56] This letter is not dated or addressed or signed, but it appears in a copy book of Walsingham's correspondence (P.R.O., S.P. xii-45) and its subject matter makes it probable that Burghley was the recipient. Cited in WARD, 97.

[57] These arrangements were apparently made when Oxford contemplated a trip overseas in the autumn of 1573. I have presumed that they were unchanged. Cf. WARD, 92. It seems likely that the document alluded to in *Cal. Salisbury MSS.*, ii, 170, which is given there a conjectural date of 1577, belongs to 1575 before Oxford left.

[58] Cecil Papers, ix, f. 91.

[59] Cited in WARD, 102.

[60] Ibid., 104.

[61] Ibid., 112. The portrait in question is probably the one reproduced in Ward. Another alleged portrait of Oxford, in the possession of the Duke of St. Albans, is reproduced, as the frontispiece, in *This Star of England*. It has been dismissed by an official of the National Portrait Gallery as too old, too early.

[62] WARD, 110.

[63] *Cal. S.P. Foreign, 1575-77*, 294.

[64] Cf. LETTENHOVE, viii, 339, and Burghley's letter of April 15th, 1576 (ibid., 340 n. 1). The French ambassador wrote April 21st, 1576, that Oxford had been stripped naked, and only escaped with his life because a Scotsman had recognized him (P.R.O. *Baschet Transcripts*, bundle 27).

[65] Note that WARD's account (p. 116) at this point is at variance with Burghley's.

[66] *Cal. Salisbury MSS.*, ii, 131-2.

[67] Cf. Master's letter of November 7th, 1575, cited in WARD, 115.

[68] This I think is the most probable explanation of Burghley's obscure statement about the matter in Cecil Papers, cxl, f. 15, quoted in *Cal. Salisbury MSS.*, xiii, 144.

[69] B.M., Lansdowne MSS., 102/2 — unsigned but in Burghley's hand.

[70] Cecil Papers, ix, f. 8, holograph.

[71] Cited in WARD, 126. WARD says that Oxford made a settlement at this time, citing as evidence *Cal. Salisbury MSS.*, ii, 170; an examination of the original in Cecil Papers, ix, f. 91, makes it clear that the document refers to a settlement made before Oxford's departure overseas. It speaks of saving some of the moneys allotted to his wife to maintain himself 'to provide necessary things for his *household against his return*'.

[72] WARD, 127.

[73] WARD, 232. Ann wrote an appealing letter to her husband on December 7th, 1581. Oxford seems to have received it and replied to it, for Ann wrote a second letter to him on December 12th. Copies of both of Ann's letters survive in Burghley's hand (B.M., Lansdowne MSS., 104, nos. 63, 64). Ward prints both of them (pp. 226-7) but without noting Burghley's connection with them. There is no way of telling whether Burghley himself drafted these letters, as seems likely, or merely copied them for his files. In any case it is very hard for any modern father to understand how Burghley could, under the circumstances, have written or even sanctioned the writing of letters from a favourite daughter to a man who had grievously wronged her.

[74] WARD, 245.

CHAPTER X

[1] READ, *Walsingham*, i, 275.

[2] FÉNÉLON, v, 351, 360, 382, 396, 403, 407, 422, 437.

[3] *Cal. S.P. Foreign, 1572-74*, 413.

[4] LETTENHOVE, vii, 6.

[5] FÉNÉLON, v, 469.

[6] *A.P.C.*, viii, 71-5.

[7] Bodleian Library, Carte MSS., 55/130-1.

[8] P.R.O., S.P., xii-45-60.

[9] MURDIN, 776.

[10] FÉNÉLON, vi, 177.

[11] *v.s.*, p. 63.

[12] FÉNÉLON, vi, 217.

[13] WRIGHT, i, 505.

[14] WRIGHT, ii, 3.

[15] FÉNÉLON, vi, 206.

[16] The statement is interesting. Among his debts to Spain Leicester enumerated:
(1) Deliverance of himself and his two brothers from prison [during Mary's reign].
(2) Restoration of his paternal inheritance.
(3) Giving him a command at St. Quentin.
(4) Offering him a pension on Elizabeth's accession.
(5) Promoting, through his ambassador De Quadra, his aspirations to marry Elizabeth.
FÉNÉLON, vi, 220ff.

¹⁷ B.M., Harleian MSS., 6991, f. 92.

¹⁸ P.R.O., S.P. xii-98-2.

¹⁹ Cf. CAMDEN, 178.

²⁰ FÉNÉLON, vi, 206.

²¹ *Cal. S.P. Domestic, Addenda, 1568-79*, 447-9.

²² So described by De Guaras in LETTENHOVE, vi, 696, 715.

²³ LETTENHOVE (vi, Introduction, i) maintains that he was a prime mover in the matter, but cites no evidence. The governor of the Merchant Adventurers, John Mersh, wrote to Burghley on September 3rd that Lee had made an offer of £74 apiece to the mariners who carried Story over (ibid., vi, 5n.).

²⁴ This correspondence is preserved in *S.P. Domestic, Addenda* and is printed rather fully in *Cal. S.P. Domestic, Addenda, 1566-79*, 338ff. Some of the letters are printed *in extenso* in LETTENHOVE, vi, *passim*.

²⁵ But in another letter Lee charged Wingfield and the Countess of Northumberland (*Cal. Salisbury MSS.*, ii, 26).

²⁶ John Engle, a friend, wrote to Burghley asking him what to do about these papers, 'if Lee do not come out as I trust he shall'. (LETTENHOVE, vi, 588).

²⁷ Cf. the correspondence of De Guaras and Alva in LETTENHOVE, vi, 696, 715, 717, 737. None of this is printed in *Cal. S.P. Spanish*.

²⁸ LETTENHOVE, vi, 756.

²⁹ Radcliffe, presuming far upon his high connections, slipped over to England late in 1575 and conferred with Burghley. Burghley informed the Queen and she sent him word by Walsingham to advise Radcliffe to slip away, 'for otherwise you doubt that her Majesty (as in justice she is bound) shall be driven for example's sake to punish him' (B.M., Harleian MSS., 6992, f. 23).

³⁰ Copley was a Surrey gentleman, distantly related to Elizabeth and a second cousin to Lady Burghley. There is an excellent life of Copley in the introduction to *Letters of Thomas Copley* (R 2248). He had sat for Gatton borough in the House of Commons in three of Mary's Parliaments and the first two Parliaments of Elizabeth.

³¹ P.R.O., S.P. xii-94-16. The original is endorsed by Burghley, 'A copy of my letter to Thos. Copley by Dr. Wilson'.

³² *v.s.*, i, 465.

³³ *Letters of Thomas Copley* (R 2248), 47.

³⁴ B.M., Harleian MSS., 6991, f. 216.

³⁵ Ibid., f. 110, printed in LETTENHOVE, vii, 403n.

³⁶ *A.P.C.*, viii, 332.

³⁷ The story is told at length in STRYPE'S *Smith*, 100ff. and appendix vii.

³⁸ It appears in the Patent Rolls, Elizabeth, under date 17th Eliz., February 14th.

³⁹ B.M., Harleian MSS., 6991, f. 112.

⁴⁰ The terms of the grant are set forth at length in B.M., Harleian MSS., 215, f. 62. The patent itself is in P.R.O., C66-1130 m.31 (11).

⁴¹ Cf. TAWNEY, *Wilson's Discourses* (R 2955),

150ff.; DE ROOVER, *Gresham on Exchange* (R 2944), 210ff.

⁴² *Tudor Economic Documents* (R 2539), ii, 169. The Privy Council had appointed a commission to hear the complaints of these merchants on November 25th, 1576. The commission included Sir Thomas Gresham and five others. It was to the commission that the Italians addressed the protest in question (*A.P.C.*, ix, 234).

⁴³ William Herle, on October 18th, 1576, wrote to Burghley an account of his interview with two Italian bankers on the subject (LETTENHOVE, viii, 482).

⁴⁴ DE ROOVER, *Gresham on Exchange*, 218.

⁴⁵ Father of the favourite.

⁴⁶ P.R.O., S.P. xii-103-26.

^{46a} Reading confirmed by Mr. Blakiston at the P.R.O., who suggests that St. George's four nights refers to the four days between the date of the letter (April 19th) and St. George's Day (23rd), the sense being perhaps, 'if I get four good nights' rest'.

⁴⁷ P.R.O., S.P. xii-103-31.

⁴⁸ Cf. *Languet-Sidney Correspondence*; London, 1845.

⁴⁹ P.R.O., S.P. xii-103-41.

⁵⁰ Parker was already dead (May 17th) when this letter was written.

⁵¹ Alexander Nowell.

⁵² P.R.O., S.P. xii-103-48.

⁵³ May 24th, 1575, at Theobalds; cf. MURDIN, 776.

⁵⁴ P.R.O., S.P. xii-103-63, holograph.

⁵⁵ Cf. Summerson's manuscript on Theobalds, p. 6. In May Leicester wrote to Burghley: 'I have to thank your L. also very heartily, perceiving by H. Hawthorn that your L. is pleased to help me that I may have some stone towards making a little banquetting house in my garden.' (B.M., Harleian MSS., 6992, f. 5).

⁵⁶ P.R.O., S.P. xii-103-68.

⁵⁷ He was about to succeed La Mothe Fénélon as French ambassador to England.

⁵⁸ P.R.O., S.P. xii-105-24.

⁵⁹ *Cal. Salisbury MSS.*, ii, 154.

⁶⁰ LODGE, ii, 52.

⁶¹ LABANOFF, iv, 369.

⁶² *Cal. Salisbury MSS.*, ii, 111.

⁶³ B.M., Harleian MSS., 6992, f. 21.

⁶⁴ Burghley was recognized as head of the Customs (*Cal. Salisbury MSS.*, ii, 130).

⁶⁵ B.M., Cotton MSS., Titus B ii, f. 233.

⁶⁶ FÉNÉLON, vi, 15, 35, 41, 56.

⁶⁷ Cf. Dale to Burghley, May 22nd, *Cal. S.P. Foreign, 1571-74*, 563.

⁶⁸ *Cal. S.P. Foreign, 1571-74*, 506.

⁶⁹ READ, *Walsingham*, i, 286.

⁷⁰ *Cal. S.P. Foreign, 1571-74*, 569.

⁷¹ READ, *Walsingham*, i, 285.

⁷² *Cal. S.P. Foreign, 1575-77*, 75.

⁷³ Cf. Harvey's letters in LETTENHOVE, vii, 575ff. Harvey wrote to Burghley on October 9th that of the money sent over, 600 angels were light weight, but he hopes they would 'be put out without loss'. LETTENHOVE, vii, 595; cf. also ibid., 260, and *Cal. S.P. Foreign, 1575-77*, 96, 118.

[74] P.R.O., S.P. xii-105-45.

[75] SHILLINGTON and CHAPMAN, *Commercial Relations, England and Portugal* (R 3011), 141; WILLIAMSON, *Hawkins* (R 3190), 38.

[76] Continuing Bishopgate Street, without. Probably the garden was the one called Spinola's Pleasure. Cf. STOW, *London* (ed. Kingsford), (R 4591), ii, 288.

[77] P.R.O., S.P. xii-105-45. For Burghley's earlier negotiations on the subject, *v.s.*, i, 428-9.

[78] In HOLINSHED, 2nd ed., iii, 1261: 'On Michelmas even at night the like impression of fire and smoke were seen in the air to flash out of the northeast, north and northwest.' Cf. FÉNÉLON, vi, 298, for other manifestations.

[79] Walsingham signed for England; Giraldi, the Portuguese ambassador, for Portugal.

[80] LETTENHOVE, vii, 526, 533, 597.

[81] Cf. LETTENHOVE, vi, 778.

[82] In 1578, when Secretary Wilson was casting about for a secret agent to send to the Low Countries, he wrote to Walsingham: 'I have thought of Herle, but he will fill our heads here with such variety of uncertain truths as I dare not adventure upon him' (LETTENHOVE, x, 703).

[83] LETTENHOVE, vi, 764, 778.

[84] Ibid., vi, 835, 843.

[85] LETTENHOVE, vii, 65, 69, 77, 89, 146.

[86] Ibid., vi, 592, 640, 740.

[87] Ibid., vii, 92, 109.

[88] MOTLEY, *Rise of the Dutch Republic* (R 940), iii, 10-13.

[89] LETTENHOVE, vii, 47, 477-9.

[90] This I gather from a letter which Rogers carried to Walsingham from Orange, dated April 17th, and another letter which he carried to Burghley, dated May 21st (LETTENHOVE, vii, 490, 510).

[91] Ibid., vii, 531.

[92] MOTLEY, op. cit., iii, 26.

[93] One of them was Count Coulemberg who, after Orange himself, was listed first among the rebels by Philip II. Cf. LETTENHOVE, vii, 489, 563n.

[94] Cf. LETTENHOVE, viii, 15, and *Cal. S.P. Foreign, 1575-77*, 425. Lettenhove's version gives £1000 for the Dutch revenues in mistake for £100,000.

[95] LETTENHOVE, vii, 598. This version does not coincide exactly with that in *Cal. S.P. Foreign, 1575-77*, 158. The advice to consult with nobles, etc. is not in LETTENHOVE.

[96] LETTENHOVE, viii, 2ff., 10ff.

[97] The draft of Corbett's is in B.M., Cotton MSS., Galba C v; those of Cobham and Hastings in P.R.O.

[98] WRIGHT, ii, 32. *Cal. S.P. Spanish, 1568-79*, 515.

[99] LODGE, ii, 60.

[100] B.M., Cotton MSS., Galba C v, f. 86; dated January 16th, 1575/6; printed in full in LETTENHOVE, viii, 121, but not quite accurately. The original is slightly damaged by fire.

[101] The phraseology is obscure, 'imparting the weightiness hereof to the chiefest of the next parliament'. It seems to suggest the sort of committee which Burghley had suggested earlier. The question was raised later by a private member in the H. of C. and called forth a rebuke from Sir J. Croft, a Privy Councillor (LETTENHOVE, viii, 249).

[102] Burghley's lucubrations (in holograph) on this subject are set forth in a memorandum entitled 'Consideration of the Case with the Hollanders', dated January 20th, 1575/6. B.M., Cotton MSS., Galba C v, f. 88, printed with many mistakes in LETTENHOVE, viii, 127. Indeed the Lettenhove version combines the Galba MS. with part of another manuscript of Burghley's dated January 21st, in LETTENHOVE, viii, 130.

[103] These are in Burghley's hand among the papers of Robert Beale (B.M., Additional MSS., 48084, ff. 24ff.). Internal evidence indicates that they belong about the beginning of 1576 (cf. LETTENHOVE, viii, 93).

[104] LETTENHOVE, viii, 104.

[105] P.R.O., S.P. xii-107-28. Printed in LETTENHOVE, viii, 137n. Burghley's reference to his contact with Champagny earlier at Brussels is interesting as his only recorded allusion to his journey to Brussels in 1554 (*v.s.*, i, 105).

[106] We are entirely dependent upon Champagny's account of this interview (LETTENHOVE, viii, 137ff.). We have nothing from Burghley.

[107] LETTENHOVE, viii, 156.

[108] *Cal. S.P. Spanish, 1568-79*, 520.

[109] Champagny thought this was her *quid pro quo* for the long delay in granting Cobham an audience in Spain.

[110] And which Champagny revealed a little later when the Spanish mutineers sacked Antwerp (MOTLEY, iii, 74ff.).

[111] LETTENHOVE, viii, 275.

[112] Ibid., viii, 257, 266, 268, 277, 284, 289, 295.

[113] Ibid., viii, 285; *Cal. S.P. Spanish, 1568-79*, 529.

[114] LETTENHOVE, viii, 257.

[115] *Cal. S.P. Spanish, 1568-79*, 523; LETTENHOVE, viii, 266.

[116] LETTENHOVE, viii, 242ff., 253.

[117] Ibid., viii, 263.

[118] Ibid., viii, 272, 328.

[119] Ibid., viii, 296, 309.

CHAPTER XI

[1] So Davison learned (LETTENHOVE, viii, 343).

[2] Ibid., viii, 303.

[3] READ, *Walsingham*, i, 326.

[4] Ibid., 326-7.

[5] LETTENHOVE, viii, 230 n.

[6] Brother of Lord Cobham, Warden of the Cinque Ports.

[7] LETTENHOVE, viii, 229, 271.

[8] Ibid., 312. At the last the Dutch seem to have seized one chest containing twelve pieces of velvet and forty pairs of silk stockings. Five members of the company were held and put in prison as enemy aliens.

[9] The suggestion in *This Star of England*, 131, that Burghley set on the pirates to attack Oxford and that he feared Oxford would reveal his knowledge that Cecil had incestuous relationship with Ann is too fantastic to be considered. The only evidence presented is Shakespeare's *Pericles* (cf. Act I, scene i).

[10] LETTENHOVE, viii, 337, 340.

[11] Ibid., viii, 367.

[12] Ibid., 396-7. In a postscript Burghley adds that the hot weather had enabled him to raise his foot from his footstool.

[13] Burghley estimated that English merchandise to the value of £200,000 was arrested at Flushing.

[14] Cf. *A.P.C.*, 75-7, 102.

[15] LETTENHOVE, viii, 340.

[16] In an interview with Orange on the 18th, Orange told a story of his visit to England in 1556, 'at which time he understood that the Queen which now is, at the coronation of Queen Mary, should have carried her train: at which time Queen Mary had at dinner with her divers ambassadors, where likewise the Queen did sit, but after the ambassadors. The French ambassador after dinner came to the Queen, which now reigneth, and declared unto her how that day Her Majesty had carried the Queen's train and sat at dinner; that he doubted not but her Majesty should wear the crown and that the other should carry her train'.

[17] LETTENHOVE, viii, 385.

[18] The same Winter who had blockaded the Firth of Forth when the English besieged Edinburgh in 1560.

[19] LETTENHOVE, viii, 399. The loan was later expressed as 253,000 florins (ibid., 468). Orange also asked for 200 gotelings (i.e. artillery pieces) (ibid., 419).

[20] Ibid., 417.

[21] READ, *Walsingham*, i, 330.

[22] B.M., Cotton MSS., Galba C v, 100 (printed in LETTENHOVE, viii, 316). Another memorandum in the P.R.O. (S.P. xii-108-82) is also ascribed to Burghley by LETTENHOVE and is printed by him (viii, 420). The sentiment expressed in this memorandum and the form of it suggests Burghley's authorship, but it is not in his hand and bears no positive indication of his authorship.

[23] Lettenhove prints 'parks' for marts. Burghley had long leaned to such a course, *v.s.*, i, 291, 295.

[24] One plan of assurances, proposed by an English merchant to the Privy Council, is printed in LETTENHOVE, viii, 491. It proposed a committee of two or three in London, appointed by Orange, which should insure English merchants against Dutch depredations by a charge of 5 or 6 per cent upon the value of the cargo.

[25] LETTENHOVE, viii, 423.

[26] Ibid., 483. The italics are my own. A hoy was a small vessel, usually sloop-rigged.

[27] READ, *Walsingham*, i, 337.

[28] Ibid., 337.

[29] He returned to England July 13th, 1577.

[30] On the relations of Alençon with the Low Countries cf. MULLER and DIEGERICK (R 905).

[31] LETTENHOVE, viii, 85.

[32] LETTENHOVE, ix, 157n. Cf. instructions of Philip to Don John in LETTENHOVE, ix, 15 (dated November 11th).

[33] Ibid., Introduction, xii. It is interesting to note that Philip II expected some such manœuvre as revealed in his instructions of November 15th (*v.s.*, n. 32).

[34] On Walsingham's part in the plot to seize Don John cf. READ, *Walsingham*, i, 349.

[35] *Cal. S.P. Spanish, 1568-79*, 464.

[36] Leader of the anti-Orange faction.

[37] LETTENHOVE, ix, 515.

[38] Ibid., 264, 284.

[39] MURDIN, 779.

[40] LODGE, ii, 83 — Roger Manners [of Uffington], Esquire of the Body to Queen Elizabeth third son of 1st Earl of Rutland. Cf. *Rutland MSS* (R 181), i, 112.

[41] LODGE, ii, 85.

[42] B.M., Cotton MSS., Titus B ii, f. 235.

[43] *Cal. S.P. Scottish, 1574-81*, 234.

[44] LODGE, ii, 87.

[45] July 28th.

[46] He married Ann Sidney, Philip Sidney's aunt; twice Lord Deputy of Ireland.

[47] B.M., Cotton MSS., Vespasian F xii, f. 127. Shrewsbury seems to have housed Burghley in a chamber reserved for Sussex.

[48] Illegible in original.

[49] B.M., Cotton MSS., Titus B ii, f. 476.

[50] Cecil Papers, 160, f. 138.

[51] *Cal. Salisbury MSS.*, ii, 157, 159.

[52] LABANOFF, iv, 369. The year following, Leicester spoke of going to Buxton again. According to the Spanish ambassador, the Privy Councillors were much concerned, 'Cecil being one of those who is most anxious about it' (*Cal. S.P. Spanish, 1568-79*, 590).

[53] Cf. Mary to De Guaras, August 25th, LETTENHOVE, ix, 483.

[54] He sat with the Privy Council at Otlands on September 2nd, but not at its previous meeting on August 21st (*A.P.C.*, x, 21, 23).

[55] Cecil Papers, ix, f. 48.

[56] *v.s.*, p. 147.

[57] PEARSON, *Cartwright* (R 2437), 97.

[58] GRINDAL, *Remains* (R 2169), 376, from Burghley's copy in B.M., Lansdowne MSS., 23, no. 12. STRYPE also prints it in his life of Grindal, p. 558. It is dated December 20th, but GRINDAL in a letter to Burghley dated December 16th (*Remains*, 391) says that he wrote it eight days ago and that Leicester had delivered it to Elizabeth.

[59] GRINDAL, *Remains*, 391.

[60] STRYPE, *Grindal* (R 2216), 574.

[61] *Annals*, ed. 1635, 256. This same view is taken in *Leicester's Commonwealth* (ed. 1641), 21, which makes Julio out to have been Leicester's expert on poisoning.

[62] Mandell Creighton in the life of Grindal in

D.N.B. accepts Camden's story. Strype is doubtful.

[63] In the same place he named Walsingham as his good friend, and left him 'a standing cup'.

[64] B.M., Lansdowne MSS., 103, no. 8; printed in large part in STRYPE, *Grindal*, 348.

[65] Dispatches of October 9th, November 24th to the King, November 24th to Catherine de Medicis. P.R.O., *Baschet Transcripts*, bundle 27.

[66] November 24th to the King. De Guaras remained a prisoner until the following year in May when he was allowed to leave the country. We hear of him later in Paris in July (*Cal. S.P. Spanish, 1568-79*, 663ff.).

[67] B.M., Cotton MSS., Galba C vi, ff. 119-20, 122-3. LETTENHOVE, x, 125, 127, 152, prints the memorandum as three separate documents. I have arranged the various parts of it in what seems to me to be the logical order.

[68] LETTENHOVE, x, 832.

[69] *Cal. S.P. Foreign, 1577-78*, 203.

[70] On February 2nd, Lawrence Tomson, writing for Walsingham to Davison observed: 'Of late such as incline more to the faction of Spain than to her Majesty's safety and the quiet estate of the realm, have persuaded her that she cannot in honour do anything to help the Estates either with men or money till she have some answer from the King and Don John' (*Cal. S.P. Foreign, 1577-78*, 484).

[71] B.M., Cotton MSS., Galba C vi, pt. 1, f. 30.

[72] January 31st, 1578.

[73] His instructions are in LETTENHOVE, x, 274. A note in Burghley's hand of 'Points to be answered by Mr. Leighton' is in B.M., Cotton MSS., Galba C vi, f. 121.

[74] READ, *Walsingham*, i, 365.

[75] LETTENHOVE, x, 340. Cf. on the same subject Elizabeth to Casimir of April 10th, 1578 (*Cal. S.P. Foreign, 1577-78*, 610).

[76] READ, *Walsingham*, i, 365ff.

[77] Ibid., 368n.

[78] *Cal. S.P. Spanish, 1568-79*, 553n.

[79] READ, *Walsingham*, i, 368-9.

[80] *Cal. S.P. Spanish, 1568-79*, 565.

[81] Ibid., 572.

[82] Ibid., 586.

[83] *Cal. S.P. Spanish, 1568-79*, 610, 668. In February Lawrence Tomson, one of Walsingham's secretaries, wrote to Davison that the Spanish faction at Court were opposing direct intervention and favouring mediation; he does not indicate who these were (*Cal. S.P. Foreign, 1577-78*, 485). Sussex and Burghley both favoured peace in the Low Countries if it could be achieved. And Sussex certainly was prepared to accept peace without religious toleration to the Dutch Protestants, provided that the Dutch recovered their 'ancient liberties' (cf. *Cal. S.P. Foreign, 1577-78*, 372). Hume says (*Cal. S.P. Spanish, 1568-79*, xlix) that Sussex and Burghley both accepted bribes in 1579, but the evidence he cites in support of this position simply says that Mendoza was recommending bribes.

[84] LETTENHOVE, x, 465, undated.

[85] B.M., Cotton MSS., Galba C vii, 34, in LETTENHOVE, x, 465, undated but probably belonging early in May. Cf. W. to D., May 11th, LETTENHOVE, x, 457. The term Monsieur, used in the sense of the King's eldest brother, was generally used in England at the time to designate Alençon.

[86] A course suggested by Henry III to the English ambassador in France in April; cf. *Cal. S.P. Foreign, 1577-78*, 608.

[87] LETTENHOVE, x, 457.

[88] Ibid., 506, 513.

[89] *Cal. S.P. Foreign, 1578-79*, 10.

[90] LETTENHOVE, x, 521.

[91] Cf. Butler in *Cal. S.P. Foreign, 1578-79*, vii.

[92] READ, *Walsingham*, i, 381.

[93] Cf. READ, *Fame of Sir Edward Stafford* (R 860); READ, *A Letter from Leicester* (R 758).

[94] LETTENHOVE, x, 659.

[95] The dispatches of Mauvissière are wanting before July 1578. Cf. TEULET (R 4929), iii, 1n.

[96] *Cal. S.P. Foreign, 1578-79*, 14.

[97] LETTENHOVE, x, 544.

[98] READ, *Walsingham*, i, 387.

[99] Her ideas on the subject of a reasonable peace are set forth at length, August 29th, in LETTENHOVE (x, 770), drafted by Burghley (cf. *Cal. S.P. Foreign, 1578-79*, 157).

[100] Walsingham and Cobham suggested later that the Queen could always at a pinch reimburse herself, 'by the sending out of a ship or two', to seize Dutch shipping (LETTENHOVE, x, 841).

[101] Ibid., 593.

[102] In Essex, where Elizabeth, on progress, was visiting Dr. Altham (*Cal. S.P. Foreign, 1578-79*, 86).

[103] LETTENHOVE, x, 659.

[104] *Cal. S.P. Foreign, 1578-79*, 14.

[105] LETTENHOVE, x, 661.

[106] Ibid., 665; in French, De Gastel may have been the writer. He wrote in French and had been twice to England.

[107] Cf. V. A. WILSON, *Elizabeth's Maids of Honour* (R 793).

[108] LETTENHOVE, x, 678.

[109] Ibid., 696.

[110] Ibid., 698.

[111] Ibid., 701.

[112] Probably a mistake for Wednesday.

[113] In LETTENHOVE's version (x, 702), 'islands' is read 'Flanders' and 'coat', 'court'. Burghley wrote from Bury St. Edmunds, 'where', he remarked, 'we find the people very sound, saving in some parts infected with the brain-sick heresy of the papistical family of love'.

[114] B.M., Cotton MSS., Galba C vi, pt. 2, 128. LETTENHOVE's version (x, 708), for 'with our intermeddling' prints 'without intermeddling', which reverses the meaning.

[115] LETTENHOVE, x, 116.

[116] Ibid., 711.

[117] Ibid., 712.

[118] READ, *Walsingham*, i, 403.

[119] LETTENHOVE, x, 734.

[120] Ibid., 713.

[121] Ascribed to Sussex in LETTENHOVE (x, 743), but cf. READ, *Walsingham*, i, 403 n.1.

[122] READ, *Walsingham*, i, 415.

[123] LETTENHOVE, X, 776.
[124] Ibid., 773.
[125] Ibid., 772.
[126] Ibid., 776.

[127] Ibid., 774. Sussex elaborates on the theme in a long letter to the Queen, dated August 28th and printed in LODGE, ii, 107-18.
[128] READ, *Walsingham*, i, 416.

CHAPTER XII

[1] NICHOLS, *Progresses*, ii, 92ff.

[2] Randolph had been to Russia in the spring of 1568.

[3] B.M., Harleian MSS., 6992, f. 104.

[4] NICHOLS, ii, 113-14.

[5] *Cal. Salisbury MSS.*, ii, 210. Sir F. Knollys wrote to Burghley on October 21st: 'Because I do hear that your L. doth go little abroad by reason of the infirmity of your legs, by means whereof you do spend your time the more within doors in reading and perusing of good matters, therefore I am so bold as to present unto your L. this little book... treating of the true understanding of the words of Christ at His last supper, touching the sacrament of His body and blood' (S.P. xii-126-12).

[6] S.P. xii-126-5. No place given.

[7] P.R.O., S.P. xii-125-73.

[8] *Cal. Salisbury MSS.*, ii, 208. The matter in question had to do with the discovery that the Master of the Mint had been making about $6\frac{1}{2}$d. more from a pound of silver than the standard permitted. The commission investigated, accepted the Mint Master's explanation and authorized him to coin silver at the rate of 60s. 3d. per pound silver and of a fineness of 11 oz. 1 dwt. pure silver to the pound, though the standard was 60s; and gold at the rate of £36 1s. $10\frac{1}{2}$d. the pound, though the standard was £36. In short, the commission authorized a slight debasement of the coinage. It appears from Hatton's letter that Burghley was instrumental in securing some enrichment of the coin. According to Ruding, the Mint Master had been coining silver at the rate of 60s. 5d., and gold at the rate of £36 3s. (*Annals of the Coinage* (R 1265), i, 91, 349), and Burghley may have been responsible for inducing the Mint Master to accept the rate as specified. In any case, Burghley was clearly a party to some authorization of debasement, though as Feavayear pointed out, it only amounted to $\frac{1}{2}$ grain in the weight of a shilling (FEAVAYEAR, *The Pound Sterling* [R 1260], 79). The justification of it was that the Mint was not receiving adequate compensation for its services. Cf. B.M., Harleian MSS., 698; B.M., Cotton MSS., Otho E x, f. 305.

[9] Mary Stuart thought this was a factor. Cf. LABANOFF, v, 94.

[10] On the dating of these cf. READ, *Walsingham*, ii, 46 n. 3. Some of Elizabeth's letters are in holograph, and there are a great many letters in French between members of Alençon's entourage. Some of Elizabeth's letters are drafts in her own hand or copies. She may have turned these over to Burghley but it looks as though many of them had been obtained through French channels. Some of Elizabeth's earlier letters she apparently passed on

to Walsingham. There is no evidence or any indications of Burghley's handling of these letters.

[11] READ, *Walsingham*, ii, 8.

[12] Of these Sussex had already committed himself in no uncertain terms to the marriage. Cf. his long letter to Elizabeth on the subject, of August 28th, in LODGE, ii, 107.

[13] READ, *Walsingham*, ii, 9, 11, 11n., 12.

[14] LODGE, ii, 147.

[15] In south-west Essex, a few miles from London.

[16] Cecil Papers, 148/23. Cf. also ibid., 25, 29, 32, 36, 39, 40v., 58.

[17] READ, *Walsingham*, ii, 14ff.

[18] The argument here follows the same line as that of a memo attributed to Sir E. Stafford, in *Cal. Salisbury MSS.*, ii, 239ff.

[19] Cecil Papers, 148/25.

[20] Cf. POLLARD, *History of England, 1547-1603*, 181n. Pollard accepts the position that the Queen was sterile. NEALE agrees with me (*Elizabeth*, 217, 242).

[21] In full in *Cal. Salisbury MSS.*, ii, 239-45. I am less certain than the editor of the Calendar that this is in Stafford's hand. There is a thrust at the Dudleys in one passage which savours of Stafford's animosity to Leicester, to wit:

'Such as impugn her [Elizabeth's] marriage with a stranger and know she will not marry with her subject, do directly mean that she should not marry with any person. To what end this meaning tendeth is to be left to the good consideration of Almighty God ... but in the sight of man it doth carry a hard construction ... and showeth a disposition of the alienating of the crown from the right succession of the body of the famous King Henry the Eighth, which can never proceed from a true English heart.'

To those who recalled that Leicester's father had attempted 'the alienating' of the Crown from the 'right succession' in the interests of his daughter-in-law, Lady Jane Grey, the implication would have been obvious — like father, like son!

[22] For his earlier views on the subject, *v.s.*, p. 60ff.

[23] The course of the negotiations is outlined by Burghley in a memo of May 3rd and 4th (*Cal. Salisbury MSS.*, ii, 253). Cf. also Burghley's summary in Cecil Papers, 148/27-8.

[24] *Cal. Salisbury MSS.*, ii, 249.

[25] LABANOFF, v, 94.

[26] *Annals*, ed. 1635, 205. Camden says that the Queen 'commanded Leicester to keep himself within the Tower of Greenwich and thought to have committed him to the Tower of London ... but Sussex dissuaded her ... He held opinion that no man was to be molested for lawful marriage'.

[27] *Cal. S.P. Foreign, 1579-80*, 8.

[28] READ, *Walsingham*, ii, 19.

[29] This from Burghley's own digest of the course of the marriage negotiations, in *Cal. Salisbury MSS.*, ii, 288ff.

[30] *Cal. S.P. Spanish, 1568-79*, 692.

[31] *A.P.C.*, xi, 243ff.

[32] On the conference cf. LETTENHOVE, xi, Introduction, xlvii n. 4, and Blok (R 933) [Putnam translation], iii, 141 n. 1. The issue turned chiefly on the old question of freedom of religion and restoration of ancient privileges. Upon the religious issue the Spaniards remained adamant.

[33] NICOLAS, *Hatton*, 121-2.

[34] *A.P.C.*, xi, 218.

[35] Wentworth had been summoned in May to appear before the Privy Council with reference to his unorthodox religious services (*A.P.C.*, xi, 132-3), but there is no evidence that he ever appeared. Since he was Walsingham's brother-in-law (he and Mildmay each married sisters of Walsingham), he may have been excused. On Wentworth cf. NEALE (R 1124).

[36] Holdenby like Theobalds was totally destroyed during the Commonwealth.

[37] NICOLAS, *Hatton*, 224.

[38] Ibid., 125-6. 'Spirit' was Elizabeth's nickname for Burghley.

[39] Printed many times. Cf. STRYPE, *Annals*, iv, 641.

[40] FROUDE, xi, 175.

[41] *Cal. S.P. Spanish, 1568-79*, 693.

[42] STEELE, i, 79; set forth in STRYPE, *Annals*, iv, 232ff.

[43] *A.P.C.*, xi, 270, 276; a copy of the letter is in STRYPE, *Grindal*, 584ff.

[44] *Cal. Salisbury MSS.*, ii, 271. It is to be noted that Henry Howard, brother of the late Duke of Norfolk, wrote in defence of the match (B.M., Harleian MSS., 180; B.M., Cotton MSS., Titus C xviii). It was never published. One wonders whether Burghley prompted it. He and Howard were at the time on intimate terms.

[45] Cf. *Cal. S.P. Spanish, 1568-79*, 704. According to the Venetian ambassador at Paris, she learned that Walsingham had some foreknowledge of STUBBS's *Gaping Gulf* (*Cal. S.P. Venetian, 1558-90*, 621).

[46] *Cal. S.P. Spanish, 1568-79*, 702.

[47] MURDIN, 322-31.

[48] *v.s.*, i, 274.

[49] Cf. MURDIN, 333-6.

[50] The Spanish ambassador said that all opposed it but Burghley and Sussex (*Cal. S.P. Spanish, 1568-79*, 702), but cf. MURDIN, 332-3, for Wilson's and Hunsdon's position.

[51] *Cal. Salisbury MSS.*, ii, 271. He does not seem to have had any inside information on the subject. He argued that if she did not favour it, she might easily have broken it off on religious grounds without seeking the advice of her Council. He added 'that she liketh him is still more probable from her having pronounced these speeches, "that she will never any, if she shall marry, but him", and also, "that she doth not mislike of him". And most of those about her know that she never speaketh of him but with great allowance of his

nature and considerations; and lastly, she seemeth not pleased with any person or with any argument appearing to mislike of the marriage'.

[52] Here again the Spanish ambassador was wrong. He says that they declared against the match and that their decision was conveyed to the Queen by the Chancellor and the Earl of Arundel (*Cal. S.P. Spanish, 1568-79*, 702). Burghley's memo tells the story recorded in the text.

[53] MURDIN, 336.

[53a] *Cal. S.P. Spanish, 1568-79*, 704-5.

[54] *Cal. S.P. Foreign, 1579-80*, 95.

[55] *Cal. Salisbury MSS.*, ii, 275.

[56] A letter not signed, and not in Burghley's hand, addressed to Elizabeth, dated January 18th, 1579-80, is among the Hatfield Papers. It is said to be in Sir Thomas Cecil's hand, which I question. Another letter in the same hand is ascribed to Sir Ed. Stafford (cf. *Cal. Salisbury MSS.*, ii, 239). In any case it certainly was not Sir Thomas's letter. From the context it can hardly be doubetd that it is a copy of a letter which Burghley himself sent to his mistress. *Cal. Salisbury MSS.*, ii, 308; MURDIN, 339 (very incorrectly printed).

[57] READ, *Walsingham*, ii, 26, 29.

[58] *Cal. S.P. Spanish, 1568-79*, 696.

[59] *Cal. S.P. Foreign, 1579-80*, 166, 183.

[60] B.M., Cotton MSS., Galba E vi, f. 6.

[61] *Cal. S.P. Foreign, 1579-80*, 202, 205.

[62] *Cal. S.P. Spanish, 1580-86*, 24-5, 33.

[63] Ibid., 38-9.

[64] B.M., Cotton MSS., Titus B ii, f. 438.

[65] Printed in full in *Cal. Salisbury MSS.*, ii, 329, and, with errors, in LODGE, ii, 172.

[66] Mauvissière wrote on July 5th that 'the Lord Treasurer and those who favour the marriage are altogether resolute for friendship between France and England. They assure me that Condé will return to France without satisfaction' (P.R.O., *Baschet Transcripts*, bundle 28).

[67] I assume this from a letter from Francis Talbot to his father of May 29th, 1580 (LODGE, ii, 167) in which he reports that she was recovering from a critical illness. Lady Sussex, Sussex's second wife, was the sister of Sir Henry Sidney and therefore the aunt of Sir Philip. In her will she provided funds for the foundation of Lady Frances Sidney-Sussex College at Cambridge.

[68] Burghley was only six years older than Sussex.

[69] In LODGE, ii, 160, and, with minor variations, in *Cal. Salisbury MSS.*, ii, 326.

[70] *v.s.*, i, 456.

[71] *Cal. S.P. Spanish, 1580-86*, 14-15.

[72] READ, *Walsingham*, ii, 32.

[73] Cf. his memorandum, endorsed by Burghley, 'Mr. Wilkes at Nonesuch' (*Cal. S.P. Foreign, 1579-80*, 348).

[74] Ibid., 360ff.

[75] As a matter of fact, she did come, but achieved nothing. Cf. MOTLEY, iii, 502.

[76] *Cal. S.P. Foreign, 1579-80*, 348.

[77] These instructions are assigned in the Calendar to September 1580, and to Daniel Rogers. More probably they were for Davison (*Cal. S.P. Foreign, 1579-80*, 433).

[78] READ, *Walsingham*, ii, 133.

[79] P.R.O., S.P. xii-103-26. Walsingham's letter to Burghley, in S.P. xii-45-27, is quoted at length in READ, *Walsingham*, ii, 136. Walsingham had heard that Morton was bending his ear towards French advances. 'The gentleman [Morton],' he wrote to Burghley, 'being noted to be over much inclined to his own gain and profit, it is to be doubted that the large offers of France draw him to revolt.'

[80] READ, *Walsingham*, ii, 143.

[81] B.M., Harleian MSS., 6992, f. 104.

[82] Nearly two years later Robert Bowes was still in doubt as to whether he should address his official letters to Burghley or to Walsingham or to them both. He put the question to Walsingham (*Cal. S.P. Scottish, 1574-81*, 404). Walsingham replied: 'For that you have begun to write jointly to my Lord Treasurer and me, and that his Lordship should peradventure think somewhat if hereafter you should not do so, I think good you hold still that course; and withal to write, as you do use, privately to me ... For the better answering her Majesty's commandment given you for addressing your intelligence specially to me, if you have any matter you think fit to impart only for her, lest, in my absence from the Court, my private letter should be opened, I wish you put therein a paper in cipher of the said intelligence' (BOWES, *Correspondence* (R 5303), 49). Froude interprets this reply as an indication that Elizabeth only half

trusted Burghley (FROUDE, xi, 296n.), but Elizabeth's attitude towards Burghley was really not in question. It was her custom to provide special channels for information intended only for herself, and all that Walsingham really said was that Bowes should follow the royal instructions in the matter. (There is nothing said on the subject in Bowes's instructions of April 17th, 1580, in *Cal. S.P. Scottish, 1574-81*, 40). Actually official letters to Bowes went off over Burghley's and Walsingham's joint signatures.

[83] LETTENHOVE, x, 660.

[84] READ, *Walsingham*, ii, 151.

[85] The English position was that James as alien born could not inherit. Arabella Stuart, another grandchild of the Countess (the offspring of the marriage between Charles Darnley and Elizabeth Cavendish, step-daughter of the Earl of Shrewsbury) put in a claim. Elizabeth referred the matter to the English Courts and meanwhile sequestered the Lennox English estates in the hands of Lord Burghley as Master of the Court of Wards.

[86] READ, *Walsingham*, ii, 151.

[87] LETTENHOVE, x, 783.

[88] Later first duke.

[89] BOWES, *Correspondence*, 111.

[90] READ, *Walsingham*, ii, 168.

[91] TEULET, iii, 88.

CHAPTER XIII

[1] B.M., Cotton MSS., Galba C v, no. 31, printed, not too accurately, in LETTENHOVE, viii, 122. Cf. Shaw's report that Burghley in 1575 admitted that for one staunch and constant Catholic at the opening of the reign there were now ten. POLLEN, *English Catholics in the Reign of Elizabeth* (R 2366), 257.

[2] B.M., Additional MSS., 48084, f. 26.

[3] MURDIN, 325.

[4] Ibid., 326, 331.

[5] MURDIN, 340.

[6] B.M., Cotton MSS., Titus B iii, f. 63. In Burghley's holograph: 'It was seen that the pain being no greater than 12d. no officer did seek to charge any offender therewith, so as the number of evil disposed persons increased herein to offend with impunity.'

[7] 5 Elizabeth c. 23.

[8] Cf. *A.P.C.*, ix, *passim*.

[9] FRERE, *English Church under Elizabeth* (R 2188b), 207.

[10] But cf. Henry Shaw, cited in POLLEN, 257.

[11] POLLEN, 316-17, citing *Baschet Transcripts*.

[12] *Cal. S.P. Spanish, 1568-79*, 607.

[13] Fénélon, the French ambassador in London, reported an interview with Stukeley in London in February 1570 (*Correspondence*, iii, 53; vii, 94). He reported earlier (ii, 81, lll) that Stukeley in Ireland was fighting on the side of the rebels and that in July 1569 he was captured and sent to

London. The Spanish ambassador in January 1570 speaks of his capture and subsequent liberation (*Cal. S.P. Spanish, 1568-79*, 226).

[14] *Cal. S.P. Rome*, ii, 361.

[15] MATHEW, *The Celtic Peoples* (R 355), 126ff.

[16] DIGGES, 41.

[17] Ibid., 45.

[18] POLLEN, 193ff.; *Cal. S.P. Spanish, 1568-79*, 305.

[19] *Cal. S.P. Spanish, 1568-79* ,315, 330.

[20] Ibid., 561; cf. *Cal. Salisbury MSS.*, ii, 173.

[21] *A.P.C.*, x, 236, 258.

[22] Pillen's report is undated, but since it records that he left Lisbon on May 28th it must be in June and not in April as conjectured in the *Cal. S.P. Domestic, Addenda, 1566-79*, 42.

[23] *Cal. S.P. Foreign, 1578-79*, 23, 28, 35.

[24] *Sidney Papers* (R 629), i, 7.

[25] Cf. MATHEW's appraisal in *The Celtic People*, 151ff.

[26] I disagree with POLLEN's description of his fighting spirit as 'chivalrous' (op. cit., 226).

[27] FALLS, *Elizabeth's Irish Wars* (R 3366), 101ff.

[28] FALLS, 127; MATHEW, 166; HOOKER in Holinshed, ed. 1587, i, 154.

[29] CODE, *Queen Elizabeth and the English Catholic Historians* (R 2315), 16.

[30] POLLEN, 304.

[31] FALLS, 126.

[32] Copies of this letter and of another letter to Walsingham of the same date appear in a letter book of Sir Christopher Hatton (NICOLAS, *Hatton*, 121ff.). How they got there is puzzling. Walsingham may have sent them to Hatton, or Burghley may have left copies with Hatton, being on the way to visit Hatton's place at Holdenby when he wrote.

[33] Sander in fact never left Ireland after his arrival, and the reinforcements which arrived the next year from Spain were wiped out to a man.

[34] Early in January 1580 Burghley dilated at large on the Irish situation, pointing out that much of the difficulty there arose from misgovernment (MURDIN, 340-1).

[35] FALLS, 100.

[36] *Cal. S.P. Ireland, 1572-85*, 206.

[37] Ibid.

[38] *Catholic Record Soc., Miscell.*, xiii, 54n.

[39] There were two proclamations against Desmond, one dated November 2nd, 1579, the other January 24th, 1580. This quotation is from the earlier one, which Burghley probably drafted (*Cal. Carew MSS.* (R 5723), ii, 63).

[40] STEELE, i, 80; printed in FROUDE, xi, 340 n. 4. Two copies of the draft in Burghley's hand are in P.R.O., S.P. xii-140-18, 19.

[41] FROUDE, xi, 341, speaks of it as a 'noble appeal'. I disagree.

[42] NEALE, *Elizabeth*, 296.

[43] *A.P.C.*, xii, 53; the letter itself is printed in PECK, *Desiderata Curiosa* (R 277), bk. iii, 8.

[44] PECK, bk. iii, 11.

[45] Ibid., 12.

[46] B.M., Harleian MSS., 360, f. 65. It is summarized, but misdated, in READ, *Walsingham*, ii, 282.

[47] D'EWES, *Journals of Parliament* (R 1037), 285ff.

[48] P.R.O., S.P. xii-147-34, 46; S.P. xii-148-5, 10.

[49] The quotation is from NEALE, *Elizabeth I and her Parliaments*, i, 391. In the main Neale's account of this Parliament is admirable, but I cannot agree with his appraisal of Burghley. He seems to find confirmation of his views in a well-known letter of advice on the subject commonly ascribed to Burghley. SPEDDING (*Life and Letters of F. Bacon*, i, 43ff.) has shown, I think, quite conclusively, that the letter in question was almost certainly Francis Bacon's composition. Even so, the position taken in the letter is far from being one of ruthless severity. I think it comes close to reflecting Burghley's own position and I wish Burghley could have stated it as well as Bacon did. After all, Bacon was Burghley's nephew. The subject was one which Bacon in his earlier years liked to play with. Cf. his notable letter to Mr. Critoy, commonly ascribed to Walsingham in SPEDDING (ibid., 97). In that letter Bacon coined the well-known phrase, describing Elizabeth's attitude as 'not liking to make windows into men's hearts and secret thoughts'.

[50] 23 Eliz. c. 1.

[51] 23 Eliz. c. 2. The controversy over this bill is well set forth in NEALE, op. cit., 392ff., in which the Puritan House of Commons, fearing that the bill might be used against Puritan pamphleteers, succeeded in mitigating its asperities.

[52] STRYPE, *Parker*, ii, 164.

[53] In SIMPSON, *Campion* (R 2376), 225.

[54] At the time of his expulsion Burghley had intervened in his favour but without success. Cf. *D.N.B.* art. Charke. For his answer cf. *S.T.C.*, 5005. A second edition appeared in 1581. Another pamphlet on the same subject by Merideth Hanmer appeared in 1581. Simpson (*Campion*, in an appendix, 491) gives a useful bibliography of Campion's works and the literature which ensued from them.

[55] WRIGHT, *ii*, 132n.

[56] SIMPSON, 492. There was a publishers' adventure afoot to translate one of these answers into English, but the idea seems to have been blocked by the Bishop of London. One gathers from Burghley's correspondence with Aylmer that Burghley was active in arranging for an answer to Campion (cf. SIMPSON, 358). WRIGHT, ii, 155.

[57] SIMPSON, 338, who does not cite his source (probably BOMBINO's *Life of Campion*).

[58] HOWELL, *State Trials* (R 1645) i, 1062.

[59] Talbot, Trans. (from Longleat), P.R.O.; cited also by SIMPSON, 345, from Kennett Transcripts, in B.M., Lansdowne MSS., 982.

[60] Cf. READ, *Walsingham*, ii, 289n. There is a letter from Walsingham to Hatton, dated Boulogne, June 17th, in Hatton's letter book (NICOLAS, *Hatton*, 179) but probably misdated. Cf. Walsingham to Burghley from Boulogne July 27th in DIGGES.

[61] *A.P.C.*, xiii, 144. His examiners were Dr. Hammond, a notable civilian and a member of the Court of High Commission; Robert Beale, Walsingham's brother-in-law; and Thomas Norton, a belligerent Puritan parliamentarian.

[62] *A.P.C.*, xiii, 149, 152-5.

[63] DIGGES, 373. Simpson seems to have missed this letter. It is interesting to compare it with Burghley's earlier letter to Shrewsbury, cited on p. 249 *supra*. Simpson's position on these revelations of Campion varies. At one point he suggests that the revelations of Campion were forgeries (p. 352); at another, that he merely confessed what was known already to his examiners from other sources (p. 353). The case for forgeries is untenable if only because of Burghley's letter cited above, added to Campion's own confession, and the records of the Privy Council. There is a page of a memorandum surviving in Burghley's own hand in which Burghley enumerates some of the places which Campion visited (B.M., Lansdowne MSS., 30, no. 75).

[64] B.M., Lansdowne MSS., 33 *passim*.

[65] SIMPSON, 377.

[66] STRYPE, *Annals*, ii, pt. 2, 360. Strype does not quote his source and I have been unable to find any such exchange of letters. But Strype is reliable.

[67] See Fleetwood's letters in WRIGHT, ii *passim*.

[68] 25 Ed. iii, c. 2. Cf. MEYER, *England and the Catholic Church under Queen Elizabeth* (Eng. trans.), 151.

[69] Cited by SIMPSON, 395, from B.M., Lansdowne MSS., 33, no. 64.

[70] For Simpson's charge that Walsingham in France was concocting a conspiracy to meet the situation, cf. READ, *Walsingham*, ii, 290n.

[71] I can find no evidence from English sources to support Simpson's story, p. 445, that Burghley had decided the matter of Campion's execution by saying that since they could not catch Sander they must hang Campion; nor the further story that he had fixed the date of execution (ibid., 446). Catholic writers were disposed to blame everything on Burghley. But there is nothing inherently probable in the stories.

[72] Cf. SIMPSON, appendix, for a detailed bibliography.

[73] *S.T.C.*, 4901.

[74] *S.T.C.*, 4902.

[75] *S.T.C.*, 4904. I have used the copy at the Folger Library. It is ascribed to Burghley in the *S.T.C.* but not in the *British Museum Catalogue*. There is no indication at all of the author or printer on the pamphlet itself. I think it was probably written by Thomas Norton, one of the commissioners employed in the examination of Campion under torture. Norton was thrown into the Tower late in 1581 because of indiscreet manifestations of Puritanism in and out of Parliament, but he was employed there by Walsingham to write an account of the torture of Campion as well as other things. He sent his report on the torture to Walsingham, March 27th, 1582, and then applied himself to other writings. On April 11th he wrote to Walsingham: 'I have here sent you another of these toys... You need not deliver my name... This trifle and one other laying by me are the fruits of a mean space.' The argument of the pamphlet in question follows closely Norton's letter of March 27th, and it is evident from his letter of April 11th that he was turning out pamphlet literature. The relevant material on Norton is printed in *Archaeologia*, xxxvi, 109ff. Cf. also NEALE, ii, 405. Norton said of Burghley in his letter to Walsingham of March 27th: 'My Lord Treasurer is the only man in whom I have and do lay the course of my relief. I have found him gracious, he will do me good in time.' There is further material on Norton in B.M., Additional MSS., 48023. His diary of adventures in Rome is in B.M., Additional MSS., 48029. He died in March 1584 and his books and papers passed into the hands of Thomas Wilkes, clerk of the Council. A list of them is preserved at Hatfield (Cecil Papers, 140/51).

[76] *S.T.C.*, 4902. Although published anonymously, there can be little doubt about its authorship. Robert Parsons wrote, December 13th, 1584: 'Cecil was esteemed the author of *Justicia Britannica*, who, being reprehended therefore by Leicester, wrote another book about the Earl relating to his wicked life.' The book about Leicester was none other than the one commonly called *Leicester's Commonwealth*, and certainly Burghley did not write it. According to Parsons, William Allen's reply to Cecil's pamphlet was so good that the heretics were sorry they ever brought it out (*Catholic Record Soc.*, xxxix, 267). We have parts of the *Execution of Justice* in Burghley's hand in P.R.O., S.P. xii-73-49 and S.P. xii-153-74; and one with his corrections in S.P. xii-164-85.

In a note among the papers of Robert Beale (B.M., Additional MSS., 48063, f. 6) are two short discourses — one on unlawfulness of excommunication of Christian princes; the other on resistance of Christian princes against excommunication. Against these in the margin Beale has written: 'These two discourses were made by Mr. Dr. Hammond at the request of the Lord Treasurer, before the setting forth of the book called *Justicia Britannica*.'

[77] *S.T.C.*, 4903.

[78] *S.T.C.*, 4904-5-6. An Italian translation appeared in 1589. All of them anonymously.

[79] Cf. *inter alia*, *Anglia Loquens*, B.M., Cotton MSS. (Caligula B iv, f. 235); S.P. xii-161-47; Caligula B iv, 229; Lansdowne MSS., 104, 49.

[80] There can be no doubt about their authenticity. Cf. particularly POLLEN, 293-4; SIMPSON, 141; MEYER, 138 and appendix xvii.

[81] MEYER, Eng. trans., 138.

[82] MEYER, 139-40, rejects this view of the matter. So does POLLEN, 295ff. Pollen argues that Gregory's dispensation was really 'of no little advantage to Elizabeth's government' since it enabled English Catholics to reconcile loyalty to their faith with loyalty to their Queen.

[83] POLLEN, 297, quotes Burghley as saying: 'This only means that you are loyal while you cannot resist and that you will rebel at the first opportunity.' But I find no evidence that Burghley said anything of the sort. Probably Father Pollen simply threw into direct discourse what he assumed to be Burghley's reaction.

[84] In the edition of 1914.

[85] Ibid., edition of 1914, ii, 56.

[86] STRYPE, *Annals*, ii, pt. 2, 306. Stubbs wrote it and Burghley had it reviewed, and the reviewers in July 1587 recommended its immediate publication. The reviewers observed: 'Touching the work, it is more than time, in our opinion, it were abroad; not only for the better staying of such weak ones as may lightly be carried away with fair shows of the adversary, but also for the repressing of some insolent vaunts, lately given out by petty pamphleteers of that Roman faction, who have dared so highly to magnify that popish libel as though it were for workmanship unmatchable and for sound matter uncontrollable by ours. But, God be thanked, it is ripped in sunder and the rottenness of every member in such sort discovered as all their shifting surgery will never recover it.'

But it was apparently never printed. Thomas Byng, Regius Professor of Civil Law, Master of Clare College, Cambridge, and Dr. John Hammond, one of the commissioners who conducted Campion's examinations, were the referees.

CHAPTER XIV

[1] TEULET, iii, 79.

[2] Cf. Mary Stuart's letter in LABANOFF, vi, 36-42.

[3] Two short memoranda on the subject from him survive: the first dated April 25th, 1581, which makes no mention of the succession (*Cal. Salisbury MSS.*, ii, 387); the other undated (*Cal. S.P. Foreign, 1582*, 530) which raises the question but not in terms of expectant issue from Elizabeth.

[4] On Hatton's attitude cf. NICOLAS, *Hatton*, 160, dated September 26th, 1580; printed also in Wright, ii, 106, where it is dated April 26th.

[5] *Cal. S.P. Spanish, 1580-86*, 136, 141, 154.

[6] *Cal. S.P. Foreign, 1580-81*, 287, 288; TEULET, iii, 74.

[7] A pool, used as refuge by hunted deer.

[8] P.R.O., S.P. xii-141-39.

[9] Probably a crossbow.

[10] July 26th, 1580; P.R.O., *Baschet Transcripts*, bundle 28.

[11] Ibid., August 8th.

[12] In HOLINSHED, ed. 1587, iii, 1315. The French commissioners kept a long and colourful account of their reception, April 24th-May 1st. P.R.O., *Baschet Transcripts*, bundle 28. For Burghley's arrangements cf. *Cal. S.P. Foreign, 1581-82*, 141.

[13] B.M., Lansdowne MSS., 31, no. 70.

[14] *Burghley's Household Accounts* (R 4090).

[15] *Diary, Camden Soc. Misc.*, vi, 42.

[16] An account of this by Henry Goldwell was published in 1581 (*S.T.C.*, 11990) and is printed in NICHOLS, *Progresses*, ii, 310. Stow's account in the second edition of HOLINSHED is clearly derived from GOLDWELL (HOLINSHED, iii, 1316). Goldwell designates i as a 'Triumph'.

[17] Burghley, Lincoln, Sussex, Bedford, Leicester, Hatton, Walsingham were named as English commissioners in the treaty, but Leicester appears to have taken little or no part. Cf. Treaty in MAUVISSIÈRE, *Mémoires*, ed. 1659, i, 706ff.

[18] *Cal. S.P. Foreign, 1581-82*, 144.

[19] Mendoza says on the 27th (*Cal. S.P. Spanish, 1580-86*, 110).

[20] *Cal. S.P. Spanish, 1580-86*, 111. Burghley urged this course in a session with the French commission in May. Cf. dispatch to French King, May 12th, 1581, P.R.O. *Baschet Transcripts*.

[21] *Cal. S.P. Foreign, 1579-80*, 97, 102; ibid., 1581-82, 169.

[22] CASTELNAU, *Mémoires*, ed. 1659, i, 706ff. The form of ceremony to be used at the wedding was also defined (ibid., i, 714).

[23] Ibid., i, 715.

[24] *Cal. S.P. Spanish, 1580-86*, 120, 131-2.

[25] *Cal. Salisbury MSS.*, ii, 394.

[26] P.R.O., S.P. xii-149-53. Bucklersbury was a street in London just south of the Poultry. STOW says of it (*London*, ed. Kingsford, i, 261): 'The whole street called Bucklersbury on both the sides throughout is possessed of grocers and apothecaries.'

[27] Cf. Nuñez to Burghley, June 28th (B.M., Lansdowne MSS., 33, no. 39).

[28] *A.P.C.*, xiii, 131.

[29] August 8th, 1581 (P.R.O., *Talbot Transcripts*).

[30] READ, *Walsingham*, ii, 51.

[31] B.M., Lansdowne MSS., 102, no. 104; printed in STRYPE, *Annals*, iii, pt. 2, 108ff.

[32] Burghley at this point gave an outline of the financial arrangements for the voyage as Drake and Hawkins revealed them to him:
(1) £5000 loaned by Elizabeth through Walsingham to Don Antonio;
(2) £2000 loaned by Walsingham;
(3) the balance, £6000 or £7000, advanced by Drake, Hawkins and other adventurers.

Spoil to be divided as follows:

Half to Don Antonio, of which he should receive half himself and the other half to go to Walsingham, Drake and the other adventurers.

Half for the rental of the ships and the reward of the ships' companies.

Burghley raised the question of the £5000 advanced by the Queen in Walsingham's name. She insisted that it should remain in his name, but should herself receive that share of the profit which its investment produced. Later when the expedition was abandoned, it looked as though Walsingham was to be charged personally with the loss of £5000. Fortunately he had secured a diamond from Don Antonio as security.

[33] In a final paragraph Burghley considered what ought to be done if the voyage were abandoned. He said that (a) Antonio should have back his jewel; (b) the preparations should be inventoried and sold and distributed; (c) the loss should be borne; (d) upon the security of the jewel or some lesser jewel the King might purchase four ships and victuals.

[34] DIGGES, 379, 388, 393-4.

[35] He died in Paris in 1595.

[36] Cf. Alençon's remarks to Walsingham in READ, *Walsingham*, ii, 62.

[37] Ibid., 59.

[38] Papers in Burghley's hand; *Cal. S.P. Foreign, 1581-82*, nos. 276-82.

[39] READ, op. cit., ii, 75, 88.

[40] DIGGES, 360. Digges prints fifteen letters from Burghley to Walsingham in France, of which I can find only one in manuscript, that of September 2nd, 1581, which is in B.M., Cotton MSS., Galba E vi, f. 119, cf. DIGGES, 415.

[41] In every list of attendance at the Privy Council from July 20th until October 1st, when Walsingham resumed his seat, Burghley's name is included (*A.P.C.*, xiii, 136-218).

[42] DIGGES, 371.

[43] DIGGES, 374, 377, 390, 397.

[44] On Walsingham's advice cf. *Cal. S.P. Foreign, 1581-82*, 307.

[45] On payments to Alençon at this time cf. READ, *Walsingham*, ii, 99 n. 2. The second payment in specie was made apparently to Du Bex, an agent of Alençon in London. Cf. Mendoza's account in *Cal. S.P. Spanish, 1580-86*, 165, who says that specie was in the form of broad angels

newly coined. Since the pound weight of gold was coined into £36 sterling we may estimate that the total shipment weighed about four hundred pounds. With regard to the second shipment, Walsingham wrote to Burghley, October 6th, 1581 (Exchequer of Receipts, Warrants, 123) that the £15,000 was to be shipped £10,305 11s. 10½d. in bullion, the balance in foreign coin.

[46] DIGGES, 422.

[47] According to a report of Marnix de St. Aldegonde, a Dutch agent in London (MULLER and DIEGERICK, *Anjou et les Pays-Bas* (R 905), iv, 258).

[48] *Cal. S.P. Spanish, 1580-86*, 226. St. Aldegonde confirms the story in MULLER and DIEGERICK, iv, 258. A few days later he had his doubts (ibid., 260).

[49] *Cal. S.P. Foreign, 1581-82*, 368, 403.

[50] *Cal. S.P. Spanish, 1580-86*, 214.

[51] Ibid., 233, 243, 249, 260.

[52] *Cal. S.P. Foreign, 1581-82*, 484. He never got it all but he did ger £30,000 in two instalments later in the year. Cf. READ, *Walsingham*, ii, 99 n. 2.

[53] *Cal. S.P. Spanish, 1580-86*, 243.

[54] P.R.O., S.P. xii-152-42.

[55] The editor of *Cal. S.P. Domestic, 1581-90*, 45, suggests that the document referred to had to do with the payment of £15,000 from Alençon to Du Bex, cf. READ, *Walsingham*, ii, 99 n. 2.

[56] *Cal. S.P. Domestic, 1581-90*, 45.

[57] *Cal. Salisbury MSS.*, ii, 345ff.

[58] P.R.O., S.P. xii-149-35.

[59] P.R.O., S.P. xii-149-36, 46.

[60] P.R.O., S.P. xii-150-7.

[61] P.R.O., S.P. xii-152-46.

[62] An account of the expenses involved is preserved in B.M., Lansdowne MSS., 31, no. 71, which is summarized by ELLIS (*Original Letters*, 3rd series, iv, 40ff.).

[63] *Cal. S.P. Domestic, 1581-90*, 74. Letters of condolence to Burghley from Hatton and Walsingham and Sussex are preserved in B.M., Lansdowne MSS., 36, nos. 6, 7, 8, 9, and one from his sister-in-law, Lady Killigrew, in P.R.O., S.P. xii-155-97.

[64] NICOLAS, *Hatton*, 280.

[65] NICOLAS, ibid., 280-1.

[66] ELLIS, *Original Letters*, 3rd series, iv, 44.

[67] WARD, 208.

[68] NICOLAS, *Hatton*, 323.

[69] Cited in OGBURN, *This Star of England*, 306. In a letter to John Thynne (*Thynne Papers* [Longleat], vi, f. 173), dated March 23rd, 1581, M. Browne wrote as follows: 'There happened a great misadventure at Court yesterday, being Tuesday, that one of the maids of honour called Mistress Vavasour was delivered of a good boy begotten by my L. of Oxford, who in consideration of the mishap by offering him that kindness, hath given her two thousand pounds and hath given the child an hundred pound-land. There is much ado and little help about the matter. The Queen's Majesty is greatly offended and it is thought my L. of Oxford shall be committed to the Tower who has absented himself from the Court.'

[70] WARD, 227-8.

[71] On May 8th, 1583, a son, born to Ann a short while before, was buried (WARD, 232).

[72] NICOLAS, op. cit., 324-6.

[73] I find no record of her death in Burghley's *Memoria Mortuorum*, though her husband's death is recorded there (MURDIN, 745). The only record of her death I have found is in a consolatory letter from Walsingham to Burghley on the subject, dated April 15th, 1583, in B.M., Lansdowne MSS., 38, no. 20, which in the catalogue is referred to as the death of Ann, who died five years later. The cause of Elizabeth's death does not appear.

[74] B.M., Lansdowne MSS., 38, no. 61, entered in catalogue as referring to the death of Lady Burghley, who died six years later.

[75] STRYPE, *Annals*, iii, pt. 1, 241. I have not found the original of this letter. Strype's copy of it is in B.M., Lansdowne MSS., 1236, no. 31, and there is another copy in B.M., Harleian MSS., 787, no. 64.

[76] WARD, 232.

[77] MURDIN, 781. NICHOLS (*Progresses*, ii, 400) says five days.

[78] WARD, 233.

[79] B.M., Lansdowne MSS., 39, no. 22; in WARD, 242.

CHAPTER XV

[1] Among others, Sir Ed. Stafford, later ambassador to France. Cf. STRYPE, *Annals*, iii, pt. 1, 161ff.

[2] HARRINGTON, *Nugae Antiquae* (ed. 1779), i, 206; cf. STRYPE, *Annals*, iii, pt. 1, 142-58.

[3] NICOLAS, *Hatton*, 315, undated.

[4] Sandys evidently thought Bernard Maude to be the contriver of the whole plot (cf. STRYPE, *Annals*, iii, pt. 2, 224). Maude was connected later with the Babington Plot (READ, *Walsingham*, iii, 18 n. 3).

[5] NICOLAS, *Hatton*, 316.

[6] Ibid., 317.

[7] STRYPE, *Annals*, iii, pt. 2, 158.

[8] Cf. *Cal. S.P. Domestic, 1581-90*, 178.

[9] DIGGES, 359, 373.

[10] READ, *Walsingham*, ii, 177.

[11] He wrote to Burghley, July 29th, 1581. Boyd assumes that the letter was written to Walsingham, but it is clear from the context that it was addressed to Burghley (*Cal. S.P. Scottish, 1581-83*, 41). The letter requested an interview with Elizabeth. There are no indications that he had any further dealings with Burghley.

[12] *Cal. S.P. Spanish, 1580-86*, 266.

[13] It may not be without significance that Walsingham sent one of his spies to interview Carey after his return; Fowler to Walsingham, January 16th, 1582/3, P.R.O., S.P. Scottish, 31, no. 12;

cf. also Bowes to Walsingham, March 10th, *Cal. S.P. Scottish, 1581-83,* 327, in which he opposes Carey's course with the King.

[14] STÄHLIN, *Der Kampf um Schottland* (R 5346), 152.

[15] P.R.O., S.P. xii-155-103, 107.

[16] *Cal. S.P. Foreign, 1582,* 499.

[17] *Cal. S.P. Spanish, 1580-86,* 421ff. Walsingham's agent, Fowler, procured a copy of La Mothe's instructions; P.R.O., S.P. Scottish, 31-16; cf. *Cal. S.P. Scottish, 1581-83,* 282, where the instructions are summarized.

[18] Why Burghley thought so does not appear. He turned out to be wrong.

[19] The Gregorian Calendar went into effect in France on January 1st, 1583 (*Cal. S.P. Foreign, 1582,* 434), which coincided with December 22nd according to the old calendar.

[20] S.P., xii-156-21.

[21] It seems likely that B.'s notes in *Cal. S.P. Scottish, 1581-83,* 229, had reference to Colville's request.

[22] READ, *Walsingham,* ii, 190.

[23] *Cal. S.P. Scottish, 1581-83,* 316.

[24] This point was raised by La Mothe Fénélon when he returned to London from Scotland in February (*Cal. S.P. Scottish, 1581-83,* 301).

[25] Ibid.

[26] *Cal. S.P. Spanish, 1580-86,* 473.

[27] Mauvissière says that the appointees were Burghley, Leicester, Hunsdon, Hatton and Walsingham.

[28] TEULET, iii, 210.

[29] P.R.O., S.P. Scottish, 31-99. This quoted sentence is omitted in the calendared version of the letter in *Cal. S.P. Scottish, 1581-83,* 378.

[30] TEULET, iii, 218ff.

[31] Fowler to Walsingham, P.R.O., S.P. Scottish, 32-51.

[32] Cf. READ, *Walsingham,* ii, 379.

[33] Cf. BOWES in *Cal. S.P. Scottish, 1581-83,* 434ff.

[34] *Cal. S.P. Spanish, 1580-86,* 471. It was during the negotiations with Mary in the autumn of 1582 that Mary wrote her well-known protest against Elizabeth's treatment of her (November 8th, 1582, in LABANOFF, v, 318-38). Walsingham sent a copy of the letter to Burghley written, as he pointed out, 'in proud and arrogant terms' (B.M., Cotton MSS., Caligula C vii, f. 72). He went on to say that Elizabeth thought it likely that Mary meant to distribute copies of the letter, and 'she doth find it very meet that the same should receive answer and for that it cannot be well performed without the knowledge of things past ... her Majesty's pleasure is that your Lordship cause a collection of those matters which upon the view of the said letter shall by you be thought necessary to be used in the answer of the same'. Walsingham suggested that Randolph and Killigrew be consulted. Killigrew wrote to Burghley on the subject (September 4th, 1583: *Cal. S.P. Domestic, 1581-90,* 119).

There is a paper corrected by Burghley in P.R.O., S.P. xii-161-47, entitled 'Against a Seditious letter dated 1583 entitled Mémoires'. It deals in the main with the defence of Q. Elizabeth's policy towards the Q. of Scots. Just what the connection was with a pamphlet to which CAMDEN refers [*Annals,* 262, cf. *D.N.B.* art. Wm. Carter] does not appear. In any case Burghley's paper is unfinished. It was apparently never published.

[35] WRIGHT, ii, 200. The offers made are in *Cal. S.P. Scottish, 1581-83,* 426.

[36] TEULET, iii, 221; cf. also Fowler to W., *Cal. S.P. Scottish, 1581-83,* 490.

[37] B.M., Cotton MSS., Caligula C vii, f. 209.

[38] P.R.O., S.P. xii-162-3.

[39] *Cal. S.P. Scottish, 1581-83,* 532.

[40] P.R.O., S.P. xii-162-19.

[41] In September a commission was set up to survey the navy (*Cal. S.P. Domestic, 1581-90,* 122) and in the same month orders, drafted by Burghley, went out to deal with horsemen (ibid., 123).

[42] Boyd is not aware of the difference. Cf. *Cal. S.P. Scottish, 1581-83,* 572; ibid., 581; and the version in STÄHLIN, 145.

[43] STÄHLIN, 149.

[44] READ, *Walsingham,* ii, 212.

[45] Ibid., 213-14, 222.

[46] Ibid., 221, 227.

[47] Cf. P.R.O., S.P. xii-163-27-8.

[48] Cf. a memo in the hand of one of his clerks, P.R.O., S.P. 12-163-17.

[49] The *A.P.C.* are missing from June 1582 to February 1586.

[50] P.R.O., S.P. xii-164-2.

[51] READ, op. cit., ii, 258.

[52] There is some doubt about her endorsement of the Scottish succession on her death-bed. Cf. CLAPHAM, *Elizabeth of England* (R 606), 99.

[53] Davison had this from Cuthbert Armourer and passed it on to Burghley (*Cal. S.P. Scottish, 1583-84,* 238).

[54] Cf. HANDOVER, *Arabella Stuart* (R 677), 62ff.

[55] Hoby, in a letter to Burghley of November 13th, complained of Walsingham's hostility (P.R.O., S.P. xii-175-7).

[56] He was Elizabeth's first cousin through her mother.

[57] READ, *Walsingham,* ii, 231. Walsingham said later that he had been 'hardly handled by Burghley and Hunsdon' during his mission to Scotland (ibid., 243) but there is no independent evidence of it.

[58] *Cal. S.P. Scottish, 1583-84,* 108.

[59] Ibid., 390.

[60] Ibid., 539, 558, 580. Fontenay wrote to Mary, August 15th, 1584, that he had told James that Burghley was one of Mary's friends and partisans in England (ibid., 267).

[61] B.M., Cotton MSS., Caligula C viii, f. 73.

[62] *Cal. S.P. Scottish, 1584-85,* 192.

[63] *Cal. S.P. Scottish, 1584-85,* 362. Some two years later, in an interview with Sir E. Wotton, James spoke warmly of Burghley again. 'He [James] hath,' Wotton wrote to Burghley, 'since my coming hither, uttered to me at sundry times so many good and honourable speeches ...

praising your great wisdom, your faithfulness towards your sovereign, your excellency of speech, quickness of dispatch and your short and plain writing.' (*Hamilton Papers* (R 4826), ii, 708, undated.)

⁶⁴ Certainly not Sir Thomas Edmonds as

suggested in *Cal. Salisbury MSS.*, iii, 104. It is, in fact, part of a longer letter to William Herle, same date, in P.R.O., S.P. xii-180-50.

⁶⁵ READ, *Walsingham*, ii, 445.

⁶⁶ Ibid., 238.

⁶⁷ *Leicester Correspondence* (R 907), 52.

CHAPTER XVI

¹ On October 21st, 1584, Burghley wrote to Walsingham: 'I will tomorrow send to you the instrument of the Association when I shall have Mr. Chancellor's hand and seal, having already the three Councillors' hands with their seals, as I am persuaded by their most earnest protestations and solemn oaths' (B.M., Cotton MSS., Caligula C viii, f. 162).

² Cf. on this Huntingdon to Walsingham, November 30th, 1584 (*Cal. S.P. Domestic, Addenda, 1580-1625*, 130).

³ This document, endorsed in Burghley's hand, is in B.M., Lansdowne MSS., 104, ff. 127-32 (printed in STRYPE's *Annals*, iii, pt. 1, 624-31). It is undated but probably belongs at this time, certainly after the Statute of 1581 and before that of 1585.

⁴ In this connection, he proposed that those banished should be branded on the hand.

⁵ These are printed in STRYPE, *Whitgift*, i, 81.

⁶ B.M., Lansdowne MSS., 396, f. 23; printed in STRYPE, *Whitgift*, iii, 104.

⁷ FULLER, *Church History*, bk. ix, 159, as corrected by STRYPE, *Whitgift*, i, 317.

⁸ B.M., Lansdowne MSS., 376, f. 112; in STRYPE, *Whitgift*, i, 323.

⁹ STRYPE, *Whitgift*, iii, 114.

¹⁰ Ibid., i, 337-8.

¹¹ B.M., Lansdowne MSS., 396, f. 16.

¹² Published in Latin, 1574, in English the same year, indubitably by Travers.

¹³ Strype supposes this to be Dr. Nicholas Bond, later president of Magdalen College, Oxford; STRYPE, *Whitgift*, i, 341.

¹⁴ FULLER, *Church History*, bk. ix, 214.

¹⁵ B.M., Lansdowne MSS., 50, f. 78; in STRYPE, *Whitgift*, i, 475.

¹⁶ FULLER, *Worthies*, ed. 1952, 133, and FULLER, *Church History*, bk. ix, 216.

¹⁷ Cf. Beale's account in B.M., Additional MSS., 48064, f. 50; *Second Part of a Register* (R 2407), i, 275-83.

¹⁸ KNAPPEN, *Puritanism*, 280; STRYPE, *Whitgift*, i, 432.

¹⁹ B.M., Additional MSS., 48039, f. 47. Beale

records his statement to B. in ibid., f. 48, which contains some interesting biographical data on both Beale and Whitgift; P.R.O., S.P. xii-173-8.

²⁰ My account on this Parliament is based upon NEALE, *Elizabeth I and her Parliaments*, ii.

²¹ It is interesting to note that Burghley at this time began a treatise which he called *The Usage of Parliament*. It ends abruptly after one and a quarter pages and contributes nothing to our knowledge of the subject. The manuscript is in Burghley's own hand and is dated November 25th, 1584, two days after the Parliament assembled (B.M., Lansdowne MSS., 103, f. 4). Curiously enough Burghley, in this fragment, always refers to the Crown as King.

²² *v.s.*, i, 268.

²³ P.R.O., S.P. xii-176-22.

²⁴ HOLINSHED (ed. 1587), iii, 1392ff. A Welshman by his own account, one of thirty children (B.M., Lansdowne MSS., 43, f. 13), Stow says that he deflowered his own step-daughter, a story confirmed by John Somer (*Cal. S.P. Scottish, 1584-85*, 585).

²⁵ B.M., Lansdowne MSS., 31, nos. 1-4, 39, 21.

²⁶ Cf. J. H. Pollen in *The Month*, June 1902, pp. 2ff.

²⁷ Burghley interested himself in the preparation of an official account of the Parry conspiracy (cf. P.R.O., S.P., xii-177-1).

²⁸ P.R.O., S.P. xii-177-1.

²⁹ NEALE, *Elizabeth I and her Parliaments*, ii, 60.

³⁰ P.R.O., S.P. xii-176-68.

³¹ This was the notorious William Overton, who had earlier regarded Burghley as his best friend (STRYPE, *Annals*, iii, 136-42) but whose covetous extravagance (STRYPE, *Whitgift*, i, 200-12) probably turned Burghley against him.

³² Those present were the Lord Chancellor, the Lord Treasurer, Leicester, Bedford, Lord Chamberlain, Walsingham and Mr. Solicitor.

³³ D'EWES, 350.

³⁴ NEALE, op. cit., 84-8.

³⁵ *v.s.*, i, 271ff.

³⁶ P.R.O., S.P. xii-177-33, in Burghley's hand.

³⁷ B.M., Lansdowne MSS., 104, f. 150.

CHAPTER XVII

¹ This takes the form of three papers (Cecil Papers, 163/50, 52, 54). They are blended into one in another copy in B.M., Cotton MSS., Caligula C ix, ff. 64ff. The version in Cecil Papers contains marginal notes in Burghley's hand.

² *Annals* (ed. 1635), 282.

³ P.R.O., S.P. Holland and Flanders, xxiii, no. 28.

⁴ READ, *Walsingham*, iii, 83n.

⁵ Ibid., 87-8.

⁶ *Cal. S.P. Foreign, 1584-85*, 352.

⁷ Cf. MOTLEY, *United Netherlands* (R 941), i, 289ff.

⁸ B.M., Harleian MSS., 168, f. 102, dated March 18th, 1584, 26 Elizabeth. Normally March 18th, 1584, would have meant 1585, but March 18th, 26 Elizabeth was in 1584. The contents of the manuscript make it clear that it was written after the assassination of Orange in July 1584. We must therefore conclude that 26 Elizabeth is a mistake.

⁹ *v.s.*, i, 295ff.

¹⁰ *Cal. S.P. Foreign, 1584-85*, 424.

¹¹ CLAPHAM, *Elizabeth*, 60-1.

¹² *Cal. S.P. Spanish, 1580-86*, 547.

¹³ CORBETT, *Drake*, ii, 14.

¹⁴ P.R.O., S.P. xii-176-19, 20.

¹⁵ On this subject, cf. READ, *Walsingham*, iii, 383ff. There is no other evidence that Burghley opposed Walsingham's farm of the Customs, though he did go over the contract as originally drawn and suggested amendments. As a matter of fact, Walsingham got his lease in August 1585.

¹⁶ B.M., Harleian MSS., 286, f. 68.

¹⁷ P.R.O., S.P. xii-180-45.

¹⁸ Lettice Knollys. Elizabeth's antipathy to her was great. What particular manifestation of it is here in question I do not know.

¹⁹ P.R.O., S.P. xii-172-37.

²⁰ Walsingham said flatly that Thos. Morgan wrote it. Cf. his letter to Leicester dated September 10th, 1584, B.M., Cotton MSS., Titus B vii, f. 10. Leslie Hotson printed this letter in the *Listener*, March 16th, 1950. His findings were questioned by Father Leo Hicks in subsequent issues of the *Listener*. I agree with Hotson.

The charge, endorsed in NICHOLS, *Progresses*, ii, 434n., that Burghley supplied the material for *Leicester's Commonwealth* is unsubstantiated.

²¹ B.M., Lansdowne MSS., 102, no. 122.

²² B.M., Lansdowne MSS., 45, no. 34; STRYPE, *Annals*, iii, pt. 2, 386.

²³ P.R.O., S.P. xii-180-23. Printed with some serious blunders in STRYPE, *Annals*, iii, pt. 2, 384.

²⁴ P.R.O., S.P. xii-180-30.

²⁵ I find no other record of a visit by Elizabeth to Theobalds at this time.

²⁶ P.R.O., S.P. xii-180-33. The letter goes on about Robert Cecil and what Burghley called a children's quarrel at Court.

²⁷ Thomas had married Northumberland's sister-in-law.

²⁸ P.R.O., S.P. xii-181-32.

²⁹ Ibid., xii-181-42; printed with many errors in STRYPE, *Annals*, iii, pt. 2, 379.

³⁰ As always in Latin; Psalm cxl, 3.

³¹ Psalm xciv, 22-3.

³² P.R.O., S.P. xii-181-60, 71; both of them are undated.

³³ Ibid., 61.

³⁴ Ibid., 70.

³⁵ The originals are in P.R.O., S.P. xii-180 and 181. Copies of many of them are in B.M., Lansdowne MSS., 103, ff. 45-52. On the back of one copy in S.P. xii-181-43, appears the following note in Burghley's hand: 'Letters to Wm. Herle from Lord Burghley ... found among his writings and

brought to the Earl of Leicester after the death of Herle.' Herle died in the summer of 1588, Leicester in September of the same year.

³⁶ MOTLEY, i, 321, quoting a Dutch account of the interview. Cf. READ, *Walsingham*, iii, 106.

³⁷ MOTLEY, i, 324.

³⁸ P.R.O., S.P. Holland, ii, f. 143.

³⁹ READ, *Walsingham*, iii, 106.

⁴⁰ Talbot Papers [Longleat], i, f. 107, misdated 1563.

⁴¹ B.M., Additional MSS., 48116, dated August 25th. The treaty was revised accordingly on September 24th.

⁴² READ, *Walsingham*, iii, 115.

⁴³ BRUCE, *Correspondence* (R 907), 8.

⁴⁴ READ, *Walsingham*, iii, 116.

⁴⁵ *Cal. S.P. Spanish, 1580-86*, 547.

⁴⁶ BRUCE, *Correspondence*, 10. Walsingham later besought Leicester to treat Sir Thomas with all kindness (ibid., 183).

⁴⁷ *Cal. S.P. Foreign, 1585-86*, 53. The letter is neither dated nor addressed.

⁴⁸ B.M., Lansdowne MSS., 102, no. 123. The damp air and the bad drinking water of Brill did not agree with Sir Thomas. He went home in the early spring on sick leave (Leicester complaining that it would not look well) but returned in June. Despite Walsingham's efforts to induce Leicester to befriend him (cf. BRUCE, 192), they did not get on well together. Leicester complained that Thomas had identified himself with Sir John Norris (BRUCE, 379-80). Walsingham wrote to Leicester on April 11th (B.M., Harleian MSS., 285, f. 149) that he feared that the ground of the Colonel's [Norris's] 'strange carriage of himself towards your Lordship groweth by practice from hence. The world seeth that we delight here in nourishing of faction both at home and abroad which I fear will one day breed some irreparable mischief'. In September Leicester reported that Sir Thomas meant to resign his post, and tried to put Lord North in his place (ibid., 411). Sir Thomas left finally in October.

⁴⁹ *Cal. S.P. Foreign, 1585-86*, 133.

⁵⁰ Ibid., 113.

⁵¹ B.M., Lansdowne MSS., 102, no. 23.

⁵² WRIGHT, ii, 271.

⁵³ P.R.O., S.P. xii-184-50.

⁵⁴ BRUCE, 21.

⁵⁵ Ibid., 25.

⁵⁶ BRUCE, 100, 103, 112, 143, 144, 152, 156.

⁵⁷ Ibid., 175.

⁵⁸ P.R.O., S.P. xii-190-10.

⁵⁹ P.R.O., S.P. xii-190-37.

⁶⁰ BRUCE, 237, 239, 269, 341.

⁶¹ Ibid., 279.

⁶² It is, however, to be noted that Buzenvals, Henry of Navarre's agent in London, wrote on May 26th that Burghley was obstructing Leicester all he could, 'and certainly without him the Queen would be engaged bravely. But the other [Leicester] swears not a little that he will revenge himself of it'. (*Cal. S.P. Foreign, 1585-86*, 672.) This probably reflects gossip at Court.

⁶³ BRUCE, 314.

⁶⁴ Cf. NEALE, *Elizabeth and the Netherlands*

(R 942), 373ff.; on army finance, cf. CRUIKSHANK, *Elizabeth's Army* (R 3327), chaps. vii and viii.

[65] BRUCE, 157, 293, 354, 357, 397.

[66] *Cal. S.P. Foreign, 1585-86,* 502.

[67] BRUCE, 153, 356.

[68] P.R.O., S.P. France, xvi, f. 139. This was in answer to a letter from Burghley of October 2nd, printed in part in MURDIN (569-70), in which Burghley had written 'The Earl of Leicester is like to be revoked with a pretence to give counsel to her Majesty'. Leicester himself, in announcing his departure to the Council of State, gave as his reason the writ of summons to Parliament (BRUCE, 443n.).

[69] B.M., Cotton MSS., Galba C xi, f. 227.

[70] B.M., Lansdowne MSS., 55, no. 33; printed in STRYPE, *Annals,* iii, pt. 2, 506.

[71] B.M., Cotton MSS., Galba C xi, f. 229. The letter is badly damaged by fire. The date and part of the postscript are burned away. What is left of it reads as follows: 'My Lord, I hope this hath brought to end the root of long uncertainty . . . Surely Beale hath been . . . ' Evidently Burghley was referring to Beale's secret mission to Fotheringhay, bearing the warrant for Mary's execution (*v.i.,* p. 367).

[72] READ, *Walsingham,* iii, 166ff.

[73] P.R.O., S.P. xii-195-54.

[74] In January or early in February 1586, the French ambassador declared that Burghley was responsible for these appointments (*Cal. S.P. Scottish, 1585-86,* 248). Thomas Morgan in a letter to Mary said the same thing (*Cal. S.P. Scottish, 1585-86,* 267). He probably had a hand in them. Walsingham, writing to Stafford on February 5th, ascribed the royal action to the fact that two councillors had died (Clinton and Bedford) and with Leicester away she found her Council 'grown somewhat naked' (*Cal. S.P. Foreign, 1585-86,* 352-3).

[75] The best account of these peace negotiations is that in *Cal. S.P. Foreign,* vols. xx and xxi, pts. 2 and 3, chiefly the work of Sophie C. Lomas. Froude's account is brief, Motley's inaccurate.

[76] *Cal. S.P. Foreign, 1585-86,* 240.

[77] *Cal. S.P. Foreign, 1585-86,* 368.

[78] Ibid., 370. This is a translation from the Italian original. All of De Loo's surviving correspondence is in Italian.

[79] *Cal. S.P. Foreign, 1585-86,* 514, 527, 545-6.

[80] BRUCE, 200.

[81] *A Declaration of the Causes moving the Queen of England to give aid to the Low Countries,* October 1585; printed in HOLINSHED (ed. 1587), iii, 1414. Burghley and Walsingham composed it.

[82] LABANOFF, vi, 280, in French.

[83] *Cal. S.P. Foreign, 1586-87,* 384.

[84] *Cal. S.P. Foreign, 1586-88,* 105.

[85] *Cal. S.P. Foreign, 1586-87,* 56, 78.

[86] Ibid., 277.

[87] Ibid., 389; March 6th, 1587; original in Burghley's hand.

[88] Ibid., 396; original in Burghley's hand in B.M., Cotton MSS., Galba C ix, 124.

CHAPTER XVIII

[1] Cf. Elizabeth's letter to Mary of May 22nd, 1585, in *Cal. S.P. Scottish, 1584-85,* 596.

[2] Ibid., 423-4.

[3] An undated letter, which probably was written in the autumn of 1581, from Burghley to Shrewsbury, conveyed a complaint that Shrewsbury had allowed Mary to take the baths at Buxton twice during the summer, though he was only authorized to allow one visit (Talbot Papers [Longleat], ii, f. 274).

[4] *Sadler Papers* (ed. 1809), (R 4958), ii, 477.

[5] Ibid., ii, 373, 424, 461, 538.

[6] P.R.O., S.P. xii-177-4.

[7] *Cal. S.P. Scottish, 1584-85,* 606.

[8] Ibid., 524.

[9] MORRIS, *Sir A. Paulet* (R 5210), 4.

[10] *Sadler Papers,* ii, 501.

[11] *Cal. S.P. Scottish, 1584-85,* 566, 577, 585.

[12] MORRIS, 65; *Sadler Papers,* ii, 436; cf. *Cal. S.P. Scottish, 1585-86,* 327.

[13] These are printed in Morris, from Paulet's letter books in the Bodleian Library.

[14] MORRIS, 35, 57, 70.

[15] Ibid., 57.

[16] POLLEN, *Babington Plot* (R 5212), civ-v. On his connection with Shrewsbury cf. POLLEN, 89.

[17] POLLEN, 26ff.

[18] Ibid., 41. Pollen rejects the argument that the paragraph was a forged interpolation (ibid., 32).

[19] J. H. POLLEN, S.J. Pollen accepts the letter but denies the implication, which in view of the passage quoted is not convincing.

[20] On this postscript cf. READ, *Bardon Papers* (R 5201), appendix, 3; also READ, *Walsingham,* iii, 42ff.

[21] Walsingham in a letter to Phelippes of August 3rd (B.M., Cotton MSS., appendix L, f. 140): 'So soon as you shall have deciphered this letter, so earnestly looked for by her Majesty, I pray you bring it with you, for I think meet you should deliver it yourself.'

[22] POLLEN, 133.

[23] *Cal. S.P. Scottish, 1585-86,* 581, dated August 2nd, but cf. STEELE, i, 85, where it is dated August 11th, from B.M., Lansdowne MSS., 49/61. It was certainly composed after Babington's flight on August 5th and before his capture on August 19th. No printed copy of the proclamation survives but HOLINSHED refers to it (ed. 1587), iii, 1553.

[24] BRUCE, 399.

[25] Cf. *Cal. S.P. Scottish, 1585-86,* 621.

[26] POLLEN, 49.

[27] Cf. POLLEN, 60, 69.

[28] Dunne had seen Mary's letter to Babington and recalled the forged postscript which was a little awkward. Cf. B.M., Cotton MSS., Caligula C ix, f. 381, summary of confessions, etc.

[29] *Bardon Papers,* 43; Psalm xviii, 3.

30 *Cal. S.P. Scottish, 1585-86*, 627, 659.

31 POLLEN, p. clxxxvii.

32 *Bardon Papers*, 45.

33 Cf. *Cal. S.P. Spanish, 1580-86*, 625ff.

34 POLLEN, p. clxxxii.

35 *Cal. S.P. Scottish, 1585-86*, 630.

36 B.M., Cotton MSS., Caligula B ix, f. 448.

37 B.M., Lansdowne MSS., 103/24.

38 P.R.O., S.P. xii-193-28 (September 10th 1586).

39 *Bardon Papers*, 50.

40 BRUCE, 412.

41 *Bardon Papers*, 50.

42 B.M., Cotton MSS., Caligula C ix, reproduced in ELLIS, 1st series, ii, frontispiece, which conforms in the main to the drawings in B.M., Additional MSS., 48027, reproduced in *B.M. Quarterly*, xix, no. 1 (1954). The chief difference is the position of the Q. of Scots; she was moved to a corner in order to make a place for the Privy Councillors.

43 Glasgow to Mary, January 1st, 1585 (*S.P. Mary Q. of Scots*, xv, f. 1) and Mary to Glasgow, July 12th, 1586 (*Cal. S.P. Scottish, 1585-86*, 256, 532), also *Cal. Salisbury MSS.*, iii, 53, 130. Thomas Morgan wrote that he had heard that Burghley's grandson, William Cecil, had been to Rome and become a Catholic (MURDIN, 475). The story was probably not true, but young Cecil, a son of Thomas, was on the continent at the time and behaving badly. He disappeared from Paris in July 1585, went to Italy in defiance of orders and was back again in Paris in July 1586, where, the English ambassador reported, 'he haunts bad company' (*Cal. S.P. Domestic, Addenda, 1580-1625*, 147, 183).

44 MORRIS, 189, from *S.P. Mary Q. of Scots*, xvii/60. Morris has misread 'solved' as 'salved' and 'point' as 'packet'. Cecil Papers, 164/114-5. MURDIN prints part of this letter, but gets his pronouns mixed (p. 569). Passages underlined in cipher. Stafford sent out 'the little mulatt' in November, describing him as 'young and little and very towardly paced which I think you desire as much as anything' (*Cal. S.P. Foreign, 1586-88*, 150).

45 Stafford answered at great length on November 6th (*Cal. S.P. Foreign, 1586-88*, 125) which is not very convincing. On the subject of Stafford's loyalty, cf. my article, 'The Fame of Sir Edward Stafford', in *A.H.R.*, xx, no. 2 (January 1915), 292ff., PROFESSOR NEALE's reply in *E.H.R.*, xliv (1929), 203ff., and my rejoinder in *A.H.R.*, xxxv (1930), 560ff.

46 The story about W. Cecil is from Morgan's letter (*v.s.*); the Bishop's letter referred to is that of March 21st, 1586 (*Cal. S.P. Scottish, 1585-86*, 255).

47 B.M., Additional MSS., 48027, f. 574A, in Beale's hand.

48 *A.P.C.*, xiv, 217.

49 Cf. list in *Cal. S.P. Scottish, 1586-88*, 44, and Beale's picture in B.M., Additional MSS., 48027, neither of which is accurate. Some of those appointed did not attend.

50 Burghley wrote to Walsingham: 'We mean to meet by 8 in the morning and I think all will not be well done before 2' (*Cal. S.P. Scottish, 1586-88*, 54).

51 B.M., Cotton MSS., appendix L, f. 146.

52 *Cal. S.P. Scottish, 1586-88*, 77. As a matter of fact they were both appointed, but neither of them sat.

53 P.R.O., S.P. xii-194-14.

54 *Cal. S.P. Domestic, 1581-90*, 361.

55 B.M., Lansdowne MSS., 102, no. 4. Wooley in a letter to Leicester of October 1st, 1586 (Cotton MSS., Galba C x, f. 47), in sending the news of his appointment and Davison's, wrote as follows: 'Which would haply have fallen out otherwise if your excellency had been in England.'

56 NICOLAS, *Davison*, 38.

57 *Cal. S.P. Scottish, 1586-88*, 82, 88, 91.

58 'then she is' in the original.

59 *Bardon Papers*, 51. Fotheringhay was in Northants., about five miles from Burghley House and about twenty-five miles south of Holdenby.

60 A copy of his report is preserved among Beale's papers in B.M., Additional MSS., 48027, ff. 540-54 with a note in Beale's hand: 'This collection was made by Mr. Ed. Barker, principal register of the delegates, who was appointed as a notary to make a note of that which passes. The notes on the margin are in the Lord Treasurer's hand.' These marginal notes are quoted in the text. Another copy without the notes is in B.M., Stow MSS., 159.

61 *Cal. S.P. Scottish, 1586-88*, 98. Elizabeth seems to have wavered in her position. Davison in a letter to Walsingham of the 15th (P.R.O., S.P. xii-194-44) reveals her doubt as to whether it would not have been better to proceed to judgment. But he added that if they had she would have liked it still less. Davison complained about the post, saying it took four days for Walsingham's letter of the 13th to reach him.

62 P.R.O., S.P. xii-194-43. He expected that sentence would be given Wednesday morning, the 12th.

63 Most of the relevant material on the trial is in the B.M., Cotton MSS., Caligula C ix and Julius F vi. Caligula C ix, ff. 631ff. is a fragment containing some details omitted in other accounts. For Barker's official account, cf. n. 60 *supra*. The account of the trial in HOWELL, *State Trials*, i, 1161ff., is based upon Barker's account. The account in Camden's *Annals* (ed. 1635), 310ff., is evidently also based upon Barker. Much of the material is summarized in *Cal. S.P. Scottish, 1586-88*.

64 A memorandum in Burghley's hand outlines the course of procedure to be followed. It does not appear that the Committee was selected as he proposed (*Cal. S.P. Scottish, 1586-88*, 100).

65 Burghley's marginal notes at this point: 'These objections were read out of a piece of paper of her handwriting which ought to be here.'

66 *Cal. S.P. Scottish, 1586-88*, 99-100.

67 HOWELL, i, 1172.

68 Ibid., i, 1186.

69 Ibid., i, 1188.

[70] *Cal. S.P. Domestic, Addenda, 1580-1625,* 188; *Cal. S.P. Scottish, 1586-88,* 70; *Cal. S.P. Foreign, 1586-88,* 120, 137.

[71] B.M., Cotton MSS., Caligula C ix, f. 576, printed in ELLIS, 1st series, iii, 12-13.

[72] ELLIS (op. cit.) reads this 'Mr. Rich'; it is obviously Mr. Vice [Chamberlain], i.e. Hatton.

[73] B.M., Cotton MSS., Caligula C ix, f. 502, in Walsingham's own hand. Walsingham wrote a longer account of the trial to Sir Ed. Stafford on October 27th (Cotton MSS., Galba E vi, f. 326).

[74] P.R.O., S.P. xii-194-44. Walsingham sent Burghley a copy of the letter which reached him on the 18th.

[75] POLLEN, 149.

[76] P.R.O., S.P. xii-194-45; in POLLEN, 150.

[77] MORRIS, 297.

[78] The most complete account of the proceedings in Star Chamber is in *Hardwicke Papers* (R 280), i, 224. Cf. also *Cal. S.P. Scottish, 1586-88,* 107-8.

[79] In 1605 Nau insisted that he had done all he could to defend Mary, but this late statement is of doubtful validity. Cf. LETTENHOVE, *Marie Stuart* (R 5248), ii, 50, and NAU, *History of Mary Stuart* (R 5194), ed. Stevenson, Introduction, lxii.

[80] WRIGHT, ii, 320. Lord Zouche seems to have demurred upon the last point. Cf. HOWELL, i, 1212.

[81] *Cal. S.P. Scottish, 1586-88,* 108.

[82] Talbot Papers [Longleat]. Copy in B.M., Lansdowne MSS., 982, f. 726.

[83] P.R.O., S.P. xii-195-68. Burghley wrote to Shrewsbury on December 1st (Talbot Papers [Longleat]): 'Though there has been a good long truce betwixt your L. common enemy and mine, yet of late he hath broken out with me, not into a full war but into a skirmishing brawl.'

[84] *Cal. S.P. Scottish, 1586-88,* 180.

[85] This from Walsingham, writing to Stafford on the 27th (WRIGHT, ii, 320). Châteauneuf had written to Elizabeth before Mary's trial (TEULET, iv, 109). He wrote a second letter on the 23rd, enclosing it in a letter to Burghley (*Cal. S.P. Foreign, 1586-88,* 119). Châteauneuf seems to have been very uncertain about the position of his master in the matter; cf. his letter to Esneval of October 10th (TEULET, iv, 112). Cf. READ, *Walsingham,* iii, 201 n. 3.

[86] *Cal. S.P. Scottish, 1586-88,* 202; *Cal. S.P. Foreign, 1586-88,* 184; and Burghley's notes in Cecil Papers, 165/19.

[87] If we are to believe Stafford, always seeking to curry Burghley's favour (*Cal. S.P. Foreign, 1586-88,* 194).

[88] B.M., Additional MSS., 48027, f. 489.

[89] B.M., Cotton MSS., Caligula B ix, f. 448.

[90] *A.P.C.,* xiv, 227.

[91] P.R.O., S.P. xii-194-4.

[92] *Cal. S.P. Scottish, 1586-88,* 78.

[93] Cf. NEALE, *Elizabeth I and her Parliaments,* ii, 103ff.

[94] Talbot Papers [Longleat].

[95] D'EWES, 273.

[96] NEALE, op. cit., ii, 114n. The draft of the petition in the Huntington Library (Ellsmere MSS.

1191) contains some verbal corrections in Burghley's hand, but no basic alterations. One gets the impression that Burghley was regarded as an expert in selecting words likely to influence Elizabeth. There is some reason to believe that Elizabeth saw the petition before it was formally presented to her and suggested to Burghley that it should contain reference to the Bond of Association (NEALE, op. cit., ii, 115).

[97] P.R.O., S.P. xii-195-7.

[98] P.R.O., S.P. xii-195-11.

[99] Talbot Papers [Longleat].

[100] There is no indication of this sudden volteface in the *Lords Journals,* which simply record the names of twenty temporal peers as appointed to the Committee (*Journals,* ii, 121). D'EWES (p. 379) in his account names eighteen. The account of the proceedings at Hatfield (published by NEALE in *E.H.R.,* xxxv, 103-13) throws no light upon the matter.

[101] P.R.O., S.P. xii-195-7.

[102] Printed in full in NEALE, op. cit., ii, 116ff.

[103] *S.T.C.,* 6052.

[104] *S.T.C.,* 6053.

[105] NEALE, op. cit., ii, 130. In the *S.T.C.* the editor is given as Richard Crompton, on what authority does not appear. Robert Beale at the end of *Notes of the Proceedings* of the Parliament in the cause of Mary Queen of Scots (B.M., Additional MSS., 48027, f. 477) wrote in his own hand: 'Other notes concerning the Parliament; look in the book published in print by Mr. R. Cecil and dedicated to the Earl of Leicester.' NEALE accepts this as decisive that Robert Cecil was the editor (ii, 129). He sat in the Parliament of 1586. If we may accept his authorship, then his dedicatory letter to Leicester indicates that Robert had wished to serve under him in the Low Countries but had been prevented 'by the overmuch tendering of me by my parents'. The letter is signed R. C. It may be rash to assume that the pamphlet was inspired by R. C.'s father, but it may at least be conjectured.

[106] P.R.O., S.P. xii-195-22.

[107] Talbot Papers [Longleat].

[108] P.R.O., S.P. xii-195-41.

[109] Ibid., xii-195-25.

[110] Ibid., xii-195-26, 40, 41.

[111] Talbot Papers [Longleat].

[112] BRUCE, 441, 447.

[113] MURDIN, 574, 576.

[114] Cf. B.M., Cotton MSS., Galba E vi, f. 353; *Cal. S.P. Domestic, Addenda, 1580-1625,* 200-1.

[115] *Cal. S.P. Foreign, 1586-88,* 185.

[116] TEULET, iv, 181.

[117] *Cal. S.P. Scottish, 1586-88,* 394.

[118] Davison's account is printed in NICOLAS, *Davison* (R 746), 221ff. It took the form of a defence of his share in what follows, the substantial accuracy of which is confirmed from other sources. Beale's account in B.M., Additional MSS., 48027, ff. 636ff., is based on Davison's. So far as what happened at Court is concerned, Walsingham set it forth in a brief summary of the matter to Stafford (*Cal. S.P. Foreign, 1586-88,* 242).

[119] NEALE, op. cit., ii, 139.

120 Probably the same members were present as those named by BEALE (*v.i.*, n. 127).

121 MORRIS, 361. Walsingham acknowledged this reply and approved of it in a letter to Paulet of February 3rd (B.M., Additional MSS., 48027, f. 644b).

122 NEALE, op. cit., ii, 138-9.

123 READ, *Walsingham*, iii, 269.

124 Cf. several examinations of Davison in NICOLAS, 293ff.; Davison's arraignment, 302ff.

125 Cf. *E.H.R.*, xliv (1929), 104-6; xlvi (1931), 632-6. Burghley and Walsingham wrote to the Lt. of the Tower, October 23rd, 1588, directing him to release Davison to the custody of Sir Robert Constable secretly and to forbear to exact from Davison 'such ordinary as prisoners . . . have occasionally yielded and to give order to inferior officers to do the like' (B.M., Additional MSS., 48027, f. 402). On the back of this letter (which is a copy made for Beale) Beale wrote in his own hand: 'Memoranda. That his fine set upon him in the Star Chamber was remitted unto him by Privy Seal, Anno 1594. Her Majesty did grant him a —— of fee farm of the yearly rental of £200 which he sold for £5000.' In another place (B.M., Additional MSS., 48027, f. 687) Beale says that the fine was remitted in June or July 1589. Some time after Burghley's death Davison wrote a long memorandum charging Burghley with constant obstruction to every effort to restore Davison to royal favour (NICOLAS, 350). The charge lacks confirmation from other sources and there is some evidence to the contrary. Cf. Gray to Davison, undated in B.M., Harleian MSS., 290, f. 243.

126 B.M., Additional MSS., 48027, ff. 636-9.

127 Beale's list agrees with the signatures on the Council's letter to Shrewsbury of February 3rd in ELLIS, 2nd series, iii, 112.

128 According to Beale, Burghley recovered these drafts at the time of Davison's committal (f. 637).

129 Cf. B.M., Additional MSS., 48027, f. 650b. According to Beale, Burghley had already written to Shrewsbury bidding him defer his visit to London, and Leicester sent off a private letter to Shrewsbury's son, bidding him attend Beale's coming. Neither of these letters appear to be extant among the Talbot Papers at Longleat or in the College of Arms Archives. Shrewsbury and Kent were present as representatives of the Trial commissioners. Walsingham wrote to Paulet on February 3rd that it had originally been intended to send three others, Derby, Cumberland and Pembroke, but it could not be arranged with sufficient secrecy (ibid., 644b).

130 This fact is noted in Beale's own hand on the margin of his account (B.M., Additional MSS., 48027, f. 637r.). It is virtually confirmed by Davison in his report to Walsingham (NICOLAS, 241).

131 Cecil Papers, 164/9.

132 It is interesting to note that Camden, writing after Mary's son had taken his place on the English throne, gives a very sympathetic account of Mary's latter end, and a flattering appraisal of her virtues.

133 Signed by Kent, Beale, Paulet and Drury (*Cal. S.P. Scottish, 1586-88*, 269ff.).

134 Cecil Papers, 165/20; printed in *Cal. Salisbury MSS.*, iii, 231, with some blunders. A comparison of this résumé with the text of the original (n. 133) can leave no doubt that it is a résumé.

CHAPTER XIX

1 WRIGHT, ii, 332; dated Sunday, 1586. Sunday fell on February 11th.

2 Cecil Papers, 164/10, 15; both in Burghley's hand. The first one is endorsed February 2nd, which is clearly a mistake, the second February 12th.

3 This letter is printed in STRYPE, *Annals*, iii, pt. 1, 540, from B.M., Lansdowne MSS., 102/4. Another draft of the same letter is in ibid., f. 8.

4 This paragraph may have been prompted by a letter from Walsingham of the same date in which Walsingham begged Burghley to intercede for Davison.

5 STRYPE, *Annals*, iii, pt. 2, 404.

6 Ibid., 408.

7 In Latin as always, *Non est sanitas in me a facie irae tuae* (Psalm xxxviii, 3). The *Vulgate* reads *Sanitas in carne mea*, etc.

8 NEALE's interpretation (*Elizabeth I and her Parliaments*, ii, 141) of this cryptic letter (B.M., Lansdowne MSS., 108/54) seems to me to be sound. It is probably, though not certainly, in the hand of Michael Hicks, who was Burghley's secretary later (we do not hear of him in that capacity before 1590). It is in cipher accompanied by a sheet of clues, and is dated February 25th, 1568, obviously a mistake for 1586.

9 Cf. p. 372 *supra*.

10 Robert Beale, in notes on Davison's trial in March 1597 (B.M., Additional MSS., 48027, f. 690b) records: 'It was thought and given forth that the Lords of the Privy Council that had sent down the commission for the execution of the Scottish Q. should be likewise called into the Star Chamber. But that cause was stayed.'

Another note by Beale (ibid., f. 402) runs as follows: 'Mr. Davison told me, Robert Beale, that Sir William Bruncke brought him word from Sir Walter Mildmay that Mr. John Popham, then her Majesty's Attorney-General, and Mr. Egerton, the Solicitor, did plainly say that they would rather leave their offices than be brought to deal against him [Davison] otherwise than in Star Chamber, where somewhat might be done to countenance the matter and satisfy her Majesty and be remitted by her as was in this case.'

11 Chief Justice of Common Pleas.

12 Walsingham, in an account of the matter to Stafford, dated March 9th (*Cal. S.P. Foreign, 1586-88*, 241), reported that the judges had told Elizabeth that she might proceed against Davison by fine and imprisonment but that the law could not touch him further.

[13] Of the Common Pleas; he had been present at Mary's trial.

[14] Another cliché from Burghley's collection (v.s., p. 372).

[15] B.M., Lansdowne MSS., 115/20.

[16] There are two drafts of this letter in Burghley's hand, one in B.M., Lansdowne MSS., 102/5, the other in Lansdowne 115/20. The first one is endorsed '15 March, a writing for Mr. Vice-Chamberlain, not delivered. I sent one by Mr. Killigrew the 20th of March whereof I received no answer'. The second is endorsed '14 of March, my writing to be delivered to her Majesty by Mr. Vice-Chamberlain'.

[17] B.M., Lansdowne MSS., 102/5.

[18] Cf. v.s., p. 332.

[19] B.M., Additional MSS., 48027, f. 402.

[20] P.R.O., S.P. xii-199-70. No signature or address. The letter contains a reference to Leicester, designating him as brother of the addressee. The letter is certainly not from Walsingham as suggested in the Cal. S.P. Domestic, 1581-90, 398. It may have been from J. Wooley, the Latin Secretary, who had participated in Davison's examination (NICOLAS, 292) and was probably present at the Star Chamber proceedings. He was a follower of Leicester and had written to him earlier in the month on the subject (v.s., n. 1).

[21] Cal. S.P. Scottish, 1586-88, 343.

[22] The French ambassador wrote to the French King in March that Leicester, Hatton and Burghley were all out of favour and excluded from the royal presence (TEULET, iv, 183). The one letter we have from Leicester to Burghley at this juncture is a friendly and sympathetic one (Cal. Salisbury MSS., iii, 242). Leicester's role is indeed hard to determine. Judging from the letters he exchanged with the King of Scotland (Warrender Papers (R 4963), i, 248, 253) he was very close in the confidence of Elizabeth during the period just before Mary's execution.

[23] Davison at his trial declared that Burghley had asked the question privately, not in conference (HOWELL, i, 1233).

[24] B.M., Additional MSS., 48027, f. 702, passages in italics underlined in the manuscript.

[25] Walsingham explained Burghley's performance in a letter to Stafford of March 9th (Cal. S.P. Foreign, 1586-88, 241-2): 'My Lord [Burghley] doth allege in his own defence that Mr. Davison was her Majesty's secretary unto whom credit was to be given, that the commission was brought to him sealed with the Great Seal and that if, in that dangerous time, he had stayed the sending of the same whereby any danger should have happened to her Majesty's person, all the realm would have accused him of high treason.'

[26] Burghley had some kind of an alibi in his sore leg. Curiously enough, Hatton seems to have escaped practically unscathed.

[27] Stafford wrote to Burghley on April 4th: 'For all she [Elizabeth] can do, cannot persuade them here [in France] that your L. could ever be brought to do anything against her express mind' (Cal. S.P. Foreign, 1586-88, 266).

[28] WRIGHT, ii, 335.

[29] Cf. Mendoza's account in Cal. S.P. Spanish, 1587-1603, 26.

[30] P.R.O., S.P. xii-200-21.

[31] B.M., Cotton MSS., Galba C xi, f. 306.

[32] P.R.O., S.P. xii-202-1.

[33] Ibid., 202-18.

[34] P.R.O., S.P. xii-203-59.

[35] Talbot Papers [Longleat].

[36] MURDIN, 786.

[37] Cal. S.P. Domestic, 1581-90, 420. The Privy Council had its first recorded meeting at Theobalds on July 9th, its last on August 13th (A.P.C., xv, 151, 193).

[38] Cf. attendance in A.P.C., xv passim.

[39] P.R.O., S.P. xii-198-29.

[40] Cf. J. D. Gould, The Crisis in the Export Trade; E.H.R., lxxii (1956), 189-211.

[41] P.R.O., S.P. xii-201-15. A copy in an early seventeenth-century hand is in Corpus Christi (Cambridge) MSS., 543/30. The letter is accurately printed in NICOLAS, Hatton, 470-2.

[42] P.R.O., S.P. xii-201-18.

[43] P.R.O., S.P. xii-201-17.

[44] Ibid., 201-45.

[45] The George in King Street (STEELE, i, 86).

[46] v.s., i, 294.

[47] A.P.C., xiv, 272-4.

[48] B.M., Lansdowne MSS., 50, no. 4. Though Buzenvals is not mentioned in this memorandum, it was clearly designed to prevent Navarre's defection.

[49] STONE (Palavicino [R 776], 117) takes this to be the French écu – worth about 6s. English.

[50] BRUCE, 360.

[51] Cal. S.P. Foreign, 1568-88, 100. On the English negotiations in Germany cf. STONE, Palavicino, 114ff.

[52] B.M., Harleian MSS., 6994, f. 96.

[53] B.M., Cotton MSS., Galba C xi, f. 317.

[54] Cal. S.P. Foreign, 1586-88, 360.

[55] B.M., Lansdowne MSS., 53, no. 60. Burghley's letter is missing but the gist of it can be gathered from Wooley's letter to Burghley of September 10th in Cal. Salisbury MSS., iii, 280.

[56] Not given in O.E.D. Mammer = to stutter.

[57] Cf. Cal. S.P. Foreign, 1586-88, 362.

[58] P.R.O., S.P. xii-203-41, 42, 47.

[59] My position on Stafford remains unchanged since I wrote my article 'The Fame of Sir Edward Stafford', notwithstanding Sir John Neale's argument to the contrary. For my article, his reply and my rejoinder cf. R 860. Professor Mattingly, who has recently reviewed the Spanish evidence from the original sources, tells me that it supports my position.

[60] The attitude of Navarre's agents is of the same tenor. Cf. Cal. S.P. Foreign, 1585-86, 672.

[61] MURDIN, 570.

[62] Ibid.

[63] P.R.O., S.P. xii-203-42, 47.

[64] Cal. S.P. Spanish, 1587-1603, 78.

[65] P.R.O., S.P. xii-203-59, undated.

[66] *Cal. S.P. Foreign, 1586-88,* 319.

[67] *Cal. S.P. Spanish, 1587-1603,* 80, 123, 197, 209.

[68] *Cal. S.P. Foreign, 1586-88,* 519; cf. *Cal. S.P. Spanish, 1587-1603,* 229, dated March 15th. This is M.'s second letter on the subject. The first appears to be missing. Walsingham heard about the conference from La Rochelle. Stafford blamed it on his old enemy the Abbot del Bene (*Cal. S.P. Foreign, 1586-88,* 564). On Stafford's promise cf. his letter to Burghley of February 26th in *Hardwicke Papers,* i, 264.

CHAPTER XX

[1] In the P.R.O. and in B.M., Cotton MSS., Galba C xi, D i, ii, and in the Harleian MSS., 287, 1582, 6994.

[2] B.M., Cotton MSS., Galba C xi, ff. 288, 292.

[3] P.R.O., S.P. xii-200-21; B.M., Cotton MSS., Galba C xi, f. 288.

[4] Walsingham wrote to Leicester on April 8th: 'The hope of peace with Spain hath put her in a most dangerous security' (B.M., Cotton MSS., Galba C xi, f. 294).

[5] *Cal. S.P. Foreign, 1587,* 203.

[6] B.M., Cotton MSS., Galba D i, f. 93; words in italics in cipher.

[7] *Cal. S.P. Foreign, 1587,* 125.

[8] P.R.O., S.P. xii-203-14.

[9] Walsingham to Leicester, April 10th, B.M., Cotton MSS., Galba C xi, ff. 292, 299.

[10] *Cal. S.P. Foreign, 1587,* 47.

[11] B.M., Harleian MSS., 6994, ff. 68, 70.

[12] *Cal. S.P. Foreign, 1587,* 121. The original shows corrections in both hands.

[13] On Wilkes cf. *Cal. S.P. Foreign, 1587,* 162. On Buckhurst, B.M., Cotton MSS., Galba D i, 93. Three months earlier Wilkes had supported Leicester's position before the Estates General. Cf. BLOK, iii, 220ff.

[14] Walsingham wrote to Burghley on July 20th: 'I fear the division between the said Earl [of Leicester] and them [the Dutch Estates] will be the loss of Sluys, or rather the loss of the whole country' (B.M., Harleian MSS., 6994/84). Needham wrote to Walsingham on July 29th (Harleian MSS., 287/41), 'I do now utterly despair to hope for any good success. The situation might be saved if L. were revoked. Etc.'

[15] *Cal. S.P. Foreign, 1587,* 200.

[16] B.M., Cotton MSS., Galba D i, 230.

[17] Herle so wrote to Leicester (B.M., Cotton MSS., Galba D ii, 27). For Essex, cf. WRIGHT, ii, 345.

[18] B.M., Cotton MSS., Galba D i, 244.

[19] B.M., Cotton MSS., Galba D ii, f. 139.

[20] *Cal. S.P. Foreign, 1587,* 327.

[21] Ibid., 423.

[22] READ, *Walsingham,* iii, 255.

[23] *Cal. S.P. Spanish, 1587-1603,* 190.

[24] *Annals,* ed. 1635, 356.

[25] *v.s.,* i passim.

[26] I find only one letter from him on the subject, to Willoughby, in the P.R.O. (*Cal. S.P. Foreign, 1588,* 482).

[27] Cf. *Cal. S.P. Foreign, 1588,* 167, 188, 189, 204.

[28] *v.s.,* i, 170, 178.

[29] MOTLEY, *United Netherlands,* ii, 386.

[30] *Armada Papers* (R 3518), i, 49; it is absurd to assume that Howard referred to Burghley.

[31] B.M., Cotton MSS., Galba D ii, f. 86.

[32] *Cal. S.P. Spanish, 1587-1603,* 166, 184.

[33] P.R.O., S.P. xii-202-56.

[34] The letter seems to be missing, but a letter from De Loo to Burghley of July 11th which came by the same carrier bears out Burghley's contention (*Cal. S.P. Foreign, 1587,* 161, 177).

[35] Needham reported from the Low Countries on July 24th but says nothing about the matter. No letters on the subject to Leicester survive in the dispatches nor any reference to them in his letters home (*Cal. S.P. Foreign, 1587,* 185, 196, 199).

[36] Walsingham to Leicester, August 7th, B.M., Cotton MSS., Galba D i, 744.

[37] *Cal. S.P. Foreign, 1587,* 228; drafted by the joint efforts of Burghley and Walsingham.

[38] Ibid., 287.

[39] P.R.O., S.P. xii-203-34.

[40] Two different drafts, corrected in Burghley's hand, of these instructions are in the P.R.O. (*Cal. S.P. Foreign, 1587,* 472; *Cal. S.P. Foreign, 1588,* 43), neither of them dated.

[41] P.R.O., S.P. xii-203-41.

[42] *Cal. S.P. Foreign, 1586-88,* 369.

[43] *Cal. S.P. Foreign, 1586-87,* 252, 256; we have no report from Rogers of the outcome of his interview with Frederick.

[44] P.R.O., S.P. xii-203-42.

[45] B.M., Harleian MSS., 6994, f. 98.

[46] Trinity Term ended early in July and Michaelman Term began early in October.

[47] *Cal. S.P. Foreign, 1587,* 375.

[48] *Cal. S.P. Foreign, 1587,* 394.

[49] B.M., Cotton MSS., Galba D ii, 178.

[50] *Cal. S.P. Foreign, 1587,* 398.

[51] *A.P.C.,* xv, 301.

[52] It is rather surprising that Croft was not present at this meeting.

[53] P.R.O., S.P. xii-206-31, dated December 13th; B.M., Lansdowne MSS., 53/11, dated December 14th. In P.R.O., S.P. xii-203-62 is a manuscript of some sixty folio pages entitled 'A brief discourse touching the Low Countries... written by Lord Burghley'. Another copy of the same is in B.M., Additional MSS., 754. Both of these are copies in a later hand. The copy in the B.M. is ascribed to Bacon in *Ayscouth's Catalogue,* 94, which SPEDDING (viii, 67) rejects on the basis of style. I reject it as Burghley's, partly for its style, partly for its content. In content it is certainly much closer to Bacon than to Burghley.

[54] *Cal. S.P. Foreign, 1587,* 432.

[55] Ibid., 452.

T

[56] *Cal. S.P. Foreign, 1588,* 10.

[57] *Cal. S.P. Foreign, 1587,* 472, 481.

[58] Unfortunately, with Leicester's return to England, we no longer can draw upon Walsingham's correspondence with him, one of the chief sources of our information earlier.

[59] Cobham's correspondence with Walsingham in B.M., Harleian MSS., 287, reveals his position very clearly.

[60] *Cal. S.P. Foreign, 1588,* 351, 363, 384, 385.

[61] *Cal. S.P. Foreign, 1588,* 413, 468, 499.

[62] *D.N.B.* art. Croft says that Burghley sent him to the Tower, but I find no evidence.

[63] STRYPE, *Annals,* iii, pt. 2, 615.

[64] *Cal. S.P. Foreign, 1588,* 116.

[65] B.M., Cotton MSS., Galba C xi, f. 812; cf. *Cal. S.P. Foreign, 1588,* 118, where these arguments were used in an answer to Dutch deputies.

[66] 'It is a job for some Dedalus to direct [us in] the maze' (reference being to Dedalus, who built the maze for the minotaur in Crete).

[67] P.R.O., S.P. xii-208-56.

[68] *Cal. S.P. Foreign, 1588,* 118.

[69] P.R.O., S.P. xii-209-83.

[70] Probably those of March 19th and March 25th (*Cal. S.P. Foreign, 1588,* 207, 225).

[71] *Cal. S.P. Foreign, 1588,* 472-4.

[72] P.R.O., S.P. xii-211-15; cf. *S.T.C.,* 368.

[73] P.R.O., S.P. xii-211-56.

[74] *Cal. S.P. Foreign, 1588,* 541, 529.

[75] P.R.O., S.P. xii-212-52.

[76] B.M., Harleian MSS., 6994/126.

[77] *Cal. S.P. Foreign, 1588* (pt. 2), 81.

[78] Talbot Papers [Longleat], ii.

[79] An account of Jane Cecil's funeral procession is in B.M., Harleian MSS., 1107, 62b. Among others the Bishop of Peterborough was there, and William Cecil, Burghley's grandson. For her portrait, *v.s.,* i, 22.

[80] *Apocrypha,* Book of Tobit, xiv, 10.

[81] B.M., Lansdowne MSS., 55, f. 75.

[82] WARD, 262. WARD (286) speaks of another daughter, Frances, who died September 12th, 1587. We know nothing about her. One wonders why there is no mention of a fourth daughter on the tomb in Westminster Abbey.

[83] P.R.O., S.P. xii-201-3.

[84] Ibid., xii-211-56.

[85] *Cal. S.P. Foreign, 1584-85,* 83.

[86] CECIL, *Life of Cecil* (R 686), 25-6.

[87] *v.s.,* i, 106.

CHAPTER XXI

[1] The document dealing with this is undated (P.R.O., S.P. xii-15-4). It is analysed by CORBETT, *Drake and the Tudor Navy* (R 3212), i, 138ff.

[2] P.R.O., S.P. xii-3-24, analysed by CORBETT, i, 133ff.

[3] CORBETT regards this as an Elizabethan innovation (i, 137); OPPENHEIM takes the view that it was part of a long development (*Monson Naval Tracts* [R 344], i, 19).

[4] OPPENHEIM, 120. To the end the prestige-value of the larger ships must have been a consideration. In the Armada fight the flagship was of 800 tons, the rear flagship (Hawkins) 800 tons, Frobisher's ship, 1100 tons. Drake, the vice-Admiral, alone among the great navigators, chose a first-rate fighting ship in the *Revenge* of 500 tons.

[5] *v.s.,* i, 272ff.

[6] On Burghley and Hawkins, cf. WILLIAMSON, *Hawkins* (R 3190); on his encouragement of Gilbert, cf. *Voyages of Gilbert* (R 3234); on his relations with Frobisher, cf. *Voyages of Frobisher* (R 3227); on his relations with Drake, CORBETT, op. cit., and WILLIAMSON, *The Age of Drake* (R 3220). The issues arising over Drake's plunder from his Pacific adventure can be followed in *Cal. S.P. Spanish* and CAMDEN's *Annals,* 225.

Burghley's renegade son-in-law, the Earl of Oxford, seems to have lost £3500 in the Frobisher adventure.

[7] B.M., Lansdowne MSS., 113/45-7, undated.

[8] CORBETT has printed most of these attacks in *Spanish War, 1585-87* (R 3451).

[9] P.R.O., S.P. x

[10] CORBETT, *Spar*

[11] Cf. CRUICKSH

3327); GLADYS SCOTT THOMSON, *The Lord Lieutenants in the 16th Century* (R 1278); and JOAN WAKE, *Musters &c. in Northants.* (R 1274). Miss Wake's introduction gives an excellent picture of the way the musters were handled.

[12] BRUCE (R 3384), cxiii; FOLJAMBE (R 138), 40. Of those who responded, Hatton added to his 100 horse, 300 foot; Warwick 150 horse, 20 foot; Essex 244 horse, 50 foot. The response from others was less impressive. Altogether 1610 horse and 1448 foot were secured this way. On Walsingham's contribution, cf. READ, *Walsingham,* iii, 316.

[13] P.R.O., S.P. xii-193-28.

[14] WAKE, lii.

[15] P.R.O., S.P. xii-201-40.

[16] Son of the Lord Admiral who had died in 1585.

[17] In the old sense of habitually used.

[18] B.M., Harleian MSS., 6994, f. 68. Burghley's principal house was, of course, not in Lincolnshire, but in Northants., just across the river and up the hill from Stamford.

[19] *v.s.,* i, 453-4.

[20] P.R.O., S.P. xii-168-3.

[21] This is MISS SCOTT THOMSON's assumption (op. cit., 74). There appears to be no concrete evidence on the subject except perhaps Burghley's memo. of December 31st, 1585 (*Cal. S.P. Domestic, 1581-90,* 293).

[22] P.R.O., S.P. xii-206-62 (printed imperfectly in BRUCE, appendix vi); S.P. xii-231-47 (in

ERRATA

See notes to Chapter XXI on pp. 578-579

Note 11, line 4:	*for* JOAN WAKE, *read* JOAN WAKE (editor),
line 5:	*for* Miss Wake's *read* J. E. Morris's
Note 22, line 3:	*for* MISS WAKE *read* J. E. MORRIS
Note 24:	*for* WAKE, *read* J. E. MORRIS
Note 38, lines 1 and 2:	*for* These are MISS WAKE's figures (ci). She does not cite her sources. *read* These are J. E. MORRIS's figures. (ci). He does not cite his sources.

Bruce it is ascribed to Essex. Probably it went out to both counties. Cf. also LODGE, ii, 394ff.

[23] *Cal. Salisbury MSS.*, iii, 297.

[24] WAKE, op. cit., xv.

[25] *Annals*, 369. LAUGHTON, *Armada Papers*, i, p. lxxvii, is sceptical, but he was not aware of Burghley's pamphlet. Leicester, in a letter to Walsingham of July 28th (WARD, 289) confirms Oxford's participation. For Burghley's pamphlet, *v.i.*, p. 431.

[26] P.R.O., S.P. xii-198-30.

[27] FOLJAMBE, 20; not recorded in *A.P.C.*

[28] *A.P.C.*, xv, 192, 212.

[29] *Cal. S.P. Domestic, 1581-90*, 394-423.

[30] He attended no meetings of the Council between October 9th and December 12th.

[31] *Spanish War Papers*, i, 197.

[32] *A.P.C.*, xv, 252.

[33] BRUCE, appendix iii.

[34] P.R.O., S.P. xii-205-11. The next day, in a memo. of 'things to be done', he noted: 'To confer with the Mayor of London for the making ready of all such powers as may serve for her Majesty's person.'

[35] Talbot Papers [Longleat], November 26th, 1587.

[36] READ, *Walsingham*, iii, 270 n. 1.

[37] The number of trained men ready in 1588 is difficult to arrive at. Aske, in his poetic effusion on Elizabeth's visit to Tilbury, puts it at 100,000 trained men (NICHOLS, *Progresses*, ii, 562). BRUCE (p. cccxxiv) gives figures three years later of 155,489, but of these only 42,887 are noted as trained and equipped. MILLER (*E.H.R.*, xxxiv, 41ff.) confuses total man power with man power trained and equipped. The best sources of information are the Muster Book in the Foljambe MSS. and Ralph Starkey's figures in B.M., Harleian MSS., 168, which are printed in Murdin. The figures on the actual musters in 1588 are given in both places. They cover only twenty-nine English and nine Welsh counties, leaving out Yorkshire and all the counties to the north of it where the armed forces were reserved to defend the east coast north of Harwich and to be a guard against a possible invasion from Scotland. The totals actually given for the area included are 48,127 trained men, 9213 pioneers and 4626 horse. The horse returned at the musters may not have included those levied upon the clergy, the recusants and those supplied by the nobility and the Court. Probably 50,000 trained foot and 10,000 horse is not far wrong.

It is unfortunate that historians in general have ignored these military preparations. Even Cruickshank confines his attention almost entirely to troops mustered for foreign service. Froude glibly accepts Aske's figures of 100,000 men. Black and Pollard say nothing. Even Fortescue and Oman, the foremost military historians, say very little, though this was the most considerable effort, up to that date, to mobilize the military strength of England.

[38] These are MISS WAKE'S figures (ci). She does not cite her sources. In *A.P.C.*, xvi, 222, the troops under Leicester are put at 18,000 foot and 2000 horse.

[39] MURDIN, 612.

[40] *Cal. S.P. Domestic, 1581-90*, 469.

[41] P.R.O., S.P. xii-168-3.

[42] B.M., Cotton MSS., Vespasian C viii, f. 12ff.; in Burghley's holograph, printed in full in *A.H.R.*, ii (1896), 93-8.

[43] Cf. CORBETT's criticism of this strategy (*Drake*, ii, 130-1).

[44] *Cal. S.P. Domestic, 1581-90*, 462.

[45] *Cal. S.P. Domestic, 1581-90*, 195, 273-84.

[46] A letter went out from the Council to the various counties to this effect on February 25th, 1585/6. The letter as sent is in P.R.O., S.P. 46-34-33. In the draft of the letter in S.P. xii-186-81 83, suggestions were made that the rich (those whose income exceeded £250) should pay one-half their income; those with income £150 to £250, one-third; those below £150, one-quarter. These suggestions were omitted in the letter as sent.

[47] *Cal. S.P. Domestic, 1581-90*, 297.

[48] P.R.O., S.P. xii-198-29.

[49] B.M., Lansdowne MSS., 53, no. 88, undated. There is much else in this volume illustrative of the effort to purify the J.P.s. In ibid., f. 184, is a list of J.P.s in twenty-nine counties which total up to 1587, Lincolnshire the most numerous, with 131.

[50] P.R.O., S.P. xii-206-85.

[51] P.R.O., S.P. xii-206-69. The letter comes from one of Burghley's few surviving letter books. It is undated, but probably of the same date as one on the same subject to the Earl of Huntingdon, in *A.P.C.*, xv, 297.

[52] B.M., Harleian MSS., 703, f. 52; cf. also WRIGHT, ii, 358; LODGE, ii, 338-44, and many letters in S.P. xii-208.

[53] P.R.O., S.P. xii-209-86; *Cal. Rutland MSS.* (R 181), i, 246.

[54] P.R.O., S.P. xii-205-33.

[55] *Cal. Salisbury MSS.*, iii, 319.

[56] READ, *Walsingham*, iii, 322.

[57] *Bardon Papers*, 103ff.

[58] B.M., Cotton MSS., Galba C iii, f. 111.

[59] P.R.O., S.P. xii-209-16. Cf. OPPENHEIM (R 3557), 140ff., and for an opposed view, LAUGHTON, *Armada Papers*, i, lviiff.

[60] READ, *Walsingham*, iii, 306.

[61] *Cal. Salisbury MSS.*, iii, 351.

[62] Two thousand four hundred and sixteen subjects in thirty-six counties. *V.C.H. Dorset*, ii, 144. A copy of the letter which went out is in WRIGHT, ii, 361.

[63] SCOTT, *Joint Stock Companies* (R 3009), i, 92.

[64] Cf. LEWIS, *Elizabethan Ship Money* (R 1224), 38ff.

[65] B.M., Harleian MSS., 6994, f. 126.

[66] P.R.O., S.P. xii-212-66.

[67] B.M., Lansdowne MSS., 56, ff. 6ff.

[68] SCOTT, i, 92.

[69] He probably included the local taxes levied to finance the requisition of ships.

⁷⁰ Exeter, for example, where the burden amounted to more than five subsidies, cf. LEWIS, 40.

⁷¹ P.R.O., S.P. xii-212-63. He refers to the grant in the Parliament of 1587 of one subsidy and two-tenths and fifteenths. In the case of the subsidy, five-eights was payable in October 1587, three-eights in November 1588. In the case of the tenths and fifteenths, one-half was payable in November 1587, one-half in November 1588. Cf. 29 Eliz. chap. viii. According to SCOTT (i, 92), only £50,000 of the subsidy was paid in November 1587, though £100,000 was due.

⁷² *Harleian Misc.* (ed. Malham), ii, 68.

⁷³ LEWIS, op. cit., 24.

⁷⁴ P.R.O., S.P. xii-213-67.

⁷⁵ P.R.O., S.P. xii-211-56.

⁷⁶ P.R.O., S.P. xii-211-15.

⁷⁷ P.R.O., S.P. xii-211-56.

⁷⁸ The proclamation as issued on July 15th is printed in STRYPE, *Annals*, iii, pt. 1, 92. It was directed specifically against those who circulated papal bulls or seditious books. It incorporated Burghley's suggestion that informers should report to the Lord Lieutenants.

⁷⁹ The Declaration is summarized in *Cal. S.P. Domestic, 1581-90*, 493.

⁸⁰ Cf. HOLDSWORTH, i, 297. On this occasion the Justices of the Peace, who generally participated, could not be called together in time.

⁸¹ B.M., Additional MSS., 48027, ff. 691bff.

⁸² Anthony Martin. Cf. *D.N.B.* art. Martin.

⁸³ *Cal. S.P. Domestic, 1581-90*, 509, 521, 523.

⁸⁴ *A.P.C.*, xvi, 221-2.

⁸⁵ LODGE, ii, 345. A Spanish informant in London reported in September that the forces raised by noblemen for the Queen's army were reviewed before her, notably those of Hatton, Burghley, Leicester and Essex (*Cal. S.P. Spanish, 1587-1603*, 418-19).

⁸⁶ B.M., Harleian MSS., 6994, f. 142; in *Armada Papers*, ii, 82.

⁸⁷ B.M., Harleian MSS., 6994, f. 140.

⁸⁸ *Armada Papers*, ii, 109.

⁸⁹ READ, *Walsingham*, iii, 324.

⁹⁰ *Armada Papers*, ii, 213.

⁹¹ B.M., Lansdowne MSS., 103, ff. 134-63v. Two English editions appeared in London, 1588 (*S.T.C.*, 15412 and 15413) both of them bound up and issued with *Certain Advertisement out of Ireland*, printed by the same printer in the same year. Both English editions were published anonymously, but with the statement that the manuscript had been found in the chamber of Richard Leigh, 'who was lately executed for high treason'. Both English editions print at the end of the text 'London — August 1588'. Both also print a supplement dated September and 'The Printer to the Reader' dated October 1588. Internal evidence indicates that the supplement was written during the week following Sunday, September 8th (Spanish banners brought to St. Paul's September 8th. Cf. STOW, *Annals*, ed. 1605, 1259. This is referred to in text as 'last Sunday'.) It contains some late news and refers to a French edition. There were at least two French editions and two

Italian editions printed in 1588. The note from the printer gives still later news, and calls attention to pamphlets put forth by Mendoza in French, Italian and Spanish claiming a victory.

The pamphlet was printed again in 1601 and again in 1746, under the title *State of England 1588*, ascribed to J. T. Phillips (LEWIS, 24). It appears in vol. ii of *Harleian Misc.* (ed. 1809).

⁹² LAUGHTON's comment is amusing (*Armada Papers*, ii, 391): 'It is little more than a pamphlet and has no special authority though its age gives it a certain respectability.' Of course Laughton was quite unaware of its author. It is worth noting that a Spanish informer in England reported that Burghley was the author of the pamphlet (*Cal. S.P. Spanish, 1587-1603*, 484).

⁹³ Dated August in the printed version. It was registered in Stationers Co. October 23rd. Cf. *S.T.C.*

⁹⁴ Cf. texts in pamphlet with texts of originals in *Armada Papers*, ii, 219ff.

⁹⁵ The book was printed before September 30th. Walsingham sent a copy to Stafford in France on that day (*Hardwicke Papers*, i, 364).

⁹⁶ P.R.O., S.P. xii-219-46. P.S. in Burghley's hand.

⁹⁷ CORBETT thinks Drake may have written it and describes the style as Drake's (287). Corbett then goes on to quote what he indicates to be a quotation from the pamphlet. Actually the words quoted are not in the pamphlet at all but are virtually word for word from RALEIGH's *Last Fight of the Revenge*. (Cf. SOMER's *Tracts*, i, 466). Curiously enough, Corbett points out that the similarity of the words he quotes to a passage in the *Last Fight of the Revenge* gives grounds for the view that Raleigh may have written *The Pack*, etc. In short, he first inserts Raleigh in the text and then suggests that it sounds like Raleigh. Homer evidently nodded on this occasion.

⁹⁸ In SOMER's *Tracts*, i, 453-63. STRYPE asserts that the Spanish book which Burghley attacked had been brought from Flanders to England by a Spaniard (*Annals*, iii, pt. 2, 32), but does not document the statement. He says also that another Spanish book, written by a Spaniard and translated by James Lea, with the title *An Answer to the untruths published in Spain in glory of their supposed victory* was also brought into England from the Low Countries. He probably had in mind the Spanish and the English versions of the same book, i.e. *S.T.C.*, 17131-2, which had nothing to do with the Armada, but with the expedition of Norris and Drake to Lisbon the year following.

I have made some search for the Spanish pamphlet which Burghley used. The one which comes closest to it, suggested by my friend, Garret Mattingly, is entitled: *Relacio del succedido a la Armada de su Majestad que entro en el Canal de Inglaterra hasta a lo que se entendio en Dunquerque los doze y treze de Agoste de 1588 . . . Impressa en Sevilla en Casa de Cosmo deLare, impressor.*

The publisher is the same as the one mentioned in the *Pack of Spanish Lies*. It is only three pages long and it does claim that, at a general engagement off Calais, Drake was captured, many ships taken, many sunk and many fled to port. But it does not sustain the details as Burghley set them forth.

[99] Quoted in STRYPE, iii, pt. 2, 551ff.

[100] P.R.O., S.P. xii-215-65.

[101] *Annals*, 373.

[102] *v.s.*, i, 252.

[103] *The Ruines of Time*. Complete works of E. S., ed. Morris (1898), 492.

[104] Cf. Walsingham to Sir Robert Sidney, September 7th, 1588 (B.M., Cotton MSS.,

Caligula D l, f. 333). Elizabeth seized Kenilworth and all other lands belonging to Leicester in Warwickshire (cf. P.R.O., E 123/17, dated October 23rd, 32 Eliz. [1590]). A Spanish agent in London wrote on September 17th: 'The Queen is sorry for his death, but no other person in the country. She was so grieved that for some days she shut herself in her chamber alone, and refused to speak to anyone, until the Treasurer and other Councillors had the doors broken open and entered to see her' (*Cal. S.P. Spanish*, *1587-1603*, 431).

CHAPTER XXII

[1] A list of these in Walsingham's hand, undated, is in P.R.O., S.P. xii-222-31i. A copy in a clerical hand (ibid., 33) is dated January 24th.

[2] Talbot Papers [Longleat].

[3] READ, *Burghley's Household Accounts*, 346.

[4] Cf. FULLER's story of Hunsdon in *D.N.B.* art. Hunsdon.

[5] *Armada Papers*, ii, 167.

[6] Cf. HARING, *Trade and Navigation* (R 3490), 208.

[7] WERNHAM, *Portuguese Expedition* (R 3372), 6.

[8] P.R.O., S.P. xii-219-37.

[9] *Cal. S.P. Foreign, July-Dec. 1588*, 372.

[10] WERNHAM, op. cit., 31ff.

[11] This loan was definitely assessed, and the amount which everyone was assessed was definitely stated. The affairs of those who refused to lend were to be investigated, their wealth appraised, and the amount of their usual assessment for the subsidy, the musters, etc. (notoriously far below their actual wealth) raised accordingly. Burghley no doubt was the active agent in the matter, but there is very little evidence on the subject. One letter from Sir John Petrie, Deputy Lieutenant of Essex, to Henry Maynard, Burghley's secretary, February 19th, 1588/9 (B.M., Lansdowne MSS., 58, no. 78), throws a little light upon the matter. Burghley (then Ld. Lieut. of Essex) had apparently directed Petrie to check the assessments in Essex and make appropriate recommendations.

[12] P.R.O., S.P. xii-219-37.

[13] P.R.O., S.P. xii-219-45.

[14] Wernham's analysis seems to me a sound one.

[15] A Spanish informer reported that Burghley, Walsingham and Hatton all favoured the enterprise, though Howard and Raleigh opposed it (*Cal. S.P. Spanish*, *1587-1603*, 525).

[16] B.M., Lansdowne MSS., 103/48.

[17] Ibid., 104/62. Cf. Hatton's speech in NEALE, *Elizabeth I and her Parliaments*, ii, 194ff.

[18] He was after all in the Lords *ex officio*, and not a peer.

[19] Cf. ALLEGRA WOODWORTH, *Purveyance* (R 1263), 21ff.

[20] WOODWORTH gives the substance of the bill, p. 23.

[21] His suggestions, in his own hand, are in B.M., Lansdowne MSS., 56, f. 85.

[22] Despite WOODWORTH, 23.

[23] D'EWES, 440.

[24] In WOODWORTH, 24.

[25] B.M., Lansdowne MSS., 56, no. 30.

[26] NEALE, op. cit., ii, 215.

[27] D'EWES, 422.

[28] Ibid., 439.

[29] Burghley, in recording debate on the subject, refers to a statute in 4 Henry viii, but no relevant law was enacted that year.

[30] Statutes at Large, ii, 395.

[31] Cf. 7 Henry vii, c. 1; 3 Henry viii, c. 5.

[32] D'EWES, 448.

[33] B.M., Lansdowne MSS., 58, no. 70.

[34] STRYPE, *Annals*, iii, pt. 2, 216-18.

[35] NEALE, op. cit., ii, 199.

[36] B.M., Lansdowne MSS., 104, no. 3.

[37] NEALE, op. cit., ii, 227.

[38] In Petyt MSS. 538/52 ff. 32v.-36; copy in B.M., Lansdowne MSS., 396, ff. 59-60. I owe this reference to Sir John Neale.

[39] He made much of 21 Henry VIII, c. 13, particularly sects. 9 and 26.

[40] As NEALE does, op. cit., ii, 227.

[41] The preamble to the subsidy was drafted by Burghley. His draft differs from the subsidy act in only one particular. Burghley speaks of one subsidy and two-tenths and two-fifteenths — whereas twice that much was granted. B.M., Lansdowne MSS., 56, 79.

[42] NEALE, op. cit., ii, 237-8.

[43] The sacrum.

[44] B.M., Lansdowne MSS., 104, no. 25.

[45] P.R.O., S.P. xii-233-34.

[46] He entered in his diary (in Latin) on April 4th: 'On Friday, between the hours of 3 and 4 in the morning, Mildred, Lady Burghley, fell asleep in the Lord' (MURDIN, 790). In another diary (*Cal. Salisbury MSS.*, v, 71) he gives the date April 5th.

[47] For her portrait, *v.s.*, i, 34.

[48] B.M., Lansdowne MSS., 103, f. 117; in STRYPE, *Annals*, iii, pt. 2, 125ff.

[49] B.M., Lansdowne MSS., op. cit.; STRYPE, op. cit., dated April 9th, 1588, evidently a mistake for 1589.

[50] Burghley's diary adds: 'Blessed are the dead who die in the Lord' (MURDIN, 790). Burghley drew up a list of mourners (*Cal. Salisbury MSS.*, iii, 462).

[51] In its earlier sense of heartfelt.

[52] At this point a passage is stricken out in Burghley's draft. It runs: 'without any unkindness to move separation or any violation of matrimony at any time'.

[53] B.M., Lansdowne MSS., 103, f. 167; printed with some deviations in STRYPE, *Annals*, iii, pt. 2, 128-9.

[54] Late in May Burghley wrote to Shrewsbury that he could not get over his sadness, which assaulted him both day and night (LODGE, iii, 372).

[55] Cecil MSS., Legal, 22/5. Exception is made of such lands as were covered by another indenture, dated May 31st, 1589, which is missing and which may have covered lands granted to Robert and his fiancée as a marriage portion.

[56] Only one attendance at Privy Council between March 2nd and June 6th.

[57] B.M., Harleian MSS., 6994, f. 168.

[58] B.M., Cotton MSS., Galba D iv, f. 195.

[59] WERNHAM (*Portuguese Expedition*, 213) says there were twenty French, sixty Hansa ships. WINGFIELD (in *Hakluyt* (ed. Maclehose), vi, 510) speaks of sixty, all Hansa.

[60] B.M., Harleian MSS., 6994, f. 187.

[61] *A.P.C.*, xvii, 447. On the controversy in general, cf. CHEYNEY (R 690), i, 447ff., and OPPENHEIM's ed. of *Monson's Naval Tracts*, i, 272ff.

[62] *S.T.C.*, 9196-7. A copy of the *Declaration* is among Beale's papers, with a draft of part of the Latin version corrected in Beale's hand (B.M., Additional MSS., 48023, ff. 220ff.).

[63] B.M., Lansdowne MSS., 104/30. It is dated in the endorsement 1591 and in the text a reference is made to the Queen 'having reigned 33 years'.

[64] *Cal. S.P. Scottish, 1586-88*, 693, 701.

[65] Walsingham had made the same point in a letter to Fowler in December 1588 (*Cal. S.P. Scottish, 1586-88*, 650).

[66] *Cal. S.P. Scottish, 1589-93*, 14, as quoted in calendar.

[67] READ, *Walsingham*, iii, 342.

[68] *Cal. S.P. Scottish, 1586-88*, 655.

[69] Burghley wrote to Shrewsbury on June 16th: 'The King of Scots wooeth the King of Denmark's daughter, but we could better like the match with the King of Navarre's sister' (LODGE, ii, 377).

[70] *Cal. S.P. Scottish, 1589-93*, 51.

[71] *Cal. S.P. Scottish, 1589-93*, 77.

[72] P.R.O., S.P. xii-225-6.

[73] *Cal. S.P. Scottish, 1589-93*, 125, 137, 144, 170-1; WILSON, *James I*, 88.

[74] *Cal. S.P. Scottish, 1589-93*, 206, 209.

[75] *Cal. S.P. Foreign, 1588*, 53.

[76] B.M., Cotton MSS., Galba E vi, f. 397.

[77] All this from WERNHAM's introduction to *Cal. S.P. Foreign, 1589*.

[78] LODGE, ii, 372-3.

[79] *Cal. S.P. Foreign, 1589*, 340.

[80] B.M., Harleian MSS., 6994, f. 187.

[81] B.M., Lansdowne MSS., 104, no. 26; CHEYNEY, i, 230, ascribes this to 1590. It is dated July 1589.

[82] WERNHAM in *Cal. S.P. Foreign, 1589*, lviii. Though Professor Wernham was apparently unaware of Burghley's memo., he surmises that Elizabeth's willingness to help Henry III was that she looked forward to some such alliance.

[83] B.M., Lansdowne MSS., 103, no. 62.

[84] B.M., Harleian MSS., 6994, f. 195.

[85] During the year following, Crown lands to the aggregate value of £126,305 were sold (DIETZ, *English Public Finance* [R 1217], 64).

[86] Thomas Howard, writing probably to Burghley, in an undated letter, sent word of corruption in the collection of the subsidy in Devonshire, adding: 'I thought good to remember your L. who in parliament house very rightly reported the abuse of justices in making their clerks petty collectors, so in truth many clerks deal so far in their masters' offices that the poor smart for it, and go away with grudging hearts, and her Majesty notwithstanding hath less than her due' (S.P. xii-224-16).

[87] *A.P.C.*, xvii, 413-14.

[88] P.R.O., S.P. xii-224-88.

[89] *A.P.C.*, xvii, 413-14. Cf. North's letters to Burghley on the subject in WRIGHT, ii, 401: 'For the subsidy matters . . . I will do all that I can with good conscience to further that service, leaving every man a good and large penny worth of his own goods and yet advance the rate.' Cf. also *Cal. Salisbury MSS.*, iii, 428.

[90] CHEYNEY, i, 216. Cf. Robert Cecil to Hicks in WRIGHT, ii, 402.

[91] *A.P.C.*, xviii, 86-129. The register is gratifyingly full at this point.

[92] For Willoughby's instructions, cf. BERTIE, *Five Generations* (R 670), 261.

[93] *Cal. Ancaster MSS.* (R 97), 298.

[94] Accounts in *Cal. S.P. Domestic, 1591-94*, 37, speak of three establishments — the first costing £134,271; the second £124,617; the third £106,162.
    DIETZ (458) dates these 1585, March 1588, December 1588. But cf. *Cal. S.P. Domestic, Addenda, 1580-1625*, 264, which dates the second (in Burghley's hand) February 1589, and (307) the third, May 1590, and attributes saving to Burghley. Dietz speaks of these as three contracts, but there was only one (1585). The change was in the English implementation, brought about by economies in operation, reduction of corruption and troop withdrawals at various times.

[95] In the spring of 1589 the Dutch began to attack him openly. He retorted with a statement in his own defence which was published in the same year under the title: *A Short and True Discourse for satisfying all those who speak indiscreetly of her Majesty* (S.T.C., 7597). There appears to be only one copy of this pamphlet in England, in the Ogden Collection at University College, London. For the Dutch attack cf. *Cal. S.P. Foreign, Jan.-July, 1589*, 205.

[96] B.M., Cotton MSS., Galba D ivff.

[97] P.R.O., S.P. xii-224-41.

[98] *Cal. S.P. Foreign, 1589*, 38.

[99] B.M., Harleian MSS., 6994, f. 191.

[100] B.M., Cotton MSS., Galba D vii, f. 357.

Burghley harped again and again on this tune in his letters to Bodley. Cf. Galba D ix, f. 130. The points at issue are well set forth in *A.P.C.*, xxii, 7ff.

¹⁰¹ Walsingham wrote to Bodley, August 2nd, 1589: 'I wish our fortune and theirs were not so straitly tied as it is, so as we cannot well untie without great hazard. And then there would be easily found some way to free us from them without peril' (B.M., Cotton MSS., Galba C v, f. 65). Cf. also Sir Walter Raleigh's comments on the Dutch in the Parliament of 1593, in D'EWES, 509

CHAPTER XXIII

¹ B.M., Lansdowne MSS., 103, f. 68.

² P.R.O., S.P. xii-231-70, 103.

³ P.R.O., S.P. xii-233-12.

⁴ *v.s.*, i, 212-17.

⁵ P.R.O., S.P. xii-233-109.

⁶ Wilkes thought Burghley would be kept on as long as he lived (*Sidney Papers* [R 629], i, 312).

⁷ Cf. WARD in *E.H.R.*, January 1929 (R 785), and WERNHAM, ibid., October 1930 (R 788), 785, 788. Essex's letters to Davison on the subject are in NICOLAS, *Davison* (R 749).

⁸ This appears from a memo., in which arrangements are outlined for the entertainment of the royal party, in Cecil Papers, 14, ff. 33-4.

⁹ MURDIN, 796. For cost of entertainment, cf. P.R.O., S.P. xii-238-157, total £998 13s. 4d., to which Burghley added in the endorsement: 'For a gown for the Queen, £100.'

¹⁰ *A.P.C.*, xxi, 109ff. Members present: (13th) Whitgift, Hatton, Burghley, Derby, Hunsdon, Howard; (16th) Hatton, Burghley, Derby, Buckhurst, Wooley; (18th) attendance not given. The famous letter, addressed by the Queen 'to the disconsolate and retired Sprite, the Hermit of Tybols' on this occasion, was called forth by a poem addressed to Elizabeth by Sir Robert Cecil, in which he called himself a hermit who had been living in a cell for ten years but was forced to change places with his father who, by reason of his mother's and his wife's death, wished to retire and grieve in solitude. In the Queen's reply she odered Robert to return 'to your old cave' and make way for the return of his father. The whole story is set forth at length in CECIL's *Cecil* (R 686), 48ff. As to Burghley's retirement, he certainly did not withdraw from his public duties. It is to be noted, however, that his 'Meditation' on the death of his wife is dated at Collyn's Lodge (B.M., Lansdowne MSS., 103, f. 117). Probably Burghley had retired, socially, to one of the smaller houses on the Theobalds estate.

¹¹ *A.P.C.*, xxi, 358, August 2nd. It is to be noted that Essex was in France at the time.

¹² The conjecture outlined in a draft letter of Thomas Phelippes (P.R.O., S.P. xii-239-159) cannot be taken seriously.

¹³ Wilkes believed that Robert's appointment would be a bar to the appointment of any Secretary during Burghley's life (*Sidney Papers*, i, 329).

¹⁴ DEVEREUX, *Earls of Essex* (R 608), i, 144. Walter wanted to name his son William, but his wife forestalled him.

¹⁵ It is unlikely that Burghley acquired the wardship. Cf. HURSTFIELD, *Burghley and the Court of Wards* (R 1704). Cf. READ, *Burghley's Household Accounts*, 347.

¹⁶ BACON's *Essay on Deformity* is relevant.

¹⁷ R. Bagot wrote to his father, May 6th, 1587, that Essex hoped to succeed Leicester as Master of Horse. (Folger Library, Bagot Papers, L.a. 87.)

¹⁸ The most important two books on Elizabethan Puritanism, PEARSON's *Cartwright* (R 2437) and KNAPPEN's *Puritanism* (R 2433), pass Essex over with a mere mention. JOHN PENRY, in his *Notebook* (R 2470a), xvi, 70, refers to Court gossip that either Essex or Sir Robert Cecil was Martin Marprelate. Penry's one letter to Essex seeks to cultivate his support by proposing confiscation of Church lands (ibid., 89.)

¹⁹ STRYPE, *Whitgift*, ii, 3. Undated but anticipating Council action in March 1590. Cf. *A.P.C.*, xviii, 407.

²⁰ *Cal. S.P. Domestic, 1581-90*, 656.

²¹ This from the proclamation. There appears to be no evidence of direct action by the Pope against England. It may be that Burghley had in mind the establishment of another college in Valladolid.

²² MEYER, *Catholics under Elizabeth* (R 2356), Eng. trans., 350n.

²³ *Annals*, 406.

²⁴ *S.T.C.*, 10005.

²⁵ On Burghley's later activities, cf. *Cal. S.P. Domestic, 1591-94*, 201, 209, 433, 453; ibid., *1595-97*, 303. Anthony Standen wrote, September 8th, 1592 (BIRCH, *Memoirs* (R 601), i, 80ff.): 'Since the death of the earl of Leicester and Sir Francis Walsingham, all these rigours, now used in England are attributed to the Lo. Treasʳ.'

²⁶ Gregory died less than a fortnight after the proclamation was issued, but his immediate successors followed his policy.

²⁷ *v.s.*, p. 464.

²⁸ Cf. PENRY's *Notebook*, xxii. The evidence is of doubtful validity, being from a letter drafted by Thomas Phelippes, a government agent, to be written to a Catholic refugee (P.R.O., S.P. xii-244-124) but is substantiated by what we otherwise know of Burghley's attitude.

²⁹ NEALE, *Elizabeth I and her Parliaments*, ii, 276.

³⁰ Even Walsingham, ardent Puritan though he was, had taken the same position in rebuking a too ardent reformer fifteen years earlier: 'What else we lack, we must seek by prayer and attend with patience' (READ, *Walsingham*, ii, 265).

³¹ STOW, *Annals*, ed. 1605, 1264.

³² *A.P.C.*, xxi, 293, 297-300, 319, 325; cf. also *Cal. S.P. Domestic, 1591-94*, 75-6.

³³ *S.T.C.*, 5823.

³⁴ B.M., Lansdowne MSS., 103, no. 63, undated, corrected in Burghley's hand. Fair copy in B.M., Cotton MSS., Galba D viii, f. 204.

[35] B.M., Harleian MSS., 6995, f. 32.

[36] The passage in the discourse, to which the Queen alluded, ran as follows: 'He [Philip of Spain] raised wars against the Q. of England . . . adding also procuration to have murdered her sacred person at divers times' (B.M., Lansdowne MSS., 103, f. 183). Apparently the copy of the discourse which the Queen saw was in Robert Cecil's handwriting. Windebank went on to say: 'Her Majesty knew the hand and [noted] your very good speeches of Mr. Cecil for his many good parts of sufficiency in him to serve her.' Evidently Burghley had seized upon the occasion to bring Robert to the royal attention.

[37] B.M., Cotton MSS., Galba D viii, f. 92, February 22nd, 1590/1. Burghley had spoken of the matter to Bodley in his letter of February 13th (ibid., f. 73).

[38] B.M., Cotton MSS., Galba D viii, f. 95v.

[39] A copy of the Dutch note on the subject is in B.M., Cotton MSS., Galba D ix, f. 130.

[40] CAMDEN, Annals, ed. 1635, 393-4; cf. STONE, Palavicino, 174. It is customary to ascribe what Camden said to Burghley's prompting. Camden himself says that Burghley, in 1597, had charged him simply with the business of writing the first beginnings of Elizabeth's reign. Probably at that time, only a year before Burghley's death, he put some of the materials at Camden's disposal. Camden himself did not begin to write until ten years after Burghley's death. Cf. Annals, 'The Author to the Reader'. Under these circumstances it seems hardly likely that Burghley played any very active part in its composition and certainly can hardly be held responsible for Camden's views on the situation in 1591.

[41] P.R.O., S.P. xii-234-11.

[42] Which were coming in very slowly. Fanshaw of the Exchequer wrote to Burghley on December 4th, 1591, that scarcely a fifth part of the third fifteenth and tenth, due in November, had been paid (P.R.O., S.P. 46/38).

[43] P.R.O., S.P. xii-238-30.

[44] Cf. DIETZ, 64. On the Queen's reluctance, cf. Windebank to Burghley, November 8th, 1590 (B.M., Harleian MSS., 6996, f. 67).

[45] Burghley to Bodley, September 10th, 1590 (B.M., Cotton MSS., Galba D vii, f. 272). The Dunkirk enterprise was still under consideration in May 1591 (Burghley to Bodley, May 7th, 1591, in Cotton MSS., Galba D viii, f. 137).

[46] B.M., Cotton MSS., Galba D vii, f. 286.

[47] P.R.O., S.P. 84-40-102.

[48] B.M., Cotton MSS., Galba D viii, f. 4a.

[49] P.R.O., S.P. 84-41-80, Burghley's holograph.

[50] CHEYNEY, i, 245.

[51] UNTON, Correspondence (R 830), 8.

[52] Ibid., 12. There is a long note on these negotiations in Burghley's hand dated January 5th, 1590-91, in P.R.O., S.P. 78-23-15.

[53] Cf. ibid., 13. Burghley wrote to that effect to Norris on July 27th (P.R.O., S.P. 78-25-101).

[54] Cf. READ, Walsingham, iii, 435 n. 1. Burghley's comment on the subject is in B.M., Lansdowne MSS., 39, no. 14. He speaks of Dee's

recommendations and of a conference with Dee on the subject. Dee maintained that the discrepancy was eleven days, not ten days (which indeed was true), but he was willing to have the English calendar made to conform with the Gregorian one, so long as the error in calculations should be spread abroad 'hoping that the truth will draw the Romanists . . . to take out of their calendar the said odd day'. The matter went so far that a Proclamation was drafted announcing the establishment of the Gregorian calendar in England (STEELE, i, 82) but the bishops objected, and the proposed reform was dropped. Burghley, quite obviously, favoured it. His report to the Privy Council on the subject is in Trinity College, Dublin, D. 2.3. It ends with the suggestion that the Queen issue a proclamation on the subject.

[55] SERGEANT, Dyer (R 769), 106.

[56] P.R.O., S.P. 81-6-3; on Palavicino's reply, cf. STONE, 243.

[57] B.M., Lansdowne MSS., 103, no. 72; in STRYPE, Annals, iv, 3-4.

[58] B.M., Lansdowne MSS., 103, no. 73; in STRYPE, Annals, iv, 4-6.

[59] STRYPE, Annals, iii, pt. 2, 617ff.

[60] Burghley drafted his instructions; cf. B.M., Lansdowne MSS., 103, no. 67; cf. also LODGE, ii, 440.

[61] Sidney Papers, ii, 317.

[62] DEVEREUX, i, 212.

[63] Ibid., 215. One English observer reported that the resident French ambassador opposed his going, believing that Essex would be more useful to Henry at the English Court than in the French field (LODGE, ii, 442).

[64] UNTON, Correspondence (R 830), 60.

[65] A.P.C., xxi, 358.

[66] Sidney Papers, i, 329; cf. also Cal. S.P. Domestic, 1591-94, 97. Wilkes himself was seriously considered for the Secretariat (LODGE, ii, 425).

[67] P.R.O., S.P. xii-240-52. A year earlier one observer at Court wrote: 'I never knew my Lord Treasurer more lusty and fresh of hue than at this hour' (LODGE, ii, 415).

[68] Cal. Salisbury MSS., iv, 151; in MURDIN, 647. Essex took no heed of the warning, and later at Cadiz he created so many knights that it passed into rhyme, 'Knight of Cales'.

[69] Unton wrote to Robert Cecil in January 1591: 'He [Essex] suspecteth my L. your father hath not so much favoured him in his absence as he expected' (UNTON, Correspondence, 264). Another blow came to Essex just before his return when the Queen blocked an effort by Essex's friends to name him Chancellor of Oxford. On this subject cf. THOMAS SMITH (Essex's secretary) in Cal. Salisbury MSS., iv, 162-3. Essex in a letter to Robert Cecil laid all the blame on the Queen (ibid., iv, 165).

[70] Sidney Papers, i, 221. Cf. Burghley to Bodley, August 27th, 1594 (B.M., Cotton MSS., Galba D x, f. 177); cf. also Willoughby to Essex, January 30th, 1591, in Cal. Salisbury MSS., iv, 131. D.N.B. places appointment of Lake as Clerk of the Signet c. 1600. He certainly held the office as

early as June 1592 (*Cal. S.P. Domestic, 1591-94,* 235). The obscure letter from Heneage to Burghley in June 1591 (*Cal. S.P. Domestic, 1591-94,* 53) may be relevant. One wonders how so much of Essex's correspondence found its way into the Cecil Papers at Hatfield. It may have been after Essex's fall.

[71] SPEDDING, viii, 108.

[72] Ibid., 143. Bacon's title was *Certain Observations made upon a Libel published this present year 1592,* printed in SPEDDING, viii, 143-208.

[73] Ibid., viii, 106.

[74] BIRCH, i, 73.

[75] SPEDDING, viii, 107.

[76] P.R.O., S.P. xii-241-2.

[77] UNTON, 348.

[78] *Cal. S.P. Domestic, 1591-94,* 41.

[79] B.M., Harleian MSS., 6995, f. 105. It was on this progress at Oxford that Elizabeth is reported to have called for a chair for Burghley. The story is probably apocryphal, though characteristic. Cf. PLUMMER, *Eliz. Oxford* (R 3768), xxviii.

[80] *Cal. S.P. Domestic, 1591-94,* 309. Passage in italics in cipher.

[81] B.M., Cotton MSS., Galba D vii-x.

[82] P.R.O., S.P. xii-243-37; UNTON, 376.

[83] UNTON, 466.

[84] Ibid., 319.

[85] CHEYNEY, i, 280, 282.

[86] *A.P.C.,* xxiii, 9-10. Two memoranda of Burghley's survive on these negotiations, in P.R.O., S.P. 78-28-199, 208, but they add nothing, except that the original offer of the English was 5000.

[87] P.R.O., S.P. 78-29-189, Burghley's holograph.

[88] UNTON, 398.

[89] *Edmondes Papers* (R 810), 24.

[90] B.M., Cotton MSS., Caligula E ix, f. 130; misdated 1593 in *Catalogue of Cotton MSS.*

[91] Psalm cxxvii, 1. Burghley takes some liberties here with his text which gives '*domus*' for '*civitas*'.

[92] In the following May, after Henry had definitely agreed to return to the Catholic faith, Edmondes wrote to Burghley urging that the Queen write to Bouillon 'to assure him of her Majesty's comfort, and because he and others of the chief of the religion in the doubtful perplexities wherein they hold themselves by this great metamorphosis, do often times demand whether

her Majesty will assist them if the storm turn towards them' (*Edmondes Papers,* 72).

[93] The relevant letter is that to Robert Cecil, May 23rd, 1593 (MURDIN, 666); but cf. letter of September 1594 to R. C. (WRIGHT, ii, 434).

[94] In CAMDEN, *Annals,* 422; the draft of the French original is in *Cal. Salisbury MSS.,* iv, 343.

[95] His difficulties about getting from the French an operating base on the Isle of Bréhac are set forth in a letter from Burghley to Edmondes of September 1593 (B.M., Stowe MSS., 166, f. 64, not printed in *Edmondes Papers*).

[96] *Cal. S.P. Domestic, 1591-94,* 348.

[97] *A.P.C.,* xxiv, 78.

[98] WRIGHT, ii, 425.

[99] *Cal. S.P. Domestic, 1591-94,* 391; cf. also his letter to Robert Cecil (PECK, v, 2).

[100] This from a letter of Howard and Robert Cecil to Sir John Hawkins, of December 11th (*Cal. S.P. Domestic, 1591-94,* 393). Burghley's letter to the Queen appears to be missing, but he wrote to Robert at length on the subject on December 7th (PECK, v, 3, misdated September 7th).

[101] B.M., Cotton MSS., Galba D x, f. 7.

[102] He wrote to Edmondes, December 5th, 1593: 'I have received sundry letters from you now during my sickness. Notwithstanding, her Majesty hath been always acquainted with them all by my direction to my son Robert Cecil, who doth now by her Majesty's commandment write unto you in my absence from the Court' (B.M., Stow MSS., 166, f. 86, not in *Edmondes Papers*).

[103] *v.i.,* p. 490.

[104] Cf. *Cal. Salisbury MSS.,* iv, 112.

[105] *Cal. S.P. Scottish, 1589-93,* 518, 823.

[106] *Cal. S.P. Scottish, 1593-95,* 44.

[107] *Cal. Salisbury MSS.,* iv, 513, misdated 1594.

[108] An early use of the word — first reference in *O.E.D.,* 1645.

[109] WRIGHT, ii, 425.

[110] *Cal. Salisbury MSS.,* iv, 319.

[111] Cambridge MSS., E e 3-56, no. 26.

[112] WRIGHT, ii, 426.

[113] *A.P.C.,* xxiv, 259, 271, 272, 298.

[114] Trinity Term, which began June 11th.

[115] After August 1593 the records of the P.C. are missing until October 1595.

[116] Cambridge MSS., E e 3-56, no. 56.

[117] WRIGHT, ii, 427.

[118] PECK, v, 2.

CHAPTER XXIV

[1] *A.P.C.,* xxiv, 78.

[2] Cf. Article for the Speaker's Speech, dated February 13th, 1592/3, corrected by Burghley, B.M., Lansdowne MSS., 73, no. 2, printed in STRYPE, *Annals,* iv, 174. The text of Puckering's speech was published in *E.H.R.,* xxxi (1916), 128-37, from Harleian MSS., 1888, f. 17ff. Burghley's outline is very brief, but it raises virtually all the points which Puckering covered, with the exception of a passing reference which he made to 'the discontentment of the papists, of the proceedings

of the Puritans'. Elizabeth in an interview with the Speaker in the course of the session observed: 'The calling of this parliament was only that the Majesty of God might be more religiously served and those that neglect this service might be compelled by some sharp means to a more due obedience and more true service of God than there hath been hitherto used' (D'EWES, 478). NEALE (ii, 274), who draws his account of this interview from another source, omits this statement.

[3] *v.s.,* p. 441.

[4] *v.s.*, n. 2.

[5] NEALE, *Peter Wentworth* (R 1124), 175ff.

[6] Notwithstanding NEALE, *Elizabeth I and her Parliaments* (p. 281) to the contrary.

[7] B.M., Cotton MSS., Titus F ii, f. 80.

[8] B.M., Lansdowne MSS., 104, no. 33; printed with some deviations in STRYPE, *Annals*, iv, 149ff.

[9] i.e. period.

[10] Burghley got his facts from copies of the confessions made by Kerr, the messenger, early in February. Ambassador Burgh was dispatched February 12th (*Cal. S.P. Scottish, 1593-95*, 45). Instructions prepared by Burghley (ibid.).

[11] Based upon the parliamentary diary of 1593, in B.M., Cotton MSS., Titus F ii.

[12] Heneage was absent from the Council meetings between February 7th and March 18th (*A.P.C.*, xxiv, 536), and he did not participate in debates in the Commons before March 5th (D'EWES, 487). On his gout, cf. NEALE, ii, 310.

[13] He had been so ill in February that Elizabeth sat with her Council at his bedside in Covent Garden (*A.P.C.*, xxiv, 41-61; *Cal. S.P. Domestic, Addenda, 1580-1625*, 351).

[14] B.M., Lansdowne MSS., 103, no. 10, holograph, undated.

[15] D'EWES, 513, 519, 521. There is no mention of the bill in the *Lords Journals*.

[16] STEELE, i, 80.

[17] Those having £5 in goods or £3 revenue in lands.

[18] SPEDDING, viii, 237.

[19] Ibid., 236; the letter is unfortunately undated. Original in B.M., Lansdowne MSS., 89, no. 209.

[20] SPEDDING, viii, 238.

[21] Between end of Easter Term, May 2nd, and beginning of Trinity Term, *c.* June 17th.

[22] *Cal. Salisbury MSS.*, iv, 116. The letter is dated at Nonesuch, June 8th, no year given. The calendar guesses 1591, but the Court was not at Nonesuch but at Greenwich on that date. It was at Nonesuch June 8th, 1593.

[23] BIRCH, i, 114-16.

[24] SPEDDING, viii, 255.

[25] Ibid., 257.

[26] According to Essex, Elizabeth said that Burghley put Bacon in second place (BIRCH, i, 125). Coke's attitude towards Burghley is reflected in a letter (B.M., Lansdowne MSS., 53, no. 53) dated October 15th, 1587. 'When I remember', Coke wrote, 'what comfort I have received by your Lordship's preferment and commendation of me in her Majesty's service, vouchsafing to direct me in all things that might turn to my good, and what cares and pains your Lordship took for my instruction in the last Parliament, and (omitting many others) what exceeding favour your Lordship extended to me lately . . . all that I can yield is a dutiful and faithful heart.'

[27] BIRCH, i, 152-3.

[28] Ibid., 150. Two interesting letters from Nicholas Fant (sometime secretary to Walsingham) to Anthony Bacon on the subject of the Lopez plot are in Lambeth 650/66-7. They record conversations on the subject with William Waad, but add nothing of moment except Waad's praise of Essex's efficiency.

[29] An obscure postscript in a letter from Burghley to his son, Robert, may refer to the Lopez plot: 'In folly (?) I see no point of treason intended to the Queen, but a readiness to make some gain to the hurt of ———.' (Cambridge MSS., E e 3-56, no. 15, January 23rd, 1593/4. The name at the end is erased.)

[30] Cf. DIMOCK in *E.H.R.*, xxiii (1894), (R 695), 440ff.; HUME, *Treason and Plot* (R 711), 115ff.; Sidney Lee in *D.N.B.* art. Roderigo Lopez. Hume and Lee cast considerable doubt on Lopez's guilt, a view generally accepted.

[31] *Cal. Salisbury MSS.*, iv, 483.

[32] *Cal. S.P. Domestic, 1591-94*, 444, 448.

[33] *Cal. S.P. Domestic, 1591-94*, 452-3. He also drafted a speech for the Queen on the subject, which apparently she never delivered (*Cal. S.P. Domestic, 1591-94*, 462).

[34] Later Waad read over the manuscript, made some suggestions, and sent it back October 7th (*Cal. Salisbury MSS.*, iv, 2). Burghley wrote to Thos. Edmondes in Paris on November 28th, 1594 (B.M., Stowe MSS., 166, f. 167) that he was sending him a book on the horrible treason of Lopez and others, come newly from the press, translated out of English into French.

[35] DIMOCK, op. cit., 453 n. 20, ascribes it to Coke; so does SPEDDING, viii, 274. There are at least three published versions of the plot, one by Francis Bacon, in SPEDDING, viii, 274ff., one in MURDIN, 669ff. and the official one which goes by the name of the publisher, Chas. Yetsweirt (HUME, op. cit., 160 n. 1). One wonders whether Bacon's account was inspired by Essex trying to steal a march on Burghley.

A draft of the printed version, copiously corrected in Burghley's hand, is in P.R.O., S.P. xii-250-10. The manuscript ends two printed pages short of the printed version. A manuscript in the Cecil Papers, 139/41-8, is evidently a second draft with further corrections in Burghley's hand, and in the hands of others, and the addition of the final passages in the printed version. Burghley submitted his draft to Wm. Waad, clerk of the Council, who made further corrections and suggested the addition of two confessions (*Cal. Salisbury MSS.*, v, 2) which Burghley accepted and added in the printed version. On these grounds there can be no doubt, I think, that Burghley was the author of the official version. Bacon's version does not appear to have been printed until 1657. Another manuscript account by Waad is in the British Museum (Additional MSS., 48029, ff. 145-184v.).

[36] *v.s.*, p. 471.

[37] Cited in SPEDDING, viii, 307.

[38] *Cal. S.P. Domestic, 1591-94*, 540.

[39] A diary of his for 1594 is preserved at Hatfield (*Cal. Salisbury MSS.*, xiii, 506) but except as a record of his movements and of his health it reveals little.

[40] STRYPE, *Annals*, iv, 224.

[41] Cambridge MSS., E e 3-56, no. 13.

[42] *Cal. S.P. Domestic, 1591-94*, 433-4; corrections in Burghley's hand.

[43] Ibid., 432, 453.

[44] *Cal. Salisbury MSS.*, xii, 506.

[45] P.R.O., S.P. xii-248-84.

[46] *Cal. Salisbury MSS.*, xii, 507.

[47] NICHOLS, *Progresses*, iii, 244. On the Hermit, *v.s.*, Chap. XXIII, n. 10.

[48] *Cal. Salisbury MSS.*, iv, 587.

[49] Ibid., 524-5; *Cal. S.P. Domestic, 1591-94*, 514.

[50] BIRCH, i *passim*. Cf. particularly STANDEN, 165, 189.

[51] WRIGHT, ii, 437. Probably the document assigned in *Cal. S.P. Domestic, 1591-94*, 264, to 1592 is a description of the proposed grant. According to Burghley's diary a large grant of lands, some of them park lands, was made to Essex in December 1594, and another grant to two of Essex's followers in February 1595 (MURDIN, 805-6). Burghley's cryptic remark in the last sentence quoted above suggests that the Queen had made some commitment to Essex which she was in honour bound to content. Maybe this has something to do with the story in BIRCH, i, 181, that she had given Essex a warrant for £4000 when she refused to allow him the leadership of the expedition against Brest.

[52] *Cal. S.P. Domestic, 1591-94*, 529.

[53] P.R.O., S.P. xii-249-34.

[54] WRIGHT, ii, 435.

[55] *Cal. Salisbury MSS.*, iv, 623-4.

[56] PECK, v, 5.

[57] WRIGHT, ii, 436, 439-40.

[58] WARD, 317.

[59] WRIGHT, ii, 440-1. Post and pare was a card game (*Shakespeare's England*, ii, 475).

[60] Ed. 1605, 1279. Though the match was of Elizabeth Vere's own making it does not appear to have been a happier one than those of her sisters. There is indication that Elizabeth, after her marriage, led a gay life at Court (*Cal. Salisbury MSS.*, vi, 387), and there was even a rumour about that she had slept with the Earl of Essex (ibid., vii, 392). Her husband was jealous and parsimonious (ibid., viii, 19). Some effort was made to keep the matter from Burghley (ibid., vii, 344). As it finally worked out, Elizabeth left the Court. Her husband provided for her living and signed a document in the presence of Burghley, Howard and Robert Cecil denying that he had ever questioned his wife's fidelity (*Cal. Salisbury MSS.*, viii, 20).

[61] *Cal. S.P. Domestic, 1591-94*, 71.

[62] *Cal. Salisbury MSS.*, iv, 527.

[63] Cambridge MSS., E e 3-56, no. 44. Oddly enough Henry Maynard wrote to Robert Cecil on the same day that Burghley was not able to write himself, 'being much pained with gout in his hand. After he had read your letter he caused me to burn it' (*Cal. Salisbury MSS.*, v, 100).

[64] *Cal. Salisbury MSS.*, v, 99.

[65] *Edmondes Papers*, 205.

[66] PECK, v, 6.

[67] B.M., Harleian MSS., 6996, f. 250. The correspondence between Willoughby and Burghley on this subject can be followed in *Cal. Ancaster MSS.* (R 97), 317ff.

[68] Cf. *Cal. Salisbury MSS.*, v, 149ff.; *Cal. S.P. Domestic, 1595-97*, 48-50, 56, 58. Oxford was not successful and complained that Burghley had not helped as much as he should.

[69] WRIGHT, ii, 442-3.

[70] Cambridge MSS., E e 3-56, no. 48.

[71] *Cal. Salisbury MSS.*, v, 203.

[72] May 26th.

[73] WRIGHT, ii, 443.

[74] P.R.O., S.P. xii-252-42.

[75] WRIGHT, ii, 445.

[76] *Cal. Salisbury MSS.*, v, 273.

[77] P.R.O., S.P. xii-253-88.

[78] A copy in his own hand of the last paragraph of the revised draft is in P.R.O., S.P. 46-21-69E.

[79] *Cal. S.P. Domestic, 1595-97*, 96.

[80] B.M., Harleian MSS., 6997, f. 84.

[81] Thomas Lake in *Sidney Papers*, i, 343.

[82] BIRCH, i, 294.

[83] *Cal. Salisbury MSS.*, v, 360.

[84] *Cal. S.P. Domestic, 1595-97*, 99.

[85] Thomas Lake wrote to R. Sidney on August 22nd that the country was very fearful of a Spanish attack.

[86] WRIGHT, ii, 446.

[87] *Cal. Salisbury MSS.*, v, 381.

[88] *Sidney Papers*, i, 347.

[89] P.R.O., S.P. xii-254-1.

[90] The *A.P.C.* resume on October 1st, 1595, vol. xxv.

[91] PECK, v, 8.

[92] *Sidney Papers*, i, 353.

[93] Cambridge MSS., E e 3-56, no. 64.

[94] P.R.O., *Baschet Trans.*, bundle 29; *Journal of de Loménie*, 1595; cf. on this mission Lake to Sidney, October 9th, *Sidney Papers*, i, 354.

[95] *Cal. S.P. Domestic, 1595-97*, 114.

[96] WRIGHT, ii, 452-3; cf. on the same subject his letter to Bodley of September 24th, in B.M. Cotton MSS., Galba D xi, f. 184.

[97] *Sidney Papers*, i, 357.

[98] *Cal. S.P. Domestic, 1595-97*, 117ff., 127ff.; STRYPE, *Annals*, vii, 309ff.

[99] WRIGHT, ii, 453. Burghley, as usual, quotes the Psalms in Latin.

[100] *Sidney Papers*, i, 376. There appears to be no confirmatory evidence.

[101] Cf. *Cal. Salisbury MSS.*, v, 457.

[102] B.M., Cotton MSS., Galba D xi, f. 221.

[103] B.M., Stowe MSS., 166, f. 285.

[104] *Sidney Papers*, i, 385.

[105] *Cal. Salisbury MSS.*, v, 511.

[106] It is undated, but several times in the text Burghley indicated that it was composed in 37 Elizabeth, that is to say between November 17th, 1594, and November 17th, 1595. Other internal evidence indicates that it was composed after the successful campaign against the Spaniards in the port of Brest (November 1594) and before the appointment of Robert Cecil as Secretary in July 1596. The date 1595 must be taken as approximate. Of Burghley's authorship there can be little doubt, though it bears no trace of his

handling. It is assigned, in a later hand, to him; the style is his and the references to himself in the text are almost indubitably his. Only one copy appears to have survived (P.R.O., S.P. xii-255-84). This copy is clearly a draft. The fact that it bears no trace of his handling suggests that he dictated it to his secretary. The handwriting is probably that of Michael Hicks.

[107] In the text he speaks of it as a 'treatise' (f. 20). The title is assigned to it in a later hand.

[108] A wide corner is torn off of the first folio.

[109] This is the second version of this paragraph (f. 191v.), of which the earlier version appears on f. 191r.

[110] He ascribes 20 to Henry, 11 to Elizabeth.

[111] The statement on Parliament ascribed to Burghley by SIR HENRY WOTTON (*Life and Letters* [R 773], ii, 498) I have found nowhere else. It runs as follows: 'The Lord Treasurer Burghley, speaking of a king's authority in parliament, sayeth: "I know not that thing a king cannot do in a course of parliament, unless it be a miracle." '

CHAPTER XXV

[1] This is concluded *ex silentio*.

[2] BIRCH, ii, 62, citing *Reliquae Bodleianae*, 8ff.

[3] Cambridge MSS., E e 3-56, no. 75.

[4] B.M., Cotton MSS., Galba D xii, f. 9.

[5] Cambridge MSS., E e 3-56, no. 77.

[6] *Sidney Papers*, i, 378; cf. *Edmondes Papers*, 275.

[7] His letters to Elizabeth, to Burghley and to Essex are in MURDIN, 701-11.

[8] WRIGHT, ii, 456; Essex's secret instructions to Unton are given in BIRCH, i, 353.

[9] *A.P.C.*, xxvi *passim*.

[10] Cambridge MSS., E e 3-56, nos. 79, 82, 84.

[11] *Cal. S.P. Domestic, 1595-97*, 181.

[12] Cambridge MSS., E e 3-56, no. 87.

[13] BIRCH, i, 331.

[14] WRIGHT, ii, 457.

[15] WRIGHT, ii, 457. Standen, in a letter to A. Bacon dated November 13th, 1596, records a rare instance of Burghley's irritability: 'The old man, upon some pet, would needs away against her [the Queen's] will, on Thursday last, saying that his business was ended and that he would, for ten days, go take physic. When she saw it booted not to stay him, she said he was a froward old fool' (BIRCH, i, 448).

[16] *Cal. S.P. Domestic, 1595-97*, 188.

[17] *Cal. S.P. Domestic, 1595-97*, 189.

[18] CHEYNEY, ii, 48.

[19] CAMDEN, *Annals*, ed. 1635, 460.

[20] WRIGHT, ii, 458-9.

[21] Ibid., 460; undated.

[22] CAMDEN, *Annals*, ed. 1635, 459.

[23] WRIGHT, ii, 460.

[24] *Cal. Salisbury MSS.*, vi, 141.

[25] The most complete account of these negotiations was written by the Sieur Guillaume du Vair, one of the French delegates. A transcription of it is in the P.R.O., *Baschet Trans.*, bundle 29, along with Du Vair's interesting description of England. Both are printed in *Les Œuvres de Messire Guillaume du Vair*, Paris, 1625. The best modern account is in CHEYNEY, ii, 142ff.

[26] Cf. Maynard's list of French bonds in *Cal. Salisbury MSS.*, vi, 191.

[27] CHEYNEY, ii, 148ff.

[28] WRIGHT, ii, 461.

[29] One wonders whether he was sending her a copy of his *Meditations* at this juncture (*v.s.*, pp. 508 ff.).

[30] Cambridge MSS., E e 3-56, no. 97.

[31] By some mistake this document has been placed among the *S.P. Domestic* (cclii) of June 1595, and it so appears in the *Cal. S.P. Domestic, 1595-97*, 167. The context makes it quite clear that it belongs a year later, after the fall of Calais in mid-April and after the certain news of the loss of Drake and Hawkins had reached England in mid-May.

[32] This part of the memo. seems to reflect points which Essex raised in his letter to the Council, undated, but probably about May 15th (BIRCH, ii, 8).

[33] BIRCH, i, 483.

[34] *Cal. Salisbury MSS.*, vi, 241.

[35] BIRCH, ii, 57.

[36] Printed in STOWE, *Annals*, ed. 1605, 1282-3. STRYPE (vii, 361ff.) prints the same from a manuscript drawn up by Burghley in B.M., Lansdowne MSS., 64, no. 77.

[37] It was also printed in English and Latin. Cf. *S.T.C.*, 9203-8.

[38] In STRYPE, *Annals*, vii, 364.

[39] *S.T.C.*, 13648-74. The one exception was the homily against sedition, added after the Rising of the North, and retained in subsequent issues.

[40] As a matter of fact, Essex had written to Burghley July 1st (DEVEREUX, i, 372), but the letter was a month in transit, if we may presume that it came by the same messenger as one of the same day to Sir Robert, which bears the endorsement, 'Received, 1 August' (*Cal. Salisbury MSS.*, vi, 241).

[41] *A.P.C.*, xxvi, 7.

[42] BIRCH, ii, 61.

[43] P.R.O., S.P. xii-259-60.

[44] Cambridge MSS., E e 3-56, no. 100.

[45] Cf. *A.P.C.*, xxvi, 15.

[46] Ibid., 21.

[47] Cf. A. Bacon to Hawkins May 9th, 1596, (Lambeth 657/25) on Puckering and Egerton.

[48] Bodleian Library, Tanner MSS., 168, ff. 211ff. I owe this reference to Sir John Neale's student, Dr. W. J. Jones.

[49] BIRCH, ii, 100.

[50] BIRCH, ii, 121, 131, 146, 176. Lake's letter is in *Cal. D'Lisle and Dudley MSS.*, ii, 227.

[51] BIRCH, ii, 147-8.

[52] *Cal. D'Lisle and Dudley MSS.*, ii, 217.

[53] *Cal. Salisbury MSS.*, vi, 418, 109.

[54] *Cal. S.P. Domestic, 1595-97*, 294.

⁵⁵ Cambridge MSS., E e 3-56, no. 107.
⁵⁶ P.R.O., S.P. xii-260-50.
⁵⁷ *Cal. Salisbury MSS.*, vi, 463-4.
⁵⁸ *Cal. Salisbury MSS.*, vi, 469.

⁵⁹ In STRYPE, *Annals*, vii, 355; the original is in B.M., Lansdowne MSS., 103, no. 85; a copy is in P.R.O., S.P. xii-260-92.
⁶⁰ *Cal. Salisbury MSS.*, vi, 547.

CHAPTER XXVI

¹ There are over a hundred of these surviving, most of them, in holograph, in the Cambridge University Library (Cambridge MSS. E e 3-56). Others are scattered through the *S.P. Domestic* in the P.R.O. and the Cecil Papers at Hatfield. A few are printed in PECK, *Desiderata Curiosa*, bk. v; many more, though by no means all, in WRIGHT, ii. We have very little of Robert's side of the correspondence. On one occasion Burghley directed his secretary to burn one of Robert's letters.
² *Cal. D'Lisle and Dudley MSS.* (R 124), ii, 248. Hatton was the elderly husband of Burghley's grand-daughter. He had himself arranged the marriage in the spring of 1594, through the medium of Roger Manners. Cf. Standen to Bacon, March 3rd, 1593/4 (Lambeth MSS. 650/81).
³ Ibid., 246, 256, 260; *A.P.C.*, xxvii, 75.
⁴ B.M., Lansdowne MSS., 83, no. 53; cf. WOODWORTH, 40ff.
⁵ *Cal. S.P. Domestic, 1595-97*, 352, 374, 521, 526, 539.
⁶ Cambridge MSS., E e 3-56, no. 112; *Cal. Salisbury MSS.*, vii, 200.
⁷ Cambridge MSS., E e 3-56, no. 129.
⁸ *Cal. Salisbury MSS.*, vii, 286.
⁹ *Cal. S.P. Domestic, 1595-97*, 390, 399, 402, 410.
¹⁰ PRICE, *Patents* (R 2907), 9.
¹¹ In STEELE, i, 100.
¹² WRIGHT, ii, 479; cf. also *Cal. Salisbury MSS.*, vii, 316-17. NICHOLS (*Progresses*, iii, 417-18) prints both Latin and English versions.
¹³ B.M., Lansdowne MSS., 85, no. 23.
¹⁴ WRIGHT, ii, 477.
¹⁵ *Cal. Salisbury MSS.*, vii, 320.
¹⁶ Ibid., 293-4.
¹⁷ DEVEREUX, i, 436.
¹⁸ *A.P.C.*, xxvii, 341.
¹⁹ In PECK, v, 19-20; and in WRIGHT, ii, 485. Wright has misread Fortescue as Forrester.
²⁰ His birthday, September 13th, misprinted as September 18th in vol. i, 22.
²¹ *A.P.C.*, xxviii, 4.
²² According to Cecil's diary the audience took place at Theobalds on September 7th, which must be wrong. The account of the interview in Nichols gives the date September 7th, the Queen's birthday. This is confirmed by a citation in Cecil's diary. This date is difficult to reconcile with Burghley's letter of the 13th cited above, and with the meeting of the Privy Council at Theobalds on September 20th. It seems to me probable that the Danish ambassadors were received at Court on the 7th and got their answer at Theobalds on the 20th. It is hardly likely that the Queen was at Theobalds both on the 7th and on the 20th.

²³ NICHOLS, iii, 419-20.
²⁴ In R. Cecil's continuation of his father's diary in B.M., Harleian MSS., 36, ff. 439-85. The record runs '7 Oct. 1597, My Master was sworn Chancellor of the Duchy in the Council Chamber at Richmond'.
²⁵ *Cal. D'Lisle and Dudley MSS.*, ii, 182.
²⁶ B.M., Lansdowne MSS., 94, no. 65; printed in ELLIS, 3rd series, iv, 148.
²⁷ *Cal. Salisbury MSS.*, vii, 425.
²⁸ *A.P.C.*, xxviii *passim*.
²⁹ The order of the procession is in NICHOLS, iii, 409ff., misdated 1596. The Lord Keeper and the Lord Treasurer were expected to walk together. (That the order was set down before the procession is clear from the fact that it was not yet certain whether the Queen would ride on horseback or in a chariot. She actually rode in a chariot [D'EWES, 523]).
³⁰ D'EWES, 523.
³¹ NEALE, ii, 333.
³² 39 Eliz., c. 7.
³³ 13 Eliz., c. 4.
³⁴ D'EWES, 528-30; Whitgift is named first, but Burghley probably presided.
³⁵ P.R.O., S.P. xii-265-30.
³⁶ D'EWES, 539.
³⁷ *Cal. D'Lisle and Dudley MSS.*, ii, 243.
³⁸ Ibid., 267.
³⁹ Ibid., 284.
⁴⁰ *Cal. S.P. Domestic, 1595-97*, 439.
⁴¹ WRIGHT, ii, 474-5.
⁴² July 6th, probably Essex to Cecil of that date in *Cal. S.P. Domestic, 1595-97*, 451, in which Essex wrote: 'If I live to return I will make you think your friendship well professed.'
⁴³ Cambridge MSS., E e 3-56, no. 118.
⁴⁴ *Cal. S.P. Domestic, 1595-97*, 469, a more accurate version than that in DEVEREUX, i, 430.
⁴⁵ DEVEREUX, i, 436.
⁴⁶ *Cal. S.P. Domestic, 1595-97*, 524.
⁴⁷ P.R.O., S.P. xii-265-6.
⁴⁸ Ibid., 265-14.
⁴⁹ Ibid., printed in DEVEREUX, i, 471. Devereux's versions are not always accurate.
⁵⁰ *Cal. D'Lisle and Dudley MSS.*, ii, 305.
⁵¹ BIRCH, ii, 363-4.
⁵² B.M., Lansdowne MSS., 84, no. 66.
⁵³ BIRCH, ii, 366.
⁵⁴ *Cal. Salisbury MSS.*, vii, 64.
⁵⁵ WRIGHT, ii, 476.
⁵⁶ Bonaventura Calatagione, general of the Cordeliers, who played a large part in the peacemaking (LAVISSE, *Histoire de France*, vi, pt. 1, 411).
⁵⁷ Psalm xxx, 1; in Latin in original.
⁵⁸ Cf. *Edmondes Papers*, 305-14.
⁵⁹ DE MAISSE, *Journal* (R 817). One wonders

whether De Maisse was inspired by Du Vair's Journal of a previous French mission. The development of French interest in the English political organization is apparent in both journals.

60 Cf. ibid., 64. 'His [Essex's] quarrel with the L. Treasurer, the Admiral and the Secretary cannot yet be settled.' Later he wrote (114): 'At my departing I went to visit Essex who sent word to me that I should go to see the L. Treasurer before going to see him. They have great respect for each other and render strange charities to each other.'

61 Cf. Cecil to Edmondes (*Edmondes Papers*, 320).

62 P.R.O., S.P. xii-266-3, Burghley's holograph.

63 *Cal. D'Lisle and Dudley MSS.*, ii, 326; B.M., Cotton MSS., Caligula E ix, pt. 2, 174; in WRIGHT, ii, 486. This letter is so badly burned that what is left of it is unintelligible. Other letters from Cecil in this volume have suffered even more. When Wright transcribed it over a century ago, the burned edges were more intact.

64 *Cal. Salisbury MSS.*, viii, 49; *Cal. S.P. Domestic, 1598-1601*, 30.

65 *Cal. Salisbury MSS.*, viii, 138.

66 *Chamberlain Letters* (R 605), i, 33.

67 PECK, v, 22-3.

68 Ibid., 23-4.

69 B.M., Lansdowne MSS., 87, no. 22.

70 P.R.O., S.P. 46-41. His letter of that date is from his house in Covent Garden.

71 *Cal. Salisbury MSS.*, viii, 244.

72 The Dutch account of the mission is in DEVENTER, *Gedenkstukken* (R 917), ii, 232ff. MOTLEY, *United Netherlands*, iii, 486ff., draws his account from this source.

73 B.M., Lansdowne MSS., 103, no. 87; printed in STRYPE, *Annals*, iv, 451, but with omission of last two pages. Other memoranda on the same subject in Burghley's hand are in B.M., Lansdowne MSS., 87, no. 7.

74 *Chamberlain Letters*, ii, 38.

75 *Annals*, 490, 492.

76 Cf. his letter of May 17th probably to Lord Henry Howard, in *Cal. Salisbury MSS.*, viii, 170.

77 WRIGHT, ii, 488; the letter itself is reproduced in facsimile.

78 PECK, v, 25, July 21st, 1598.

79 In the anonymous life printed in PECK, bk. i, and in CLAPHAM's *Observations* (R 606), 77ff.

80 In Robert Cecil's diary the time of death is given as 7 a.m., August 4th (B.M., Harleian MSS., 36, ff. 439ff.) The life in Peck says 8 a.m.

81 *Annals*, 494.

INDEX

INDEX

Thoghe I know you cont it your duty, in nature so
contynually, to shew you carefull of my state of
helth, yet war I also vnnaturall, if I shuld not
tak comfort therby, and to besek almighty God
to bles you w superply of such blessyng as I can not
in this infirmyte yeld you

only I pray you diligently and effectually, let hir
Maty vnderstand how hir syngular kyndnes doth
overcom my power to acqt it, who thowgh she will
not be a mother, yet she sheweth hir self by
fedyng me w hir own princely hand, as a carefull noris
and if I may be wayned to fede my self, I shall
be more redy to serve hir on ye erth, if not I hope
to be in heavë a svitor for hir and Gods church.
and so I thank you for your partriches.

serve God by servyng of ye Quene for
all other svice is in dede bondage to
ye devill

10 Feb 1598
Your languishyng
fath W Burghley

BURGHLEY'S LAST AUTOGRAPH LETTER

NOTES